W9-BCQ-646

THE COLLECTED WORKS OF RALPH WALDO EMERSON

"By lonely lakes to men unknown" ("May-Day")

Follansbee Pond. Photograph by William J. Stillman, 1859.

Reproduced by permission of the Adirondacks Historical Museum

The Collected Works of Ralph Waldo Emerson

VOLUME IX

POEMS: A VARIORUM EDITION

Historical Introduction, Textual Introduction, and Poem Headnotes
by Albert J. von Frank

Text Established
by Albert J. von Frank and Thomas Wortham

The Belknap Press of Harvard University Press
Cambridge, Massachusetts, and London, England
2011

ISBN 978–0–674–04915–4
Library of Congress Control Number: 70–158429

978–0–674–13970–1 (vol. 1)
978–0–674–13980–0 (vol. 2)
978–0–674–13990–9 (vol. 3)
978–0–674–13991–6 (vol. 4)
978–0–674–13992–3 (vol. 5)
978–0–674–01190–8 (vol. 6)
978–0–674–02627–8 (vol. 7)
978–0–674–03560–7 (vol. 8)

For Barbara L. Packer,
The Teacher,
The Friend,
The One Who Inspires.

PREFACE

This volume has been prepared in a scholarly collaboration be-
tween Albert J. von Frank and Thomas Wortham. The volume's
Historical Introduction, Textual Introduction, and individual
Poem Headnotes were written by Mr. von Frank; the Text of the
poems was established by Mr. von Frank and Mr. Wortham.
Throughout their preparation of this volume, the editors reviewed
and made substantive contributions to each other's work; at cru-
cial junctures along the way to their final presentation of *Poems,*
the editors solicited and profited from the advice of members of
the Editorial Board of *The Collected Works of Ralph Waldo Emerson*
and from members' reading of and commentary on individual
portions of this volume. As with all previous volumes of the *Col-
lected Works,* the General Editor has primary responsibility for the
edition and for certification of individual volumes.

Ever since the *Collected Works* edition was first conceived of by a
generation of elder Emerson scholars in the early 1960s, the ques-
tion of how to present in print Emerson's lifelong achievement as
a poet has been a constant and sometimes contested subject of
discussion among members of the Editorial Board and others. By
one standard, an approach that brought together in one volume
the works gathered by Emerson in *Poems* (1847), *May-Day and
Other Pieces* (1867), and *Selected Poems* (1876), and that might also
include the texts of his otherwise uncollected poems, seemed ap-
propriate to the task; by another standard, however, this approach
seemed wanting, especially in accounting for the substantial body
of poetic works—some in reasonably complete form, some in

vii

progress, and some in a fragmentary state—which remained un-published at Emerson's death in the manuscript journals and notebooks he affectionately referred to as his "savings bank." For lack of a better word, until recent years this editorial "impasse" between two approaches to Emerson's poetic achievement char-acterized the state of thinking about this volume through a gen-eration of previous general and textual editors of the *Collected Works;* it certainly represents the nature of the discussion about what this volume should be in the 1970s, when Thomas Wortham, who was assigned to work on the poems volume, and I were first appointed to the Editorial Board.

There is perhaps no small irony or surprise in the fact that the last two volumes of the *Collected Works, Poems,* volume IX, and *Un-collected Prose Writings: Addresses, Essays, and Reviews,* volume X, which is forthcoming under the editorship of Ronald A. Bosco, Glen M. Johnson, and Joel Myerson, have been the most antici-pated but proven in their execution to be the most complex of the entire series. With respect to *Poems,* the completion of *The Journals and Miscellaneous Notebooks* (1960–1982), *The Poetry Note-books* (1986), and *The Topical Notebooks of Ralph Waldo Emerson* (1990–1994) collectively created the conditions for a definitive account of Emerson's poetic achievement from initial manuscript form through to the form Emerson ultimately placed into print. At a meeting in Denver, Colorado, in September 2005, Mr. Wortham, Mr. Myerson (who by then had been appointed to the Editorial Board and would be named Textual Editor of the *Col-lected Works* in 2007), and I agreed that the only appropriate and adequate presentation of *Poems* in the *Collected Works* would be as a variorum edition, and that judgment was unanimously affirmed by the Editorial Board. Subsequently, Mr. von Frank, who had pre-viously served as an editor of *The Poetry Notebooks* and as Chief Edi-tor of *The Complete Sermons of Ralph Waldo Emerson* (1989–1992), graciously accepted appointment to the *Collected Works* and the as-signment to join with Mr. Wortham in the preparation of a vario-rum edition of *Poems.* Each editor has brought a lifetime of devo-tion to Emerson scholarship to this collaboration. Of particular note, Mr. Wortham's special contribution to the collaboration is that he brought to it three decades of discovery and significant research into all of Emerson's extant poetic manuscripts.

The appropriateness of a variorum edition for *Poems* is fully articulated in the Textual Introduction that follows below; A Note to the Reader, meant to guide the reader in the use of the special documentation associated with this variorum edition, immediately follows the table of contents. As explained in the Textual Introduction, for the first time since Emerson's death readers are given access, in this edition, to all of the poems that Emerson thought finished and fit to print and in the form he wished to see them in print. His decision to publish a particular poem being the criterion for its inclusion here, it follows that the individual poem and not any of Emerson's collections is the principal focus of editorial attention. The complete history of each poem determines its treatment here. Thus, as employed and followed in this volume, the term variorum refers to the presentation of a given text in immediate association with all the variants found in all authorized printings or editions, as well as in printings and editions, including posthumous ones, that arguably might reflect the author's intentions. By compiling a chronological list of these variants for each poem, the editors have produced a history of the changes in the poetic text. This is the evidentiary heart of the volume, and it is the evidence that makes this volume, this edition, unique.

In the 1970s and 1980s, the National Endowment for the Humanities, initially through the Center for Editions of American Authors, provided support for the planning of the *Collected Works* edition as a whole and the work of the edition's early editors.

The present editors' access to the archival holdings of many institutions has been crucial in bringing this volume to conclusion. Foremost, we gratefully acknowledge the Ralph Waldo Emerson Memorial Association and the Houghton Library, Harvard University, for permission to quote from Emerson's poetic manuscripts, marginalia and corrections in his personal copies of various printings of his poems, and other materials contained in Ralph Waldo Emerson Memorial Association deposit at the Houghton Library, and the Houghton Library, Harvard University, for permission to quote from manuscript and print materials in other of its collections. Members of the staff of the Houghton Library have been generous in providing the editors with courteous and expert assistance throughout their preparation of this volume; here we should like to acknowledge, in particular, Dr. Leslie A. Morris, Curator, and Denison Beach, James Capobianco, Mary Haegert, Susan Halpert, Rachel Howarth, Jennie Rathbun, Marte Shaw, and Emily Walhout, current and past research providers in the Houghton Reading Room.

In addition, the editors' timely access to manuscript and print holdings relating to Emerson's career as a poet by officers and librarians of the following institutions has been essential to their work: The Trustees of the Boston Public Library/Rare Books, Boston, Massachusetts; The John Hay Library, Brown University; Rutherford B. Hayes Presidential Center, Fremont, Ohio; The Huntington Library, San Marino, California; The Lilly Library, Indiana University, Bloomington, Indiana; Special Collections, Lehigh University Libraries, Bethlehem, Pennsylvania; Sterling Library, Senate House Library, University of London, London, U.K.; Longfellow National Historic Site, Cambridge, Massachusetts; Massachusetts Historical Society, Boston, Massachusetts; The Pierpont Morgan Library, New York, New York; The Henry W. and Albert A. Berg Collection, New York Public Library, New York, New York; Rare Book and Manuscript Library, University of Pennsylvania, Philadelphia, Pennsylvania; Robert H. Taylor Collection, Manuscript Division, Department of Rare Books and Special Collections, Princeton University Library, Princeton, New Jersey; Joel Myerson Collection of Nineteenth-Century American Literature, University of South Carolina, Columbia, South Carolina; Harry Ransom Humanities Research Center, University of Texas at Austin, Austin, Texas; Special Collections, University of Virginia Library, Charlottesville, Virginia; Special Collections, Wake Forest University, Winston-Salem, North Carolina; Yale Collection of American Literature, Beinecke Rare Book and Manuscript Library, Yale University, New Haven, Connecticut. As appropriate, permission to use and print materials from each of these institutions is formally and fully acknowledged in the headnotes, texts, and/or annotations contained in this volume.

Albert J. von Frank gratefully acknowledges David M. Robinson for his independent reading of the poem headnotes, texts, and annotations included in this volume; Barbara L. Packer for her critical reading of the Historical Introduction; Ralph H. Orth for his assistance with the translations of Persian poets into German by Joseph von Hammer Purgstall, and Paul Edward Losensky for his assistance with Emerson's Persian poetry; Robert E. Burkholder for his insights into Emerson's "Adirondacs"; Nicolas Kiessling for various forms of help and support; and, as always, Jane von Frank for her immense good will and good cheer and for her smart reading of nearly everything printed in this volume.

Thomas Wortham wishes to acknowledge at the outset his long association as an editor of Emerson's poems with the late Douglas Emory Wilson, who for many years served as a textual editor and a general editor of the *Collected Works;* he also gratefully acknowledges the following persons for their personal support and scholarly assistance as well as their intellectual exchanges with him over the course of his work on this volume: Nan Card, Sean Casey, Anne Garner, Sara Hodson, Megan Mulder, Stephen F. Railton, Joseph M. Thomas, the late Wallace E. Williams, Leslie Perrin Wilson, Elizabeth Hall Witherell, and especially the Rev. John M. Kauffman for his patient companionship. He also expresses appreciation to the American Council of Learned Societies, the American Philosophical Society, and the Committee on Research, UCLA Academic Senate, for their support of his research on this volume.

I am grateful to President George M. Philip, Provost and Vice President for Academic Affairs Susan M. Phillips, Dean of Arts and Sciences Edelgard Wulfert, and Chair (interim) of English Stephen M. North at the University at Albany, State University of New York, for providing me with the intellectual space to fulfill my responsibilities as General Editor of the *Collected Works*. A point of great pride among modern editors of Emerson's writings is that their scholarship is invariably a collaborative venture; in this as well as in earlier volumes of the *Collected Works,* the editors' dependence upon the editorial scholarship evident in *The Journals and Miscellaneous Notebooks, The Letters, The Early Lectures, The Later Lectures, The Poetry Notebooks,* and *The Topical Notebooks of Ralph Waldo Emerson,* and upon that of the editor of *The Letters of Ellen Tucker Emerson,* will be clear. Finally, on behalf of the Editorial Board, I wish to acknowledge the continuing commitment of Harvard University Press to the successful completion of the *Collected Works* edition as a whole. That commitment has been admirably demonstrated by the dedication of the Press's staff to the edition, and by the professionalism with which Executive Editor-at-Large John Gregory Kulka, who is our Press editor, Production Editor Alexander W. Morgan, and book-designer Lisa Roberts have worked with us to see this volume, with all its complexities, into print.

Ronald A. Bosco

CONTENTS

POEMS (1847)

Contents

Contents

MAY-DAY AND OTHER PIECES (1867)

Contents

Contents

SELECTED POEMS (1876)

xvii

Contents

Contents

A NOTE TO THE READER

The entries for each poem in this edition consist of five parts:

1. POEM HEADNOTE. Following the title is a discussion of the poem's sources and composition, including its historical and biographical context. It does not, of course, present a comprehensive critical account, but emphasizes instead the factual background required for an informed study of the poem.

2. THE POEM. The text of the poem has been critically established from a study of all available relevant evidence, among which the most important is the complete historical collation given in the Variants list. See the Textual Introduction below for a full discussion of the methods by which the text has been established.

3. TEXTS. Immediately following the poem itself is a chronological list of the various texts, manuscript and/or printed, that constitute the historical collation, beginning in each case with the copy-text, designated (A). When a text proves to be identical to its immediate predecessor, it is given the same alphabetical designation, but is distinguished serially by superscript numbers. Thus, for example, texts designated (B^2) and (B^3) present no variants compared with text (B), which in turn differs textually from (A), or copy-text. All readings of (B) as given in the list of Variants are to be understood as applying equally to the identical texts (B^2) and (B^3). This use of superscript numbers may be thought of as a way of reporting negative results (the absence of variants), but it will serve also to reassure the reader that these editions and reprintings have in fact been collated rather than ignored, and that,

as a historical matter, they do not exhibit variants, whether the text in question is an unaltered reprint from the same plates as its predecessor or is itself a new edition—that is, a new setting of type. This way of reporting invariant texts also gives the editors an opportunity to provide the location (page numbers) of poems in readily available and historically important collections, including the Riverside and Centenary editions.

The TEXTS section also includes two sub-headings, one dealing with *pre-copy-text forms* (generally referring the reader to relevant sections of *The Poetry Notebooks* or *The Journals and Miscellaneous Notebooks*), and the other summarizing information about historical variations in the *format* of the poem (often having to do with variant patterns of indentation or stanza divisions). The guide to pre-copy-text forms takes the place of the listing of "Parallel Passages," a feature common to all the other volumes in the *Collected Works*.

4. VARIANTS. It is important to note that the editorially adopted reading, keyed to the particular line in the poem, is always given first, and so will always correspond to the reading in the established text. The adopted reading may or may not be that of copy-text (A). In cases where the (A) reading is adopted, all the rejected emendations follow in the list in chronological order, separated one from another by a single vertical line. Where the adopted reading represents an authoritative post-copy-text revision, it is cited first, followed by copy-text form, then by all others in chronological order. If more than one variant occurs in a line the records of each are separated by double vertical lines. Emendations that Emerson entered (or were entered on his behalf) in his personally maintained correction copies (designated CC1 through CC11) are included in the list of variants (see the discussion of these sources in the Textual Introduction, pp. cxiii–cxvii).

5. NOTES. Informational notes keyed to corresponding lines in the poem explain such of Emerson's allusions as are not self-evident or such as are not discussed in the headnote. By and large notes are not provided in explanation of terms included in standard dictionaries.

ABBREVIATIONS

AM	*The Atlantic Monthly Magazine.*
Capper	Charles Capper, *Margaret Fuller: An American Romantic Life.* 2 vols. New York: Oxford University Press, 1992–2007.
CC	Emerson's correction copies. See the list in the Textual Introduction, pp. cxiv–cxvii, below.
CEC	*The Correspondence of Emerson and Carlyle.* Ed. Joseph Slater. New York: Columbia University Press, 1964.
Chronology	Albert J. von Frank. *An Emerson Chronology.* New York and Toronto: G. K. Hall, 1994.
CS	*The Complete Sermons of Ralph Waldo Emerson.* Ed. Albert J. von Frank et al. 4 vols. Columbia: University of Missouri Press, 1989–1992.
CW	*The Collected Works of Ralph Waldo Emerson.* Ed. Alfred R. Ferguson, Joseph Slater, Douglas Emory Wilson, and Ronald A. Bosco, general editors; Robert E. Burkholder, Jean Ferguson Carr, Glen M. Johnson, Joel Myerson, Philip Nicoloff, Barbara L. Packer, Albert J. von Frank, Wallace E. Williams, and Thomas Wortham, editors. 9 vols. to date. Cambridge: The Belknap Press of Harvard University Press, 1971—.
EAW	*Emerson's Antislavery Writings.* Ed. Len Gougeon and Joel Myerson. New Haven: Yale University Press, 1995
EL	*The Early Lectures of Ralph Waldo Emerson, 1833–1842.* Ed. Stephen E. Whicher, Robert E. Spiller, and Wallace E. Williams. 3 vols. Cambridge: The Belknap Press of Harvard University Press, 1959–1972.
ETE	*The Letters of Ellen Tucker Emerson.* Ed. Edith E. W. Gregg. 2 vols. Kent: Kent State University Press, 1982.
FuL	*The Letters of Margaret Fuller.* Ed. Robert N. Hudspeth. 6 vols. Ithaca: Cornell University Press, 1983–1994.
J	Henry David Thoreau, *Journal.* Ed. John C. Broderick et al. 8 vols. to date. Princeton: Princeton University Press, 1981—.
JMN	*The Journals and Miscellaneous Notebooks of Ralph Waldo Emerson.* Ed. William H. Gilman and Ralph H. Orth, chief editors; Linda Allardt, Ronald A. Bosco, George P. Clark, Merrell R. Davis, Harrison Hayford, David W. Hill, Glen M. Johnson, J. E. Parsons, A. W. Plumstead, Merton M. Sealts, Jr., and

	Susan Sutton Smith, editors; Ruth H. Bennett, associate editor. 16 vols. Cambridge: The Belknap Press of Harvard University Press, 1960–1982.
L	*The Letters of Ralph Waldo Emerson.* Ed. Ralph L. Rusk and Eleanor M. Tilton. 10 vols. New York: Columbia University Press, 1939–1995.
LL	*The Later Lectures of Ralph Waldo Emerson, 1843–1871.* Ed. Ronald A. Bosco and Joel Myerson. 2 vols. Athens: University of Georgia Press, 2001.
LLet	*The Letters of Henry Wadsworth Longfellow.* Ed. Andrew Hilen. 6 vols. Cambridge: The Belknap Press of Harvard University Press, 1966–1982.
Myerson	Joel Myerson. *Ralph Waldo Emerson: A Descriptive Bibliography.* Pittsburgh: University of Pittsburgh, 1982.
OED	*The Oxford English Dictionary.* (All references are to the current [2008] online edition.)
OFL	*One First Love: The Letters of Ellen Louisa Tucker to Ralph Waldo Emerson.* Ed. Edith W. Gregg. Cambridge: The Belknap Press of Harvard University Press, 1962.
PN	*The Poetry Notebooks of Ralph Waldo Emerson.* Ed. Ralph H. Orth, Albert J. von Frank, Linda Allardt, and David W. Hill. Columbia: University of Missouri Press, 1986.
Richardson	Robert D. Richardson, Jr., *Emerson: The Mind on Fire.* Berkeley: University of California Press, 1995.
SAR	*Studies in the American Renaissance.* Ed. Joel Myerson. 20 vols. New York: Twayne Publishers, and Charlottesville: University Press of Virginia, 1977–1996.
Strauch, Diss.	Carl F. Strauch, "A Critical and Variorum Edition of the Poems of Ralph Waldo Emerson." Ph.D. Diss., Yale University, 1946.
TN	*The Topical Notebooks of Ralph Waldo Emerson.* Ed. Ralph H. Orth, chief editor; Ronald A. Bosco, Glen M. Johnson, and Susan Sutton Smith, editors; Douglas Emory Wilson, consulting editor. 3 vols. Columbia: University of Missouri Press, 1990–1994.
W	*The Complete Works of Ralph Waldo Emerson.* Ed. Edward Waldo Emerson. Centenary Edition. 12 vols. Boston and New York: Houghton, Mifflin and Company, 1903–1904.

SYMBOLS

(Used in transcribing manuscript text)

↑ ↓   Inserted matter
< >   Deleted matter

Note. Words following a deletion without a space after the second angle bracket are to be understood as occupying the same space as the canceled word or phrase. E.g., <word>phrase. When the canceled matter is followed by a space and the added text is enclosed between up and down arrows, the new wording is to be understood as having been supplied above the line. E.g., <word> ↑phrase↓.

HISTORICAL INTRODUCTION
Albert J. von Frank

At the time of his death on 27 April 1882, Ralph Waldo Emerson was regarded, along with Henry Wadsworth Longfellow, who had died a month earlier, and John Greenleaf Whittier, who had yet another decade to live, as one of America's greatest and most popular poets. Few supposed that Oliver Wendell Holmes or James Russell Lowell were of that class; Walt Whitman labored under a taint of scandal, and Emily Dickinson was unknown. The names of these last two would eventually eclipse the first five, whose public acclaim seemed, especially after the turn of the century, a lingering effect of New England's Victorian past. Yet in many respects Emerson was *sui generis:* he had been held in highest regard as a poet by Longfellow and Whittier, had been ostentatiously hailed as "Master" by Whitman, and had been the subject of a biography by Holmes that included a very appreciative chapter on the poetry. Emerson continued to be crucially important to major twentieth-century poets such as E. A. Robinson, Robert Frost, and Wallace Stevens. And yet, from the very beginning, and in the face of the admiration of the poets, there has been a counter-tradition of critical objection, a long-sustained insistence that as a poet Emerson had too often been technically incompetent, an author of hobbled rhythms and impossible rhymes, a man incapable of writing concretely imagistic, sensuous, and impassioned verse. Although Emerson had at all times numerous enthusiastic critical defenders, he was, for a surprising number of those who took the trouble to comment, not really a poet at all.

Such, for example, was the opinion of Matthew Arnold, who came to Boston in 1883 to announce that while Emerson's poetry "is interesting [and] makes one think," still "it is not the poetry of one of the born poets," and Emerson himself, indeed, was not to be counted as "one of the legitimate poets." Emerson disappointed many readers whose notions of what constituted "legitimate" poetry were either tightly bound to one or another traditional view or else simply arbitrary or idiosyncratic. In his Boston address, Arnold averred that all of Emerson's poetry, taken together, was not worth so much as "The Bridge" by Longfellow or "In School Days" by Whittier, two narrative poems of male nostalgia for the lost romance of childhood. It may be that these very popular poems helped sustain Arnold's announced thesis that American culture not only possessed but celebrated the virtues of youth and immaturity; they also, according to Arnold, satisfied Milton's idea of poetry by being what Emerson's verse never was: "simple, or sensuous, or impassioned."[1] Yet in a way that Arnold could scarcely have imagined, Emerson had long since accepted the Miltonic touchstone, confiding to his journal in 1846, as he assembled his first collection of poems: "There is an unwritten law of Criticism respected by all good scholars, this namely, that when a good book of poems has been once written, say Milton's Minor Poems, no man shall print anything thereafter in that kind less excellent" (*JMN*, IX, 432). In elaborating this idea, he noted that "Wordsworth dismisses a whole regiment of poets from their vocation" (*TN*, II, 185). Emerson's characteristically thoughtful demand for independence and originality—his deliberate aim to do something new in verse—vastly increased the chances that he would disappoint the expectations of many readers (for simplicity, for example, or for the avoidance of what "makes one think"). His approach to the vocation of the poet made it likely that he

1 "Emerson," in *Discourses in America* (London: Macmillan, 1885), 153–154.

would be misunderstood in his aims and that his work would be misjudged in precisely the way that Matthew Arnold misjudged it.

Emerson knew, of course, that his practice of the art was grounded in the same ideas that went to make up his "Transcendentalism," and that it could never be better understood than his philosophy in general. More than any other American poet of the nineteenth century Emerson felt the need to bring explicitly to his audience, in lectures, essays, and poems, the subject of poetics. Beyond trying to make his own practice intelligible, he meant to combat the besetting narrowness of popular critical judgment, which, in his view, never asked enough of the artist in verse or prose. His essay "The Poet" (1844) is a theoretical statement unmatched in the challenges it posed to the conventional assessments of the art of poetry. Emerson's dramatically aggrandized figure of the Poet is the point on which the conceptual ambition of his essay may be seen to exceed that of other manifestos of the period, including Whitman's own very Emersonian Preface to *Leaves of Grass* (1855). And yet, like the "Language" chapter of *Nature* (1836), "The Poet" has a presence, as a locus of American romantic theory, that does not so much serve to illuminate as to overshadow the poetry—even to preempt its place as a satisfactory object of the reader's attention. It has often seemed, in short, that the theory was in many respects finer than the practice, "The Poet" than the poetry.

And yet, this is precisely Emerson's contention. Poetry is not "ideal" in anything like the way that theory is, but always and necessarily a useful betrayal of the ideal: "For poetry was all written before time was, and whenever we are so finely organized that we can penetrate into that region where the air is music, we hear those primal warblings, and attempt to write them down, but we lose ever and anon a word, or a verse, and substitute something of our own, and thus miswrite the poem" (*CW,* III, 5–6). To assume that such statements amount to a disavowal of the work of authorship or to infer that Emerson endorses a literal notion of inspiration is seriously to misconstrue the place and function of theory in his poetics, which is frequently, as here, to express how the poet participates in heaven (or "that region where the air is music") by a specific kind of openness to it, including the ability, in the first place, to posit its existence as a useful conceptual space. Were it not for the fallen (or short-fallen) language of poets, we might never become conscious of the perfect realm of meaning with which such language is in compromise. In the sequential experience of reading "The Poet," one understands that the oddity of the sentence about transcribing the music of the spheres is that its meaning is not contained within the sentence but is in a process of evolution not unlike a living thing: if there is at first the slightly comic suggestion that the poet is a secretary poorly taking dictation, the notion soon makes way for a model of organic relations involving a necessary "abandonment to the nature of things," for when the "pre-cantations" are once again overheard some pages later in the essay, then "the intellect is released from all service," and in that preconditional freedom of abandonment "new passages are opened for us into nature, the mind flows into and through things hardest and highest, and the metamorphosis is possible" (*CW,* III, 15–16). The process that a moment earlier had been figured as passive and slightly comic has now become active and heroic. In a characteristically Emersonian contradiction, what was first impressed now in turn impresses. Emerson of course had many ways of saying this, of asserting the rule of the mind (or the "Me") over that which can at times seem intransigently opposite to mind—physical nature (or the "Not-Me"). In "Monadnoc," he observed that "Adamant is soft to wit" (line 271), implying that mind may bring the very stones to life. In one of the most interesting of Emerson's unpublished quatrains, he said:

> Ever the Rock of Ages melts
> Into the mineral air
> To be the quarry whence to build
> Thought & its mansion fair[.] (*TN,* III, 341–342)

The lines make a metaphor out of chemistry and theology, implying that processes of transformation and subliming—of the sort that in certain versions poets are concerned with—may turn the spiritual elements of Christianity no less than the mineral elements of earth into thought, the stuff of life and growth.[2]

Against the background of a popular culture in which the uses of poetry were almost entirely decorative or commemorative, comfortingly moralistic, reassuringly sentimental, or bracingly regulatory, the uses that Emerson announced might well seem eccentric and in need of careful explanation. In a certain sense the explanations embedded in his theoretical statements were indeed carefully crafted, though in another and perhaps more obvious sense they were deliberately extravagant and provocative. The poet is "the man without impediment" (*CW*, III, 5); poets are "liberating gods" (17). Emerson tasks his reader with understanding how these propositions are more than mere approving enthusiasm. The poet "unfixes the land and the sea, makes them revolve around the axis of his primary thought, and disposes them anew. Possessed himself by a heroic passion, he uses matter as symbols of it" (*Nature, CW*, I, 31). In regard to such language two observations might be made: first, that Emerson speaks of the Poet, rhetorically, much as Jonathan Edwards had spoken of the majesty of God, not incorrectly, but on the understanding that no form of exaltation or tall talk can overstate the miracle or be even so much as adequate to the amazing facts; and, second, that no actual poetry, written under the sponsorship of these exaltations, could ever be supposed to vindicate the claims. It is a mistake, however, to be scandalized by this gulf between theory and practice, promise and performance, though being so scandalized has always of-

2 Emerson's quatrain develops a frequently illustrated topos: for example, love may melt "boundary mountains . . . into air" (*JMN*, V, 294), or, in the conversation of idealists, according to Emerson's brother Charles, "the world begins to dislimn" (*JMN*, V, 99). See *PN*, 783–784, for additional examples. Such speculation may ultimately derive from the myth of Orpheus, who, as Margaret Fuller noted, "understood nature, and made her forms move to his music" (*Woman in the Nineteenth Century* [New York: Greeley & McElrath, 1845], 12). In her poem on this topic—at the same location—Fuller says that "Each Orpheus . . . Must melt all rocks free from their primal pain, / Must search all nature with his one soul's fire, / Must bind anew all forms in heavenly chain."

fered an easy way to express a lack of sympathy with Emerson's project. If there had been no theory there would have been no practice, just as any performance arises from a prior promise. It is much more useful, then, to understand that Emerson's poetry is what it is because, in the decade between 1834 and 1844, he developed an exquisitely nuanced and elegant theory of expression that was also, in relation to the corresponding positions of his contemporaries, almost entirely original. Its purpose was not to describe a process scientifically (as Poe pretended to do in the hyper-rationalist "Philosophy of Composition"), but to provide a way—indeed an essentially poetic way—of representing the importance of the process and of what was at stake in its conduct.

There can be no mistaking the fact that before the crucial decade leading up to the publication of his first book of poems in 1846, a decade prolific in theoretical statements and associated poems, Emerson's poetic sensibility was transformed, such that a clear line of demarcation may be drawn between the juvenile and apprentice verse that predominated before 1830 and the mature work that began to appear in 1834. Carl F. Strauch first identified this sea-change in an essay published in 1955, and although his conclusions have not been seriously challenged since, the reasons *why* 1834 should have been "The Year of Emerson's Poetic Maturity," as Strauch called it, continue to be explored.[3]

I. The First Period

The earliest poem by Ralph Waldo Emerson of which evidence survives is a composition called "The Sabbath." It was drafted in the author's ninth year, in 1812 or 1813, and sounds very much as one would expect a poem to sound written at that time and place by a boy of that age, living in the household of the widow of a protestant minister. Its seventh and concluding stanza reads:

3 Carl F. Strauch, "The Year of Emerson's Poetic Maturity: 1834," *Philological Quarterly*, XXXIV (October 1955): 353–377.

Make resolutions on this day,
Do what is right without delay,
And after death you'll have reward,
And live forever with the Lord.[4]

The remarkable thing is that while Emerson moved on to more ambitious topics and to more complex poetic structures, and while he clearly at all times delighted in the writing of poetry, what he wrote did not, with few exceptions, exceed "what one would expect" for another twenty years. If there was, in poetry, a "stairway of surprise," Emerson was not precocious in finding it.[5]

Most of these early poems were meant to be performed, either in declamatory recitation or in song, and the point of the eloquence was, by sounding well, to stir an audience. It was a good indicator of what Emerson's earliest interest in writing came to that he would say, in 1816, that "even Nonsense sounds good if cloth'd in the dress of Poetry" (*L*, I, 25). This rather cynical point was not thrown away even on older hands, for when William Cullen Bryant came to write his Phi Beta Kappa Poem for the 1821 Harvard commencement, he was cannily reassured that "an indifferent poem, if it could be spoken in a fine manner, would achieve an undoubted success."[6] In the raw culture of early Federalist New England poetry was apt to be confused with oratory, its success bound up in alien traits and extrinsic glories. Estimable poetry was neither "written" nor "being written," but typically came bound in tidy leather volumes, either from the holds of English ships or from the native publisher who dealt in reprints: in either case it naturally came to hand with a classic Old World pedigree. In 1841 Emerson recalled how astonished he had been

---

4 See Albert J. von Frank, "Emerson's Boyhood and Collegiate Verse: Unpublished and New Texts Edited from Manuscript," *SAR 1983*, pp. 1–56. Poem on p. 21. Subsequent quotations from the juvenile verse are from this edition.

5 For "the stairway of surprise," see "Merlin, I," line 38.

6 Quoted in Parke Godwin, *A Biography of William Cullen Bryant, with Extracts from His Private Correspondence*, 2 vols. (New York: D. Appleton, 1883), I, 171.

at college by hints of an authentic domestic culture, "by tidings that genius had appeared in a youth who sat near me at table," who had written "hundreds of lines," by which, for him, "all was changed, man, beast, heaven, earth, & sea" (*JMN*, VIII, 83). Only rare "genius" commanded the metamorphosis, as he would eventually believe. He would discover that the youthful eloquence he had courted was no more, after all, than a fine-sounding game, one that showed its fault precisely by leaving everything in place and quite unchanged. "Talent may frolic and juggle," Emerson would say; "genius realizes and adds" (*CW*, III, 7).

That insight was won over the course of a long apprenticeship to eloquence, the one attainment most prominently held out by an educational system that tried to culminate in lawyers and preachers. Benjamin Apthorp Gould, Emerson's teacher at the Boston Latin School, had cast at his own expense bronze medals inscribed "Palma Eloquentiæ" to encourage worthy students.[7] Ralph, as he was then still called, though he wrote and delivered the formal "English Poem" for the Latin School's public exercises in 1815 and again in 1816, never received the award. Both poems, the first on "Independence," the second on "Eloquence," contrived to feature Emerson's classical hero, Demosthenes, "great Prince of Eloquence sublime, / Whose name shall triumph o'er the wreck of time" (30). In both poems Demosthenes personified eloquence as a public and political force—the kind of useful, worldly, rhetorical power that Emerson would later find concentrated in Daniel Webster, but never in Jesus or Hafiz or Shakespeare or Swedenborg—never in any poet, expansively defined, whom he admired. Emerson's mature view, given in the "Ode Inscribed to W. H. Channing" (1846), was that political eloquence tends to be morally suspect (a "trick") and is regularly—one might say "constitutionally"—antithetical to the eloquence of real poets.

During his early years Emerson regarded his passion for poetry as essentially unserious on the one hand—as an infatuation he

7 Ralph L. Rusk, *The Life of Ralph Waldo Emerson* (New York: Charles Scribner's Sons, 1949), 57.

would soon have to give up—yet also, on the other hand, as providing a kind of shelter from the horrors of ordinary life. In 1817, as he began his Harvard studies, he wrote to his brother William some lines of anxious complaint in doggerel:

> That is—poor Ralph must versify,
> Through College *like a thousand drums*
> But when well *through* then then oh my
> The dark dull *night* of *Business* comes. (*L*, I, 42)

These homely, half-embarrassed lines are perhaps the earliest indication that, for Emerson, poetry would serve throughout his life in ever more subtle ways its purpose of rebuke to the unimaginative and unexpressive life. His ideas about poetry and its place in the world would be continuously in dialogue with his feelings about what presented itself as *not* poetry. In this way genuine eloquence is always as much a protest as a celebration. What he could not imagine at this early period was the combination of poetry and any reputable vocation. In late 1824 or early in 1825, as he was about to enter the Harvard Divinity School, he bade farewell to the "Books, Muses, Study, fireside, friends and love" that he had known—because

> . . . I, the bantling of a country Muse,
> Abandon all those toys with speed to obey
> The King whose meek ambassador I go. (*W*, IX, 385; cf. *JMN*,
>   II, 404–405)

Eloquence, to which in March 1823 he dedicated his journal Wide World 10 (*JMN*, II, 104–105), had been, since the days of his preoccupation with Demosthenes, an attribute of secular oratory and was never strongly connected either to prose or to poetry—and even less to the public performance of ministers in sermons. Beginning about 1823, however, Emerson was more attuned to the religious uses of eloquence, as instanced in his reaction to hearing a "discourse upon Revelation" by William Ellery Channing, in which the language "was a transparent medium, conveying with the utmost distinctness, the pictures in his mind, to the minds of the hearers" (*JMN*, II, 160–161). It was as if the stunning efficiency of expression emanating from Channing in the Federal Street pulpit on 12 October 1823 exemplified the sermon's thesis, which was that God's word of revelation was more to be relied upon as a vehicle of truth than nature itself. Words, it turned out, could be more to the purpose than things, even if (as the reference to "pictures" implies) language had been understood (following John Locke) as a system of abstract and arbitrary counters for things that are concretely real and not arbitrary. The effect of Channing on Emerson at this time was significant for offering a reformulated and more pertinent model of eloquence. That Channing's language was admirably "a transparent medium," transferred Emerson's approval at once away from the attention-centering trumpery of classical rhetoric and attached it to the interior, character-based resources that romantic theory stressed. In a long stock-taking journal entry, written as he entered on his "professional studies" in the spring of 1824, Emerson acknowledged that there was very little in his temperament or intellect to qualify him for the ministry, but he hoped that his "strong imagination & . . . keen relish for the beauties of poetry" would be compensations on which to rely—given that "the highest species of reasoning upon divine subjects is rather the fruit of a sort of moral imagination, than of the 'Reasoning Machines' such as Locke & Clarke & David Hume." Eloquence was now to be lavished on the poetic qualities of prose, particularly in the sermon form. "Dr. Channing's Dudleian Lecture is the model of what I mean, and the faculty which produced this is akin to the higher flights of the fancy. I may add that the preaching most in vogue at the present day depends chiefly on imagination for its success, and asks those accomplishments which I believe are most within my grasp" (*JMN*, II, 238).[8] Channing's own position, as Emerson

8 The campaign of New England ministers to appropriate the prestige of classical (literary) eloquence in the study of the Bible is well treated by Lawrence Buell in "Unitarian Aesthetics and Emerson's Poet-Priest," *American Quarterly*, XX (Spring 1968): 3–20, and in his *New England Literary Culture: From Revolu-*

well knew, was that the expressive power of ministers was a function of how well and how feelingly they could represent their own experience:

> In such an age [as the present], earnestness should characterize the ministry; and by this I mean, not a louder voice or a more vehement gesture; I mean no tricks of oratory, but a solemn conviction that religion is a great concern, and a solemn purpose that its claims shall be felt by others. To suit such an age, a minister must communicate religion, not only as a result of reasoning, but as a matter of experience, with that inexpressible character of reality, that life and power, which accompany truths drawn from a man's own soul. We ought to speak of religion as something which we ourselves know.[9]

The birth of Unitarianism in the 1820s had much to do with the influence of the Second Great Awakening, which also and more particularly underlay Channing's concern with the need for a special enlivening power in the language of preaching. He was alert, as some of his Unitarian colleagues were not, to conceptions of power broached by the new European romanticism and saw that these must eventuate in a modernizing revision of taste. Thus he advised ministers to make use of the resources of contemporary poetry, which, he said, "has a deeper and more impressive tone than comes to us from what has been called the Augustan age of English literature."[10] In fact, despite the earliest influence on Emerson of Alexander Pope and John Dryden, Edward Young and William Cowper, by way of the popular taste, his strongest enthusiasms in poetry actually lay on either side of this "Augustan

---

tion through Renaissance (Cambridge and New York: Cambridge University Press, 1986), 166–190.

9 "The Demands of the Age on the Ministry: Discourse at the Ordination of the Rev. E. S. Gannett. Boston, 1824." *The Works of William E. Channing, D. D.* 8th ed., 6 vols. (Boston: James Munroe, 1848), III, 147–148.

10 Ibid., III, 146.

age": he had a reputation in college, for example, as an expert reader of Shakespeare, and came then and later to an appreciation of Byron and (more permanently) of Wordsworth. His aunt Mary Moody Emerson had a strong, shaping influence on his taste in poetry, both by encouraging his boyhood composition of hymns and later (and more importantly) by pointing him to Wordsworth's evocative meditations on nature. Self-taught as she was, she had nevertheless been an appreciative reader of the *Lyrical Ballads* as early as 1805. She managed as well to communicate to her nephew an enthusiasm for Milton. According to a well known story she had become enamored of a poem that she knew only from an old, tattered copy, lacking spine and title-page, that she discovered in the rubbish of an attic—and only much later found that it was *Paradise Lost*. But, important as these influences were, it was finally Channing and the force of his timely example that had become the wedge to separate Emerson from the aesthetics of the foregoing generations (*JMN*, II, 239). Lawrence Buell has pointed out the importance to Emerson of Channing's great essay on Milton, which carried an encouraging endorsement of his subject's view that "of all God's gifts of intellect . . . poetical genius [is] the most transcendent."[11]

II. The Transition

In 1830 Emerson was an earnest, occasionally interesting, but essentially unremarkable young Unitarian minister. By the winter of 1834–1835, when he declared himself a poet in a letter to his future second wife, Lydia Jackson, he was well positioned to be, for the rest of his career, the central voice of American literary Romanticism. This brief five-year period of transformation included most of his ministry at the Second Church, where he had been

11 Buell, *Literary Transcendentalism: Style and Vision in the American Renaissance* (Ithaca: Cornell University Press, 1973), 37. For Mary Moody Emerson and the English poets see Phyllis Cole, *Mary Moody Emerson and the Origins of Transcendentalism: A Family History* (New York: Oxford University Press, 1998), 87–88, 119–120.

ordained in March 1829 and which he left in December 1832 following a dispute with his congregation over formalism in religion. It included also most of his first marriage: he had wed Ellen Louisa Tucker in September 1829 and she had died after an extended period of debility, from tuberculosis, on 8 February 1831 at the age of nineteen. The period included as well Emerson's physically and spiritually restorative first trip to Europe (1832–1833), at which time he met Wordsworth, Coleridge, and Carlyle—and, distinctly unintimidated, laid plans for a life in literature. Immediately upon his return to Boston, in November 1833, he began his nearly fifty-year career as a lecturer, intending at first only that these performances should contribute to the already projected "book about Nature" that he hoped might make his reputation as a man of letters. At the outset of this period he was a novice minister, shrewdly introspective but otherwise of seemingly limited talents, who aspired to poetic flourishes in his sermons. He emerged from it not so much a Transcendentalist as *the* Transcendentalist —and a major American poet.

If Emerson achieved his mature poetic voice by the conclusion of this tumultuous interval, it was principally owing, as Carl F. Strauch argued, to his immersion in the writings of Joseph de Gérando, Ralph Cudworth, Emanuel Swedenborg, J. W. von Goethe, and Samuel Taylor Coleridge, who, along with Victor Cousin and Thomas Carlyle, effected a revolution in the young minister's thinking, and comprised the principal sources of his new, platonically inflected "First Philosophy," out of which *Nature* (1836) would be written.[12] Emerson undertook his ambitious program of study once he had satisfactorily arranged his circumstances—that is to say, as soon as he was happily married and set-

12 Strauch, "The Year of Emerson's Poetic Maturity: 1834," 353–377. On Emerson's writing of *Nature,* see Albert J. von Frank, "The Composition of *Nature:* Writing and the Self in the Launching of a Career," in James Barbour and Tom Quirk, eds., *Biographies of Books: The Compositional Histories of Notable American Writings* (Columbia: University of Missouri Press, 1996), 11–40, and Merton M. Sealts, Jr., and Alfred R. Ferguson, eds., *Emerson's* Nature: *Origin, Growth, Meaning,* 2nd ed., enl. (Carbondale and Edwardsville: Southern Illinois University Press, 1979).

tled at a prestigious Boston church (the one at which Increase and Cotton Mather had anciently officiated). He shared this charged atmosphere of venturesome modern thought with his favorite intellectual companion, his brilliant brother Charles. The immediate effect of Emerson's new European teachers—especially of Coleridge and Carlyle—was to weaken the authority of external (i.e., traditional or historically sanctioned) precepts and to cultivate a nearly (at times an entirely) Antinomian confidence in the subjective realm of individual consciousness. It also directed his researches toward Kant and J. G. Fichte, who regarded the world as, for all intents and purposes, a mental construct. These men, along with theologian Friedrich Schleiermacher and "subversive" biblical scholars such as Johann Gottfried von Herder and Jacob Eichhorn (associated in the new "Higher Criticism"), conveyed what seemed to the ministerial profession in New England —the Unitarian ranks in particular—like a dangerous challenge to the preeminence of John Locke and the Scottish Commonsense philosophers in Anglo-American thought.[13]

13 On the German background the best sources are, first, the pioneering work of Octavius Brooks Frothingham in *Transcendentalism in New England* (New York: Putnam's, 1876), 1–59, then, in the current scholarship, Barbara L. Packer, *The Transcendentalists* (Athens: University of Georgia Press, 2007), Elisabeth Hurth, *Between Faith and Unbelief: American Transcendentalism and the Challenge of Atheism* (Leiden: Brill, 2007), and two works by Philip F. Gura: *The Wisdom of Words: Language, Theology, and Literature in the New England Renaissance* (Middletown, Conn.: Wesleyan University Press, 1981) and *American Transcendentalism: A History* (New York: Knopf, 2007). See also Robert D. Richardson, Jr., "Schleiermacher and the Transcendentalists," in Charles Capper and Conrad Edick Wright, eds., *Transient and Permanent: The Transcendentalist Movement and Its Contexts* (Boston: Massachusetts Historical Society, 1999), 121–147. The differential bearing of the German "Higher Criticism" on the Transcendentalists and on conservative Unitarians such as Andrews Norton is a complicated issue: see Packer, "Origin and Authority: Emerson and the Higher Criticism," in Sacvan Bercovitch, ed., *Reconstructing American Literary History* (Cambridge, Mass.: Harvard University Press, 1986), 67–92. The relevant fact for Emerson's poetry is that Herder and Eichhorn chose to study the Bible as if it signified in the same way that other works of literature or of the mythic imagination did: that is to say, not as the inerrant word of God or as an inevitable rallying point for historical and theological orthodoxy, but rather as Oriental fable, with a good deal of

Because the influence of Locke and the Scottish philosophers was concentrated (and more than a little consecrated) at Harvard, and because the insurgent German influences were being developed by a cadre of Harvard students and young ministers, a conflict soon arose between what looked like a powerful, entrenched, time-honored, profession-protecting institution on the one hand and obstreperous young heretics on the other. The conflict, which Emerson rehearsed in his poem "Uriel," did not break out into the open until 1836, but it had been simmering quietly for years before that, and this simmering was a main context for the transition in Emerson's thinking from Arminianism to Antinomianism.[14] Being a heretic is not altogether disadvantageous, especially to a poet, though it does not generally conduce to good reviews, as Emerson would eventually discover. Mainly it promotes independent thought. It fosters and makes a value of original relations to the universe. But more to the point, as shown by the invariant history of heretical movements, it entails thinking differently at an especially deep level. "Inspiration" or "enthusiasm" is the typical hallmark of Antinomian, Gnostic, and transcendental positions, so that, whether it is Anne Hutchinson claiming direct communication with God, the Quaker determined to follow an "inner light," the ecstatic Sufi poet-teacher, or the ancient Valentinian heretic guided by some "gnosis" or esoteric doctrine of the pneumatic elect, all evoke an epistemology of unassailable inwardness, an aspiration after a perfect, apocalyptic understanding, a suspension of respect for historic precedent and public institutions, and a reliance instead on a poetic or deliberately non-standard, indirect, or elliptical mode of expression. The aim was to teach not as one had carefully learned, *ab extra,* from the past, but, as Emerson declared in 1830, "as one having authority" in the present (*JMN,*

"play" in it. See, for example, on this point, *EL,* III, 274. Arguably, this change in perspective applied the same kind of shock to the text as the Gnostics achieved with their creatively subversive reworkings of canonical narratives.

14 "The first Emerson was an Arminian." See Daniel B. Shea, "Emerson and the American Metamorphosis," in David Levin, ed., *Emerson: Prophecy, Metamorphosis, and Influence* (New York: Columbia University Press, 1975), 35.

III, 185; Matt. 7:29). The idea was to speak, as Jesus had, a language of the kingdom of God.[15]

The crisis that separated Emerson from his church was just such an epistemological reorientation away from conventional, conformable ways of being in the world and toward the heretical stance. His advancing Antinomianism is fully documented in the journals and sermons of this period, including the well known—not to say notorious—"Lord's Supper Sermon," in which he defended his preference for an inward and active as opposed to a memorial and formal faith. On 1 October 1832, as he was deciding to resign his pastorate, he wrote accusingly of himself:

> Instead of making Christianity a vehicle of truth you make truth only a horse for Christianity. It is a very operose way of making people good. You must be humble because Christ says, "Be humble." "But why must I obey Christ?" "Because God sent him." But how do I know God sent him? "Because your own heart teaches the same thing he taught." Why then shall I not go to my own heart at first? (*JMN*, IV, 45)

He was learning that to speak originally and not from an accurate or inaccurate recollection of what some other person had once said involved a less deferential and therefore heightened management of meaning—a process consistent with (though certainly more radical than) Channing's intent of renovation in his advice that "We ought to speak of religion as something which we ourselves know." One might offer this advice, as Channing did, on the ground that the interests of religion would thereby be served, or, one might receive it, as Emerson the incipient poet likely did, on the ground that language would thereby gain power.

Indeed this last—the relation of authentic language to poetry—was the point from which Emerson's journal entry had taken off. He had extemporized his parable of Christian truth-speaking in response to raw materials far-fetched from *The Edinburgh Review*—from Thomas Carlyle's essay on the verse of Ebenezer Elliott, the

15 Gura, *The Wisdom of Words,* 77.

"Corn-Law Rhymer." Carlyle had praised the poetry by saying of its author that he was "*genuine,*" an "earnest, truth-speaking man" who "has used his eyes for seeing [and] his tongue for declaring what he had seen." "The thing that he speaks is not a hearsay," Carlyle insisted, "but a thing which he has himself known, and by experience become assured of." He "has worked himself loose from cant, and conjectural halfness, idle pretenses and hallucinations, into a condition of Sincerity."[16] The impressive energy of Carlyle's language on this point testifies to his disgust at the blight of falseness in modern discourse. Channing, as we have seen, had earlier voiced an identical lament, and by 1832 Emerson had reason to feel the same about the linguistic practices (including his own) that upheld a merely formal religion. The last sermon Emerson delivered as pastor of the Second Church, on 21 October 1832, was not "The Lord's Supper," but one entitled "The Genuine Man" (*CS*, IV, 201–208). It is hard to estimate the effect that these matters had on Emerson's view of poetry and language, but clearly sincerity and authenticity had come to replace formal rhetoric as the hallmark of the highest eloquence. The power of language reflected the absolute amount of life implicated in it.

No event in Emerson's personal crisis of the early 1830s was more shattering or more fraught with long-term consequences than the death of his young wife Ellen, nor was any event more closely connected with poetry. During the courtship and marriage (1828–1830) Emerson wrote no fewer than eleven amatory poems, including two ("To Ellen, at the South" and "To Eva") that he would publish some years later, first in the *Dial,* and again in *Poems* (1847).[17] Following Ellen's death in February 1831 he wrote twenty additional poems, many of them fragments, expressing his profound grief and a bewildered sense of loss.[18] This body of po-

16 "Corn-Law Rhymes" (1832), *Critical and Miscellaneous Essays* (Philadelphia: A. Hart, 1850), 368.

17 The unpublished verses may be found in *PN*, 10–11, 61, 69; *JMN*, II, 410–411, III, 151, 181–182; and *OFL*, 25, and 127.

18 For these, mostly written in the summer of 1831, see *PN*, 14–15, 18, 36–37, 47, 121–122, 342; *JMN*, III, 228–235, 285–286; and four additional manuscript fragments first published in *Ralph Waldo Emerson: Collected Poems and Trans-*

etry, both the lover's addresses and the elegiac laments, are essential documents in their author's emotional life, but they also play a pivotal role in the development of Emerson's mature poetic style. Because they are the first of his poems to be deeply occupied with the intimate sphere, Emerson was compelled to adapt his language to the near audience, matching, as it were, the unpretentious diction of Ellen's own poems.[19]

> She promised in my secret ear
> When none but God & I could hear
> That she would cleave to me forever[.] (*JMN*, III, 285)

In 1847 Emerson said of her poetry that it was "very sweet, and on the way to all high merits and yet as easy as breathing to her who wrote it" (*OFL*, 147)—strangely forgetting that for her, at that time, breathing had often been the hardest thing of all. Death figured largely and persistently in her verse, as, for example, in her lines "To the South Wind":

> O come not now to lure
> Me back to earth again
> That moment I was sure
> I felt the latest pain.
> And yet ye're heaven's messenger
> And bear soft words to me;
> But breathe not yet, but wait until
> My spirit is set free.
>
> Then whisper round my grave
> The tale of my release—(*OFL*, 159)

---

lations, ed. Harold Bloom and Paul Kane (New York: Library of America, 1994), 333–335.

19 The first verses that Emerson ever published ("Fame" and "William Rufus and the Jew" appeared in an 1829 gift-book edited by Andrews Norton of the Harvard Divinity School) were also the last that he thought suitable for presentation to a teacher—the last, that is to say, in the category of juvenile poems essentially designed for public display. Ellen's quiet, sentimental poems were published in *OFL*, 147–161.

The meaning of the tale of her release was terrifically difficult to declare, though most of Emerson's poetic fragments of 1831 struggle with the task. In these broken laments her death astonishes, leaving him bereft and perplexed because it has defeated their communion, defeated the real life of words that more than all else had made them one. Even the fragmentary character of the poems has meaning. In the midst of his "one first love" he had said,

> . . . never shall the hour appear
> In sunny joy, in sorrow's gloom,
> When aught shall hinder me from telling
> My ardent love, all loves excelling. (*PN*, 10)

But in the supervention of death he would say,

> She never comes to me
> Sits never by my side
> I never hear her voice
> She comes not even to my dreams[.] (*JMN*, III, 285)

As noted by Robert D. Richardson, Jr., Emerson's faith, going into this event, was, like Ellen's, "time-honored and conventionally Christian."[20] Visions of bright heaven and interceding angels softened the blow for both, and Ellen died beautifully and resignedly. His fantasy that she was still somehow an alert benefactor, a hovering presence, was almost too comforting to relinquish: "Teach me I am forgotten by the dead / And that the dead is by herself forgot / And I no longer would keep terms with me" (*JMN*, III, 228). But the implied or assumed imperative from Ellen, "Do this in remembrance of me," faded along with the hallucinations of a theologically reified personhood. Communion could no longer be predicated on history or embodiment, even though Emerson is said to have walked out every day to her grave in Roxbury. In the event, as Henry F. Pommer concluded, "Immortality

20 *Emerson: The Mind on Fire* (Berkeley: University of California Press, 1995), 108–109.

was left sadly unpropped," and Emerson's hold on a conventional Christianity was released forever.[21]

The argument that these events precipitated Emerson's "second birth" (Richardson, 110) seems sound, however unorthodox and complex the meaning one must assign to it. The events were undeniably a baptism in Eros and Thanatos and from this point forward Emerson would importantly rely on a sort of Shekinah, or female principle of creative inspiration, represented to him in one sense, and most commonly, by "Muse," but more specifically by actual women, by such proximate New England "nuns" as Elizabeth Hoar, Mary Moody Emerson, Margaret Fuller, and, most powerfully of all, by Caroline Sturgis, figures that of necessity make their many crucial appearances in the headnotes to the poems that follow.

The period of transition closed as Emerson found ways of coming to terms with Ellen's death. Late in 1831 he recorded an accusation by certain of his Second Church parishioners that "I treat death with unbecoming indifference and do not make the case my own, or, if I do, err in my judgment" (*JMN*, III, 312). On 29 March 1832, by then more than a year a widower, Emerson "visited Ellen's tomb & opened the coffin" (*JMN*, IV, 7). By then he was reading Plotinus, embracing that writer's Neoplatonic view of the spirit and sympathizing readily with his contempt for the flesh and corresponding devotion to the mind. It was an anti-cosmic position frequently associated with Gnostic circles, and it led Emerson deeper into that repertoire of heresy with which the Transcendentalist movement would soon be charged—including, for example, the view that the soul after death "is merged or reabsorbed into the infinite" or that no human attribute but "selfishness . . . desires an individual immortality."[22] The death that was so

21 *Emerson's First Marriage* (Carbondale and Edwardsville: Southern Illinois University Press, 1967), 75.

22 [William J. Pabodie], "The Dial," *Providence Daily Journal*, 27 July 1840, p. 2. He is apparently recalling Emerson's 1837 lecture on "Religion" (see *EL*, II, 83–97, esp. 91). On Emerson's reading of *The Select Works of Plotinus*, in the translation by Thomas Taylor, see Richardson, 110, and Harding, 217.

busy around Emerson in the early to mid 1830s (claiming also his brothers Edward, in 1834, and Charles, in 1836) greatly clarified the point that art could only be in the service of life: "Genius," as he said in "The Poet," "is the activity which repairs the decays of things" (*CW,* III, 13). In consequence of the increasingly radical idealism of his outlook, thought and meaning would dominate in his poetry over persons and narratives and the concrete sensual imagery of external nature.

III. Metamorphosis

In December 1834 Emerson began to enter fair copies of recently written poems in a new notebook, entitled "P" (for Poetry), fulfilling a plan to "save my <live> verse" (*JMN,* IV, 353; *PN,* 16). This notebook would be his principal repository of rough drafts and fair copies for more than ten years—all through the period of the *Dial* and down to the moment when he first determined to collect his poems in a book.[23] His typical procedure, especially for short poems, was to begin by versifying some prose germ, generally lifted from the journals, writing a draft in pencil and correcting as he went along. There is reason to believe that in some cases he extemporized poems during walks in the woods or, in at least one case ("The Problem"), while sitting in his pew at church, and only later wrote them down. Most often he would open his notebook at random, so that, unfortunately, little can now be inferred from the relative positions of the drafts. As a rule, the earlier the draft in the sequence of a poem's composition the less punctuation it had, though it is not unusual to find that even final fair copies are only lightly pointed. Evidently, in his verse Emerson used punctu-

---

23 Over the course of his life Emerson devoted nine notebooks to this purpose. Their titles and the approximate respective dates of use are as follows: Charleston, S.C., St. Augustine, Fla. (1827–1834), P (1834–1845), X (1845–1851), EF (1846–1853), EL (1849–1867), Rhymer (1851–1864), NP ("New Poetry") (1857–1868), KL[A] (used for "May-Day" in 1865), and ETE Verses (1867–1875). Published and analyzed in *PN,* these notebooks offer a superb view of Emerson's compositional habits and are an indispensable resource for students of his poetry.

ation as much to indicate rhythms as to manage syntax, which is not at all to say that it was a matter of indifference to him. Since a notebook draft would be seen only by its author, commas and the like could easily be dispensed with, the tune continuing reliably in his head.[24] In some cases ("Each and All," for instance), Emerson might leave a first draft and not return to it until years later; he might then begin again on a new page, using the text of the first draft for a kind of running start—in which case, frugal Yankee that he was, he would often erase the preceding draft and use the page once more for something else. The taking up of pen and ink meant that the poem was to him in satisfactory, if not always final, shape.

Although he sometimes implied that true poets wrote fluently under a kind of inspiration and although some of his own poems came easily, Emerson at least revised and revised carefully. All but a few of his poems exist, reworked, in multiple drafts. He understood workmanship and deplored the lack of it in other poets, including his friend the younger William Ellery Channing, whose great genius, he believed, was crossed with a lazy indifference to criticism and correctness. Jones Very likewise leaned a bit too conspicuously on inspiration—often at the expense of good spelling and decent grammar.[25] Emerson never denied that the effect a work of art aims at—a perfectly organic grace and wholeness, or

24 Poems that Emerson published in the *Dial* (1840–1844) tend likewise to be underpunctuated relative to the revised form they had in *Poems* (1847). This phenomenon may best be understood in terms of the need to control other people's readings or to conform them to Emerson's intended patterns, in which case the additional punctuation (the heart of the system is the promotion of commas to semicolons) becomes a direct measure of the alienation of the poem from the poet. As a separate matter Emerson contended that "a perfect sentence," because it "makes its own feet, [and] creates its own form," stands in no real need of punctuation (*JMN*, IV, 290). "Write solid sentences & you can even spare punctuation" (*JMN*, IV, 273).

25 "New Poetry," *Dial*, I (October 1840): 220–232. Joel Myerson's sketch of Channing in *The New England Transcendentalists and the* Dial: *A History of the Magazine and Its Contributors* (Rutherford, N.J.: Fairleigh Dickinson University Press, 1980), 107–114, provides a fine short account of Channing's stubborn eccentricities and Emerson's tried patience.

fitness of form to meaning—is often the product of much laborious chisel-work. "The poem, the oration, the book are superhuman," Emerson said, "but the wonder is out when you see the manuscript" (*JMN*, IV, 285).

The wonder goes back in, however, when the deeper sources rather than the means of production are considered. Emerson's well known poem "The Snow-Storm," for example, one of the four works on which Carl Strauch based his argument for the importance of 1834 as a turning point in the poet's development, grew out of a series of experiences—internal and, as it were, external—that took place from mid to late December of that year. Emerson was then living in the Old Manse, the Concord home of his step-grandfather, the Reverend Ezra Ripley. It had been a snowy month. On Sunday morning 14 December he drove alone by sleigh eleven miles to the town of East Sudbury to preside over morning and afternoon services at the Unitarian church, delivering sermons he had written two years before. On his way there, passing in earliest morning through the woods on cold and Sabbath-still country lanes, Emerson looked out at the landscape:

I pleased myself with the beauties & terrors of the snow; the oak-leaf hurrying over the banks is fit ornament. Nature in the woods is very companionable. There, my Reason & my Understanding are sufficient company for each other. I have my glees as well as glooms, alone. (*JMN*, IV, 359)

It is possible to know that he was at that moment thinking of Ellen—and now, too, of his brother Edward, a mere two months dead—and of the relation of these persons to his altered faith:

Confirm my faith (& when I write the word, Faith looks indignant.) pledge me the word of the Highest that I shall have my dead & my absent again, & I could be content & cheerful alone for a thousand years. . . . The moment we indulge our affections, the earth is metamorphosed; all its tragedies & ennuis vanish, all duties even, nothing remains to fill eternity with but two or three persons. But then a person is a *cause*.

What is Luther but Protestantism? or Columbus but Columbia? And were I assured of meeting Ellen tomorrow would it be less than a world, a personal world? Death has no bitterness in the light of that thought. (*JMN*, IV, 359–360).

The meaning of this difficult, much-compressed passage is that Ellen, having ceased as a person, is now felt as a cause—no less truly a cause, indeed, than Luther or Columbus. Cut off early in life, she nevertheless bequeaths a potential to be developed by others in her name. She has come to be understood in terms of the distinctive way her life and presence had taught her husband to see the world, including its snow and its dead leaves. She remains to him, permanently, a cause of consciousness, by the invocation of which at any moment "the earth is metamorphosed." This is perhaps an anticipation of what he would say two years later in *Nature* (1836), prompted by the recent death of his brother Charles, about the use of "friends":

When much intercourse with a friend has supplied us with a standard of excellence, and has increased our respect for the resources of God who thus sends a real person to outgo our ideal; when he has, moreover, become an object of thought, and, whilst his character retains all its unconscious effect, is converted in the mind into solid and sweet wisdom,—it is a sign to us that his office is closing, and he is commonly withdrawn from our sight in a short time. (*CW*, I, 28–29).

In both passages there is an implication that vision may be instructed (as it is the office of poets to do), that we are responsible for the world we see, and that in some real sense it is the affections—love in particular—that teach us the use of the eye. In the sermon that Emerson delivered that December morning in East Sudbury, he gave the people a simpler version of the principle on which poets rely when he referred to "the story of two children who walked in the same road and one found it full of pleasing objects and the other very dull, disagreeable. It is a good illustration of the truth we are considering. In the very same objects at the very same time two persons with different minds see, one a world of beauty, and the other a series of vexations" (*CS*, IV, 104).[26] He would later say that "Nature is a setting that fits equally well a comic or a mourning piece" (*CW*, I, 9), making the world a useful partner and adjunct to the mind. The snow he rode to church on thus turned symbolic—become, through thoughts of Ellen, a thing of "beauties & terrors," and through the "affections" become an agent of metamorphosis. Now it was true for Emerson, as it had been true for the youth years earlier "who sat near me at table," that "all was changed."

It seems likely that Emerson deliberately cultivated this ability to see more intelligently and advantageously. On 17 December, three days after his drive to East Sudbury, he attended a lecture on anatomy where a brain was dissected. It was a "grim compost of blood & mud," as he reported, but it variously served his purpose in the concurrent writing of his lecture on Michelangelo (who saw differently from other men in part because he knew anatomy so well), and, in a somewhat contrary direction (as also, perhaps, with his opening of Ellen's coffin) in the project of weaning himself from nature's body (*JMN*, IV, 362). "The Snow-Storm," written in the immediate aftermath of the great blizzard of 28–29 December, announced a doctrine central to Emerson's poetics—the doctrine, already several times cited, of "metamorphosis," or the far-ramifying belief that the constant change of everything is the

---

26 Compare "The lover walks in miracles, and the man beside him sees none," from "Religion," *EL*, III, 279, and a journal notation from 1863: "In every company in which a poem is read, you may be sure, a part hear the exoteric, and a part the esoteric sense" (*JMN*, XV, 400). Emerson's conviction that the universe is in this way consistently doubled might seem to imply a preference for the spiritual or "upper" half, but in fact he was devoted to seeing the two as (of course) harmoniously joined and so celebrated the doubling itself. The parallax between two views, nearly explicit in a poem like "Two Rivers," not only supplies a special kind of energy to the poetry, but is implicated in the generic desire of reformers (in the sense that Emerson was a reformer) that things should be "on earth as they are in heaven."

law of life.[27] In "Woodnotes, II" Emerson would point out that "The rushing metamorphosis, / Dissolving all that fixture is, / Melts things that be to things that seem, / And solid nature to a dream" (lines 167–170). In "The Snow-Storm," the overnight transformation of the familiar to the wonderful is nature's metamorphic model of human art, done after the divine fashion, in "Parian" perhaps, but altogether hiding Angelo's scaffold and chisel-work.

The idea of metamorphosis came to Emerson from numerous sources and was all the richer for that fact. Ovid was the first source, from whom Emerson knew the Pythagorean theory of the transmigration of souls and the many magic changes thus explained on which classical myth so much depended. But Goethe's "Metamorphosis of Plants," known to him at first through Sarah Austin's three-volume *Characteristics of Goethe* (London, 1833), seems to have been a revelation of this transitional period of concentrated reading, such that "metamorphosis," with its crypto-evolutionary overtones, is as clearly a contribution from the botany of Goethe as, at the same time, "Reason" and "Understanding" are from the psychology of Coleridge, or "correspondence" from the theology of Swedenborg.[28] But the larger meaning that Emerson gave to the concept—what made "metamorphosis" so evocative for the poetry—had from the start to do with its assertion of a distinct principle of life that, almost as a logical sequel, put death properly in its place. Thus, as Emerson said, "early hints are given that we are not to stay here; that we must be making ready to go;— a warning that this magnificent hotel and conveniency we call Nature is not final. First innuendoes, then broad hints, then smart taps, are given, suggesting that nothing stands still in nature but death; that the creation is on wheels, in transit, always passing into something else, streaming into something higher; that matter is

27 "Metamorphosis is the law of the Universe" (1845; *JMN*, IX, 301).

28 Precisely this point is made by Strauch in "The Year of Emerson's Poetic Maturity," 360. Austin's volumes are in Emerson's library; see Harding, 116–117.

not what it appears" (*CW*, VIII, 1–2). In consequence of this insight, poetry would become for Emerson a way of "Chasing with words fast-flowing things" (*PN*, 440).[29]

In the end one can only speculate about the connection between the mysterious process whereby Emerson came to be a genuine poet and the no less mysterious process by which he managed his grief over the loss of Ellen. But it seems not altogether coincidental that within a month of inaugurating his poetry notebook P (expressing a commitment of some depth and extension), he proposed marriage to Lydia Jackson of Plymouth. It is clear that Emerson, with much deliberation, was now organizing the elements of a new life: his marriage, his purchase of a large house in ancestral Concord, his gathering into that house not only his bride, but his mother as well, expecting, indeed, that his brother Charles would live there also, when, as he was expected shortly to do, he married his fiancée Elizabeth Hoar. By 1835 the "second birth" was accomplished; he had re-centered himself. Just two years earlier, while sailing back from Europe, he had confessed in his journal that he wished he "knew where & how I ought to live" (*JMN*, IV, 237). Now, it would appear, he was the author of the answer.

---

29 The first few pages of "Poetry and Imagination" (*CW*, VIII, 1–42) are especially concerned with the implications of the doctrine of metamorphosis, as, for example, in the observation that "power and purpose ride on matter to the last atom" and that "interest [therefore] is gradually transferred from the forms to the lurking method" (2). Metamorphosis became one rationale for privileging thought over its medium, form: "the thoughts of God pause but for a moment in any form" (7). "The endless passing of one element into new forms, the incessant metamorphosis, explains the rank which the imagination holds in our catalogue of mental powers. The imagination is the reader of these forms" (7–8). The concept may be found at the core of poems as diverse as "Threnody" and "Terminus." See Michael H. Cowan, "The Loving Proteus: Metamorphosis in Emerson's Poetry," in Carl Ferdinand Strauch, ed., *Characteristics of Emerson, Transcendental Poet: A Symposium* (Hartford: Transcendental Books, 1975), 11–22, and Daniel B. Shea, "Emerson and the American Metamorphosis," 29–56 (op. cit., n. 14).

IV. Theory and Practice

On 1 February 1835, Emerson expressed to Lydia Jackson his strong preference that the marital home be set on the rocky loam of the inland river town of Concord, not by the sandy streets of her sea-side Plymouth. Of the former, his own home, he said to her, "I must win you to love it."

> I am born a poet, of a low class without doubt yet a poet. That is my nature & vocation. My singing be sure is very 'husky,' & is for the most part in prose. Still am I a poet in the sense of a perceiver & dear lover of the harmonies that are in the soul & in matter, & specially of the correspondences between these & those. A sunset, a forest, a snow storm, a certain river-view, are more to me than many friends & do ordinarily divide my day with my books. (*L*, I, 435)

One suspects that this famous passage of self-definition has been taken seriously fewer times than it has been quoted. When it was written Emerson had composed a scant handful of competent poems, of which none had yet been published. That he knew his voice was "husky" suggests that he anticipated the charge that would in fact be lodged against his work on account of its lack of musicality. Saying that his singing was "for the most part in prose" acknowledged that if his poetry was at times unmelodic or downright prosaic, he had always been at pains to make his prose poetic—at least from the time ten years earlier when he began deliberately to write "literary" sermons. It is a measure of his theoretical sophistication that as early as this letter of 1835 he was productively attentive to the relation of prose to poetry, especially given that prose passages from the journals would so often provide the starting points for his poems. The self-deprecating tone of Emerson's declaration could be read as conceding most of what hostile critics (including, down the line, Matthew Arnold) would eventually say about his performance and standing as a poet. Or it could be interpreted more sympathetically to mean that he had already, on his own authority, made some counter-popular decisions about what did and did not belong to the essential nature of poetry—in which case canny Emerson, for all his nineteenth-century idealism, places himself more squarely than Matthew Arnold among the moderns.

If the "second birth" has any heuristic value in understanding Emerson's career at this point, the implication has to be owned up to that although he was "born a poet," he becomes one in fact only now, at the age of thirty-two. The sincerity of the claim he makes to Miss Jackson—that he is not a minister or a public lecturer or a generalized man of letters, but, in a completely undeluded sense, one who has embraced poetry as a vocation—is the warrant for taking it seriously. In an essay entitled "The Problem of Emerson," Joel Porte effectively acknowledges this point and insists on the benefits of approaching Emerson accordingly:

> Emerson, as he himself frequently insisted, is fundamentally a poet whose meaning lies in his manipulations of language and figure. The best guide to change, or growth, or consistency in Emerson's thought, is his poetic imagination and not his philosophical arguments or discursive logic. The alert reader can discover, and take much pleasure in discovering, remarkable verbal strategies, metaphoric patterns, repetitions and developments of sound, sense, and image throughout Emerson's writing. One finds an impressively unified consciousness everywhere in control of its fertile meanings.[30]

In declaring poetry absolutely and explicitly central to his new life (identifying his personal life with his expression in poetry, just as Walt Whitman would do), Emerson makes the unity and consistency of the one a function of the same traits in the other, such

---

30 In *Emerson's Prose and Poetry*, ed. Joel Porte and Saundra Morris (New York: Norton, 2001), 685. The passage is explicitly offered as the thesis of the article (679–697). It is a thesis that attentive readers of Emerson's poetry—few as these may have been—have always found attractive and have occasionally ventured to defend. Another, earlier instance is to be found in the chapter on the poetry in George Edward Woodberry's *Ralph Waldo Emerson* (New York: Macmillan, 1907), 158–177.

that vision, character, and expression synergistically refine each other as they engage mutually in a project of matching nature. It is a way of becoming "genuine" after the model derived by Carlyle from Ebenezer Elliott and explored in Emerson's own "Genuine Man" sermon. This is all by way of saying that Emerson endorses an "organic" view of his function as a poet, and yet that unelaborated term fails to convey how much more is at issue in his verse than the simple privileging of natural imagery prompted by an entirely understandable fascination with "a sunset, a forest, a snow storm, a certain river-view." The genuineness and underived originality that he sought was partly bound up in a sense of place, so that he could say of the personified "genius of Poetry" that he is, despite all reports to the contrary, "here. He worships in this land also, not by immigration but he is Yankee born" (*EL*, III, 362).

From about 1835 on through the *Dial* years, there is an important synergy between Emerson's theory and practice of the art of poetry, the former most substantially represented in three locations: the "Language" chapter of *Nature* (1836), the lecture entitled "The Poet" (1841), and the famous essay of the same title but with very different content, published in *Essays: Second Series* (1844). A thorough examination of these documents might well be the subject of a book. In the discussion that follows only a few topics will be alluded to, and these for the light they shed on Emerson's practice.

Emerson's theory of language, the subject of the fourth chapter of *Nature* (*CW*, I, 17–23), amounts to a tracing out of the implications of a belief that language is, from the first, radically metaphoric, that it is a provision of nature whereby spiritual and ethical meanings become possible. This idea turns up as early as Emerson's very first lecture, "The Uses of Natural History," delivered on 5 November 1833:

> The strongest distinction of which we have an idea is that between thought and matter. The very existence of thought and speech supposes and is a new nature totally distinct from the material world; yet we find it impossible to speak of it and its laws in any other language than that borrowed from our ex-

perience in the material world. We not only speak in continual metaphors of the morn, the noon and the evening of life, of dark and bright thoughts, of sweet and bitter moments, of the healthy mind and the fading memory; but all our most literal and direct modes of speech—as right and wrong, form and substance, honest and dishonest etc., are, when hunted up to their original signification, found to be metaphors also. And this, because the whole of Nature is a metaphor or image of the human Mind. The laws of moral nature answer to those of matter as face to face in a glass. "The visible world," it has been well said, "and the relations of its parts is the dial plate of the invisible one." (*EL*, I, 24–25)

Language, rooted in the brute material world, becomes our only means of access to the immaterial world, a realm that Emerson calls "spiritual," but understands metaphysically as the locale—the only locale—of meaning. The "strong distinction" is between thought and matter: these are as distinct as the "Me" and the "Not-Me" into which, as Emerson proposed, the universe might be comprehensively divided (*CW*, I, 8), but they are also united—or they become united—in the system of metaphor called language.

Among the several illustrations of this theory that Emerson offers in the "Language" chapter is one that would shortly pose significant hermeneutical difficulties: "That which, intellectually considered, we call Reason," Emerson explained, "considered in relation to nature, we call Spirit. Spirit is the Creator. Spirit hath life in itself. And man in all ages and countries, embodies it in his language, as the FATHER" (*CW*, I, 19). His claim is that the generative role of the father, as a familiar fact of nature or biology, is made use of to express (or to "embody" and so make comprehensible) the purely immaterial fact of creative power. The capacity to bring into existence must arise from a force that "hath life in itself." So, by analogy (or by metaphor), the Creator is the Father.[31]

---

31 Again, according to Emerson, words are poems (*CW*, III, 11): "father" is nature's contribution (through a poetic transfer of application) to the human ability to think about, and ultimately to express, the creator concept. Why not,

The difficulty in all this is that culture almost inevitably corrupts the natural connections and the poem that language intrinsically is soon enough comes to be misread. Emerson, quoting the Quaker George Fox, noted that "the fundamental law of criticism" is that "every scripture is to be interpreted by the same spirit which gave it forth" (*CW*, I, 23). Arguably, the spirit that "gave forth" the fact of the father did not simultaneously authorize the bundling of traits only accidentally related to creation, such as disciplinary power or parental affection, as metaphors of (abstract) creation are misread as denoting the very features and human appeal of a personal God. In this way theological disputes such as that between the Transcendentalists and the Unitarian establishment at Harvard, culminating in Emerson's "heresy" in the 1838 Divinity School Address, are reducible to questions of competence in the reading of metaphor. Indeed this is what Emerson meant when he contended in that address that the churches were in crisis precisely to the extent that they had been built not on the principles of Jesus, but on his tropes (*CW*, I, 81). The capacity to read poetry, in other words, is not some luxurious attainment, but a way of clearing one's relation to the world and all meaning.[32]

The important 1841 lecture on "The Poet" upholds the theory of language articulated in *Nature,* but makes it subordinate to an overarching concern with "expression."[33] "Poetry," says Emerson,

---

one might ask, simply avoid metaphor and use "creator" instead? It turns out that "creator" (likewise a word) is no less metaphorical, deriving originally from the same root as "Ceres," the goddess of agriculture, which permits us, at need, to come at the idea from the botanical rather than the biological side.

32 It is a fascinating gloss on this issue that Emerson's rejection of personality as a feature of God, Reason, spirit, and even of highest friendship was the point of ultimate concern to Henry Ware, Jr., his erstwhile senior colleague at the Second Church, in the wake of the Divinity School Address. Emerson's heresy, according to Ware, was his rejection of God as a father to be worshipped and a figure to be the dutiful, protected child of. See Kenneth Walter Cameron, "Henry Ware's Divinity School Address—A Reply to Emerson's," *American Transcendental Quarterly*, XIII (Winter 1972): 84–91, which includes a reprint of Ware's *The Personality of the Deity*.

33 Here Emerson portrays nature as the facilitator of human expression, "so changeable, so fruitful in names and methods and metres that it appears to be a sympathetic cipher or alphabet, and to exist that it may serve man with a lan-

"finds its origin in that *need of expression* which is a primary impulse of nature" (*EL,* III, 348–349). Although the observation is cast in historical terms, Emerson's effort is primarily to account for the relevance of poetry to life and to offer a theory of its power. Not improbably thinking still of the lesson of Ellen's death, he asserts in this lecture that "Expression is prosperity"; without it, "I must disappear, and the brute form must crowd the soul out of nature" (349). Any defense of meaning, as in the activity of the poet, any enlargement of the amount of available meaning in the world, is to be construed as an act of self-defense; indeed it is the defense of spirit (which "hath life in itself") against the prospect of being overwhelmed by and entombed in a wholly material world.[34] Emerson is in this way constantly alert to the restorative, life-preserving function of poetry, and everywhere he bears out the sense of a claim already quoted—that "Genius is the activity which repairs the decays of things" (*CW,* III, 13). There is, throughout, an undeniable grandeur and elevation in Emerson's claims about poetry—or about poetry's claims on its audience—that sets him permanently apart from all other theorists and practitioners of the period.

"Who knows but more is meant than yet appears?" (*EL,* III, 354). It is the purpose of expression to discover the fuller meaning of the common appearances (as, for example, of a rhodora or a humble-bee) so as to facilitate domestication in a truer, richer world, a world not of forms merely, but of forms as they are connected to human thoughts.[35] "What does all this love for signs de-

---

guage." The included theory of metaphor is enlarged, however, by a new sense of the range of possible meanings. Adducing, as it were, the "each in all" principle that he had worked out in 1834, Emerson asserts that "there is no word in our language that can not become to us typical of nature by giving it emphasis. The world is an animal; it is a bird; it is a boat; it is a shadow; it is a torrent, a mist, a spider's snare; it is what you will, and the metaphor will hold, and it will give the imagination keen pleasure" (*EL,* III, 352).

34 "When you assume the rhythm of verse & the analogy of nature it is making proclamation 'I am now freed from the trammels of the Apparent; I speak from the Mind'" (*JMN,* V, 51).

35 "All the facts in natural history taken by themselves, have no value, but are barren like a single sex. But marry it to human history, and it is full of life. Whole Floras, all Linnæus' and Buffon's volumes, are but dry catalogues of facts; but

note, if not that the relation of man to these forms in nature is more intimate than the understanding yet suspects; and that perhaps the metamorphoses which we read in Latin or in Indian literature are not quite so fabulous as they are accounted?" (354). Poetry provides a benefit not only in giving outlet to the human need for expression, but in making life larger by expanding the scope of meanings that might be expressed, and in convincing us (as in the case of Shakespeare, for example) that "the range of human articulation reaches higher and lower than we had yet found" (350).

Emerson's thesis in the lecture is that "we love, we worship the expressors of that which we have at heart" (355). It is not always a simple matter to trace the practical connection between Emerson's theory of poetics (which is never, of course, entirely present in any of its propositions) and its issue in the poems, but his extended probing of the idea of expression may provide an unexpectedly helpful context for one moment in the 1846 poem "Monadnoc." In the first (London) edition of that work, at line 369, Emerson addresses Mount Monadnoc as "Thou grand expressor of the present tense," which is the reading also of the printer's copy and, behind that, of the prose source entered in journal O on 27 June 1846:

> We [evidently Emerson and Bronson Alcott] had conversation today concerning the poet & his problem. He is there to see the type & truly interpret it; O mountain, what would your highness say? thou grand expressor of the present tense; of permanence; yet is there also a taunt at the mutables from old Sitfast. If the poet could only forget himself in his theme, be the tongue of the mountain, his egotism would subside and that firm line which he had drawn would remain like the

---

the most trivial of these facts, the habit of a plant, the organs, or work, or noise of an insect, applied to the illustration of a fact in intellectual philosophy, or, in any way associated to human nature, affects us in the most lively and agreeable manner" (*Nature*, *CW*, I, 19).

names of discoverers of planets, written in the sky in letters which could never be obliterated." (*JMN*, IX, 432–433)

It is not quite certain that Emerson's variant spelling *expressor* signifies the variant or specialized meaning that the word had for him, compounding, as he did, the expressive capacity of natural forms with the expressive capacity of poets.[36] That specialized meaning can be recovered by paying attention to the contextual usage in the prose. The term itself is unusual for Emerson. He used it only in the 1840s and then on no more than half a dozen occasions, always with reference to a specific conception of poetry. In the 1841 lecture, in which Emerson alludes to the extreme rarity of "adequate intellectual expression," the "expressors," as we have seen, are objects of love and worship. In an 1847 journal entry, in the course of thinking about "expression" as "tantamount to life," Emerson noted that "there are great expressors with little stuff; as Byron," whereas "Shakspeare is nothing but a wonderful expressor" (*JMN*, X, 91). It is possible as a reader, even without a concordance, to pick up something of the special resonance of this word, the new-making supplement of meaning that Emerson has privately given it, on encountering the term in "Monadnoc."[37] The London edition follows the original manu-

---

36 In a private communication to the author, 28 May 2010, Barbara Packer suggested that Emerson may have preferred the Latinate ending, which one finds in such words as "councillor" or "malefactor," for example, to the more usual Germanic ending, as better implying a human-like agent. An "expresser" could be something like a French press in coffee-making, whereas to call Monadnoc an "expressor" would be to find the mountain in speech, if not exactly in the act of uttering words.

37 The oddity that concentrates around particular words when, as here, a term that Emerson has privately or publicly cogitated is inserted into a context of comparatively neutral public speech, will often have an unsettling effect on the reader; in his review of *Poems*, Francis Bowen, a critic consistently unsympathetic to Emerson, pointed to this line in "Monadnoc" as an instance of "inimitable bathos" ("Nine New Poets," *North American Review*, LXIV [April 1847]: 413). One may choose to regard Bowen's objection as the prejudice opposite to that expressed in Joel Benton's exclamation: "with what pure selection he chooses every word!" (*Emerson as a Poet* [New York: M. L. Holbrook, 1883], 39).

script spelling, but the Boston edition avoids the helpful strangeness by adopting the conventional spelling, *expresser,* which may be Emerson's concession to the correcting hand of an editor. Such, in any event, was the form the word maintained until 1863, when Emerson replaced it with "affirmer," perhaps because at some level he had lost touch with the sixteen-year-old linguistic structure of its original form, so long obscured by the Boston emendation.

"The Poet" in *Essays: Second Series* (1844; *CW,* III, 3–24) comes a decade after Emerson's avowal to his wife-to-be that he was "born a poet." This essay, especially in its last paragraph, invites being read in personal and vocational terms as a confirmation of what it means to be "a devout lover of the Muse" (*EL,* III, 348):

> Thou shalt leave the world, and know the muse only. . . . Thou shalt lie close hid with nature, and canst not be afforded to the Capitol or the Exchange. The world is full of renunciations and apprenticeships, and this is thine; thou must pass for a fool and a churl for a long season. . . . And this is the reward: that the ideal shall be real to thee, and the impressions of the actual world shall fall like summer rain, copious, but not troublesome, to thy invulnerable essence. Thou shalt have the whole land for thy park and manor, the sea for thy bath and navigation, without tax and without envy; the woods and the rivers thou shalt own; and thou shalt possess that wherein others are only tenants and boarders. Thou true land-lord! sea-lord! air-lord! (*CW,* III, 23–24)

If there is a monkish or religious-ascetic quality to being a devotee of the Muse—an entailed retirement from the worldly affairs of politics or reform or money-getting, as Emerson would shortly suggest in the "Ode to Channing"—there is also, in compensation, a genuine joy in the poet's cleared title to nature. "There is a property in the horizon," Emerson wrote in *Nature,* "which no man has but he whose eye can integrate all the parts, that is, the poet" (*CW,* I, 9.) The poet alone knows the world he lives in, and knowing it, can genuinely speak it. "The world being thus put under the mind for verb and noun, the poet is he who can articulate it" (*CW*, III, 12). Nowhere else in nineteenth-century literature does one find this sort of exuberance and exaltation about the mind's capacity for creation: not until Wallace Stevens' poet came in 1922 to dazzle the high-toned old Christian woman was this pitch of feeling again set down. Between times only Whitman approached it.

V. Assembling *Poems*

Ten years elapsed between the publication of Emerson's last apprentice verses and his first mature poems. After "Fame" and "William Rufus and the Jew" made their anonymous appearance in the anonymously-edited *Offering for 1829,* Emerson published no more poetry until 1839 with the exception of two commissioned hymns—the "Hymn for the Ordination of Chandler Robbins" (1833) and the "Hymn" for the dedication of the Concord Monument (1837), both printed as broadsides. Emerson would never be in a hurry to publish his verse. Over the decade he had written sparingly yet with increasing power and confidence, accumulating finished drafts in poetry notebook P and sharing them only with family and closest friends. One of the earliest and most constant of these privileged readers was Elizabeth Hoar, daughter of a leading family in Concord, whose marriage to Emerson's brother Charles had been thwarted by his death in 1836. According to Emerson it was she who first encouraged him to publish (*L*, II, 78, and *L*, VII, 592), specifically urging him to grant the request made in the spring of 1837 by James Freeman Clarke, then the editor of the *Western Messenger,* for a contribution to the journal. Clarke, a graduate of Harvard College and the Divinity School, had been called to a church in Louisville, Kentucky, where he also took up the journal editorship in part to advocate Boston Unitarianism and, increasingly, Transcendentalist ideas to a trans-Alleghany audience. Beginning in 1836 Emerson encountered him mainly at meetings of the Transcendental Club during Clarke's summer visits to Boston. Before then he knew him as an intelligent reader of Goethe and Carlyle; afterward as a friend of Margaret Fuller. Emerson complied by sending "Each and All" and "To the Humble-Bee," poems that, as he said, "have pleased some of my friends, and so may please some of your readers" (*L*, VII, 327). As soon as Clarke received them, he wrote to ask permission to publish two more—"The Rhodora" and "Good-Bye"—which just happened to be in his possession, having been accidentally gathered up in a parcel of papers given him some time earlier by Margaret Fuller.[38]

Although the *Western Messenger* never had many subscribers (probably, indeed, no more than 400), under Clarke's editorship it exerted a disproportionate influence for being, simply, the most distinguished of the Western literary magazines. The enthusiastic publicity it gave to the writings of the Transcendentalists, and to those of Emerson in particular, would prove significant. In the end, however, only four of Emerson's poems appeared in its pages —all in 1839. By the next year, Clarke gave up journal editing in favor of marriage and a return to Boston. The movement's attention turned at this time to a new vehicle, the *Dial*, edited in Boston by Margaret Fuller.

During the *Dial* years (1840–1844) Emerson published two dozen poems in that journal, then not a single one in any magazine until 1857, when *The Atlantic Monthly* was founded. This thirteen-year interval included, of course, the publication of *Poems* in December 1846, first in London, then a fortnight later in Boston, but the fact is that Emerson would not submit his poems to any journal not closely identified with the Transcendentalists. If between 1844 and 1857 no such journal existed, he was perfectly content to let his poems quietly accumulate in the notebooks.

Emerson's poetic contributions to the *Western Messenger* and *Dial* were immediately noticed, however—especially and with

38 See Clarke, *Autobiography, Diary and Correspondence*, ed. Edward Everett Hale (Boston: Houghton Mifflin, 1891), 123–127. The best discussion of the *Western Messenger* is Robert D. Habich, *Transcendentalism and the Western Messenger: A History of the Magazine and Its Contributors, 1835–1841* (Rutherford, N.J.: Fairleigh Dickinson University Press, 1985), but see also Clarence L. F. Gohdes, *The Periodicals of American Transcendentalism* (Durham, N.C.: Duke University Press, 1931), 17–37.

greatest consequence by Rufus Wilmot Griswold, best known, by the end of the 1840s, as the friend and betrayer of Edgar Allan Poe. A New Englander by birth, Griswold had succeeded Poe as editor of *Graham's,* a Philadelphia magazine, in 1842, but he achieved his greatest success that year as a pioneering anthologist of American literature. His *Poets and Poetry of America* (1842) contained, among a great many others, five poems by Emerson. The enormous commercial success of this project enhanced Griswold's critical reputation with the general public and tended for a time to fix the canon of American poetry. Griswold tried to parlay this success with other more or less similar compilations, all of which included poems by Emerson: *Gems from American Poets* (1842, with an expanded edition in 1844), *Readings in American Poetry* (1843), and *The Illustrated Book of Christian Ballads* (1844). These publications—particularly the first—undoubtedly brought Emerson's poems to the attention of more readers than the *Dial* ever did.[39]

It was in the wake of this kind of publicity that publishers began to inquire about Emerson's interest in collecting his poems in a volume. In a letter of 3 December 1843 to his brother William, Emerson mentioned that he had the day before—"for the second time"—fielded an application of that sort from a "bookseller" (*L,* III, 227). He responded with a characteristic diffidence (at least to his brother), wondering whether he had, after all, "one true spark of that fire which burns in verse." Not improbably the very grandeur of his conception of the Poet, still in the course of being laid out in lecture and essay, required him to hesitate—though the letter to William also shows that he intended to finish *Essays: Second Series* before he would entertain the notion of collecting his

---

39 Griswold had noted "The Humble-Bee" in the *Western Messenger* and in September 1841 made inquiries with its author about additional poems; see Emerson's reply of 25 September (*L,* III, 472–473), in which he supplied information about Jones Very and Henry Thoreau as well. Interestingly, Emerson did not have a file of the *Messenger* or the *Dial* in his personal library and so could not recover the titles of all his poems; in October 1842, however, he entered a list in poetry notebook P (*PN,* 105) that included 18 poems—all that had been published to that date, with the exception of three very short pieces in the *Dial,* "Silence," "Grace," and "Tact."

verse. William, in reply, said that if Waldo really meant to publish a volume of poems, then "I will take leave to recommend that you appoint some musical friend (of course not an Emerson) to trim your metres according to some canon" (*L*, III, 234 n. 4). It would be ten months more before William could read in the essay "The Poet" that "it is not metres, but a metre-making argument, that makes a poem" (*CW*, III, 6).

Most of 1844 would be given to the finishing up of *Essays: Second Series,* of which the lead essay, the second longest in the volume and the first written, was "The Poet." Soon after this book appeared, Emerson commended the neatness and accuracy of the work of his new London publisher, John Chapman, in bringing it out, at the same time looking to new projects in a casual postscript: "Our booksellers have repeatedly asked me to collect my verses into a volume, which perhaps I shall adventure" (*L*, III, 274). No doubt Chapman signified his interest by return mail, for on 7 February 1845 Emerson could report to his old friend, William Henry Furness, that "I have been spirited up lately from several sides to collect my verses" (*L*, VIII, 7).[40]

That summer, Nathaniel Hawthorne, living in Concord's Old Manse, was asked by his literary agent, Evert A. Duyckinck, to see if Emerson could be persuaded to publish with Wiley & Putnam, the New York firm with which Duyckinck was connected. On 1 July Hawthorne reported the results:

> I sounded Emerson on the subject of a contribution to the series of American Books; but he seems to think it preferable to publish on his own account—which has always been his method hitherto. I doubt, moreover, whether he is prepared with any prose, or likely soon to be so. He contemplates col-

40 Emerson and Furness had known each other from earliest childhood in Boston, where they had gone to school together. Both entered the Unitarian ministry at about the same time, though Furness spent the whole of a long and distinguished career in his pulpit at Philadelphia. In the 1840s he edited several gift-books to which, at Furness's request, Emerson contributed a total of six poems, "The Apology," "Dirge," "Loss and Gain," "A Fable," "Fore-Runners," and "The World-Soul," all before their inclusion in *Poems* (1847).

lecting his poetry into a volume, including much that is still in manuscript; but I know not whether this idea has taken the consistency of a purpose. I wish he might be induced to publish this volume in New York. His reputation is still, I think, provincial, and almost local, partly owing to the defects of the New England system of publication.[41]

Hawthorne's sense of the shortcomings of the Boston booksellers reinforced Emerson's own increasing dissatisfaction with James Munroe, the printer-bookseller with whom he had dealt for the past ten years, and particularly with Munroe's old-fashioned, uncommercial indifference to making sales outside the region (where he missed the retail commission he got for dealing over his own counter). Munroe's phlegmatic business practices were a far cry from the aggressive tactics of the upstart New Yorkers, who commanded a national market by routinely distributing their wares via canal barge and railroad. In many respects Wiley & Putnam typified this vigorous, democratic approach to selling books, not only by courting a large audience with cheap prices, but also by adopting the cultural politics of the nationalist Young America movement, led by Democrats John L. O'Sullivan, Cornelius Mathews, and Evert A. Duyckinck.

Duyckinck initiated a correspondence with Emerson in August, and over the next three months they explored a variety of possible projects and arrangements (*L*, III, 296–297, 301–302, 307–308, 310). Emerson conceded certain advantages in publishing at New York, but insisted that he would come out ahead financially if he published on his own account, selling fewer books of better quality at a higher price and giving Munroe his standard 30% commission for printing. It is clear from this exchange that Emerson, who had taken personal charge of his publications from the beginning, was quite shrewd about the literary marketplace and confident in his ability to manage his own affairs. He kept the negotia-

41 Nathaniel Hawthorne, *The Letters, 1843–1853*, ed. Thomas Woodson et al., volume XVI of The Centenary Edition of the Works of Nathaniel Hawthorne (Columbus: Ohio State University Press, 1985), 105–106.

tions with Duyckinck open as long as he did mainly, it would seem, to learn of conditions at the heart of American publishing, but he broke off the correspondence when he learned that John Wiley meant, dishonorably in Emerson's view, to bring out a pirated edition of Carlyle (*CEC*, 403). Emerson's instinct had all along been to remain in his comfortable relations with Munroe, Whiggish and unprofessional as those relations were. But had he taken Hawthorne's advice and been more concerned to cultivate a national reputation, had he joined Poe and Hawthorne and Melville in Duyckinck's "Library of American Books," his development as a poet might have been somewhat different.[42]

As late as September 1845 Emerson hoped to have the book of poems ready for sale by the end of the year to take advantage of the New Year's gift-giving (*L*, VIII, 60). That schedule, however, did not prove feasible, as he became wholly occupied with the writing of his "Representative Men" lectures. The need to prepare for the winter lecture season led Emerson to announce that he would suspend work on the poems for two months, though he also cited as a further reason for postponement, the intervention of "a critical friend of mine" (almost certainly Caroline Sturgis) who "discovered so many corrigible & repairable places" that the job of revision loomed suddenly larger than he had supposed (*L*, III, 310). As it happened, the delay lasted the better part of a year, and yet it was probably just as well, since many of the best poems that eventually made their way into the volume, such as "Mithridates," Alphonso of Castile," the two "Merlin" poems, the "Ode, Inscribed to W. H. Channing," and "Bacchus," were composed during the spring and summer of 1846.

42 The New York firm of D. Appleton also wanted to publish Emerson's book of poems (*L*, III, 350n). Part of the difficulty here, as also in the negotiation with Wiley and Putnam, was that Emerson already had an understanding with John Chapman and so could not offer English rights to any American publisher. Emerson's decision to go with Munroe has recently been interpreted as a refusal to engage the emergent national-scale literary marketplace: see Ronald J. Zboray and Mary Saracino Zboray, "Nineteenth-Century Print Culture" in Joel Myerson et al., eds., *The Oxford Handbook of Transcendentalism* (New York: Oxford University Press, 2010), 106–107.

Of the sixty distinct works that made up *Poems* (1847), nearly half had not been published before. Although a few of these "new" poems had been written much earlier—"Thine Eyes Still Shined," for example, a poem about Ellen, was composed in 1830, while "Compensation" and "Xenophanes" dated to 1834 and 1836 respectively—most of the others were composed during intense creative outbursts in the spring and summer of 1845 and 1846, almost certainly more in the latter year than the former. As one who was "born a poet," he had written from time to time when the spirit moved him, but he was virtually a professional poet in the two years before his volume appeared, half full, as it were, with the fruits of a more deliberate application.

The causes of this creativity are not mysterious: it is an almost adequate explanation to say that he knew he needed more matter to fill out the book. And yet other poets had published volumes more slender than the 251-page book that Munroe issued on Christmas Day, 1846.[43] A more interesting and no less accurate explanation for Emerson's creative outpouring at this time involves his discovery of the Persian Sufi poet, Hafiz. The discovery itself was intoxicating, and Emerson ever afterwards recognized Hafiz as, along with Shakespeare and Dante, one of the greatest poets of world literature. An entry for 9 April 1846 in the MS Account Book for 1845–1849 shows that Emerson purchased Joseph von Hammer's German translation of the *Diwan von Mohammed Schemsed-din Hafis*, 2 vols. (Stuttgart and Tübingen, 1812–1813), at Elizabeth Peabody's West Street bookshop. Immediately he began to fill up his notebooks (especially notebook Orientalist: see *TN*, II, 37–141) with fragmentary English translations as he explored the range of his new poet. *Poems* (1847) would include two of these works, "From the Persian of Hafiz" and "Ghaselle," but the oriental influence is discernible as well in a number of Emerson's own compositions throughout the book. As Oliver Wendell Holmes observed, "his Persian and Indian models betray themselves in many of his poems, some of which, called translations,

43 Myerson, A 18.2.a, pp. 156–157; *L*, III, 366, n. 167; see *JMN*, IX, 456–457, 461–464, and 468–469, for lists of recipients of complimentary copies.

sound as if they were original."[44] In a letter to Elizabeth Hoar of 27 July 1846 (*L*, III, 341) Emerson mentioned "Bacchus" as among the poems he had written lately, adding that it was "not however translated from Hafiz"—suggesting that she well knew of his current fascination, and asserting, at the same time, an important Persian influence in his own verses. The poem was a favorite with Caroline Sturgis, who said to Emerson, on first reading it in manuscript, that it "made the day wider, as your words always do" (*L*, VIII, 89).

The significance to Emerson of Hafiz and the other Persian poets has not been adequately explored. When the matter is referred to it is often subsumed under a generalized conception of "oriental" influences. The slight justification for doing so is that the Transcendentalists were at this period especially open to the literature of Hinduism, Confucianism, and the mystical tradition in Islam known as Sufism. They gratefully received these works as "Ethnical Scriptures" self-evidently on a par with (though in general less patently "theological" than) the familiar Christian documents. The Transcendentalists prized these ancient but newfound writings for the challenge they posed to the imagination—which is to say, for their capacity to relax the mental stranglehold that a steady diet of Anglo-American Protestantism seems to have created. In performing this function the Eastern scriptures helped to recover the widest possibilities, creative and spiritual, inherent in the religious sensibility.

From an early date Emerson had been alert to literary orientalism, having been sufficiently impressed by Robert Southey's fatuous but very popular *Curse of Kehama* (1817) to compose his own derivative "Indian Superstition" for a Harvard Exhibition in 1821.[45] A very different vision of Hindu literature came to him

44 Holmes, *Ralph Waldo Emerson* (Boston: Houghton Mifflin, 1884), 338.

45 See "Young Emerson's Orientalism at Harvard," in Kenneth Walter Cameron, ed., *Indian Superstition* (Hanover, N.H.: Friends of the Dartmouth Library, 1954), 12–14. Emerson had a more permanent regard for Thomas Moore's extremely popular *Lalla Rookh* (1817). The copy of this work in Emerson's library (Harding, 193) belonged to his first wife, Ellen.

the next year from the least predictable of sources, Mary Moody Emerson, who in writing to her nephew quoted without attribution the "Hymn to Narayena" from the *Works* of the Sanscrit scholar and pioneer orientalist, Sir William Jones. Like his aunt, Emerson valued this poem for its striking expression of a most intense religious idealism, one that is prepared to regard all of nature as "Delusive pictures! Unsubstantial shows! / My soul absorbed, one only Being knows." As Phyllis Cole has suggested, the "Hymn to Narayena" was an important introduction to the concept of maia, or illusion, and primed Emerson to accept more readily the neo-platonic and Gnostic elements in the poetry of Eastern mysticism.[46]

We hear little of the Persians, however, until October 1842 when the poem "Saadi" appeared in the *Dial*. Even then, Emerson had merely appropriated the name for a meditation on the figure of the ideal poet, and betrays no very detailed knowledge of the historical Saadi or his works, regarding which he did some research in the Harvard College library a year afterwards (see the headnote to "Saadi," below). Well or poorly known, Saadi remained to Emerson for a very long time a sort of allegorical representation of what an Emersonian poet might be. In a late essay used to preface a reissue of Saadi's *Gulistan or Rose Garden*, Emerson conceded that Saadi lacked the lyrical gifts of Hafiz, and, surprisingly, compared him, in his "cheerfulness" and "benevolent wisdom," to Benjamin Franklin.[47] But if he had Franklinian qualities of character, he was nevertheless also a Sufi. Acknowledging that in his poems one found "a pure theism," Emerson noted that "the poet or thinker must always be, in a rude nation, the

---

46 See *The Selected Letters of Mary Moody Emerson*, ed. Nancy Craig Simmons (Athens: University of Georgia Press, 1993), 157; *L*, I, 116, and *JMN*, I, 153–154; Emerson never forgot the verses and quoted them toward the end of his life in *Parnassus*, 2nd ed. (Boston: James R. Osgood, 1875), 180, from which the poem is here quoted. See Cole, *Mary Moody Emerson*, 169 and 245.

47 "Preface to the American Edition," *The Gulistan or Rose Garden. By Musle-Huddeen Sheik Saadi, of Shiraz*. Trans., Francis Gladwin (Boston: Ticknor and Fields, 1865), vii-viii. The essay had earlier appeared in *AM*, XII (July 1864): 33–37.

chief authority on religion" (ix). There is a valuable hint here that Emerson never ceased to identify the power of his own poetic eloquence with the religious sentiment, broadly or liberally construed. In other words, the Sufism of the old Persian poets, stronger in Hafiz than in Saadi, retained an undiminished spiritual power. This was the liveliness, exuberance, and immediacy that in the "Lord's Supper" sermon and the Divinity School Address Emerson implied had been lost to modern religion by the preference of orthodoxy for ritual and ceremony.

The discovery of Hafiz was clearly energizing in precisely this way and at an absolutely crucial time, just months before Emerson's first book of poems took shape. In the "Ghaselle," one of the two translations from Hafiz in *Poems,* Emerson foregrounded the antinomian spirit of Persian Sufism. Here Hafiz urges a strictly observant hermit fakir, a self-mortifying Arminian companion, to "renounce" with him the thought of Paradise. The evidence of their own "names of sin" suggests (as the hermit, a figure of justice, must assume) that they are not worthy of heaven. The business of the poem is to make an efficient traverse from this introductory hypothesis of guilt and anxiety to a conclusion in which, at least for Hafiz, "Heaven is secure." Each of the five intervening stanzas makes its contribution to this process, but the most telling comes in the midmost quatrain: here it is pointed out that while the hermit's mind requires fasting and prayer, and these in an institutional setting of "mosque and cool kiosk,"

> Mine me allows the drinking-house,
>   And sweet chase of the nuns.

The frequent references to drinking, which might lead one on a first acquaintance to confuse Hafiz with Anacreon, are of course all symbolic and therefore not quite deliberate affronts to Islamic proscriptions—though they do, nevertheless, connote a joyous freedom. As so often in ancient Gnostic symbologies, drinking represents divine inspiration, and (as in "Bacchus") is thus connected to poetry. The "sweet chase of the nuns" invokes the charge of sexual licentiousness traditionally brought against all antinomian movements, on the assumption that a religiosity grounded in self-reliance—as opposed to fear of the law—must be friendly to self-indulgence, celebration, and a love of God in nature.

The hermit needed to learn "abandonment" or yielding to the whole, of the sort that Emerson had commended as early as 1834 in "Each and All"; he needed to become, in the drama of the "Ghaselle," like the Sufi Hafiz, whose faith, centered on God exclusively and the unquestionable satisfactions of his providence, will not permit ungrateful doubts or any meddling in the ways of the universe for outcomes favorable to oneself.[48]

Who dear to God on earthly sod
    No rice or barley plants,
The same is glad that life is had,
    Though corn he wants.

Emerson noted in his journal that "Orientalism is Fatalism, resignation: Occidentalism is Freedom & Will" (*JMN*, X, 90). He understood the Persians somewhat allegorically, through the lens of his own mythopoeic purposes. He needed this philosophical parallax of cultural difference.[49]

48 See, on this point, Reynold A. Nicholson, *The Mystics of Islam* (1914; rpt. Arkana/Penguin: London and New York, 1989), 37–38. Nicholson also stresses the relation between Sufism and Christian Gnosticism, indicating a historical nexus in the region near Basra, home of the Sabaeans or Mandaeans (14–16), whose literature figures prominently in the classic work of Hans Jonas, *The Gnostic Religion*, 2nd ed. (Boston: Beacon, 1963). The point is worth noting because Sufism and Gnosticism are, as it were, ideological cousins to Transcendentalism in their repudiation of forms, ceremonies, and legalism in general in favor of an immediate and inward knowledge of God. See also Albert J. von Frank, "Emerson and Gnosticism," in *Emerson: Bicentennial Essays*, ed. Ronald A. Bosco and Joel Myerson (Boston: Massachusetts Historical Society, 2006), 289–314.

49 In 1850 Theodore Parker suggested that Emerson had no historically accurate understanding of "that curious philosophy" embodied in "the ancient oriental literature." "Hence his oriental allies are brought up to take a stand which no man dreamed of in their time, and made to defend ideas not known to men till long after these antediluvian sages were at rest in their graves" ("The Writings of Ralph Waldo Emerson," *Massachusetts Quarterly Review*, III [March 1850]: 211–212). Emerson's scholarly interest in the Sufi poets had its limits, though Parker's pedantry (he was a founding member of the American Oriental Society) probably makes too much of them. Emerson was better informed before he

Such Eastern mysticism was a resource in Emerson's effort to move poetry constantly further from the linear, not to say mechanical logic of the Understanding which, as in the "Rational religion" of Anglo-American Unitarianism, obscured the truths that he felt were available only to the Reason. "Wonderful," said Emerson in 1864, "is the inconsecutiveness of the Persian poets. European criticism finds that the unity of a beautiful whole is everywhere wanting. Not only the story is short, but no two sentences are joined." Since the same criticisms had been leveled at Emerson's writing (echoing, indeed, his own judgment), he would seem to have found a welcome precedent for his expressive practices in "the loose and irrecoverable ramble of the Oriental bards."[50]

VI. *Poems* (1847)

Emerson's English publisher was John Chapman, an early and enthusiastic reader of *Nature* and the first book of *Essays*. He had initially come to Emerson's attention as the English distributor of the *Dial,* having, late in 1843 or early in 1844, bought out the publishing house of John Green. Although the *Dial* ceased publi-

---

published his essay "Persian Poetry" in the *Atlantic Monthly* in 1858 (note that the version of the essay collected in *Letters and Social Aims* [1876] is an abridgment: *CW*, VIII, 124–149). What did not seem to have limits was Emerson's sympathetic appropriation of the Sufi poets, novel as their expressions were to Western ears, for his own poetic purposes.

50 "Preface to the American Edition," xi. In 1890 the critic Maurice Thompson, a friend of Thomas Wentworth Higginson, thought the influence of Emerson on Emily Dickinson was obvious: "She has his curious scorn of continuity and his way of appearing ignorant of absurd discords, setting them just where the finest accord is imperatively demanded." Since Thompson attributed the oddity of her manner to "a superb brain that has suffered some obscure lesion," it is likely that his diagnosis would have been the same for Emerson. The appearance in Emerson or Dickinson of what might be thought of as "modern" or "difficult" elements was at times offensive to Victorian aesthetic values and in certain instances, as here, registered as psychopathology. Thompson's remarks are quoted in Millicent Todd Bingham, *Ancestors' Brocades* (New York: Harper and Row, 1945), 79–80, and again in Joseph Morgan Thomas, "Harnessing Proteus: Publishing the Canon of Emerson's Poetry," Ph.D. diss., Rutgers, 1994, p. 54.

cation shortly after this change was made, Chapman's helpfulness to its erstwhile editor persisted. On the recommendation of Bronson Alcott's Fruitlands partner, the English reformer Henry G. Wright, Emerson accepted Chapman's offer to publish his works, and sent him, in 1844, the pamphlets on *The Young American* and the *Address . . . on . . . Emancipation . . . in the British West Indies* in addition to *Essays: Second Series*. Emerson was pleased with Chapman's work on these items, even though the arcane laws of England had prevented the securing of a usable copyright. Nearly three years later, hoping to fare better with arrangements for *Poems*, Emerson entrusted him with that work as well. The securing of copyright in fact required that the book be published first in England, so Emerson produced a set of fair copies of the sixty poems he had selected, finishing up the work of transcription in Bangor, Maine, where he had gone to lecture. The packet of manuscripts was bundled up and sent on 13 October by coastal schooner to James Munroe's office in Boston, to be forwarded thence by steamer to Chapman. In the accompanying note to Munroe, Emerson said:

> In this parcel I send Chapman all the Copy of my poems, but the few last, which will go in the next steamer. I tell him that he must act in concert with you in reference to the time of publication. . . . Now that I have got the right readings settled for him, I shall be able to finish & send you your Copy immediately on my return home, which should be on Saturday next [17 October]. I have duplicates of all but a few which I think to print directly from the Dial, indicating the *errata*. Monday or Tuesday we can begin to print. (*L*, III, 356–357)

Work progressed a little more slowly than Emerson predicted, however, so as not to preempt Chapman.[51] On the Wednesday fol-

---

51 See Robert J. Scholnick, "Boston and Beyond," in Joel Myerson et al, eds., *The Oxford Handbook of Transcendentalism* (New York: Oxford University Press, 2010), 497–505, for an overview of Chapman's involvement with Emerson and the Transcendentalist circle.

lowing Emerson's return home, he signed his contract with Munroe.[52]

A month later, on 27 November, Emerson reported to his brother William that he had received the first hundred pages of Munroe's proofs (*L,* III, 362). The letter gave no hint of alarm, but he must have discovered by this time or shortly afterwards that he was making a great many corrections, sometimes to repair Munroe's misreading of the manuscript, but more often to revise the text he had submitted. By the time he got through with this process he realized that Chapman's edition, lacking the benefit of his supervision and corrections, must be teeming with errors and with innumerable newly rejected readings. A few days after the publication of the Boston edition, but before the arrival of the first copy from England, Emerson wrote to Chapman with instructions to conform any future printing to the text as established in Munroe's edition.

> The printing of it has convinced me that I was guilty of a great rashness in sending you the work in manuscript: for I see how impossible it is in printing from a manuscript so far from the author to avoid a hundred blunders. So I assure myself that with all your superior intelligence & best heed, I shall yet find a multitude of errata in your edition, for which I shall be obliged to thank my own bad writing: to say nothing of corrections more or less material which I have made on my own text, in the course of printing. May I then request of you, before a single copy more is printed from your office, that an exact comparison should be made, page for page, & letter for letter, between your book & ours, and your edition corrected from ours. (*L,* VIII, 100)

The comparison made by the present editors between the surviving pages of printer's copy and the text of the English first edition shows that Chapman's typesetters had little difficulty with Emer-

52 The text of the contract is quoted in the Textual Introduction below, see p. cxxiii.

son's handwriting and were, on the whole, quite accurate. Emerson's strong preference for the Boston edition thus involves no aspersion on the quality of the work in Chapman's shop but reflects instead the numerous authorial changes made after the first, hurriedly prepared set of manuscripts had been sent off to England. The book was published in London on 12 December and in Boston on 25 December, 1846, though each bore the date 1847 on the title page (Myerson, A 18.1.a and A 18.2.a, respectively).

Many of the reviews, including some that were strongly negative, conceded that here, in the words of a first brief notice in the *Boston Courier,* was "one of the most peculiar and original volumes of poetry ever published in the United States."[53] Not all the early commentary, however, meant to imply that peculiarity and originality were estimable traits. Indeed the consensus was that Emerson's verse, being markedly difficult, had, disappointingly and unpoetically, more to do with the head than with the heart. There were complaints of obscurity, vagueness, and abstraction. To many in that sentimental age the philosophical character of Emerson's efforts seemed a betrayal of the fundamental aims and purposes of poetry, the conventional limits of which were often asserted by reviewers with a smug and knowing precision. It was a position not far removed from that which Matthew Arnold would later adopt, and yet to a modernist or post-modernist sensibility, it involves an arbitrary and rather Victorian set of expectations. The most abusive of these reviewers, unable to read Emerson as they had been accustomed to reading Scott or Byron or Mrs. Hemans, simply gave up, falling back on the pretense that Emerson offered "a mere hubbub and jumble of words," a mere concoction of "mystical nonsense." The conservative Unitarian philosopher Francis Bowen, the author of this opinion, had published a similarly adverse review of *Nature* a decade earlier, where the complaint centered, as it did here again, on the sheer unintelligibility

---

53 29 December; quoted in Ralph L. Rusk, *The Life of Ralph Waldo Emerson* (New York: Columbia University Press, 1949), 322. In the *Christian Examiner,* XLII (March 1847): 255, Cyrus A. Bartol wrote that Emerson's book was "the most original and peculiar" of the ten volumes of poetry he had under review.

of Transcendental discourse.[54] It is worth noting that the word "mysticism" or "mystical" crops up in virtually every review of Emerson's poetry—it tends to be strongly pejorative when used in connection with *Poems* and, twenty years later, appreciative when used in connection with *May-Day.* The term defies strict contextual definition, but it seems to be covering a religious anxiety over Emerson's antinomianism that the culture had largely resolved— or got past—by 1867.

The novelty of Emerson's writings, including its indifference to sectarian religion, clearly challenged the assumptions of his readership, but more was involved in Emerson's giving offense than a simple doctrinal disagreement. The reviews show time and again that the ability of readers to appreciate or even to comprehend poetry depended on finding approved religious positions, as if on these the reading experience itself radically depended. Absent such points of agreement, it was often the case that no positive sense could be made out at all. Surely the single most vituperative review was that by the Catholic convert and ex-transcendentalist Orestes Brownson, who admitted that he would gladly assign to his old friend's poems "the highest rank among our American attempts at poetry"—but for the fact that they were blasphemous and formally incompetent. He would like to praise their excellence as poems, but there was a nagging difficulty about discussing the excellence of "poetry which chants falsehood and evil." Brownson managed to contradict his own finding of dangerous meanings by suggesting elsewhere that Emerson, as a poet, dealt in "words, words with no distinct meaning, with scarcely any meaning at all." For this reason, for this way of avoiding being a Christian in "Threnody," for example, the consolations of that poem failed, which in turn contributed to making *Poems* "the saddest book we ever read."[55]

54 Bowen, "Nine New Poets," *North American Review,* LXIV (April 1847): 407, 413. Bowen was the editor of the *North American Review* at this time and wrote most of its articles; his review of *Nature* appeared in the *Christian Examiner,* XXI (January 1837): 371–385.

55 Orestes A. Brownson, "R. W. Emerson's Poems," *Brownson's Quarterly Review,* IV (April 1847): 262, 263, 273, 264.

A far more nuanced objection arose in quarters nearer at hand (indeed among friends) from the perception that Emerson was, if not quite in the way that Brownson supposed, nevertheless still a heretic. Both John Sullivan Dwight and Cyrus A. Bartol, graduates of the Harvard Divinity School in 1835 and, subsequently, Transcendental Club attendees, wrote reviews including generous claims for Emerson's performance, but they both ended by sharply qualifying the praise, advancing a concern that, because Emerson notoriously rejected the personality and fatherhood of the Deity, he could have, in consequence, no feel for the brotherhood of suffering Humanity. For this reason he was forced to sit apart and aloof in an age justifiably preoccupied with reform. What Dwight and Bartol had to say on this subject seems offered in support of the associationist and communitarian William Henry Channing in the simmering dispute best known through Emerson's Ode to Channing. Although offered in behalf of reform, it was nevertheless a seriously conservative argument that was being urged against Emerson: that some form of organized religion— even Unitarianism—was in fact the only point of access to the organized or social world, the only originator of moral responsibility. The defensive anxiety that Emerson's positions provoked—in poetry as in prose—was not confined to the conservative churches, but operated to a surprising extent within Transcendentalist circles as well.[56]

Ironically, the reviews from New York were more positive on average than those from New England, as they were less likely to invoke the sort of religious scruples that bedeviled the Yankees. In

56 Thus Bartol's question: "And not taking cordially to his heart the Christian doctrines of a Father and a particular Providence, how can he strongly embrace the dependent doctrine of human brotherhood, or feel the unlimited sympathy which this doctrine inspires?" Such enabling faith in the exclusive reform efficacy of Christian doctrines seems to Bartol to be impaired by Emerson's having "no preference of Jesus over any other great and good man," and by his objectionable habit of speaking of "'the gods' as an old Roman would do" (op. cit., 258). Dwight's review, with its very similar opinions, appeared in *The Harbinger, Devoted to Social and Political Progress*, IV (16 January 1847): 91–94, and (23 January 1847): 106–109.

another irony, the Democratic papers seemed to like the poems better than the Whig journals did. The founder of the so called Young Americans, Cornelius Mathews, writing in *The Literary World,* shrewdly disposed of what seemed problematic in Emerson's poems by quoting at length Samuel Johnson's equivocally negative comments on the metaphysical poets—first the violent yoking together of the most heterogeneous ideas, then the fact that "their learning instructs, and their subtlety surprises; but the reader commonly thinks his improvement dearly bought, and though he sometimes admires, is seldom pleased." Having bracketed Emerson with Herbert, Donne, and Cowley, Mathews then turned to Emerson's "substantial and distinctive merits" (something few reviewers bothered to particularize). He instanced "The Apology" as being, in an entirely characteristic way, more about Emerson's relation to nature than about nature itself—as nature might figure in more conventional or less thoughtful descriptive poems. "Here, it will be noticed, [referring to "The Apology,"] there is more about the thing than of the thing itself." Emerson's

> chief capital as a poetical writer consists in the profound belief of a mighty secret in nature, animating, connecting, irradiating, solving all things, which is worth all external things in a mass, which pervades and transcends them all, which it is worth the world and all the best effort of the world to discover, and to discover which all other business, callings, avocations, should be laid aside; and he has an Ideal Man who is constantly on the search, and whom to delineate so engaged, is the pleasure, and the chief success of our author.

Conceiving of nature as Emerson did "in relation to the intellect, in its creative and constructive qualities, in reference to beauty and proportion and fitness," manages to present "the aspect of nature remotest from the general interest of mankind"—which explains, on the one hand, why Emerson was unlikely to be popular, and why, on the other, he had accomplished something new and valuable. Mathews ended the review by announcing that "we have in Mr. Emerson one of the finest, as he is certainly one of the most singular, poetical spirits of the time."[57]

That view was shared by an anonymous writer for *The United States Magazine and Democratic Review,* a journal long associated with Mathews' colleague and Hawthorne-promoter, John Louis O'Sullivan. The emphasis of this commentary was once again on the sheer novelty of the contents of *Poems.* Early and late, Emerson was able to surprise the critics: as O. W. Firkins noted, Emerson was "always doing something not quite like other people and not quite like himself."[58] Where so many other poets were conventional and derivative, Emerson was regularly taken notice of for his startling self-reliance. He was, according to the *Democratic Review,* "the most original, not only of American poets, but of living writers. He is no vendor of second-hand notions, but a man on his own account, who gives you jewels from his own mines, and of his own setting."[59] And, once again, this large acknowledgment of genuineness was not inconsistent with the noting of deficiencies. Truth to self seems to have included, for example, an indifference to musicality: "He lacks too much that peculiar sense which is the origin of rhythm and number, to pay much attention to either. Not endowed with the perception and love of music, he feels no need of it, and generally does not aim at it. . . .The meaning and not the melody is what he thinks of."[60] The reviewer notes, as oth-

---

57 *The Literary World,* I (3 April 1847): 197–199. Ralph L. Rusk, in his *Life of Ralph Waldo Emerson,* 323, identified Mathews as the author of this anonymous review. Evert Duyckinck, Mathews' close friend and collaborator in the literary nationalism of Young America, had soured on Emerson when he failed to get his book under contract to Wiley and Putnam; in "Bad News for Transcendental Poets," *Literary World,* I (20 February 1847): 53, Duyckinck foretold the imminent collapse of that school of poetry.

58 Firkins, *Ralph Waldo Emerson* (Boston: Houghton Mifflin, 1915), 287.

59 "New Poetry in New England," *The United States Magazine, and Democratic Review,* XX (May 1847): 393. Subsequent quotations in this paragraph are from pp. 396–397.

60 Emerson's allegedly (and sometimes actually) faulty metrics were routinely made a subject of commentary. It seems that he could never dissociate regularity of rhythm from the triteness of popular magazine verse: "By and by [the ear]

ers had also, that by including the poem "Merlin" Emerson seemed to present the key to his poetics, from which one could sensibly infer that he valued the rough and natural over the smooth and artificial. The idea that Emerson courted imperfection and made a virtue of it helped to explain, if it did not extenuate, the occasionally grating rhythms and awkward rhymes, while at the same time contributing to the impression that as a poet he relied on the raw, unprocessed inspiration that had been given to him and not on "the Jacob's ladder of preparatory toil."[61] The whole notion that the poet Emerson somehow communed directly

---

learns the secret, that love and thought always speak in measure or music,—that with the elevation of the soul, the asperities and incoherence of speech disappear, and the language of truth is always pure music. . . . The finer poet, the finer ear. Each new poet will as certainly invent new metres as he will have new images to clothe. In true poetry, the thought and the metre are not painfully adjusted afterward, but are born together, as the soul and the body of a child. The difference between poetry and what is called 'stock poetry,' I take to be this, that in *stock poetry* the metre is given and the verses are made to it, and in poetry the sense dictates the tune or march of the words" ("The Poet," *EL*, III, 358–359). These views may help to account for Emerson's dismissal of Edgar Allan Poe, in 1860, as "the jingle-man" (William Dean Howells, *Literary Friends and Acquaintances* [New York: Harper & Brothers, 1900], 63). Those who heard the poems read in Emerson's own voice were much less inclined to fault the rhythms: "Of me, Alcott said, 'some of the organs were free, some fated; the voice was entirely liberated; And my poems or Essays were not rightly published, until I read them!'" (*JMN*, XV, 339).

61 A surprisingly large and often quite useful fraction of the critical commentary on Emerson's poetry has organized itself around this binary of conscious and unconscious artistry (if the latter is not an oxymoron). How, in Emerson, is the inspired romantic artist compounded with the realist workman who respects composition and counts syllables? "Any account of his poetics," writes Joseph M. Thomas, "should recognize a competing set of social and skeptical ideas, attitudes, and performances that lie alongside his talk of oracular passivity [as in "The Problem"], indeed pulling against it and giving primacy to the writer's worldly limitations and practice." See Thomas's "Poverty and Power: Revisiting Emerson's Poetics," in Ronald A. Bosco and Joel Myerson, eds., *Emerson: Bicentennial Essays* (Boston: Massachusetts Historical Society, 2006), 213–246, an essay that surveys the criticism on this topic and provides a perceptive analysis (quotation on p. 216).

with God and (unlike the rest of us) dispensed with "preparation" belonged with the logical inferences from his antinomianism.

Poems (1847) has scarcely ever been read as a single performance, and yet it will reward the reader who, with patience and attention, moves through the whole book consecutively. It opens with "The Sphinx," the very name of challenge, the very name of puzzle, a poem that on its first appearance in the *Dial* elicited a sustained intelligent response from Thoreau, who thus acknowledged its demands (see Appendix A at the end of this volume). It also, however, elicited a pained and outraged lament from Orestes Brownson, in the review mentioned above, who charged Emerson with the dangerous immorality of confounding the "love of the Best" with the mortal sin of pride. This difficult poem put readers on notice and prepared them to accept the series of short poems that followed, linking abstract philosophical issues with ordinary experience. The longer meditative poems toward the middle of the book, clustered around the symphonic "Woodnotes, II" and the argumentative "Ode, Inscribed to W. H. Channing," further clarified themes introduced earlier. Distinct clusters dominated later in the book, pursuing themes of love and poetry, while the conclusion is given to an intimate, quiet, and melancholy combination of history and personal memorial.

VII. Interlude

The English edition of *Poems*, with its many errors, attracted relatively little public attention. Several British journals, by way of noticing it, doubted that it would add much to the favorable opinion that readers had already formed of the author from his essays.[62]

---

62 This was about the sum total of what was said in the *Westminster Review*, XLVII (April 1847): 250, and in *The Daguerreotype*, I (4 September 1847): 142–143. A few longer reviews were not especially perceptive or noteworthy. A writer for *The Athenæum*, no. 1006 (6 February 1847), praised Emerson's "tone of independent thinking, . . . which begets respect for the author," but found wanting, in most of the poems, the "decision of outline and form necessary to a finished work" (144–145). A writer for *The Christian Remembrancer*, ser. 2, XV (April 1848),

On 31 May 1847 Emerson wrote to Chapman to express regret on learning "that my book of Poems is to be the occasion of loss to you, which I had ventured to hope might be a benefit" (*L*, VIII, 118).

But if *Poems* was not a critical or commercial success in England, it nevertheless helped to solidify a small circle of devoted readers, and provoked Chapman and Carlyle in London and Alexander Ireland in Manchester to invite Emerson to come to England to give lectures. During the ensuing tour (1847–1848) Emerson met a great many notables, including, among the poets, Arthur Hugh Clough, David Thom, Henry S. Sutton, Thomas H. Gill, Bryan Waller Procter ("Barry Cornwall"), Richard Monckton Milnes, Coventry Patmore, Philip James Bailey (author of *Festus*), William Wordsworth (renewing an old acquaintance), and Alfred Tennyson. Emerson often gave these new acquaintances copies of the corrected "Fourth" Boston edition of *Poems* that they might have the proper readings.[63] It may be that Emerson's introduction to the literary and scientific talent of England inclined him all the more to take seriously John Chapman's proposal for an "'Atlantic Journal,' which," Emerson explained after returning home, would "be written from London & Boston" (*L*, VIII, 186). Theodore Parker was at this time urging Emerson to help with the new *Massachusetts Quarterly Review* that he and James Elliot Cabot were busily filling with matter of their own, but this publishing venture,

---

after bestowing measured praise on William Cullen Bryant and Nathaniel Parker Willis, was unable to follow up on a critically disarming verdict that Emerson's poems were "the most unequivocal nonsense which was ever gravely brought before the world" (346).

63 Henry Sutton alluded to this circumstance: "Up to that date we in this country had only had them as published by John Chapman; and, on minutely comparing the two books, I found swarms of errors of the press in the English edition, and was afterwards careful to supply my friend William Allingham, the poet, with a full list of these, enabling him to correct his own copy thereby" ("Emerson. Reminiscences of His Visits to Manchester. II," *Manchester City News*, 27 May 1899, 14). The editors thank Joel Myerson for calling this article to our attention.

stuffy and dull as it seemed to Emerson, and more concerned with theology and politics than with literature, was not an eligible medium for his poetry and did not in other respects engage his interest. Young Wentworth Higginson agreed, telling Emerson that what was needed was a revival of the defunct *Dial*.[64] The existence of such a journal earlier in the decade had provided social cohesion to the Transcendental movement, with the added benefit that it kept Emerson's muse employed. Now, without a convenient periodical venue, without a magazine that Emerson could cordially support, his energies reverted to lecturing and to the publishing of prose works, notably *Nature, Addresses and Lectures* (1849), *Representative Men* (1850), *Memoirs of Margaret Fuller Ossoli* (1852), and *English Traits* (1856). His productivity as a poet during this period fell off, not to revive again in full strength until the founding of *The Atlantic Monthly* in 1857. During the decade after *Poems* appeared, he published no more than eight poems: half a dozen very brief translations from the Persian in *The Liberty Bell* (1851), edited by the anti-slavery activist Edmund Quincy; one poem, "Freedom," in the anti-slavery anthology *Autographs for Freedom* (1854), edited by Frederick Douglass's assistant Julia Griffiths; and a single quatrain, "S.H.," in an obituary notice for Emerson's friend and fellow Concordian Samuel Hoar. Privately and in a very desultory manner he continued to compose poems, mostly rather short, as the journals and poetry notebooks show, but he was for the time being wholly unconcerned about publishing them.

Still, his fascination with Hafiz and the poets of ancient Persia continued unabated. In October 1850 he purchased from Theodore Parker a copy of Joseph von Hammer's *Geschichte der schönen redekünste Persiens, mit einer Blüthenlese aus zweyhundert persischen Dichtern* (Wien: Heubner und Volke, 1818), which reinforced Emerson's appreciation for this "light out of the east" (*L*, VIII, 249 n.66; Harding, 125; *TN*, II, 39). In notebook Orientalist through-

---

64 *L*, VIII, 185–186; *JMN*, XI, 59–60; Tilden G. Edelstein, *Strange Enthusiasm: A Life of Thomas Wentworth Higginson* (New York: Athenaeum, 1970), 90–91.

out the 1850s Emerson entered draft translations from this work as well as from the *Diwan* of Hafiz, interspersed with notes from his extensive reading in the literary history of India and Persia (*TN*, II, 37–141). The major consequence of this study was "Persian Poetry," one of Emerson's first prose contributions to the *Atlantic Monthly*. Although this essay included references to a number of Sufi poets, it is mainly occupied with Hafiz, who, in Emerson's estimation, exemplified all the traits of a great poet, becoming thereby a theoretical or explanatory convenience.

> That hardihood and self-equality of every sound nature, which result from the feeling that the spirit in him is entire and as good as the world, which entitle the poet to speak with authority, and make him an object of interest, and his every phrase and syllable significant, are in Hafiz, and abundantly fortify and ennoble his tone. (*CW*, VIII, 131)

A great merit of Hafiz was his independence from religious orthodoxy. Such "intellectual liberty," Emerson observes, "is a certificate of profound thought."

> We accept the religions and politics into which we fall; and it is only a few delicate spirits who are sufficient to see that the whole web of convention is the imbecility of those whom it entangles,—that the mind suffers no religion and no empire but its own. It indicates this respect to absolute truth by the use it makes of the symbols that are most stable and reverend, and therefore is always provoking the accusation of irreligion. (132)

Emerson implicitly refers this "complete intellectual emancipation" to traits of character in Hafiz or to his individual genius, but as Emerson knew, the Sufi mystics quite generally asserted the claims of an antinomian spirituality as against the legal and ceremonial aspects of orthodox Islam. So, indeed, had the Gnostics with respect to orthodox Christianity or the Transcendentalists with respect to a conservative and often formalist Unitarianism. Hafiz did not often sound like an approved follower of Mohammad, any more than Emerson had avoided the charge that his first book of poems was "a directly infidel work."[65]

The *Atlantic Monthly*, under the genial editorship of James Russell Lowell, a fellow member with Emerson of the Saturday Club, provided a new audience for the poems, but the publication of "Brahma" in the first number (November 1857) gave occasion for much public hilarity over a poem so allegedly esoteric and gnomic. The popular press for a while teemed with parodies.[66] Between November 1857 and October 1858 Emerson published six strong poems in the new journal: in addition to "Brahma" there appeared "The Romany Girl," "Days," "The Chartist's Complaint" (companion piece to "Days"), "Two Rivers," and "Waldeinsamkeit," mostly selected from poems written some years earlier. In 1859 Emerson's American publisher, Phillips and Sampson, failed, and Emerson, hesitating only briefly, acted on Lowell's urging that he sign with Ticknor and Fields, who would then bring out *The Conduct of Life* in 1860. His work on that book, following a heavy schedule of lecturing in the spring, kept him from publishing anything in the *Atlantic* until November. It was during this hiatus that Emerson contributed a dozen of his remarkable quatrains and one of the most important of his oriental translations ("The Song of Seid Nimetollah of Kuhistan") to Moncure Conway's Cincinnati journal, the *Dial*. By the time he returned to the *Atlantic* as a place to publish his poems, beginning with "The Titmouse" in

65 The accusation was made by the anonymous reviewer for the English high church journal the *Christian Remembrancer,* 349 (see fn. 60, above), and less directly by many others. In "Persian Poetry" Emerson proceeded to commend the boundlessness of Hafiz's antinomian freedom: "Wrong shall not be wrong to Hafiz, for the name's sake. A law or statute is to him what a fence is to a nimble schoolboy,—a temptation to jump" (132).

66 Robert E. Burkholder and Joel Myerson, *Emerson: An Annotated Secondary Bibliography* (Pittsburgh: University of Pittsburgh Press, 1985), 735–737, lists 27 parodies published before the end of the year.

May 1862, the journal had been purchased by Ticknor and Fields and James T. Fields himself had succeeded Lowell as editor. Emerson's much increased activity as a poet in the public eye after 1857 coincided with a renewal of interest in the theoretical aspects of poetic composition, as evidenced by the extensive gathering of notes in journal PY at this time (*TN*, II, 256–329).

The publishing firm of Ticknor and Fields was unlike any Emerson had dealt with before. The sequence from James Munroe to Phillips and Sampson and on to Ticknor and Fields represented a steady increase in professionalism and aggressive marketing. Hawthorne's old concerns about the regional limitation of Emerson's reputation had now been as fully addressed as the choice of a publisher could address them. (Neither before the Civil War nor after would Emerson have sympathetic readers in the South). Initially the work of the new publisher centered on *The Conduct of Life* and the reissuing of older collections, including the first two series of *Essays*. Such reprints were often identified as volumes of "Emerson's Writings" by gold-stamping that phrase on the spine to encourage sales of the seven volumes as a set. With respect to *Poems,* they followed the lead of Phillips and Sampson and simply used the stereotype plates that Emerson owned to issue new printings. These plates were by now worn and battered, but the plan to bring out a new edition (that is, a complete resetting of type) seems to have been formed not to supplant the older edition, but simply to have an edition to sell in a format matching other Ticknor and Fields poets. This was the so-called "Blue and Gold" edition the firm had inaugurated in 1857 for American authors long since under contract, such as Whittier and Longfellow, and for the numerous British poets they published, such as Tennyson, Arthur Hugh Clough, and Gerald Massey. The small trim size, attractive blue cloth binding, and gilt edges made these handy volumes instant classics of book design, but the authors had very little to do in any instance with their production. There is no indication that Emerson read proofs for his "Blue and Gold" volume, issued in the spring of 1865. Reprintings from the old 1847 plates continued to be made at regular intervals throughout Emerson's lifetime, since this format realized a 25¢ per copy return to the author compared to only 10¢ for the Blue and Gold. Copies from the old plates were last struck off in 1882.[67]

Although the "Blue and Gold" edition possesses little intrinsic interest for the bibliographer or textual editor, its appearance marked a notable shift in Emerson's standing with the public. His adoption into this conspicuous series immediately placed Emerson in a galaxy of approved Anglo-American poets, a fact that in some measure mooted the "outsider" or heretical reputation created in the late 40s by the first reviews. More specifically, it bracketed Emerson with fellow Saturday Club members Lowell, Holmes, Longfellow, and Whittier, all of whom had their Blue and Gold incarnations, so that the designation Fireside or Schoolhouse Poets quickly became a benchmark context for thinking about an otherwise individualistic and self-reliant Emerson. Through the last quarter of the nineteenth century Emerson floated in and out of affiliation, in the public's mind's eye, with this popular group, though attentive critics continued in various ways to affirm Emerson's distinguishing traits. As John Timberman Newcomb has suggested, the poet and anthologist Edmund Clarence Stedman was "the first [in 1900] to form a transcendentalist canon for American poetry by reorienting Emerson away from the Fireside group and toward Whitman."[68]

As notices in the Boston *Commonwealth* suggest, the Blue and Gold edition proved a convenient rallying point for an especially emphatic group of young disciples, a group that Carl F. Strauch referred to, for the extravagance of its appreciation, as a "cult." The *Commonwealth* had been a Free-Soil paper during the previous decade, but in 1862 it was reorganized by Emerson's friend George Luther Stearns to agitate for immediate emancipation. Stearns, a wealthy Medford industrialist, had been one of

67 Myerson, 160. See also Houghton Library "Contract File," MS Am2346 (914), folder 3.

68 *Would Poetry Disappear? American Verse and the Crisis of Modernity* (Columbus: Ohio State University Press, 2004), 112.

the earliest and most important financiers of Free State forces in Kansas and, as an outgrowth of that activity, became one of the "Secret Six" of John Brown's backers. Putting the *Commonwealth* into business, Stearns hired two young men as editors: Franklin B. Sanborn and Moncure D. Conway, the first a fellow member of the "Secret Six," a Kansas Committeeman, and a resident of Concord (where he taught the Emerson children), the second the erstwhile editor of the Cincinnati *Dial*, an acolyte of Emerson, and, though a native of Virginia, a very active abolitionist. By the spring of 1865 when the Blue and Gold *Poems* appeared, Conway had already left the journal, the freedom of the slaves having been achieved. Sanborn, however, continued on as editor and made the paper into something of an opinion-shaper in literary matters. On 15 April he published his "Appraisal of Emerson's Prose and Poetry," noting that Emerson was now a universally popular writer, though still far more recognized for the morality of the prose than for the under-appreciated mysticism of the poetry. The aggressiveness of Sanborn's claims for the verse would set the tone for the "cult": "There are those who think that even in the metrical form of his poems, Mr. Emerson has equalled any modern poet; but in the poetic spirit—a much nobler quality—he has certainly done so, and, as we hold, gone far beyond any one. . . . The verses of other poets seem tame and vapid compared with his masterly lines" (p. 1, col. 5). A month later a similarly effusive notice appeared from the pen of John A. Dorgan, a member of Conway's circle from Cincinnati and a contributor of poetry to the *Dial*. Like Sanborn, he argued that Emerson's poetry was much superior to the prose works, though scarcely so well known. More important than any of these early notices in the *Commonwealth*, however, is the way they anticipate more ambitious critical and appreciative works by subsequent members of the cult, extending from Joel Benton's *Emerson as a Poet* (1883) to William Sloane Kennedy's "Clews to Emerson's Mystic Verse" (1899), and including much miscellaneous popular commentary by Charles Malloy and F. B. Sanborn. Among the lasting effects of this body of material was the transformation of that old *bête noir* of Emerson's first critics—his "mysticism"—into something approachable and even admirable, though perhaps at the cost of making it also seem ordinary and innocuous.[69]

VIII. *May-Day*

On 4 October 1866 Emerson's daughter Ellen wrote to her brother Edward, then sojourning in the West, to announce that plans were under way for a new volume of poems. She noted that Edith, the younger daughter,

> discourses upon the binding of the new Poems, for prominent among our present interests is the fact that Mr Papa has actually undertaken to finish the Spring poem ["May-Day"] and publish the second volume this autumn. Isn't it delightful? Two nights he has read to us out of them and we have had perfect evenings. "Voluntaries" is to be in it you know, and the Mottoes that are best from the books, and all that have been in the Atlantic, with Spring, and one or two others that never were printed. (*ETE*, I, 406)

Within a few weeks Emerson was examining the earliest proof sheets in what became an unusually drawn-out process of publication (*L*, IX, 244; *The Commonwealth*, 20 October 1866, p. 3, col. 3). Months later—toward the end of February 1867—Emerson explained to an inquiring correspondent that it had been James

---

69 On the original "cult" and its recrudescence in the 1880s and 90s see Strauch, diss., 223–229, 269–274. For the connection of F. B. Sanborn, Joel Benton, and John Dorgan with Conway's *Dial*, see Gohdes, *The Periodicals of American Transcendentalism*, 205–206. Dorgan's authorship of the *Commonwealth* article ("Mr. Emerson as Poet and Essayist," 27 May 1865, p. 1, cols. 3–4, signed "D") was revealed by Benton in *Emerson as a Poet* (New York: M. L. Holbrook, 1883), 89. Two copies of Dorgan's volume of poetry, *Studies*, 2nd ed. (Philadelphia: C. H. Marot, 1864) are in Emerson's library (Harding, 83). Kennedy and Malloy combined close readings of Emerson's poetry with the commendatory delight of the effective popularizer. Kennedy's "Clews" was serialized in *Poet-Lore* in 1899 and 1900; Malloy's commentary, of approximately the same period, was gathered from five periodicals by Kenneth Walter Cameron as *A Study of Emerson's Major Poems* (Hartford: Transcendental Books, 1973).

T. Fields who first urged the new collection, only then, in mid-production, to put the project on hold:

> At his own instance long ago, I began in the autumn to collect my own scattered verses not hitherto published in a book, & added of quite unpublished verses about half the volume & when it was all in type about the 1 December [1866], he [Fields] said he was sorry but it would be madness to print it for New Year's for all his western correspondents had written to him, "Send us no new book, least of all poetry." So it was put aside, with the chance of better times in April. (*L*, V, 506–507)

Emerson had taken proofs with him on his western lecture tour (9 January to 23 March), but it was quite impossible, in the bustle of railroad life, to find the time to correct them. "It is very awkward," he wrote to Ellen from Chicago, "as my Poems are promised for 1 April, that I should be eleven hundred miles & more from the printers, & with so many *errata* that I am bound to correct. I shall have to pray Mr Fields to postpone a little, now that he has postponed so much" (*L*, V, 505). At last, on 2 April, he gave Fields permission to publish (Myerson, 297). Although the book was announced as published on 29 April (*Boston Daily Advertiser*), the presentation copies, in a handsome white linen binding, were inscribed and sent out on 1 May (see *JMN*, XVI, 56–61, for the list of recipients).

The order and arrangement of the poems within the volume were, again, as in the 1847 volume, carefully thought out. An opening section comprising a full thirty percent of the whole consisted of the two poems "May-Day" and "The Adirondacs." The central section, under the heading "Occasional and Miscellaneous Pieces," contained all of the *Atlantic Monthly* poems, augmented by four that had appeared elsewhere and a dozen poems previously unpublished. The *Atlantic* items were not arranged in a precisely chronological order, but they do all fall between "Brahma," the earliest published, and "Terminus," the last published. The decision to open the section with "Brahma" likely reflects the same determination to put difficulty in the foreground that twenty years earlier in *Poems* had given pride of place to "The Sphinx." A section of "Elements" (the chapter mottoes from the prose works) is followed by sections of "Quatrains" and "Translations"—most of the latter having been culled from the *Atlantic* essay on "Persian Poetry."

The reviews this time were less dismayed by Emerson's heterodoxy and more willing to be charmed by the title poem's long meditative celebration of spring in New England, which was several times praised for its realism. Given the non-authorial reshufflings that "May-Day" rather notoriously underwent in 1876 (directed by Ellen) and again for the 1884 Riverside edition (directed by Edward), it might be supposed to have been a failure on its first appearance, and yet such was by no means the case. Rufus Ellis, minister at Boston's First Unitarian Church, said of "May-Day" that "amongst many jewels" to be found in the book, "it is the gem"; he particularly commented on the poem's authenticity as a record of impressions: it was not dependent on "pretty words about spring from old poets. [Emerson] is in the midst of the world he tells of, and what comes to him through every open sense he reports, as one might fetch a rose, all dripping with the morning dew."[70] An anonymous writer for the major bookseller's trade publication opined that the title poem was "fresh and vigorous in its style" and "one of the author's most successful efforts in courting the muses."[71] A young writer and sub-editor at the *Atlantic Monthly*, William Dean Howells, judged that "no one has yet been allowed to speak so well for the spring of our New World as this poet." Howells generously conceded that "the very irregularity of Mr. Emerson's poem seems to be part of its verisimilitude," its "pauses and impulses and mysterious caprices" being those of

70 Ellis, Review of *May-Day and Other Pieces, Monthly Religious Magazine*, XXXVIII (July 1867): 79.

71 *American Literary Gazette and Publishers' Circular,* IX (15 May 1867): 45. "May-Day" was also highly praised by the second-generation Transcendentalist David A. Wasson in the *Radical*, II (August 1867): 760–762, an organ of the Free Religious Association.

the variable season itself and not indicative of "the deliberation and consequence of art." Which was, of course, an elegantly delicate way of saying that the poem, however much enjoyed by many and however eloquent with "tenderness and beauty," had at best a merely superficial kind of coherence.[72]

The review by Howells was nearly the only one of any critical distinction or discernment—the only one that had anything new to say of Emerson's achievement in poetry. Slighting the mottoes ("we do not expect to live long enough to enjoy some of them"), Howells preferred "The Romany Girl," "Voluntaries," and "The Boston Hymn," pointing out how the first of these exemplified an important, constantly recurrent theme of the poet's: "wild nature's gleeful consciousness of freedom, and exultant scorn of restraint and convention." In speaking of "Voluntaries," Howells praised what so many critics of Emerson found lacking—an impressive and dignified musicality, promised by the title and borne out in the verse.

A brief reference to "The Boston Hymn" becomes an occasion to point out Emerson's "sublime colloquiality in which the commonest words of every-day parlance seem cut anew, and are made to shine with a fresh and novel lustre." In pointing to the so-frequently overlooked matter of Emerson's diction, Howells indicates in what ways and to what extent the romantic poet satisfies a realist aesthetic.[73] Howells also lavishes high praise on "Terminus" in a way that might suggest what is missing in the contention—reiterated elsewhere to the point of triteness—that Emerson's po-

72 *AM*, XX (September 1867): 376.

73 "Words used in a new sense & figuratively, dart a diamond lustre that delights; & *every* word admits a new use, & heaven beyond heaven. Almost it is not even friends, but this power of words that is best" (*JMN*, XV, 230). O. W. Firkins gives an example from "May-Day": "Where in English is there a word more pedestrian, more lounging and unambitious, than the word 'fellows'? Emerson can dilate it to cosmic dimensions, and make it orchestral with music:—

The caged linnet in the Spring
Hearkens for the choral glee,
When his *fellows* on the wing
Migrate from the Southern Sea" (*Ralph Waldo Emerson*, 293).

ems lack feeling: "'Terminus' has a wonderful didactic charm, and must be valued as one of the noblest introspective poems in the language. The poet touches his reader by his acceptance of fate and age, and his serene trust of the future, and yet is not moved by his own pathos." What is valuable and distinctive in Howells's comment is all in that last clause.

Howells was not much taken with "The Adirondacs," which he found "one of the prosiest" of the poems. And yet, as indicated below in the poem headnote, the work has not lacked admirers. In the context of Emerson's canon, it is so unusual in so many respects that it is perhaps best regarded as deliberately experimental. The undeniable impression of prosiness comes from its colloquial and at times mock heroic blank verse, by which Emerson's nearly unprecedented excursion into narrative has been accommodated. The poem seems to test Emerson's own dictum that "poetry needs little history.—It is one part history & ninety nine parts music; or, shall I say, fact & affection" (*JMN*, X, 144). The performance gives the impression that Emerson may have been exploring to see what territory, if any, might lie between his always poetic prose and the compressed lyricism of his poetry. It is likely in any event that in "The Adirondacs" Emerson projected an American poem somewhat in the comic mode of Chaucer or Boccaccio (as the epigraph more than hints), but, in turning aside from that aim, accomplished something rather differently valuable.

The Chapman edition of *Poems* (1847) had been a lesson in how not to publish poetry in England. This time no manuscript crossed the Atlantic, but fully proof-read printed sheets instead, with instructions to match the Ticknor and Fields text. The result was that the Routledge first English edition of *May-Day and Other Pieces* differs only in the introduction of a few British spellings. Once again, though Emerson's poetry was prized by a few select readers in England, the general response was not enthusiastic and the few reviews of the book were divided. The *Athenæum* found here and there "a very fascinating strain of mystic thought," but mostly the verse seemed to "hover rather hopelessly between prose and music." *The London Review,* on the other hand, thought

"May-Day" "an exquisite spring cantata," interwoven with "threads of mystical suggestion." Emerson's first collection, in the reviewer's opinion, had been less polished and musical; the impression it created had in the intervening years been "eclipsed" by the essays, so that *May-Day* would "probably raise the general estimate of its author as a poet." By and large, however, Emerson tended to antagonize British taste, perhaps because, as Richard Garnett said in one of the earliest English biographies, his importance lay in being "the harbinger of distinctively American poetry."[74]

IX. *Selected Poems* and Posthumous Collections

May-Day and Other Pieces marks the effective end of Emerson's career as a poet. What little he published thereafter originated in writings composed much earlier. The only poem of his to appear in the *Atlantic Monthly* after the issuance of *May-Day*—the only poem, indeed, that he published anywhere between 1867 and 1876—was "Boston," which he had mostly written in the 1850s and then abandoned. He revised it at the request of Annie Fields for delivery in 1873 at a ceremony marking the hundredth anniversary of the Boston Tea Party—and then waited three years to print it in the *Atlantic*.

The project that mainly occupied Emerson as poet during these last years was the effort to define the canon of his best poems—that is, to indicate the work on which he wished his reputation as a poet permanently to rest. A major element, therefore, in the project that became *Selected Poems* was a process of winnowing. Of three draft tables of contents the earliest occurs on a sheet of paper laid in poetry notebook ETE Verses (*PN*, 588–590). It nominates 24 titles from the 60 in *Poems* and 11 from the 44 in *May-Day* (exclusive of the Quatrains and Translations, which were not chosen). A separate list of "Questionable" items included "The World-Soul," "Alphonso of Castile," "Mithridates," "Fate," "Guy,"

74 "A Shoal of Verse-Writers," *The Athenæum*, no 2114 (2 May 1868): 626; "Emerson's Poems," *The London Review*, XIV (1 June 1867): 629; Richard Garnett, *Life of Ralph Waldo Emerson* (London: Walter Scott, 1888), 135.

"Woodnotes, I and II," "Monadnoc," "A Fable," "Astræa," "Compensation," "The Amulet," and the "Hymn at the Second Church." Of these all but "Compensation" were finally admitted along with two items listed as "Proposed Additions" ("April" and "The Nun's Aspiration"), which had not been published before. Interestingly, "May-Day," the title poem from his second collection, was nowhere mentioned, not rising even into the "Questionable" category.[75]

Emerson had no shortage of advice in choosing the poems. Apart from the children, who all took an active interest, Elizabeth Hoar, Franklin Benjamin Sanborn, James Russell Lowell, and James Elliot Cabot were those most frequently mentioned as offering opinions. Emerson had always been open to suggestions from friends and friendly editors, as his relationship to Lowell and Fields had shown; conversely, he had been appalled by the obstinacy in the face of criticism of such as Jones Very and Ellery Channing. He welcomed advice, but in the end—even as late as 1876—it was his own opinion that settled matters. It was his decision, for example, to retain "The Sphinx" in the lead position and to exclude "Good-Bye" altogether, overriding in both cases the strongly stated preferences of his children.[76]

---

75 There was perhaps a slight note of alarm in Ellen's tone when she informed her sister on 18 February 1876 that "Father is for leaving out May Day" (*ETE*, II, 194). Eventually the poem was included in *Selected Poems*, though only after Ellen abridged and rearranged the text. There is some evidence that the children (Ellen and Edward) agreed with Howells as to there being a certain disorganization of topics in the first-edition form, a coincidence of opinion that may have contributed to Emerson's disappointment with the piece (see Joseph M. Thomas, "Late Emerson: *Selected Poems* and the 'Emerson Factory,'" *ELH*, LXV [1998]: 985). The second and third tables of contents for the 1876 volume occur in an unpublished manuscript at the Houghton Library, bMS Am1280.235 (31), and in notebook ETE Verses (*PN*, 582–583). The process of selection is also reflected in the principal correction copies (see list in the Textual Introduction), in which, probably in 1873 or later, Emerson identified the poems he preferred, marked them with a "yes," and canceled the others.

76 See Thomas, "Harnessing Proteus," 186–189. In 1883, while preparing the Riverside edition of *Poems*, Edward learned from Ellen that the arrangement of *Selected Poems* had been his father's choice "longer ago than I had supposed,"

But *Selected Poems* involved revision and not selection merely. One of the most difficult issues that a modern editor of Emerson faces is how to gauge the authority of particular revisions undertaken so late in Emerson's life and under well documented conditions of failing mental acuity. The onset of the dementia that clouded Emerson's last years has been variously dated—most often it has been connected to the fire that nearly destroyed his house in 1872—but Emerson may have caught the first impressions of diminished powers in an unpublished couplet entitled "Old Age" that he wrote in April 1861 as the Civil War commenced:

The brook sings on, but sings in vain
    Wanting the echo in my brain. (*W*, IX, 332; cf. *JMN*, XV, 135, and *PN*, 883–884)

By 1864 he would observe in his journal, "I have heard that the engineers in the locomotives grow nervously vigilant with every year on the road until the employment is intolerable to them: and I think writing is more and more a terror to old scribes" (quoted in *W*, VII, 445). This was the terror brought front and center in 1870 by the prospect of working on a new collection of essays, the volume published, with much assistance, as *Letters and Social Aims* in 1876, the same year that *Selected Poems* appeared. The story of this protracted and anguish-provoking effort (along with the history of Emerson's cognitive decline) has for the first time been fully told by Ronald A. Bosco in the Historical Introduction to Volume VIII in the present series. The crisis, prompted by Emerson's advancing dementia in combination with the strong desire of family and friends that his reputation be kept up, was the occasion for organizing the so-called Emerson factory, in which, unbeknownst to the public, the late works were manufactured, mostly by Ellen

---

which might mean that its contents were largely settled when Emerson was in better health (Edward to Cabot, 30 January 1883; bMS Am 1280.226 [262], Ralph Waldo Emerson Memorial Association deposit, Houghton Library, Harvard University).

Emerson and James Elliot Cabot, from the raw materials of old manuscript lectures. According to Joseph M. Thomas, the efforts resulted in a kind of "collaborative authorship which produced virtually all of [Emerson's] work from 1875 until his death." Ellen and Cabot "were helping in their editorial work to create a more benign Emerson for posterity."[77]

A great deal of uncertainty surrounds the history and publication of *Selected Poems* in 1876, since it is not confidently known just how far Emerson's impairment had progressed at this time or whether the disability that manifestly prevented him from composing new works—in prose or in poetry—also ruled out the making of authoritative particular revisions. In a letter of 22 July 1876, written to Emma Lazarus in the midst of preparing *Selected Poems*, Emerson explained his difficulty:

> I send you warm thanks for your kind letter & invitation;—but an old man fears most his best friends. It is not them that he is willing to distress with his perpetual forgetfulness of the right word for the name of a book or fact or person he is eager to recall, but which refuses to come. I have grown silent to my own household under this vexation, & cannot afflict dear friends with my tied tongue. Happily this embargo does not reach to the eyes, and I read with unbroken pleasure. (*L*, VI, 296)

The complaint is sufficiently eloquent. It has been noted, too, that certain forms of aphasia leave oddly intact, amid the general ruin of the intellect, an aptitude for poetry and song. As late as April 1882, for example, just two weeks before his death, Emerson was able to offer intelligent praise of Bronson Alcott's recent book,

77 Ibid., 181. Thomas argues that *Selected Poems* was an exception to the method by which Emerson's late publications were produced. Scholarship on "the Emerson factory" commenced with the work of Nancy Craig Simmons, and particularly with her essay "Arranging the Sibylline Leaves: James Elliot Cabot's Work as Emerson's Literary Executor," *SAR 1983*, pp. 335–389, which is mostly concerned with the preparation of *Letters and Social Aims*. See, further, Ronald A. Bosco, "Historical Introduction" to *Letters and Social Aims* (*CW*, VIII, xix–ccxviii).

Sonnets and Canzonets, and to read some of the poems aloud "with emphasis."[78]

Emerson could and did labor independently on *Selected Poems.* Aside from the treatment of the poem "May-Day," the Emerson factory played a much smaller role in its production than in the prose works of the same period. On 29 September 1876, Ellen wrote that "Father is still working on the new poems, and I am not helping" (*ETE,* II, 226), implying both that she did sometimes "help" and that she was relatively nonchalant about her father's making changes on his own. There is reason to think, however, that Ellen was concerned that the public might become aware of her assistance and she then be blamed for meddling—a concern that, with respect to *Letters and Social Aims,* extended to Cabot's involvement as well. Cabot gallantly reassured her, pointing out that "there is much more danger that my exertions in behalf of the book will be overestimated rather than the contrary. The only comfort is that any shortcomings in point of revision will probably be attributed to me—a position wh[ich] I am naturally well qualified to sustain."[79]

Selected Poems, issued on 30 October 1876, did not accomplish its purpose of defining a limited canon of Emerson's best poems, principally because it was so soon overtaken and made obsolete by the posthumous Riverside edition of 1883–1884, edited by Edward with, in the case of the *Poems* volume, only slight assistance from Cabot. Between 1876 and 1884 several small printings of *Selected Poems*—generally no more than 270 copies each—were issued by James R. Osgood and Company and its successors, Houghton, Osgood, and Houghton, Mifflin. Following Emerson's death in 1882, however, a need was felt for the fullest record of the poet's work. Edward satisfied this demand in the *Poems* volume of the comprehensive new edition by including all but twelve of the previously published poems (seven from *Poems* and five from *May-*

78 *The Journals of Bronson Alcott,* ed. Odell Shepard (Boston: Little, Brown, 1938), 533.

79 Cabot (Brookline) to Ellen Emerson, 18 December 1875; bMS Am 1280.226 (3221), Ralph Waldo Emerson Memorial Association deposit, Houghton Library, Harvard University.

Day), and supplementing these with a 62-page Appendix of drafts and fragments drawn from the notebooks.

Cabot, who had overall responsibility for the Riverside edition, had been appointed literary executor in Emerson's will, but he had been instructed by the same instrument to cooperate with the children in any work of publication. Edward inherited the literary rights and was entitled to whatever income the books might generate. Following his father's death in 1882 Edward retired from the practice of medicine—a vocation he never enjoyed—and became a hard-working and generally conscientious amateur editor, consulting Cabot at all points in the preparation of the new edition, but assuming the lead role often, most especially when it came to the poems. In view of the vast extent of disorganized unpublished material (mainly but not exclusively the nine poetry notebooks, together with a large folder that Emerson had entitled "Verses not entirely finished"), it is surprising how well Edward did once the decision was taken to invade and plunder this territory. He made mistakes, often misdated poems and fragments, did not distinguish much between the finished and the nearly finished works, provided his own titles where these seemed called for, and in one spectacular instance manufactured a single gerrymander monster out of numerous granular fragments on the subject of "The Poet." Still he brought forward much new and interesting material and was, by the lax and unprofessional standards of late-Victorian editing, respectful of his texts.[80]

As had been the case with *Selected Poems,* so again in the Riverside edition the main opening for editorial intervention was the poem "May-Day," now, it would seem, regarded less as a crippled poem than a standing problem. Edward agreed with the criticism of its structure advanced first by William Dean Howells in 1867, but he may have supposed that Ellen's refashioning of the text in

---

80 Joseph M. Thomas points out that Edward argued with Cabot in favor of conserving Emerson's sometimes erratic punctuation, preferring that to a policy of normalizing. Likewise he warned the publisher against imposing house style. See Thomas, "Harnessing Proteus," 226. Nevertheless, certain liberties were taken, like the elimination of the serial comma, evidently because it struck someone (most likely Edward) as old-fashioned.

1876 had solved the difficulty. If so, he was undoubtedly dismayed by Joel Benton's assessment of the *Selected Poems* text as expressed in his 1883 book, *Emerson as a Poet:*

> The poem has itself undergone in its new guise, in addition to this long elision [the removal and separate publication of "The Harp"], a variety of permutations similar to that which would happen if half its paragraphs were to be taken and shuffled like a pack of cards. The traditional critic would signal this as evidence of invalidity in the poem, but the admirer of Emerson sees in the fact that it survives such a shock the deep spiritual content of it, and feels that it has filaments which secure its unity against all accidents of disrupted logical succession or mere verbal welding.[81]

In October 1883 Edward reminded Cabot of what they had agreed to do about re-editing that text for the new edition:

> As for those changes in arrangement, the authority was this. Father saw that the order was not quite true to nature and sanctioned <the> ↑a change of↓ arrangement in Selected Poems which Ellen made and says that you too were called into counsel, she thinks, also Miss Emma Lazarus who made some verbal changes which Father assented to. Th<es>e change of arrangement improved the likeness to nature in some places, but made it worse in others. I therefore considered that if Father allowed one of his children to make a different arrangement it might not be going too far if another of them, who perhaps knew more than the first of out-door events, should revise it. I presented this argument to you and you consented.[82]

---

81 Benton, *Emerson as a Poet*, 43. As Strauch notes (diss., 272), Benton delivered a portion of this book as a lecture at the Concord School of Philosophy in 1882.

82 Edward to Cabot, 19 October 1883; bMS Am 1280.226 (295), Ralph Waldo Emerson Memorial Association deposit, Houghton Library, Harvard University.

In the brief "Prefatory Note" to *Poems* in the Riverside edition—a note written by Edward but signed by Cabot—the approval Emerson had originally bestowed on Ellen's revisions (whatever that may have been) was now, disingenuously, extended to cover Edward's: "A change in the arrangement of the stanzas of 'May-Day,' in the part representative of the march of Spring, received his sanction as bringing them more nearly in accordance with the events in Nature" (vi).

The Riverside Edition remained in print for thirty years (Myerson, 549), superseded at last by Houghton Mifflin's Centenary Edition issued (1903–1904) to celebrate the hundredth anniversary of Emerson's birth. The text of the poems that Emerson had published during his lifetime, again constituting the core of the volume, remained nearly unaltered from the Riverside, but the ancillary material was expanded, mainly by the inclusion of a section of seventeen unpublished "Poems of Youth and Early Manhood."[83] As that title suggests, and as Edward in fact explained in his new "Preface," these were offered, a little doubtfully, on the score of their historical and autobiographical interest. The Centenary was the most inclusive collection yet published (reversing Emerson's own impulse toward a selective edition) and remained so for nearly a century, or until the publication of the *Collected Poems and Translations* by the Library of America in 1994, which adds to the 233 poems that Emerson published, another 450 that he did not.[84]

It may be said of the Centenary edition that its most remarkable feature was the lengthy section of "Notes" (*W*, IX, 403–518) in which Edward provided what information he had regarding the origin and date of composition of each poem, its relation to journal sources or to parallels in the published prose. These notes are often quite valuable and the present edition has taken advan-

---

83 Responsibility for the editorial decisions involved in preparing the Centenary edition, together with the labor of annotating its twelve volumes, were all Edward's, since Cabot died on 16 January 1903, and Ellen and Edith did not participate. See Thomas, "Harnessing Proteus," 238.

84 This most recent collection reprints first-edition texts of the published poems or, in the case of the unpublished verse, diplomatic transcripts, and includes a modest sampling of authorial emendations among the volume's end-notes.

tage of them as appropriate. But as the elder Emerson knew full well, the work of explanation, for all its rewards, all its filiopietistic satisfactions, is in an important sense futile. As he said in 1841, "When we have told all our anecdotes of detail, there yet remains the total wonder. We must add then the fact that no enumeration of particulars brings us nearer to an explanation; for poetry is always a miracle not to be explained or disposed of, a miracle to the hearer; a miracle to the poet; he admires his verses as much as you do, when they are the right inspiration: he cannot tell where or how he had them" (*EL*, III, 360).

STATEMENT OF EDITORIAL
PRINCIPLES

The intention of the *Collected Works* is to provide for the first time critically edited texts of those works of Emerson which were originally published in his lifetime and under his supervision. The canon and order follow the physical arrangement which Emerson himself suggested in 1869 when he sent his first six volumes of prose to the printer as text for the first American edition of his collected prose. Two subsequently published volumes, *Society and Solitude* (1870) and *Letters and Social Aims* (1876), appeared as volumes seven and eight in the Little Classic edition of 1876. Volume nine, specially prepared for that edition, was *Selected Poems* (1876), a sampling of Emerson's best work as a poet. After the author's death, in the Riverside and all later collected editions, it was replaced by a more comprehensive gathering, entitled *Poems,* largely compiled by Edward Waldo Emerson, with the assistance, initially, of James Elliot Cabot.

The editorial challenges presented by the poetry differ considerably from those confronted by the editors of the prior volumes of prose, and yet, while the presentation of the text in the present volume has been adapted to the genre, the underlying editorial principles remain substantially identical to those of the volumes preceding. The decision to offer a variorum edition—discussed in greater detail in the Textual Introduction—does not relieve the editors of the responsibility to produce the kind of critical and unmodernized text of the poems that has been produced in the volumes of prose to date. As in the earlier volumes, the editors have adapted the theories of Sir Walter Greg to the particular problems of nineteenth-century American printed texts, and more particularly still, to the case of Emerson's dealings, as a poet, with a succession of publishers and publishing venues. While, as a variorum, the present volume offers all the evidence needed to reconstruct the history of each poem, it is centrally concerned to establish the text of each poem, first selecting copy-text, then emending from later texts when the variants are judged to be authorial.

Building on Greg's work and the subsequent applications of it to the editing of American literary documents by Fredson Bowers and G. Thomas Tanselle, the central editorial principles of this edition are that the copy-text is the text closest to the author's initial coherent intention and that determining his subsequent intention depends on the use of evidence from other relevant forms of the text according to conservative editorial principles. The rationale of copy-text assumes that in printed works each resetting is likely to introduce additional non-authorial corruption into the text, both in substantives and in accidentals, even when such resetting of type is supervised by the author.[1] The earliest feasible

---

1 "Substantives" are the words themselves, the word-order, and any punctuation that affects the author's meaning; "accidentals" are matters of punctuation, spelling, word-division, capitalization and the like that affect mainly the formal presentation of the text. Greg, whose distinction this is ("The Rationale of Copy-Text," *Studies in Bibliography,* III [1950–1951]: 19–36), argued that editors should, as a general rule, follow copy-text in accidentals and emend the substantives where variants in later texts seem to have been introduced by the author. The argument, one notes, was derived from Elizabethan and Jacobean dramatic works—which is to say, it has reference to a time when there were few generally accepted grounds for being particular about punctuation and orthography. The argument is also informed by a sense of how infrequently the popular dramatists of the sixteenth and seventeenth centuries arranged for and personally supervised editions after the first printing—if, indeed, they had much to do even with that. In the nineteenth century, it is fair to say, when increasingly the standards of competence in punctuation were a routine element of primary education, even casual writers paid more attention to the "accidentals" of their texts—an observation that applies *a fortiori* to writers like Emerson who were self-consciously engaged in the production of "literature." While Greg's distinction

form, therefore, is normally chosen as copy-text. In cases where manuscript printer's copy or printer's proof has not survived, this edition chooses the first printed form as copy-text.

Copy-text may be emended to correct errors, as in the case of obvious misprints, or to acknowledge a revision by the author. It has for the most part been the policy of the earlier prose volumes in the *Collected Works* to retain the accidentals of the copy-text on the grounds that "there is generally no evidence on which to base emendation . . . even though this means, in the case of printed copy-text, following much house styling" (*CW,* V, lv). There are several good reasons for modifying this policy when it comes to the poetry. First, while house style may sometimes be in play, it tends for good and comprehensible reasons to bear far more lightly on verse than on prose. Second, it is clear that Emerson, who often omitted punctuation in early drafts, as we find these in *The Poetry Notebooks,* tended to rely on punctuation to convey the rhythm of his lines in print. In other words, he had the melody sufficiently in mind as he wrote and revised, but needed punctuation as much or more to bring the tune intact to the reader as to coordinate the grammar of his sentences. The accidentals of the poetry are integral to the literary effect in ways that punctuation in prose is not. There is arguably more evidence on which to base emendation of accidentals in the poetry (some of which is discussed in the Textual Introduction), but in the end—as Greg foresaw would always be necessary—a large reliance is to be had on the informed judgment of the editors. Such expertise is indispensable as well in the emendation of substantives, where, however, clearer evidence is usually available to assist in discriminating authorial revision from variants that lack authority.

In practical terms there are three principal classes of evidence for emendation of copy-text: the author's handwritten corrections and revisions in extant texts; external authorial instructions concerning the text; and subsequent variants which correct, modify, add, or delete. The first and second classes apply to both substan-

---

between substantives and accidentals remains sound and, indeed, foundational, editors must be alert to authorial practice that, particularly in the case of poetry, takes matters of punctuation as seriously as word-choice.

tives and accidentals. The third applies primarily to substantive emendation, and even so must be justified as authorial: known similar revision, context, kind of revision, and the like must be weighed as probabilities against non-authorial emendation (sophistication) or printer's error. In emendation, pre-copy-text forms (which for the poems are usually drafts in the journals and poetry notebooks) as well as Emerson's established usage and preference may cautiously be adduced as supporting evidence in furtherance of the primary editorial responsibility.

It had been a desideratum in previous volumes "to preserve a clear page, free of all subsidiary information except Emerson's own footnotes" (*CW,* VII, lxix); consequently, much relevant textual and contextual matter—explanatory notes, parallel passages, lists of emendations, and the like—was gathered at the back of the volume. As will immediately be apparent, the somewhat different purposes of the present volume, and indeed the somewhat different requirements of the reader of the poems, have suggested a different scheme. In order better to facilitate the study of individual poems, all relevant materials are gathered adjacent to the text. This is accomplished by the division into five parts of each poem's presentation, as summarized and explained in the prefatory "Note to the Reader" (pp. xxi–xxii, above): these are the headnote, the text of the poem, the list of collated editions, the variants, and the explanatory notes. It should be mentioned that the list of variants takes the place of the list of "Emendations in Copy-Text" in earlier volumes of the *Collected Works,* and it provides the reader with the information needed to reconstruct the textual evolution of the poem and at the same time makes it clear what the editors have done in establishing the text. As in previous volumes, variants in the Riverside and Centenary editions are included even though these texts are not authoritative. Variants in British editions which are not authoritative are not normally included, although some are cited (principally in "May-Day") to illustrate for those interested the sort of non-authorial changes that took place.

It has not been found necessary to include a list of line-end hyphenations, common to other volumes in the *Collected Works,* since no instance occurs in Emerson's printed poetry. Finally, a list of stanza breaks that occur at the bottom of the page in the present edition is given in Appendix D.

The Textual Introduction includes a history of the texts of *Poems* (beginning with the London edition brought out in late December 1846, but dated 1847), *Poems* (the "Blue and Gold" edition of 1865), *May-Day and Other Pieces* (beginning with the Boston edition of 1867), *Selected Poems* (1876), and the posthumous editions of 1884 and 1904, the Riverside and the Centenary. The Textual Introduction also provides a rationale for the variorum presentation adopted in this edition, discusses matters both theoretical and practical relating to copy-text decisions, and identifies and locates those copies of the books actually used in the collation.

TEXTUAL INTRODUCTION

Albert J. von Frank

This volume in *The Collected Works of Ralph Waldo Emerson,* like the others in the series, is a critical and unmodernized edition of its text, but it differs otherwise in a number of respects. It does not, for example, correspond to the text of any single book published by Emerson, but presents instead edited texts of all the poems, regardless of date of composition or first printing, that were published by Emerson in any book, periodical, or other format during his lifetime. The first of Emerson's poems to reach print ("William Rufus and the Jew" and "Fame") appeared in 1829, the last (a quatrain entitled "Alms") more than fifty years later in 1880. Thus, instead of a single title, such as *Essays: First Series,* for example, or *The Conduct of Life,* the present volume offers, as it were, a poet's whole career. Volume IX differs in this respect from all the previous volumes, but anticipates the situation of Volume X, which will gather Emerson's uncollected prose works, written over a comparable period of time.

Restricting the present edition to poems actually published by Emerson immediately distinguishes it from the very popular and influential Riverside and Centenary editions (1883–1884 and 1904, respectively), which, edited by the poet's son, Edward Waldo

Emerson, included a generous sampling of fragments and drafts of varying degrees of completeness taken from the then unpublished poetry notebooks. More will be said shortly of these posthumous collections, but for now the point is that the present edition is the first to include no more and no less than all the poems that Emerson thought finished and fit to print. His decision to publish a particular poem, his extending his imprimatur to it, being the criterion for its inclusion here, it follows that the poems individually and not any of Emerson's collections (*Poems* in 1847, *May-Day* in 1867, or *Selected Poems* in 1876) are the immediate objects of editorial attention. Decisions about the choice of copy-text, in other words, refer to the poems individually and not, as in the case of previous volumes, to whole books. Immediately related to this fact—indeed following from it—is the decision to produce a *variorum* edition.

I. A Variorum Edition

The term variorum, as here employed, refers to the presentation of a given text together with all the variants found in all authorized editions and printings, as well as editions and printings, including posthumous ones, that arguably might reflect the author's intentions. Such variants arise from a number of causes, including printer's errors, the correction of printer's errors, damage to standing type or to stereotype plates, the imposition of a publisher's house style or other editorial intervention—or, of course, in many cases, deliberate authorial emendation, for good or ill, whether carried out by the author or by an authorized surrogate. To compile a chronological list of these variants is to produce a history of the changes in the text. Indeed such lists are sometimes called "historical collations," as implying the evolutionary character of the text but also as revealing the state of the text at any particular moment in its history. "May-Day," for example, was one poem in 1867, a quite different poem in 1876, and different yet again in 1883. A variorum edition allows us to study these differences and to reconstruct the poem's text at various points in time.

In the present edition the heading used to identify these lists is not "Historical Collation," however, but simply "Variants," in part to acknowledge that another, relatively ahistorical purpose is also served: the construction of the poem's text according to the author's intention. The lists give in tabular form the evidence from which the editor derives a critical edition of the poem, emending copy-text or declining to emend based on judgments about the degree to which a variant is meaningful—that is, whether it represents a deliberate authorial revision or the eruption of error or mere chance into the order of the poem. The lists put the reader in possession of the same evidence the editor has, which means that all of the editor's activity in ascertaining the author's intention is open to scrutiny and may be dissented from or corroborated at the reader's discretion. Indeed, the reader is given the opportunity to consider the effect of a wide range of possible editorial decisions.

These implications of the variorum presentation may be illustrated in a brief look at the first poem in this edition, "The Sphinx." The variants list for this poem shows that the word "Sphinx" is consistently rendered as "Sphynx" in the (B) text. Reference to the text list shows that (B) is the first English edition of *Poems* (1847), so the easy inference is that "Sphynx" is a British spelling imposed on the text by compositors working for the publisher John Chapman—and, furthermore, that such is not Emerson's own preferred spelling. There is no reason, then, to emend copy-text, the January 1841 *Dial* text—listed as (A)—which, like all subsequent American printings, has "Sphinx." As clear as this conclusion would appear to be, the editors often have supplementary evidence on which to draw, including the form of the word in manuscript rough drafts (generally published in *PN* or *JMN*), or, sometimes, in the printer's copy sent to London (which happens not to have survived in the particular case of "The Sphinx").

A somewhat more ambiguous, but still not difficult situation involves the punctuation in the poem's second line. In the variants list we find the following notation:

2 furled; (C-H) | furled, (A-B) | furled: (I-J)

Copy-text—always given first in the chronologically arranged list of collated texts and so assigned the letter (A)—reads as follows:

Her wings are furled,

The variants list shows that this was the reading also of the first English edition of *Poems* (B), but that the comma became a semi-colon in the first American edition (C), issued two weeks later in December 1846, and that it remained a semi-colon in all five subsequent editions and printings issued during Emerson's lifetime. Finally, it became a colon in the posthumous Riverside and Centenary editions. The variants list gives these facts, but how are they to be construed? The persistence of any given form is unremarkable (as the attention to "variants" implies), so the alignment of the first English with the earlier *Dial* printing requires no explanation. One could hypothesize that the alteration of the comma to a semi-colon in the first American edition reflected house style at publisher James Munroe's shop and did not embody Emerson's intention. Indeed, classical editorial theory tends to preserve the "accidentals" of copy-text (that is, punctuation and other features of the text that do not significantly affect meaning) on the assumption that printers and publishers have their own way of dealing with these matters and that authors, so often inexpert in this area of arcane trivia, are glad to be relieved of the responsibility. That theoretical generality is, however, always a rebuttable assumption. Weighing against its relevance here is that Emerson declined numerous opportunities to restore his comma if comma he continued to mean: even though the Boston *Poems* was quickly stereotyped, making alterations relatively difficult and expensive, Emerson did from time to time make revisions, including revisions to punctuation, in later printings. But he also declined to restore the comma when the poem was reset in new editions, first in 1865 in the "Blue and Gold" edition, and then again in *Selected Poems* in 1876. Of perhaps similar evidentiary weight with the persistence of the semi-colon is the fact that we know that in December 1846 Emerson very carefully read proofs for the Boston edition of *Poems,* whereas he was, of course, unable to supervise the

London edition at all. Given the care he lavished on the Boston edition, the presumption has to be that if he was not himself the proximate cause of the change (as seems likely), it almost certainly met with his conscious approval. This conclusion is further buttressed by the appearance of a distinct pattern of revision involving verse that Emerson reprinted from the *Dial* or the *Western Messenger* in the Boston *Poems*—a pattern created by the liberal introduction of semi-colons (most often, in fact, the promotion of numerous commas to semi-colons) the better to indicate, with the resultant two-tier system of rhetorical pauses, the rhythms that Emerson no doubt felt in the lines to begin with.[1] The clearly unauthorized substitution of a colon for the semi-colon in the Riverside edition (continued in the Centenary) appears to have been a misguided but conscientious effort on Edward Waldo Emerson's part to preserve the stronger pause at this point while evading the awkwardness of having rejected one series comma out of three, which appear to set off independent clauses. Even though such posthumous changes lack authority, they do help to indicate how the poems were being treated by the editor—the poet's son—who was, in fact, responsible for the form of the texts most commonly read and quoted throughout the twentieth century.

Although none of the points raised in the preceding paragraph may be supposed to have great intrinsic significance, they do illustrate certain of the deeper issues that practically guide the editors as they move from the raw data of the variants list to the construction of a critical edition of the poem.

---

1 During the nineteenth century the rationale for punctuation was in transition from a rhetorical to a syntactical system. "Punctuation," declared the influential Lindley Murray, "is the art of dividing sentences, by points or stops, for the purpose of marking the different pauses which the sense, and an accurate pronunciation require. The Comma represents the shortest pause; the Semicolon, a pause double that of the comma; the Colon, double that of the semicolon; and a Period, double that of the colon" (*English Grammar, Adapted to the Different Classes of Learners* [1795; New York: Samuel Raynor, 1855], 176.

II. Correction Copies

The variorum presentation also proves a convenience in dealing with an otherwise troublesome and in any event a complicating class of variants: emendations that Emerson entered in his correction copies. It was his habit to maintain a number of copies of various editions, both of his prose works and his poetry, in which, from time to time as they occurred to him, Emerson would record potential emendations in advance of new printings or editions. These emendations are troublesome in several respects. Since they are almost without exception very brief—usually single-word substitutions or changes in punctuation, and sometimes mere crossings-out—it is not always clear whose handwriting they are in. Certainly in some cases they are not by Emerson, but even when the handwriting can be determined to be that of his daughter Ellen (who served as a kind of private secretary during her father's last years), the likelihood is very great that the inscriptions were made at Emerson's immediate direction and not on anyone else's independent or assumed authority.[2]

It must be stressed that entries in these volumes were nothing more than memoranda to be acted upon or not at such time as the poems they refer to might be reprinted. Most of the entries do in fact correspond with emendations made in later printings and editions, but in some cases they were either overlooked or rejected on Emerson's second thought. For this reason no emendation has

---

2 As is now well known, Ellen had few qualms about manufacturing new publications from old prose manuscripts, especially when this course of action had the support of Emerson's literary executor, James Elliot Cabot. Such indeed was the main business of the "Emerson factory" that operated during Emerson's mental decline over the last six or so years of his life. But apart from her documented intervention to rescue the problematic "May-Day" (discussed further below), there is simply no evidence that she interfered in the slightest with any other poem. Indeed, her work on "May-Day" involved excision and rearrangement, which, though drastic, managed to avoid almost entirely any change in wording. On her labors with Cabot, see Nancy Craig Simmons, "Arranging the Sibylline Leaves: James Elliot Cabot's Work as Emerson's Literary Executor," *SAR 1983*, pp. 335–389, and Ronald A. Bosco's "Historical Introduction" to *Letters and Social Aims* (*CW*, VIII, xix–ccxviii).

been adopted into the text of any poem in this edition solely on the basis of its appearance in a correction copy. It is quite impossible to tell when a particular entry might have been made in a correction copy. One can only say that it was done at some time between the date of publication of the book in which the hand-written correction appears and the date of the printing in which the revision was actually incorporated. For example, in the variants list for "The Sphinx," at line 64, the adopted reading is "my child's head?'"—an emendation that occurs in the earliest and most important of the correction copies (referred to in this edition as CC1), but that is not incorporated until the 1876 *Selected Poems* text. Since CC1 is Emerson's personal copy of the first printing of *Poems,* the line could have been marked for alteration at any time between the last days of 1846 and the fall of 1876. Still, it is a reasonable working hypothesis that the later the incorporation, the later the emendation.[3]

Emerson's Correction Copies and Errata Lists

CC1: *Poems* (Boston: James Munroe, 1847). *AC85. Em345.846pba (D), Ralph Waldo Emerson Memorial Association deposit, Houghton Library, Harvard University.

> This copy of the first printing, subsequently rebound and the title-page rebacked, has the most extensive corrections and emendations, in both ink and pencil, of any of the correction copies, the majority of which can be attributed with some certainty to Emerson's own hand. Since a number of poems are

---

3 For an example of a correction-copy emendation that was never incorporated, see "The Sphinx," line 80. Such emendations are always given last in the variants list as being effectively removed from the chronology of actual (as opposed to potential) variants. Those that actually were incorporated (the vast majority) are listed immediately before the published text in which they first appear, on the assumption that they are the cause of that appearance. The poet's son Edward recalled these "copies of the poems which my father kept for corrections and changes," and which he "marked carefully and repeatedly" (quoted in Joseph M. Thomas, "Late Emerson: *Selected Poems* and the 'Emerson Factory,'" *ELH,* LXV (1998): 980.

marked for cancellation and others marked "yes," it would appear that this volume was used, as others were also, in the preparation of *Selected Poems* (1876).

CC2: *Poems* (London: Chapman, Brothers, 1847). *AC85. Em345.846p (C), Ralph Waldo Emerson Memorial Association deposit, Houghton Library, Harvard University.

According to Emerson's note on the front fly-leaf: "This book, thus marked throughout with pencil, was brought to me by its owner Mr. Dockray, at the door of the hall in Edward St. Marylebone, in London, on the day of my first Lecture there in June, 1848. R.W.E." Written on the front end-paper: "B Dockray / April 21. 1847. / Dalton Square / Lancaster" (see *L*, IV, 98). Except for Emerson's correction of "hovered" to "honored" at line 40 in "Guy," all the other corrections (transcribed from the errata slip pasted in this copy) and its copious annotations and cross references appear to be in the hand of Benjamin Dockray.

CC3: *Poems* ["Fifth Edition"] (Boston: Phillips, Sampson & Co., 1856). *AC85.Em345.846pe, Ralph Waldo Emerson Memorial Association deposit, Houghton Library, Harvard University.

Signed on front fly-leaf: "Lidian Emerson." Ten emendations and cancellations, both in the text and noted on the end paper, appear to be in Emerson's hand. Of these emendations one was adopted in the 1860 printing and three in the 1864 printing. None of the four is reflected in the 1865 "Blue and Gold" edition.

CC4: *Poems* ["Sixth Edition"] (Boston: Phillips, Sampson & Co., 1857). *AC85.Em345.846pf, Ralph Waldo Emerson Memorial Association deposit, Houghton Library, Harvard University.

Signed on the front fly-leaf—"R W Emerson / copy for correction"—this copy was also used at some point during Emerson's planning of his *Selected Poems* volume.

CC5: *Poems* (Boston: Ticknor and Fields, 1865). *AC85. Em345.846pm, Ralph Waldo Emerson Memorial Association deposit, Houghton Library, Harvard University.

> A copy of the so-called "Blue and Gold" edition of Emerson's poems, in a publisher's presentation binding of green cloth. Other than Emerson's signature on the recto of front fly-leaf and the notation "Poems corrected" on the recto of the frontispiece portrait, few of the emendations in this volume can be identified with certainty as being in Emerson's handwriting. Ellen's testimony (*ETE*, II, 68) is that the cancellations are Emerson's. A few of the changes appear to be in Ellen's hand. Emerson took this volume with him when he traveled with Ellen to Europe in 1872–1873; notations entered at that time (and subsequently transferred to CC1) belong to the earliest stage of planning for *Selected Poems*.

CC6: *May-Day and Other Pieces* (Boston: Ticknor and Fields, 1867). *AC85.Em345.867ma (C), Ralph Waldo Emerson Memorial Association deposit, Houghton Library, Harvard University.

> A presentation copy bound in violet cloth and inscribed by James T. Fields: "For Mrs Emerson from J. T. F. / (the first copy bound of that / lovely Spring Volume.)" Two corrections ("Damsels" to "Daughters" in "Days" and "flowers" to "hours" in "Botanist") are probably by Emerson, as is the addition of two titles to the translations from von Hammer.

CC7: *May-Day and Other Pieces* (Boston: Ticknor and Fields, 1867). *AC85.Em345.867m (B), Ralph Waldo Emerson Memorial Association deposit, Houghton Library, Harvard University.

> Other than the two-line correction at the end of the volume (emending "spread" to "shoot" at line 7 in "Terminus," and "flowers" to "hours" in line 4 of "Botanist"), corrections appear not to be in Emerson's hand. Marks in the table of con-

tents suggest choices for *Selected Poems*. Some tentative revisions to "May-Day" are indicated, but not the major rearrangement of paragraphs.

CC8: Emerson's copies of the *Dial*. *AC85.Em345.Zy841d, Ralph Waldo Emerson Memorial Association deposit, Houghton Library, Harvard University.

Emerson emended lines in three poems published in the *Dial* for October 1841 ("Fate"), for October 1842 ("Saadi"), and for January 1844 ("Blight").

CC9: Two manuscript lists of nearly identical contents (MS Am 1280.217 [1] and [2]), Ralph Waldo Emerson Memorial Association deposit, Houghton Library, Harvard University.

The emendations recorded in list [1] (six pages written on two leaves) were adopted in the 1863 printing; those unique to list [2] (two pages written on one leaf) were adopted in the 1866 printing.

CC10: Errata list in Journal GH (*JMN*, X, 127).

A list of 23 corrections to the London printing of *Poems* (1847).

CC11: Errata slip tipped into some copies of the London 1847 edition of *Poems*.

Apparently added after Chapman received Emerson's letter dated 29 December 1846 (but mailed after 31 December), in which the English publisher was asked to make "an exact comparison . . . , page for page, & letter for letter, betwee[n] your book & ours, and your edition correc[ted] from ours" (*L*, VIII, 100). Other than the insertion of the errata slip (which lists 19 corrections, only ten of which are in CC10), no changes were made in the text of the two English printings. A copy with the errata slip is at the Houghton Library, *AC85.Em345.846pa.

III. Copy-Text and Pre-Copy-Text Forms

As indicated in the "Statement of Editorial Principles," the earliest feasible form of the text is normally chosen as copy-text. In most cases this has meant the first printing of a poem, whether in a periodical or in a book, although, following the practice established in previous volumes of this edition, preference is given to printer's copy whenever such holograph documents survive, on the grounds that they provide better and more direct evidence of Emerson's intentions. In a very few instances, the "earliest feasible form" of a poem is an authorized fair copy that did not in fact serve as printer's copy but circulated to a limited audience at or near the time of first publication. "Waldeinsamkeit" illustrates such a choice of copy-text: the version that in September 1858 Emerson inscribed in the guest-book at the Naushon Island estate of his friend John Murray Forbes is a less mediated witness of the poet's intentions than is the text published in the *Atlantic Monthly* in October, which, as the evidence shows, he did not proofread. There are only two similar examples among the sixty poems in *Poems* (1847): copy-text for "Mithridates" is a manuscript version sent to Caroline Sturgis; copy-text for "Bacchus" is likewise a manuscript read by friends. These exceptional decisions regarding copy-text are further explained in the respective poems' editorial apparatus.

Printer's copy prepared by Emerson for the London edition survives for 43 of the 60 poems included in *Poems* (1847). In 22 of these 43 instances the manuscripts are the earliest complete form of the poems and are therefore selected as copy-text. In 21 other instances a first printing in the *Dial* serves as copy-text. Printer's copy for three of the four poems that Emerson published in the *Western Messenger* in 1839 were preserved by that journal's editor, James Freeman Clarke, and still survive ("Good-Bye," "The Rhodora," and "The Humble-Bee"); for the fourth, "Each and All," the manuscript having been lost, the journal printing itself serves as copy-text. Of the six poems first published in the Philadelphia annuals *The Diadem* and *The Gift*, edited by Emerson's friend William H. Furness ("The Apology," "Dirge," "Loss and Gain," "A Fable," "The Forerunners," and "The World-Soul"), the last two are represented in printer's copy. Copy-text for the "Concord Hymn" is that poem's first printing, in broadside form. In the remaining four cases first printings in the London edition serve as copy-text ("To J. W.," "Compensation," "Give All to Love," and "Merops"), though only because, by chance, their manuscripts happen to have disappeared.

The notion of copy-text is especially crucial to this edition of the poems. The definition embraced by the *Collected Works* project ("the earliest feasible form of the text") fortunately marks the line dividing the public artifact from the private performance, the seen from the unseen in the development and dissemination of the text. Copy-text may be thought of as the end-point of the drafting process, even if revision never altogether ceases during the author's lifetime. Copy-text is the name for what literary effort struggles to realize, an impulse elevated to an accomplishment. As a theoretical or conceptual boundary, copy-text had simply not existed in the nineteenth century because nothing but mystery was supposed to be anterior to the finished work of art. Readers who then marveled at the fine poem did so precisely to the extent that it seemed to have no seams, no parts, no history, indeed no susceptibility to analysis; often the poem was regarded as a discovered rather than a constructed thing, an effect not of work but of inspiration. To have heard about rough drafts would have been unpleasant, impertinent, disillusioning. What passed for criticism was actually, in most cases, competitive admiration.

It is a fact of some consequence that important Victorian editions of Emerson's poems—the Riverside in 1883–1884 and the Centenary in 1904, both edited by Edward Waldo Emerson—were compiled, in the absence of a practical theory of copy-text, on essentially this view of the nature of the poem as object. The Riverside edition included an "Appendix" that offered 134 previously unpublished "poems"—some explicitly called "Fragments," some with early dates, others pieced together in the manner of the Emerson factory to form a spurious whole, some few genuine poems, but mostly rejected or abandoned drafts from Emerson's original notebooks or drawn from a file that the poet had called "Verses not entirely finished."[4] This "Appendix" constituted section III of the volume, where "Poems" and "May-Day and Other Pieces" comprised sections I and II, respectively. This equivalence by segregation makes no room for the distinction maintained by modern editors between a finished or a "feasible" poem and related pre-copy-text forms. The total effect of Edward's "Appendix" (repeated with some expansion and subdivision in the Centenary edition) was not helpful in advancing Emerson's reputation as a poet.

Nor did it facilitate planning for a better edition. During the mid twentieth century the pioneer Emerson scholar Carl Ferdinand Strauch (1908–1989), a founding member of the Editorial Board of this edition, with a main responsibility for the *Poems* volume, began his career with a dissertation under Yale professor Stanley T. Williams, entitled "A Critical and Variorum Edition of the Poems of Ralph Waldo Emerson."[5] It is 719 pages long and edits a total of 46 poems, of which only 13 had been published in Emerson's two collections, *Poems* and *May-Day;* the other 33 were "Appendix" poems or verses previously unpublished. The main

4 The file of "Verses not entirely finished" is alluded to in James Elliot Cabot to Edward Waldo Emerson, 10 July 1882, bMS Am 1280.226 (3244), Ralph Waldo Emerson Memorial deposit, Houghton Library, Harvard University, and again by Joseph M. Thomas in his dissertation, "Harnessing Proteus: Publishing the Canon of Emerson's Poetry," Rutgers the State University of New Jersey, 1994, 219.

5 Joseph M. Thomas correctly places Strauch's dissertation in the context of important efforts by pioneer Americanist scholars including Williams, Henry Pochman, Willard Thorp, and others, beginning in the 1920s, to raise the academic study of American literature to professional standards. Among the earliest requirements identified in this effort were reliable editions of the works of American authors. See Thomas's discussion of "Professionalizing the Profession: Carl F. Strauch's Critical and Variorum Edition" in his dissertation, "Harnessing Proteus," 252–267. By no means the least of Strauch's accomplishments was to have been "instrumental in the Emerson family's decision to make available to scholars the original manuscripts of both the journals and the verse-books" (255).

difficulty, it would seem, is that the dissertation was completed in 1946, four years before Sir Walter Greg's classic essay on "The Rationale of Copy-Text." Initially, for Strauch, the proper editing of Emerson's poems (and his idea of a "Variorum") required an exhaustive tracking from first draft through all the manuscript revisions in the journals and poetry notebooks, to printer's copy and other loose manuscripts, and on to first publication and all the subsequent variants discoverable in later printings. Even if the manuscripts had been straightforward and orderly, this would have posed an enormous challenge to the energies and talents of a graduate student, but in fact Strauch found the manuscript background more often than not "in a state of inconceivable chaos" ("A Critical and Variorum Edition," 3). For the next forty years, he neither gave up his expectation of completing a full edition, nor did he, lacking a clear concept of copy-text, find a way to present the poems without the opaque complications and overwhelming detail of their full textual history.

This impasse was broken in 1986 toward the very end of Strauch's life with the publication of *The Poetry Notebooks of Ralph Waldo Emerson* under the general editorship of Ralph H. Orth, a work that simply presented and clearly organized the pre-copy-text forms of nearly all the poems. Thus at a single stroke, half the subject matter of the edition Strauch envisioned was taken off the table to be treated as a subject unto itself. As a practical matter, the ground-clearing publication of *The Poetry Notebooks* has made the present edition possible, while Greg's theory of copy-text, by enforcing the distinction between the private compositional history of a poem and the history of its presentation to a public, not only put an end to the lackadaisical methodologies of Victorian editing, but also gave a theoretical legitimacy to the subject of the *Poetry Notebooks* and so made the planning and execution of that volume possible.

Since the textual history of each poem is treated in both the *Poetry Notebooks* and in the notes to the individual poems in this edition, the remainder of the Textual Introduction will address, in chronological order, the major authorized collections of Emerson's poems.

IV. *Poems* (1847)

Emerson maintained that the idea of publishing a book of poems was not his own, but grew from the urging of friends. The modesty and selflessness of this explanation amount almost to a literary convention: tributes to the forcing clamor of friends occur frequently in the prefaces to books of all kinds during the nineteenth century. Clearly Elizabeth Hoar was the immediate cause of the start of Emerson's periodical publication of verse, and Margaret Fuller and Caroline Sturgis were, in private, enthusiastic readers of the manuscript poems. Undoubtedly the pieces that Emerson had been publishing, first in the *Western Messenger*, then in the *Dial*, had met with the kind of praise, especially from within the circle of his Transcendental acquaintance, that, though at times measured and judicious, favored book publication. In January 1845, for example, Frederic Henry Hedge published the opinion that "with a little more activity of feeling, and a little less activity of speculation, Mr. Emerson would have made a first-rate poet. As it is, the little poetry he has published possesses rare merit. In point of vividness, melody, and force of expression, it is unsurpassed."[6] But Emerson had heard as much before: when Rufus W. Griswold in 1842 included him in the pantheon of contemporary American poets, noting that "Mr. EMERSON has a poetical mind, and has written much true poetry besides his verses," a book was bound to appear.[7]

In fact it is unlikely that Emerson needed such critical encouragement to collect his fugitive verse. Others in his circle whom he admired but who were clearly less accomplished were publishing books of poems. In 1839 Emerson had edited the *Essays and Poems* of Jones Very, published in Boston by Charles C. Little and James Brown. In 1843 Emerson advised Christopher Pearse Cranch on

---

6 "Writings of R. W. Emerson," *Christian Examiner*, XXXVIII (January 1845): 101–102. Hedge noted, further, that "He does not dilute his verse with the washy sentimentality which floods the pages of his contemporaries" and went so far as to compare Emerson with John Milton and Andrew Marvell (102–103).

7 *The Poets and Poetry of America*, ed. Rufus W. Griswold (Philadelphia: Carey and Hart, 1842), 237.

the publication of his book of poems, though he seems to have had nothing more to do with the volume, issued a year later by Carey and Hart of Philadelphia, than to praise its "sweetness and elegance of versification." Cranch had also been included by Griswold in *The Poets and Poetry of America,* and, like Emerson, had later published poems in the annual *The Gift,* edited by Emerson's friend and Cranch's cousin, William Henry Furness.[8] Emerson had also been a strong advocate for the poems of the younger William Ellery Channing. In an important 1840 *Dial* essay entitled "New Poetry," he had praised their intellectual character and defended their rough, unpolished quality as *"Verses of the Portfolio."* Subsequently, he arranged publication of Channing's *Poems: Second Series* (1847) by attaching it to the contract he negotiated with Munroe for his own book of poems.[9]

Whatever else was accomplished by Emerson's interest in the

8 See Joel Myerson, *The New England Transcendentalists and the* Dial: *A History of the Magazine and Its Contributors* (Rutherford, N. J.: Fairleigh Dickinson University Press, 1980), 139.

9 The contract (bMS Am1280.235 [190], Ralph Waldo Emerson Memorial Association deposit, Houghton Library, Harvard University) reads as follows:

> Memorandum of an Agreement made this Twenty First day of October 1846 by & between R. W. Emerson of Concord and James Munroe & Co of Boston, Witnesseth—
>
> Said R. W. Emerson is to furnish Copy for a Volume of Poems, which J. M. & Co are to have printed 16mo size on a paper a sample of which is selected by said E. J. M. & Co are to charge all the expenses of the manufacture of the Book to said E. & all the copies given to Editors are to be charged to the Author.
>
> J. M. & Co are to a/c for all copies sold at 30 pr ct discount from the retail price, whatever that price may <agree> be & give twenty pr ct disct to the trade—settlements to be made every six months the first one to be made on July1st 1847, by notes at 3 months from such settlement.
>
> The first edition to be fifteen hundred copies & stereotyped.
>
> James Munroe & Co
R Waldo Emerson
>
> It is also agreed between said Emerson & said Munroe & Co that said Emerson shall furnish a Volume of Poems by W. E. Channing to be printed on the same terms as above—with exception of last clause.
>
> James Munroe & Co
R. Waldo Emerson.

poetry of his contemporaries, it afforded an important schooling (along with Emerson's involvement in the American publications of Thomas Carlyle and of Margaret Fuller's *Summer on the Lakes* in 1844) in the ways of the literary marketplace. As indicated above in the Historical Introduction, Emerson's choice of a publisher for *Poems* was by no means a foregone conclusion, even though he had been using the services of James Munroe for the better part of a decade. His restiveness on this point did not so much signify a dissatisfaction with his old and relatively comfortable relations with that company (he continued, he said, to "feel safe in their hands" [*L*, III, 249]), but had to do instead with recent changes in the ways of commercial publishing and in particular with the emergence of an aggressively democratic and nationalistic style in the New York book business.[10] These developments and the energies they betokened had effectively lured Margaret Fuller to New York just a few years earlier and turned her literary career in a dramatically different direction. "How can you publish anywhere but in New York?" was the question posed to Emerson by Margaret's brother Richard.[11]

Emerson's sounding out of Evert Duyckinck, agent for the New York firm of Wiley & Putnam, was an effort to learn if the promised larger sale of cheaper books might realize a greater net income. It was a natural question for New England writers of the time. As Lawrence Buell has pointed out:

> The crucial literary institutions [in Boston] were still slow in developing. . . . Before midcentury, no one was able to make a living from creative writing published in the Boston area.

10 The ideological context of New York's "Young America" movement is well told in Perry Miller's *The Raven and the Whale* (New York: Harcourt, Brace, 1956), while its more particular meanings for Emerson as a writer in search of a publisher are accurately traced by Joseph M. Thomas in "'The Property of My Own Book': Emerson's *Poems* (1847) and the Literary Marketplace," *New England Quarterly*, LXIX (September 1996): 406–425.

11 Richard F. Fuller to Emerson, 26 December 1845, bMS Am 1280.1162, Ralph Waldo Emerson Memorial Association deposit, Houghton Library, Harvard University.

(Emerson told Edward Everett Hale that *Representative Men* [1850] was the first book that yielded him any income.) William Charvat makes the point cogently: "Up to 1850, the publishers of the [New York-Philadelphia] axis were the discoverers and interpreters of American literary taste"; "Boston publishers did not even know they had a renaissance on their hands until Ticknor & Fields woke up in the late forties," and when they did, they essentially emulated the marketing and distribution methods that the New York and Philadelphia houses had devised. Boston publishing, then, remained anachronistically and obstinately localized; New England authors who wanted a national hearing were forced, until 1850, to go to the "axis" to get it; the so-called flowering of New England was made possible by entrepreneurs in Philadelphia and New York.[12]

But when Emerson got a "very liberal offer" from Duyckinck (six cents on each book retailed at 31 cents), he did the arithmetic and discovered that "it does not in fact promise me the advantage I had expected." "If I print my Poems in Boston," he told Duyckinck, "I suppose the book will cost 75 cents [in fact it cost 87 cents when printed two years later]; and if we sell 2000 copies, I should receive more money than by the sale of 2500 on the scale you propose" (*L*, III, 307, 308). Emerson understood that poetry had some cultural prestige in Boston, that readers preferred the costlier binding, the better paper and wider margins. In commercial New York, it seemed, poetry was a vendible commodity. But it may be, as Joseph M. Thomas has argued, that the final decision in favor of Munroe came down to Emerson's desire to control the circumstances of publication and thereby protect "the property in my own book." Instead of accepting royalties, Emerson would employ Munroe simply as a printer and retailer, have the work ste-

12 Lawrence Buell, *New England Literary Culture: From Revolution Through Renaissance* (Cambridge: Cambridge University Press, 1986), 35–36. See also Ezra Greenspan, *George Palmer Putnam: Representative American Publisher* (University Park: The Pennsylvania State University Press, 2000), 165–176.

reotyped, retain ownership of the plates, and compensate Munroe at a rate of 30% for his trouble.[13]

The story of Emerson's dealings with the London publisher, John Chapman, has fewer interesting complications. They first crossed paths when Chapman bought out John Green, "the Unitarian & Transcendental Bibliopole for all England," as Theodore Parker called him, thereby succeeding in 1844 to the London distributorship of the *Dial.* Chapman was, if anything, a more efficient businessman and a more enthusiastic promoter of Emerson than Green had been. In 1844 he published a pamphlet edition of *The Young American* and the book *Essays: Second Series,* the latter reset from "ten or more signatures" made up of proofsheets from Munroe's Boston edition and sent by Emerson to England. Emerson was delighted with the quality of Chapman's work on these projects, and in the letter saying so (30 December 1844), he all but promised that Chapman could have the *Poems,* too, whenever that should be ready.[14]

The problem was that copy for that volume was sent, less than two years later, a little before it was actually "ready"—sent, that is,

13 See Thomas, "'The Property of My Own Book,'" 416. Emerson had other reasons for breaking off negotiations with Duyckinck: when Wiley and Putnam brought out what Emerson supposed was a pirated edition of his friend Thomas Carlyle's work on Oliver Cromwell, he decided, a little hastily, that the New Yorkers were not gentlemen (see *CEC*, 386–390, Greenspan, 123–128, and Ronald A. Bosco and Joel Myerson, *The Emerson Brothers: A Fraternal Biography in Letters* [Oxford and New York: Oxford University Press, 2006], 345–346). Moreover, Emerson had to give up the idea of publishing for the Christmas and New Year's trade when he became occupied with preparations for the winter's lecture series. As he explained to Duyckinck, this consideration led him to put off the volume for another year (*L*, III, 308), but shortly afterward he wrote to his brother William to say that "a critical friend of mine" (evidently Caroline Sturgis) had come for a visit, looked over the poems, and convinced Emerson that they needed more revision than he had supposed (*L*, III, 310).

14 Theodore Parker quoted in Robert J. Scholnick, "Boston and Beyond," in Joel Myerson et al., eds, *The Oxford Handbook of Transcendentalism* (Oxford and New York: Oxford University Press, 2010), 497; Myerson, 117; *L*, III, 273–274. Scholnick's essay also provides a discussion of Chapman and his importance to the Transcendentalists.

not in the form of printed sheets from Munroe, but as holograph manuscript, written out, strangely enough, while Emerson was in Bangor, Maine, delivering his "Representative Men" lectures. The intention was to supply Chapman with "a copy that he can copyright" (*L*, III, 351), and so this procedure must have seemed at the time the best way to satisfy the requirements of English copyright law.[15] More than half this manuscript survives.[16] And except in cases where the poems had been published previously in periodicals, it serves as copy-text, being, in the remaining instances, the "earliest feasible form" of the texts it contains, even though, as we shall see, Emerson effectively repudiated its authority.

On 13 October, Emerson sent a parcel containing "all but the few last" pages of manuscript by boat to Munroe in Boston (through a storm) to be forwarded by steamer to Chapman. In the cover letter to Munroe, Emerson wrote, "Now that I have got the right readings settled for him, I shall be able to finish & send you your Copy immediately on my return home, which should be on Saturday next [17 October]. I have duplicates of all but a few which I think to print directly from the Dial, indicating the *errata*. Monday or Tuesday we can begin to print" (*L*, III, 356–357). One assumes from this that, apart from the *Dial* verses, Emerson produced two nearly identical fair copies of each poem ("duplicates") as he became satisfied with the effect of last revisions. The fact that he leaves himself no additional working time after his return to Concord implies that as of 13 October he has a nearly com-

15 Chapman's edition in fact contains a "NOTICE" on the half-title verso that reads, in part: "The Publishers of this work, which is printed from the Author's manuscript, beg to state that it is Copyright, according to the late Copyright, Act 5 & 6 Victoria," and goes on to warn against infringement (see Myerson, 152).

16 Each poem was copied on one or more sheets of its own, so that their order could be fixed after the copying was done; it is probably more accurate, therefore, to speak of manuscripts in the plural. In a note at *L*, III, 356, Ralph L. Rusk mentions that "the MS for Chapman's London edition" was then (1939) in the personal collection of Owen D. Young, founder of the Radio Corporation of America and chairman at the time of General Electric. Many of the manuscripts were included in Young's 1941 donation to the Berg Collection of the New York Public Library, but others seem to have scattered and are now in various major research libraries.

plete set of manuscript fair copies for Munroe to print from. The point is significant, because it suggests that the many differences between the London text (both manuscript and printed) and the Boston text (for which no manuscript evidence survives) are attributable in the main to corrections and emendations that Emerson made during the process of seeing the Munroe edition through the press.

Each time Emerson made a change in the Boston proofs—and he made hundreds—he would have known that the English edition was bound to preserve the reading he was now rejecting. Also, as he corrected the local printer's occasional misreadings of his own occasional illegibilities, he knew that some ludicrous error was likely going uncaught across the ocean. And, indeed, it was only because Emerson did not read proofs for Chapman's edition that line 79 of "Woodnotes, I," where a part of the description of the Maine wilderness ought to have read, "Where feeds the moose, and walks the surly bear," confounded some Cockney compositor, who knew not the animal nor its Algonquian-derived name, and so made it "mouse" instead.

The Boston edition was published on Christmas Day 1846. Four days later Emerson sent a copy to Chapman with instructions to conform all future printings of his edition to this approved American text. He had not yet seen a copy of the London edition, published on 12 December (Myerson, 153), but knew nevertheless that he would "find a multitude of errata in your edition" (*L,* VIII, 100).[17] An errata slip was tipped into unsold copies at some point, but none of the errors was ever actually corrected in the text. Only one additional printing was issued, unaltered, by George Routledge in 1850, ending the English history of Emerson's *Poems.*

---

17 See also the discussion of these same matters in the Historical Introduction, above. Some commentators have given 26 December as the date the publication of Munroe's edition, but Emerson inscribed and sent out the presentation copies on 25 December, the date, moreover, that he assigned to the publication in a memorandum in *JMN,* VII, 483. Longfellow received his copy in the mail on the 26th and responded to the gift with generous praise in a letter of 27 December (see *L,* III, 364).

The presence or absence of manuscript printer's copy and the temporal priority of the English first edition determine our choice of copy-text, but the circumstances of publication and Emerson's reasons for rejecting the English text explain our frequent acceptance of emendations from the first American edition.

As called for in the contract with Munroe, plates were prepared at the Boston Type and Stereotype Foundry and after the first printing of 1500 copies was exhausted, further printings from these plates were issued, on Emerson's order, as follows:[18]

2. April 1847. This printing can be distinguished from the first by the absence of brackets around the words "its counterpart," at line 58 of "The Dæmonic Love," a correction requested by Emerson in his letter to Munroe of 29 December 1846 (*L*, VIII, 98).
3. 28 December 1847. See *JMN*, VII, 483.[19]
4. 1847 [actual date of issue uncertain, perhaps 1848]; stated "Fourth Edition" on title page; Myerson notes copies with Munroe's ads dated 1 January 1847 and September 1849.
5. 1850. Again called the "Fourth Edition" but issued by Emer-

---

18 Information in the following list is partly drawn from Joel Myerson, *Ralph Waldo Emerson: A Descriptive Bibliography* (Pittsburgh: University of Pittsburgh Press, 1982), and Myerson, *Supplement to Ralph Waldo Emerson: A Descriptive Bibliography* (Pittsburgh: University of Pittsburgh Press, 2005). The history of Longfellow's publications during this period is too essentially different to permit meaningful comparison, and yet it may be worth mentioning that the two-volume set of Longfellow's *Poems,* first issued by Ticknor, Reed and Fields in 1850, was reprinted 26 times by 1864, and repeatedly updated by the inclusion of the poet's later work (see *The Cost Books of Ticknor and Fields and Their Predecessors, 1832–1858,* ed. Warren S. Tryon and William Charvat (New York: The Bibliographical Society of America, 1949), 155.

19 At this location, the end of journal E, Emerson listed several debits and credits relating to the first several printings of *Poems.* The figures are confusing and probably incomplete, but they seem to suggest that the book sold very well in the week following publication (i.e., between Christmas and New Year's). Allowing for 86 presentation and review copies (*L*, VIII, 102) and the sale of 693 copies by the time of Munroe's first semi-annual reckoning, enough of the first printing of 1500 copies had been disposed of warrant the new printing in April.

son's new publisher, Phillips, Sampson; some copies made up with sheets from Munroe's stock in a Phillips, Sampson casing and with a cancel title leaf.

6. "Fifth Edition." Phillips, Sampson, 1856. 500 copies printed September 1856 (*JMN*, XIV, 452).
7. "Sixth Edition." Phillips, Sampson, 1857. 500 copies printed 2 April 1857. The record of this printing at *JMN*, XIV, 452, also includes reference to a printing of 250 copies on "fine" paper in December 1856. No copies of this printing have been located.
8. "Seventh Edition." Phillips, Sampson, 1858. 500 copies printed July 1858.

Phillips, Sampson failed in September 1859. New printings from Emerson's plates, generally of 280 copies only, were issued by his new publisher, Ticknor and Fields, in 1860, 1863, 1864, 1866, and 1868. No textual changes have been noted in the ten printings issued between 1868 and 1883 by the successor firms of Fields, Osgood, James R. Osgood, or Houghton, Mifflin. Wear to the plates began to be noticeable in the mid-1850s; by the late 1860s much punctuation had been lost at line ends.

V. The "Blue and Gold" *Poems* (1865)

The "Blue and Gold" format had been introduced by Ticknor and Fields in 1856 for an edition of Tennyson's *Poetical Works*. The innovative design was an enormous marketing success, combining a conveniently small trim size of 3 ½ x 5 ½ inches with legible, well-spaced type, all bound in royal blue with gilt edges. The books were so popular that competing publishers closely imitated their appearance; by 1869 Ticknor and Fields had 41 titles in 57 volumes in the series.[20] James T. Fields proposed on 7 May 1864 that Emerson approve the inclusion of the first and second series of

---

20 *The Cost Books of Ticknor and Fields*, 362–363. See also Michael Winship, *American Literary Publishing in the Mid-Nineteenth Century: The Business of Ticknor and Fields* (Cambridge: Cambridge University Press, 1995), 124.

Essays in a single Blue and Gold volume. When he agreed, in a letter of 13 May, Fields responded on the 18th with an offer to publish a new edition of the *Poems* in the same series. Emerson agreed on the 19th (*L,* V, 376–377), authorizing an initial printing of 2500 copies, 500 fewer than for the prose volume.[21] Although he supplied "a short list of *errata*" for the edition of the *Essays,* it seems that he made no such corrections in the *Poems* text, which collation shows must have been set from an 1857 copy, since emendations done in printings later than that were not incorporated. As in the prose volume, there are numerous changes in the accidentals, which appear to be the effect of an unhindered imposition of house style. The fact that these changes often ran counter to Emerson's preferences prompted the conclusion in the case of the prose volume (*CW,* II, xlv–xlvi) that Emerson almost certainly did not read proofs. The same conclusion is warranted in the case of the 1865 *Poems.*

This edition was unusual in that Ticknor and Fields paid for and retained the plates and paid Emerson a royalty of ten cents per copy, on a retail price of $1.50. It would seem that neither the author nor the publisher expected to profit greatly from this venture; in 1868 Emerson lamented that Ticknor and Fields had probably lost money on it (*L,* VI, 39).

VI. *May-Day and Other Pieces* (1867)

If Emerson did not pay close attention to the 1865 second edition of his *Poems,* it may have been because the book was far more his publisher's project than his own. It is also likely, however, that by 1865 he had begun to focus his attention on a new collection,

21 It was subsequently determined that the first printing should be 2800 copies; the only other printing, in March or April 1865, consisted of 280 copies (Myerson, 160; see also the Emerson "Contract file" in the Houghton Library, Harvard University [MS Am 2346 (914), folder 3]). Plans for a "Cabinet Edition" of *Poems,* for which Emerson would have received a slightly higher royalty, were evidently abandoned. See *L,* V, 377, and *The Round Table* (New York), 7 October 1865, p. 74, where the Cabinet Edition is described by Boston correspondent Justin Windsor as a large-paper version of the blue and gold.

May-Day and Other Pieces (1867). Since the founding of the *Atlantic Monthly* in 1857, Emerson had published thirteen poems in its pages, including "The Romany Girl," "Days," "Brahma," "Two Rivers," "The Titmouse," "The Boston Hymn," "Voluntaries," and "Terminus."[22] He had also, in 1860, published a dozen quatrains in Moncure Conway's Cincinnati *Dial,* together with "The Sacred Dance" (collected as "The Song of Seid Nimetollah of Kuhistan"), the most important of Emerson's Persian translations. *May-Day* would also include a section called "Elements," made up of thirteen of the best poetic epigraphs to the essays. Only thirty of the volume's 92 poems were appearing for the first time. These new poems, however, included the two uncharacteristically long works, "May-Day" and "The Adirondacs," with which the book opened.

In letters of 5 and 7 October 1866 to James T. Fields and Charles Eliot Norton, Emerson mentions that he is "working away at my last pages of rhyme" and "trying to make an end of my second collection of poems (so called)" (*L*, V, 480). Both letters express anxiety, first about trying to do this work in the "quarters of hours" of free time between interruptions from visitors, then about the looming prospect of an ambitious western lecture tour that he sees will keep him from closely supervising the proofing and printing. From a letter by Ellen to Edward on 4 October, it is clear that the project had only recently been announced in the Emerson home. Ellen tells her brother that "Mr. Papa has actually undertaken to finish the Spring poem ["May-Day"] and publish the second volume this autumn. Isn't it delightful? Two nights he has read to us out of them and we have had perfect evenings. 'Voluntaries' is to be in it you know, and the Mottoes that are best in the books, and all that have been in the Atlantic, with Spring, and one or two others that never were printed." Emerson's daughter Edith Emerson Forbes, meanwhile, "discourses upon the binding of the

22 Although Emerson enjoyed close and cordial relations with the editors at the *Atlantic*—Lowell (1857–1861) and Fields (1861–1871)—he was never tempted to be relaxed or casual about reading proofs, as the episode involving "Waldeinsamkeit" in 1858 demonstrated (see the headnote to that poem, below).

new Poems" (*ETE,* I, 406). On 12 October Emerson declined an invitation to lecture because "I am held fast at present by a little printing" (*L,* IX, 244). Not for another month, however, was all the manuscript copy ready for the printers. In a letter of 17 November he alluded to work on "a task that must be finished on Monday night." Eleanor M. Tilton suggested that this reference is to "completing the proofs for *May-Day.* . . , which would be printed by December 1" (*L,* IX, 253). In fact, according to Emerson the book was "all in type about the 1 December" (*L,* V, 507), so that proofs only became available at that time, in advance of the stereotyping process. He informed Anne Botta on 7 December that he had hoped by this time to be able to send her a copy of the volume, "but though it is printed, Fields will not let it be published; for which, no doubt, we ought both to thank him" (*L,* IX, 255).

It would seem, based on Emerson's explanation to Seneca Dorr the following February (*L,* V, 506–507), that at some time between 1 and 7 December, Fields halted publication at the proof stage, deciding that, as Emerson recalled, "it would be madness to print it for New Year's for all his western correspondents had written to him, 'Send us no new book, least of all poetry.'" At this point a 1 April publication date seemed more reasonable, Fields hoping that the market would have improved by then. Undoubtedly the post-war book trade was still uncertain, but since we have no independent evidence of Fields' motives, it may also be that he felt the book would be improved if its author had more time. From early January through the middle of March 1867, Emerson was on the road, carrying the unread proofs with him in his trunk as he traveled to lecture at such places as Faribault, Minnesota, and Keokuk, Iowa. From Chicago on 24 February he wrote to Ellen pointing out how awkward it was, "as my Poems are promised for 1 April, that I should be eleven hundred miles from the printers, & with so many errata that I am bound to correct. I shall have to pray Mr Fields to postpone a little, now that he has postponed so much" (*L,* V, 505). The proofs adamantly refused to be read on the fly. He asked Fields for a delay beyond 1 April in a letter sent on 6 March from St. Louis (*L,* IX, 266–267), and on 26 March, after his long-delayed return home, he informed Fields, with what sounds like exhaustion, "I have no keen edge now to publish, since looking again at the rhymes; but neither have I much resistance to withstand it" (*L,* IX, 269). On 2 April, he at last gave Fields permission to publish, and included "a few *errata* to be at once corrected on the plates" (*L,* IX, 270). *May-Day and Other Pieces* was published on 29 April in an edition of 2000 copies, though the very first copy off the press, inscribed by Fields to Mrs. Emerson, had arrived in Concord the day before.[23]

The English edition, which followed the American by two months, was published in both cloth and wrappers by George Routledge and Sons, who had also issued the second printing of *Poems* in 1850. Emerson's arrangement with this London firm evidently continued the relation he had personally negotiated for the publication of *English Traits* in 1856 (see *CW,* V, lxi–lxii, and *L,* IV, 528). At that time recent changes in English copyright law made it difficult for an American author to secure legal protection, so Emerson settled for a token payment in exchange for an advance copy of the American proof-sheets. Although Emerson entered into a more lucrative arrangement with Smith, Elder for *The Conduct of Life* in 1860 (Myerson, 275), apparently the earlier arrangement with Routledge was reinstated in 1867. As with *English Traits,* the London edition of *May-Day* was set from the American sheets and differed in the end by the omission of half-titles and blank pages and the adoption of national usage in spelling and punctuation. In fact there are no differences between the two editions that cannot be set down either to error or to house styling. There were no reprintings.

Emerson had spent considerable time reading proofs for the Boston edition of *May-Day,* but he complained that the effort was broken up, and, toward the end, rushed. On 6 May he had a letter from James Elliot Cabot thanking him for the gift copy of the vol-

---

23 This volume is in the Houghton Library, Harvard University. See CC6 in the list of correction copies above. For a list of recipients of presentation copies, which were inscribed and sent out on 1 May, see *JMN,* XVI, 56–61. Emerson had arranged to have 100 copies in a special white linen presentation binding (Myerson, 297).

ume and inquiring about an odd revision in the first line of "Days": the familiar reading from the *Atlantic* text, "Daughters of Time" had inexplicably become "Damsels of Time." Emerson was abashed. "I read with amazement the word 'Damsels' which slipped into the text I know not how," he told Cabot: "'Daughters' was right & shall be" (*L*, V, 518). A correction was attempted in the 1868 second printing, but it came out "Daughter." There were seven more printings between 1868 and 1883, totaling perhaps 1500 copies. In all these printings "Daughter" was allowed to stand.

VII. *Selected Poems* (1876)

One of the most difficult issues which the editors of the present work had to confront was how to estimate the authority of Emerson's revisions in *Selected Poems* and, indeed, how to decide which ones were the author's own. By the mid-1870s the aphasia that descended on Emerson during his last years had taken hold and demonstrably made any significant original writing impossible and the revision of old lectures into new essays so laboriously difficult for him that a collaboration was established among Emerson, his daughter Ellen, and a trusted outside advisor, James Elliot Cabot. Of the three the last two often seemed to be the most active. But the question is still worth asking, as Joseph M. Thomas has done, whether the effects of Emerson's dementia "applied equally to poetry late in his life."[24] Without going into clinical detail (which would unavoidably involve speculation and could not, in any event, offer usefully conclusive answers), it is worth saying, at a minimum, that Emerson had good days and bad and that the mental acuity required to improve a phrase is different from that needed to construct large arguments. The medical literature has

24 Thomas, "Late Emerson," 972. Thomas alludes to the "collaboration" first referred to as "the Emerson factory" by Nancy Craig Simmons, who discusses it mainly in relation to the late prose works. The history of that collaboration is most thoroughly detailed by Ronald A. Bosco in the Historical Introduction to *CW*, VIII (for Simmons and Bosco, see n. 2, above).

long recognized that in many cases of aphasia a capacity for song and poetry may long outlast sharpness of memory and recall. Emerson's decline was progressive: between 1872, when his house burned, and 1876, when *Selected Poems* was published, his symptoms, always more or less intermittent, were noticeable (and annoying to Emerson), but clearly they were not as severe as they would become over the course of the remaining six years of his life.

The idea for *Selected Poems* was entirely Emerson's. After the Concord house burned in July 1872, he and Ellen undertook an extended trip to Europe and Egypt to be out of the way while repairs were made and also for the purpose of recruiting Emerson's strength. While at Florence, Italy, in March 1873, he took the first steps in planning the volume. As Ellen explained it in a letter to Edith, written from Paris,

> His hands are as cold & as numb as ever, he remembers no better, he feels the same inability to write the smallest note. But in Florence one day [where they stayed from 10 to 14 March] he sat in his room for some hours, and when I came in he said he had been looking over the green book of poems, and to some purpose [the reference is to Emerson's copy of the 1865 *Poems;* see CC5 in the list of correction copies, above]. He had struck out several poems entire, and corrected many lines. That is the first work he has done, and it cheered me very much—him too, no doubt. (*ETE,* II, 68)

The notation shows that the decision in favor of a less than comprehensive edition of the poems was, spontaneously, Emerson's, and that it preceded by more than a year James R. Osgood's project of the "Little Classic" edition of Emerson's works, in which *Selected Poems* would appear as the ninth volume. As Ellen's contemporary description of the book's inception indicates, her father's interest in it was looked upon as a sign of his returning vigor, and eventually the Emerson children—and Ellen especially—would involve themselves so as further to encourage it. In that respect the project developed some of the same motives that lay behind

Edith's supportive involvement in the production of *Parnassus,* an anthology of favorite passages from other poets, published in December 1874.[25] A year later work on *Selected Poems* began in earnest, Emerson writing to his son-in-law William Hathaway Forbes, who oversaw his financial affairs, that he consented to Osgood's terms and that he would "give immediate attention to the new edition of Poems which is chiefly to be improved by careful sinking of the poorer & poorest matter, rather than by much addition, though I have a few which I shall like to add. I think the new volume of selected poems will not excede [*sic*] the size of one of the old" (*L,* VI, 268–269).[26]

Two weeks later, on 10 January 1876, Ellen was inquiring in a letter to Edith about just when "Mr Osgood wants the poems," adding that "if we are put up to a date, we can be ready" (*ETE,* II, 193). Her concern about a deadline accurately reflects her administrator's role: she would organize and facilitate the process, but would for the most part leave the actual editing and revising to her father. Others, such as Franklin B. Sanborn, James Russell Lowell, James Elliot Cabot, and Elizabeth Hoar, were either permitted or encouraged to express opinions regarding omissions and inclusions, but their advice seems to have been adopted only

25 For *Parnassus,* see Ronald A. Bosco, "'Poetry for the World of Readers' and 'Poetry for Bards Proper': Poetic Theory and Textual Integrity in Emerson's *Parnassus," SAR 1989,* pp. 257–312. Joseph M. Thomas ("Late Emerson," 977) suggested that the working relationship formed among Emerson and his daughters for *Parnassus* supplied a model for the immediately subsequent work on *Selected Poems.* In particular he instanced Ellen's letter of 8 December 1875 to Edith saying that she had been "instructing Father to bring materials for making up the new book of poems" at a gathering at Edith's home in Milton (*ETE,* II, 192).

26 William Hathaway Forbes, husband of Edith, had taken on responsibility to negotiate with publishers and more generally to look after Emerson's financial and contractual affairs. The letter is dated "Wednesday Eve. 23, Dec^r." Rusk assigned it conjecturally to 1874, pointing out that the 23rd fell on a Wednesday in that year, but allowing that the year remained uncertain. In fact, Emerson went to visit Mr. and Mrs. Forbes at their home in Milton on December 24 to spend the holiday, so a letter is hardly likely. More probably Emerson's dateline was mistaken and the note was written in 1875, since he did not in fact spend Christmas in Milton that year (see *ETE,* II, 192).

when it coincided with Emerson's own preferences. A significant instance involved the poem "Good-Bye," a favorite with all the bystanders, who were nevertheless gravely disappointed when Emerson stood firm against including it. In his careful study of the composition of *Selected Poems* it was Thomas's conclusion that, despite the author's compromised mental acuity, "Emerson's was the primary voice in each of two areas of importance—the selection of works and the revision of the texts" ("Late Emerson," 979). Conceding that matters were quite different in the Emerson factory's concurrent handling of the prose volumes, Thomas convincingly argues that those who built essays by piecing together lecture fragments did not feel sufficiently bold or sufficiently competent to meddle with the poems—at least not while Emerson was alive. Although numbers of "new" essays were being turned out by the factory, it is significant that no "new" or inauthentic poems are to be found in the 1876 volume.

The one place where a hand other than Emerson's did manifestly intrude was the poem "May-Day." This poem was shortened and rearranged by Ellen, who had been quite reasonably alarmed by her father's threats to leave it out altogether (*ETE*, II, 194). What she did with "May-Day" is fully indicated in the commentary on the poem, below. There are several possible explanations for why she did it, though it is not a matter about which certainty is attainable. It would seem that her father had come to believe that the poem was not successful, and may well have taken to heart the adverse criticism of William Dean Howells in his *Atlantic Monthly* review.[27] The assertion that the poem lacked a credible structure may have sapped his confidence in other long poems, such as "Woodnotes" and "The Adirondacs," as well as the long translation from Hafiz in the 1847 *Poems*. In Florence in 1873, Emerson had made major excisions to "Woodnotes" in the "green book," and had determined to omit altogether "The Adirondacs" and "From the Persian of Hafiz." The letter to Will Forbes declares Emerson's intention that this new volume would be no longer than either of the two previous collections. Such a consideration

27 Review of *May-Day and Other Pieces*, AM, XX (September 1867): 376–378.

independently militated against the longer poems, but Emerson had for some time known about himself what Howells openly averred—that he was not a master of the long form. "I am a bard least of bards," he had complained in 1863:

> I cannot, like them, make lofty arguments in stately continuous verse, constraining the rocks, trees, animals, & the periodic stars to say my thoughts,—for that is the gift of great poets; but I am a bard, because I stand near them, & apprehend all they utter, & with pure joy hear that which I also would say, &, moreover, I speak interruptedly words & half stanzas which have the like scope & aim. (*JMN*, XV, 308)

Emerson was inclined to credit Howells's criticism by omitting "May-Day"; Ellen was determined to save it, no doubt feeling that the title poem of her father's second collection was too important to omit, and certainly feeling a real fondness for the poem whose draft fragments had charmed her childhood.[28]

Ellen's reorganization of the poem "May-Day" is well documented, yet it is just as clear that she performed no similar operation on any other of her father's poems. The textual emendations introduced in 1876 (apart from the situation with "May-Day," which has required separate treatment in Appendix B) fall into two major classes. First are the changes corresponding to notations in the correction copies. This category in turn includes emendations of two sorts: those made in desultory fashion as they occurred to Emerson during the period from 1847 to 1873 and those made between 1873 and 1876 in immediate contemplation of *Selected Poems*. As noted above, the latter revisions were first made in the green book (CC5) in Florence. Most of these were

---

28 When the poet Emma Lazarus visited in 1876, while *Selected Poems* was being assembled, she suggested certain verbal changes to which, according to Edward's later recollection, Emerson assented (Edward Waldo Emerson to James Elliot Cabot, 19 October 1883, bMS Am 1280.226 (297), Ralph Waldo Emerson Memorial Association deposit, Houghton Library, Harvard University). It is probably significant that these changes were limited to the text of "May-Day," the one poem singled out as an object of special concern.

subsequently transferred to the main correction copy of the 1847 *Poems* (CC1), no doubt to consolidate early corrections with the recent ones. Alterations to the poems of the first collection were predictably much more numerous than for the *May-Day* poems. The significance of these facts for the editing process lies in the rule derived from the empirical evidence: that textual changes first appearing in *Selected Poems* have a greater or more obvious authority if they correspond to notations in the correction copies, some portion of which were made prior to 1873.[29]

That leaves the second class of variants in the 1876 texts: those lacking precedent in the correction copies—which is to say, those that appear to have been made (by someone) in 1876. Although there is no evidence whatsoever (again apart from "May-Day") that anyone other than Emerson himself contributed to the text, the imperfectly knowable extent of Emerson's mental impairment at this time raises the possibility, first, that undocumented assistance might actually have been rendered, and, second, that changes personally and entirely made by Emerson might be, in fact, less than authoritative. Unfortunately, the editors have no practical or theoretically defensible way to deal with the ambiguities inherent in these possibilities. The best that can be done is to present all the evidence (as a variorum presentation requires), and allow the reader a full view of the editor's textual choices. In the limited class of choices involving 1876 variants lacking correction-copy authority, the editors have given weight to their impression (where such impressions arise) that a given emendation is the work of a poet and not of a grammarian or an "improver."

Although *Selected Poems* is a relatively accurate edition—especially in comparison to the 1865 "Blue and Gold"—whoever read

---

29 It is not always certain whether the handwriting in a particular correction-copy notation is Emerson's or Ellen's, but the presumption must be that wherever Ellen happened to be responsible for an inscription, she wrote at her father's direction. Indeed, she often served as Emerson's "secretary" during his last decade. A more difficult question involves the possibility that some of the holograph emendations might have been made by Edward as he prepared copy for the Riverside edition. This possibility scarcely affects the text in the present edition, however, since almost no Riverside variants have been adopted.

proofs missed one especially blatant error: the transposition of pages 129 and 130, affecting the end of "Woodnotes, I" and the beginning of "Woodnotes, II." This error, almost certainly in the imposition, went uncorrected until the Houghton, Osgood printing of 1880. It is probable that Emerson himself read the proofs, since he is known to have done so for other works in 1877 (*L*, X, 195) and 1878 (*CW*, VIII, ccv), though he was surely not the only reader in any of these instances. *Selected Poems* was separately reprinted seven times between 1876 and 1884 and five times in combination with *Letters and Social Aims* as volume IV of the five-volume "Fireside Edition" of the collected works (Myerson, 160–162).

VIII. The Riverside (1883–1884) and Centenary *Poems* (1904)

Following Emerson's death on 27 April 1882, James Elliot Cabot became literary executor by a provision in Emerson's will. The same will required that he act in concert with the children, principally Edward, in whom the copyrights vested. Over the next two years, Cabot labored to produce a "New and Revised Edition" of the complete works—known as the Riverside edition—but the surviving correspondence of this period shows that Edward was an equally active silent partner. In fact, with respect to the poems, a matter of particular interest to him, he clearly took the editorial lead.[30] The first eight volumes of the Riverside edition essentially reproduced the contents of the corresponding volumes in the

---

30 Thomas was undoubtedly correct in asserting of the *Poems* volume in the Riverside edition that "Cabot was . . . involved in the work, but in the main the book was Edward's" ("Harnessing Proteus," 218). Forty-two of Edward's letters to Cabot, owned by the Ralph Waldo Emerson Memorial Association, are preserved at the Houghton Library, Harvard University, bMS Am 1280.226 (260–301). The daughters were less involved in the edition, but seem to have taken an interest nevertheless: among the Edith Emerson Forbes and William Hathaway Forbes Papers and Additions at the Massachusetts Historical Society are a number of letters from Edith to Ellen, including one dated 4 March 1883 in which she says she is "reading & studying Father's poems" (Carton 3 SH 17PL D, quoted by permission). According to the contract with Houghton, Mifflin dated 15 March 1883, the Emerson heirs were to receive a 20% royalty (Myerson, 549).

1876 Little Classic edition, but it was Edward's decision not to reprint *Selected Poems* as the ninth volume, but to offer in its place a more nearly comprehensive work, entitled *Poems,* which would restore the omitted verses, rearrange "May-Day" for a second time, and add a great many poems and fragments that their author had never been inclined to publish.

Edward was conflicted about this decision. In January 1883 he wrote to Cabot regarding a brief draft Preface to the edition: "I see no objection to the introductory note which seems to cover the ground. Something more must be said in the preface to the Poems justifying our allowing those omitted from Selected Poems to stand, for since I have been at home Ellen has told me that Father meant that to be his final choice longer ago than I had supposed. I still believe, however, that we are right in preserving many of the old ones and putting in some of the unpublished ones."[31] The "something more" that duly appeared in the "Prefatory Note" to volume 9, written by Edward but signed by Cabot, downplays the significance and authority of *Selected Poems:*

> This volume contains nearly all the pieces included in the Poems and May-Day of former editions. In 1876, Mr. Emerson published a selection from his Poems, adding six new ones, and omitting many. Of those omitted, several are now restored, in accordance with the expressed wishes of many readers and lovers of them. Also, some pieces never before published are here given in an Appendix; on various grounds. Some of them appear to have had Mr. Emerson's approval, but to have been withheld because they were unfinished. These it seemed best not to suppress, now that they can never receive their completion. Others, mostly of an early date, re-

31 Edward Waldo Emerson to James Elliot Cabot, 30 January 1883, bMS Am 1280.226 (262), Ralph Waldo Emerson Memorial Association deposit, Houghton Library, Harvard University. In the end, Edward omitted seven poems from the first collection ("Tact," "Suum Cuique," "Loss and Gain," "The House," "Painting and Sculpture," "From the Persian of Hafiz," and "Ghaselle") and five from *May-Day* ("Nemesis," "Love and Thought," "Lover's Petition," "Una," and "Merlin's Song"). None of these had appeared in *Selected Poems.*

mained unpublished doubtless because of their personal and private nature. Some of these seem to have an autobiographical interest sufficient to justify their publication. Others again, often mere fragments, have been admitted as characteristic or as expressing in poetic form thoughts found in the Essays.

In coming to a decision in these cases it seemed on the whole preferable to take the risk of including too much rather than the opposite, and to leave the task of further winnowing to the hands of Time.

As stated in the preface to the first volume of this edition . . . the readings adopted by him in the Selected Poems have not always been followed here, but in some cases preference has been given to corrections made by him when he was in fuller strength than at the time of the last revision. (*Poems* [Boston, 1884], v–vi)

Coming out only seven years after *Selected Poems,* the Riverside *Poems* effectively superseded it, submerging Emerson's own effort to define his canon in the broad documentary aim of the posthumous collection.[32]

Joseph M. Thomas has pointed to these statements as important evidence that Emerson had in fact been responsible for the choice of poems in 1876 and responsible, as well, for the readings that Edward and Cabot now felt free to challenge ("Harnessing Proteus," 190). More important, however, than the eclipse of *Selected Poems* was the canon-shaping effect of the magisterial Riverside edition, with which Houghton, Mifflin began to consolidate

---

32 The Riverside *Poems* is consistently referred to in the present edition as having been published in 1884, which is the date that appears on the title page of the trade edition. Five hundred numbered copies of the American Large Paper "edition" (actually printing) bear the title-page date of 1883 (Myerson, 548–549). Edward's letters to Cabot show that he was working on proofs all through October and into November of that year. The completion of the edition, with the publication of volumes 9–11, was noticed in "The Books of the Month," *AM,* LIII (February 1884): 295.

its position as the purveyor, par excellence, of America's standard authors.[33]

The approaching hundredth anniversary of Emerson's birth and the planned celebrations at Concord and Boston markedly revived interest in the writings and provided the immediate impetus for a new collected edition, the Centenary, published in 1903–1904 by Houghton, Mifflin and edited once more by Edward.

The edition, which sold well and immediately became standard, has been aptly characterized as "only a modification of its Riverside Press precursor" (Thomas, "Harnessing Proteus," 237). Edward added somewhat to the number of poems, particularly in the Appendix, and rearranged slightly as he added. But the texts themselves were very little altered from the form they had achieved in the 1884 collection. The distinguishing fact about the Centenary edition, however, and its great advantage over its predecessor, lay in the 115-page section of notes that Edward provided. According to Edward, supplying such annotation for all of the edition's twelve volumes had been the publisher's idea (*W*, I, vi). Edward presented the plan to Cabot, who approved it, but, citing advanced age and poor health, declared that he was simply not in a position to help (in fact, he died on 16 January 1903). Edward, having long since given up his medical practice, having decided that he lacked the talent to be a painter (as for many years he wished to be), turned with no reluctance to the advancement of his father's literary reputation, taking up almost the only remunerative work that, at the age of sixty, he was clearly fitted for.[34]

List of Collated Editions

The first column of the following table gives the identifying number of each edition or printing, taken from Joel Myerson, *Ralph*

---

33 See Ellen Ballou, *The Building of the House: The Formative Years of Houghton, Mifflin* (Boston: Houghton, Mifflin, 1970), 308–314, and John Tebbel, *A History of Book Publishing in the United States* (New York: R. R. Bowker, 1972), I, 211–212.

34 On the history of the Centenary edition, see Joel Myerson, "Introduction to the AMS Edition," *The Complete Works of Ralph Waldo Emerson*, ed. Edward Waldo Emerson, 12 vols. (New York: AMS Press, 1979), I, v–xliv, and Thomas, "Harnessing Proteus," 235–243.

Waldo Emerson: A Descriptive Bibliography; the second column gives the place and date of publication; the third column indicates the use made by the editors of each edition or printing (M = machine collation; S = sight collation; Sp = spot collation); the fourth column indicates the ownership of the books (TW = Thomas Wortham; AvF = Albert von Frank; JM = Joel Myerson; Houghton = Houghton Library, Harvard University; Widener = Widener Library, Harvard University; CWRWE = books collected by previous editors, now owned by the edition, to be deposited in the Ralph Waldo Emerson Society Collection at the Thoreau Institute Library, Lincoln, Massachusetts).

Poems 47 (London)

A18.1.a	London, 1847	M, S	TW
A18.1.a	London, 1847	M, S	CWRWE
A18.1.a	London, 1847	M	Houghton
A18.1.a	London, 1847	M	Houghton
A18.1.b	London, 1850	M	CWRWE
A18.1.b	London, 1850	M, S	TW
A18.1.b	London, 1850	M	Houghton

Poems 47 (Boston)

A18.2.a	Boston, 1847	M, S	TW
A18.2.a	Boston, 1847	M, S	CWRWE
A18.2.a	Boston, 1847	S	Houghton
A18.2.a	Boston, 1847	M, S	Houghton
A18.2.b	Boston, 1847	M, S	Houghton
A18.2.d	Boston, 1847 ["Fourth Edition"]	S	TW
A18.2.d	Boston, 1847 ["Fourth Edition"]	M, S	CWRWE
A18.2.d	Boston, 1847 ["Fourth Edition"]	M	Houghton
A18.2.e	Boston, 1850 ["Fourth Edition"]	M, S	TW
A18.2.e	Boston, 1850 ["Fourth Edition"]	M	Houghton
A18.2.f	Boston, 1856	M, S	CWRWE
A18.2.f	Boston, 1856	S	TW
A18.2.g	Boston, 1857	S	CWRWE
A18.2.g	Boston, 1857	Sp	TW
A18.2.h	Boston, 1858	M, S	TW
A18.2.h	Boston, 1858	S	CWRWE
A18.2.i	Boston, 1860	Sp	TW

A18.2.j	Boston, 1863	S	TW
A18.2.k	Boston, 1864	Sp	TW
A18.2.l	Boston, 1866	Sp	JM
A18.2.m	Boston, 1868	Sp	TW
A18.2.s	Boston, 1877	M, S	TW

Poems ("Blue and Gold")

A18.3	Boston, 1865	S	TW
A18.3	Boston, 1865	S	TW
A18.3	Boston, 1865	S	AvF
A18.3	Boston, 1865	Sp	AvF

May-Day and Other Pieces (Boston)

A28.1.a	Boston, 1867	M	Houghton
A28.1.a	Boston, 1867	M	Houghton
A28.1.a	Boston, 1867	M, S	CWRWE
A28.1.a	Boston, 1867	M	TW
A28.1.a	Boston, 1867	M, S	TW
A28.1.a	Boston, 1867	S	AvF
A28.1.b	Boston, 1868	M, S	Houghton
A28.1.b	Boston, 1868	M, S	TW
A28.1.b	Boston, 1868	S	AvF
A28.1.c	Boston, 1871	Sp	TW
A28.1.e	Boston, 1875	M	TW

May-Day and Other Pieces (London)

A28.2	London, 1867	M	Houghton
A28.2	London, 1867	M	Houghton
A28.2	London, 1867	S	TW
A28.2	London, 1867	S	TW
A28.2	London, 1867	S	AvF
A28.2	London, 1867	Sp	AvF

Selected Poems

A18.4.a	Boston, 1876	M	Houghton
A18.4.a	Boston, 1876	S	AvF
A18.4.a	Boston, 1876	S	AvF

A18.4.b	Boston, 1878	M	Houghton
A18.4.f	Boston, 1880	Sp	AvF
A18.4.h	Boston, 1881	M	Widener
A18.4.i	Boston, 1882	Sp	AvF

Poems (Riverside)

B7	Boston, 1884	M, S	TW
B7	Boston, 1884	S	AvF
B7	Boston, 1894 [*sic*]	M	TW
B8	Boston, 1883	S	TW
B8	Boston, 1883	Sp	AvF

Poems (Centenary)

B18	Boston, 1904	M, S	TW
B18	Boston, 1904	S	AvF
B18	Boston, n.d.	M	TW

POEMS (1847)

THE SPHINX.

Emerson's regard for "The Sphinx" is evidenced by his having given it first position in the 1847 *Poems* and again in the 1876 *Selected Poems*. It remains, as it was meant to be, a richly challenging and rewarding poem rather than an easy welcome to the writer's poetical canon. Edward Emerson can thus be forgiven his decision to dislodge it from its leading place when he came to edit his father's poems for the 1904 Centenary Edition on the grounds that the "Sphinx has no doubt cut off, in the very portal, readers who would have found good and joyful words for themselves, had not her riddle been beyond their powers" (*W,* IX, 403). In taking this position Edward was endorsing the earlier opinion of Oliver Wendell Holmes that the poem was "for the adept and not for the beginner" (*Ralph Waldo Emerson* [Boston, 1884], 330).

Emerson began composing "The Sphinx" in May 1840 in a draft that comprises most of the first eight and last two of the poem's seventeen stanzas, and he seems to have added four more by 21 July when he reported to Margaret Fuller that "The 'Sphinx' has fourteen verses & wants one to complete it, but that is unluckily in the middle & like Aladdin's window" (*L,* II, 317). On 24 November, when it was finally transmitted to Fuller for printing in the *Dial,* Emerson made a special request for page proofs, "as I have not quite settled two or three words in the piece" (*L,* II, 361).

Thematically the poem is characteristic of the period at which it was written, a period that also includes the composition of *Essays* (1841). Indeed, in that book's first essay, "History," Emerson alludes to the Sphinx legend:

Poems (1847)

As near and proper to us also is that old fable of the Sphinx, who was said to sit in the roadside and put riddles to every passenger. If the man could not answer she swallowed him alive. If he could solve the riddle, the Sphinx was slain. What is our life but an endless flight of winged facts and events! In splendid variety these changes come, all putting questions to the human spirit. Those men who cannot answer by a superior wisdom these facts or questions of time, serve them. Facts encumber them, tyrannize over them, and make the men of routine, the men of *sense*, in whom a literal obedience to facts has extinguished every spark of that light by which man is truly man. But if the man is true to his better instincts or sentiments, and refuses the dominion of facts, as one that comes of a higher race, remains fast by the soul and sees the principle, then the facts fall aptly and supple into their places; they know their master, and the meanest of them glorifies him. (*CW*, II, 18–19; cf. *EL*, III, 48–49)

As a gloss on "The Sphinx" these comments ally the poem with Emerson's broader assault on Lockean empiricism; they help us to see how the implications of that assault were coming into focus for Emerson at this time. A journal entry written many years later (1859) expresses the same point with some slight retrospective differences in emphasis:

I have often been asked the meaning of the "Sphinx." It is this,— The perception of identity unites all things and explains one by another, and the most rare and strange is equally facile as the most common. But if the mind live only in particulars, and see only differences (wanting the power to see the whole—all in each), then the world addresses to the mind a question it cannot answer, and each new fact tears it in pieces, and it is vanquished by the distracting variety. (Unpublished Notebook BL [Book of Lectures], 241, quoted by Edward Emerson at *W*, IX, 412; see also the note to line 1 below)

The poem seems to have been especially important to Henry David Thoreau, who studied it carefully following its publication in the third number of the *Dial*. In his journal, under the date of 7–10 March 1841, he wrote a detailed and appreciative explica-

4

tion, picking up especially on its congenial moral-allegorical construction of ancient myth, in which, during the 1840s, all the Transcendentalists were much interested (*J*, I, 279–286, reprinted in Appendix A below).

THE SPHINX.

The Sphinx is drowsy,
    Her wings are furled;
Her ear is heavy,
    She broods on the world.
"Who'll tell me my secret,   5
    The ages have kept?—
I awaited the seer,
    While they slumbered and slept;—

"The fate of the man-child;
    The meaning of man;   10
Known fruit of the unknown;
    Dædalian plan;
Out of sleeping a waking,
    Out of waking a sleep;
Life death overtaking;   15
    Deep underneath deep?

"Erect as a sunbeam,
    Upspringeth the palm;
The elephant browses,
    Undaunted and calm;   20
In beautiful motion
    The thrush plies his wings;
Kind leaves of his covert,
    Your silence he sings.

"The waves, unashamed,   25
    In difference sweet,
Play glad with the breezes,
    Old playfellows meet;

The journeying atoms,
    Primordial wholes,   30
Firmly draw, firmly drive,
    By their animate poles.

"Sea, earth, air, sound, silence,
    Plant, quadruped, bird,
By one music enchanted,   35
    One deity stirred,—
Each the other adorning,
    Accompany still;
Night veileth the morning,
    The vapor the hill.   40

"The babe by its mother
    Lies bathed in joy;
Glide its hours uncounted,—
    The sun is its toy;
Shines the peace of all being,   45
    Without cloud, in its eyes;
And the sum of the world
    In soft miniature lies.

"But man crouches and blushes,
    Absconds and conceals;   50
He creepeth and peepeth,
    He palters and steals;
Infirm, melancholy,
    Jealous glancing around,
An oaf, an accomplice,   55
    He poisons the ground.

"Out spoke the great mother,
    Beholding his fear;—
At the sound of her accents
    Cold shuddered the sphere:—   60

'Who has drugged my boy's cup?
    Who has mixed my boy's bread?
Who, with sadness and madness,
    Has turned my child's head?'"

I heard a poet answer,   65
    Aloud and cheerfully,
"Say on, sweet Sphinx! thy dirges
    Are pleasant songs to me.
Deep love lieth under
    These pictures of time;   70
They fade in the light of
    Their meaning sublime.

"The fiend that man harries
    Is love of the Best;
Yawns the pit of the Dragon,   75
    Lit by rays from the Blest.
The Lethe of nature
    Can't trance him again,
Whose soul sees the perfect,
    Which his eyes seek in vain.   80

"Profounder, profounder,
    Man's spirit must dive;
To his aye-rolling orbit
    No goal will arrive;
The heavens that now draw him   85
    With sweetness untold,
Once found,—for new heavens
    He spurneth the old.

"Pride ruined the angels,
    Their shame them restores;   90
And the joy that is sweetest
    Lurks in stings of remorse.

7

Have I a lover
    Who is noble and free?—
I would he were nobler   95
    Than to love me.

"Eterne alternation
    Now follows, now flies;
And under pain, pleasure,—
    Under pleasure, pain lies.   100
Love works at the centre,
    Heart-heaving alway;
Forth speed the strong pulses
    To the borders of day.

"Dull Sphinx, Jove keep thy five wits!   105
    Thy sight is growing blear;
Rue, myrrh, and cummin for the Sphinx—
    Her muddy eyes to clear!"—
The old Sphinx bit her thick lip,—
    Said, "Who taught thee me to name?   110
I am thy spirit, yoke-fellow,
    Of thine eye I am eyebeam.

"Thou art the unanswered question;
    Couldst see thy proper eye,
Alway it asketh, asketh;   115
    And each answer is a lie.
So take thy quest through nature,
    It through thousand natures ply;
Ask on, thou clothed eternity;
    Time is the false reply."   120

Uprose the merry Sphinx,
    And crouched no more in stone;
She melted into purple cloud,
    She silvered in the moon;

The Sphinx

She spired into a yellow flame;   125
    She flowered in blossoms red;
She flowed into a foaming wave;
    She stood Monadnoc's head.

Thorough a thousand voices
    Spoke the universal dame: 130
"Who telleth one of my meanings,
    Is master of all I am."

TEXTS

(A) *Dial*, 1 (January 1841): 348–350; (B) *Poems* (London, 1847), 1–6; (C) *Poems* (Boston, 1847), 7–13; (D) *Poems* ["Fourth Edition"] (Boston, 1847), 7–13; (E) *Poems* (Boston, 1857), 7–13; (F) *Poems* (Boston, 1858), 7–13; (G) *Poems* (Boston, 1865), 7–13; (H) *Selected Poems* (Boston, 1876), 7–11; (I) *Poems* [Riverside] (Boston, 1884), 9–13; (J) *Poems* [Centenary] (Boston, 1904), 20–25.

Format: (A-B) lack the alternating indentation. Because the verse form shifts slightly at l. 105, the two resulting sections, each centered on its longest line, have different general indentations. This feature, like the alternating line indentations, was introduced in (C) and maintained thereafter.

Pre-copy-text forms: The earliest draft of the poem occurs in Journal E (*JMN*, VII, 354–357), which was extensively revised in Notebook P (*PN*, 51–56). No complete manuscript survives.

VARIANTS

Title: THE SPHINX. (A, C-J) | THE
SPHYNX. (B)

1   Sphinx (A, C-J) | Sphynx (B)
2   furled; (C-H) | furled, (A-B) |
furled: (I-J)
4   world. (A, C-J) | world.— (B)
5   "Who'll (A, C-G, I-J) | 'Who'll
(B, H) ‖ secret, (C-J) | secret (A-B)
6   kept?— (C-J) | kept? (A-B)

7   I (A, C-J) | —I (B) ‖ seer, (B-H) |
seer (A, I-J)
8   slept;— (B-H) | slept. (A) |
slept:— (I-J)
9   "The (A, C-G, I-J) | The (B) |
'The (H) ‖ man-child; (C-H) |
manchild,— (A) | manchild, (B, I-J)
10   man; (B-J) | man,— (A)
11   unknown; (C-G, I-J) |

9

unknown,— (A) | unknown, (B) | Unknown; (H)

12 plan; (B-J) | plan. (A)

14 sleep; (C-J) | sleep, (A-B)

15 Life (A-F, H-J) | Like (G) | <Like> ↑Life↓ (CC5) || overtaking; (C-J) | overtaking, (A-B)

16 deep? (C-J) | deep. (A-B)

17 "Erect (A, C-G, I-J) | Erect (B) | 'Erect (H) || sunbeam, (C-J) | sunbeam (A-B)

19 browses, (C-J) | browses (A-B)

22 wings; (B-D, H-J) | wings, (A) | wings: (E-G) [*readings in* E *and* F *caused by damage to the plates*]

23 covert, (C-G, I-J) | covert! (A-B) | covert (H)

25 "The (A, C-G, I-J) | The (B) | 'The (H) || waves, unashamed, (C-J) | waves unashamed (A-B) [J *has* "unashamèd,"]

28 meet; (C-J) | meet. (A-B)

33 "Sea, (A, C-G, I-J) | Sea, (B) | 'Sea, (H)

36 stirred,— (C-J) | stirred, (A-B)

38 still; (B-J) | still, (A)

40 vapor (A, C-J) | vapour (B)

41 "The (A, C-G, I-J) | The (B) | 'The (H) || babe (B-J) | babe, (A)

42 bathed (A-F, H-I) | bathëd (G) | bathèd (J) || joy; (C-J) | joy, (A-B)

43 uncounted,— (C-J) | uncounted, (A-B)

45 being, (C-J) | being (A-B)

46 cloud, (C-J) | cloud (A-B) || eyes; (C-J) | eyes, (A-B)

49 "But (A-G, I-J) | But (B) | 'But (H) || [*The comma after* "blushes" *is lost in some of the last printings from the plates made for* (C).]

50 conceals; (A, C-J) | conceals, (B)

57 "Out spoke (D-G, I-J) | "Outspoke (A, C) | Out spoke (B) |

'Out spoke (H) || mother, (C-J) | mother (A-B)

58 fear;— (A, C-J) | fear, (B)

60 sphere:— (C-J) | sphere;— (A-B)

61 'Who (A, C-G, I-J) | Who (B) | "Who (H) || cup? (C-J) | cup (A) | cup, (B)

63 Who, (A, C-J) | Who (B) || madness, (A, C-J) | madness (B)

64 my child's head?'" (CC1, H-J) | the manchild's head?'" (A) | the manchild's head?'— (B) | the man-child's head?'" (C-G)

65 answer, (C-H) | answer (A-B, I-J)

67 "Say (A, C-G, I-J) | 'Say (B, H) || Sphinx! thy (C-J) | Sphinx!—thy (A) | Sphynx! thy (B)

68 me. (A-D, H-J) | me (E-F) [*result of plate damage*] | me; (G) | me: (CC4)

70 time; (C-J) | time, (A-B)

73 "The (A, C-G, I-J) | The (B) | 'The (H) || harries (A, C-J) | harries, (B)

74 Best; (B-J) | Best, (A)

75 pit (C-J) | Pit (A-B) || Dragon, (C-J) | Dragon (A-B)

76 Blest. (B-J) | Blest; (A)

77 nature (C-H) | Nature (A-B, CC4, I-J)

79 perfect, (C-J) | Perfect (A) | Perfect, (B)

80 Which his (A-J) | Which (CC4)

81 "Profounder, (A, C-G) | Profounder, (B) | 'To insight (H) | "To vision (I-J) || profounder, (B-G, I-J) | profounder (A, H) | To vision (CC1) | "In deeper abysses (CC4)

82 dive; (B-I) | dive: (A)

83 To his (A-G) | His (H-J) | his (CC1) || orbit (A-H) | orb (I-J) | <↑orb↓> (CC1)

84 No (A-G) | ↑At↓ No (CC1) | At no (H-J) || arrive; (C-J) | arrive. (A-B)

85   that now draw (A, C-J) | that draw (B)

89   "Pride (A, C-G, I-J) | Pride (B) | 'Pride (H)

90   restores; (C-J) | restores: (A) | restores, (B)

91   And (A-H) | Lurks (CC4, I-J)

92   Lurks in (A-H) | in (CC4) | In (I-J)

95   free?— (C-J) | free,— (A-B)

97   "Eterne (A, C-G, I-J) | Eterne (B) | 'Eterne (H)

98   flies; (C-J) | flies, (A-B)

101   centre, (B-J) | centre (A)

102   Heart-heaving (B-J) | Heart heaving (A) || alway; (B-J) | alway, (A)

105   "Dull (A, C-G, I-J) | Dull (B) | 'Dull (H) || Sphinx, (A, C-J) | Sphynx, (B) || wits! (A-D) | wits. (E-F [*result of plate damage*]) | wits: (G-H) | wits; (I-J)

106   blear; (A, C-J) | blear, (B)

107   Rue, myrrh, and cummin for the Sphinx— (C-F) | Hemlock and vitriol for the Sphinx (A) | Rue, myrrh, and cummin for the Sphynx, (B) | Rue, myrrh, and cumin for the Sphinx— (G) | Rue, myrrh, and cummin for the Sphinx,— (H) | Rue, myrrh and cummin for the Sphinx, (I-J)

108   clear!"— (C-G) | clear." (A) | clear.' (B) | clear!'— (H) | clear!" (I-J)

109   Sphinx (A, C-J) | Sphynx (B)

110   Said, "Who (A, C-G, I-J) | 'Who (B) | Said, 'Who (H)

111   I am thy spirit, yoke-fellow, (C-I) | Manchild! I am thy spirit; (A) | I am thy spirit, yoke-fellow! (B) | I am thy spirit, yoke-fellow; (J)

113   "Thou (A, C-G, I-J) | Thou (B) | 'Thou (H) || question; (B-J) | question:— (A)

115   asketh, asketh; (C-J) | asketh, asketh, (A-B)

118   ply; (C-H, J) | ply, (A-B) | ply: (I)

119   eternity; (C-J) | eternity, (A) | eternity,— (B)

120   reply." (A, C-G, I-J) | reply.' (B, H)

121   Sphinx, (A, C-J) | Sphynx, (B)

122   stone; (C-J) | stone, (A-B)

123   melted into purple cloud, (B-J) | hopped into the baby's eyes, (A)

124   silvered in the moon; (C-J) | hopped into the moon, (A) | silvered in the moon, (B)

125   flame; (C-J) | flame, (A-B)

126   red; (C-J) | red, (A-B)

127   wave; (C-I) | wave, (A-B) | wave: (J)

130   dame: (C-H) | dame, (A-B) | dame; (I-J)

131   "Who (A, C-G, I-J) | 'Who (B, H) || meanings, (B-F, H-I) | meanings (A, G, J)

132   am." (A, C-G, I-J) | am.' (B, H)

NOTES

1.   In his Ph.D. dissertation, "Harnessing Proteus: Publishing the Canon of Emerson's Poetry" (Rutgers, 1994), 113–114, Joseph M. Thomas plausibly suggests that the source of Emerson's familiarity with "Sphinx lore"—evidently a topic

of discussion between Emerson and his brother Charles in the mid-1830s—was Francis Bacon's *De Sapientia Veterum or Wisdom of the Ancients* (1609). See also *JMN*, XIV, 322.

12. Dædalus in Greek mythology was an artificer of such surpassing cunning and intricacy as to be able to create almost as nature does, as in the wings he devised for his son Icarus. Dædalus was also the architect of the Labyrinth of Minos on Crete, the devious windings of which concealed the Minotaur.

107–108. In "Emerson's Adaptation of a Line from Spenser," *MLN*, XLIX (April 1934): 265–67, Arthur E. Bestor suggested that the source of these lines is verse 188 of Edmund Spenser's "Muiopotmos, or the Fate of the Butterflie" ("Ranke smelling Rue, and Cummin good for eyes"), which Emerson had been reading in the late summer of 1846 (see *JMN*, IX, 453), about the time he was revising this poem for the collected edition.

128. Monadnoc is the name of a mountain in southern New Hampshire: see the headnote to Emerson's poem of that title below. The reference here, however, may also involve a pun on *monad* (from Greek μονάς, meaning unit or alone), a term employed by Pythagoras and his followers—as well as by Gnostic theologians influenced by them—to refer to the "good" or first God, from which all of creation was believed to have emanated.

EACH AND ALL.

The philosophical issues raised by this poem were much on Emerson's mind in the early to mid-1830s, when, in preparation for writing *Nature,* he began to study theories of natural history, including especially those of Coleridge and Goethe, both of whom struggled against an encroaching scientific tendency, under the Baconian model, to an objectified and materialistic understanding of nature. In the Spring of 1834, for example, Emerson, under the influence of Coleridge's discussion of "Classification" in

The Friend (1818), reacted against the work of Linnaeus and other materialistic systematizers, concluding that "The Classification of all Nat. Science is arbitrary I believe, no Method philosophical in any one. And yet in all the permutations & combinations supposable, might not a Cabinet of shells or a Flora be thrown into one which should flash on us the very thought? We take them out of composition & so lose their greatest beauty. The moon is an unsatisfactory sight if the eye be exclusively directed to it & a shell retains but a small part of its beauty when examined separately" (*JMN*, IV, 288). The impulse of science to sever and analyze (or "murder to dissect" in Wordsworth's phrase) ran counter to Emerson's prejudice in favor of the central position of human subjectivity, including its aesthetic capacities, and counter likewise to the Platonic notion, dear to Emerson, that man and nature were unified as microcosm and macrocosm. As Emerson would write in "Compensation" (1841), "Pleasure is taken out of pleasant things, profit out of profitable things, power out of strong things, as soon as we seek to separate them from the whole. We can no more halve things and get the sensual good, by itself, than we can get an inside that shall have no outside, or a light without a shadow" (*CW*, II, 61). His formulation of this idea in *Nature* had been even more obviously Platonic: "Every particular in nature, a leaf, a drop, a crystal, a moment of time, is related to the whole, and partakes of the perfection of the whole. Each particle is a microcosm, and faithfully renders the likeness of the world" (*CW*, I, 27).

A cluster of journal sources dating from the Spring of 1834 stands behind the first half of the poem, but a few of slightly later date may well be implicated in the poem's second half (see *PN*, 778–779); if so, it would be unsafe to conclude, as Carl F. Strauch did, that "Each and All" was composed in 1834 ("The Year of Emerson's Poetic Maturity: 1834," *Philological Quarterly*, XXXIV [October 1955]: 369–373). Indeed it may have been written at any time between 1834 and 1838, shortly before it was solicited by James Freeman Clarke for his Louisville, Kentucky, *Western Messenger*. An early printing of the poem by Rufus W. Griswold in his popular *Poets and Poetry of America* (Philadelphia, 1842) simply reproduced the *Western Messenger* text with some inconsequential light copy-editing. The provenance, however, of the text published by Longfellow in *The Waif* (dated 1845, but published in December 1844) is something of a mystery. The fact that it includes the reading "club-moss burrs" in line 42 (consistent with Emerson's drafts in Notebook P) shows that it was not based on either of the two preceding published texts. When Longfellow later compared the *Waif* text with the version in *Poems* (Boston, 1847), he could only confess his puzzlement in a letter to Emerson, adding that he had never before seen—and so did not intentionally omit—the lines on the lover and his graceful maid (*L*, III, 364n). A comparison of variants shows that the *Waif* text influenced Emerson's decisions when he produced copy for the London edition of *Poems* (1847), and yet without knowing more about the source of the *Waif* text it is impossible to ascribe these changes confidently to Longfellow's editorial hand.

EACH AND ALL.

Little thinks, in the field, yon red-cloaked clown
Of thee from the hill-top looking down;
The heifer that lows in the upland farm,
Far-heard, lows not thine ear to charm;
The sexton, tolling his bell at noon,   5
Deems not that great Napoleon
Stops his horse, and lists with delight,
Whilst his files sweep round yon Alpine height;
Nor knowest thou what argument
Thy life to thy neighbor's creed has lent.   10
All are needed by each one;
Nothing is fair or good alone.
I thought the sparrow's note from heaven,
Singing at dawn on the alder bough;
I brought him home, in his nest, at even;   15
He sings the song, but it pleases not now,
For I did not bring home the river and sky;—
He sang to my ear,—they sang to my eye.
The delicate shells lay on the shore;
The bubbles of the latest wave   20

Fresh pearls to their enamel gave;
And the bellowing of the savage sea
Greeted their safe escape to me.
I wiped away the weeds and foam,
I fetched my sea-born treasures home;   25
But the poor, unsightly, noisome things
Had left their beauty on the shore,
With the sun, and the sand, and the wild uproar.
The lover watched his graceful maid,
As 'mid the virgin train she strayed,   30
Nor knew her beauty's best attire
Was woven still by the snow-white choir.
At last she came to his hermitage,
Like the bird from the woodlands to the cage;—
The gay enchantment was undone,   35
A gentle wife, but fairy none.
Then I said, 'I covet truth;
Beauty is unripe childhood's cheat;
I leave it behind with the games of youth.'—
As I spoke, beneath my feet   40
The ground-pine curled its pretty wreath,
Running over the club-moss burrs;
I inhaled the violet's breath;
Around me stood the oaks and firs;
Pine-cones and acorns lay on the ground;   45
Over me soared the eternal sky,
Full of light and of deity;
Again I saw, again I heard,
The rolling river, the morning bird;—
Beauty through my senses stole;   50
I yielded myself to the perfect whole.

TEXTS

(A) *Western Messenger,* VI (February 1839): 229–230; (B) *The Waif: A Collection of Poems,* ed. H. W. Longfellow (Cambridge, 1845), 73–75; (C) Yale MS, printer's copy for D, by permission of the Yale University Library; (D) *Poems* (London,

Poems (1847)

1847), 7–9; (E) *Poems* (Boston, 1847), 14–16; (F) *Poems* "Fourth Edition" (Boston, 1847), 14–16; (G) *Poems* (Boston, 1865), 14–16; (H) *Selected Poems* (Boston, 1876), 12–13; (I) *Poems* [Riverside] (Boston, 1884), 14–15; (I²) *Poems* [Centenary] (Boston, 1904), 4–6.

Format: Emerson eventually rejected stanza breaks and patterns of indentation. In (A, C-D) line spaces occur before ll. 13, 29, and 37; in (B) before ll. 19 and 37. In (B) ll. 14, 16, 38, 40, 42, and 44 were indented, probably by Longfellow, to acknowledge the deviation in rhyme scheme.

Pre-copy-text forms: See *PN*, 778–779.

VARIANTS

Title: EACH AND ALL. (D-I) | EACH IN ALL; / BY RALPH WALDO EMERSON. For the Western Messenger. / [Those of our readers who enjoy fine poetry, will thank the author of the following verses, for communicating them, as well as those on "The Humble Bee," to the reading public. The same antique charm, the same grace and sweetness, which distinguish the prose writings of our author, will be found in his verse. These are almost the first poetical specimens of his writing which have appeared in print. There are others, as we know, behind, not inferior to them in beauty of thought and expression. May we not hope also that these gems may be given to the lovers of "the blameless Muse?"] (A) | EACH IN ALL. (B) | Each & All (C)

1 thinks, (B-I) | thinks (A) || field, (B-I) | field (A) || clown (A, H-I) | clown, (B-G)

2 thee (A, E-I) | thee, (B-D)

3 The heifer (E-I) | And the heifer (A) | And the heifer, (B-D) || farm, (B-I) | farm (A)

4 Far-heard, (C-I) | Far heard, (A-B)

5 sexton, (B, E-I) | sexton (A, C-D) || his bell (A, E-I) | the bell (B-D) || noon, (B-I) | noon (A)

6 Deems (CC11, E-I) | Dreams (A-D)

7 lists (A-C, CC11, E-I) | lifts (D)

8 Whilst (A, D-I) | As (B) | <As>Whilst (C) || Alpine (A, C-I) | distant (B)

10 neighbor's (A, C, E-I) | neighbour's (B, D) || has lent. (E-I) | hath lent, (A) | has lent: (B-D)

11 one; (A, E-I) | one, (B-D)

13 thought (A, C-I) | sought (B) [*Corrected in Emerson's hand to* thought *in his personal copy of* The Waif (Houghton Library, *AC85 Em 345 Zy845l; Ralph Waldo Emerson Memorial Association deposit, Houghton Library, Harvard University).*]

15 home, . . . nest, (E-I) | home . . . nest (A-D) || even; (E-I) | even,— (A) | even;— (B-D)

16 pleases (A-G) | < ↑ charms ↓ > ↑ cheers ↓ (CC1) | cheers (H-I) | thrills (CC5) || now, (A, E-I) | now; (B-D)

17 sky;— (E-I) | sky, (A) | sky; (B-D)

18 He . . . ear,—they (E-I) | He . . .

ear, these (A) | *He . . . ear; they* (B) |
He . . . ear; they (C-D)
19 shore; (B-I) | shore— (A)
21 gave; (B-H) | gave, (A, I)
23 me. (A, E-I) | me; (B-D)
25 I fetched (A, E-I) | And fetched
(B-D) || home; (B-I) | home, (A)
26 poor, unsightly, (B-I) | poor
unsightly (A)
27 shore, (A, E-H) | shore (B-D, I)
28 sun, and the sand, (A-E, H) | sun
and the sand (G, I) || uproar. (C-I) |
uproar! (B) | uproar, / Nor rose, nor
stream, nor bird is fair, / Their
concord is beyond compare. (A)
[*These two lines in* (A), *together with
lines 29–36, are omitted in* (B): *see
headnote.*]
29 maid, (E-I) | maid (A, C-D)
30 As (A, C-I) | While (CC1) || 'mid
(C-G, I) | mid (A, H)
32 the . . . choir. (E-I) | that . . .
quire. (A) | the . . . quire; (C-D)
33 last (C-I) | last, (A)

34 cage;— (E-I) | cage,— (A, C-D)
35 undone, (C-I) | undone,—(A)
37 'I (A, D-F, I) | "I (B-C, G-H) ||
truth; (A, E-I) | Truth; (B-D)
38 cheat; (A, E-I) | cheat,— (B-D)
39 youth.'— (E-F) | youth;' (A) |
youth." (B-C) | youth.' (D) |
youth."— (G-H) | youth:'— (I)
40 As (B-I) | —As (A)
42 club-moss burrs; (B-I) | hair-cap
burs: (A)
45 Pine-cones (A, E-I) | Pine cones
(B-D) || ground; (B-D, F-I) | ground.
(A) | ground, (E)
46 Over (A, E-I) | Above (B-D) ||
sky, (B-I) | sky (A)
47 and of deity; (A, E-I) | and Deity;
(B) | and <of> deity; (C) | and deity;
(D)
48 saw, again (B-I) | saw—again (A)
49 bird;— (B-I) | bird: (A)
50 stole; (E-I) | stole,— (A) | stole,
(B-D)
51 whole. (B-I) | Whole. (A)

NOTES

Title: A translation of εν καί παν, a phrase associated with Xenophanes that Emerson encountered in writings by Ralph Cudworth and J. W. von Goethe (see *JMN*, V, 128).

2. During his tour through northern Italy in 1833 Emerson noted the picturesque effect of the red cloaks worn by the peasants (*JMN*, IV, 188). He recalled this impression in a journal entry of late November 1834: "The shepherd or the beggar in his red cloak little knows what charm he gives to the wide landscape that charms you on the mountain top . . . & I no more the part my individuality plays in the All" (*JMN*, IV, 345–346).

8. "Napoleon sat back on his horse in the midst of the march to catch the fine tone of a bell" (12 July 1834; *JMN*, IV, 304). Emerson probably found the anecdote in John Kidd, *On the Adaptation of External Nature to the Physical Condition of Man* (London, 1833), 143; see Kenneth Walter Cameron, "Notes on the Early Lectures," *Emerson Society Quarterly*, no. 20 (3d Quarter 1960): 37–38. Cf. *CS*, II, 39.

12. "The river flowed brimful & I philosophised upon this composite collective beauty which refuses to be analysed. Nothing is beautiful alone. Nothing but is beautiful in the Whole" (28 March 1835; *JMN*, V, 26).

28. "I remember when I was a boy going upon the beach & being charmed with the colors & forms of the shells. I picked up many & put them in my pocket. When I got home I could find nothing that I gathered—nothing but some dry ugly mussel & snail shells. Thence I learned that Composition was more important than the beauty of individual forms to effect. On the shore they lay wet & social by the sea & under the sky" (16 May 1834; *JMN*, IV, 291). Cf. *EL*, I, 73–74, 317.

36. "In life all finding is not that thing we sought, but something else. The lover on being accepted, misses the wildest charm of the maid he dared not hope to call his own. The husband loses the wife in the cares of the household" (12 April 1837; *JMN*, V, 297). Emerson, who was married on 14 September 1835, may have derived this idea from his brother Charles. In the months following the death of Charles on 9 May 1836 (on the eve of his planned marriage to Elizabeth Hoar), Emerson went through his brother's private papers intending to write a memorial; shocked to discover an unsuspected sadness in these writings, Emerson confided to his journal that "The horror of the housekeeper pervades his views of marriage" (*JMN*, V, 157).

THE PROBLEM.

That Emerson resigned as minister of Boston's Second Church in 1832 is well known; what is less well known is that he continued for years thereafter to be an accredited Unitarian minister, taking informal charge for a while of the church at East Lexington and acting as a supply minister at various other churches in the area. He last delivered a sermon during Sunday services at his hometown Concord church on 20 January 1839, the year in which he wrote "The Problem." Between 1832 and 1839 the option of returning to the active ministry remained open. Even though the duties of the office had not, for Emerson, grown more congenial, the profession, along with the interest of religion, had attractions that endured. On 28 August 1838, in the wake of the controversy over the Divinity School Address—indeed the day after Andrews Norton attacked him in the *Boston Daily Advertiser*—Emerson wrote in his journal, "It is very grateful to my feelings to go into a Roman Cathedral, yet I look as my countrymen do at the Roman priesthood. It is very grateful to me to go into an English Church & hear the liturgy read. Yet nothing would induce me to be the English priest. I find an unpleasant dilemma in this, nearer home. I dislike to be a clergyman & refuse to be one. Yet how rich a music would be to me a holy clergyman in my town. It seems to me he cannot be a man, quite & whole. Yet how plain is the need of one, & how high, yes highest, is the function. Here is Division of labor that I like not. A man must sacrifice his manhood for the social good. Something is wrong, I see not what" (*JMN*, VII, 60). On 10 November 1839 Emerson composed this poem while sitting in his pew at the Concord church as the Reverend Barzillai Frost held forth from the pulpit.

The poem, however, seems not to have been ready to enclose as a submission in Emerson's letter of 14 November to Margaret Fuller, who was then eagerly collecting verses for the inaugural issue of the *Dial* (*L*, II, 234). When he first mentioned it to her on 12 December, he described it has having been written "one Sunday lately at church: the better place not always the better poetry." He explained that he could not enclose the verses just yet, "for I let Henry Thoreau carry them away . . . when he brought me poetry" (*L*, II, 242–43).

"The Problem," one of Emerson's strongest poems, was especially highly regarded by his admirers. Toward the end of Emerson's life, at a time when praise for his work was more than usually robust, Frederic Henry Hedge commented: "Wholly unique, and transcending all contemporary verse in grandeur of style, is the piece entitled 'The Problem.' When first it appeared in the *Dial* forty years ago come July, I said: 'There has been nothing done in English rhyme like this since Milton.' All between it and Milton seemed tame in comparison" ("Emerson the Philosopher and the Poet," *The Literary World,* XI [22 May 1880]: 177).

THE PROBLEM.

I like a church; I like a cowl;
I love a prophet of the soul;
And on my heart monastic aisles
Fall like sweet strains, or pensive smiles;
Yet not for all his faith can see   5
Would I that cowled churchman be.

Why should the vest on him allure,
Which I could not on me endure?

Not from a vain or shallow thought
His awful Jove young Phidias brought;   10
Never from lips of cunning fell
The thrilling Delphic oracle;
Out from the heart of nature rolled
The burdens of the Bible old;
The litanies of nations came,   15
Like the volcano's tongue of flame,
Up from the burning core below,—
The canticles of love and woe;
The hand that rounded Peter's dome,
And groined the aisles of Christian Rome,   20
Wrought in a sad sincerity;
Himself from God he could not free;
He builded better than he knew;—
The conscious stone to beauty grew.

Know'st thou what wove yon woodbird's nest   25
Of leaves, and feathers from her breast?
Or how the fish outbuilt her shell,
Painting with morn each annual cell?

Or how the sacred pine-tree adds
To her old leaves new myriads? 30
Such and so grew these holy piles,
Whilst love and terror laid the tiles.
Earth proudly wears the Parthenon,
As the best gem upon her zone;
And Morning opes with haste her lids, 35
To gaze upon the Pyramids;
O'er England's abbeys bends the sky,
As on its friends, with kindred eye;
For, out of Thought's interior sphere
These wonders rose to upper air; 40
And Nature gladly gave them place,
Adopted them into her race,
And granted them an equal date
With Andes and with Ararat.

These temples grew as grows the grass; 45
Art might obey, but not surpass.
The passive Master lent his hand
To the vast soul that o'er him planned;
And the same power that reared the shrine,
Bestrode the tribes that knelt within. 50
Ever the fiery Pentecost
Girds with one flame the countless host,
Trances the heart through chanting choirs,
And through the priest the mind inspires.
The word unto the prophet spoken 55
Was writ on tables yet unbroken;
The word by seers or sibyls told,
In groves of oak, or fanes of gold,
Still floats upon the morning wind,
Still whispers to the willing mind. 60
One accent of the Holy Ghost
The heedless world hath never lost.
I know what say the fathers wise,—

Poems (1847)

The Book itself before me lies,
Old *Chrysostom,* best Augustine,   65
And he who blent both in his line,
The younger *Golden Lips* or mines,
Taylor, the Shakspeare of divines.
His words are music in my ear,
I see his cowled portrait dear;   70
And yet, for all his faith could see,
I would not the good bishop be.

TEXTS

(A) *Dial,* I (July 1840): 122–23; (B) *The Estray,* ed. H. W. Longfellow (Boston, 1847), 54–57; (C) MS, Ralph Waldo Emerson Collection, Harry Ransom Center, University of Texas at Austin, printer's copy for D, by permission of the University of Texas at Austin; (D) *Poems* (London, 1847), 9–12; (E) *Poems* (Boston, 1847), 17–20; (E²) *Poems* (Boston, 1865), 17–20; (F) *Selected Poems* (Boston, 1876), 14–16; (G) *Poems* [Riverside] (Boston, 1884), 15–17; (H) *Poems* [Centenary] (Boston, 1904), 6–9. Longfellow wrote to Emerson on 25 November 1846 asking for a corrected copy of "The Problem," which he meant to include in *The Estray* (Longfellow, *Letters,* 3:124). No reply survives, but it is likely that there was one.

Format: There is no verse paragraph break in (G-H) following line 54, no doubt because in (E-F)—though not (E²)—this break occurs at the bottom of the page and is therefore not readily apparent.

Pre-copy-text forms: On or around 10 December 1839 Emerson loaned a manuscript of the poem to Thoreau (*L,* II, 242–243), who copied it into his commonplace book (unpublished MS, Morgan Library, M.A. 594). This text, intermediate between the draft in Emerson's Notebook P (*PN,* 42–44) and the *Dial* printing, differs from the latter in the omission of line-end punctuation in twelve instances and the inclusion of four misreadings of substantives.

VARIANTS

1   church; (E-H) | church, (A-D) ||
cowl; (E-H) | cowl, (A-D)
2   soul; (E-H) | soul, (A-D)
4   strains, (E-H) | strains (A-D) ||

smiles; (B, D-F, H) | smiles, (A, C) |
smiles: (G)
5   see (A-B, E-H) | see, (C-D)
6   cowled (A-F) | cowlèd (G-H)

10   brought; (A-E, G-H) | brought, (F)

13   rolled (A-C, E-H) | rolled, (D)

17   below,— (A-B, E-H) | below, (C-D)

18   woe; (E-F) | wo. (A, C) | woe. (B, D) | woe: (G-H)

19   dome, (A-F) | dome (G-H)

20   Rome, (A-F) | Rome (G-H)

21   sincerity; (E-H) | sincerity. (A-B) | sincerity, (C-D)

23   knew;— (E-H) | knew, (A-D)

25   [*Flush*] Knows't (A-B, D-H) | [*Inset*] Know'st (C) || woodbird's (C-H) | wood-bird's (A-B)

26   leaves, (A-B, E-H) | leaves (C-D) || breast? (E-H) | breast; (A-D)

27   her (A-B, E-H) | <her> ↑its↓ (C) | its (D)

28   cell? (E-H) | cell; (A-D)

29   pine-tree (B, E-H) | pine tree (A) | pinetree (C-D)

33   Parthenon, (E-H) | Parthenon (A-D)

34   zone; (A, C-F) | zone, (B, G-H)

35   lids, (E-F) | lids (A-D, G-H)

37   abbeys (C-H) | Abbeys (A-B) || sky, (B, E-H) | sky (A, C-D)

38   its (A-B, D-H) | <her>its (C) || friends, (B, E-H) | friends (A, C-D)

39   For, (A-B, E-F) | For (C-D, G-H) || sphere (A-D, G-H) | sphere (E-F)

40   air; (E-H) | air, (A-D)

41   Nature (E-H) | nature (A-D)

45   [*Flush*] These (A-B, D-H) | [*Inset*] These (C) || grass; (B, E-H) | grass, (A, C-D)

46   obey, (B, E-H) | obey (A, C-D)

48   soul (C-H) | Soul (A-B) || planned; (E-H) | planned, (A-D)

49   shrine, (A, C-E) | shrine (B, F-H)

51   Ever (A-C, E-H) | Even (D)

52   countless (A-C, E-H) | Countless (D)

53   choirs, (B, E-H) | quires, (A, C-D)

55   spoken (B-H) | spoken, (A)

57   sibyls (B, D-H) | sybils (A) | s<y>ibyls (C) || told, (E-H) | told (A-D)

58   oak, (C-H) | oak (A-B) || fanes (A-B, D-H) | <flames>fanes (C) || gold, (A, C-D) | gold (B)

63   fathers (E-H) | Fathers (A-D) || wise,— (A-B, E-H) | wise, (C-D)

64   lies, (C-H) | lies,— (A-B)

65   *Chrysostom,* (A, C-E, G-H) | Chrysostom, (B, F)

67   *Golden Lips* (A, E-H) | Golden Lips (B) | *Golden-Lips* (C) | *Golden-lips* (D)

68   divines. (E-H) | divines; (A-B) | divines, (C-D)

70   cowled (A-F) | cowlèd (G-H) || dear; (E-H) | dear, (A-D)

71   yet, (B, E-H) || yet (A, C-D)

NOTES

10.   Phidias (c. 480–430 B.C.), one of the greatest sculptors of classical Greece, received numerous commissions from Pericles. Among his greatest works were the Parthenon and colossal statues of Athena and Zeus (Jove), the latter regarded as one of the Seven Wonders of the World. In a journal entry of 11 April 1839, Emerson wrote, "That is the best part of each [artist] which he does not

know; that which flowed out of his constitution, & not from what he called his talents. . . . Phidias it is not but the work of Man in that early Hellenic World that I would know. The name & circumstance of Phidias, however convenient for history, embarrasses merely when we come to the highest criticism. We are to see that which Man was tending to do in a given period & was hindered or . . . modified in doing by the interfering volitions of Phidias, of Dante, of Shakspear, the Organ whereby Man at the moment wrought" (*JMN*, VII, 185; cf. "Compensation," *CW*, II, 63).

19–24.   The reference is to Michelangelo. Franklin B. Newman ("Emerson and Buonarroti," *New England Quarterly*, XXV [December 1952]: 534–535) has argued that Emerson is here influenced by Michelangelo's aesthetic theories, especially as expressed in his sonnets, which Emerson is known to have admired and, in one instance, to have translated.

32.   "Love & fear laid the stones in their own order" (*JMN*, V, 196; 20 September 1836), said in explanation of the artistic achievement of medieval cathedral-building.

51–52.   See Acts 2:1–4.

65.   St. John (c. 347–407), Archbishop of Constantinople, was called Chrysostom (or "Golden Mouth") for his eloquence. He pursued a moral rather than dogmatic interpretation of Christianity in his homiletic commentaries on the books of the Bible. In the draft in Notebook P (*PN*, 44) Emerson first wrote "Golden Mouth" in line 66 before emending it to "Golden Lips." Emerson owned several editions of the *Confessions* and *Meditations* of St. Augustine, bishop of Hippo (354–430); numerous journal references testify to Emerson's high regard for his writings and especially for the element of Platonism of which he often took notice (Harding, *Emerson's Library*, 17).

68.   Jeremy Taylor (1613–1667), personal chaplain to Archbishop Laud, became himself bishop of Down and Connor after the Restoration. Emerson obtained a copy of Taylor's best-known work, *The Rule and Exercise of Holy Dying*, as early as 1824 (Harding, *Emerson's Library*, 268), and read through most of a fifteen-volume collected edition between 1827 and 1829, at which time Emerson "thought him a Christian Plato; so rich & great was his philosophy" (*JMN*, VI, 8n, 68).

TO RHEA.

The germ of this poem may be a journal entry written on or very shortly after 18 May 1843: "Nature lives by making fools of us all, adds a drop of nectar to every man's cup" (*JMN*, VIII, 397). The first draft (*JMN*, VIII, 472–73), written on or shortly after 21 May, begins with a version of line 35 ("Who drinketh of this nectar cup") and continues, with a number of false starts, to the end. Emerson worked out the poem's first half in a complete draft in Journal R that follows an entry for 20 May (*JMN*, VIII, 408–10). This was further revised in a third draft, also in Journal R (*JMN*, VIII, 414–16). "To Rhea" was very likely the poem that Emerson enclosed in a letter of 24 May 1843 to Margaret Fuller (*L*, III, 176), who was to leave the next day on her journey to the West (Capper, II, 124). The close timing of this transmittal was such that Fuller expressed her relief, on seeing the poem published in the July *Dial*, that the manuscript had not been lost (4 August 1843: *FuL*, III, 137).

Edward Emerson insisted that the poem "is not to be regarded as personal," and assigned it, in its generality, to "the cold heights of pure intellect" (*W*, IX, 407). Certainly the "dear friend" to whom it appears to be sympathetically addressed has never been identified. More than a few of its lines effectively rule out Margaret Fuller as the addressee in all but the most literal—or postal—sense, though it remains tempting to associate the work with the extended discussion of love and friendship that had occupied Emerson, Fuller, and Caroline Sturgis in 1840 and 1841. The fact that "To Rhea" appeared in the issue of the *Dial* that also contained Fuller's "Great Lawsuit," with its characteristic invocation of Minerva, may offer another context for interpretation, in which both works may figure, as if in conversation, as Transcendental recommendations of divine behavior. Theodore Parker, neither an especially acute nor always a sympathetic critic of Emerson's poetry, nevertheless found "To Rhea" very much to his liking. It had, he suggested, "seldom been equalled in depth and beauty of thought"; he added that "it has sometimes been complained of as obscure, we see not why" ("The Writings of Ralph Waldo Emerson," *Massachusetts Quarterly Review,* III [March 1850]: 249).

TO RHEA.

Thee, dear friend, a brother soothes,
Not with flatteries, but truths,
Which tarnish not, but purify
To light which dims the morning's eye.
I have come from the spring-woods,   5
From the fragrant solitudes;—
Listen what the poplar-tree
And murmuring waters counselled me.

If with love thy heart has burned;
If thy love is unreturned;   10
Hide thy grief within thy breast,
Though it tear thee unexpressed;
For when love has once departed
From the eyes of the false-hearted,
And one by one has torn off quite   15
The bandages of purple light;
Though thou wert the loveliest
Form the soul had ever dressed,
Thou shalt seem, in each reply,
A vixen to his altered eye;   20
Thy softest pleadings seem too bold,
Thy praying lute will seem to scold;
Though thou kept the straightest road,
Yet thou errest far and broad.

But thou shalt do as do the gods   25
In their cloudless periods;

For of this lore be thou sure,—
Though thou forget, the gods, secure,
Forget never their command,
But make the statute of this land.   30
As they lead, so follow all,
Ever have done, ever shall.
Warning to the blind and deaf,
'Tis written on the iron leaf,
Who drinks of Cupid's nectar cup   35
Loveth downward, and not up;
He who loves, of gods or men,
Shall not by the same be loved again;
His sweetheart's idolatry
Falls, in turn, a new degree.   40
When a god is once beguiled
By beauty of a mortal child,
And by her radiant youth delighted,
He is not fooled, but warily knoweth
His love shall never be requited.   45
And thus the wise Immortal doeth.—
'Tis his study and delight
To bless that creature day and night;
From all evils to defend her;
In her lap to pour all splendor;   50
To ransack earth for riches rare,
And fetch her stars to deck her hair:
He mixes music with her thoughts,
And saddens her with heavenly doubts:
All grace, all good his great heart knows,   55
Profuse in love, the king bestows,
Saying, 'Hearken! Earth, Sea, Air!
This monument of my despair
Build I to the All-Good, All-Fair.
Not for a private good,   60
But I, from my beatitude,
Albeit scorned as none was scorned,
Adorn her as was none adorned.

I make this maiden an ensample
To Nature, through her kingdoms ample,   65
Whereby to model newer races,
Statelier forms, and fairer faces;
To carry man to new degrees
Of power, and of comeliness.
These presents be the hostages   70
Which I pawn for my release.
See to thyself, O Universe!
Thou art better, and not worse.'—
And the god, having given all,
Is freed forever from his thrall.   75

TEXTS

(A) *Dial*, IV (July 1843): 104–06; (B) MS HM 7628, by permission of the Huntington Library, San Marino, California, printer's copy for C; (C) *Poems* (London, 1847), 13–16; (D) *Poems* (Boston, 1847), 21–24; (E) *Poems* (Boston, 1863), 21–24; (F) *Poems* (Boston, 1865), 21–24; (G) *Selected Poems* (Boston, 1876), 21–23; (H) *Poems* [Riverside] (Boston, 1884), 18–20; (H²) *Poems* [Centenary] (Boston, 1904), 9–11.

Format: Line 9 indented (A). Line 25 indented, with no white line (A). White line following line 73 (A).

Pre-copy-text forms: Drafts occur in journals Books Small and R (*JMN*, VIII, 472–473, and 408–410, 414–416).

VARIANTS

1   soothes, (B-H) | soothes (A)
2   flatteries, (B-H) | flatteries (A)
5   spring-woods, (B-H) | spring woods, (A)
6   solitudes;— (D-H) | solitudes, (A) | solitudes; (B-C)
7   poplar-tree (D-H) | poplar tree (A) | poplar tree, (B-C)

9   [*Flush*] (B-H) | [*Inset*] (A) || burned; (D-H) | burned, (A-C)
10   unreturned; (D-H) | unreturned, (A-C)
12   unexpressed; (D-H) | unexpressed. (A-C)
13   For (A, D-H) | For, (B-C)
14   false-hearted, (B-H) | falsehearted (A)

28

16   light; (D-H) | light, (A-C)

18   soul (A-B, D-H) | Soul (C) ||
dressed, (D-H) | drest, (A-C)

19   seem, (D-H) | seem (A-C) ||
reply, (D-H) | reply (A-C)

20   eye; (B-H) | eye, (A)

22   will (A, D-H) | shall (B-C) ||
scold; (D-H) | scold. (A-C)

26   periods; (A, D-H) | periods:
(B-C)

27   this lore be thou sure,— (D-H) |
this be thou assured, (A) | this lore
be thou sure, (B-C)

28   gods, secure, (D-H) | gods
secured (A) | gods secure (B-C)

30   land. (A, D-H) | land: (B-C)

34   'Tis (A, C-H) | Tis (B)

35   *cup* (A-E, G-H) | *cup,* (F)

36   *downward,* (A, D-H) | *downward*
(B-C) || *up;* (B, D-H) | *up.* (A, C)

37   He (CC4, CC9, E, G-H) |
Therefore, (D, F) | Therefore (A-C)
|| loves, (B-H) | loves (A)

38   the same (A-H) | his nymph
(CC1)

40   Falls, in turn, (D-H) | Falls in
turn (A-C)

41   When (B-H) | But when (A)

42   child, (A-G) | child (H)

44   knoweth (A, D-H) | knoweth,
(B-C)

45   requited. (D-H) | requited, (A) |
requited; (B-C)

46   doeth.— (D-G) | doeth. (A-C) |
doeth,— (H)

47   'Tis (C-H) | It is (A) | Tis (B)

48   creature (D-H) | creature, (A-C)
|| night; (D-F, H) | night, (A-C) |
night. (G)

49   her; (D-H) | her, (A-C)

50   splendor; (D-H) | splendor, (A) |
splendour, (B-C)

52   hair: (D-H) | hair; (A-C)

54   doubts: (D-H) | doubts; (A-C)

55   good (B-E, G-H) | good, (A, F) ||
knows, (B-F, H) | knows (A, G)

56   love, (D-H) | love (A-C) ||
bestows, (B-C, H) | bestows; (A) |
bestows: (D-G)

57   'Hearken! (D-E, G-H) |
"Hearken! (A, F) | Hearken, (B-C) ||
Earth, Sea, Air! (A, D-H) | Earth!
Sea! Air! (B-C)

61   I, (D-H) | I (A-C)

65   Nature, (D-H) | Nature (A) |
nature (B-C)

67   forms, (B-G) | forms (A, H) ||
faces; (D-H) | faces, (A-C)

69   power, (B-G) | power (A, H)

71   release. (D-H) | release; (A-C)

72   Universe (A, D-H) | universe
(B-C)

73   better, (D-H) | better (A-C) ||
worse.'— (D-E, G-H) | worse." (A) |
worse.— (B-C) | worse."— (F)

74   god, (D-H) | god (A-C)

75   forever (A-B, D-H) | for ever
(C)

NOTES

34.   On the subject of fate, Emerson wrote in an 1847 journal entry, "But the
Asiatics believe it is writ on the iron leaf & will not turn on their heel to save
them from famine, plague, or sword" (*JMN*, X, 30).

THE VISIT.

Emerson wrote the first draft of this poem (*JMN,* IX, 12) in the midst of a week-long visit from Caroline Sturgis, 28 August to 4 September 1843. His contemporaneous comments about the visit, both in a letter to Elizabeth Hoar (*L,* III, 203) and in his journals (*JMN,* IX, 16, 19–20), convey a very different tone and describe nothing so much as a pleasant visit from a valued and interesting friend. Edward Emerson saw the poem as a development of the comedy of the antisocial host, which his father had invoked in an 1842 journal entry regarding a certain "Professor Fortinbras," whose patience with house-guests regularly shut down at nine o'clock (*W,* IX, 407).

THE VISIT.

Askest, 'How long thou shalt stay?'
Devastator of the day!
Know, each substance, and relation,
Thorough nature's operation,
Hath its unit, bound, and metre;   5
And every new compound
Is some product and repeater,—
Product of the earlier found.
But the unit of the visit,
The encounter of the wise,—   10
Say, what other metre is it
Than the meeting of the eyes?
Nature poureth into nature
Through the channels of that feature.
Riding on the ray of sight,   15
Fleeter far than whirlwinds go,

The Visit

Or for service, or delight,
Hearts to hearts their meaning show,
Sum their long experience,
And import intelligence.   20
Single look has drained the breast;
Single moment years confessed.
The duration of a glance
Is the term of convenance,
And, though thy rede be church or state,   25
Frugal multiples of that.
Speeding Saturn cannot halt;
Linger,—thou shalt rue the fault;
If Love his moment overstay,
Hatred's swift repulsions play.   30

TEXTS

(A) *Dial*, IV (April 1844): 528; (B) MS HM 7630, by permission of the Hunting-ton Library, San Marino, California, printer's copy for C; (C) *Poems* (London, 1847), 16–17; (D) *Poems* (Boston, 1847), 25–26; (E) *Poems* ["Fourth Edition"] (Boston, 1847), 25–26; (F) *Poems* (Boston, 1857), 25–26; (G) *Poems* (Boston, 1858), 25–26; (H) *Poems* (Boston, 1865), 25–26; (I) *Selected Poems* (Boston, 1876), 17–18; (J) *Poems* [Riverside] (Boston, 1884), 20–21; (J²) *Poems* [Centenary] (Boston, 1904), 12–13.

Pre-copy-text forms: See *PN*, 958.

VARIANTS

1   'How (A-G, I-J) | "How (H) ||
stay?' (A-C, E-G, J) | stay,' (D) | stay?"
(H) | stay'? (I)
2   day! (A-C, E-J) | day? (D)
3   substance, (D-I) | substance (A-C, J) || relation, (D-J) | relation (A-C)
4   Thorough nature's operation, (B-J) | In all Nature's operation (A)

5   bound, (A-I) | bound (J) || metre; (D-J) | metre, (A-C)
7   repeater,— (D-J) | repeater, (A-C)
8   Product (B-J) | Some frugal product (A) || earlier (CC1, F-J) | early (A-E)
10   wise,— (D-J) | wise, (A-C)
11   Say, (A, D-J) | Say (B-C)

14   feature. (A-H) | feature (I) | feature, (J)

15   sight, (B, D-J) | sight (A) | Sight, (C) [*a plausible misreading of the MS*]

16   Fleeter far than (CC1, CC3 ["far" *canceled in red pencil in* (CC1)], G, I-J) | More fleet than waves or (A-F, H)

17   service, (D-J) | service (A-C)

21   breast; (D-J) | breast, (A-C)

27   halt; (B-J) | halt, (A)

28   Linger,— (B-J) | Linger, (A) || fault; (D-I) | fault: (A, J) | fault, (B-C)

URIEL.

When Emerson sent a copy of "Uriel" to Caroline Sturgis sometime in 1845 or 1846, it had the following preamble: "You have heard news from Saadi, that the most baleful heresy has been broached in heaven at some Epoch not fixed. It seems some body said words like these, that Geometers might say what they pleased, but in Uranometry there was no right line" (*PN*, 711–712). In other words, what appears straight or "right" from an earth-bound perspective is actually, from a superseding or heaven-regarding position, curved. To mark the difference is precisely to separate "what subsisteth" from "what seems" (l. 14); and to announce the Uranometrical truth to an audience of Geometrical fabulists is to invite the charge of heresy. This is what Emerson famously did in the Divinity School Address of 15 July 1838, and the School authorities, led by Andrews Norton, did not fail to level just that charge at Emerson. That the poem is a comment on the Address and its hostile aftermath has been generally acknowledged, at least since 1904, when Edward called it "an account of that event generalized and sublimed" (*W,* IX, 409).

Some months after the Address, on 30 October, Emerson wrote in his journal, "At the first entering ray of light, society is shaken with fear & anger from side to side. Who opened that shutter? they cry, Wo to him! They belie it, they call it darkness that comes in, affirming that they were in light before. Before the man who has spoken to them the dread word, they tremble & flee" (*JMN*, VII, 126). At this time Emerson was noticing instances of calmly heroic adversarial truth-telling, which may have helped him to see his experience not only as a part of the ongoing "miracles controversy" between young Transcendentalists and older conservatives at the Divinity School, but also of the general history of heresy. Two days earlier, on 28 October, Emerson had been amazed and delighted at the way Jones Very had opposed the conservative dogmatizing of Concord pastor Ezra Ripley (Emerson's step-grandfather) during a meeting at Emerson's home (*JMN*, VII, 127–128; *L*, II, 171). Likewise, though in a rather different context, he saw how the truth of the abolitionists was discomfiting aristocratic slaveholders (*JMN*, VII, 125–126). The astronomical references in "Uriel" forcibly imply the model heresies of Galileo and Copernicus—as Edward Emerson noted (*W*, IX, 408).

Robert Frost called "Uriel" "the greatest Western poem yet" ("A Masque of Reason," *Complete Poems of Robert Frost* [New York, 1967], 601).

URIEL.

It fell in the ancient periods
    Which the brooding soul surveys,
Or ever the wild Time coined itself
    Into calendar months and days.

This was the lapse of Uriel,   5
Which in Paradise befell.
Once, among the Pleiads walking,
SAID overheard the young gods talking;
And the treason, too long pent,
To his ears was evident.   10
The young deities discussed
Laws of form, and metre just,

Orb, quintessence, and sunbeams,
What subsisteth, and what seems.
One, with low tones that decide, 15
And doubt and reverend use defied,
With a look that solved the sphere,
And stirred the devils everywhere,
Gave his sentiment divine
Against the being of a line. 20
'Line in nature is not found;
Unit and universe are round;
In vain produced, all rays return;
Evil will bless, and ice will burn.'
As Uriel spoke with piercing eye, 25
A shudder ran around the sky;
The stern old war-gods shook their heads;
The seraphs frowned from myrtle-beds;
Seemed to the holy festival
The rash word boded ill to all; 30
The balance-beam of Fate was bent;
The bounds of good and ill were rent;
Strong Hades could not keep his own,
But all slid to confusion.

A sad self-knowledge, withering, fell 35
On the beauty of Uriel;
In heaven once eminent, the god
Withdrew, that hour, into his cloud;
Whether doomed to long gyration
In the sea of generation, 40
Or by knowledge grown too bright
To hit the nerve of feebler sight.
Straightway, a forgetting wind
Stole over the celestial kind,
And their lips the secret kept, 45
If in ashes the fire-seed slept.
But now and then, truth-speaking things

Uriel

Shamed the angels' veiling wings;
And, shrilling from the solar course,
Or from fruit of chemic force,   50
Procession of a soul in matter,
Or the speeding change of water,
Or out of the good of evil born,
Came Uriel's voice of cherub scorn,
And a blush tinged the upper sky,   55
And the gods shook, they knew not why.

TEXTS

(A) MS HM 7629, by permission of the Huntington Library, San Marino, California, printer's copy for B; (B) *Poems* (London, 1847), 18–20; (C) *Poems* (Boston, 1847), 27–29; (D) *Poems* ["Fourth Edition"] (Boston, 1847), 27–29; (E) *Poems* (Boston, 1865), 27–29; (F) *Selected Poems* (Boston, 1876), 19–20; (G) *Poems* [Riverside] (Boston, 1884), 21–23; (G²) *Poems* [Centenary] (Boston, 1904), 13–15. No variants occur in printings from the 1847 plates after (D).

Format: (A-B) indents lines 1–4; all later editions indent lines 2 and 4 only. Line spaces appear after lines 4, 34, and 42 in (A-B); (C) has a line space after line 4 only, while (D-G) have spaces after lines 4 and 34, the scheme adopted here.

Pre-copy-text forms: Fragmentary drafts of the poem are discussed in *PN*, 956; the fair copy that Emerson sent to Caroline Sturgis, now among the Tappan Papers at Harvard, is printed in *PN*, 711–713.

VARIANTS

1   periods (A-B, D-G) | periods, (C)
6   befell. (C-G) | befel. (A-B)
7   Once, (C-G) | Once (A-B)
8   Said (A-E) | Sayd (F) | Seyd (G) | Seyd (CC1) | Sayd (CC5) || talking; (C-G) | talking, (A-B)
9   treason, (C-G) | treason (A-B) || pent, (C-G) | pent (A-B)
12   form, (C-G) | form (A-B)
20   line. (C-G) | line: (A-B)
21   'Line (A-D, F-G) | "Line (E) || found; (C-G) | found, (A-B)
23   return; (C-G) | return, (A-B)
24   burn.' (A, C-D, F-G) | burn,' (B) | burn." (E)
27   heads; (C-F) | heads, (A-B, G)
29   festival (C-G) | festival, (A-B)

35

32   bounds (A, C-G) I bonds (B)

33   own, (A, C-G) I own. (B)

35   self-knowledge, (C-G) I self-knowledge (A-B) II withering, (C-G) I withering (A-B)

36   Uriel; (C-G) I Uriel. (A-B)

38   Withdrew, (C-G) I Withdrew (A-B) II hour, (C-G) I hour (A-B) II cloud; (C-G) I cloud, (A-B)

43   Straightway, (C-G) I Straightway (A-B)

47   then, (C-G) I then (A-B)

48   wings; (C-G) I wings, (A-B)

54   of cherub scorn, (C-G) I of <godlike> ↑cherub↓ scorn; (A) I of cherub scorn; (B)

NOTES

42.   Cf. Milton, "Il Penseroso": "Hail, divinest Melancholy, / Whose saintly visage is too bright / To hit the sense of human sight" (ll. 12–14).

THE WORLD-SOUL.

When Emerson sent this poem to William H. Furness for publication in the Philadelphia *Diadem,* he referred to it as "a piece, which, for want of a better name, I call 'the World Soul.' *Anima mundi* was the name, but we are bound at least in poetry to speak English" (10 June 1846: *L,* VIII, 77). The concept of the world-soul, introduced by Plato in the *Timaeus,* was also important to such followers as Plotinus and Porphyry, because it served to explain the dependence of matter on antecedent spirit and to support the belief that the genesis of nature in spirit meant that the world was everywhere alive or ensouled ("animated"). John S. Harrison, in *The Teachers of Emerson* (New York, 1910), quoted Plotinus's observation that "soul by the power of essence has dominion over bodies in such a way, that they are generated and subsist, just as she leads them, since they are unable from the first to oppose her will" (141; cf. lines 73–80). Emerson's dismay over the wayward culture of cities, of steam-power and railroads, of brutalizing factories, base politics, and the vacuous telegraph, is overmatched by the belief that because the world is an effect of "Thought's causing stream" (line 70), a larger and better Destiny awaits.

THE WORLD-SOUL.

Thanks to the morning light,
    Thanks to the foaming sea,
To the uplands of New Hampshire,
    To the green-haired forest free;
Thanks to each man of courage,   5
    To the maids of holy mind,
To the boy with his games undaunted,
    Who never looks behind.

Cities of proud hotels,
    Houses of rich and great,   10
Vice nestles in your chambers,
    Beneath your roofs of slate.
It cannot conquer folly,
    Time-and-space-conquering steam,
And the light-outspeeding telegraph   15
    Bears nothing on its beam.

The politics are base;
    The letters do not cheer;
And 'tis far in the deeps of history,
    The voice that speaketh clear.   20
Trade and the streets ensnare us,
    Our bodies are weak and worn;
We plot and corrupt each other,
    And we despoil the unborn.

37

Yet there in the parlor sits 25
    Some figure of noble guise,—
Our angel, in a stranger's form,
    Or woman's pleading eyes;
Or only a flashing sunbeam
    In at the window-pane; 30
Or Music pours on mortals
    Its beautiful disdain.

The inevitable morning
    Finds them who in cellars be;
And be sure the all-loving Nature 35
    Will smile in a factory.
Yon ridge of purple landscape,
    Yon sky between the walls,
Hold all the hidden wonders,
    In scanty intervals. 40

Alas! the Sprite that haunts us
    Deceives our rash desire;
It whispers of the glorious gods,
    And leaves us in the mire.
We cannot learn the cipher 45
    That's writ upon our cell;
Stars help us by a mystery
    Which we could never spell.

If but one hero knew it,
    The world would blush in flame; 50
The sage, till he hit the secret,
    Would hang his head for shame.
But our brothers have not read it,
    Not one has found the key;
And henceforth we are comforted,— 55
    We are but such as they.

Still, still the secret presses;
    The nearing clouds draw down;

The crimson morning flames into
    The fopperies of the town.   60
Within, without the idle earth,
    Stars weave eternal rings;
The sun himself shines heartily,
    And shares the joy he brings.

And what if Trade sow cities   65
    Like shells along the shore,
And thatch with towns the prairie broad,
    With railways ironed o'er?—
They are but sailing foam-bells
    Along Thought's causing stream,   70
And take their shape and sun-color
    From him that sends the dream.

For Destiny does not like
    To yield to men the helm;
And shoots his thought, by hidden nerves,   75
    Throughout the solid realm.
The patient Dæmon sits,
    With roses and a shroud;
He has his way, and deals his gifts,—
    But ours is not allowed.   80

He is no churl nor trifler,
    And his viceroy is none,—
Love-without-weakness,—
    Of Genius sire and son.
And his will is not thwarted;   85
    The seeds of land and sea
Are the atoms of his body bright,
    And his behest obey.

He serveth the servant,
    The brave he loves amain;
He kills the cripple and the sick,   90
    And straight begins again.

For gods delight in gods,
    And thrust the weak aside;
To him who scorns their charities,   95
    Their arms fly open wide.

When the old world is sterile,
    And the ages are effete,
He will from wrecks and sediment
    The fairer world complete.   100
He forbids to despair;
    His cheeks mantle with mirth;
And the unimagined good of men
    Is yeaning at the birth.

Spring still makes spring in the mind,   105
    When sixty years are told;
Love wakes anew this throbbing heart,
    And we are never old.
Over the winter glaciers,
    I see the summer glow,   110
And, through the wild-piled snowdrift,
    The warm rosebuds below.

TEXTS

(A) MS, Furness Papers, Van Pelt Library Special Collections, by permission of the University of Pennsylvania, printer's copy for B; (B) *The Diadem for MDCCCX-LVII* (Philadelphia, 1847), 76–78; (C) MS Am 82.5, Ralph Waldo Emerson Memorial Association deposit, Houghton Library, Harvard University, printer's copy for D; (D) *Poems* (London, 1847), 21–25; (E) *Poems* (Boston, 1847), 30–35; (F) *Poems* ["Fourth Edition"] (Boston, 1847), 30–35; (G) *Poems* (Boston, 1857), 30–35; (H) *Poems* (Boston, 1858), 30–35; (I) *Poems* (Boston, 1865), 30–35; (J) *Selected Poems* (Boston, 1876), 24–28; (K) *Poems* [Riverside] (Boston, 1884), 23–27; (L) *Poems* [Centenary] (Boston, 1904), 15–19.

Format: All printings separate the eight-line, or double-quatrain, stanzas with line spaces, except that the first space, after line 8, is omitted in (D). The pattern of alternating indentation was introduced in (E) and maintained in all later printings.

The World-Soul

Pre-copy-text forms: Drafts of portions of the poem (stanzas 6 through 14) occur in Notebook X, pp. 32–37, and are discussed at *PN*, 973–975; these were preliminary to an ink fair copy that is known to have circulated at different times to Elizabeth Hoar, Margaret Fuller, and Caroline Sturgis. Fuller made a copy from this manuscript and, without explicit authorization from Emerson, quoted ll. 9–32 in her article, "Asylum for Discharged Female Convicts," *New-York Tribune*, 19 June 1845, p. 1 (see *L*, VIII, 77–78; Fuller's article is reprinted in *Margaret Fuller, Critic: Writings from the* New-York Tribune, *1844–1846*, ed., Judith Mattson Bean and Joel Myerson [New York, 2000], 135–136). The poem text as Fuller printed it differs from her source only slightly in the punctuation and has no independent authority. The manuscript she copied from, which survives among the Tappan Papers at Harvard (bMS Am 1221 [41]), is missing one or more leaves at the end and so contains only ll. 1–60 and 65–88. It is transcribed at *PN*, 715–718. This text was in turn the basis for the fair copy inscribed by Emerson in Notebook X, pp. 44–49, where it received further revision and the addition of the missing half stanza (ll. 61–64). Finally, this text was the basis for the printer's copy (A) that Emerson supplied to his old friend, William Henry Furness, editor of *The Diadem*, in his letter of 10 June 1846: see *L*, VIII, 77–81, for the letter and a transcription of the poem manuscript.

VARIANTS

1	light, (C-L) | light! (A-B)
2	foaming (E-L) | seething (A-D)
3	New Hampshire, (A-F, J-L) | New-Hampshire, (G-I) | New-Hampshire (CC1)
4	green-haired (B, D-L) | greenhaired (A, C)
6	To the (A-L) | To (CC5) || mind, (A-D, K-L) | mind; (E-J)
7	undaunted, (A-G, I) | undaunted (H, J-L)
8	behind. (C-L) | behind! (A-B)
11	your chambers, (B, D-L) | your <chimneys> ↑chambers↓, (A) | your chambers (C)
13	folly, (C-J) | folly— (A-B) | folly,— (K-L)
14	steam, (A-B, CC1, G-J) | steam,— (C-D, K-L) | steam (E) | steam; (F)
16	on (A, C-L) | in (B)
17	base; (E-L) | base, (A-D)
18	cheer; (E-L) | cheer, (A-D)
19	'tis (B, D-L) | tis (A, C) || history, (E-L) | history (A-B) | history— (C-D)
20	clear. (C-L) | clear; (A-B)
22	worn; (E-L) | worn, (A, C-D) | torn, (B)
23	plot (C-L) | plot, (A-B)
25	parlor (B, E-L) | parlour (A, C-D)
26	guise,— (E-L) | guise, (A-D)
27	angel, (E-L) | angel (A-D)
28	eyes; (C-L) | eyes, (A-B)
30	window-pane; (C, E-L) | window-pane, (A-B) | window pane; (D)
31	Music (A-B, E-L) | music (C-D)
34	be; (E-L) | be, (A-D)
35	Nature (A-B, D-L) | <n>Nature (C)
38	walls, (C-L) | walls (A-B)

39　wonders, (E-J) I wonders (A-D, K-L)

41　Alas! (E-L) I Alas, (A-D) II Sprite (A-B, E-L) I sprite (C-D)

42　desire; (E-L) I desire, (A-D)

44　mire. (E-L) I mire; (A-B) I mire: (C-D)

46　That's writ (A-L) I engraved (CC5) II cell; (E-L) I cell, (A-D)

47　help (A-I) I <help> [*canceled in red pencil*] ↑ taunt ↓ (CC1) I taunt (J-L)

50　flame; (E-L) I flame, (A-D)

51　sage, (C-L) I sage (A-B)

52　shame. (C-L) I shame; (A-B)

53　But our (A-J) I <But> our (CC5) I Our (K-L)

54　key; (E-L) I key, (A-D)

55　comforted,— (E-L) I comforted, (A-D)

56　they. (C-L) I they.— (A-B)

57　Still, still (C-L) I Still, still, (A-B) II presses; (F-L) I presses, (A-E)

58　down; (E-L) I down, (A-D)

60　town. (C-L) I town; (A-B)

61　earth, (A-B, E-L) I earth (C-D)

62　rings; (E-L) I rings, (A-D)

63　heartily, (C-L) I heartily (A-B)

65　Trade (A-C, E-L) I trade (D) II cities (C-L) I cities, (A-B)

67　broad, (E-I) I broad (A-D, J-L)

68　o'er?— (E-L) I o'er;— (A-D)

69　foam-bells (B, E-L) I foambells (A, C-D)

71　sun-color (B, E-L) I sun-colour (A, C) I Sun-colour (D)

73　Destiny (A-C, E-L) I destiny (D) II does not like (A-I) I never swerves (J, L) I never swerves, (K) I does not swerve, (CC5)

74　To yield (A-I) I Or yields (J) I Nor yields (K-L) I Or yield (CC5) II helm; (E-L) I helm, (A-D) I [*In CC1 Emerson first revised to* "For Destiny

does not stoop / To yield" *then revised again to* "For Destiny never swerves / Nor yields"]

75　And (A-I) I He (J-L) II thought, (E-L) I thought (A-D) I will (CC1) II nerves, (E-L) I nerves (A-D) I nerve (CC1)

76　realm. (C-L) I realm; (A-B)

77　sits, (E-L) I sits (A-D)

78　shroud; (E-L) I shroud, (A-D)

79　way, (A, C-L) I way (B) II gifts,— (A-B, E-L) I gifts— (C-D)

81　nor (E-L) I or (A-D)

82　none,— (E-L) I none, (A-D)

83　Love-without-weakness,— (E-L) I Love-without-weakness, (A-D)

84　son. (A, E-L) I son, (B) I son; (C-D)

85　thwarted; (A-B, E-L) I thwarted, — (C-D)

90　amain; (E-L) I amain, (A-D)

92　straight begins (A-L) I rears new lords (CC1) II again. (E-F, I) I again; (A-D, J-L) I again (G-H) [*probably damage in the plate*]

94　aside; (C-L) I aside, (A-B)

95　charities, (A-J) I charities (CC4, K-L)

97　sterile, (A-J) I sterile (CC4, K-L)

101　despair; (E-L) I despair, (A-D)

102　mirth; (E-L) I mirth, (A-D)

105　Spring still makes (A, C-L) I Spring makes (B) II mind, (C-J) I mind (A-B, K-L)

106　told; (C-L) I told, (A-B)

108　old. (A-K) I old; (L)

109　glaciers, (C-J) I glaciers (A-B, CC4, K-L)

111　And, (E-J) I And (A-D, CC4, K-L) II snowdrift, (E-K) I snowdrift (A, C-D) I snow-drift (B, L)

112　rosebuds (A-C, E-L) I rose buds (D)

NOTES

15. Emerson first encountered "the newly invented electric Telegraph" in Washington, D.C., in January 1843 (*L*, III, 120).

91–100. Edward Emerson (*W*, I, 458) suggested that this portion of the poem reflects the early evolutionary thinking found, for example, in "The Young American" (1844); see the reference there to "*amelioration in nature*" (*CW*, I, 231).

105–112. Shortly after his sixty-ninth birthday Emerson wrote in his journal, "If I should live another year, I think I shall cite still the last stanza of my own poem, 'The World-Soul'" (*JMN*, XVI, 274).

ALPHONSO OF CASTILE.

Alphonso X, king of Castile, León, and Galicia (1221–1284), was a prodigiously gifted scholar in a variety of fields, literary, scientific, and legal. According to a popular apocryphal story, Alphonso expressed his criticism of the convoluted reasoning and complicated mathematics by which Ptolemaic astronomers sought to patch and save their theory by saying that if he (Alphonso) had been present at the creation, he could have recommended to the Almighty a simpler, more elegant plan. Modern scholarship has shown that the story of Alphonso's offer of help at the creation was a deliberate libel, invented years after his death, by which the king's alleged arrogance might be magnified into blasphemy. Indeed medieval and Renaissance versions of the anecdote cite the remark as the cause of the king's downfall and death. Later versions occur in sources that Emerson knew, including Pierre Bayle's *Dictionary*, Voltaire's *Essai sur les moeurs*, and Bernard de Fontenelle's *Discourse on the Plurality of Worlds* (see Bernard R. Goldstein, "The Blasphemy of Alphonso X: History or Myth?" in *Revolution and Continuity: Essays in the History and Philosophy of Early Modern Science,* ed. P. Barker and R. Areiw [Washington, D.C., 1991], 143–153). Emerson follows these sources (rather than earlier ones) in regarding Alphonso's observation as a witty pleasantry, especially in the 1839 lecture on "Comedy" (*EL,* III, 130) and in the 1844 essay "Nominalist and Realist" (*CW,* III, 140). To whatever extent the suppressed suggestion of blasphemy may operate as a trace in the poem, the effect would be to align the work thematically with "Uriel." In "Nominalist and Realist" Emerson noted that "nature has her maligners," and in journal entries of this period developed an array of attitudes, comic and heroic, toward reformers who would revise the natural order. No "parallel passage" among the prose writings, however, illuminates the poem so thoroughly as a paragraph toward the end of the "Montaigne" chapter in *Representative Men:*

> Charles Fourier announced that "the attractions of man are proportioned to his destinies;" in other words, that every desire predicts its own satisfaction. Yet all experience exhibits the reverse of this; the incompetency of power is the universal grief of young and ardent minds. They accuse the divine Providence of a certain parsimony. It has shown the heaven and earth to every child, and filled him with a desire for the whole; a desire raging, infinite, a hunger as of space to be filled with planets; a cry of famine as of devils for souls. Then for the satisfaction;—to each man is administered a single drop, a bead of dew of vital power, *per day,*—a cup as large as space, and one drop of the water of life in it. Each man woke in the morning with an appetite that could eat the solar system like a cake; . . . but on the first motion to prove his strength, hands, feet, senses, gave way, and would not serve him. He was an emperor deserted by his states, and left to whistle by himself or thrust into a mob of emperors all whistling: and still the sirens sung, "The attractions are proportioned to the destinies." In every house, in the heart of each maiden and of each boy, in the soul of the soaring saint, this chasm is found,—between the largest promise of ideal power, and the shabby experience. (*CW,* IV, 103–104)

The journal entry on which this passage is based (*JMN*, VII, 474–476; December 1842) responds to theories of communal living, as exemplified in conversations conducted by Bronson Alcott and his Fruitlands colleague Charles Lane, as well as Fourierist ideas being debated at the same time at Brook Farm. The premise here —involving, probably, an allusion to the economic depression following the Panic of 1837—was that "the parsimony which for a long time had characterized the government of Olympus, could not be sufficiently reprobated. It was stingy, it was shabby, it deserved worse names." Further along in this entry, Emerson quoted Thoreau's lines: "Ask! must I ask? The gods above should give; / They have enough, & we do poorly live." The entry ends (as the poem does) with the point that a longer life would better accommodate the great labors to which the human spirit aspires.

Emerson's letter of 27 July 1846 to Elizabeth Hoar mentions "Alphonso" as among the poems he had recently completed (*L*, III, 341). The appearance of a few relevant detached phrases in the journals, such as "American debility," "Double the dose," and a reference to Alphonso (*JMN*, IX, 384, 388, and 397), are consistent with Emerson's having written the poem within, at most, a few months of this letter. He sent a copy, along with copies of the other new poems, to Caroline Sturgis in August, and she responded with some characteristic impatience about its excessively intellectual quality, noting that "Philosophy is still philosophy although delivered in rhyme by Alphonso" (*L*, VIII, 89).

ALPHONSO OF CASTILE.

I, Alphonso, live and learn,
Seeing Nature go astern.
Things deteriorate in kind;
Lemons run to leaves and rind;
Meagre crop of figs and limes;   5
Shorter days and harder times.
Flowering April cools and dies
In the insufficient skies.

Imps, at high midsummer, blot
Half the sun's disk with a spot: 10
'Twill not now avail to tan
Orange cheek or skin of man.
Roses bleach, the goats are dry,
Lisbon quakes, the people cry.
Yon pale, scrawny fisher fools,   15
Gaunt as bitterns in the pools,
Are no brothers of my blood;—
They discredit Adamhood.
Eyes of gods! ye must have seen,
O'er your ramparts as ye lean,   20
The general debility;
Of genius the sterility;
Mighty projects countermanded;
Rash ambition, brokenhanded;
Puny man and scentless rose   25
Tormenting Pan to double the dose.
Rebuild or ruin: either fill
Of vital force the wasted rill,
Or tumble all again in heap
To weltering chaos and to sleep.   30

Say, Seigniors, are the old Niles dry,
Which fed the veins of earth and sky,
That mortals miss the loyal heats,
Which drove them erst to social feats;
Now, to a savage selfness grown,   35
Think nature barely serves for one;
With science poorly mask their hurt,
And vex the gods with question pert,
Immensely curious whether you
Still are rulers, or mildew?   40

Masters, I'm in pain with you;
Masters, I'll be plain with you;
In my palace of Castile,

46

I, a king, for kings can feel.
There my thoughts the matter roll,   45
And solve and oft resolve the whole.
And, for I'm styled Alphonse the Wise,
Ye shall not fail for sound advice.
Before ye want a drop of rain,
Hear the sentiment of Spain.   50

You have tried famine: no more try it;
Ply us now with a full diet;
Teach your pupils now with plenty;
For one sun supply us twenty.
I have thought it thoroughly over,—   55
State of hermit, state of lover;
We must have society,
We cannot spare variety.
Hear you, then, celestial fellows!
Fits not to be overzealous;   60
Steads not to work on the clean jump,
Nor wine nor brains perpetual pump.
Men and gods are too extense;
Could you slacken and condense?
Your rank overgrowths reduce   65
Till your kinds abound with juice?
Earth, crowded, cries, 'Too many men!'
My counsel is, kill nine in ten,
And bestow the shares of all
On the remnant decimal.   70
Add their nine lives to this cat;
Stuff their nine brains in his hat;
Make his frame and forces square
With the labors he must dare;
Thatch his flesh, and even his years   75
With the marble which he rears.
There, growing slowly old at ease,
No faster than his planted trees,
He may, by warrant of his age,

47

In schemes of broader scope engage.   80
So shall ye have a man of the sphere,
Fit to grace the solar year.

TEXTS

(A) MS Am 1347.1, Houghton Library, Harvard University, printer's copy for B; (B) *Poems* (London, 1847), 26–29; (C) *Poems* (Boston, 1847), 36–40; (D) *Poems* ["Fourth Edition"] (Boston, 1847), 36–40; (E) *Poems* ["Fourth Edition"] (Boston, 1850), 36–40; (F) *Poems* (Boston, 1858), 36–40; (G) *Poems* (Boston, 1865), 36–40; (H) *Selected Poems* (Boston, 1876), 29–31; (I) *Poems* [Riverside] (Boston, 1884), 27–29; (J) *Poems* [Centenary] (Boston, 1904), 25–28.

Pre-copy-text forms: A fair copy (Houghton MS Am 1221 [39]) intermediate between the drafts in Notebook X and the printer's copy for (B) is given in *PN*, 618–620.

VARIANTS

Title: CASTILE (B-J) I *Castille* (A)

1   I, Alphonso, (C-J) I I Alphonso (A-B)

2   Nature (C-J) I nature (A-B)

3   kind; (C-J) I kind, (A-B)

4   rind; (C-J) I rind, (A-B)

5   limes; (C-J) I limes, (A-B)

7   skies. (C-J) I skies; (A-B)

9   Imps, (C-J) I Imps (A-B) II midsummer, (C-J) I midsummer (A) I Midsummer (B)

10   disk (C-J) I disc (A-B) II spot: (C-I) I spot; (A-B, J)

12   cheek (C-J) I cheek, (A-B) II man. (C-J) I man: (A-B)

15   pale, (C-J) I pale (A-B)

17   blood;— (C-J) I blood,— (A-B)

21   general (A-G, I-J) I cosmical (CC1, H) II debility; (C-J) I debility, (A-B)

22   sterility; (C-J) I sterility, (A-B)

23   countermanded; (C-J) I countermanded, (A-B)

24   ambition, (C-J) I ambition (A-B) II brokenhanded; (C-G, I-J) I broken-handed, (A-B) I broken-handed; (H)

29   Or (C-J) I Or, (A-B)

30   chaos (C-I) I Chaos, (A) I chaos, (B) I Chaos (J)

31   Seigniors, (C-J) I Seigneurs, (A-B)

33   heats, (C-J) I heats (A-B)

34   feats; (C, E-J) I feats, (A-B) I feats (D) [*In some copies of* (D) *the semicolon faintly shows.*]

35   Now, (C-J) I Now (A-B)

37   hurt, (A-I) I hurt; (J)

40   mildew? (C-I) I Mildew. (A-B) I Mildew? (J)

41   I'm (B, D-J) I I am (A, C) II with (A-J) I for (CC1)

42   you; (C-J) I you. (A-B)

48

43 Castile, (B-J) | Castille, (A)
44 feel. (C-J) | feel; (A-B)
46 whole. (C-J) | whole, (A-B)
48 advice. (C-G, I-J) | advice, (A-B) | advice: (H)
51 it; (A-E, G-J) | it, (F) [*Evidently plate damage*]
53 plenty; (C-G) | plenty, (A-B, H-J)
54 twenty. (C-J) | twenty: (A-B)
55 over,— (C-J) | over, (A-B)
59 celestial (B-J) | Celestial (A)
60 overzealous; (A, C-F, H-J) | over zealous; (B) | over-zealous; (G)
62 pump. (C-J) | pump; (A-B)
63 extense; (C-J) | extense,— (A-B)
65 reduce (C-J) | reduce, (A-B)
66 juice? (C-J) | juice. (A) | juice; (B)
67 Earth, (C-J) | Earth (A-B) || crowded, (C-J) | crowded (A-B) || men!' (C-J) | men.' (A) | men,'— (B)
68 kill (C-J) | Kill (A-B)
72 his (A-G) | one (CC1, H-J)
74 labors (C-J) | labours (A-B)
76 rears. (C-J) | rears; (A-B)
77 There, (C-J) | There (A-B) || ease, (A-I) | ease (J)
80 engage. (A, C-J) | engage: (B)

MITHRIDATES.

Mithridates VI, king of Pontus, claimed descent from Alexander the Great and offered the principal military challenge to the Roman Empire in the first century B.C. He is supposed to have been an accomplished scholar, botanist, and linguist, and yet at the same time a thoroughly ruthless military chieftain. His name is most often associated with his invention of a universal antidote to poison, with the assistance of which he was said to have taken daily sub-lethal doses of those poisons he thought most likely to be used by plotters against his life—of which there seem to have been not a few. Edward Emerson judged that his father deployed Mithridates "as symbolic of the wise man who can find virtue in all things and escape the harm" (*W*, IX, 414). As A. E. Housman correctly said of Mithridates, "he died old."

MITHRIDATES.

I cannot spare water or wine,
    Tobacco-leaf, or poppy, or rose;
From the earth-poles to the line,
    All between that works or grows,
Every thing is kin of mine.   5

Give me agates for my meat;
Give me cantharids to eat;
From air and ocean bring me foods,
From all zones and altitudes;—

From all natures, sharp and slimy,   10
    Salt and basalt, wild and tame:
Tree and lichen, ape, sea-lion,
    Bird, and reptile, be my game.

Ivy for my fillet band;
Blinding dog-wood in my hand;   15
Hemlock for my sherbet cull me,
And the prussic juice to lull me;
Swing me in the upas boughs,
Vampyre-fanned, when I carouse.

Too long shut in strait and few,   20
Thinly dieted on dew,
I will use the world, and sift it,
To a thousand humors shift it,
As you spin a cherry.
O doleful ghosts, and goblins merry!   25
O all you virtues, methods, mights,
Means, appliances, delights,
Reputed wrongs and braggart rights,

Mithridates

Smug routine, and things allowed,
Minorities, things under cloud!   30
Hither! take me, use me, fill me,
Vein and artery, though ye kill me!

TEXTS

(A) MS Am 1221 (40), Houghton Library, Harvard University; (B) *Poems* (London, 1847), 30–31; (C) *Poems* (Boston, 1847), 41–42; (D) *Poems* (Boston, 1865), 41–42; (E) *Selected Poems* (Boston, 1876), 32–33; (F) *Poems* [Riverside] (Boston, 1884), 30–31; (G) *Poems* [Centenary] (Boston, 1904), 28–29. No variants occur in later printings made from the plates for (C). In the 1847 correction copy Emerson canceled lines 33–34, then canceled the whole poem with a vertical line in pencil, indicating an intention, subsequently reversed, to exclude "Mithridates" from *Selected Poems*.

Format: Lines 2, 4, 11, 13 inset in (C–G); all lines flush left (A–B)

Pre-copy-text forms: Drafts of the poem in Notebook X are discussed in *PN,* 861. The Houghton manuscript listed as (A) above is not printer's copy for (B), but apparently was circulated to one or more of Emerson's friends (most likely Caroline Sturgis) in the summer of 1846. It is chosen as copy-text because it is the earliest coherent form of the poem. It has not previously been published.

VARIANTS

2   Tobacco-leaf, (B-G) | Tobacco leaf (A) || rose; (B-G) | rose, (A)
3   earth-poles (B-G) | earthpoles (A) || line, (C-F) | Line, (A-B, G)
5   Every thing (A-C, F-G) | Everything (D-E)
6   meat; (C-G) | meat, (A-B)
7   eat; (C-G) | eat, (A-B)
9   altitudes;— (C-G) | altitudes. (A-B)
10   natures, (B-G) | natures,— (A)
11   tame: (C-G) | tame, (A-B)
12   Tree (C-G) | Tree, (A-B)
13   Bird, (C-G) | Bird (A-B) ||

reptile, (C-G) | reptile (A-B) || game. (B-G) | game (A)
14   band; (C-G) | band, (A-B)
15   dog-wood (C-D, F-G) | dogwood (A-B, E) || hand; (C-G) | hand, (A-B)
17   me; (C-G) | me, (A-B)
19   Vampyre-fanned, (C-G) | Vampire-fanned (A-B)
23   humors (C-G) | humours (A-B)
25   merry! (C-G) | merry, (A-B)
26   mights, (A, C-G) | mights; (B)
27   delights, (A, C-G) | delights; (B)

28   wrongs (C-G) I wrongs, (A-B) II   [*Two lines canceled in* (CC1) *and*
     rights, (A, C-G) I rights; (B)   *omitted in* (E-G):] God! I will not be
29   allowed, (A, C-G) I allowed; (B)   an owl, / But sun me in the Capitol. I
30   cloud! (B-G) I cloud, (A)   ["God!" *canceled in* (CC5)]
32   me! (C-G) I me, (A) I me; (B) II

TO J. W.

Edward Emerson identified "J. W." as John Weiss, "a young cler-
gyman and an able writer, who had seemed to Mr. Emerson to
dwell overmuch on Goethe's failings" (*W*, IX, 414). Edward no
doubt had this information from an unimpeachable source, and
yet Emerson encountered Weiss, an 1843 graduate of Harvard Di-
vinity School, only very rarely before the publication of the *Poems*
in December 1846. Minister at Watertown following his gradua-
tion, Weiss would become known as a protégé of Theodore Parker
and eventually—and mainly—as his biographer. He was early in-
terested in German literature, however, and published transla-
tions of Novalis (1842) and Schiller (1845), but if he developed
an opinion about Johann Wolfgang von Goethe (1749–1832), it
must have reached Emerson orally. Even so, Weiss seems an odd
choice as addressee, since there were other more prominent fig-
ures who notably expressed indignation over the moral cast of
Goethe's life. George Bancroft, for example, had advertised his
disapproval as early as 1824 in an article in the *North American Re-
view* and again in the *Christian Examiner* for July 1839. In an 1841
review in the *Dial* Theodore Parker rejected the "unmannerly hos-
tility to Goethe" ("insane as it obviously is") contained in Wolf-
gang Menzel's *German Literature,* a volume in George Ripley's *Spec-*

imens of Foreign Standard Literature. Even so, Parker's defense was equivocal, since he felt obliged to admit that "Goethe, as a man, was selfish to a very high degree, a debauchee and well-bred epicurean, who had little sympathy with what was highest in man, so long as he could crown himself with rose-buds" (332). The disfavor in which Goethe was held, especially in proper New England Unitarian circles, was a problem for the Transcendentalists generally, as Perry Miller has noted (*The Transcendentalists* [Cambridge, 1950], 369–370), but most especially for Margaret Fuller, translator of Eckermann's *Conversations with Goethe* (1839), to whom he was a literary hero. She reacted to Menzel's "abuse" (*Dial*, I [January 1841]: 345), in a supplement to Parker's review, with an apology that explored the question of the standards by which literary genius was to be valued and, in so doing (as Charles Capper has said), "raised the ongoing debate over Goethe to a new intellectual plane" (II, 60). Still, in an 1844 Phi Beta Kappa Address, George Putnam, who had attended early sessions of the Transcendental Club, annoyed Emerson by his strictures on Goethe, whose main failing seemed to be that he was "not a New England Calvinist" (*JMN*, IX, 145–146). The controversy, in other words, was widespread and troublesome: that Emerson should entail it upon the young, unknown, virtually anonymous John Weiss makes his statement seem the more broadly theoretical and impersonal.

In the summer of 1842 Emerson advised himself in his journal to "husband your criticism on J. W. for a few days & he will have demonstrated his insufficiency to all men's eyes & give you no farther trouble" (*JMN*, VIII, 192–193). If this rather strong language actually refers to an obscure Divinity School student, then Emerson may well have delayed writing the poem; the fact that it did not appear in the *Dial* almost certainly means that it was written between 1844 and 1846.

TO J. W.

Set not thy foot on graves:
Hear what wine and roses say;

The mountain chase, the summer waves,
The crowded town, thy feet may well delay.

Set not thy foot on graves; 5
Nor seek to unwind the shroud
Which charitable Time
And Nature have allowed
To wrap the errors of a sage sublime.

Set not thy foot on graves: 10
Care not to strip the dead
Of his sad ornament,
His myrrh, and wine, and rings,
His sheet of lead,
And trophies buried: 15
Go, get them where he earned them when alive;
As resolutely dig or dive.

Life is too short to waste
In critic peep or cynic bark,
Quarrel or reprimand: 20
'Twill soon be dark;
Up! mind thine own aim, and
God speed the mark!

TEXTS

(A) *Poems* (London, 1847), 32–33; (B) *Poems* (Boston, 1847), 43–44; (C) *Poems* ["Fourth Edition"] (Boston 1847), 43–44; (D) *Poems* (Boston, 1857), 43–44; (E) *Poems* (Boston, 1865), 43–44; (F) *Poems* [Riverside] (Boston, 1884), 31–32; (G) *Poems* [Centenary] (Boston, 1904), 29–30. The only alteration in the plates after (C) is in (D), line 2, as noted below. The poem was not included in *Selected Poems* (Boston, 1876). In the 1847 correction copy Emerson canceled "To J. W." with a vertical line in pencil and tore out most of the leaf containing pp. 43–44, evidently signifying that the poem was not to be included in *Selected Poems*.

Format: (F-G) have a line space after l. 13.

Pre-copy-texts forms: The drafts in Notebook X are discussed in *PN*, 949.

VARIANTS

[*In* (CC4) *Emerson indicated by a line that the last stanza (p. 44) should be first*]

1   graves: (B-D) | graves; (A, E-G)
2   say; (A, D-G) | say (B) | say: (C)
7   Time (B-G) | time (A)
8   Nature (B-G) | nature (A)
10   graves: (B-E) | graves; (A, F-G)
12   ornament, (B-G) | ornament; (A)
15   buried: (B-F) | buried; (A) | burièd: (G)

16   Go, (B-G) | Go (A) ‖ alive; (B-G) | alive, (A)
19   In critic peep (B-G) | The critic bite (A) | [(CC10) *substitutes* "In" *for* "The"]
20   Quarrel (B-G) | Quarrel, (A) ‖ reprimand: (B-G) | reprimand; (A)
22   Up! mind (A, C-G) | Up, heed (B)
23   mark! (B-G) | mark. (A)

FATE.

On a visit to Boston on 16 June 1841 Emerson obtained from Convers Francis the loan of James Philip Bailey's *Festus* (London, 1839), a book-length poem on the Faust theme, popular in Britain but not yet reprinted in America (*L*, II, 406). He read the book at once and in response composed this poem, a version of which he sent in a letter to an unidentified correspondent, who received it on the 27th of the same month (*L*, VII, 458; *PN*, 661–663). "You shall have the rest of my thought on Festus," Emerson had written, "which lies by me in numbers somewhat rude, I own, for the topic." It was a rather more polished version that Emerson shortly thereafter sent to Margaret Fuller for publication in the *Dial,* where it appeared in the October number along with Fuller's own favorable thirty-page review of Bailey's work. By a convoluted system of loans and recoveries, documented with some comedy in Emerson's letters (*L*, II, 417–419, 435–436, 439), Francis's copy was read in quick succession by Emerson, Elizabeth Hoar, her brother Ebenezer Rockwood Hoar, Bronson Alcott, Caroline Sturgis, and Fuller. Sturgis, one of the later readers, wrote to Emerson to say that *Festus* was "like a vast cloud, full of gorgeous lights & gloomy shadows"; she further expressed a doubt that Emerson would understand the half of it (Joel Myerson, *The New England Transcendentalists and the* Dial [Rutherford, N.J.,1980], 243 n. 67).

The association of Emerson's poem with Bailey's would have been hard to make out had it not been for the accidental survival of the manuscript giving Emerson's testimony. And yet "Fate" makes its way quite apart from this connection. In his note to the poem in the Centenary Edition, Edward quotes Oliver Wendell Holmes's praise of Emerson's "subtle selective instinct" in the pathetic language of the portrait in lines 18–26, and his appreciation as well for the surprising effect of the "grand hyperbole" in the two lines following (*W*, IX, 414–415; Holmes, *Ralph Waldo Emerson*, 331–332). The title of the poem was changed in the Riverside and Centenary editions to "Destiny," perhaps because the earlier title had been used, over the years, for several shorter pieces.

FATE.

That you are fair or wise is vain,
Or strong, or rich, or generous;
You must add the untaught strain
That sheds beauty on the rose.
There's a melody born of melody,   5
Which melts the world into a sea.
Toil could never compass it;
Art its height could never hit;
It came never out of wit;
But a music music-born   10
Well may Jove and Juno scorn.

Thy beauty, if it lack the fire
Which drives me mad with sweet desire,
What boots it? what the soldier's mail,
Unless he conquer and prevail?   15
What all the goods thy pride which lift,
If thou pine for another's gift?
Alas! that one is born in blight,
Victim of perpetual slight:
When thou lookest on his face,   20
Thy heart saith, 'Brother, go thy ways!
None shall ask thee what thou doest,
Or care a rush for what thou knowest,
Or listen when thou repliest,
Or remember where thou liest,   25
Or how thy supper is sodden;'
And another is born
To make the sun forgotten.
Surely he carries a talisman
Under his tongue;   30
Broad his shoulders are and strong;
And his eye is scornful,
Threatening, and young.
I hold it of little matter
Whether your jewel be of pure water,   35
A rose diamond or a white,
But whether it dazzle me with light.
I care not how you are dressed,
In coarsest weeds or in the best;
Nor whether your name is base or brave;   40
Nor for the fashion of your behavior;
But whether you charm me,
Bid my bread feed and my fire warm me,
And dress up Nature in your favor.
One thing is forever good;   45
That one thing is Success,—
Dear to the Eumenides,

And to all the heavenly brood.
Who bides at home, nor looks abroad,
Carries the eagles, and masters the sword.   50

TEXTS

(A) *Dial,* II (October 1841): 205–206; (B) MS HM 7627, by permission of the Huntington Library, San Marino, California, printer's copy for C; (C) *Poems* (London, 1847), 33–35; (D) *Poems* (Boston, 1847), 45–47; (E) *Poems* ["Fourth Edition"] (Boston, 1847), 45–47; (F) *Poems* (Boston, 1858), 45–47; (G) *Poems* (Boston, 1863), 45–47; (H) *Poems* (Boston, 1865), 45–47; (I) *Poems* (Boston, 1866), 45–47; (J) *Selected Poems* (Boston, 1876), 88–89; (K) *Poems* [Riverside] (Boston, 1884), 32–33; (L) *Poems* [Centenary] (Boston, 1904), 31–32.

Pre-copy-text forms: No drafts occur in the poetry notebooks or the journals; the version sent to the unidentified correspondent and endorsed 27 June 1841, is now in the Alderman Library, University of Virginia. This text is transcribed in *PN,* 661–663.

VARIANTS

Title: FATE. (A-J) I DESTINY. (K) I DESTINY (L)

3   You must add (J-L) I You must have also (A-I) I < ↑ Still you want ↓ > You must add (CC1)

5   There's (CC4, CC9, G, I-L) I There is (A-F, H) II of melody, (B-L) I of melody (A)

6   sea. (A-C, E-L) I sea: (D)

7   it; (D-L) I it, (A-C)

8   hit; (D-L) I hit, (A-C)

9   wit; (A, D-L) I wit, (B-C)

12   Thy beauty, (A-L) I <Thy> beauty, (CC4)

14   what the (B-J) I What the (A, K-L) II soldier's (A-B, D-L) I soldiers (C)

19   slight: (D-L) I slight;— (A-C)

20   on (A, D-L) I in (B-C)

21   'Brother, (D-L) I Brother! (A-C) II ways! (B-L) I ways; (A)

23   a rush (C-L) I an apple (A) I <<an> <apple> ↑ acorn ↓ > ↑ a rush ↓ (B)

26   sodden;' (D-I, K-L) I sodden,— (A-C) I sodden'; (J)

30   tongue; (B-L) I tongue, (A)

31   Broad his shoulders are and strong; (CC9, G, I-L) I Broad are his shoulders, and strong, (A-C) I Broad are his shoulders and strong; (D-E, H) I Broad his shoulders are and young; (F) I Broad his shoulders are and strong (CC1, CC4, CC5) I Broad his shoulders are, & strong, (CC3)

33   Threatening, (B-J) I Threatening (A, K-L)

34   matter (D-L) I matter, (A-C)

36   white, (A, D-L) | white,— (B-C)
38   how (A, C-L) | <whether>
↑how↓ (B) || dressed, (D-L) | drest,
(A-C)
39   coarsest weeds or in the best;
(CC4, CC5, CC9, I-L) | the coarsest
or in the best, (A) | the coarsest, or in
the best, (B-C) | the coarsest or in the
best; (D-H)
40   brave; (D-J) | brave, (A-C) |
brave: (K-L) [*In* CC1 *the words* "or
vile" *are written in the margin, canceled;
then the entire line canceled*]
40–41   [*In poetry notebook* ETE Verses,
among "Corrections of New Edition
of Poems," *Emerson wrote:* "Nor
whether your name is baser or braver
/ Nor for the fashion of your

behavior / Whether your name's
renowned or low"; *see* PN, *584*]
41   behavior; (D-L) | behavior, (A) |
behaviour,— (B-C)
43   feed (A, D-L) | feed, (B-C) || me,
(A-K) | me (L)
44   Nature (D-L) | nature (A-C) ||
favor. (A, E-L) | favour. (B-C) | favor
(D)
45   forever (A-B, D-L) | for ever (C)
|| good; (D-L) | good,— (A) | good,
(B-C)
46   Success,— (B, D-L) | Success,
(A) | success,— (C)
50   Carries (B-L) | He carries (A) ||
eagles, and masters (B-L) | eagles
—he masters (A) | <he> ↑and↓
(CC8)

NOTES

46–47.   In the *Eumenides* by Æschylus the Erinyes (or Furies), ancient avengers
of blood, are baulked in their pursuit of Orestes, but find a productive place
among the younger gods in the new, more rational order of divinity when Ath-
ena enlists them in support of the success of Athens. In taking up this role they
become the Eumenides, or "the Kindly Ones."

50.   In the Roman legions it was the responsibility of the Aquilifer to carry the
insignia of the eagle (Aquila) into battle.

GUY.

Although it seems to have been written a number of years later
—perhaps as late as 1846—"Guy" is clearly a companion to "Fate,"
a kind of gloss on the fortunate man "born / To make the sun
forgotten." The source of the name "Guy" is obscure (see *EL,* III,
350, for evidence that its selection was entirely arbitrary); never-
theless the character appears in several journal passages as an Em-
ersonian heuristic for thinking about the paradoxical threat that
envy poses for self-reliance (see, e.g., *JMN,* X, 38). In 1840 Emer-
son noted that "Guy wished all his friends dead on very slight oc-
casion" (*JMN,* VII, 333). The source of the acrimony is more fully
indicated in an earlier, cross-referenced passage: the ordinary
feeling that "The superiority in him is inferiority in me" (*JMN,*
VII, 99), though in both locations Emerson acknowledged that,
however tempting a course of action, murder would not effectu-
ally remedy the case. In this dramatizing, however, the protagonist
is dual: Guy the malignant envier presents a stark contrast to what
he becomes—Guy the redeemed, the possessor of "the talisman /
That all things from him began." The choice of the word "talis-
man" is crucial: it is etymologically related to the Greek root *telos*
and implies fulfillment. Possessing this, Guy becomes the fortu-
nate man, one who would seem to have no need of "amulets" as
protection against external threats.

Edward Emerson said of this poem that it was the portrait of
"the balanced soul in harmony with Nature" (*W,* IX, 415), but the
tone is significantly complicated, not to say darkened, by the ref-
erence in line 7 to Polycrates, tyrant of Samos, the subject of a well
known moral fable by Herodotus (*History,* III, 40–43; cf. *JMN,* V,
93–94) and of a poem by Schiller (see *FuL,* II, 179–180). As Ed-
ward gives the story, "Fortune so constantly smiled on [Polycrates]
that Amasis, king of Egypt, bade his friend make some great sacri-

fice to avert the disaster that must come to balance unbroken prosperity. Polycrates flung his wonderful emerald into the sea. It returned to him in a fish on his table the next day. Amasis at once broke off his alliance, and soon overthrow and cruel death befel Polycrates" (*W,* IX, 416). This "cruel death" involved the fulfillment of a prophecy that he should be washed by Jove and anointed by the Sun—when it transpired that his crucified corpse was long exposed to the elements.

In the Riverside edition Edward interpolated some lines originating in Notebook X ("Vain against him were hostile blows") that his father had at some point written out on the page containing the first lines of "Guy" in a correction copy of the 1865 "Blue and Gold" edition (see variants list at line 16). Emerson's intention in copying this passage is unclear, especially since the six lines are written in the bottom margin of the page, with no particular direction given as to their placement—if, indeed, they were to be inserted at all. Opinions will differ as to their fitness. In the notes to the Centenary edition Edward seemed to want to expand the poem still further, and suggested that another fragment from the same page in notebook X ("Fine presentiments controlled him") was likewise "destined for this poem" (see *PN,* 790–791, 957).

GUY.

Mortal mixed of middle clay,
Attempered to the night and day,
Interchangeable with things,
Needs no amulets nor rings.
Guy possessed the talisman   5
That all things from him began;
And as, of old, Polycrates
Chained the sunshine and the breeze,
So did Guy betimes discover
Fortune was his guard and lover;   10
In strange junctures, felt, with awe,
His own symmetry with law;
That no mixture could withstand

The virtue of his lucky hand.
He gold or jewel could not lose,   15
Nor not receive his ample dues.
In the street, if he turned round,
His eye the eye 'twas seeking found.
It seemed his Genius discreet
Worked on the Maker's own receipt,   20
And made each tide and element
Stewards of stipend and of rent;
So that the common waters fell
As costly wine into his well.
He had so sped his wise affairs   25
That he caught Nature in his snares:
Early or late, the falling rain
Arrived in time to swell his grain;
Stream could not so perversely wind
But corn of Guy's was there to grind;   30
The siroc found it on its way,
To speed his sails, to dry his hay;
And the world's sun seemed to rise,
To drudge all day for Guy the wise.
In his rich nurseries, timely skill   35
Strong crab with nobler blood did fill;
The zephyr in his garden rolled
From plum-trees vegetable gold;
And all the hours of the year
With their own harvest honored were.   40
There was no frost but welcome came,
Nor freshet, nor midsummer flame.
Belonged to wind and world the toil
And venture, and to Guy the oil.

TEXTS

(A) MS m.b., Berg Collection, by permission of the New York Public Library, printer's copy for B; (B) *Poems* (London, 1847), 35–37; (C) *Poems* (Boston, 1847), 48–50; (D) *Poems* ["Fourth Edition"] (Boston, 1847), 48–50; (D²) *Poems*

Guy

(Boston, 1865), 48–50; (E) *Selected Poems* (Boston, 1876), 90–91; (F) *Poems* [Riverside] (Boston, 1884), 33–35; (G) *Poems* [Centenary] (Boston, 1904), 33–34. No variants occur in later printings from the 1847 plates after (D).

Format: Line 5 is indented (A-B). (A) has a line space following l. 34, which, falling at the bottom of p. 36 in (B), disappears. It does not occur in any subsequent printing.

Pre-copy-text forms: None.

VARIANTS

5   Guy possessed (B-G) I Guy
<had> ↑ possessed ↓ (A)
6   began; (C-G) I began, (A-B)
11   felt, with awe, (C-G) I felt with awe (A-B)
12   law; (C-G) I law, (A-B)
13   That (B, D-G) I <So t>That (A) I So that (C)
16   dues. (C-G) I dues; (A-B).
[*Followed in* (CC5, F-G) *by six lines of verse:*

    Fearless Guy had never foes,
    He did their weapons
        decompose.
    Aimed at him, the blushing
        blade
    Healed as fast the wounds it
        made.
    If on the foeman fell his gaze,
    Him it would straightway blind
        or craze.

(G) *has* "craze," *in the last line* I *The text at* (CC5) *has* <Did> He did *in the second line, and the* <assailant>

↑ foeman ↓ *in the fifth: see the headnote above*]
26   Nature (C-G) I nature (A-B) II snares: (C-D) I snares; (A-B, E) I snares. (F-G)
29   wind (C-G) I wind, (A-B)
30   grind; (A-E) I grind: (F-G)
31   The siroc (C-G) I <Each wind> ↑ The whirlwind ↓ (A) I The whirlwind (B) II way, (C-G) I way (A-B)
33   rise, (C-E) I rise (A-B, F-G)
37   zephyr (C-G) I <[*illegible*]>Zephyr (A) I Zephyr (B)
38   plum-trees (C-G) I plum trees (A-B)
39   And all the hours of the (A-G) I All hours of the plenteous (CC4) I And all the seasons of the (CC5)
40   honored were. (C-G) I honored were: (A) I hovered were: (B) I <hovered> ↑ honored ↓ were: (CC2, CC10)
42   flame. (C-G) I flame; (A-B)

NOTES

15.   "The terror of cloudless noon, the emerald of Polycrates, the awe of prosperity, the instinct which leads every generous soul to impose on itself tasks of

noble asceticism and vicarious virtue, are the tremblings of the balance of justice through the heart and mind of man" ("Compensation," *CW*, II, 65).

36. An obscure reference, but perhaps an allusion to the fact that the blood of crabs is blue, as it is based on hemocyanin, a copper compound, rather than on hemoglobin, in which iron conveys the oxygen. The phrase "blue blood," denoting nobility, is said to have entered the language in 1834, when Maria Edgworth translated the Spanish *sangre azul*, the traditional self-characterizing boast of the Castillian aristocracy.

TACT.

This poem was first published in a group with "Holidays" and "The Amulet" in the *Dial* for July 1842. There is almost no direct evidence as to the date of its composition, but Edward Emerson, in his note to "The Amulet" (*W*, IX, 436) plausibly implied that all three were written about the same time, shortly before publication. His further comment, however, that all three develop "the same subject" casts some doubt on his information.

TACT.

What boots it, thy virtue,
    What profit thy parts,
While one thing thou lackest,—
    The art of all arts?

The only credentials,   5
    Passport to success;
Opens castle and parlor,—
    Address, man, Address.

Tact

The maiden in danger
   Was saved by the swain;   10
His stout arm restored her
   To Broadway again.

The maid would reward him,—
   Gay company come,—
They laugh, she laughs with them;   15
   He is moonstruck and dumb.

This clinches the bargain;
   Sails out of the bay;
Gets the vote in the senate,
   Spite of Webster and Clay;   20

Has for genius no mercy,
   For speeches no heed;
It lurks in the eyebeam,
   It leaps to its deed.

Church, market, and tavern,   25
   Bed and board, it will sway.
It has no to-morrow;
   It ends with to-day.

TEXTS

(A) *Dial*, III (July 1842): 72–73; (B) *Poems* (London, 1847), 37–38; (C) *Poems* (Boston, 1847), 51–52; (D) *Poems* ["Fourth Edition"] (Boston, 1847), 51–52; (E) *Poems* (Boston, 1865), 51–52. "Tact" was not included in *Selected Poems* (Boston, 1876), nor did it appear in the posthumous editions of 1884 and 1904. There are no variants in the 1847 plates after (D). Plate damage affecting terminal punctuation in ll. 20 and 27 in *Poems* (Boston, 1857) was repaired in *Poems* (Boston, 1858).

Format: The spacing and indentation adopted here were introduced in (C) and adhered to thereafter. (A-B) lack indentation and (B) omits the line space after l. 4.

Pre-copy-text forms: None.

VARIANTS

1 virtue, (B-E) | virtue? (A)
2 parts, (B-E) | parts? (A)
3 While (B-E) | The (A) ||
lackest,— (C-E) | lackest (A) | lackest,
(B)
4 The (B-E) | Is the (A) || arts? (C-
E) | arts. (A) | arts! (B)
6 success; (C-E) | success, (A-B)
7 parlor,— (C-E) | parlour,—
(A-B)
10 swain; (C-E) | swain: (A) | swain,
(B)
12 Broadway again. (C-E) | her
palace again; (A) | Broadway again:
(B)
14 come,— (A-B, D-E) | come; (C)

15 them; (C-E) | them, (A-B)
17 clinches (C-E) | clenches (A-B) ||
bargain; (A, C-E) | bargain, (B)
18 bay; (A, C-E) | bay, (B)
19 senate, (A, C-E) | Senate, (B)
20 Clay; (A-D) | Clay. (E)
22 heed; (A, C-E) | heed,— (B)
24 deed. (B-E) | deed; (A)
25 Church, market, and tavern, (C-
E) | It governs the planet, (A) |
Church, tavern, and market, (B)
26 Bed and board, it will sway. (C-
E) | Church and State it will sway; (A)
| Bed and board it will sway; (B)
27 to-morrow; (C-E) | to-morrow,
(A-B)

NOTES

20. Daniel Webster (1782–1852) of Massachusetts and Henry Clay (1777–1852) of Kentucky were the two most powerful Whig politicians of the period, though, somewhat coincidentally, neither was in the Senate when Emerson's poem was published.

HAMATREYA.

In July 1845 Emerson borrowed James Elliot Cabot's copy of Horace Hayman Wilson's translation of *The Vishńu Puráńa*, read it on a trip to Vermont, and entered extracts in Notebook Y (*L*, III, 293). The following passage is the germ of "Hamatreya":

Hamatreya

I have now given you a summary account of the sovereigns of the earth.—These, & other kings who with perishable frames have possessed this ever-during world, & who, blinded with deceptive notions of individual occupation, have indulged the feeling that suggests 'This earth is mine,—it is my son's,—it belongs to my dynasty, —' have all passed away. So, many who reigned before them, many who succeeded them, & many who are yet to come, have ceased or will cease to be. Earth laughs, as if smiling with autumnal flowers to behold her kings unable to effect the subjugation of themselves. I will repeat to you, Maitreya, the stanzas that were chanted by Earth, & which the Muni Asita communicated to Janaka, whose banner was virtue.

'How great is the folly of princes who are endowed with the faculty of reason, to cherish the confidence of ambition when they themselves are but foam upon the wave. Before they have subdued themselves, they seek to reduce their ministers, their servants, their subjects, under their authority; they then endeavour to overcome their foes. "Thus," say they, "will we conquer the ocean-circled earth;" &, intent upon their project, behold not death, which is not far off. But what mighty matter is the subjugation of the sea girt earth, to one who can subdue himself. Emancipation from existence is the fruit of self-control. It is through infatuation that kings desire to possess me, whom their predecessors have been forced to leave, whom their fathers have not retained. Beguiled by the selfish love of sway, fathers contend with their sons, & brothers with brothers, for my possession. Foolishness has been the character of every king who has boasted, "All this earth is mine—every thing is mine —it will be in my house forever;"—for he is dead. How is it possible that such vain desires should survive in the hearts of his descendants, who have seen their progenitor absorbed by the thirst of dominion, compelled to relinquish me whom he called his own, & tread the path of dissolution? When I hear a king sending word to another by his ambassador, "This earth is mine; resign your pretensions to it,"—I am at first moved to violent laughter; but it soon subsides in pity for the infatuated fool.'

These were the verses, Maitreya, which Earth recited & by listening to which ambition fades away like snow before the sun. (*JMN*, IX, 321)

When Emerson read the poem to Bronson Alcott on 28 June 1846, it had the title "Concord" (Alcott, *Journals*, ed. Odell Shep-

67

ard [Boston, 1938], 182). In bringing home the Hindu source, Emerson drew on research he had done ten years earlier for his "Historical Discourse at Concord," delivered on the occasion of the town's bicentennial (*W,* XI, 27–86). In that commemorative address Emerson had a rather different perspective on the evanescence of the landlords:

> Yet the race survives whilst the individual dies. In the country, without any interference of the law, the agricultural life favors the permanence of families. Here are still around me the lineal descendants of the first settlers of this town. Here is Blood, Flint, Willard, Meriam, Wood, Hosmer, Barrett, Wheeler, Jones, Brown, Buttrick, Brooks, Stow, Hoar, Heywood, Hunt, Miles,—the names of the inhabitants for the first thirty years; and the family is in many cases represented, when the name is not. If the name of Bulkeley is wanting, the honor you have done me this day, in making me your organ, testifies your persevering kindness to his blood. (*W,* XI, 30)

Emerson had a more certain sense of his own fugacity as landlord:

> When I must leave land, house, & Lidian,
> Of all my planted trees & shade
> Will none but funeral firs & cypresses
> Follow their shortlived lord. (*TN,* III, 355)

HAMATREYA.

Bulkeley, Hunt, Willard, Hosmer, Meriam, Flint,
Possessed the land which rendered to their toil
Hay, corn, roots, hemp, flax, apples, wool, and wood.
Each of these landlords walked amidst his farm,
Saying, ''Tis mine, my children's, and my name's: 5
How sweet the west wind sounds in my own trees!
How graceful climb those shadows on my hill!
I fancy these pure waters and the flags
Know me, as does my dog: we sympathize;
And, I affirm, my actions smack of the soil.'   10

Hamatreya

Where are these men? Asleep beneath their grounds;
And strangers, fond as they, their furrows plough.
Earth laughs in flowers, to see her boastful boys
Earth-proud, proud of the earth which is not theirs;
Who steer the plough, but cannot steer their feet   15
Clear of the grave.
They added ridge to valley, brook to pond,
And sighed for all that bounded their domain.
'This suits me for a pasture; that's my park;
We must have clay, lime, gravel, granite-ledge,   20
And misty lowland, where to go for peat.
The land is well,—lies fairly to the south.
'Tis good, when you have crossed the sea and back,
To find the sitfast acres where you left them.'
Ah! the hot owner sees not Death, who adds   25
Him to his land, a lump of mould the more.
Hear what the Earth says:—

EARTH-SONG.

'Mine and yours;
Mine, not yours.   30
Earth endures;
Stars abide—
Shine down in the old sea;
Old are the shores;
But where are old men?   35
I who have seen much,
Such have I never seen.

'The lawyer's deed
Ran sure,
In tail,   40
To them, and to their heirs
Who shall succeed,
Without fail,
Forevermore.

'Here is the land,   45
Shaggy with wood,
With its old valley,
Mound, and flood.
But the heritors?
Fled like the flood's foam,—   50
The lawyer, and the laws,
And the kingdom,
Clean swept herefrom.

'They called me theirs,
Who so controlled me;   55
Yet every one
Wished to stay, and is gone.
How am I theirs,
If they cannot hold me,
But I hold them?'   60

When I heard the Earth-song,
I was no longer brave;
My avarice cooled
Like lust in the chill of the grave.

TEXTS

(A) MS, m.b., Berg Collection, by permission of the New York Public Library, probably printer's copy for (B), though it lacks the usual page numbers; (B) *Poems* (London, 1847), 39–41; (C) *Poems* (Boston, 1847), 53–56; (D) *Poems* (Boston, 1857), 53–56; (E) *Poems* (Boston, 1858), 53–56; (F) *Poems* (Boston, 1865), 53–57; (G) *Selected Poems* (Boston, 1876), 70–72; (H) *Poems* [Riverside] (Boston, 1884), 35–37; (I) *Poems* [Centenary] (Boston, 1904), 35–37. No variants occur in printings from the plates for (C) until the 1857 "Sixth Edition" (D).

Format: (H-I) have a line space after 1. 10. (B) lacks the line space after l. 37.

Pre-copy-text forms: None.

Hamatreya

VARIANTS

1 Bulkeley, Hunt, (CC5, G-I) |
Minott, Lee, (A-F) | Bulkeley, <Jones>
Hunt (CC1) || Flint, (A-B, F-I) | Flint
(C-E)

2 land (C-I) | land, (A-B)

5 children's, (A-G) | children's (H-
I) || name's: (C-G) | name's.
(A-B, H-I)

6 How (C-I) | 'How (A-B) || west
wind (A-F, H-I) | west-wind (G) ||
sounds (A-I) | murmurs (CC5) || my
own (A-I) | my (CC5) || trees! (C-I) |
trees; (A-B)

7 How (C-I) | 'How (A-B) || hill!
(C-I) | hill; (A-B)

8 I (C-I) | 'I (A-B) || these (C-I) |
those (A-B)

9 Know me (C-I) | 'Know me, (A) |
'Know me (B) || sympathize; (C-I) |
sympathize, (A-B)

10 And, (C-I) | 'And, (A-B)

10–11 soil.' / Where (A-I) | soil.' / #
/ Where ["Space, & new paragraph"]
(CC1)

11 these (C-I) | those (A-B) ||
grounds; (C-G) | grounds, (A-B) |
grounds: (H-I)

13 flowers, (C-I) | flowers (A-B)

14 Earth-proud, (A, C-I) | Earth
proud, (B)

16 grave. (C-I) | grave.— (A-B)

18 domain. (A, C-F) | domain, (B) |
domain; (G-I)

19 pasture; (B-I) | pasture, (A) ||
park; (C-I) | park, (A-B)

20 We (C-I) | 'We (A-B)

21 And (C-I) | 'And (A-B) ||
lowland, (C-I) | lowland (A-B)

22 The (C-I) | 'The (A-B)

23 'Tis (C-I) | 'Tis (A) | ''Tis (B)

24 To (C-I) | 'To (A-B)

27 says:— (C-I) | says; (A) | says: (B)

28 EARTH-SONG. (A-H) | EARTH-
SONG (I)

29 'Mine (C-F, H-I) | Mine (A-B, G)
|| yours; (C-I) | yours, (A-B)

30 Mine, (C-I) | Mine (A-B)

31 endures; (C-I) | endures, (A-B)

32 abide— (C-I) | abide, (A-B)

33 Shine down in (B-I) | Shine
↑ down ↓ in (A) || sea; (C-I) | sea,
(A-B)

34 shores; (C-I) | shores, (A-B)

38 'The (C-F, H-I) | The (A-B, G)

39 sure, (C-I) | sure (A-B)

40 tail, (C-I) | tail (A-B)

41 them, (C-I) | them (A-B)

42 succeed, (C-I) | succeed (A-B)

43 fail, (C-I) | fail (A-B)

44 Forevermore. (A, C-I) | For
evermore. (B)

45 'Here (C-F, H-I) | Here (A-B, G)

48 mound, (A-G) | mound (H-I) ||
flood. (C-I) | flood.— (A-B)

49 heritors? (C-G) | heritors— (A-
B) | heritors?— (CC1, H-I)

50 foam,— (C-G) | foam; (A-B) |
foam. (H-I)

54 'They (C-F, H-I) | They (A-B, G)

57 gone. (A-G) | gone, (H-I)

60 them?' (C-F, H-I) | them? (A-B,
G)

61 Earth-song, (A-H) | Earth-song
(I)

64 grave. (A-C, E-I) | grave (D)
[*Evidently plate damage.*]

NOTES

1.   The 1876 substitution of "Bulkeley, Hunt," for "Minott, Lee," among the names prominent in the settlement of Concord, may reflect the urging of the Emerson children to include reference to Peter Bulkeley (1583–1659), Puritan leader of the pioneer community, author of *The Gospel-Covenant* (1646), and an Emerson ancestor (see *W*, IX, 417–18). Emerson may have avoided it originally because so few knew that the name was properly pronounced "Buckley." He may have avoided the name "Hunt" in 1846 because of the notorious suicide of Martha Hunt the year before, memorably evoked by Nathaniel Hawthorne in his journal (*The American Notebooks*, ed. Claude M. Simpson [Columbus, Ohio, 1972], 261–267).

17–18.   Emerson alluded to this point in an 1852 journal entry that makes the anti-imperialist position explicit: "The farmer said, he should like to have all the land that joined his own. Bonaparte who had the same appetite, endeavoured to make the Mediterranean a French lake. The Russian czar Alexander was more expansive, & wished to call the Pacific *My ocean,* and the Americans were obliged to resist energetically his attempts to make it a close sea. But if he got the earth for his cowpasture & the sea for his fishpond, he would be a pauper still. He only is rich who owns the day" (*JMN*, XIII, 90).

GOOD-BYE.

Of all the poems that Emerson chose to collect, "Good-Bye" was the earliest written, and perhaps for that reason was never among his favorites. It belongs, if loosely, to the old monastic tradition of *contemptus mundi,* updated for the age of Wordsworth and Byron. Under that distinctively Platonic rubric it may be seen to have points of connection with such divers works as Sir Walter Ralegh's "The Lie," Shakespeare's Sonnet 66, Alexander Pope's "Solitude," and portions of Byron's *Childe Harold's Pilgrimage* (see Kendall B.

Taft, "The Byronic Background of Emerson's 'Good-Bye,'" *New England Quarterly*, XXVII [December 1954]: 525–527). A year before he wrote the poem, Emerson quoted in his journal a line from *Romeo and Juliet:* "The world is not thy friend, nor the world's law" (*JMN*, II, 101), but the theme is and has been so universally popular that a singular source is not to be insisted upon. W. H. Beable found the matter and some of the manner embedded in the popular culture, expressed in a much imitated epitaph quoted from the 1707 tombstone of one James Marshall, of Oakham, Rutland (*Epitaphs: Graveyard Humour & Eulogy* [New York, 1925], 31):

> Farewell poor world, I must be gone,
> Thou art no home, no rest for me,
> I'll take my staff and travel on
> Till I a better world may see.
> Put on, my soul, put on with speed,
> Tho' the way be long, the end is near:
> Once more, poor world, farewell indeed.

A close variant of this epitaph, quoted from "the Church-yard of Westminston, in Sussex," was reported in Stephen Collet [pseudonym of Thomas Byerley], ed., *Relics of Literature* (London, 1823), 316, and reprinted the next year in the London periodical *Saturday Night*, I (1824): 96. Both this epitaph and Marshall's derive from the very popular hymn "The Pilgrim's Farewel to the World" by Samuel Crossman (1624–1683), first published in 1664 in *The Young Man's Meditation*.

Emerson wrote "Good-Bye" in the winter and spring of 1824 at the age of twenty, shortly after his family, consisting of his mother and four brothers, moved for the first time out of Boston, to the bucolic setting of Light Lane in the Canterbury section of Roxbury. This was a "picturesque wilderness of savin, barberry bush, catbrier, sumach and rugged masses of pudding stone," all within three miles of downtown Boston, where Emerson, with his brother William, went each morning, on foot or doubled up on horseback, to teach at a school for young ladies (Edward Emerson, *Em-*

erson in Concord: A Memoir [Boston, 1889], 29). Emerson chafed at life as a schoolmaster, especially after William left to pursue his studies in Germany, and the poem testifies to the complex emotional pressures and sense of vocational disappointment that grew upon him after his graduation from Harvard two years earlier. The rustication at Canterbury was undoubtedly an economy measure for his hard-pressed family, but it was also an expedient strongly recommended by Aunt Mary Moody Emerson, who did not want her nephews to become, from their urban upbringing, like the "coarse thrifty cit [who] profanes the grove by his presence." As Emerson noted at the time, "she was anxious that her nephew might hold high & reverential notions regarding [nature] as the temple where God & the Mind are to be studied & adored" (*L*, I, 133). After months of skeptical resistance and environmental adjustment, Emerson began to find in nature "a serene superiority to man & his art in the thought of which man dwindles to pigmy proportions" (134).

James Freeman Clarke had seen the poem in manuscript before he asked permission to publish it in his Louisville, Kentucky, journal, *The Western Messenger.* In a letter of 27 February 1839 (*L*, VII, 332–334), Emerson obliged with a "corrected copy," which perhaps accounts for the revisions found in notebook P (see *PN*, 38–39). In the letter of transmittal Emerson apologized for the verses as being among his "juvenilities," explaining that "They have a slight misanthropy,—a shade deeper than belongs to me." When he came to collect the poem in 1846, he again revised with many small touches, some of which, interestingly, seem to have been back in the direction of the original manuscript drafts. In later life Emerson remained uncomfortable with the poem. In 1876 he held out against the wishes of his children (with whom it seems to have been a favorite) and forbade its republication in *Selected Poems* (*ETE*, II, 245). Edward explained his father's prejudice saying that he had been "both annoyed and amused" that the poem had so often been construed as a representation of his abandonment of the ministerial profession in 1832 and his removal to Concord in 1835, implying that the poem had to have been written ten years later than it actually was (*Emerson in Concord*, 29).

GOOD-BYE.

Good-bye, proud world! I'm going home:
Thou art not my friend, and I'm not thine.
Long through thy weary crowds I roam;
A river-ark on the ocean brine,
Long I've been tossed like the driven foam;   5
But now, proud world! I'm going home.

Good-bye to Flattery's fawning face;
To Grandeur with his wise grimace;
To upstart Wealth's averted eye;
To supple Office, low and high;   10
To crowded halls, to court and street;
To frozen hearts and hasting feet;
To those who go, and those who come;
Good-bye, proud world! I'm going home.

I am going to my own hearth-stone,   15
Bosomed in yon green hills alone,—
A secret nook in a pleasant land,
Whose groves the frolic fairies planned;
Where arches green, the livelong day,
Echo the blackbird's roundelay,   20
And vulgar feet have never trod
A spot that is sacred to thought and God.

O, when I am safe in my sylvan home,
I tread on the pride of Greece and Rome;
And when I am stretched beneath the pincs,   25
Where the evening star so holy shines,
I laugh at the lore and the pride of man,
At the sophist schools, and the learned clan;

For what are they all, in their high conceit,
When man in the bush with God may meet?   30

TEXTS

(A) MS Am 1569.7 (206), Houghton Library, Harvard University, printer's copy for B, misdated "1823" by Emerson; (B) *Western Messenger,* VI (April 1839): 402; (C) *Poems* (London, 1847), 42–43; (D) *Poems* (Boston, 1847), 57–58; (D²) *Poems* (Boston, 1865), 58–59; (E) *Poems* [Riverside] (Boston, 1884), 37–38; (E²) *Poems* [Centenary] (Boston, 1904), 3–4. No variants occur in later printings from the plates made for (D). "Good-Bye" was not included in *Selected Poems* (Boston, 1876). Rufus Wilmot Griswold reprinted the poem from (B) on three occasions: in *The Poets and Poetry of America* (New York, 1842), 237–238; in *Gems from the American Poets* (New York, 1842), 109–110; and in *Readings in American Poetry, for the Use of the Schools* (New York, 1843), 176–177. Variants in the punctuation of these texts are to be attributed to house styling and have no authority.

Pre-copy-text forms: The drafts, in *JMN,* II, 223–224 and 243, as well as in two of the early poetry notebooks, are discussed in *PN,* 804.

VARIANTS

Title: GOOD-BYE. (D-E) | [*Untitled*] (A) | "GOOD-BYE, PROUD WORLD!" (B) | GOOD BYE. (C)

1 Good-bye, (B, D-E) | Good bye, (A, C) ‖ world! (A-B, D-E) | world, (C) ‖ home: (D-E) | home; (A-B) | home, (C)

2 Thou art (A-B, D-E) | Thou'rt (C) ‖ friend, and I'm (C-E) | friend; I am (A-B) ‖ thine. (D-E) | thine: (A-B) | thine; (C)

3 Long through thy (C-E) | Too long through (A-B) ‖ roam; (C-E) | roam:— (A-B)

4 river-ark (C-E) | river ark (A-B) ‖ ocean (C-E) | Ocean (A-B)

5 Long I've been (C-E) | Too long I am (A-B) ‖ foam; (D-E) | foam: (A-B) | foam, (C)

6 world! (D-E) | world, (A-C)

7 Good-bye (B, D-E) | Good bye (A, C) ‖ face; (A-B, D-E) | face, (C)

8 Grandeur (A, D-E) | grandeur (B) | Grandeur, (C) ‖ grimace; (D-E) | grimace: (A-B) | grimace, (C)

9 eye; (A-B, D-E) | eye, (C)

10 Office, (A, D-E) | office, (B) | Office (C) ‖ high; (A-B, D-E) | high, (C)

11 court (A-B, D-E) | court, (C) ‖ street; (D-E) | street, (A-C)

12 hearts (D-E) | hearts, (A-C) ‖ feet; (D-E) | feet, (A-C)

13 come; (D-E) | come,— (A-B) | come, (C)

14 Good-bye, (B, D-E) | Good bye, (A, C) ‖ world! (D-E) | world, (A-C)

15 I am going to (D-E) | I go to seek

(A-B) | I'm going to (C) || hearth-stone, (D-E) | hearthstone (A) | hearth-stone (B-C)

16   Bosomed (A, C-E) | Bossomed (B) || hills alone,— (D-E) | hills alone; (A-B) | hills, alone, (C)

17   nook (C-E) | lodge (A-B)

18   planned; (C-E) | planned, (A-B)

19   green, (B, D-E) | green (A, C) || livelong day, (D-E) | livelong day (A) | live long day (B-C)

21   vulgar feet (C-E) | evil men (A-B)

23   O, (D-E) | O (A-C)

24   tread on (C-E) | mock at (A-B)

25   pines, (D-E) | pines (A-C)

27   the pride (A, C-E) | pride (B)

28   schools, (A-D) | schools (E)

29   all, (D-E) | all (A-C)

30   meet? (D-E) | meet. (A-C)

THE RHODORA:

ON BEING ASKED, WHENCE IS THE FLOWER?

According to a notation in Emerson's poetry notebook CSA, "The Rhodora" was composed in 1834 in Newton, Massachusetts, presumably in May (*PN,* 10). In late April Emerson had moved from his rented quarters in Franklin Place, Boston, to take up a summer's residence with his mother at the home of Mrs. Emerson's sister, Mary Haskins Ladd, and her husband William. Despite the mills at Newton's Upper and Lower Falls on the Charles River, the region away from the river was exceptionally quiet— "calm as eternity," as Emerson noted (*L,* I, 414)—a place where, as he also said, nothing moved but the sun and the moon, the thrushes, and once in a great while a cow (411). "The muses love the woods & I have come hither to court the awful Powers in this sober solitude" (*JMN,* IV, 280). Here was an environment that answered his needs, fit for reading, contemplation, and long walks in the pine woods near Baptist Pond, now called Crystal Lake

Poems (1847)

(*JMN*, IV, 272). The journals show that Emerson was just then much occupied with botanizing, an interest connected both to his scientific lectures of 1833 and 1834 and ultimately to his preparation for writing *Nature* (1836). In pursuing the "one aim" of all science, "namely, to find a theory of nature" (*CW*, I, 8), Emerson skeptically probed the implications of Linnaean classification, relying on Goethe, Coleridge, and various older writers to arrive at a more subjective conception of man's relation to natural phenomena. For Emerson, the meaning of the flora and fauna would not lie in their distinctive physical characteristics, as Linnaeus insisted, but in those important relations of mutuality which, in the nature of things, they sustained to man the observer. As first noted by Kenneth Walter Cameron (*Emerson the Essayist*, 2 vols. [1945; rpt. Hartford, 1972] I, 62 n. 25) and reaffirmed by Carl F. Strauch in his 1946 dissertation (523–524), Emerson's understanding of the observer's position as expressed in "The Rhodora" was indebted to the seventeenth-century Cambridge Platonist Ralph Cudworth. In *The True Intellectual System of the Universe* (1678), Cudworth had conjectured that "the eye, whose structure and fabric consisting of many parts (humours and membranes), is so artificially [i.e., artfully] composed, no reasonable person, who considers the whole anatomy thereof, and the curiosity of its structure, can think otherwise of it, but that it was made out of design for the use of seeing; and did not happen accidentally to be so made, and then the use of seeing follow. . . . [E]yes were made for the sake of seeing, and ears for the sake of hearing" (*The True Intellectual System of the Universe*, ed. Thomas Birch, 4 vols. [London, 1820], III, 284). The bearing of this passage on lines 11–12 of "The Rhodora" is obvious, and yet Emerson did not acquire his copy of Cudworth's great work until April 1835 (Walter Harding, *Emerson's Library* [Charlottesville, 1967], 73; *JMN*, V, 34; Carl F. Strauch, "The Year of Emerson's Poetic Maturity: 1834," *Philological Quarterly*, XXXIV [October 1955]: 359–365). He may have known the passage from acquaintance with another copy, but given the general popularity of the argument from design and Emerson's long fascination with ocular imagery, it is entirely possible that his formulation here was independent. What is more significant is the way in which the poem—especially in its strong last line—anticipates the observation in *Nature* that "The greatest delight which the fields and woods minister, is the suggestion of an occult relation between man and the vegetable. I am not alone and unacknowledged" (*CW*, I, 10). Knowing something of Emerson's situation in secluded Newton in May of 1834, "when sea-winds pierced our solitudes," will inevitably suggest a "relation" between, on the one hand, the observer's own sense of undeserved obscurity (*JMN*, IV, 274–275), now manifested in his retirement to the countryside (in a larger sense, what "brought [him] there"), and, on the other, the uncomplaining hiddenness in nature of one suddenly meaningful, suddenly eloquent representative of *Rhododendron canadense.*

THE RHODORA:

ON BEING ASKED, WHENCE IS THE FLOWER?

In May, when sea-winds pierced our solitudes,
I found the fresh Rhodora in the woods,
Spreading its leafless blooms in a damp nook,
To please the desert and the sluggish brook.
The purple petals, fallen in the pool,   5
Made the black water with their beauty gay;
Here might the red-bird come his plumes to cool,
And court the flower that cheapens his array.
Rhodora! if the sages ask thee why
This charm is wasted on the earth and sky,   10
Tell them, dear, that if eyes were made for seeing,
Then Beauty is its own excuse for being:
Why thou wert there, O rival of the rose!
I never thought to ask, I never knew;
But, in my simple ignorance, suppose   15
The self-same Power that brought me there brought you.

TEXTS

(A) MS Am 1569.7 (205), Houghton Library, Harvard University, printer's copy for B; (B) *Western Messenger,* VII (July 1839): 166; (C) MS, m.b., Berg Collection,

Poems (1847)

by permission of the New York Public Library, printer's copy for D; (D) *Poems* (London, 1847), 44; (E) *Poems* (Boston, 1847), 59; (F) *Poems* (Boston, 1858), 59; (G) *Poems* (Boston, 1865), 60–61; (H) *Selected Poems* (Boston, 1876), 58; (I) *Poems* [Riverside] (Boston, 1884), 39; (I²) *Poems* [Centenary] (Boston, 1904), 37–38. Rufus Wilmot Griswold reprinted the poem from (B) in *The Poets and Poetry of America* (Philadelphia, 1842), 238, and again in *The Poetry of Flowers* (Philadelphia, 1844), 62.

Pre-copy-text forms: Early fair copies are preserved in notebooks CSA and P (see *PN*, 902).

VARIANTS

Title: THE RHODORA: ON BEING ASKED, WHENCE IS THE FLOWER? (C, E-I) I THE RHODORA. LINES ON BEING ASKED, WHENCE IS THE FLOWER? (A-B) I THE RHODORA, ON BEING ASKED, WHENCE IS THE FLOWER. (D)
1   sea-winds (C-I) I seawinds (A) I sea winds (B)
3   nook, (B-I) I nook (A)
4   desert (A-B, D-I) I desart (C) II brook. (A, C-E, G-I) I brook; (B) I brook (F)
5   petals, (E-I) I petals (A-D) II pool, (E-I) I pool (A-D)
6   water (A, C-I) I waters (B)
7–8 Here . . . array. (C-I) I—Young Raphael might covet such a school; /

The lively show beguiled me from my way. (A-B; *dash omitted in* B)
10   earth (C-I) I marsh (A-B)
11   Tell them, dear, (A, C-I) I Dear, tell them, (B) II that (A-B, E-I) I that, (C-D)
12   Beauty (E-I) I beauty (A-D) II being: (A, E-I) I being. (B) I being; (C-D)
14   ask, (A, E-I) I ask; (B-D) II knew; (C-G) I knew (A) I knew, (B) I knew: (H-I)
15   But, (E-J) I But (A-D) II ignorance, (E-J) I ignorance (A-D)
16   self-same (A-G, I) I selfsame (H) II Power (A-C, E-I) I power (D) II there (A-B, E-I) I there, (C-D)

NOTES

10.   The line recalls Thomas Gray's "Elegy Written in a Country Churchyard" (1751): "Full many a flower is born to blush unseen, / And waste its sweetness on the desert air" (lines 55–56); but it may also recall Edward Young's lines from *The Love of Fame*, "Satire V" (1728): "In distant wilds, by human eyes unseen, / She rears her flowers, and spreads her velvet green; / Pure gurgling rills the lonely desert trace, / And waste their music on the savage race" (lines 230–233).

THE HUMBLE-BEE.

Two months into the presidency of Martin Van Buren, American banks started collapsing, the result of years of unrestrained speculation during the boom times of Andrew Jackson. As Emerson would shortly discover, the personal meaning of the Panic of 1837 was that the regular quarterly dividends from his bank stocks —a welcome supplement to his income from lecturing—failed to appear. On 14 May he declared that "The humblebee & the pine warbler seem to me the proper objects of attention in these disastrous times" (*JMN*, V, 327), while the actual writing of the poem is acknowledged in the entry for 9 May: "Yesterday in the woods I followed the fine humble bee with rhymes & fancies fine" (ibid.). The poem was an especial favorite with Elizabeth Hoar, who, as Emerson acknowledged, "first persuaded me to print some rhymes" (*L*, VII, 592; see also *L*, II, 78). "The Humble-Bee," along with "Each and All," were the first of Emerson's poems to appear in a magazine—in the February 1839 issue of James Freeman Clarke's *Western Messenger* (see *L*, VII, 327–328).

In January 1844 the manuscript that had served as printer's copy for the *Western Messenger* figured in a private demonstration of the mesmeric powers of Anna Q. T. Parsons, held at the Boston home of the manuscript's owner, James Freeman Clarke, lately returned from the West. According to Margaret Fuller, Parsons, upon touching the document, declared the writer to be "holy, true, and brave," which Fuller took to be strong evidence of Parsons' clairvoyance (*FuL*, III, 177).

In 1846, lines 44–47 were transferred to the poem from Emerson's unfinished and eventually abandoned composition, "Where the fungus broad & red" (*PN*, 820, 968–69). Elizabeth Hoar particularly admired these lines and urged Emerson to preserve them by adding them to "The Humble-Bee" (*ETE*, I, 553–554). The poem—one of Emerson's most popular—bears a striking resemblance to Alfred Tennyson's "The Grasshopper," which Emerson knew from the rare first edition of *Poems, Chiefly Lyrical* (London, 1830) that he had acquired as early as 1831 (*L*, I, 341).

THE HUMBLE-BEE.

Burly, dozing humble-bee,
Where thou art is clime for me.
Let them sail for Porto Rique,
Far-off heats through seas to seek;
I will follow thee alone,   5
Thou animated torrid-zone!
Zigzag steerer, desert cheerer,
Let me chase thy waving lines;
Keep me nearer, me thy hearer,
Singing over shrubs and vines.   10

Insect lover of the sun,
Joy of thy dominion!
Sailor of the atmosphere;
Swimmer through the waves of air;
Voyager of light and noon;   15
Epicurean of June;
Wait, I prithee, till I come
Within earshot of thy hum,—
All without is martyrdom.

When the south wind, in May days,   20
With a net of shining haze
Silvers the horizon wall,
And, with softness touching all,
Tints the human countenance
With a color of romance,   25
And, infusing subtle heats,
Turns the sod to violets,
Thou, in sunny solitudes,

Rover of the underwoods,
The green silence dost displace   30
With thy mellow, breezy bass.

Hot midsummer's petted crone,
Sweet to me thy drowsy tone
Tells of countless sunny hours,
Long days, and solid banks of flowers;   35
Of gulfs of sweetness without bound
In Indian wildernesses found;
Of Syrian peace, immortal leisure,
Firmest cheer, and bird-like pleasure.

Aught unsavory or unclean   40
Hath my insect never seen;
But violets and bilberry bells,
Maple-sap, and daffodels,
Grass with green flag half-mast high,
Succory to match the sky,   45
Columbine with horn of honey,
Scented fern, and agrimony,
Clover, catchfly, adder's-tongue,
And brier-roses, dwelt among;
All beside was unknown waste,   50
All was picture as he passed.

Wiser far than human seer,
Yellow-breeched philosopher!
Seeing only what is fair,
Sipping only what is sweet,   55
Thou dost mock at fate and care,
Leave the chaff, and take the wheat.
When the fierce north-western blast
Cools sea and land so far and fast,
Thou already slumberest deep;   60
Woe and want thou canst outsleep;
Want and woe, which torture us,
Thy sleep makes ridiculous.

Poems (1847)

TEXTS

(A) MS Am 1569.7 (204), Houghton Library, Harvard University, printer's copy for B; (B) *Western Messenger* 6 (February 1839): 239–241; (C) MS Am 1280.221, Ralph Waldo Emerson Memorial Association deposit, Houghton Library, Harvard University, printer's copy for D; (D) *Poems* (London, 1847), 45–47; (E) *Poems* (Boston, 1847), 60–63; (F) *Poems* ["Fourth Edition"] (Boston, 1847), 60–63; (G) *Poems* (Boston, 1865), 62–65; (H) *Selected Poems* (Boston, 1876), 59–61; (I) *Poems* [Riverside] (Boston, 1884), 39–41; (I²) *Poems* [Centenary] (Boston, 1904), 38–40. Printings in 1850 and 1857 are identical to (F) except that plate damage to the end of l. 61 in the former is corrected in the latter. Reprinted from (B) by Rufus Wilmot Griswold first in *The Notion* (1841), then in *The Poets and Poetry of America* (Philadelphia, 1842), 238. Emerson's letter to Griswold of 25 September 1841 (*L*, VII, 472) shows that he did not offer revisions.

Pre-copy-text forms: An erased draft and a fair copy occur in poetry notebook P (see *PN*, 819–820). A copy that Emerson wrote out for Richard Henry Stoddard in 1858, now in the New York Public Library, is textually identical to (F).

VARIANTS

Title: THE HUMBLE-BEE. (E-G, I) | To the Humble-bee. (A) | TO THE HUMBLE-BEE (B) | ↑ The ↓ Humble-Bee. (C) | THE HUMBLE BEE. (D) | THE HUMBLEBEE. (H)

1 Burly, dozing humble-bee, (F-G, I) | Fine humble-bee! fine humble-bee! (A-B) | <Portly> ↑ Burly ↓ dozing humblebee! (C) | Burly dozing humble bee! (D) | Burly, dozing, humble-bee, (E) | Burly, dozing humblebee, (H)

4 Far-off (E-I) | Far off (A-D) || seek; (E-I) | seek,— (A-B) | seek, (C-D)

6 torrid-zone! (C-I) | torrid zone! (A-B)

7 Zigzag (E-I) | Zig-zag (A-D) || desert cheerer, (A-B, E-I) | desart-cheerer, (C) | desert-cheerer (D)

8 lines; (E-G, I) | lines, (A-D) | lines: (H)

10–11 vines. / [*white line*] / Insect (D-I) | vines. / [*white line*] / Flower bells, / Honied cells,— / These the tents / Which he frequents. / [*white line*] / Insect (A-C) [B has "Flower-bells,"; C, *in which the lines are canceled, omits the dash in the second line*]

13 atmosphere; (E-I) | atmosphere, (A-D)

14 air; (E-I) | air, (A-D)

15 noon; (E-I) | noon, (A-D)

16 June; (E-I) | June, (A-D)

17 Wait, (A-C, E-J) | Wait (D)

18 earshot (A-C, E-I) | ear shot (D)

20 south wind, (B, D-G, I) | South wind, (A) | southwind, (C) | south-wind, (H) || May days (A-B, D-I) | May-days (C)

21 haze (E-I) | haze, (A-D)

23 And, (C-H) | And (A-B, I)

25 color (A-B, E-I) | colour (C-D)

26 And, (C-H) | And (A-B, I) || heats, (C-I) | heats (A-B)

The Humble-Bee

27 violets, (C-I) | violets,— (A-B)

28 Thou, (E-I) | Thou (A-D) ||
sunny (A-B, D-I) | su<mmer>nny (C)

30 displace (A-C, E-I) | displace,
(D)

31 mellow, (E-I) | mellow (A-D)

33 tone (E-I) | tune, (A-D)

34 Tells (E-I) | Telling (A-D)

35 flowers; (E-I) | flowers, (A-D)

37 found; (E-I) | found, (A-D)

38 leisure, (A, C-I) | leisure. (B)

39 cheer, (A-B, E-I) | cheer (C-D)

40 unsavory (A-B, E-I) | unsavoury
(C-D) || unclean (A-C, E-I) | unclean,
(D)

41 seen; (E-I) | seen, (A-D)

42 violets (C-I) | violets, (A-B)

43 Maple-sap, (E-H) | Maple sap,
(A-B) | Maple-sap (C, I) | Maple sap
(D) || daffodels, (A-G, I) | daffodils,
(H)

44–47 [*Four lines added in* (C) *and
continued without alteration thereafter*]

48 adder's-tongue, (F-H) |
adderstongue, (A) | adders-tongue
(B) | adders-tongue, (C-D) | adder's
tongue, (E) | adder's-tongue (I)

49 brier-roses, (F-I) | briar roses (A,
C) | brier-roses (B) | briar-roses (D) |
brier roses, (CC1, E) || among; (C-I) |
among. (A-B)

53 philosopher! (C-I) | philosopher,
(A-B)

55 sweet, (A, C-I) | sweet (B)

57 chaff, (E-I) | chaff (A-D)

58 north-western (D-F) |
northwestern (A-C, G-I)

59 fast, (C-I) | fast,— (A-B)

60 deep; (E-I) | deep, (A-B) | deep,
— (C-D)

61 Woe (E-I) | Wo (A-D) || outsleep;
(A-B, E-I) | outsleep,— (C) | out-
sleep,— (D)

62 woe, (E-I) | wo (A-D)

NOTES

3. During the ante-bellum period, New England sufferers from tuberculosis often sought relief in travelling to Puerto Rico. Among these were Emerson's brothers, Charles and Edward; Edward died there in 1834. At the time "The Humble-Bee" was written Emerson's own health was precarious, and he thought of making a similar trip (*L*, II, 83).

38. "Syrian peace" may allude to the Hebrew Bible's representation of Canaan (or Syria) as "a land of milk and honey," or perhaps to the enervating climate of the extensive Syrian Desert.

48. Emerson recorded Thoreau's opinion that "The adderstongue arethusa smells exactly like a snake" (*TN*, I, 560).

BERRYING.

An erased pencil draft of this poem occurs in a journal that Emerson kept between April 1846 and February 1847. If composed during the regular season for blackberry-picking, it would date, as Edward suggests (*W,* IX, 419), to late summer, either August or September. "Berrying" evidently owes its origin to a journal entry of September 1841, featuring Emerson's autobiographical persona "Osman":

> Osman said that when he went a-berrying the devil got into the blueberries & tempted him to eat a bellyful, but if he came into a spring of water he would wash his hands & mouth & promise himself that he would eat no more. Instantly the devil would come to him again in the shape of larger & fairer berries than any he had yet found, & if he still passed them by, he would bring him blackberries, and if that would not serve, then grapes. He said, of one thing he was persuaded, that wisdom & berries grew on the same bushes, but that only one could ever be plucked at one time. (*JMN,* VIII, 50).

In 1855 Emerson read this poem to his twenty-three year old protégé, Franklin Benjamin Sanborn, and asked him what he thought it meant. "I hardly knew what to reply," recalled Sanborn, "where several meanings were possible; but said that he must have meant that Nature does not leave her least particle without a lesson for Man; that the moral of the delicious flavor of the low blackberry was, 'Even so, what seems black to you in Man's destiny may have as fair an issue.'" Emerson smiled at this interpretation, but did not comment. Sanborn, an earnest young school-teacher at this time, understood that his impromptu statement no doubt revealed more about himself than about the poem (Sanborn, *The Personality of Emerson* [Boston, 1903], 79).

BERRYING.

'May be true what I had heard,—
Earth's a howling wilderness,
Truculent with fraud and force,'
Said I, strolling through the pastures,
And along the river-side.   5
Caught among the blackberry vines,
Feeding on the Ethiops sweet,
Pleasant fancies overtook me.
I said, 'What influence me preferred,
Elect, to dreams thus beautiful?'   10
The vines replied, 'And didst thou deem
No wisdom from our berries went?'

TEXTS

(A) MS HM 7625, by permission of the Huntington Library, San Marino, California, printer's copy for B; (B) *Poems* (London, 1847), 48; (C) *Poems* (Boston, 1847), 64; (D) *Poems* (Boston, 1863), 64; (E) *Poems* (Boston, 1865), 66; (F) *Poems* [Riverside] (Boston, 1884), 41–42; (F²) *Poems* [Centenary] (Boston, 1904), 41. "Berrying" was omitted from *Selected Poems* (Boston, 1876), evidently at the suggestion of Franklin B. Sanborn and over the objections of James Elliot Cabot (*ETE*, II, 197).

Pre-copy-text forms: A draft of the poem occurs in erased pencil in Journal O (*JMN*, IX, 420–421).

VARIANTS

1 heard,— (C-F) | heard, (A-B)
2 wilderness, (C-F) | wilderness (A-B)
8 me. (C-F) | me: (A-B)
9 influence (B-F) | <fortune>

↑influence↓ (A) ‖ preferred, (C-F) | preferred (A-B)
10 Elect, (C-F) | Elect (A-B)
12 from (CC4, CC9, D, F) | to (A-C, E) ‖ went?' (B-F) | went? (A)

NOTES

2. The phrase, from Deuteronomy 32:10, had been appropriated by New England's Puritan settlers to convey their antagonistic sense of nature in the New World.

7. Perhaps a recollection of Keats, *Endymion,* II, 412–413: "the ivy mesh, / Shading its Ethiop berries."

10. According to the old Puritan doctrine, only a fraction of mankind would be among the "elect": those who experienced saving grace, a free and arbitrary gift of God.

THE SNOW-STORM.

When the heavy snowfall of 29 December 1834 struck Concord, Emerson was living in the upstairs back room of the Old Manse, the home of his step-grandfather, the Reverend Ezra Ripley. That evening he wrote in his journal:

> The great willowtree over my roof is the trumpet & accompaniment of the storm & gives due importance to every caprice of the gale and the trees in the avenue announce the same facts with equal din to the front tenants. Hoarse concert: they roar like the rigging of a ship in a tempest. (*JMN,* IV, 384)

The language about the trumpet and the annunciation, as Alan D. Hodder has pointed out (*Emerson's Rhetoric of Revelation* [University Park, Pa., 1989], 47)—and as the full context of the journal passage shows—reflects Emerson's adverse response to his grandfather's dutifully apocalyptic preaching (cf. Matthew 24:29–

31). A paragraph written earlier the same evening, in which Emerson hoped that he might eventually clarify "the distinction between a spiritual & a traditional religion," begins, oddly, with an allusion to the storm: "To the music of the surly storm that thickens the darkness of the night abroad & rocks the walls & fans my cheek through the chinks & cracks, I would sing my strain though hoarse & small" (*JMN*, IV, 382). The journal entries of that day suggest that Emerson's awareness of the end-of-the-world weather and the character of his religious speculations were closely conjoined, even as they would be again when, in a famous passage from the Divinity School Address, another formalist Concord preacher, Barzillai Frost, appeared in the pulpit as a merely "spectral" figure in counterpoint to the real snow-storm evident through the window behind him (*CW*, I, 85).

Probably within a day or two of the blizzard (after emerging into the transfigured landscape of the morning after) Emerson wrote "The Snow-Storm," first in prose form (not his usual practice), yet with such intermittent capitalization as to show that he knew it was poetry already (*JMN*, VI, 246). Here the power that descends out of "heaven" to transform the world is no less the divine architect than the figure envisioned in traditional apocalypses. The prehistory of architecture, as of the other arts, lay for Emerson in the primary forms of nature, an insight that guided all his aesthetic theorizing of the period, as, for example, in his consideration, in the first lecture he ever gave, of the beauty and usefulness of falling and fallen snow (*EL*, I, 15; cf. *JMN*, IV, 60–62). A brief but concentrated discussion of this natural artistry occurs also in the essay "History" (1841), in the course of which he mentions having seen "a snow-drift along the sides of the stone wall which obviously gave the idea of the common architectural scroll to abut a tower" (*CW*, II, 11).

The treatment of the poem by Carl F. Strauch in "The Year of Emerson's Poetic Maturity: 1834" (*Philological Quarterly*, XXXIV [October 1955]: 373–377) mainly concerns Emerson's dependence on the writings of the Cambridge Platonist Ralph Cudworth, from which "spring directly" the poem's "central ideas": that "nature, in a frolic mood and in the briefest span of time, has created an architecture which the art of man can laboriously mimic only through long ages" (374).

THE SNOW-STORM.

Announced by all the trumpets of the sky,
Arrives the snow, and, driving o'er the fields,
Seems nowhere to alight: the whited air
Hides hills and woods, the river, and the heaven,
And veils the farm-house at the garden's end.   5
The sled and traveller stopped, the courier's feet
Delayed, all friends shut out, the housemates sit
Around the radiant fireplace, enclosed
In a tumultuous privacy of storm.

    Come see the north wind's masonry.   10
Out of an unseen quarry evermore
Furnished with tile, the fierce artificer
Curves his white bastions with projected roof
Round every windward stake, or tree, or door.
Speeding, the myriad-handed, his wild work   15
So fanciful, so savage, nought cares he
For number or proportion. Mockingly,
On coop or kennel he hangs Parian wreaths;
A swan-like form invests the hidden thorn;
Fills up the farmer's lane from wall to wall,   20
Maugre the farmer's sighs; and, at the gate,
A tapering turret overtops the work.
And when his hours are numbered, and the world
Is all his own, retiring, as he were not,
Leaves, when the sun appears, astonished Art   25
To mimic in slow structures, stone by stone,
Built in an age, the mad wind's night-work,
The frolic architecture of the snow.

The Snow-Storm

(A) *Dial,* I (January 1841): 339; (B) MS, m.b., Berg Collection, by permission of the New York Public Library, printer's copy for C; (C) *Poems* (London, 1847), 49–50; (D) *Poems* (Boston, 1847), 66–67; (E) *Selected Poems* (Boston, 1876), 66–67; (F) *Poems* [Riverside] (Boston, 1884), 42–43; (F²) *Poems* [Centenary] (Boston, 1904), 41–42. No variants occur in later printings from the plates made for (D), nor in *Poems* (Boston, 1865), 67–68, a new setting of type. Rufus W. Griswold reprinted the poem from (A) in *Poets and Poetry of America* (Philadelphia, 1842), 238.

Format: Line 1 indented (D). No white line after line 9 (B-C).

Pre-copy-text forms: The earliest draft, in *JMN,* VI, 246, is lightly revised in two drafts in notebook P, one of which is dated "29 Dec" (see the discussion at *PN,* 918).

VARIANTS

Title: THE SNOW-STORM. (A, D-F) | *The snow-storm.* (B) | THE SNOW STORM (C)

1 sky, (D-F) | sky (A-C)

2 and, (B-F) | and (A)

4 river, (A, D-F) | river (B-C)

5 farm-house (A, C-F) | farmhouse (B)

6 sled (A-B, D-F) | steed (C)

8 fireplace, (B, D-F) | fire-place, (A, C)

10 Come (A, D-F) | Come, (B-C) || north wind's (C-D, F) | north-wind's (A, E) | northwind's (B)

16 nought (A-D, F) | naught (E)

17 Mockingly, (D-F) | Mockingly (A-C)

19 thorn; (A-F) | thorn, (CC5)

21 sighs; (D-F) | sighs, (A-C) || and, (D-E) | and (A-C, F) || gate, (D-E) | gate (A-C, F)

22 work. (A-D, F) | work: (E)

26 structures, (A, C-F) | structures (B) || by stone, (A, D-F) | by stone (B-C)

NOTES

1–9. John Greenleaf Whittier chose this passage as the epigraph for his popular *Snow-Bound* (1866).

18. Since the white, unglazed bisque porcelain known as Parian ware, which became a popular Victorian decorative item, was introduced by Staffordshire

potters a year after Emerson's poem was published, the reference has to be to the fine marble mined at the island of Paros and favored by Greeks and Romans for their classic sculpture—after which the English pottery was named.

WOODNOTES.

I.

Drafts of the several sections of "Woodnotes," likely dating to 1835, are to be found in early pages of Notebook P, which Emerson began to use in December 1834 (see *PN*, 16, 972–973). The poem—or at least its third and fourth sections—hearkens back to Emerson's excursions into the forest north of Bangor, Maine, during July 1834. Probably it was this work that Emerson sent to Margaret Fuller toward the end of April 1840 for publication in the *Dial*, saying in the cover letter that he was enclosing "the old rhymes you asked for—You will see I have tacked them together so as to form a sort of whole—but it is so rude & unwieldy that it is not worth preserving if you prefer to print only one of them or two at two times. It was E[lizabeth] H[oar] & not I who said they wd. pass muster" (*L*, II, 288; cf. Myerson, *The New England Transcendentalists and the* Dial [Rutherford, N.J., 1980], 238 n. 9). Fuller declined to break up this suite of poems, with the result that it was crowded out of the *Dial*'s first issue and appeared in the second (*FuL*, II, 147). Included in *Selected Poems* (1876), "Woodnotes I" was abridged by the omission of the third section and by the trimming and revising of the opening; the former intervention has to be accounted unfortunate, the latter less so. As with other revisions introduced in this late collection, it is unclear just whose aesthetic judgment was at work.

WOODNOTES.

I.

1.

For this present, hard
Is the fortune of the bard,
   Born out of time;
All his accomplishment,
From Nature's utmost treasure spent,   5
   Booteth not him.
When the pine tosses its cones
To the song of its waterfall tones,
He speeds to the woodland walks,
To birds and trees he talks: 10
Cæsar of his leafy Rome,
There the poet is at home.
He goes to the river-side,—
Not hook nor line hath he;
He stands in the meadows wide,—   15
Nor gun nor scythe to see;
With none has he to do,
And none seek him,
Nor men below,
Nor spirits dim.   20
Sure some god his eye enchants:
What he knows nobody wants.
In the wood he travels glad,
Without better fortune had,
Melancholy without bad.   25
Planter of celestial plants,
What he knows nobody wants;
What he knows he hides, not vaunts.

Knowledge this man prizes best
Seems fantastic to the rest: 30
Pondering shadows, colors, clouds,
Grass-buds, and caterpillar-shrouds,
Boughs on which the wild bees settle,
Tints that spot the violets' petal,
Why Nature loves the number five,   35
And why the star-form she repeats:
Lover of all things alive,
Wonderer at all he meets,
Wonderer chiefly at himself,—
Who can tell him what he is?   40
Or how meet in human elf
Coming and past eternities?

                    2.

And such I knew, a forest seer,
A minstrel of the natural year,
Foreteller of the vernal ides,   45
Wise harbinger of spheres and tides,
A lover true, who knew by heart
Each joy the mountain dales impart;
It seemed that Nature could not raise
A plant in any secret place,   50
In quaking bog, on snowy hill,
Beneath the grass that shades the rill,
Under the snow, between the rocks,
In damp fields known to bird and fox,
But he would come in the very hour   55
It opened in its virgin bower,
As if a sunbeam showed the place,
And tell its long-descended race.
It seemed as if the breezes brought him;
It seemed as if the sparrows taught him;   60
As if by secret sight he knew
Where, in far fields, the orchis grew.
Many haps fall in the field

Seldom seen by wishful eyes,
But all her shows did Nature yield,   65
To please and win this pilgrim wise.
He saw the partridge drum in the woods;
He heard the woodcock's evening hymn;
He found the tawny thrush's broods;
And the shy hawk did wait for him;   70
What others did at distance hear,
And guessed within the thicket's gloom,
Was showed to this philosopher,
And at his bidding seemed to come.

3.

In unploughed Maine he sought the lumberers' gang,   75
Where from a hundred lakes young rivers sprang;
He trode the unplanted forest floor, whereon
The all-seeing sun for ages hath not shone;
Where feeds the moose, and walks the surly bear,
And up the tall mast runs the woodpecker.   80
He saw beneath dim aisles, in odorous beds,
The slight Linnæa hang its twin-born heads,
And blessed the monument of the man of flowers,
Which breathes his sweet fame through the northern bowers.
He heard, when in the grove, at intervals,   85
With sudden roar the aged pine-tree falls,—
One crash, the death-hymn of the perfect tree,
Declares the close of its green century.
Low lies the plant to whose creation went
Sweet influence from every element;   90
Whose living towers the years conspired to build,
Whose giddy top the morning loved to gild.
Through these green tents, by eldest Nature dressed,
He roamed, content alike with man and beast.
Where darkness found him he lay glad at night;   95
There the red morning touched him with its light.
Three moons his great heart him a hermit made,
So long he roved at will the boundless shade.

The timid it concerns to ask their way,
And fear what foe in caves and swamps can stray,   100
To make no step until the event is known,
And ills to come as evils past bemoan.
Not so the wise; no coward watch he keeps
To spy what danger on his pathway creeps;
Go where he will, the wise man is at home,   105
His hearth the earth,—his hall the azure dome;
Where his clear spirit leads him, there's his road,
By God's own light illumined and foreshowed.

4.

'Twas one of the charmed days,
When the genius of God doth flow,   110
The wind may alter twenty ways,
A tempest cannot blow;
It may blow north, it still is warm;
Or south, it still is clear;
Or east, it smells like a clover-farm;   115
Or west, no thunder fear.
The musing peasant lowly great
Beside the forest water sate;
The rope-like pine roots crosswise grown
Composed the network of his throne;   120
The wide lake, edged with sand and grass,
Was burnished to a floor of glass,
Painted with shadows green and proud
Of the tree and of the cloud.
He was the heart of all the scene;   125
On him the sun looked more serene;
To hill and cloud his face was known,—
It seemed the likeness of their own;
They knew by secret sympathy
The public child of earth and sky.   130
'You ask,' he said, 'what guide
Me through trackless thickets led,
Through thick-stemmed woodlands rough and wide?'—

I found the water's bed.
The watercourses were my guide;   135
I travelled grateful by their side,
Or through their channel dry;
They led me through the thicket damp,
Through brake and fern, the beavers' camp,
Through beds of granite cut my road,   140
And their resistless friendship showed.
The falling waters led me,
The foodful waters fed me,
And brought me to the lowest land,
Unerring to the ocean sand.   145
The moss upon the forest bark
Was polestar when the night was dark;
The purple berries in the wood
Supplied me necessary food;
For Nature ever faithful is   150
To such as trust her faithfulness.
When the forest shall mislead me,
When the night and morning lie,
When sea and land refuse to feed me,
'Twill be time enough to die;   155
Then will yet my mother yield
A pillow in her greenest field,
Nor the June flowers scorn to cover
The clay of their departed lover.

TEXTS

(A) *Dial*, I (October 1840): 242–245; (B) MS, m.b., Berg Collection, by permission of the New York Public Library, printer's copy for C; (C) *Poems* (London, 1847), 50–56; (D) *Poems* (Boston, 1847), 67–74; (E) *Poems* ["Fourth Edition"] (Boston, 1847), 67–74; (F) *Poems* (Boston, 1865), 69–77; (G) *Selected Poems* (Boston, 1876), 126–28, 130; (H) *Poems* [Riverside] (Boston 1884), 43–47; (I) *Poems* [Centenary] (Boston, 1904), 43–48. The discontinuous pagination in (G) is the result of an error of imposition whereby the last full page of text was transposed with the first page of "Woodnotes II." "Woodnotes I" was reprinted from (A) in

Poems (1847)

Our Pastors' Offering (Boston, 1845), 70–76, a volume edited by Chandler Robbins, Emerson's successor as minister at the Second Church. In a letter of 2 March 1845 (*L*, VIII, 11–12) Emerson explained why he could not oblige Robbins, on short notice, with an original contribution, but allowed him to choose among poems in print. It is highly unlikely, therefore, that Emerson was responsible for the altered punctuation in lines 34 ("violet's"), 95 ("him," and "night."), 106 ("earth;"), 132 ("led:"), and 147 ("dark;"), or for the substitution of "traveled" for "travelled" in line 136.

Format: The use of Arabic numerals to designate poem sections, introduced in (B), has been adopted. Lines 3 and 6 set flush (B-C).

Pre-copy-text forms: See *PN*, 972–973.

VARIANTS

Title: WOODNOTES. / I. / 1. (D-E, G-H) I WOODNOTES. / I. (A) I Woodnotes. / I. (B) I WOOD NOTES. / I. (C) I WOOD-NOTES. / I. / I. (F) I WOODNOTES / I / I (I)

1–6 [*Lines canceled in* (CC1, CC5), *not present in* (G-H); *present in* (I) *only in the note at pp. 419–420*]

1 present, (A-F) I present (I)

2 bard, (D-F) I bard (A-C, I)

4 accomplishment, (D-F) I accomplishment (A-C, I)

5 Nature's (D-F, I) I nature's (A-C) II spent, (D-F) I spent (A-C, I)

6 <Booteth> ↑ /Avails/Helpeth/ Contents/Filleth/ ↓ [*Emendation precedes cancellation of ll. 1–6*] (CC1) I <Booteth> ↑ Contenteth ↓ [*Emendation precedes cancellation of ll. 1–6*] (CC5)

9 He (A-F) I Who (CC1, CC5, G-I) II walks, (A-F) I walks? (G-I)

10 he (A-F) I who (G-I) II talks: (A, D-F) I talks (B) I talks. (C) I talks? (G-I) I ↑ Who ↓ To birds and <trees he> ↑ the forest ↓ talks<:> ↑ ? ↓

(CC1) I trees <he> ↑ who ↓ talks<;> (CC5)

12 poet (A, C-I) I Poet (B)

13 river-side,— (D-I) I river side,— (A-C)

14 he; (D-I) I he: (A-C)

16 see; (A-F) I see: (G) I see. (H-I)

17–20 [*Lines canceled in* (CC1, CC5), *not present in* (G-H); *present in* (I) *only in the note at p. 420, where it is quoted without variation from* (A)]

21 enchants: (D-I) I enchants:— (A) I enchants, (B-C)

22 knows (D-I) I knows, (A-C) II wants. (B-I) I wants: (A)

23 glad, (D-I) I glad (A-C)

26–28 [*Lines canceled in* (CC1, CC5), *not present in* (G-H); *present in* (I) *only in the note at p. 420, where it is quoted without variation from* (A)]

27 knows (A, D-F) I knows, (B-C) II wants; (A, D-F) I wants,— (B-C)

28 knows (D-F) I knows, (A-C)

30 rest: (D-I) I rest; (A) I rest, (B-C)

31 colors, (A-B, D-I) I colours, (C)

32 Grass-buds, (D-G) I Grass buds,

Woodnotes, I

(A-C) I Grass-buds (H-I) II caterpillar-shrouds, (D-I) I caterpillars' shrouds, (A-C)

34 violets' (A, D-E) I violets (B) I violet's (C, F-I)

35 Nature (D-I) I nature (A-C)

36 repeats: (D-I) I repeats;— (A) I repeats, (B-C)

39 himself,— (A-F) I himself, (G-I)

40 is? (D-I) I is; (A) I is, (B-C)

47 true, (A, D-I) I true (B-C)

49 Nature (D-I) I nature (A-C)

54 fox, (A-C, E-H) I fox (D) I fox. (I)

57 sunbeam (A-B, D-I) I sun-beam (C)

58 long-descended (B-I) I long descended (A)

59 him; (D-H) I him, (A-C, I)

60 him; (D-I) I him, (A-C)

62 where, (D-I) I where (A-C) II fields, (D-I) I fields (A-C)

63 Many haps fall (D-I) I There are many events (A-C) II field (B-I) I field, (A)

64 Seldom seen by wishful (D-I) I Which are not shown to common (A-C) II eyes, (A-G, I) I eyes; (H)

65 Nature yield, (D-I) I nature yield (A-C)

67 woods; (D-I) I woods, (A-C)

68 hymn; (D-I) I hymn, (A-C)

69 thrush's (A-F) I thrushes (CC1) I thrushes' (CC5, G-I) II broods; (D-I) I broods, (A-C)

70 him; (D-I) I him. (A-C)

73 showed (A-G) I shown (H-I)

75–108 [*Entire third section canceled* (CC1); *not present* (G), *with following section renumbered* "3"]

75 Maine (A, D-F, H-I) I Maine, (B) I maine, (C) II lumberers' (A, D-I) I lumberer's (B-C) II gang, (A-D) I gang (E-F, H-I) [*Some copies of* Poems

["Fourth Edition"*] (Boston, 1850) have the comma*]

76 sprang; (B-F, H-I) I sprang, (A)

77 trode (A-B, D-F, H-I) I trod (C) II forest floor, (D-F, H-I) I forest floor (A) I forest-floor, (B-C)

78 shone; (A, D-F, H-I) I shone, (B-C)

79 moose, (A-B, CC10, CC11, D-F, H-I) I mouse, (C)

81 saw (A, D-F, H-I) I saw, (B-C) II aisles, (B-F, H-I) I aisles (A) II beds, (B-F, H-I) I beds (A)

84 northern (A-B, D-F, H-I) I Northern (C)

85 heard, (D-F, H-I) I heard (A-C) II grove, (B-F, H-I) I grove (A) II intervals, (B-F, H-I) I intervals (A)

86 pine-tree (C-F, H-I) I pinetree (A-B)

87 crash, (A, D-F, H-I) I crash (B-C) II perfect (A, C-F, H-I) I <falling>perfect (B)

92 gild. (A-B, D-F, H-I) I guild. (C)

93 Nature dressed, (D-F, H-I) I nature drest, (A-C)

94 roamed, (B-F, H-I) I roamed (A) II beast. (B-F, H-I) I beast: (A)

95 him (A, D-F, H-I) I him, (B-C) II night; (B-F, H-I) I night, (A)

99 way, (A-E, H-I) I way; (F)

100 can stray, (A, C-F, H-I) I <may> ↑can ↓ stray, (B)

102 bemoan. (A, D-F, H-I) I bemoan: (B-C)

103 keeps (A-B, D-F, H-I) I keeps, (C)

106 earth,— (D-F, H-I) I earth;— (A-C) II dome; (B-F, H-I) I dome, (A)

107 road, (A-F, H) I road (I)

109 'Twas (A, C-I) I Twas (B) II charmed (A-F, H) I charméd (CC1, G) I charmèd (I) II days, (A, D-G) I days (B-C, H-I)

110   flow, (A-H) I flow; (I)
112   blow; (D-I) I blow: (A-C)
115   clover-farm; (D-E, G-I) I clover farm (A-C, F)
117   peasant (A-H) I peasant, (I) II great (A-H) I great, (I)
118   sate; (D-I) I sat: (A) I sate: (B-C)
119   pine roots (A, D-F, H) I pine-roots (B-C, G, I)
120   throne; (B-I) I throne, (A)
121   lake, (D-I) I lake (A-C) II grass, (D-I) I grass (A-C)
123   proud (A-E, G-I) I proud, (F)
125   scene; (A, D-I) I scene, (B-C)
126   serene; (D-I) I serene, (A-C)
127   known,— (D-I) I known, (A-C)
128   own; (A, D-I) I own. (B-C)
131   'You ask,' (D-I) I You ask, (A-C) II 'what (D-I) I what (A-C) II guide (A-B, D-I) I guide, (C)
133   thick-stemmed (A, C-I) I

thickstemmed (B) II wide?'— (G) I wide; (A) I wide? (B-F) I wide. (H-I)
134   water's bed. (A, D-I) I water ↑ s ↓ '<s> bed: (B) I waters' bed: (C)
135   watercourses (A, D-F, H-I) I water-courses (G) II guide; (D-I) I guide, (A) II [*Line not present* (B-C)]
139   fern, (B-I) I fern (A)
141   showed. (B-C, I) I showed; (A, D-F) I showed: (G-H)
147   polestar (A-B, D-E, G) I pole-star (C, F, H-I) II dark; (B-E, G-I) I dark, (A, F) [*The comma in* (F) *reproduces the form of the damaged semicolon in post-1856 copies of* Poems]
149   food; (D-I) I food. (A-C)
150   Nature (D-I) I nature (A-C)
155   'Twill (C-E) I 'T will (A, F-I) I T'will (B)
159   lover. (A-G) I lover.' (CC1, H-I)

NOTES

31–34.   These lines were used by Louisa May Alcott as the epigraph to her first book, *Flower Fables* (1855), a volume dedicated to Emerson's daughter Ellen.

35–36.   "Why am I more curious to know the reason why the star form is so oft repeated in botany or why the number five is such a favorite with nature, than to understand the circulation of the sap & the formation of buds?" (*JMN,* V, 42, 15 May 1835).

43.   In later years this reference was frequently assumed to be an allusion to young Henry David Thoreau. Edward's note (*W,* IX, 420) indicates an uncertainty as to the fact, but cites a family tradition that the passage was written "before he knew Thoreau's gifts and experiences." Franklin Benjamin Sanborn likewise denied the connection, apparently on direct information from Emerson (*The Personality of Emerson* [Boston, 1903], 70).

73.   This was an acceptable form of the past participle at the time of composition, according to *An American Dictionary of the English Language* (New York, 1843), but it had come to seem archaic by the time of the posthumous Riverside and Centenary editions, and was there changed to "shown."

75–76. Emerson spent most of July 1834 in Bangor, Maine, where he had gone to preach at the recently established Unitarian church. As he explained in a letter to Frederic Henry Hedge, the city "subsists by the lumber trade which brings all the timber from a vast territory through a hundred lakes & small streams down the Penobscot river" (*L*, VII, 227). He recorded his visit to the sawmills on 7 July (*JMN*, IV, 389).

77–78. These lines were taken from Emerson's "Poem, Spoken Before the Phi Beta Kappa Society, August, 1834": see Carl F. Strauch, "Emerson's Phi Beta Kappa Poem," *New England Quarterly* XXIII (March 1950): 84.

82. "8 July [1834]. Walked in the forest but found there some old acquaintances—the Medeola, Uraspermum, a new Pyrola, the Linnaea, Diervilla, & some unknown plants" (*JMN*, IV, 389). *Linnæa borealis americana,* or "twinflower," has five petals on each of its two blossoms (see line 35).

83–84. Carl von Linné, or Linnaeus (1707–1778), Swedish botanist and zoologist, devised the modern system of plant and animal taxonomy. Thoreau refers to Linnaeus as "the man of flowers" in an 1852 journal entry (*J*, V, 97).

85–90. "The pride of the forest—White pines of four feet diameter which it cost a hundred years of sun & rain & cold to rear must end in a sawmill at last" (*JMN*, IV, 389).

105. Emerson's journals contain several versions of the Spanish proverb he first recorded in 1832: "A good man is ever at home wherever he chance to be" (*JMN*, IV, 17; cf. *JMN*, V, 260 and VII, 332).

WOODNOTES.

II.

Emerson referred to an early draft of this work as "The Walden or Waldonian poems" and also as "The Pine-Tree" (*L*, II, 405; *L*, VII, 458) in contexts implying that it was known in this form to both Caroline Sturgis and Margaret Fuller. In mid-June 1841 he promised Fuller that she should have a revised and enlarged version for printing in the *Dial* by the twentieth. Completing the poem on 21 June, however, and conscious that he had overshot the deadline, Emerson rode to Cambridge to hand-deliver the manuscript, only to find that the July issue had already been made up (*L*, II, 407). Emerson seems at this point to have retained the manuscript, thinking that he might expand it further, but by mid-August when he returned it to Fuller, the poem had received no additions (*L*, II, 442). "Woodnotes II" would appear in the October number.

It seems likely that the earlier version derived from drafts in Emerson's notebook "Dialling" (*JMN*, VIII, 504–509), in which most of the poem's middle portion is represented, extending, with omissions, from line 188 to line 312. The event that prompted Emerson to expand "The Pine-Tree" was an outing to the "Cliff" (a hill near Walden Pond on the shore opposite the spot where Thoreau would build his hut) that according to Eleanor M. Tilton most likely took place on 7 June (*L*, VII, 458 and 455–456, n. 49). This picnic was attended by Emerson, Thoreau, and a number of ladies, including Caroline Sturgis—"my summer harp," as Emerson called her (*L*, VII, 457). In the notebook entitled "Books Small" are verses (cf. lines 251–273) based on an entry made at this time in "Dialling": "At the Cliff & charged nature with emptiness. That was the expression of the wide amphitheatre to the blank eye. It seemed as if the curtain should every moment rise & this maternal cluck which filled the groves & all this ado & flutter of small creatures give place to what is truly great. But thus is the particular & near ever standing in eternal <satire> contrast to the grand horizon of sun & stars that shuts down or shuts never down above it" (*JMN*, VIII, 458–459, 461–463, 494–495).

Regarding the central conceit of the arboreal narrator, Theodore Parker observed that "a pine-tree which should talk as Mr. Emerson's tree talks would deserve to be plucked up and cast into the sea" (reported, perhaps in paraphrase, by Thomas Wentworth Higginson, *Contemporaries* (Boston, 1899), 19, and quoted in Joel Myerson, *The New England Transcendentalists and the* Dial [Rutherford, N.J., 1980], 238, n. 9, which records as well the positive re-

sponses of Margaret Fuller and James Russell Lowell). The poem
is a strong advance on "Woodnotes I" and a work of notable philo-
sophical depth and nuance.

WOODNOTES.

II.

As sunbeams stream through liberal space,
And nothing jostle or displace,
So waved the pine-tree through my thought,
And fanned the dreams it never brought.

'Whether is better the gift or the donor?   5
Come to me,'
Quoth the pine-tree,
'I am the giver of honor.
My garden is the cloven rock,
And my manure the snow;   10
And drifting sand-heaps feed my stock,
In summer's scorching glow.
Ancient or curious,
Who knoweth aught of us?
Old as Jove,   15
Old as Love,
Who of me
Tells the pedigree?
Only the mountains old,
Only the waters cold,   20
Only moon and star
My coevals are.
Ere the first fowl sung
My relenting boughs among,
Ere Adam wived,   25
Ere Adam lived,
Ere the duck dived,
Ere the bees hived,

Ere the lion roared,
Ere the eagle soared,   30
Light and heat, land and sea,
Spake unto the oldest tree.
Glad in the sweet and secret aid
Which matter unto matter paid,
The water flowed, the breezes fanned,   35
The tree confined the roving sand,
The sunbeam gave me to the sight,
The tree adorned the formless light,
And once again
O'er the grave of men   40
We shall talk to each other again
Of the old age behind,
Of the time out of mind,
Which shall come again.

'Whether is better the gift or the donor?   45
Come to me,'
Quoth the pine-tree,
'I am the giver of honor.
He is great who can live by me.
The rough and bearded forester   50
Is better than the lord;
God fills the scrip and canister,
Sin piles the loaded board.
The lord is the peasant that was,
The peasant the lord that shall be;   55
The lord is hay, the peasant grass,
One dry, and one the living tree.
Genius with my boughs shall flourish,
Want and cold our roots shall nourish.
Who liveth by the ragged pine   60
Foundeth a heroic line;
Who liveth in the palace hall
Waneth fast and spendeth all.
He goes to my savage haunts,

With his chariot and his care;   65
My twilight realm he disenchants,
And finds his prison there.

'What prizes the town and the tower?
Only what the pine-tree yields;
Sinew that subdued the fields;   70
The wild-eyed boy, who in the woods
Chants his hymn to hills and floods,
Whom the city's poisoning spleen
Made not pale, or fat, or lean;
Whom the rain and the wind purgeth,   75
Whom the dawn and the day-star urgeth,
In whose cheek the rose-leaf blusheth,
In whose feet the lion rusheth,
Iron arms, and iron mould,
That know not fear, fatigue, or cold.   80
I give my rafters to his boat,
My billets to his boiler's throat;
And I will swim the ancient sea,
To float my child to victory,
And grant to dwellers with the pine   85
Dominion o'er the palm and vine.
Westward I ope the forest gates,
The train along the railroad skates;
It leaves the land behind like ages past,
The foreland flows to it in river fast;   90
Missouri I have made a mart,
I teach Iowa Saxon art.
Who leaves the pine-tree, leaves his friend,
Unnerves his strength, invites his end.
Cut a bough from my parent stem,   95
And dip it in thy porcelain vase;
A little while each russet gem
Will swell and rise with wonted grace;
But when it seeks enlarged supplies,
The orphan of the forest dies.   100

Whoso walketh in solitude,
And inhabiteth the wood,
Choosing light, wave, rock, and bird,
Before the money-loving herd,
Into that forester shall pass,   105
From these companions, power and grace.
Clean shall he be, without, within,
From the old adhering sin.
Love shall he, but not adulate
The all-fair, the all-embracing Fate;   110
All ill dissolving in the light
Of his triumphant piercing sight.
Not vain, sour, nor frivolous;
Not mad, athirst, nor garrulous;
Grave, chaste, contented, though retired,   115
And of all other men desired.
On him the light of star and moon
Shall fall with purer radiance down;
All constellations of the sky
Shed their virtue through his eye.   120
Him Nature giveth for defence
His formidable innocence;
The mounting sap, the shells, the sea,
All spheres, all stones, his helpers be;
He shall never be old;   125
Nor his fate shall be foretold;
He shall meet the speeding year,
Without wailing, without fear;
He shall be happy in his love,
Like to like shall joyful prove;   130
He shall be happy whilst he woos,
Muse-born, a daughter of the Muse.
But if with gold she bind her hair,
And deck her breast with diamond,
Take off thine eyes, thy heart forbear,   135
Though thou lie alone on the ground.
The robe of silk in which she shines,

It was woven of many sins;
And the shreds
Which she sheds   140
In the wearing of the same,
Shall be grief on grief,
And shame on shame.

'Heed the old oracles,
Ponder my spells;   145
Song wakes in my pinnacles
When the wind swells.
Soundeth the prophetic wind,
The shadows shake on the rock behind,
And the countless leaves of the pine are strings   150
Tuned to the lay the wood-god sings.
    Hearken! Hearken!
If thou wouldst know the mystic song
Chanted when the sphere was young.
Aloft, abroad, the pæan swells;   155
O wise man! hear'st thou half it tells?
O wise man! hear'st thou the least part?
'Tis the chronicle of art.
To the open ear it sings
Sweet the genesis of things,   160
Of tendency through endless ages,
Of star-dust, and star-pilgrimages,
Of rounded worlds, of space and time,
Of the old flood's subsiding slime,
Of chemic matter, force, and form,   165
Of poles and powers, cold, wet, and warm:
The rushing metamorphosis,
Dissolving all that fixture is,
Melts things that be to things that seem,
And solid nature to a dream.   170
O, listen to the undersong—
The ever old, the ever young;
And, far within those cadent pauses,

The chorus of the ancient Causes!
Delights the dreadful Destiny   175
To fling his voice into the tree,
And shock thy weak ear with a note
Breathed from the everlasting throat.
In music he repeats the pang
Whence the fair flock of Nature sprang.   180
O mortal! thy ears are stones;
These echoes are laden with tones
Which only the pure can hear;
Thou canst not catch what they recite
Of Fate and Will, of Want and Right,   185
Of man to come, of human life,
Of Death, and Fortune, Growth, and Strife.'

    Once again the pine-tree sung:—
'Speak not thy speech my boughs among;
Put off thy years, wash in the breeze;   190
My hours are peaceful centuries.
Talk no more with feeble tongue;
No more the fool of space and time,
Come weave with mine a nobler rhyme.
Only thy Americans   195
Can read thy line, can meet thy glance,
But the runes that I rehearse
Understands the universe;
The least breath my boughs which tossed
Brings again the Pentecost;   200
To every soul resounding clear
In a voice of solemn cheer,—
"Am I not thine? Are not these thine?"
And they reply, "Forever mine!"
My branches speak Italian,   205
English, German, Basque, Castilian,
Mountain speech to Highlanders,
Ocean tongues to islanders,
To Fin, and Lap, and swart Malay,
To each his bosom-secret say.   210

'Come learn with me the fatal song
Which knits the world in music strong,
Whereto every bosom dances,
Kindled with courageous fancies.
Come lift thine eyes to lofty rhymes,   215
Of things with things, of times with times,
Primal chimes of sun and shade,
Of sound and echo, man and maid,
The land reflected in the flood,
Body with shadow still pursued.   220
For Nature beats in perfect tune,
And rounds with rhyme her every rune,
Whether she work in land or sea,
Or hide underground her alchemy.
Thou canst not wave thy staff in air,   225
Or dip thy paddle in the lake,
But it carves the bow of beauty there,
And the ripples in rhymes the oar forsake.
The wood is wiser far than thou;
The wood and wave each other know.   230
Not unrelated, unaffied,
But to each thought and thing allied,
Is perfect Nature's every part,
Rooted in the mighty Heart.
But thou, poor child! unbound, unrhymed,   235
Whence camest thou, misplaced, mistimed?
Whence, O thou orphan and defrauded?
Is thy land peeled, thy realm marauded?
Who thee divorced, deceived, and left?
Thee of thy faith who hath bereft,   240
And torn the ensigns from thy brow,
And sunk the immortal eye so low?
Thy check too white, thy form too slender,
Thy gait too slow, thy habits tender
For royal man;—they thee confess   245
An exile from the wilderness,—
The hills where health with health agrees,
And the wise soul expels disease.

Hark! in thy ear I will tell the sign
By which thy hurt thou may'st divine.   250
When thou shalt climb the mountain cliff,
Or see the wide shore from thy skiff,
To thee the horizon shall express
Only emptiness and emptiness;
There lives no man of Nature's worth   255
In the circle of the earth;
And to thine eye the vast skies fall,
Dire and satirical,
On clucking hens, and prating fools,
On thieves, on drudges, and on dolls.   260
And thou shalt say to the Most High,
"Godhead! all this astronomy,
And fate, and practice, and invention,
Strong art, and beautiful pretension,
This radiant pomp of sun and star,   265
Throes that were, and worlds that are,
Behold! were in vain and in vain;—
It cannot be,—I will look again;
Surely now will the curtain rise,
And earth's fit tenant me surprise;—   270
But the curtain doth *not* rise,
And Nature has miscarried wholly
Into failure, into folly."

'Alas! thine is the bankruptcy,
Blessed Nature so to see.   275
Come, lay thee in my soothing shade,
And heal the hurts which sin has made.
I will teach the bright parable
Older than time,
Things undeclarable,   280
Visions sublime.
I see thee in the crowd alone;
I will be thy companion.
Quit thy friends as the dead in doom,

And build to them a final tomb;   285
Let the starred shade that nightly falls
Still celebrate their funerals,
And the bell of beetle and of bee
Knell their melodious memory.
Behind thee leave thy merchandise,   290
Thy churches, and thy charities;
And leave thy peacock wit behind;
Enough for thee the primal mind
That flows in streams, that breathes in wind.
Leave all thy pedant lore apart;   295
God hid the whole world in thy heart.
Love shuns the sage, the child it crowns,
And gives them all who all renounce.
The rain comes when the wind calls;
The river knows the way to the sea;   300
Without a pilot it runs and falls,
Blessing all lands with its charity;
The sea tosses and foams to find
Its way up to the cloud and wind;
The shadow sits close to the flying ball;   305
The date fails not on the palm-tree tall;
And thou,—go burn thy wormy pages,—
Shalt outsee seers, and outwit sages.
Oft didst thou thread the woods in vain
To find what bird had piped the strain;—   310
Seek not, and the little eremite
Flies gaily forth and sings in sight.

'Hearken once more!
I will tell thee the mundane lore.
Older am I than thy numbers wot;   315
Change I may, but I pass not.
Hitherto all things fast abide,
And anchored in the tempest ride.
Trenchant time behoves to hurry
All to yean and all to bury: 320

All the forms are fugitive,
But the substances survive.
Ever fresh the broad creation,
A divine improvisation,
From the heart of God proceeds,   325
A single will, a million deeds.
Once slept the world an egg of stone,
And pulse, and sound, and light was none;
And God said, "Throb!" and there was motion,
And the vast mass became vast ocean.   330
Onward and on, the eternal Pan,
Who layeth the world's incessant plan,
Halteth never in one shape,
But forever doth escape,
Like wave or flame, into new forms   335
Of gem, and air, of plants, and worms.
I, that today am a pine,
Yesterday was a bundle of grass.
He is free and libertine,
Pouring of his power the wine   340
To every age, to every race;
Unto every race and age
He emptieth the beverage;
Unto each, and unto all,
Maker and original.   345
The world is the ring of his spells,
And the play of his miracles.
As he giveth to all to drink,
Thus or thus they are and think.
He giveth little or giveth much,   350
To make them several or such.
With one drop sheds form and feature;
With the next a special nature;
The third adds heat's indulgent spark;
The fourth gives light which eats the dark;   355
Into the fifth himself he flings,
And conscious Law is King of kings.

Pleaseth him, the Eternal Child,
To play his sweet will, glad and wild;
As the bee through the garden ranges,   360
From world to world the godhead changes;
As the sheep go feeding in the waste,
From form to form he maketh haste;
This vault which glows immense with light
Is the inn where he lodges for a night.   365
What recks such Traveller if the bowers
Which bloom and fade like meadow flowers
A bunch of fragrant lilies be,
Or the stars of eternity?
Alike to him the better, the worse,—   370
The glowing angel, the outcast corse.
Thou metest him by centuries,
And lo! he passes like the breeze;
Thou seek'st in globe and galaxy,
He hides in pure transparency;   375
Thou askest in fountains and in fires,
He is the essence that inquires.
He is the axis of the star;
He is the sparkle of the spar;
He is the heart of every creature;   380
He is the meaning of each feature;
And his mind is the sky,
Than all it holds more deep, more high.'

TEXTS

(A) *Dial*, II (October 1841): 207–214; (B) MS, m.b., Berg Collection, by permission of the New York Public Library, printer's copy for C; (C) *Poems* (London, 1847), 57–72; (D) *Poems* (Boston, 1847), 75–93; (E) *Poems* ["Fourth Edition"] (Boston, 1847), 75–93; (F) *Poems* (Boston, 1856), 75–93; (G) *Poems* (Boston, 1863), 75–93; (H) *Poems* (Boston, 1865), 78–96; (I) *Selected Poems* (Boston, 1876), 129, 131–40; (J) *Poems* [Riverside] (Boston, 1884), 48–57; (K) *Poems* [Centenary] (Boston, 1904), 48–59. The discontinuous pagination in (I) is the result of an error of imposition whereby the last page of "Woodnotes I" (p. 130) has been transposed with the first page of "Woodnotes II."

Poems (1847)

Format: The verse break following line 100 in (A, C) is not present in (I-K); it coincides with a page break in (B, D-H). Line 101 is indented in (B-C), but in no instance does line 101 begin with a quotation mark. The editors conclude that Emerson did not insist on a new verse paragraph at this point. There is no verse break after line 210 in (A, D-I).

Pre-copy-text forms: See *JMN*, VIII, 458–459, 461, 463, 504–506, 508–509.

VARIANTS

Title: WOODNOTES. / II. (D-G, I-K) I
WOODNOTES. / NUMBER II. (A) I
Woodnotes / II. (B) I WOOD
NOTES. / II. (C) I WOOD-NOTES. /
II. (H)

1   *space,* (B-H) I *space* (A, I-K)

3   *pine-tree* (C-K) I *pinetree* (A-B) II
thought, (A-H) I *thought* (I-K)

5   'Whether (B-K) I "Whether (A)
II better (A-I) I better, (J-K)

6   me,' (B-K) I me," (A)

7   pine-tree, (C-K) I pinetree (A-B)

8   'I (B-K) I "I (A) II honor. (A-B,
D-K) I honour. (C)

10   snow; (D-K) I snow, (A-C)

11   sand-heaps (D-K) I sandheaps
(A-B) I sand heaps (C) II stock, (B-K)
I stock (A)

13–48 [*Lines canceled* (CC1, CC5);
not present (I-J); *also not present in* (K),
*but lines 13–44 printed in note at
pp. 421–422.*]

19   old, (A-E, K) I old [*plate damage*]
(F-G) I old. (H)

22   coevals (A-H) I coævals (K)

24   among, (B-C) I among; (A, D, K)
I among (E-H) [*plate damage?*]

31   sea, (D-H) I sea (A-C, K)

35   fanned, (A-D, K) I fanned (E-H)

37   sight, (A, C-H, K) I <l>sight, (B)

38   light, (A-H) I light; (K)

40   O'er (A, C-H, K) I Oer (B)

41   again (B-H, K) I again, (A)

44   again. (A-B, D-H, K) I again.'
(C)

45   'Whether (B-H) I "Whether
(A)

46   me,' (C-H) I me," (A) I me' (B)

47   pine-tree, (C-H) I pinetree,
(A-B)

48   'I (B-H) I "I (A) II honor. (A-B,
D-H) I honour. (C)

49   He (A-H, J-K) I 'He (I) II me. (A,
D-J) I me; (B-C) I me: (K)

55   be; (D-K) I be: (A) I be, (B-C)

57   dry, (A, D-K) I dry (B-C)

58–59 [*Lines canceled* (CC5); *not
present* (I-K)]

59   nourish. (A, D-H) I nourish;
(B-C)

60   pine (D-K) I pine, (A-C)

62   hall (D-K) I hall, (A-C)

63   all. (A, D-K) I all: (B-C)

64   haunts, (B-K) I haunts (A)

65   care; (D-K) I care, (A-C)

68   'What (D-K) I What (A-C)

69   pine-tree (C-K) I pinetree (A-B)
II yields; (A, D-K) I yields, (B-C)

70   fields; (A, D-K) I fields, (B-C)

71   boy, (A, D-K) I boy (B-C)

72   Chants (D-K) I Chaunts (A-C) II
hills (A-B, D-K) I hill (C)

74   lean; (A, D-K) I lean, (B-C)

75–78 [*Lines canceled* (CC1, CC5);
not present (I)]

76   day-star (B-H, J-K) I daystar (A)

77   rose-leaf (A-B, D-H, J-K) | rose leaf (C)

79   Iron arms, (A, D-H, J-K) | Iron arms (B-C) | Whose iron arms, (I) | < ↑ His ↓ > ↑ Whose ↓ iron arms (CC1) | ↑ Whose ↓ Iron arms (CC5)

80   That know (A-H, J-K) | Know (I) | know (CC1, CC5)

82   throat; (D-I) | throat, (A-C, J-K)

83   sea, (D-I) | sea (A-C, J-K)

85   pine (A, D-K) | pine, (B-C)

87–92 [*Lines canceled* (CC1, CC5); *not present* (I-K)]

88   railroad (A, D-H) | rail-road (B-C) || skates; (D-H) | skates, (A-C)

89   behind (A, D-H) | behind, (B-C)

90   fast; (D-H) | fast, (A, C) | fast. (B)

91   Missouri (B-H) | Missouri, (A)

93   pine-tree, (C-K) | pinetree, (A-B)

98   grace; (A, D-K) | grace, (B-C)

101   walketh (A-H) | walks (CC1, I-K) || solitude, (A-I) | solitude (J-K)

105   pass, (A, D-H, J-K) | pass (B-C, CC5, I)

106   companions, (D-K) | companions (A-C) || grace. (A, D-H, J-K) | grace; (B-C, I)

107   be, (A, D-K) | be (B-C)

108   sin. (A, D-H) | sin; (B-C) | sin, (CC5, I-K)

109–110 [*Lines canceled* (CC1, CC5); *not present* (I-K)]

109   adulate (D-H) | adulate, (A-C)

110   Fate; (A, D-H) | Fate, (B-C)

112   sight. (A-I) | sight: (J-K)

113   frivolous; (D-K) | frivolous, (A-C)

114   garrulous; (D-K) | garrulous, (A-C)

121   Nature (D-K) | nature (A-C)

122   innocence; (A, D-K) | innocence, (B-C)

123   mounting (A, CC10, D-K) |

mountain (B-C) | <mountain> ↑ mounting ↓ (CC2)

125–126 [*Lines canceled* (CC1); *not present* (I-K)]

125   old; (A, D-I) | old, (B-C)

127   meet (CC1, I-K) | see (A-H)

130   prove; (A, D-K) | prove, (B) | prove. (C)

131   woos, (D-H) | woos (A-C) | wooes (I) | wooes, (J-K)

132   Muse-born, (D-K) | Muse-born (A-C) || Muse. (D-K) | Muse; (A-C)

136   ground. (A, D-K) | ground: (B-C)

137–143 [*Lines canceled* (CC1, CC5); *not present* (I-K)]

138   sins; (D-H) | sins, (A-C)

144   'Heed (D-K) | Heed (A-C) || oracles, (B-K) | oracles (A)

145   spells; (D-K) | spells, (A-C)

147   pinnacles (A, D-K) | pinnacles, (B-C)

151   wood-god (A, C-K) | woodgod (B)

152   Hearken! Hearken! (A, D-K) | Hearken! hearken! (B-C) [*This line is flush left in* (A-C)]

153   wouldst (A, D-K) | would'st (B-C)

154   Chanted (D-K) | Chaunted (A-C) || young. (A, D-K) | young, (B-C)

155   swells; (A, D-K) | swells, (B-C)

156   man! (A-B, D-K) | man, (C)

157   man! (A, D-K) | man, (B) | man? (C) || part? (A-C, E-K) | part (D) | part? (CC1)

158   'Tis (A, C-K) | Tis (B)

159   sings (B-K) | sings, (A)

160   Sweet the (CC1, F-K) | The early (A-E) | The <early> ↑ sweet ↓ (CC2) || things, (A, D-K) | things; (B-C)

163   space (A, D-K) | space, (B-C)

165   force, (B-I) | force (A, J-K)

166   wet, (A-I, K) | wet (J) || warm: (D-K) | warm; (A) | warm, (B-C)

167 metamorphosis, (A, D-H) I metamorphosis (B-C, CC1, CC5, I-K)

171 O, (D-K) I O (A-C) II undersong— (D-H) I undersong, (A-B, J-K) I under song, (C) I undersong,— (I)

172 ever old, (A, D-K) I ever-old, (B-C) II ever young; (A, D-K) I ever-young, (B-C)

173 And, (D-K) I And (A-C) II pauses, (B-K) I pauses (A)

174 Causes! (A, D-K) I Causes. (B-C)

175 Destiny (B, D-K) I Destiny, (A) I destiny (C)

178 throat. (A, C-K) I throat— (B)

180 Nature (D-K) I nature (A-C)

182 tones (B-K) I tones, (A)

183 hear; (A, D-K) I hear, (B-C)

184 recite (B-K) I recite, (A)

185 Fate (A, D-K) I Fate, (B-C) II Want (A, D-K) I Want, (B-C)

187 Death, (A-I) I Death (J-K) II Growth, (A-I) I Growth (J-K) II Strife.' (B-K) I Strife. (A)

188 pine-tree (C-K) I pinetree (A-B) II sung:— (D-K) I sung;— (A-C) [*This line is flush left in* (B-C)]

189 'Speak (B-K) I "Speak (A) II among; (A, D-I) I among, (B-C) I among: (J-K)

190 breeze; (A, D-K) I breeze, (B-C)

191 centuries. (B-K) I centuries! (A)

192 tongue; (B-K) I tongue, (A)

198 universe; (A, D-K) I Universe. (B) I universe. (C)

199 tossed (B-K) I tossed, (A)

200 Pentecost; (A-H, J-K) I Pentecost, (I) [*Due to plate damage, the upper element in the semicolon is all but lost in printings from the 1847 plates after* (E)]

201 resounding (CC1, CC5, I-K) I it soundeth (A-H) II clear (B-K) I clear, (A)

202 cheer,— (D-K) I cheer, (A-C)

203 "Am (D-K) I 'Am (A-C) II Are (A-B, D-K) I are (C) II thine?" (D-K) I thine?' (A-C)

204 "Forever (D-K) I 'Forever (A-B) I 'For ever (C) II mine!" (D-K) I mine?' (A) I mine.' (B-C)

209 Fin, and Lap, (B-I) I Fin and Lap (A, J-K)

210 bosom-secret (G, CC4, CC9, I-K) I bosom secret (A-F, H)

211 'Come (I) I Come (A-H) II song (B-I) I song, (A)

213–214 [*Lines canceled* (CC1) *after* "bosom" *was emended to* "listener"; *canceled* (CC5); *not present* (I-K)]

213 dances, (A, D-H) I dances (B-C)

214 fancies. (D-H) I fancies, (A) I fancies: (B-C)

215 rhymes, (A, D-K) I rhymes (B-C)

218 maid, (A, D-K) I maid; (B-C)

219 flood, (A, D-K) I flood; (B-C)

220 pursued. (B-K) I pursued; (A)

221 Nature (D-K) I nature (A-C)

229 thou; (A-B, D-K) I thou: (C)

230 know. (A-I) I know (J-K)

233 Nature's (D-K) I nature's (A-C)

234 Heart. (A-B, D-K) I heart. (C)

236 mistimed? (A-I) I mistimed, (J-K)

239 deceived, (A-I) I deceived (J-K) II left? (D-K) I left; (A-C)

244 tender (A, D-K) I tender, (B-C)

245 man;—they (D-K) I man; they (A-C)

247 hills (A, C-K) I hills<,> (B)

254 Only emptiness and (A-H) I But emptiness on (CC1, CC5, I-K) II emptiness; (C-K) I emptiness: (A-B)

255 lives (CC4, CC9, G, I-K) I is (A-F, H) II Nature's (D-K) I nature's (A-C)

256 earth; (D-K) I earth, (A-C)

257 fall, (D-K) I fall (A-C)

258   satirical, (D-H, J-K) | satirical (A-C, I)

259   hens, (A-I) | hens (J-K)

260   drudges, (A-I) | drudges (J-K)

261   Most (B-K) | most (A)

262   "Godhead! (D-K) | 'Godhead! (A-C) || astronomy, (B-K) | astronomy (A)

263   fate, and practice, (D-I) | Fate, and practice (A-C) | fate and practice (J-K)

264   art, (A-I) | art (J-K)

268   again; (D-I) | again, (A-B) | again,— (C) | again. (J-K)

270   surprise;— (A-B, D-K | surprise; (C)

272   Nature (D-K) | nature (A-C)

273   folly." (D-K) | folly.' (A-C)

274   'Alas! (D-K) | Alas! (A-C)

275   Nature (D-K) | nature (A-C)

276   Come, (A, D-K) | Come (B-C)

278–281   [*Lines canceled* (CC1, CC5); *not present* (I-K)]

284   Quit thy friends (CC4, CC9, G, I-K) | Let thy friends be (A-F, H)

286   nightly (A-B, CC10, CC11, D-K) | mighty (C)

287   funerals, (A, C-K) | funerals; (B)

288   beetle and of (A, C-K) | <the> beetle & of <the> (B)

291   churches, (B-I) | churches (A, J-K) || charities; (D-K) | charities, (A-C)

294   wind. (A-I) | wind; (J) | wind: (K)

298   And gives them all (A-H) | Gives all to them (I-K) | gives all to them (CC1)

299   calls; (D-K) | calls, (A-C)

300   sea; (D-K) | sea, (A-C)

302   charity; (D-K) | charity. (A-C)

304   wind; (D-K) | wind. (A-B) | wind, (C)

305   ball; (D-K) | ball, (A-C)

306   palm-tree (C-K) | palmtree (A-B) || tall; (D-K) | tall, (A-C)

307   thou,— (B-K) | thou— (A)

308   Shalt (B-K) | Shall (A) || outsee seers, and outwit sages. (D-K) | outsee the seer, outwit the sages. (A-C)

309   thread (A-H, J-K) | search (CC1, CC5, I)

310   strain;— (D-J) | strain,— (A-C) | strain:— (K)

313   'Hearken once more! (D-K) | Hearken! once more; (A-C)

314   tell thee the (A, D-K) | tell <thee> the (B) | tell the (C)

315   wot; (D-I) | wot, (A-C, J-K) [*The semicolon in* (G) *is nearly reduced to a comma by plate damage.*]

316   not. (D-K) | not; (A-C)

319   Trenchant (A-B, CC10, CC11, D-K) | Trendrant (C) || behoves (A-G, J-K) | behooves (H-I)

320   bury: (D-K) | bury; (A-C)

329   "Throb!" (D-K) | Throb; (A-C) || motion, (A-I) | motion (J-K)

331   Pan, (D-K) | Pan (A-C)

333   never (A, C-K) | <ev>never (B)

336   plants, (A-B, D-K) | plants (C)

337   today (B) | to-day (A, C-K) [*Emerson's preference for the unhyphenated form of this word is clear in his MS practice, though he did not generally resist house styling.*]

341   race; (A, D-K) | race, (B-C)

349   think. (A-H, J-K) | think; (I)

350–351   [*Lines canceled* (CC1); *not present* (J-K)]

352   feature; (D-K) | feature, (A-C)

353   next (CC4, CC9, G, I-K) | second (A-F, H) || nature; (D-K) | nature, (A-C)

354   spark; (D-K) | spark, (A-C)

355   dark; (D-K) | dark, (A) | dark. (B-C)

356 Into the fifth (CC1, F-K) | In the fifth drop (A-E) | In the fifth <drop> (CC2)

357 kings. (A-B, D-K) | Kings. (C)

358–359 [*Lines canceled* (CC1, CC5); *not present* (I-K)]

358 him, (D-H) | him (A-C) || Child, (D-H) | Child (A-C)

362 in (A, D-K) | through (B-C)

363 form to (A, C-K) | <world to>form to (B) || he (A-H) | He (CC1, CC5, I-K) || haste; (D-K) | haste, (A) | haste. (B-C)

364 This (B-K) | And this (A)

367 meadow (A, D-K) | summer (B-C) || flowers (D-K) | flowers, (A-C)

370 worse,— (D-K) | worse;— (A) | worse, (B-C)

372 metest (A-H, J-K) | meetest (I)

376 fires, (A-F, H-I) | fires,— (I)

378 star; (A-H, J-K) | star, (I)

379 spar; (A-H, J-K) | spar, (I)

380 creature; (A-H, J-K) | creature, (I)

382 sky, (D-I) | sky (A-C) | sky. (J-K)

383 high.' (B-K) | high. (A)

NOTES

161. Edward Emerson noted the influence on this line of Wordsworth, *The Excursion*, IX, 87, "To hear the mighty stream of Tendency," as Emerson slightly misquoted the line in an early journal (see *JMN*, III, 80).

162. The earliest citation for "star-dust" in the *OED* dates to 1844.

167–170. "Metamorphosis is nature. The foetus does not more strive to be man than yonder bur of light we call a nebula tends to be a ring, a comet, a solid globe, a sun, & the parent of new stars" (*JMN*, VII, 428).

222. In 1850 Emerson wrote: "I praised the rhymes of sun & shade, man & maid, in my Woodnotes. But how far that can be carried! inasmuch as every substance is only the reflection or rhyme of some truth" (*JMN*, XI, 271).

MONADNOC.

Mount Monadnoc (or Monadnock, as it is more usually written) is an isolated peak in Cheshire County, in southern New Hampshire, near the towns of Troy, Jaffrey, Dublin, and Peterborough. Though sixty miles distant from Concord, it is just barely visible from a number of elevated points in or near the town. In 1835, while looking for a home, Emerson briefly thought to build on a site across from the Old Manse "on Grandfathers hill facing Wachusett & Monadnoc & the setting sun" (*L,* I, 445). As late as 1846, when "Monadnoc" was written, he had not quite abandoned the dream of a house with a mountain view, having just purchased his Walden acres with the included Cliff (A. B. Alcott, *The Journals,* ed. Odell Shepard [Boston, 1938], 178; *CEC,* 399). Over the years he took a number of tours to the mountain—first, perhaps, in 1838 on his way to deliver his oration on "Literary Ethics" at Dartmouth (*L,* II, 144), but it was undoubtedly the excursion to Monadnoc in early June of 1846 that allowed him to write the poem—or at least to complete it—for he read the finished work to Alcott on 28 June (Alcott, *Journals,* 182; *L,* VIII, 77, n. 36; see also *PN,* 862, for the suggestion that Emerson had written the last sixty lines just the day before). If there may have been a little haste in the composition, Emerson revised at leisure, as shown by the unusual number of authorial corrections in later printings.

The poem draws on experiences that Emerson had with a number of New England mountains. Ralph Rusk thought the genesis of the poem lay with Emerson's response to "the meanness & Mud of the population" he found in taverns round about the White Mountains, of which he complained in a letter of 3 September 1839 to Margaret Fuller (*L,* II, 220). The landscape of Northern New Hampshire, "though savage & stern," did not, for Emerson, "reach the surprising & overwhelming grandeur that in some spots of this world draws a man as by the hair of his head into awe & poetry" (221). The more permanently interesting Monadnoc would eventually do that, but in the meantime Emerson found it important to make dramatic use of this contrast between sublime scene and paltry actor. Its earliest working out took the form of a poem entitled "Wachusett," referring to a closer and tamer eminence, near the town of Princeton in Worcester County, Massachusetts, that Emerson had visited in April 1845 and again, a month later, with Caroline Sturgis (*L,* VIII, 107, n. 10). This poem, an address by Mount Wachusett to Grand Monadnoc, was only twenty-five lines in the incomplete version composed on 3

April 1845 (see *PN*, 713–714), and it proved an inadequate vehicle for Emerson's protest against American militarism in the run-up to the Mexican War. "Wachusett" was a late deletion from a manuscript table of contents for *Poems* (1847), and "Monadnoc" (the drafts of which in the poetry notebooks are intertwined with those of "Wachusett") was substituted (see *L*, III, 358 n. 140). The overtly political content of the earlier version had by this time all but disappeared, lingering alone in such traces as the reference to mountain-affiliated nationalist heroes in line 97, and in the harsh depiction (toned down over the course of later printings) of the disappointing Yankee indigenes of the Monadnoc region. Emerson's impulse to political protest was instead channeled into his "Ode, Inscribed to W. H. Channing" (q.v.), composed during the same brief visit to Monadnoc in June of 1846.

Mount Monadnoc seems to have been a point of attraction for all the Transcendentalists. It was, for example, the last peak that Thoreau climbed before his death in 1862. On one or another ascent of the mountain during the preceding decade he had been accompanied by Ellery Channing and H. G. O. Blake. Theodore Parker very agreeably passed the summer of 1855 in the mountain's shadow at the town of Dublin, a place he commended for its culture and sobriety. There, in 1880, Thomas Wentworth Higginson built a summer home, by which time the town had become something of an artists' colony. Indeed, Emerson's son Edward long maintained a painter's studio nearby on one of Monadnoc's southern spurs (George Willis Cooke, "Old Times and New in Dublin, New Hampshire," *New England Magazine* n.s. 20 [August 1899]: 759).

MONADNOC.

Thousand minstrels woke within me,
   'Our music's in the hills;'—
Gayest pictures rose to win me,
   Leopard-colored rills.
'Up!—If thou knew'st who calls   5
To twilight parks of beech and pine,

High over the river intervals,
Above the ploughman's highest line,
Over the owner's farthest walls!
Up! where the airy citadel   10
O'erlooks the surging landscape's swell!
Let not unto the stones the Day
Her lily and rose, her sea and land display.
Read the celestial sign!
Lo! the south answers to the north;   15
Bookworm, break this sloth urbane;
A greater spirit bids thee forth
Than the gray dreams which thee detain.
Mark how the climbing Oreads
Beckon thee to their arcades!   20
Youth, for a moment free as they,
Teach thy feet to feel the ground,
Ere yet arrives the wintry day
When Time thy feet has bound.
Take the bounty of thy birth,   25
Taste the lordship of the earth.'

   I heard, and I obeyed,—
Assured that he who made the claim,
Well known, but loving not a name,
   Was not to be gainsaid.   30

Ere yet the summoning voice was still,
I turned to Cheshire's haughty hill.
From the fixed cone the cloud-rack flowed,
Like ample banner flung abroad
To all the dwellers in the plains   35
Round about, a hundred miles,
With salutation to the sea, and to the bordering isles.

In his own loom's garment dressed,
By his proper bounty blessed,
Fast abides this constant giver,   40

Pouring many a cheerful river;
To far eyes, an aerial isle
Unploughed, which finer spirits pile,
Which morn and crimson evening paint
For bard, for lover, and for saint;   45
The people's pride, the country's core,
Inspirer, prophet evermore;
Pillar which God aloft had set
So that men might it not forget;
It should be their life's ornament,   50
And mix itself with each event;
Gauge and calendar and dial,
Weatherglass and chemic phial,
Garden of berries, perch of birds,
Pasture of pool-haunting herds,   55
Graced by each change of sum untold,
Earth-baking heat, stone-cleaving cold.

The Titan heeds his sky-affairs,
Rich rents and wide alliance shares;
Mysteries of color daily laid   60
By morn and eve in light and shade;
And sweet varieties of chance,
And the mystic seasons' dance;
And thief-like step of liberal hours
Thawing snow-drift into flowers.   65
O, wondrous craft of plant and stone
By eldest science wrought and shown!

'Happy,' I said, 'whose home is here!
Fair fortunes to the mountaineer!
Boon Nature to his poorest shed   70
Has royal pleasure-grounds outspread.'
Intent, I searched the region round,
And in low hut my monarch found:—
Woe is me for my hope's downfall!
Is yonder squalid peasant all   75

That this proud nursery could breed
For God's vicegerency and stead?
Time out of mind, this forge of ores;
Quarry of spars in mountain pores;
Old cradle, hunting-ground, and bier   80
Of wolf and otter, bear and deer;
Well-built abode of many a race;
Tower of observance searching space;
Factory of river and of rain;
Link in the alps' globe-girding chain;   85
By million changes skilled to tell
What in the Eternal standeth well,
And what obedient Nature can;—
Is this colossal talisman
Kindly to plant, and blood, and kind,   90
But speechless to the master's mind?
I thought to find the patriots
In whom the stock of freedom roots:
To myself I oft recount
Tales of many a famous mount,—   95
Wales, Scotland, Uri, Hungary's dells;
Bards, Roys, Scanderbegs, and Tells.
Here Nature shall condense her powers,
Her music, and her meteors,
And lifting man to the blue deep   100
Where stars their perfect courses keep,
Like wise preceptor, lure his eye
To sound the science of the sky,
And carry learning to its height
Of untried power and sane delight: 105
The Indian cheer, the frosty skies,
Rear purer wits, inventive eyes,—
Eyes that frame cities where none be,
And hands that stablish what these see;
And by the moral of his place   110
Hint summits of heroic grace;
Man in these crags a fastness find

To fight pollution of the mind;
In the wide thaw and ooze of wrong,
Adhere like this foundation strong,   115
The insanity of towns to stem
With simpleness for stratagem.
But if the brave old mould is broke,
And end in churls the mountain folk,
In tavern cheer and tavern joke,   120
Sink, O mountain, in the swamp!
Hide in thy skies, O sovereign lamp!
Perish like leaves, the highland breed!
No sire survive, no son succeed!

Soft! let not the offended muse   125
Toil's hard hap with scorn accuse.
Many hamlets sought I then,
Many farms of mountain men.
Rallying round a parish steeple
Nestle warm the highland people,   130
Coarse and boisterous, yet mild,
Strong as giant, slow as child,
Smoking in a squalid room
Where yet the westland breezes come.
Masked in those rough guises lurk   135
Western magians,—here they work.
Sweat and season are their arts,
Their talismans are ploughs and carts;
And well the youngest can command
Honey from the frozen land;   140
With cloverheads the swamp adorn,
Change the running sand to corn;
For wolves and foxes, lowing herds,
And for cold mosses, cream and curds;
Weave wood to canisters and mats;   145
Drain sweet maple juice in vats.
No bird is safe that cuts the air
From their rifle or their snare;

No fish, in river or in lake,
But their long hands it thence will take;   150
And the country's flinty face,
Like wax, their fashioning skill betrays,
To fill the hollows, sink the hills,
Bridge gulfs, drain swamps, build dams and mills,
And fit the bleak and howling place   155
For gardens of a finer race.
The World-soul knows his own affair,
Forelooking, when he would prepare
For the next ages, men of mould
Well embodied, well ensouled,   160
He cools the present's fiery glow,
Sets the life-pulse strong but slow:
Bitter winds and fasts austere
His quarantines and grottos, where
He slowly cures decrepit flesh,   165
And brings it infantile and fresh.
Toil and tempest are the toys
And games to breathe his stalwart boys:
They bide their time, and well can prove,
If need were, their line from Jove;   170
Of the same stuff, and so allayed,
As that whereof the sun is made,
And of the fibre, quick and strong,
Whose throbs are love, whose thrills are song.

Now in sordid weeds they sleep,   175
In dulness now their secret keep;
Yet, will you learn our ancient speech,
These the masters who can teach.
Fourscore or a hundred words
All their vocal muse affords;   180
But they turn them in a fashion
Past clerks' or statesmen's art or passion.
I can spare the college bell,
And the learned lecture, well;

Spare the clergy and libraries,   185
Institutes and dictionaries,
For that hardy English root
Thrives here, unvalued, underfoot.
Rude poets of the tavern hearth,
Squandering your unquoted mirth,   190
Which keeps the ground, and never soars,
While Jake retorts, and Reuben roars;
Scoff of yeoman strong and stark,
Goes like bullet to its mark;
While the solid curse and jeer   195
Never balk the waiting ear.

On the summit as I stood,
O'er the floor of plain and flood,
Seemed to me the towering hill
Was not altogether still,   200
But a quiet sense conveyed;
If I err not, thus it said:—

'Many feet in summer seek,
Oft, my far-appearing peak;
In the dreaded winter time,   205
None save dappling shadows climb,
Under clouds, my lonely head,
Old as the sun, old almost as the shade.
And comest thou
To see strange forests and new snow,   210
And tread uplifted land?
And leavest thou thy lowland race,
Here amid clouds to stand?
And wouldst be my companion,
Where I gaze, and still shall gaze,   215
Thro' tempering nights and flashing days,
When forests fall, and man is gone,
Over tribes and over times,

At the burning Lyre,
Nearing me,   220
With its stars of northern fire,
In many a thousand years?

'Ah! welcome, if thou bring
My secret in thy brain;
To mountain-top may Muse's wing   225
With good allowance strain.
Gentle pilgrim, if thou know
The gamut old of Pan,
And how the hills began,
The frank blessings of the hill   230
Fall on thee, as fall they will.
'Tis the law of bush and stone,
Each can only take his own.

'Let him heed who can and will;
Enchantment fixed me here   235
To stand the hurts of time, until
In mightier chant I disappear.
    'If thou trowest
How the chemic eddies play,
Pole to pole, and what they say;   240
And that these gray crags
Not on crags are hung,
But beads are of a rosary
On prayer and music strung;
And, credulous, through the granite seeming,   245
Seest the smile of Reason beaming;—
Can thy style-discerning eye
The hidden-working Builder spy,
Who builds, yet makes no chips, no din,
With hammer soft as snowflake's flight;—   250
Knowest thou this?
O pilgrim, wandering not amiss!

Already my rocks lie light,
And soon my cone will spin.

'For the world was built in order,   255
And the atoms march in tune;
Rhyme the pipe, and Time the warder,
The sun obeys them, and the moon.
Orb and atom forth they prance,
When they hear from far the rune;   260
None so backward in the troop,
When the music and the dance
Reach his place and circumstance,
But knows the sun-creating sound,
And, though a pyramid, will bound.   265

'Monadnoc is a mountain strong,
Tall and good my kind among;
But well I know, no mountain can,
Zion or Meru, measure with man.
For it is on zodiacs writ,   270
Adamant is soft to wit:
And when the greater comes again
With my secret in his brain,
I shall pass, as glides my shadow
Daily over hill and meadow.   275

'Through all time, in light, in gloom,
Well I hear the approaching feet
On the flinty pathway beat
Of him that cometh, and shall come;
Of him who shall as lightly bear   280
My daily load of woods and streams,
As doth this round sky-cleaving boat
Which never strains its rocky beams;
Whose timbers, as they silent float,
Alps and Caucasus uprear,   285
And the long Alleganies here,

And all town-sprinkled lands that be,
Sailing through stars with all their history.

'Every morn I lift my head,
See New England underspread,   290
South from Saint Lawrence to the Sound,
From Katskill east to the sea-bound.
Anchored fast for many an age,
I await the bard and sage,
Who, in large thoughts, like fair pearl-seed,   295
Shall string Monadnoc like a bead.
Comes that cheerful troubadour,
This mound shall throb his face before,
As when, with inward fires and pain,
It rose a bubble from the plain.   300
When he cometh, I shall shed,
From this wellspring in my head,
Fountain-drop of spicier worth
Than all vintage of the earth.
There's fruit upon my barren soil   305
Costlier far than wine or oil.
There's a berry blue and gold,—
Autumn-ripe, its juices hold
Sparta's stoutness, Bethlehem's heart,
Asia's rancor, Athens' art,   310
Slowsure Britain's secular might,
And the German's inward sight.
I will give my son to eat
Best of Pan's immortal meat,
Bread to eat, and juice to drain;   315
So the coinage of his brain
Shall not be forms of stars, but stars,
Nor pictures pale, but Jove and Mars.
He comes, but not of that race bred
Who daily climb my specular head.   320
Oft as morning wreathes my scarf,
Fled the last plumule of the Dark,

Pants up hither the spruce clerk
From South Cove and City Wharf.
I take him up my rugged sides,   325
Half-repentant, scant of breath,—
Bead-eyes my granite chaos show,
And my midsummer snow;
Open the daunting map beneath,—
All his county, sea and land,   330
Dwarfed to measure of his hand;
His day's ride is a furlong space,
His city-tops a glimmering haze.
I plant his eyes on the sky-hoop bounding:
"See there the grim gray rounding   335
Of the bullet of the earth
Whereon ye sail,
Tumbling steep
In the uncontinented deep."
He looks on that, and he turns pale.   340
'Tis even so; this treacherous kite,
Farm-furrowed, town-incrusted sphere,
Thoughtless of its anxious freight,
Plunges eyeless on forever;
And he, poor parasite,   345
Cooped in a ship he cannot steer,—
Who is the captain he knows not,
Port or pilot trows not,—
Risk or ruin he must share.
I scowl on him with my cloud,   350
With my north wind chill his blood;
I lame him, clattering down the rocks;
And to live he is in fear.
Then, at last, I let him down
Once more into his dapper town,   355
To chatter, frightened, to his clan,
And forget me if he can.'

As in the old poetic fame
The gods are blind and lame,
And the simular despite   360
Betrays the more abounding might,
So call not waste that barren cone
Above the floral zone,
Where forests starve:
It is pure use;—   365
What sheaves like those which here we glean and bind
Of a celestial Ceres and the Muse?

Ages are thy days,
Thou grand affirmer of the present tense,
And type of permanence!   370
Firm ensign of the fatal Being,
Amid these coward shapes of joy and grief,
That will not bide the seeing!

Hither we bring
Our insect miseries to thy rocks;   375
And the whole flight, with folded wing,
Vanish, and end their murmuring,—
Vanish beside these dedicated blocks,
Which who can tell what mason laid?
Spoils of a front none need restore,   380
Replacing frieze and architrave;—
Yet flowers each stone rosette and metope brave;
Still is the haughty pile erect
Of the old building Intellect.

Complement of human kind,   385
Having us at vantage still,
Our sumptuous indigence,
O barren mound, thy plenties fill!
We fool and prate;
Thou art silent and sedate.   390

To myriad kinds and times one sense
The constant mountain doth dispense;
Shedding on all its snows and leaves,
One joy it joys, one grief it grieves.
Thou seest, O watchman tall, 395
Our towns and races grow and fall,
And imagest the stable good
For which we all our lifetime grope,
In shifting form the formless mind,
And though the substance us elude, 400
We in thee the shadow find.

Thou, in our astronomy
An opaker star,
Seen haply from afar,
Above the horizon's hoop, 405
A moment, by the railway troop,
As o'er some bolder height they speed,—
By circumspect ambition,
By errant gain,
By feasters and the frivolous,— 410
Recallest us,
And makest sane.
Mute orator! well skilled to plead,
And send conviction without phrase,
Thou dost succor and remede 415
The shortness of our days,
And promise, on thy Founder's truth,
Long morrow to this mortal youth.

TEXTS

(A) bMS Am 1280.240, Ralph Waldo Emerson Memorial Association deposit, Houghton Library, Harvard University, printer's copy for B; (B) *Poems* (London, 1847), 73–90; (C) *Poems* (Boston, 1847), 94–114; (D) *Poems* ["Fourth Edition"] (Boston, 1847), 94–114; (E) *Poems* (Boston, 1856), 94–114; (F) *Poems* (Boston, 1858), 94–114; (G) *Poems* (Boston, 1863), 94–114; (H) *Poems* (Boston, 1865), 97–117; (I) *Selected Poems* (Boston, 1876), 141–154; (J) *Poems* [Riverside] (Boston 1884), 58–70; (K) *Poems* [Centenary] (Boston, 1904), 60–75.

Monadnoc

Format: Lines 2, 4, 27, 30 flush left (A-B); line 238 flush left (B); lines 175, 197 indented (J-K); line 368 indented (A). Verse break following line 30 at page bottom in (J), lost in (K); following line 318 at page bottom in (A) present in (B); following line 37 not present (J-K); following line 254 not present (A-B); following line 357 not present (B); following 373 not present (A-B). A verse break in (B) following line 91 was prompted by the ambiguous appearance of a space in (A). It is not present in any American printing.

Pre-copy-text forms: See *PN*, 861–862.

VARIANTS

Title: MONADNOC. (B-H, J) | Monadnoc (A) | MONADNOCK. (I) | MONADNOC (K)

2   hills;'— (A-G, J-K) | hills';— (H-I)

4   -colored (C-K) | -coloured (A-B)

5   'Up!— (C-K) | Up!— (A-B)

9   walls! (C-K) | walls;— (A-B)

11   surging (A, CC10, CC11, C-K) | purging (B) | <p>↑s↓urging (CC2) || swell! (C-K) | swell. (A-B)

12   Day (C-K) | day (A-B)

13   display. (C-H, J-K) | display; (A-B, I)

15   south (C-K) | South (A-B) || north; (C-K) | North; (A-B)

17   spirit (C-K) | Spirit (A-B) || forth (C-K) | forth, (A-B)

18   gray (C-H, J-K) | grey (A-B) | gay (I)

20   arcades! (C-I) | arcades; (A-B, J-K)

23   arrives (C-K) | arrive (A-B)

25   Take (CC1, CC2, E-K) | Accept (A-D) || birth, (C-K) | birth; (A-B)

26   earth.' (C-K) | earth. (A-B)

27   heard, (C-K) | heard (A-B) || obeyed,— (C-K) | obeyed, (A-B)

28   Assured that he (A-K) | Sure that the /sprite/gnome/ (CC5) || made (C-K) | pressed (A-B)

29   Well known, (C-K) | Well-known, (A-B)

33   flowed, (C-E, H-K) | flowed (A-B, F-G)

35   [*Line omitted, perhaps inadvertently, in* (A-B). *While it may have been deliberately suppressed for lacking a complementary rhyme, the line occurs in all later printings and in the drafts in poetry notebook X, pp. 15 and 28: see PN, 120 and 130.*]

37   salutation (CC1, E-K) | invitation (A-D) || sea, (A-I) sea (J-K)

38   dressed, (C-K) | drest, (A-B)

39   proper (CC1, E-K) | own (A-D) || blessed, (C-K) | blest, (A-B)

42   aerial (A, CC2, C-K) | ærial (B) | aërial (CC1) || isle (C-K) | isle, (A-B)

44   Which (A-K) | That (CC1)

45   lover, (A-I) | lover (J-K)

46   The people's pride, the (E-I) | The (A-D) | An eye-mark & The (CC1) | An eyemark and the (J-K)

47   evermore; (C-K) | evermore, (A-B)

49   forget; (C-K) | forget, (A-B)

52   Gauge and (CC4, CC5, CC9, G, I-K) | Their (A-D) | This their (CC1, E-F, H) | ↑And↓ Their (CC2)

133

53   Weatherglass (CC1, CC2, E-K) |
Barometer, (A-B) | Barometer (C-D)

54   Garden of berries, (A-K) | Berry
garden (CC2)

58   heeds (C-K) | minds (A-B) || sky-
affairs, (A-B, D-K) | own affairs, (C)

59   Rich (A-B, D-K) | Wide (C) ||
wide (A-B, D-K) | high (C)

60   Mysteries (A-K) | <Mysteries>
↑ Coats ↓ (CC1, CC2) [*Emendation in*
(CC1) *reversed with* "Stet"] || color (C-
K) | colour (A-B)

61   morn and eve (CC1, I-K) | the
great sun (A-D) | the sun (E-H) ||
shade; (C-K) | shade, (A-B)

62   chance, (A-B, D-K) | chance
(C)

63   dance; (C-K) | dance, (A-B)

65   Thawing snow-drift (C-K) |
Which thawed the snow drift (A-B)

66   O, (C-K) | O (A-B)

67   science wrought (CC1, CC4,
CC5, CC9, G, I-K) | science done (A-
F, H) | art contrived (CC3)

68   'Happy,' (C-K) | Happy, (A-B) ||
'whose (C-K) | whose (A-B) || here!
(C-K) | here, (A-B)

70   Nature (C-K) | nature (A-B)

71   outspread.' (C-K) | outspread.
(A-B)

72   Intent, (C-K) | Intent (A-B)

73   my monarch (A-H) | the dweller
(CC1, I-K) || found:— (CC1, E-I) |
found. / He was no eagle and no
earl, / Alas! my foundling was a
churl, / With heart of cat, and eyes
of bug, / Dull victim of his pipe and
mug; (A-B) | found [found. (D)] /
He was no eagle, and no earl;—/
Alas my foundling was a churl, /
With heart of cat and eyes of bug, /
Dull victim of his pipe and mug. (C-
D) | found: (J-K)

74   Woe (H-K) | Wo (A-G) || hope's

(C-K) | hopes' (A-B) || downfall! (B-
K) | downfal! (A)

75   Is yonder (E-K) | Lord! is yon (A-
D) | <Lord!> < ↑ And ↓ > is yon<der>
(CC1)

78   mind, (C-K) | mind (A-B) || ores;
(C-K) | ores, (A-B)

79   pores; (C-K) | pores, (A-B)

80   hunting-ground, (A, C-I) |
hunting ground, (B) | hunting-
ground (J-K)

81   bear (C-K) | bear, (A-B)

84   river (A, C-K) | river, (B)

85   alps' (A-J) | Alps' (K)

88   Nature can;— (C-K) | nature
can, — (A-B)

90   plant, and (CC9, G, I) | creature,
(A-F, H) | plant and (CC5, J-K) |
plant &, (CC4) || blood, (A-I) | blood
(J-K)

91   But (CC4, CC5, I-K) | And (A-D)
| Yet (CC1, E-H)

92–93   [*Lines canceled then restored*]
(CC1)

93   roots: (C-I) | roots. (A-B) | roots;
(J-K)

94   To (A-K) | ↑ When ↓ To (CC1)

95   Tales (A-B, E-K) | The tale (C-D)
| tales (CC1) || mount,— (A, C-K) |
mount.— (B)

96   dells; (C-J) | dells, (A-B) | dells:
(K)

97   Bards, Roys, (E-K) | Roys, and
(A-D) | ↑ Bards ↓ Roys, <and> (CC1)
|| Scanderbegs, and Tells. (A-I) |
Scanderbegs and Tells; (J-K)

98   Here Nature shall condense (C-
I) | Here now shall nature crowd
(A-B)

98–99   [*In* (J-K) *the following lines are
substituted:*] And think how Nature in
these towers / Uplifted shall
condense her powers,

100   And (C-K) | And, (A-B)

102 preceptor, (C-K) | preceptor (A-B)

105 delight: (A, C-K) | delight; (B)

106 skies, (C-K) | skies (A-B)

107 Rear (C-K) | Breed (A-B) || eyes, — (C-K) | eyes, (A-B)

109 see; (C-I) | see: (A-B, J-K)

110 And (C-K) | And, (A-B) || place (C-K) | place, (A-B)

119 churls (C-K) | clowns (A-B) || mountain folk, (C-I) | mountain-folk, (A-B) | mountain folk (J-K)

120 joke, (C-K) | joke,— (A-B)

121 mountain, (C-K) | mountain! (A-B) || swamp! (C-K) | swamp, (A-B)

123 leaves, (C-K) | leaves (A-B) || breed! (A-D, H, CC4) | breed (E-G, J-K) | breed: (I) [*The loss of the exclamation point in* (E) *was due to plate damage.*]

127 then, (B-K) | then; (A)

128 men. (CC4, CC5, CC9, G, I-K) | men; [men;— (A-B)] / Found I not a minstrel seed, / But men of bone, and good at need. (A-F, H)

129 steeple (B-K) | <steeple> ↑ steeple ↓ (A)

132 child, (A-H) | child. (I-K)

133–136 [*Lines canceled in* (CC1, CC5); *not present in* (I-K)]

133 room (C-H) | room, (A-B)

135 Masked (CC4, CC5, CC9, G) | Close hid (A-F, H) || lurk (B-H) | <work>lurk (A)

136 magians,— (C-H) | <sorcerers,> ↑ magians; ↓ (A) | magians, (B) || work. (C-H) | work; (A-B)

140 land; (C-K) | land, (A-B)

141 cloverheads (CC1, CC9, G, I-K) | sweet hay (A-F, H) | clover-heads (CC4) || the swamp (A-B, CC1, CC4, CC9, G, I-K) | the wild swamp (C-F, H)

142 corn; (C-K) | corn, (A-B)

143 For wolves and foxes, (A-H) | For wolf and fox bring (CC1, CC5, I) | For wolf and fox, bring (J-K)

144 curds; (A-H) | curds: (I-K)

145 mats; (C-K) | mats, (A-B)

146 maple juice (C-K) | maple-juice (A-B) || vats. (B-K) | vats, (A)

147 air (C-K) | air, (A-B)

149 fish, (C-K) | fish (A-B)

151 And (A-H) | Whilst (CC1, CC5, I-K) || flinty (CC1, E-K) | iron (A-D) || face, (CC1, C-K) | face (A-B)

152 wax, (C-K) | wax (A-B)

155 place (A-H) | waste (CC1, I-K)

156 gardens of a finer race. (B-H) | gardens of a finer race<:—>. (A) | homes of virtue, sense, and taste. (CC1, I) | homes of virtue, sense and taste. (J-K)

157 World-soul (C-K) | world-soul (A-B)

158 Forelooking, (C-K) | Forelooking (A) | Fore-looking (B) || he would (C-K) | his hands (A-B)

159 ages, (C-K) | Ages (A-B) || mould (C-K) | mould, (A-B)

162 life-pulse (C-K) | life pulse (A-B) || strong (C-K) | strong, (A-B) || slow: (C-K) | slow <,>. (A) | slow. (B)

163 austere (A, C-K) | austere. (B)

164 grottos, (B-I) | grotto<s>es, (A) | grottoes, (J-K)

167 Toil and tempest (CC4, CC5, CC9, G, I-K) | These exercises (A-F, H)

168 to breathe his stalwart boys: (CC1, E-K) | with which he breathes his boys. (A-B) | with which he breathes his boys: (C-D)

170 Jove; (C-K) | Jove, (A-B)

172 the sun (B-K) | ↑ the ↓ sun <glow> (A) || made, (C-K) | made; (A-B)

173 the (CC1, E-K) | that (A-D) ||

fibre, (C-K) | fibre (A-B) || strong, (C-K) | strong (A-B)

176   In dulness now their secret keep; (CC1, CC2, E-K) | Their secret now in dulness keep. (A-B) | Their secret now in dulness keep; (C-D)

178   teach. (A, C-K) | teach, (B)

180   affords; (C-K) | affords, (A-B)

181–182 But they turn . . . art or passion. (CC1, E-K) | These they turn in other fashion / Than the writer or the parson. (A-D) | But they turn them in a fashion / Past the wit of clerk or parson (CC2)

183   college bell, (C-K) | college-bell, (A-B)

184   lecture, well; (C-K) | lecture well, (A) | lecture well. (B)

187   that (C-H, J-K) | the (A-B) | what (I) || English (A-H, J-K) | Saxon (I)

188   here, unvalued, (C-K) | here unvalued (A-B)

189   Rude (A-K) | <Rude> (CC2)

190   your (A-K) | <your> (CC2)

191   ground, (C-I) | ground (A-B, J-K)

192   retorts, (C-I) | retorts (A-B, J-K) || roars; (C-H, J-K) | roars, (A-B) | roars: (I)

193   Scoff of yeoman strong and stark, (E-K) | Tough and screaming as birch-bark, (A-B) | Tough and screaming, as birch-bark, (C-D) | Scoff of yeomen strong & stark (CC1)

194   mark; (CC1, C-K) | mark, (A-B)

196   balk (C-H, J-K) | baulk (A-B, I) || ear. (CC1, CC4, CC5, CC9, G, I-K) | ear. [ear: (A-B)] / To student ears keen relished [keen-relished (A-B)] jokes / On truck, and stock, and farming folks,—[farming-folks,— (A-B)] / Nought the mountain yields thereof, [thereof (A-B)] / But savage health and sinews tough. (A-F, H)

[*Note that in the correction copies the lines are canceled.*]

197   ["new paragraph"] (CC5)

198   floor (CC1, CC2, E-K) | wide floor (A-D) || flood, (A-B) | flood (C-K)

199   me (A-B) | me (C-K)

201   conveyed; (A-I) | conveyed: (J-K)

202   said:— (C-K) | said; (A) | said: (B)

203   'Many (C-K) | Many (A-B) || seek, (C-K) | seek (A-B)

204   Oft, (CC9, G, I-K) | Betimes, (C-F, H) | Betimes (A-B) | /Betimes/ Oft/, (CC4)

205   winter time, (C-K) | wintertime, (A) | winter-time, (B)

206   climb, (C-H, J-K) | climb (A-B, I)

207   clouds, (C-K) | clouds (A-B)

208   shade. (A-I) | shade; (J-K)

213   stand? (C-K) | stand, (A-B)

214   wouldst (C-K) | would'st (A-B) || companion, (A-H) | companion (I-K)

215–216 Where I gaze, and still shall gaze, / Thro' tempering nights and flashing days, (E-G) | Where I gaze / And shall gaze (A-B) | Where I gaze, / And shall gaze, (C-D) | Where I gaze, and still shall gaze, / Through tempering nights and flashing days, (H, J-K) | Where I gaze, and still shall gaze, / Through hoarding nights and spending days, (I) | [*In* (CC1) *Emerson first revised in pencil:* Where I gaze, ↑ & still shall gaze ↓ / <And shall gaze> ↑ moony nights & <[*illegible*]> flashing days, ↓ *then copied the revision in ink, altering* "moony" *to* "moon<y> ↑ -lit ↓ . *Also, a second revision, at the bottom of the page, in pencil:* Thro' /hoarding/tempering/ night & /spending/chequered/ cheerful/ days]

217   fall, (A-G, I-K) | fall (H)

218   times, (C-K) | times (A-B)

219   At (A, CC10, C-K) | As (B) ‖ Lyre, (C-K) | Lyre (A-B)

222   years? (C-K) | years. (A-B)

223–226   [*Lines canceled in* (CC4); *not present in* (J-K)]

223   'Ah! (C-I) | Ah! (A-B)

225   Muse's (A, C-I) | muse's (B)

227   Gentle (A-I) | 'Gentle (J-K)

232–233   [*Lines canceled in* (CC1, CC5), *bracketed in* (CC4) *with notation* "X rec"; *not present in* (I-K)]

232   'Tis (B-H) | Tis (A) ‖ stone, (C-H) | stone,— (A) | stone— (B)

234   'Let (C-K) | Let (A-B) ‖ will; (C-K) | will,— (A-B)

238   'If (C-H) | <Pilgrim, i>If (A) | If (B, I-K)

239   play, (C-K) | play (A-B)

240   pole, (B-K) | pole (A) ‖ say; (C-G, I-K) | say, (A-B) | say (H)

245   seeming, (C-K) | seeming (A-B)

246   beaming;— (C-K) | beaming; (A-B)

250   snowflake's (A, C-G, I-K) | snow-flake's (B, H) ‖ flight;— (C-K) | flight; (A-B)

253   lie (B-K) | <are> ↑lie↓ (A)

255   'For (C-K) | For (A-B)

256   tune; (C-K) | tune, (A-B)

257   Time (A, C-K) | time (B)

258   The sun obeys them, and (I) | Cannot forget the sun, (A-H) | The sun obeys them and (CC5, J-K) | the sun obeys them, and (CC1)

260   rune; (C-K) | rune, (A-B)

266   'Monadnoc (C-H, J-K) | Monadnoc (A-B) | 'Monadnock (I)

267   among; (C-K) | among, (A-B)

268   can, (G, I-K) | can (A-F, H)

269   Zion or Meru, measure with man. (CC1, CC5, CC9, G, I-K) | Measure with a perfect man; (A-B) |

Measure with a perfect man. (C-F, H) | "a perfect" *is circled,* "Zion or Meru" *added in margin* (CC4)

270   zodiacs (D-K) | Zodiacks (A) | Zodiack's (B) | temples (C) | Zodiacs (CC1)

271   wit: (C-K) | wit; (A-B)

272   again (C-K) | again, (A-B)

273   secret (CC10, C-K) | music (A-B)

274   pass, (C-K) | pass (A-B)

276   'Through all time, in light, in gloom, (E-I) | Through all time <I hear> (A) | Through all time (B) | 'Through all time (C-D) | 'Through all time, in light, in gloom (J-K) | 'Through all time, ↑in light, in gloom,↓ (CC1) [*Preceded by two drafts in pencil:* ' ↑In day & darkness,↓ Through all time, *and* 'Through all time, ↑in shine, in gloom,↓]

277   Well I (CC1, E-K) | I (A-D)

278   On (CC1, E-K) | Along (A-D)

279   cometh, (B-K) | cometh (A) ‖ come; (C-K) | come,— (A-B)

282   doth this (CC1, F-K) | now the (A-E)

283   beams; (C-K) | beams, (A-B)

286   Alleganies (A, G, I) | Alleghanies (B-F, H, J-K) | Alleg<h>anies (CC4, CC9)

289   'Every (C-K) | Every (A-B)

290   See (CC4, CC5, CC9, G, J-K) | Gaze oer (A) | Gaze o'er (B-F, H) ‖ underspread, (C-K) | underspread (A-B)

292   Katskill (A, C-K) | Katshill (B)

295   Who, (C-K) | Who (A-B)

299   when, (C-K) | when (A-B) ‖ pain, (C-K) | pain (A-B)

301   shed, (C-K) | shed (A-B)

302   wellspring (A, C-K) | well-spring (B) ‖ head, (C-K) | head (A-B)

303   Fountain-drop (CC1, E-K) | Fountain drop (A-D)

306   oil. (C-K) | oil; (A-B)

308   Autumn-ripe, (C-K) | Autumn-ripe (A-B) || hold (A, C-K) | hold, (B)

310   rancor, (C-K) | rancour, (A-B) || Athens' (A, CC11, C-K) | Athen's (B)

312   sight. (C-K) | sight; (A-B)

315   eat, (C-G, I-K) | eat (A-B, H) || drain; (J-K) | drink, (A-B) | drink; (C-H) | drain, (I) | drain (CC1)

316   coinage of his brain (CC1, I-K) | thoughts that he shall think (A-H)

322   Dark, (A, C-K) | dark, (B)

324   South Cove (C-K) | South-Cove (A-B) || City Wharf. (C-K) | City-wharf; (A-B)

328   snow; (A-I) | snow: (J-K)

333   city-tops (CC1, E-K) | city tops (A-D) || haze. (C-K) | haze<,>: (A) | haze: (B)

334   bounding: (C-H) | bounding;— (A-B) | bounding; (I-K)

335   "See (C-K) | See (A-B) || gray (C-K) | grey (A-B)

339   deep." (C-K) | deep;— (A-B)

340   pale. (C-K) | pale: (A-B)

341   'Tis (B-K) | Tis (A) || so; (C-H) | so, (A-B, I-K) || kite, (A-I, K) | kite (J)

344   forever; (C-K) | forever, (A) | for ever, (B)

345   parasite, (C-K) | parasite,— (A-B)

346   steer,— (C-K) | steer, (A-B)

351   north wind (B-H, J-K) | northwind (A) | north-wind (I) || blood; (C-K) | blood, (A-B)

352   him, (C-K) | him (A-B) || rocks; (C-K) | rocks, (A-B)

356   chatter, frightened, (C-K) | chatter frightened (A-B) || clan, (A-I) | clan (J-K)

357   me (C-K) | me, (A-B) || can.' (C-K) | can. (A-B)

365   use;— (C-K) | use; (A-B)

366   bind (C-K) | bind, (A-B)

367   Ceres (C-K) | Ceres, (A-B)

369   affirmer (CC1, CC3, CC4, CC9, G, I-K) | expressor (A-B) | expresser (C-F, H)

370   permanence! (C-K) | permanence, (A-B)

372   grief, (C-K) | grief (A-B)

373   seeing! (C-K) | seeing. (A-B)

375   thy (CC1, I-K) | the (A-H) || rocks; (C-K) | rocks, (A-B)

376   flight, (C-K) | flight (A-B) || folded wing, (I-K) | pestering wing (A-B) | pestering wing, (C-H) | / pestering/folded/ wing, (CC1)

377   Vanish, (C-K) | Vanish (A-B) || murmuring,— (C-K) | murmuring, (A-B)

379   Which (C-K) | Which, (A-B)

381   architrave;— (C-K) | architrave; (A-B)

382   Yet (A-I) | Where (CC1, J-K) || brave; (C-K) | brave, (A-B)

386   Having (A-H) | Holding (CC1, I-K)

387   sumptuous (A-K) | (boastful?) (CC1)

388   mound, (C-K) | mound<,>↑!↓ (A) | mound! (B) || fill! (C-K) | fill. (A-B)

389   prate; (C-K) | prate,— (A-B)

391   myriad (C-K) | million (A-B)

392   dispense; (C-K) | dispense, (A-B)

395   tall, (C-K) | tall! (A-B)

397   good (C-H, J-K) | Good (A-B) | good, (I)

398   [*Line canceled* (CC1); *not present in* (I)]

399   shifting (B-K) | <dancing> ↑shifting↓ (A) || mind, (C-K) | mind; (A-B)

402   Thou, (C-K) | Thou (A-B)

404   Seen haply (C-K) | Seen, haply, (A-B)

405   hoop, (A, C-K) | hoop. (B)

406   moment, (C-K) | moment (A-B)

407   o'er (B-K) I oer (A)
408   ambition, (B-K) I Ambition, (A)
409   gain, (C-K) I Gain, (A-B)
410   feasters (C-K) I feasters, (A-B)
413   well skilled (C-K) I well-skilled
      (A-B)

415   succor and remede (CC1, CC4,
      CC5, CC9, G, I-K) I supply (A-F, H)
417   truth, (A, C-K) I truth. (B)

NOTES

97.   The opposition of the Welsh Bards to the English king Edward I, together with their association with Mount Snowdon, the highest peak in Great Britain, is described in "The Bard: A Pindaric Ode" by Thomas Gray. The subject is also treated by Felicia Hemans in "Chant of the Bards before Their Massacre by Edward I" (1822) and by Henry Gilpin in *The Massacre of the Bards* (1839). Rob Roy, title character of Walter Scott's popular 1817 novel (and subject as well of William Wordsworth's "Rob Roy's Grave"), was a Highland chieftain, outlaw, and Jacobite. Gjevgj Kastrioti Skanderbeg (1405–1486), called "the Dragon of Albania," took up arms against the Ottoman hegemony. William Tell, of the Canton of Uri, fought against the Habsburg Empire in the fourteenth century, in a conflict that led to the Swiss Confederation.

124.   Emerson's depiction of the locals as rough and stolid frontiersmen may more directly reflect his tour of Franconia Notch and the White Mountains in 1839 (see headnote). In any event the description seems unfair to the people of the region around Monadnoc and to Dublin in particular. Under the leadership of the Unitarian minister Levi Washburn Leonard, "the Oberlin of Monadnock," the Dublin schools were from a very early period the envy of the state (George Farber Clark, "Rev. Levi Washburn Leonard, D. D.," *Memorial Biographies of the New-England Historic and Genealogical Society,* VI [Boston, 1905]: 67–68). The first public library in America, established in nearby Peterborough in 1828, seems to have been conceptually influenced by the circulating library for which Leonard was responsible (Leonard, *History of Dublin* (Boston, 1855), 243–264; Clark, 66–70). Theodore Parker rejoiced in 1855 that the tavern bar in Dublin had been converted to a newsstand and that the farmers all read the Boston papers.

255–256.   John Tyndall, the preeminent nineteenth-century British physicist, was fond of quoting these, along with many other lines of Emerson's poetry, in conversation as well as in writing, to illustrate his scientific observations and arguments. See *L,* X, 16–18, and Raychal A. Haugrud, "Tyndall's Interest in Emerson," *American Literature,* XLI (January 1970): 507–517 (515).

286.   The more familiar spelling of Alleghanies was probably an imposition of house style; Emerson's preferred form, Alleganies, was an acknowledged variant.

317.   "When he spoke of the stars, he should be innocent of what he said; for it seemed that the stars, as they rolled over him, mirrored themselves in his mind as in a deep well, & it was their image & not his thought that you saw" (*JMN*, IX, 27; 1843).

318.   In the letter that Emerson wrote to Caroline Sturgis from Mount Wachusett on 1 April 1845, he described the effect of looking out from the mountaintop: "At once all is changed, & all assumes a planetary air, & I begin to see the shining of it, when a little further withdrawn, like Mars & Jupiter" (*L*, VIII, 18).

364.   Monadnoc's unusually low tree line was in fact artificially created when, early in the century, nearby sheepherders fired the mountaintop in an effort to eradicate wolves. The summit burned for three weeks. Thoreau learned these facts in 1852 (*J*, V, 339); it is doubtful that Emerson knew the story at the time he wrote the poem. See also Leonard, who cites an old resident's youthful recollection of Monadnoc "clothed with verdant foliage to the very summit" (106).

FABLE.

After several times promising to send contributions for the Philadelphia gift-book annual *The Diadem,* Emerson at last, on 9 May 1845, posted to its editor, his old friend William Henry Furness, three recently composed short poems, "Loss and Gain," "Fore-Runners," and "A Fable." It is evident from the reiteration of the promises and their last-minute fulfillment (*L*, VIII, 7, 20, 26) that the poems were written very shortly before they were sent.

Emerson's decision to place this short, comic poem immediately after the long, imposing "Monadnoc" in *Poems* (1847) is itself an instance of the dramatic conflict rehearsed in the parable. As he had said, "it is the right & property of all natural objects, of all genuine talents, of all native properties whatsoever, to be for their moment the top of the world, to exclude all other objects, & themselves monopolize the attention. A squirrel or a rabbit as I watch him bounding in the wood, not less than a lion fills the eye, is beautiful, sufficing, & stands then & there for nature; is the world" (*JMN*, VII, 199–200). Emerson's "all-in-each" principle advantages the poet by showing that importance and triviality are never "given," never fatal attributes of the subject, but always a product of the seer's commanding point of view.

The "Fable" was in general very well received: Edgar Allan Poe singled it out in a review of the *Diadem* as "exceedingly *piquant* and *naive*" (*The Poe Log*, Dwight Thomas and David K. Jackson, comps. [New York, 1987], 605). It was first introduced to a young audience when it was reprinted by the Universalist publishers of the *Boston Gospel Teacher, and Sabbath School Contributor* in its issue for 1 March 1846 (p. 74). Known informally as "The Mountain and the Squirrel," the poem seems to have been a favorite with children for many years thereafter, which may have something to do with James Russell Lowell's recommendation that it be dropped from *Selected Poems* (1876). The suggestion was overruled, however, by James Elliot Cabot and his wife, with strong support from the Emerson children (*ETE*, II, 196–197).

FABLE.

The mountain and the squirrel
Had a quarrel;
And the former called the latter 'Little Prig.'
Bun replied,
'You are doubtless very big;   5
But all sorts of things and weather
Must be taken in together,
To make up a year
And a sphere.
And I think it no disgrace   10
To occupy my place.
If I'm not so large as you,
You are not so small as I,

Poems (1847)

And not half so spry.
I'll not deny you make   15
A very pretty squirrel track;
Talents differ; all is well and wisely put;
If I cannot carry forests on my back,
Neither can you crack a nut.'

TEXTS

(A) *The Diadem for MDCCCXLVI* (Philadelphia: Carey & Hart, 1846), 38; (B) MS, Private Collection, printer's copy for C; (C) *Poems* (London, 1847), 91; (D) *Poems* (Boston, 1847), 115–16; (E) *Poems* ["Fourth Edition"] (Boston, 1847), 115–16; (F) *Poems* (Boston, 1865), 118–19; (G) *Selected Poems* (Boston, 1876), 155; (H) *Poems* [Riverside] (Boston, 1884), 71; (H²) *Poems* [Centenary] (Boston, 1904), 75. No variants occur in later printings from the Boston plates after (E).

Format: Lines 17 and 19 indented (A-B).

Pre-copy-text forms: The first and only surviving draft of the poem occurs in journal W (*JMN,* IX, 205).

VARIANTS

Title: FABLE. (C-H) I A FABLE. (A) I
Fable. (B)
2   quarrel; (D-G) I quarrel, (A-C, H)
3   latter (D-H) I latter, (A-C) II 'Little Prig.' (D-F) [*The second quotation mark is lost to plate damage in* (E).] I I "little Prig:" (A) I 'little prig:'

(B-C) I 'Little Prig'; (G) I 'Little Prig;' (H)
5   'You (D-H) I You (A-C) II big; (D-H) I big, (A-C)
7   together, (D-H) I together (A-C)
8   year (A, D-H) I year, (B-C)
14   spry. (D-H) I spry: (A-C)
19   nut.' (D-H) I nut. (A-C)

ODE,

INSCRIBED TO W. H. CHANNING.

One of the most challenging and rewarding of Emerson's poems, the "Ode, Inscribed to W. H. Channing" was written in the first week of June 1846 while the poet was on an excursion to New Hampshire's Mount Monadnoc. The poem's New Hampshire setting, prominently indicated not only in the references to the river Contoocook and the valleys of Agiochook (Mount Washington), but also in the explicit reference to the "lofty land" and "little men" of that state, serves several purposes beyond those he developed in "Monadnoc." By allying the speaker with the sublime landscape of the White Mountains, Emerson increases the contrast between his own situation and that of his friend, the Boston minister William Henry Channing, who had immediately provoked the poem by an eloquently angry disunionist speech delivered on 29 May at the annual meeting of the Massachusetts Anti-Slavery Society, at Faneuil Hall. The anger and excitement of that occasion had much to do with America's declaration of war with Mexico on 13 May (portending a vast enlargement of the American Slave Power) and with the still more recent Boston funeral of the Reverend Charles Turner Torrey, a Unitarian minister from Salem who had died in the Maryland State Prison, to which he had been consigned for having helped escaped slaves. Emerson attended the funeral, which took place at the Masonic Temple on 19 May after the Park Street Church, taking a political stance, refused its facilities. Apart from a dignified eulogy from the Rev. Joseph Lovejoy that Emerson admired, the event had, predictably, the character of an indignation meeting. Emerson wrote that "the skeptics have got into the Abolition society, & make believe to be enraged" (*JMN*, IX, 410). Channing had been one of the hotter speakers on this occasion, and it would seem that Emerson was becoming increasingly disturbed by the outraged tone and escalating fierceness of the abolitionists' public discourse. It was "skeptical," Emerson felt, desperately to resort to violent language, as if the good to which one otherwise bore witness had in itself no positive power. The logic was the same as Emerson had followed earlier in thinking about the peace reform: "if a nation of men is exalted to that height of morals as to refuse to fight & choose rather to suffer loss of goods & loss of life than to use violence, they must be not helpless but most effective and great men; they would overawe their invader, & make him ridiculous; they would communicate the contagion of their virtue & inoculate all mankind" (*JMN*, V, 378). The example of the peaceful, non-resistant Torrey, who had suffered "loss of life" for principle, jarred with the aggressive language of resentment broadcast over the gentle martyr's coffin-lid. The abolitionist Henry Bowditch, who had staged the funeral as political theatre, later said he had "reason to believe" that Emerson's poem referred to this event (quoted in Len Gougeon, "The Anti-Slavery Background of Emerson's 'Ode Inscribed to W. H. Channing,'" *SAR 1985*, p. 68).

Channing had a few years earlier offered a critique of Emerson's passivity on social questions (including his failure to embrace Brook Farm and its associationist strategies) that clearly stung Emerson. On 29 May 1842 he wrote to Margaret Fuller to say that Channing "charges me with universal homicide, nothing less. According to me there is no human race" (*L*, III, 58; Octavius Brooks Frothingham, *Memoir of William Henry Channing* [Boston, 1886], 464–465). He seems to have written several letters to Channing at this time in an effort to explain himself, but what survives from his side of the dialogue is a journal entry: "I should write again to W. H. C. & say, He that unites himself to the race separates himself from the Father but he who by love & contemplation dwells with the father, from him the Race always proceeds filially & new, and the actual race feel in his presence their degeneracy & his salutary redeeming force. Keep thyself pure from the race. Come to them only as saviour, not as companion" (*JMN,* VIII, 186; cf. *L,* VII, 503). However this argument may have adjusted itself in 1842, its philosophical premises reappear in Emerson's "Ode" of 1846. Emerson respected Channing's many talents, and yet tensions of various kinds persisted between them, as, for example, after a meeting in June 1845, which ended "unsatisfactorily" (*L,* III, 290).

The Channing Ode is often read as Emerson's apologia for his relative disengagement from organized anti-slavery work, but the positive of the same case might as truly be put: it is the expression of a fundamental belief in the moral efficacy of the poet's vocation and the value of a clear, sane, even dispassionate view of things. It is a point he made many times.

> The reason why I pound so tediously on that string of the exemption of the writer from all secular works is our conviction that his work needs a frolic health to execute. . . . In that prosperity he is sometimes caught up into a perception of means & materials, of feats & fine arts, of faery machineries & funds of poetic power, . . . which . . . he can . . . reduce into iambic or trochaic, into lyric or heroic rhyme. . . . Now at this small elevation above his usual sphere, he has come into new circulations, the marrow of the world is in his bones, the opulence of forms begins to pour into his intellect, & he is permitted to dip his brush into the old paint pot with which birds, flowers, the human cheek, the living rock, the ocean, the broad landscape, & the eternal sky were painted. (*JMN,* IX, 407; cf. "The Poet," *CW,* III, 5)

It is interesting to find that Thoreau, who shared this valuation of the "frolic-healthy" point of view, expressed it once in terms of W. H. Channing's violation of it: "My objection to Channing and all that fraternity," he wrote in 1843, "is that they need and deserve sympathy themselves rather than are able to render it to others. They want faith and mistake their private ail for an infected atmosphere, but let any one of them recover hope for a moment, and right his *particular* grievance, and he will no longer train in that company. To speak or do any thing that shall concern mankind, one must speak and act as if well, or from that grain of health which he has left" (*Correspondence,* 147). This non-resistant posture, which will not go rhetorically to war even to oppose a war, seems, like Torrey's, built of the same stuff as the position of St. Paul, who could say that "God is not the author of confusion, but of peace, as in all churches of the saints" (I Corinthians 14:33; cf. line 11 below).

The "Ode" may possibly have grieved Channing, "the evil time's sole patriot," but it certainly disappointed Channing's friends from Brook Farm, where he had been accustomed to preach (John Thomas Codman, *Brook Farm: Historic and Personal Memoirs* [Boston, 1894], 108). Although it is one of Emerson's very best poems, the "Ode" was given an inconspicuous place toward the middle of *Poems* in 1847 and was omitted entirely from *Selected Poems* in 1876, over the objections of James Elliot Cabot (*ETE,* II, 197).

ODE,

INSCRIBED TO W. H. CHANNING.

Though loath to grieve
The evil time's sole patriot,
I cannot leave
My honied thought
For the priest's cant,   5
Or statesman's rant.

If I refuse
My study for their politique,
Which at the best is trick,
The angry Muse   10
Puts confusion in my brain.

But who is he that prates
Of the culture of mankind,
Of better arts and life?
Go, blindworm, go,   15

Behold the famous States
Harrying Mexico
With rifle and with knife!

Or who, with accent bolder,
Dare praise the freedom-loving mountaineer?   20
I found by thee, O rushing Contoocook!
And in thy valleys, Agiochook!
The jackals of the negro-holder.

The God who made New Hampshire
Taunted the lofty land   25
With little men;—
Small bat and wren
House in the oak:—
If earth-fire cleave
The upheaved land, and bury the folk,   30
The southern crocodile would grieve.

Virtue palters; Right is hence;
Freedom praised, but hid;
Funeral eloquence
Rattles the coffin-lid.   35

What boots thy zeal,
O glowing friend,
That would indignant rend
The northland from the south?
Wherefore? to what good end?   40
Boston Bay and Bunker Hill
Would serve things still;—
Things are of the snake.

The horseman serves the horse,
The neatherd serves the neat,   45
The merchant serves the purse,
The eater serves his meat;
'Tis the day of the chattel,

Web to weave, and corn to grind;
Things are in the saddle,   50
And ride mankind.

There are two laws discrete,
Not reconciled,—
Law for man, and law for thing;
The last builds town and fleet,   55
But it runs wild,
And doth the man unking.

'Tis fit the forest fall,
The steep be graded,
The mountain tunnelled,   60
The sand shaded,
The orchard planted,
The glebe tilled,
The prairie granted,
The steamer built.   65

Let man serve law for man;
Live for friendship, live for love,
For truth's and harmony's behoof;
The state may follow how it can,
As Olympus follows Jove.   70

   Yet do not I implore
The wrinkled shopman to my sounding woods,
Nor bid the unwilling senator
Ask votes of thrushes in the solitudes.
Every one to his chosen work;—   75
Foolish hands may mix and mar;
Wise and sure the issues are.
Round they roll till dark is light,
Sex to sex, and even to odd;—
The over-god   80
Who marries Right to Might,
Who peoples, unpeoples,—

Ode

He who exterminates
Races by stronger races,
Black by white faces,— 85
Knows to bring honey
Out of the lion;
Grafts gentlest scion
On pirate and Turk.

The Cossack eats Poland, 90
Like stolen fruit;
Her last noble is ruined,
Her last poet mute:
Straight, into double band
The victors divide; 95
Half for freedom strike and stand;—
The astonished Muse finds thousands at her side.

TEXTS

(A) MS, m.b., Berg Collection, by permission of the New York Public Library, printer's copy for B; (B) *Poems* (London, 1847), 92–96; (C) *Poems* (Boston, 1847), 117–122; (D) *Poems* ["Fourth Edition"] (Boston, 1847), 117–122; (E) *Poems* (Boston, 1865), 120–125; (F) *Poems* [Riverside] (Boston, 1884), 71–74; (F²) *Poems* [Centenary] (Boston, 1904), 76–79. No variants occur in later printings from the plates of *Poems* (1847) after (D) other than continued progressive type damage affecting punctuation. (A) has "Monadnoc, June 1846" canceled after the title, and "Monadnoc" inscribed after the poem.

Format: Verse break following line 31 (A-B) coincides with page break (C-E); no verse break at this point in (F, F²). No verse break following line 70 in (B). Line 71 flush (A-B).

Pre-copy-text forms: Drafts occur in poetry notebook X (see *PN*, 881).

VARIANTS

1	loath (C-F) l loth (A-B)	10	Muse (C-F) l muse (A-B)
4	honied (A, CC2, CC10, CC11,	15	blindworm, (A, C-F) l blind
C-D, F) l buried (B) l honeyed (E)		worm (B)	

18   knife! (C-F) | knife. (A-B)

20   mountaineer? (A, C-F) | mountaineer, (B)

22   valleys, (C-F) | vallies, (A-B)

23   negro-holder (B-F) | negroholder (A)

26   men;— (C-F) | men. (A-B)

28   oak:— (C-F) | oak. (A-B)

29   earth-fire (C-F) | earthfire (A) | earth fire (B)

31   southern (A-D, F) | Southern (E)

32   palters; (C-F) | palters, (A-B) || Right (C-F) | right (A-B) || hence; (C-F) | hence, (A-B)

33   praised, (C-F) | praised (A-B)

39   northland (A-D, F) | Northland (E) || south? (A-D, F) | South? (E)

40   to (C-F) | To (A-B)

42   still;— (C-F) | still: (A-B)

43   snake. (B-F) | Snake. (A)

45   neatherd (C-F) | neat-herd (A-B)

48   'Tis (B-F) | Tis (A)

49   grind; (C-F) | grind, (A-B)

52   discrete, (C-F) | discrete (A-B)

53   reconciled,— (C-F) | reconciled, (A-B)

58   'Tis (B-F) | Tis (A)

61   sand (A, C-F) | land (B)

63   glebe (A, CC10, C-F) | globe (B)

64   granted (C-F) | planted (A-B)

66   man; (C-F) | man, (A-B)

69   state (B-F) | State (A)

71   implore (A-B, D-F) | invite (C)

75   work;— (C-F) | work. (A-B)

76   mar; (C-F) | mar, (A-B)

78   roll (C-F) | roll, (A-B)

79   odd;— (C-F) | odd; (A-B)

80   over-god (C-F) | Over-God, (A) | over-God, (B)

82   Who (B-F) | <He w>Who (A) || unpeoples,— (C-F) | unpeoples, (A-B)

85   faces,— (C-F) | faces, (A-B)

87   lion; (C-F) | lion, (A-B)

89   pirate (C-F) | Pirate (A-B)

93   mute: (C-F) | mute; (A-B)

94   Straight, (C-F) | Straight (A-B)

95   victors (B-F) | Victors (A) || divide; (C-F) | divide, (A-B)

96   stand;— (C-F) | stand, (A-B)

97   Muse (A, C-F) | muse (B)

NOTES

Title: William Henry Channing (1810–1884), nephew of the Unitarian leader William Ellery Channing, was himself a minister, though rarely settled for long in any one place. Through his friendships with James Freeman Clarke, Margaret Fuller, and Frederic Henry Hedge, he sustained important connections with *The Western Messenger,* the *Dial,* the *Present,* Brook Farm, and the Boston Religious Union of Associationists. In the 1840s he was intensely involved with Fourierism and anti-slavery.

6.   In 1844, the year he delivered his important anti-slavery "Address on West Indian Emancipation," Emerson wrote in his journal: "I do not & can not forsake my vocation for abolitionism" (*JMN,* IX, 64n).

9. "What satire on government can equal the severity of censure conveyed in the word *politic,* which now for ages has signified *cunning,* intimating that the State is a trick?" ("Politics," *CW,* III, 122).

11. "At times the whole world seems to be in conspiracy to importune you with emphatic trifles. Friend, client, child, sickness, fear, want, charity, all knock at once at thy closet door and say,—'Come out unto us.' But keep thy state; come not into their confusion" ("Self-Reliance," *CW,* II, 41).

12. It is tempting to identify the statesman as New Hampshire native Daniel Webster, as Carl F. Strauch has done. But Len Gougeon, offering a rebuttal, finds "no compelling reason to identify Webster with the poem in any direct or specific way" ("The Anti-Slavery Background of Emerson's 'Ode Inscribed to W. H. Channing,'" 76). Indeed, Emerson's journal references to Webster were, as late as 1846, still quite laudatory. There is nevertheless the following journal entry of that year: "To know the virtue of the soil, we do not taste the loam, but we eat the berries & apples; and to mend the bad world, we do not impeach Polk & Webster, but we supersede them by the Muse" (*JMN,* IX, 357).

15. The blindworm (*Anguis fragilis*) has the appearance of a snake but is actually a lizard; it is native to Europe and west Asia.

26. "In New Hampshire the dignity of the landscape made more obvious the meanness of the tavern-haunting men" (*JMN,* VII, 236). The comment was prompted by Emerson's trip to the White Mountains in September, 1839; see the headnote to "Monadnoc," above.

39. At the "Anniversary Week" convention of the Anti-Slavery Society held in Faneuil Hall on 1 June 1846, Channing vociferously protested the commencement of the Mexican War—and the extension of slavery it augured—with a call for disunion, as he had earlier done when the subject of Texas annexation was introduced in 1837 (Frothingham, *Memoir of William Henry Channing* [Boston, 1886], 199–200, 258–259). Emerson knew of Channing's position at least as early as 1 August 1845 when both men spoke at an open-air protest meeting in Waltham (*EAW,* pp. xxxii, 35–38, and Henry Wilson, *History of the Rise and Fall of the Slave Power in America,* 3 vols. [Boston, 1872], I, 640–41).

44. Emerson's neighbor Edmund Hosmer thought there was "a great deal of unnecessary labor spent to feed the animals—especially the pig & horse. Many a farmer is but a horse's horse or a pig's pig" (*JMN,* VIII, 278).

51. "If a man live in the saddle the saddle somehow will come to live in him" (*JMN,* VII, 102).

54. "Things have their laws, as well as men" ("Politics," *CW,* III, 120).

57. This idea was familiar to the New England Puritans. See, for example, Urian Oakes in *A Seasonable Discourse* (Cambridge, Mass., 1682): "Man is de-

throned, and become a servant and slave to those things that were made to serve him, and he puts those things in his heart, that God hath put under his feet" (27).

58. Emerson grudgingly reconciled himself to the new railroad that had snaked through Concord woods: it "was very odious to me when it began, but it is hard to resist the joy of all one's neighbours, and I must be contented to be carted like a chattel in the cars & be glad to see the forest fall. This *rushing* on your journey is plainly a capital invention for our spacious America, but it is more dignified & manlike to walk barefoot" (*CEC*, 355).

65. The due observance of the "law for thing" amounts to a kind of human self-provisioning that Emerson invariably commended and frequently figured as a taming and civilizing of brute nature. See, for example, his praise of the "Western magians" in "Monadnoc," ll. 135ff. For another, earlier, and more conventional instance of this approval of progress, see *CS*, I, 72.

84. Emerson's thinking about "weaker races" was complicated. In an 1838 journal entry, in which he correctly predicted the extinction of the St. Michael's pear, he extended his proto-evolutionary speculation to the human situation: "Each race of man resembles an apple or a pear, the Nubian, the Negro, the Tartar, the Greek, he vegetates, thrives, & multiplies, usurps all the soil & nutriment, & so kills the weaker races, he receives all the benefit of Culture under many zones & experiments, but his doom was in nature as well as his thrift, & overtakes him at last with the certainty of gravitation" (*JMN*, VII, 90).

87. Samson's encounter with the lion at Timnah is narrated in Judges 14:5–9.

88. "You see, sweet maid, we marry / A gentler scion to the wildest stock / And make conceive a bark of baser kind / By bud of nobler race. This is an art / Which does mend nature—change it rather; but / The art itself is nature" (Shakespeare, *A Winter's Tale*, IV, iv, 92–97).

90. The Russian empire was the main beneficiary in the three distinct partitions of Poland that occurred in the late eighteenth century, but the country was beset by neighboring powers, Russia, Prussia, and Austria, through much of the nineteenth century as well. This standing violation of Polish statehood was a painful inspiration to such nationalist poets as Adam Mickiewicz. It is possible that Emerson was influenced by a series of unsigned articles in *The American Whig Review* written by Polish expatriate Felix Paul Wierzbicki (1815–1860) entitled "Three Chapters on the History of Poland" (III [May 1846]: 488–496; [June 1846]: 631–640; and IV [July 1846]: 45–52). An additional essay, "Brighter Days for Poland," IV (August, 1846): 188–199, though it contains several apposite passages linking poetry and patriotism, would seem to have been published too late to have affected Emerson's Ode. Margaret Fuller wrote a lengthy notice of the New York celebration of the fifteenth anniversary of the failed Polish Revolu-

tion, held by a number of expatriates, including Wierzbicki, whose address she extensively quoted (*New York Daily Tribune*, 1 December 1845, p. 2.

97. "Nature is always gainer, & reckons surely on our sympathy. The Russians eat up the Poles. What then? when the last Polander is gone, the Russians are men, are ourselves, & the Pole is forgotten in our identification with Russian parties. A philosopher is no philosopher unless he takes lively part with the thief who picks his pocket and with the bully that insults or strikes him" (*JMN*, IX, 383, c. June 1846). Elsewhere, in his 1840 lecture on "Reforms" (*EL*, III, 257), Emerson explained the ironically salutary effect that aggression (logically including the aggression of "Cossacks" against Poles) may—and perhaps must— have: "The fury with which the slavetrader defends every inch of his bloody deck and howling auction only serves as a trump of doom to alarum the ear of mankind to wake the dull sleepers and drag all neutrals to take sides and listen to the argument and verdict which justice shall finally pronounce." A journal entry composed in September 1843 shows that Emerson thought the English "have not treated Russia as they ought in the affair of Poland," and that this was because they took their lead from "the antislavery papers and Whig papers . . . & all other committed organs" (*JMN*, IX, 17).

ASTRÆA.

Astræa ("Star maiden") was the virgin daughter of Zeus and Themis, goddess of Truth and Chastity, but preeminently of Justice. At the conclusion of the Greek Golden Age, she was the last of the immortals to consort with humans, who had begun to grow evil, and was installed in the heavens by Zeus as the constellation Virgo. Edward Emerson's suggestion (*W*, IX, 428) that his father had considered "ΓΝΩΘΙ ΣΕΑΥΤΟΝ" (the Greek maxim, "Know Thyself") as a possible title is supported by notations in two late correction copies (CC4 and CC5).

ASTRÆA.

Thou the herald art who wrote
Thy rank, and quartered thine own coat.
There is no king nor sovereign state
That can fix a hero's rate;
Each to all is venerable,   5
Cap-a-pie invulnerable,
Until he write, where all eyes rest,
Slave or master on his breast.

I saw men go up and down,
In the country and the town,   10
With this tablet on their neck,—
'Judgment and a judge we seek.'
Not to monarchs they repair,
Nor to learned jurist's chair;
But they hurry to their peers,   15
To their kinsfolk and their dears;
Louder than with speech they pray,—
'What am I? companion, say.'
And the friend not hesitates
To assign just place and mates;   20
Answers not in word or letter,
Yet is understood the better;
Each to each a looking-glass,
Reflects his figure that doth pass.
Every wayfarer he meets   25
What himself declared repeats,
What himself confessed records,
Sentences him in his words;
The form is his own corporal form,
And his thought the penal worm.   30

Yet shine forever virgin minds,
Loved by stars and purest winds,
Which, o'er passion throned sedate,

Astræa

Have not hazarded their state;
Disconcert the searching spy,   35
Rendering to a curious eye
The durance of a granite ledge
To those who gaze from the sea's edge.
It is there for benefit;
It is there for purging light;   40
There for purifying storms;
And its depths reflect all forms;
It cannot parley with the mean,—
Pure by impure is not seen.
For there's no sequestered grot,   45
Lone mountain tarn, or isle forgot,
But Justice, journeying in the sphere,
Daily stoops to harbor there.

TEXTS

(A) MS HM 7626, by permission of the Huntington Library, San Marino, California, printer's copy for B; (B) *Poems* (London, 1847), 96–98; (C) *Poems* (Boston, 1847), 123–125; (D) *Poems* ["Fifth Edition"] (Boston, 1856), 123–25; (E) *Poems* (Boston, 1863), 123–25; (F) *Poems* (Boston, 1865), 126–128; (G) *Selected Poems* (Boston, 1876), 74–75; (H) *Poems* [Riverside] (Boston, 1884), 75–76; (I) *Poems* [Centenary] (Boston, 1904), 80–81.

Format: White line omitted following lines 8 and 30 (H-I).

Pre-copy-text forms: Drafts occur in poetry notebook X (see *PN*, 738).

VARIANTS

Title: ASTRÆA (A-I) I /ASTRÆA /
ΓΝΩΘΙ ΣΕΑΤΤΟΝ/ (CC4, CC5)
  1   Thou the herald art (CC4, CC5,
CC9, E) I Himself it was (A-C) I Each
the herald is (CC1, D, F-I)
  2   Thy (CC4, CC5, CC9, E) I His
(A-D, F-I)) II thine (CC4, CC5, CC9,
E) I his (A-D, F-I)

  6   Cap-a-pie (B-I) I Capapie (A)
  8   down, (C-I) I down (A-B)
  11   tablet on (CC1, D-I) I prayer
upon (A-C) II neck,— (C-H) I neck,
(A-B, I)
  14   chair; (C-I) I chair, (A-B)
  16   dears; (C-I) I dears, (A-B)
  17   pray,— (C-I) I pray, (A-B)

18   'What (C-I) | What (A-B) ||
companion, (A, C-I) | companion;
(B) || say.' (C-I) | say, (A-B)
20   mates; (C-I) | mates, (A-B)
22   better; (C-I) | better;— (A-B)
23   Each to each (CC1, D-I) | Is to
his friend (A-C)
26   declared repeats, (C-I) |
declared, repeats; (A-B)
27   confessed records, (C-I) |
confessed, records; (A-B)
28   words; (C-I) | words, (A-B)
30   his (A-F, H-I) | his own (G)

31   forever (A, C-I) | for ever (B)
34   state; (C-I) | state, (A-B)
37   ledge (A-G) | ledge. (H-I)
38   edge. (A-G) | edge (H-I)
39   benefit; (C-I) | benefit, (A-B)
40   light; (C-I) | light, (A-B)
41   storms; (C-I) | storms, (A-B)
43   mean,— (C-I) | mean, (A-B)
45   grot, (B-I) | <spot,> grot, (A)
47   Justice, (C-I) | Justice (A) |
justice (B) || sphere, (C-I) | sphere
(A-B)
48   harbor (C-I) | harbour (A-B)

NOTES

6.   Perhaps more correctly cap-à-pie, meaning armed head to foot.

42.   Edward Emerson's note to this line in *W,* IX, 429 misleadingly indicates that "lakes" is a "First Edition" variant for "depths." In fact that reading occurs only in the manuscript draft in notebook X (*PN,* 124), where it is merely one of several variants.

ÉTIENNE DE LA BOÉCE.

The celebrated essay on "Friendship" (1841) is only the most famous expression of Emerson's perennial engagement with this subject. Accounting friendship among the greatest of the good things in life, Emerson was always curious about how it came to be, how it worked, and what its pleasures and conditions precisely were. This fascination led him not only into realms of theory, but, often enough, into a parsing analysis of his own relationships. The inevitably intellectual cast of this reaction led some of his friends —the women most particularly—to regard him as rather more aloof than they would have preferred. Characteristically, Emerson made even this fact (an effect of friendly dialogue) further grist for his poetic mill, as in such poems as "Rubies" and "Give All to Love."

In 1843 Emerson was delighted to discover a new work by a favorite author: the *Journey into Italy* by Montaigne, recently translated and published by the younger Hazlitt in his edition of the *Complete Works* (*L*, III, 212; VII, 570–71, 573). Here Emerson found the story of the writer's friendship with Étienne de la Boétie, and of the death of the latter at the age of 33. Even prior to this discovery, Emerson had marveled at the coincidence that a shared delight in Montaigne's *Essays* had been a special hallmark of his own friendships, as with Henry James, Sr., William Tappan, Ellery Channing, Caroline Sturgis, and John Sterling (*JMN*, VIII, 376). Thus it may have been partly for this reason that when Emerson found the *Journey into Italy,* he could easily persuade himself that the style of his own friendships fell in with Montaigne's model.

In a note to the poem (*W*, IX, 429) Edward pointed to a journal source: "Do not mince your speech. Power fraternizes with power & wishes you not to be like 'them' but yourself. Echo them & they will see fast enough that you have nothing for them. They came to you for somewhat new. A man loves a man" (*JMN*, VIII, 375). This comment, as Edward noted, occurs in close proximity to the entry about the importance of Montaigne to him and to his friendships, but he assigned these passages, quite mistakenly, to 1833 and assumed that the poem was of the same date. In fact the passages occur in Journal R and were certainly written in 1843, though they predate by some months Emerson's acquaintance with the crucial *Journey into Italy.* Evidence of the drafts in poetry notebook X suggests that "Étienne" was begun in 1843, but the couplet finally figuring as lines 21–22 appears, by itself, in a textually complicated setting in journal Books Small (*JMN*, VIII, 463), the date of which seems to be 1846. The fact that "Étienne" was not pub-

lished in the *Dial* may also be taken to imply that while the first
drafts belong to 1843, the poem was not finished until three years
later.

ÉTIENNE DE LA BOÉCE.

I serve you not, if you I follow,
Shadowlike, o'er hill and hollow;
And bend my fancy to your leading,
All too nimble for my treading.
When the pilgrimage is done,   5
And we've the landscape overrun,
I am bitter, vacant, thwarted,
And your heart is unsupported.
Vainly valiant, you have missed
The manhood that should yours resist,—   10
Its complement; but if I could,
In severe or cordial mood,
Lead you rightly to my altar,
Where the wisest Muses falter,
And worship that world-warming spark   15
Which dazzles me in midnight dark,
Equalizing small and large,
While the soul it doth surcharge,
That the poor is wealthy grown,
And the hermit never alone,—   20
The traveller and the road seem one
With the errand to be done,—
That were a man's and lover's part,
That were Freedom's whitest chart.

TEXTS

(A) MS HM 7623, by permission of the Huntington Library, San Marino, California, printer's copy for B; (B) *Poems* (London, 1847), 99–100; (C) *Poems* (Boston, 1847), 126–127; (C²) *Poems* (Boston, 1865), 129–30; (C³) *Selected Poems* (Boston, 1876), 76; (D) *Poems* [Riverside] (Boston, 1884), 76–77; (D²) *Poems*

[Centenary] (Boston, 1904), 82. No variants occur in later printings from the plates made for (C).

Pre-copy-text forms: See *PN,* 781–782.

VARIANTS

Title: ÉTIENNE DE LA BOÉCE. (D) | ETIENNE DE LA BOÉCE. (A, C) | ETIENNE DE LA BOECE. (B)

2 Shadowlike, (C-D) | Shadow-like, (A-B) || o'er (B-D) | oer (A) || hollow; (C-D) | hollow, (A-B)

10 yours (A, C-D) | your's (B) || resist,— (C-D) | resist, (A-B)

11 could, (C-D) | could (A-B)

12 severe or cordial (B-D) | <a grave> ↑severe↓ or <frolic> ↑cordial↓ (A) || mood, (C-D) | mood (A-B)

14 Muses (A, C-D) | muses (B)

15 And worship (B-D) | ↑And↓ Worship (A) || world-warming (A, CC10, C-D) | world-warning (B)

19 That (A-C) | Till (CC1, CC4, CC5, D)

20 alone,— (C-D) | alone, (A-B)

22 done,— (C-D) | done;— (A-B)

23–24 In (A) lines 23 and 24 occur in reverse order, marked for transposition; as part of the transposition the comma after "chart" is revised to a period, and the period after "part" to a comma. (B-D) reflect the final order, as given.

NOTES

Title: The spelling of Montaigne's friend's name varies and is now most commonly given as Boétie, though its form in Emerson's source (the Hazlitt translation) was Boëtie. Emerson's rendering is idiosyncratic. Étienne de la Boëtie (1530–1563) was the author of *Discours de la servitude volontaire,* a work often cited as having laid the philosophical groundwork for passive resistance or civil disobedience. An edition published in 1835 carried a preface by Félicité de Lamennais, a Christian socialist and reformer in whom several of the Transcendentalists were interested (see *CW,* IV, 212).

21–22. John S. Harrison, in *The Teachers of Emerson* (New York, 1910), explained the couplet in terms of the philosophy of Plotinus, who, in "On Suicide," said of the mystic devotee that "he will be ignorant of the manner in which he sees it [the One]; but the vision filling the eyes with light, will prevent him from seeing anything else, since the light itself will be the object of his vision." Harrison comments: "It is an experience in which the traveler, or the soul of the devotee, the errand, or the vision of the One, and the road, or the light from the One, are one" (162–163).

SUUM CUIQUE.

"Suum cuique" was in Emerson's day a familiar Latin tag meaning "to each his own." The fair copy of the verses in poetry notebook P carries the dateline "Newton, 1834," and probably dates from April of that year, given that on 26 April Emerson noted in his regular journal, "Rain rain. The good rain like a bad preacher does not know when to leave off" (*JMN,* IV, 281).

SUUM CUIQUE.

The rain has spoiled the farmer's day;
Shall sorrow put my books away?
   Thereby are two days lost:
Nature shall mind her own affairs;
I will attend my proper cares,   5
   In rain, or sun, or frost.

TEXTS

(A) *Dial,* I (January 1841): 347; (B) *Poems* (London, 1847): 100; (C) *Poems* (Boston, 1847), 128; (C²) *Poems* (Boston, 1865), 131. No variants occur in the later printings from the plates made for (C). The poem was not included in *Selected Poems* (1876), nor in the Riverside or Centenary editions.

Format: Lines 3 and 6 flush (A-B)

Pre-copy-text forms: Manuscript fair copies occur in poetry notebook P (*PN,* 18), journal B (*JMN,* V, 194), and in the manuscript of the 1839 lecture "The Tragic" (*EL,* III, 116). Of these the first is textually identical to the *Dial* printing, while the other two—the latter quoted from the former—lack punctuation. Each of these has "will speed" for "shall mind" in line 4, and "Come" for "In" in line 6. The poem does not appear in the 1844 *Dial* publication of "The Tragic."

Compensation

VARIANTS

Title: SUUM CUIQUE. (A, C) | "SUUM
    CUIQUE." (B)

3   lost: (B, C) | lost. (A)
4   affairs; (C) | affairs, (A-B)

COMPENSATION.

Emerson wrote this poem in New York City in November 1834, according to the dateline in the manuscript fair copy (*PN*, 19–20). He had gone there to preach for four weeks at the city's Second (Unitarian) Church in advance of the installation of New Bedford's Orville Dewey as permanent pastor. On 18 October, the day of Emerson's arrival, he received word that his brother, Edward Bliss Emerson, had passed away on 1 October in San Juan, Puerto Rico, where he had gone in hopes of recovering from tuberculosis. "So falls one pile more of hope for this life" (*JMN*, IV, 325). Emerson was at this time still recovering from the shock occasioned by the unexpected death of his close friend George Adams Sampson, of Boston, less than three months earlier.

It was in this melancholy mood that Emerson observed the unusually raucous election of 1834 (*JMN*, IV, 330–333). The race for governor between the Democrat William L. Marcy and the Whig William H. Seward mobilized a good deal of class hatred, the Jacksonians crying "Down with the aristocracy!" while the "gentlemen of property and standing," not without reason, feared mob violence (Philip Hone, *Diary,* ed. Allan Nevins [New York, 1927], 139–142). Days before Emerson left New York on 9 No-

161

vember, it was clear that the party of Jackson had won a great victory.

COMPENSATION.

Why should I keep holiday
    When other men have none?
Why but because, when these are gay,
    I sit and mourn alone.

And why, when mirth unseals all tongues,   5
    Should mine alone be dumb?
Ah! late I spoke to silent throngs,
    And now their hour is come.

TEXTS

(A) *Poems* (London, 1847), 101; (B) *Poems* (Boston, 1847), 129; (B²) *Poems* (Boston, 1865), 132; (B³) *Poems* [Riverside] (Boston, 1884), 77; (B⁴) *Poems* [Centenary] (Boston, 1904), 83. The poem was not included in *Selected Poems* (Boston, 1876).

Format: All lines flush left (A).

Pre-copy-text forms: There are two drafts in poetry notebook P, an erased pencil draft and an ink fair copy, both deriving, in that order, from a pencil draft in journal A (*JMN,* IV, 347), which is partly overwritten by an ink entry of 1 December 1834. Margaret Fuller sent a copy of these verses to Caroline Sturgis in a letter of 18 June 1837 (*FuL,* I, 285); her text closely approximates the second P draft, but has a reading in the final line ("their turn has come") unattested elsewhere. Printer's copy for the London edition has not been located, though an untraced manuscript was offered for sale in 1919. See *PN,* 762–763 for a further discussion of these matters.

VARIANTS

1   holiday (B) | holiday, (A)
3   because, (B) | because (A)
4   alone. (A) | alone? (B)

5   why, (B) | why (A) || tongues, (B) | tongues (A)

7.   The "silent throngs" are presumably Emerson's audience at New York's Second Church.

FORBEARANCE.

Edward Emerson's note to this poem (*W*, IX, 430) suggests that it may refer to James Elliot Cabot or Henry Thoreau. It is unlikely, however, that Emerson meant the poem for a portrait. He did not know Cabot until 1844, and the verses do not very clearly fit Thoreau. "Forbearance" is, rather, about friendship and the qualities, moral and social, that ideally attend it. It was published with two other short poems, "The Park" and "Grace," all on the same page in the January 1842 issue of the *Dial*.

FORBEARANCE.

Hast thou named all the birds without a gun?
Loved the wood-rose, and left it on its stalk?
At rich men's tables eaten bread and pulse?
Unarmed, faced danger with a heart of trust?
And loved so well a high behavior,   5
In man or maid, that thou from speech refrained,
Nobility more nobly to repay?
O, be my friend, and teach me to be thine!

TEXTS

(A) *Dial,* II (January 1842): 373; (B) *Poems* (London, 1847), 102; (C) *Poems* (Boston, 1847), 130; (C²) *Poems* (Boston, 1865), 133; (C³) *Selected Poems* (Boston, 1876), 77; (C⁴) *Poems* [Riverside] (Boston, 1884), 78; (C⁵) *Poems* [Centenary] (Boston, 1904], 83.

Pre-copy-text forms: A pencil fair copy occurs in poetry notebook P (*PN,* 103).

VARIANTS

1   gun? (C) I gun, (A) I gun; (B)

2   wood-rose, (B-C) I woodrose (A) II stalk? (C) I stalk, (A) I stalk; (B)

3   pulse? (C) I pulse, (A) I pulse; (B)

4   Unarmed, (B-C) I Unarmed

(A) II trust? (C) I trust, (A) I trust; (B)

5   behavior, (C) I behavior (A) I behaviour (B)

7   repay? (C) I repay?— (A-B)

8   O, (C) I O (A-B)

NOTES

2.   That is, any wild rose found in the woods; "wood-rose" was not, in 1842, the name of any particular variety native to Massachusetts.

3.   Pulse is a porridge made from peas or beans—humble fare.

THE PARK.

"The Park" was almost certainly composed in the fall or winter of 1841, since line 9 was evidently taken from the rejected opening of a poem entered into journal F 2 on 18 August of that year (*JMN,* VII, 510). On or about November 19 Emerson sent "The

Park," together with "Grace" and "Forbearance," as "my little contingent of particolored light infantry" to Margaret Fuller for publication in the *Dial* for January 1842 (*L*, II, 462, 464).

Several prose parallels from the journals have been suggested (see *PN*, 891), none closer or more pertinent than an entry for 6 June 1841: "The chief is the chief all the world over, & not his hat or his shoes, his land, his title or his purse. He who knows the most,—he who knows what sweets & virtues are in the ground beneath him, the waters before him, the plants around him, the heavens above him,—he is the enchanter, he is the rich & the royal man" (*JMN*, VII, 454). This passage is followed by a lengthy appreciation of the park-like satisfactions of nature, as shown to him by Thoreau during an evening's boating on the Concord River.

THE PARK.

The prosperous and beautiful
    To me seem not to wear
The yoke of conscience masterful,
    Which galls me everywhere.

I cannot shake off the god;   5
    On my neck he makes his seat;
I look at my face in the glass,—
    My eyes his eyeballs meet.

Enchanters! enchantresses!
    Your gold makes you seem wise;   10
The morning mist within your grounds
    More proudly rolls, more softly lies.

Yet spake yon purple mountain,
    Yet said yon ancient wood,
That Night or Day, that Love or Crime,   15
    Leads all souls to the Good.

Poems (1847)

TEXTS

(A) *Dial*, II (January 1842): 373; (B) Berg MS, by permission of the New York Public Library, printer's copy for C; (C) *Poems* (London, 1847), 103; (D) *Poems* (Boston, 1847), 131–132; (E) *Poems* (Boston, 1857), 131–132; (F) *Poems* (Boston, 1865), 134–135; (F²) *Poems* [Riverside] (Boston, 1884), 78; (G) *Poems* [Centenary] (Boston, 1904), 84. There are no variants in later printings from the plates made for (D) before 1857. The poem was not included in *Selected Poems* (Boston, 1876).

Format: All lines set flush left (A-C).

Pre-copy-text forms: Two drafts of the poem occur in erased pencil in poetry notebook P (*PN*, 78–79), the second overwritten by a draft in ink. In the Houghton library is an ink fair copy closely related to these drafts (MS Am 1221 [46], discussed in *PN*, 891). Like the first of the P drafts, it contains only lines 1–12. It shows the following variants from the text as printed above:

1   the *for* and
3   masterful *for* masterful,
5   god: *for* god;
6   seat: *for* seat;
8   eyebeams *for* eyeballs
9   Enchanters! [*repeated*] *for* enchantresses!

VARIANTS

3   masterful, (B-G) | masterful (A)

4   everywhere. (A-D, F-G) | everywhere (E) | everywhere↑.↓ (CC4)

7   glass,— (D-G) | glass, (A-C)

8   eyeballs (A-B, D-G) | eye-balls (C)

9   enchantresses! (B-F) | Enchantresses! (A, G)

10   wise; (D-G) | wise: (A-C)

15   Night or Day, (A-B, D-G) | night or day (C) ‖ Love or Crime, (D-G) | Love or Crime (A) | love or crime, (B-C)

16   Leads (D-G) | Lead (A-C)

FORERUNNERS.

According to a notation accompanying the erased first draft of this poem it was written at 4:10 A.M. on 3 May 1845 (*PN,* 130). Family tradition held that the verses "came to him as he walked home from Wachusett" (*W,* IX, 430; cf. a notation to the same effect in the hand of Ellen Emerson at CC5, p. 137). The evidence is clear that Emerson indeed took such an excursion at that time. Whatever the precise circumstances may have been, Emerson knew that he had, months earlier, promised to send some poems to his old friend William Henry Furness, in Philadelphia, for publication in Furness's annual, *The Diadem,* and that he was now up against the deadline. He sent "The Forerunners," as he then called the poem, together with "A Fable" and "Loss and Gain," in a letter of 9 May, hoping, as he said, that it was not "too late" (*L,* VIII, 26). Shortly afterwards, on 22 May, Emerson sent a copy of the poem (together with copies of "The House" and "Loss and Gain") to poet and *Dial* contributor Ellen Sturgis Hooper, Caroline's sister (unpublished letter and accompanying poems in the Beinecke Library, Yale University). Furness's annual was published that fall, and Emerson acknowledged receipt of it on 15 October (*L,* VIII, 59).

In a note in the Centenary edition (*W,* IX, 431), Edward shrewdly suggested that the poem relates thematically to a passage in the essay "Nature" (1844): "I have seen the softness and beauty of the summer-clouds floating feathery overhead, enjoying, as it seemed, their height and privilege of motion, whilst yet they appeared not so much the drapery of this place and hour, as forelooking to some pavilions and gardens of festivity beyond. It is an odd jealousy: but the poet finds himself not near enough to his object. The pine-tree, the river, the bank of flowers before him, does not seem to be nature. Nature is still elsewhere. This or this is but outskirt and far-off reflection and echo of the triumph that has passed by, and is now at its glancing splendor and heyday, perchance in the neighboring fields, or, if you stand in the field, then in the adjacent woods. The present object shall give you this sense of stillness that follows a pageant which has just gone by" (*CW*, III, 111; compare the 1840 journal source for this passage at *JMN*, VII, 392).

FORERUNNERS.

Long I followed happy guides,
I could never reach their sides;
Their step is forth, and, ere the day,
Breaks up their leaguer, and away.
Keen my sense, my heart was young,   5
Right good-will my sinews strung,
But no speed of mine avails
To hunt upon their shining trails.
On and away, their hasting feet
Make the morning proud and sweet;   10
Flowers they strew,—I catch the scent;
Or tone of silver instrument
Leaves on the wind melodious trace;
Yet I could never see their face.
On eastern hills I see their smokes,   15
Mixed with mist by distant lochs.
I met many travellers
Who the road had surely kept;
They saw not my fine revellers,—
These had crossed them while they slept.   20
Some had heard their fair report,
In the country or the court.
Fleetest couriers alive
Never yet could once arrive,
As they went or they returned,   25
At the house where these sojourned.

Forerunners

Sometimes their strong speed they slacken,
Though they are not overtaken;
In sleep their jubilant troop is near,—
I tuneful voices overhear;   30
It may be in wood or waste,—
At unawares 'tis come and past.
Their near camp my spirit knows
By signs gracious as rainbows.
I thenceforward, and long after,   35
Listen for their harp-like laughter,
And carry in my heart, for days,
Peace that hallows rudest ways.

TEXTS

(A) MS Am 1280.235 (33), Ralph Waldo Emerson Memorial Association deposit, Houghton Library, Harvard University, printer's copy for B; (B) *The Diadem for MDCCCXLVI* (Philadelphia, 1846 [i.e., October 1845]), 95–96; (C) MS Barrett 6248-a, Clifton Waller Barrett Library, by permission of the University of Virginia, printer's copy for D; (D) *Poems* (London, 1847), 104–105; (E) *Poems* (Boston, 1847), 133–134; (E²) *Poems* (Boston, 1865), 136–137; (F) *Selected Poems* (Boston, 1876), 68–69; (G) *Poems* [Riverside] (Boston, 1884), 79–80; (H) *Poems* [Centenary] (Boston, 1904), 85–86.

Pre-copy-text forms: Two untitled drafts occur in poetry notebook X, indexed by Emerson with the word "Guides." See the discussion at *PN,* 795.

VARIANTS

Title: FORERUNNERS. (E-H) I THE FORE-RUNNERS. (B) I THE FORERUNNERS. (A, C-D)
1 guides, (A-B, E-H) I guides,— (C-D)
2 sides; (E-H) I sides. (A-D)
3 forth, (A, C-H) I forth (B) II day, (A-E) I day (F-H)
4 leaguer, (C-H) I leaguer (A-B)
6 good-will (E-H) I goodwill (A, C-D) I good will (B)

10 sweet; (E-H) I sweet. (A-D)
11 strew,— (A [*dash added in pencil*], E-H) I strew, (B-D) II scent; (E-H) I scent, (A-D)
13 trace; (E-H) I trace, (A-D)
15 eastern (A-B, D-H) I <morni[ng]> eastern [*evidently an eye-skip error*] (C) II smokes, (E-H) I smokes (A-D)
18 kept; (E-H) I kept, (A-B) I kept,— (C-D)

19   revellers,— (C-H) | revellers,
(A-B)
21   report, (A-B, E-H) | report (C-D)
28   overtaken; (E-H) | overtaken:
(A-D)
29   sleep (A-B, E-H) | sleep, (C-D) ||
near,— (E-H) | near, (A-D)
30   overhear; (E-H) | overhear,
(A-D)

32   'tis (A-B, D-H) | tis (C) || past.
(E-H) | passed. (A-D)
35   thenceforward, (E-F) |
thenceforward (A-D, G-H) || after,
(A-B, E-G) | after (C-D, H)
36   laughter, (A-F, H) | laughter (G)
37   heart, (E-H) | heart (A-D) ||
days, (E-H) | days (A-D)
38   ways. (A-B, E-H) | ways.— (C-D)

NOTES

4.   A leaguer is an encampment of besieging forces. The word survives as metaphor in the term "beleaguered."

SURSUM CORDA.

Edward Emerson's note to this poem (*W,* IX, 431) suggests that he did not much care for the form the poem had before 1876, and, furthermore, that he may not have understood its meaning very precisely. It is at least open to question whether the poem can rightly be said to express, as Edward claims, "the exaltation that comes with utter humility." His feeling that this sense "did not find quite satisfactory utterance in the poem as printed in early editions" bears on the authority of the small but crucial revisions introduced in *Selected Poems* and in the posthumous Riverside edition.

SURSUM CORDA.

Seek not the spirit, if it hide
Inexorable to thy zeal:
Baby, do not whine and chide:
Art thou not also real?
Why shouldst thou stoop to poor excuse?   5
Turn on the accuser roundly; say,
'Here am I, here will I abide
Forever to myself soothfast;
Go thou, sweet Heaven, or at thy pleasure stay!'
Already Heaven with thee its lot has cast,   10
For only it can absolutely deal.

TEXTS

(A) MS, Beinecke Library, by permission of Yale University, printer's copy for B; (B) *Poems* (London, 1847), 106; (C) *Poems* (Boston, 1847), 135; (D) *Poems* (Boston, 1858), 135; (E) *Poems* (Boston, 1865), 138; (F) *Selected Poems* (Boston, 1876), 79; (G) *Poems* [Riverside] (Boston, 1884), 80; (G²) *Poems* (Boston, 1904), 86.

Pre-copy-text forms: None.

VARIANTS

Title: SURSUM CORDA. (A, C-G) | "SURSUM CORDA." (B)
1   spirit, (C-G) | Spirit, (A-B) ‖ hide (A, C-G) | hide, (B)
3   Baby, (A-E) | Trembler, (F-G) | <Baby> < ↑ Coward ↓ > ↑ Pilgrim ↓ (CC1) | <Baby> ↑ Pilgrim ↓ (CC4, CC5) ‖ chide: (C-G) | chide; (A-B)
5   Why shouldst thou stoop to poor excuse? (C-F) | Why should'st thou

stoop to poor excuse? (A-B) | Stoop not then to poor excuse; (G) | Why should'st thou stoop to poor / excuse/<delay>/ (CC1) | Stoop not then to poor excuse (CC4, CC5)
6   accuser (C-G) | Accuser (A-B)
7   abide (F-G) | remain (A-E) | <I remain> (CC1) [*With notation:* "Unless this can be mended, cancel the page."]

8   soothfast; (C-G) I soothfast, (A-B)

9   or (C-G) I or, (A-B) II stay!' (C, E, G) I stay.' (A-B) I stay! (D, F)

11   only it (A, C-G) I it only (B)

NOTES

Title: "Mr. Emerson had reference in this title to the chanting by the priest, in the introduction to the celebration of the Mass, of the words *Sursum Corda!* (Up, hearts!) to the worshippers" (*W,* IX, 431).

ODE TO BEAUTY.

On 25 September 1843 Margaret Fuller wrote to Henry Thoreau (who was then at Staten Island tutoring the children of Emerson's brother William) and mentioned that Emerson "has written a fine poem, you will see it in the Dial" (*FuL,* III, 148). When the "Ode to Beauty" duly appeared in the October issue, however, Thoreau, perhaps in part reacting to Fuller's advance praise, wrote to Emerson to say that "I have a good deal of fault to find with your ode to Beauty. The tune is altogether unworthy of the thoughts. You slope too quickly to the rhyme, as if that trick had better be performed as soon as possible or as if you stood over the line with a hatchet and chopped off the verses as they came out— some short and some long. . . .It sounds like a parody. 'Thee knew I of old' 'Remediless thirst' are some of those stereotyped lines. . . . Yet I love your poetry as I do little else that is near and recent—

especially when you get fairly around the end of the line, and are not thrown back upon the rocks" (*Correspondence*, ed. Walter Harding and Carl Bode [New York, 1958], 145–146). Of the two lines objected to, Emerson eventually rewrote the second and kept the first.

ODE TO BEAUTY.

Who gave thee, O Beauty,
The keys of this breast,—
Too credulous lover
Of blest and unblest?
Say, when in lapsed ages   5
Thee knew I of old?
Or what was the service
For which I was sold?
When first my eyes saw thee,
I found me thy thrall,   10
By magical drawings,
Sweet tyrant of all!
I drank at thy fountain
False waters of thirst;
Thou intimate stranger,   15
Thou latest and first!
Thy dangerous glances
Make women of men;
New-born, we are melting
Into nature again.   20

Lavish, lavish promiser,
Nigh persuading gods to err!
Guest of million painted forms,
Which in turn thy glory warms!
The frailest leaf, the mossy bark,   25
The acorn's cup, the raindrop's arc,
The swinging spider's silver line,
The ruby of the drop of wine,

The shining pebble of the pond,
Thou inscribest with a bond,   30
In thy momentary play,
Would bankrupt nature to repay.

Ah, what avails it
To hide or to shun
Whom the Infinite One   35
Hath granted his throne?
The heaven high over
Is the deep's lover;
The sun and sea,
Informed by thee,   40
Before me run,
And draw me on,
Yet fly me still,
As Fate refuses
To me the heart Fate for me chooses.   45
Is it that my opulent soul
Was mingled from the generous whole;
Sea-valleys and the deep of skies
Furnished several supplies;
And the sands whereof I'm made   50
Draw me to them, self-betrayed?
I turn the proud portfolio
Which holds the grand designs
Of Salvator, of Guercino,
And Piranesi's lines.   55
I hear the lofty pæans
Of the masters of the shell,
Who heard the starry music
And recount the numbers well;
Olympian bards who sung   60
Divine Ideas below,
Which always find us young,
And always keep us so.
Oft, in streets or humblest places,

I detect far-wandered graces, 65
Which, from Eden wide astray,
In lowly homes have lost their way.

Thee gliding through the sea of form,
Like the lightning through the storm,
Somewhat not to be possessed, 70
Somewhat not to be caressed,
No feet so fleet could ever find,
No perfect form could ever bind.
Thou eternal fugitive,
Hovering over all that live, 75
Quick and skilful to inspire
Sweet, extravagant desire,
Starry space and lily-bell
Filling with thy roseate smell,
Wilt not give the lips to taste 80
Of the nectar which thou hast.

All that's good and great with thee
Works in close conspiracy;
Thou hast bribed the dark and lonely
To report thy features only, 85
And the cold and purple morning
Itself with thoughts of thee adorning;
The leafy dell, the city mart,
Equal trophies of thine art;
E'en the flowing azure air 90
Thou hast touched for my despair;
And, if I languish into dreams,
Again I meet the ardent beams.
Queen of things! I dare not die
In Being's deeps past ear and eye, 95
Lest there I find the same deceiver,
And be the sport of Fate forever.
Dread Power, but dear! if God thou be,
Unmake me quite, or give thyself to me!

Poems (1847)

TEXTS

(A) *Dial*, IV (October 1843): 257–259; (B) MS, m.b., Berg Collection, by permission of the New York Public Library, probable printer's copy for C; (C) *Poems* (London, 1847), 107–111; (D) *Poems* (Boston, 1847), 136–140; (E) *Poems* (Boston, 1865), 139–143; (F) *Selected Poems* (Boston, 1876), 80–83; (G) *Poems* [Riverside] (Boston, 1884), 81–84; (H) *Poems* [Centenary] (Boston, 1904), 87–90.

Format: Lines 13–16, 33–51, and 68–99 are inset in (A). Lines 21, 33, 68, and 82 are inset in (B).

Pre-copy-text forms: The principal draft of the poem occurs on pages 263–268 of poetry notebook X. In several other places (e.g., *JMN*, VIII, 527; IX, 26) Emerson drafted revisions of the *Dial* text: see *PN*, 882.

VARIANTS

1   Beauty, (D-H) | Beauty! (A-C)

2   breast,— (D-H) | breast; (A) | breast, (B-C)

3   Too credulous lover (B-H) | To thee who betrayed me (A)

4   Of blest and unblest? (B-H) | To be ruined or blest? (A)

5   Say, (D-H) | Say (A-C)

6   old? (D-H) | old; (A-C)

7   service (B-H) | service, (A)

13   I drank at thy fountain (B-H) | Love drinks at thy banquet (A)

14   False waters of thirst; (B-H) | Remediless thirst; (A)

15   stranger, (B-H) | stranger! (A)

17–20   [*Lines added in* (B)] (B-H)

19   New-born, (D-H) | Newborn (B) | New-born (C)

21   promiser, (B-H) | promiser! (A)

22   err! (D-H) | err; (A-B) | err, (C)

23   forms, (D-H) | forms (A-C)

24   warms! (D-H) | warms, (A-C)

26   raindrop's (B-D, F-H) | rain drop's (A) | rain-drop's (E)

27–28   [*Lines added in* (B)] (B-H)

30   bond, (A, D-H) | bond (B-C)

31   play, (A, D-H) | play (B-C)

32   nature (A, D-H) | Nature (B-C)

33   Ah, (D-H) | Ah! (A, C) | Ah (B)

38   lover; (D-H) | lover. (A) | lover, (B-C)

39   sea, (A, D-H) | sea (B-C)

41   run, (B-F) | run (A, G-H)

45   chooses. (A-B, D-H) | chooses, (C)

47   whole; (D-H) | whole,— (A) | whole, (B-C)

48   Sea-valleys (A-B, D-H) | Sea valleys (C)

49   supplies; (D-H) | supplies, (A-C)

51   them, (D-H) | them (A-C) || self-betrayed? (B-H) | self-betrayed. (A)

52   portfolio (CC5, F-H) | portfolios, (A) | portfolios (B-E)

53   holds (CC5, F-H) | hold (A-E)

55   lines. (B-H) | lines; (A) | lines; (CC1)

56   pæans (A, D-G) | paeans (B) | Pæans (C)

58   music (A, D-H) | music, (B-C)

59 well; (A, D-H) | well: (B-C)
62 young, (A-F) | young (G-H)
63 so. (A-H) | so; (CC1)
64 Oft, (D-H) | Oft (A-C) || places,
(D-H) | places (A-C)
65 far-wandered (A, D-H) | far
wandered (B-C)
66 Which, (D-H) | Which (A-C) ||
astray, (D-H) | astray (A-C)
69 Like (B-H) | As (A)
74 Thou (B-H) | Thou, (A) ||
fugitive, (A, D-H) | fugitive (B-C)
77 Sweet, (D-H) | Sweet (A-C)
78 lily-bell (D-H) | lily bell (A-C)
82 great (B-H) | great, (A)
83 Works in close (D-H) | Stands in

deep (A-C) || conspiracy; (D-H) |
conspiracy, (A) | conspiracy. (B-C)
87 adorning; (A, D-H) | adorning,
(B-C)
89 art; (A, D-H) | art, (B-C)
90 E'en (A, C-H) | Een (B)
91 despair; (A, D-H) | despair,
(B-C)
92 And, (D-H) | And (A-C)
95 eye, (A-C, F) | eye; (D-E, G-H)
96 deceiver, (B-G) | deceiver
(A, H)
97 sport (B-H) | game (A)
98 Power, (A-B, D-H) | power, (C)
99 me! (A-B, D-H) | me. (C)

NOTES

52–55. In June 1838 Margaret Fuller brought to Emerson a portfolio of prints including works by Giovanni Guercino (1591–1666) and Giambattista Piranesi (1720–1778) (*JMN*, VII, 6–7). Three months later he saw a second portfolio, assembled by Samuel Gray Ward in Italy (*JMN*, VII, 46–47, 62; cf. *L*, X, 229–232).

60–63. On 1 February 1834 Emerson wrote: "Some thoughts always find us young, and keep us so. Such a thought is the love of the universal & eternal beauty" (*JMN*, IV, 260). Emerson had drawn on this entry in "The Over-Soul" (*CW*, II, 162). At several points in *Sartor Resartus* Thomas Carlyle had made conspicuous use of the phrase "Divine Idea," which he had appropriated from J. G. Fichte (see, e.g., *Sartor Resartus*, ed. Charles Frederick Harrold [New York, 1937], 209). The quatrain occurs, canceled, in the manuscript of Emerson's 1836 lecture on "Modern Aspects of Letters" (*EL*, I, 534), and was used in 1844 as the second motto for "The Poet" in *Essays: Second Series*. Emerson complained about a misprint ("keeps" for "keep") in the London edition of this work (*CW*, III, 293–294); in both the London and Boston editions, "ideas" was not capitalized.

68. "Nature is a sea of forms radically alike and even unique. A leaf, a sunbeam, a landscape, the ocean, make an analogous impression on the mind. What is common to them all,—that perfectness and harmony, is beauty. Therefore the

standard of beauty is the entire circuit of natural forms" (*Nature* [1836], *CW,* I, 17).

71.   A journal entry for 3 September 1843 shows that a visit from Caroline Sturgis—the same that inspired Emerson's poem, "The Visit"—prompted discussions of beauty: "there is that in beauty which cannot be caressed, but which demands the utmost wealth of nature in the beholder properly to meet it" (*JMN,* IX, 14 n. 25, 16).

GIVE ALL TO LOVE.

From the late 1830s through the completion of the essays on "Love" and "Friendship" (1841), Emerson weighed the implications of a Platonic view of love. His thinking tended to subordinate the circumstantial aspects of courtship and marriage to an elevated conception of the value of their purpose, which was the education of the soul. One of the earliest of several meditations on this theme occurs in a journal entry for 16 April 1837:

> How little think the youth & maiden who are glancing at each other across a mixed company with eyes so full of mutual intelligence—how little think they of the precious fruit long hereafter to proceed from this now quite external stimulus. . . . By all the virtues that appear, by so much kindness, justice, fortitude &c, by so much are they made one. But all the vices are negations on either part & they are by so much two. At last they discover that all that at first drew them together was wholly caducous, had merely a prospective end like the scaffolding by which a house is built, & the unsuspected & wholly unconscious growth of principles from year

to year is the real marriage foreseen & prepared from the first but wholly above their consciousness. (*JMN,* V, 297–298)

A journal passage of 21 November 1840—too long to be quoted here in full—returns to this theme, evidently precipitated by the realization that "Swedenborg exaggerates the Circumstance of marriage":

> All loves, all friendships are momentary. *Do you love me?* means at last *Do you see the same truth I see?* If you do, we are happy together: but when presently one of us passes into the perception of new truth, we are divorced and the force of all nature cannot hold us to each other. . . . No, Heaven is the marriage of all souls. We meet & worship an instant under the temple of one thought & part as though we parted not, to join another thought with other fellowships of joy. (*JMN,* VII, 532)

The sentiment that fastens on persons commonly opposes the law of change and growth. The worthy injunction to "give all to love" has thus to be discriminated from the unworthy injunction to "give all to the beloved."

GIVE ALL TO LOVE.

Give all to love;
Obey thy heart;
Friends, kindred, days,
Estate, good-fame,
Plans, credit, and the Muse,—   5
Nothing refuse.

'Tis a brave master;
Let it have scope:
Follow it utterly,
Hope beyond hope: 10
High and more high
It dives into noon,

With wing unspent,
Untold intent;
But it is a god,   15
Knows its own path,
And the outlets of the sky.

It was not for the mean;
It requireth courage stout,
Souls above doubt,   20
Valor unbending;
Such 'twill reward,—
They shall return
More than they were,
And ever ascending.   25

Leave all for love;
Yet, hear me, yet,
One word more thy heart behoved,
One pulse more of firm endeavor,—
Keep thee to-day,   30
To-morrow, forever,
Free as an Arab
Of thy beloved.

Cling with life to the maid;
But when the surprise,   35
First vague shadow of surmise
Flits across her bosom young
Of a joy apart from thee,
Free be she, fancy-free;
Nor thou detain her vesture's hem,   40
Nor the palest rose she flung
From her summer diadem.

Though thou loved her as thyself,
As a self of purer clay,

Though her parting dims the day, 45
Stealing grace from all alive;
Heartily know,
When half-gods go,
The gods arrive.

TEXTS

(A) *Poems* (London, 1847), 111–113; (B) *Poems* (Boston, 1847), 141–143; (B²) *Poems* (Boston, 1865), 144–146; (B³) *Selected Poems* (Boston, 1876), 84–85; (C) *Poems* [Riverside] (Boston, 1884), 84–85; (C²) *Poems* [Centenary] (Boston, 1904), 90–92. There are no variants in later printings from the plates made for (B), though the 1857 and 1858 printings exhibit plate damage, with loss of punctuation at the ends of lines 43 and 45, as Emerson noted in (CC4). The poem was reprinted in *The Harbinger,* IV (9 January 1847): 77–78, from (B).

Pre-copy-text forms: A draft in poetry notebook EF was revised, probably in the fall of 1846, in notebook X. See *PN,* 802.

VARIANTS

4 good-fame, (B-C) I good fame, (A)
5 credit, (A-B) I credit (C) II Muse,— (B-C) I muse; (A)
7 master; (B-C) I master, (A)
8 scope: (B-C) I scope, (A)
10 hope: (B-C) I hope; (A)
11 high (B-C) I high, (A)
15 it is (B-C) I 'tis (A)
16 path, (A-B) I path (C)
18 It was not (B) I 'Tis not (A) I It was never (C, CC4, CC5) II mean; (B-C) I mean, (A)
19 stout, (A-B) I stout. (C) I stout<,>. (CC4, CC5)
21 Valor (B-C) I Valour (A) II unbending; (A-B) I unbending, (C, CC4) I unbending (CC5)
22 Such 'twill (A-B) I It will (C, CC4, CC5) II reward,— (B-C) I reward, (A)
26 love; (B-C) I love;— (A)
29 endeavor,— (B-C) I endeavour, (A)
30 to-day, (B-C) I to day, (A)
31 forever, (B-C) I for ever, (A)
36 First vague (B-C) I Vague (A)
37 young (A-B) I young, (C)
39 fancy-free; (B-C) I fancy-free, (A)
40 Nor thou detain her vesture's (B-C) I Do not thou detain a (A)
45 Though (B-C) I Tho' (A)
46 alive; (B-C) I alive, (A)

NOTES

48–49.   "We cannot part with our friends. We cannot let our angels go. We do not see that they only go out that archangels may come in" ("Compensation," *CW*, II, 72). Emerson's poetic rendering of this idea may have been influenced by I Corinthians 13: 8–10: "Charity [or "Love," as the Greek αναπη is now commonly translated] never faileth. . . . But when that which is perfect is come, then that which is in part shall be done away."

TO ELLEN, AT THE SOUTH.

When Emerson first met Ellen Louisa Tucker on Christmas Day 1827 at the Concord, New Hampshire, home of her mother and step-father, she was sixteen years old and he, a new minister, as yet unsettled, was twenty-four. They were engaged less than a year later and married on 30 September 1829, by which time Emerson had become the junior pastor at Boston's Second Church. Their engagement, like their marriage, was darkly overshadowed by the irregularly recurring but ever-worsening symptoms of Ellen's illness, the consumption that would take her life, at the age of nineteen, on 8 February 1831.

The longest of several trips undertaken by the couple for Ellen's health lasted from early March to mid-May 1830, spent mostly in Philadelphia. Emerson himself could not be away for such a length of time, and so, leaving Ellen with her mother and sister and "troops of friends," he returned to Boston alone at the end of March (Henry F. Pommer, *Emerson's First Marriage* [Carbondale, Ill., 1967], 40). "To Ellen, at the South," was written in April 1830. Some months after Ellen died Emerson remarked that William Cullen Bryant's lugubrious "Death of the Flowers" had been among her favorite poems (*L*, I, 326). Emerson's tone here is very nearly the opposite of Bryant's.

TO ELLEN,
AT THE SOUTH.

The green grass is bowing,
    The morning wind is in it;
'Tis a tune worth thy knowing,
    Though it change every minute.

'Tis a tune of the spring;   5
    Every year plays it over
To the robin on the wing,
    And to the pausing lover.

O'er ten thousand thousand acres
    Goes light the nimble zephyr;   10
The Flowers—tiny sect of Shakers—
    Worship him ever.

Hark to the winning sound!
    They summon thee, dearest,—
Saying, 'We have dressed for thee the ground,   15
    Nor yet thou appearest.

'O hasten; 'tis our time,
    Ere yet the red Summer
Scorch our delicate prime,
    Loved of bee,—the tawny hummer.   20

'O pride of thy race!
    Sad, in sooth, it were to ours,
If our brief tribe miss thy face,
    We poor New England flowers.

'Fairest, choose the fairest members   25
  Of our lithe society;
June's glories and September's
  Show our love and piety.

'Thou shalt command us all,—
  April's cowslip, summer's clover,   30
To the gentian in the fall,
  Blue-eyed pet of blue-eyed lover.

'O come, then, quickly come!
  We are budding, we are blowing;
And the wind that we perfume   35
  Sings a tune that's worth the knowing.'

TEXTS

(A) *Dial*, III (January 1843): 327–328; (B) *Poems* (London, 1847), 114–115; (C) *Poems* (Boston, 1847), 144–146; (C²) *Poems* (Boston, 1865), 147–149; (D) *Poems* [Riverside] (Boston, 1884), 86–87; (D²) *Poems* [Centenary] (Boston, 1904), 93–94. No variants are introduced in later printings from the plates made for (C). The poem was not included in *Selected Poems* (Boston, 1876).

Format: All lines printed flush left in (A-B).

Pre-copy-text forms: The fair copy in poetry notebook P, entitled "To E.T.E. at Philadelphia" and misdated "Apr. 1829" (*PN*, 23–24), is the source for the second manuscript copy given at *PN*, 710–711. The latter is very close to the *Dial* text and may possibly have served as printer's copy for that publication. The few corrections in the P text were clearly made after the *Dial* printing and reflect Emerson's emendations for (B).

VARIANTS

Title: TO ELLEN, | AT THE SOUTH. (C) |
TO EVA AT THE SOUTH. (A) | TO
ELLEN, AT THE SOUTH. (B) | TO
ELLEN | AT THE SOUTH. (D) | TO
ELLEN AT THE SOUTH (D²)

1 bowing, (A, C-D) | growing, (B)
2 it; (C-D) | it, (A-B)
3 thy (A, C-D) | the (B)
5 spring; (C) | spring, (A-B) |
Spring; (D)

6   over (A, C-D) | over, (B)

7   robin (B-D) | robins (A)

8   And to (A, C-D) | To (B)

9   thousand thousand acres (A-B) | thousand, thousand acres, (C-D)

10   zephyr; (C-D) | Zephyr, (A) | zephyr, (B)

11   Flowers—tiny sect of Shakers— (C-D) | Flower,—tiny sect of Shakers, (A) | flowers, tiny feet ["sect" (CC10)] of shakers, (B)

14   dearest,— (C-D) | dearest, (A-B)

15   Saying, 'We (C-D) | Saying, "We (A) | Saying; 'We (B) || dressed (C-D) | drest (A-B)

17   'O hasten; (C) | O hasten! (A) | O hasten, (B) | 'O hasten;' (D)

18   Summer (C-D) | summer (A-B)

19   prime, (B-D) | prime (A)

20   bee,— (C-D) | the bee,— (A) | bee, (B) | bee, (CC1)

21   'O (C-D) | O (A-B)

22   Sad, (C-D) | Sad (A-B) || sooth, (C-D) | sooth (A-B)

23   face, (A, C-D) | face,— (B)

24   poor (A, C-D) | pour (B)

25   'Fairest, (C-D, CC11) | Thou shalt (A) | Fairest! (B)

28   Show (B-D) | Shalt show (A)

29   'Thou (C-D) | Thou (A-B) || all, — (C-D) | all, (A-B)

30   April's cowslip, summer's (B-D) | From April's early (A)

32   pet of blue-eyed (B-D) | favorite of thy (A)

33   'O (C-D) | O (A-B) || come! (C-D) | come, (A-B)

34   blowing; (C-D) | blowing, (A-B)

35   that (A, C-D) | which (B) || perfume (B-D) | perfume, (A)

36   the knowing.' (C-D) | the knowing. (A) | thy knowing.' (B)

NOTES

11.   Emerson, together with Ellen and her mother, Margaret Tucker Kent, had visited the Shaker community at Canterbury, New Hampshire, in August 1829. Early in April 1830 Ellen wrote to Emerson's brother Edward, then in New York, describing her situation in Philadelphia: "There is little of natural beauty I think in the environs of Phil—the little wildflowers look as if Dame Quaker rather than Dame Nature had arranged them and hardly condescend to nodd [*sic*] to Zephyrus as he passes by" (*OFL*, 128).

TO EVA.

"To Eva," another poem to Ellen, was probably written in 1829. Its form—a Spanish sestet, or sextilla—is uncommon in nineteenth-century verse.

TO EVA.

O fair and stately maid, whose eyes
Were kindled in the upper skies
   At the same torch that lighted mine;
For so I must interpret still
Thy sweet dominion o'er my will,   5
   A sympathy divine.

Ah! let me blameless gaze upon
Features that seem at heart my own;
   Nor fear those watchful sentinels,
Who charm the more their glance forbids,   10
Chaste-glowing, underneath their lids,
   With fire that draws while it repels.

TEXTS

(A) *Dial,* I (July 1840): 84; (B) MS in the Joel Myerson Collection of Nineteenth-Century American Literature, University of South Carolina, by permission of the University of South Carolina, printer's copy for C; (C) *Poems* (London, 1847), 116; (D) *Poems* (Boston, 1847), 147; (D²) *Poems* (Boston, 1865), 150; (D³) *Selected Poems* (Boston, 1876), 92; (D⁴) *Poems* [Riverside] (Boston, 1884), 87; (D⁵) *Poems* [Centenary] (Boston, 1904), 95.

Format: All lines flush left (A-C).

Pre-copy-text forms: An untitled fair copy occurs in poetry notebook P (*PN,* 37).

VARIANTS

Title: TO EVA. (B-D) | TO * * * * (A)
1   eyes (D) | eye (A-C)
2   Were (D) | Was (A-C) || skies (D) | sky (A-C)
5   will, (B-D) | will (A)
8   at (D) | in (A-C) || own; (D) | own, (A-C)

9   sentinels, (D) | sentinels (A-C)
10   Who (D) | Which (A-C)
11   Chaste-glowing, (D) | Chaste-glowing (A-B) | Chaste glowing (C) || lids, (D) | lids (A-C)

THE AMULET.

"The Amulet" was written within two months prior to its publication in the July 1842 issue of the *Dial*, where it appeared along with "Tact" and "Holidays." It develops a journal entry belonging to the first days of the preceding April: "Although you content me in all ways, I content you only in your memory, never in your presence. The inconvenience of love is that we are always tormented by the fear that it expired in the last expression of it" (*JMN*, VIII, 219). The subject recalls the close, mutually interrogatory attention paid by Emerson, Fuller, and Sturgis to the nature of their affectionate relationships during the years just past. It is tempting to suppose that Emerson has Caroline Sturgis in mind here, but in fact no evidence supports the conjecture.

THE AMULET.

Your picture smiles as first it smiled;
    The ring you gave is still the same;
Your letter tells, O changing child!
    No tidings *since* it came.

Give me an amulet   5
    That keeps intelligence with you,—
Red when you love, and rosier red,
    And when you love not, pale and blue.

Alas! that neither bonds nor vows
    Can certify possession;   10
Torments me still the fear that love
    Died in its last expression.

TEXTS

(A) *Dial,* III (July 1842): 73–74; (A²) MS, Beinecke Library, by permission of Yale University, printer's copy for A³; (A³) *Poems* (London, 1847), 117–118; (B) *Poems* (Boston, 1847), 148; (B²) *Poems* (Boston, 1865), 151; (B³) *Selected Poems* (Boston, 1876), 93 (B⁴) *Poems* [Riverside] (Boston, 1884), 88; (B⁵) *Poems* [Centenary] (Boston, 1904), 98–99.

Format: All lines flush left (A).

Pre-copy-text forms: The complete and titled fair copy in P (*PN,* 96) is preceded by an erased first draft in journal Books Small (*JMN,* VIII, 469) and by a second draft only partly recovered from a mutilated page in journal Dialling (*JMN,* VIII, 515–516).

VARIANTS

1	smiled; (B) ǀ smiled, (A)		6	you,— (B) ǀ you, (A)
2	same; (B) ǀ same, (A)		9	Alas! (B) ǀ Alas, (A)
3	child! (B) ǀ child, (A)			

THINE EYES STILL SHINED.

Henry F. Pommer (*Emerson's First Marriage* [Carbondale, Ill., 1967], 40) is probably correct in assigning this poem to April 1830, around the time that Emerson wrote "To Ellen, at the South." The date is all the more likely because Ellen's sojourn in Philadelphia was the couple's only extended period of separation. In one of the stanzas rejected from the poem Emerson refers to the miniature portrait of Ellen painted a year earlier probably by Sarah Goodridge (*L*, I, 269), but possibly by Goodridge's friend, Caroline Schetky Richardson:

> I need not hide beneath my vest
> Thy picture, the pride of art,
> Thy picture burns within my breast,
> And the chain is round my heart. (*PN*, 27)

THINE EYES STILL SHINED.

Thine eyes still shined for me, though far
    I lonely roved the land or sea:
As I behold yon evening star,
    Which yet beholds not me.

This morn I climbed the misty hill,   5
    And roamed the pastures through;
How danced thy form before my path
    Amidst the deep-eyed dew!

When the redbird spread his sable wing,
    And showed his side of flame;   10
When the rosebud ripened to the rose,
    In both I read thy name.

Poems (1847)

TEXTS

(A) MS, m.b., Berg Collection, by permission of the New York Public Library, printer's copy for B; (B) *Poems* (London, 1847), 117; (C) *Poems* (Boston, 1847), 149; (C²) *Poems* (Boston, 1865), 152; (D) *Poems* [Riverside] (Boston, 1884), 88–89; (D²) *Poems* [Centenary] (Boston, 1904), 99. No variants occur in later printings from the plates made for (C). The work was not included in *Selected Poems* (Boston, 1876).

Format: All lines flush left (A-B).

Pre-copy-text forms: The draft at poetry notebook P, pp. 28–29 consists of eight stanzas, of which the poem as published comprises the third, sixth, and seventh. The first stanza is abandoned and heavily canceled; the second was published for the first time by Edith E. W. Gregg in *One First Love: The Letters of Ellen Louisa Tucker to Ralph Waldo Emerson* [Cambridge, 1962], 47–48, along with the remainder of the P text; the disused stanzas (the fourth, fifth, and eighth) were first published in Edward Emerson's note to the poem (*W*, IX, 436). See *PN*, 940–941, for a further discussion of these matters and the location of additional partial drafts. The Berg MS printer's copy is untitled, as is the text in (B), where the title is given only in the Table of Contents.

VARIANTS

Title: THINE EYES STILL SHINED. (C-D) | [*No title*] (A-B)

2 sea: (C-D) | sea, (A-B)

5 hill, (A-C) | hill (D)

7 path (C-D) | path, (A)

9 redbird (C-D) | red bird (A-B)

10 flame; (C-D) | flame, (A-B)

11 rosebud (C-D) | rose-bud (A-B)

NOTES

11–12. "The name of those we love seems written on the leaves of every flower." Quoted from Mme. de Staël, *Germany* (London, 1813), III, 285, in *JMN*, VI, 37.

EROS.

This brief poem appears to have been written during the period immediately following Emerson's work on "Friendship" and "Love" for *Essays* (1841), at which time his correspondence with Margaret Fuller and Caroline Sturgis was much occupied with these themes.

EROS.

The sense of the world is short,—
Long and various the report,—
   To love and be beloved;
Men and gods have not outlearned it;
And, how oft soe'er they've turned it,   5
   'Twill not be improved.

TEXTS

(A) *Dial*, IV (January 1844): 401; (B) *Poems* (London, 1847), 118; (C) *Poems* (Boston, 1847), 150; (D) Poems (Boston, 1863), 150; (E) *Poems* (Boston, 1865), 153; (F) *Poems* [Riverside] (Boston, 1884), 89; (F²) *Poems* [Centenary] (Boston, 1904), 100. "Eros" was not included in *Selected Poems* (Boston, 1876).

Format: All lines flush left (A-B).

Pre-copy-text forms: The earliest trace of the poem is a version of line 1 toward the end of a draft fragment of "Saadi" in P, p. 231 (*PN*, 88). Drafts of the whole poem occur at pages 157 and 210 of P as well as in the unpublished notebook L Camadeva (reported in *TN*, III, 343), and, finally, in a separate manuscript textually identical to the *Dial* printing: see, further, *PN*, 781. As Edward observed (*W*, IX, 509), the context at P, p. 157, associates this work with another poem on the same subject, never published by Emerson, "Love / Asks nought": see *PN*, 849–850.

VARIANTS

1   short,— (C-F) I short, (A-B)
3   beloved; (B-F) I beloved;— (A)
4   it; (C-F) I it, (A-B)
5   And, (C-F) I And (A-B) II soe'er
(B-F) I so e'er (A)

6   'Twill not (D) I Tis not to (A) I
'Tis not to (B-C, E) I Not to (F) I
T'will not (CC4) I <<'>T'will> 'T will
not (CC5) I T'will not (CC9)

HERMIONE.

Edward Emerson admits, perhaps a little coyly, that "The history of this poem does not appear" (*W*, IX, 436). We do know, however, that his father used the name "Hermione" on at least one occasion to refer to Caroline Sturgis. In a journal entry of September 1841 he noted "An engagement between Mr Vise and the beautiful Miss Vane! But of that other maiden, that counterweight of all her sex, Hermione, no engagement, no gossip. News of all others, no news of her" (*JMN*, VIII, 51). The identification of Hermione (the name is that of the daughter of Menelaus and Helen of Troy) with Sturgis is secure because Emerson referenced this journal entry in a gathering of passages relating to her in notebook OP Gulistan (*TN*, III, 39). The engagement announced in September 1841 was that between the poet Ellery Channing and Ellen Kilshaw Fuller, an alliance that deeply worried Ellen's older sister Margaret (*FuL*, II, 230–233), and one that many, including Emerson, thought would wound Sturgis, who had been romantically involved with Channing just a few years earlier. The analysis of the composition of "Hermione" in *PN*, 814–815, demonstrates that the first draft of the poem had been written and erased at some point before mid-June 1841, so the poem cannot turn on the fact of the engagement, but rather on another point involved: the nature of Emerson's relationship with the twenty-two-year-old Sturgis.

Emerson had met Caroline Sturgis casually as early as 1835, but their friendship, under the sponsorship of mutual acquaintance Margaret Fuller, began in earnest in 1838 (*Chronology*, 99, 134–137). Emerson biographer Robert D. Richardson, Jr., notes that this friendship, in its quickly developed depths and richness, "was colored, if not actually created by Bettina von Arnim's *Goethe's Correspondence with a Child*" (*Emerson: The Mind on Fire* [Berkeley, 1995], 327), which offered the model of a very unconventional relationship—ardent, flirtatious, and intellectual—between the young Bettina and the old philosopher-poet. Emerson and Sturgis were fascinated by the book and adopted its style in their correspondence and in the affectionate character of their personal relationship. Indeed the style dominated in Emerson's friendships with other new acquaintances whom Fuller brought forward, including Anna Barker Ward and extending as well to Fuller herself. Richardson's conclusion was that "in the early 1840s Emerson was living emotionally, though not physically, in what would now be called an open marriage" (329). Emerson, who "worshipped" friendship despite a constitutional need for privacy and a certain coolness of personality that he frequently regretted, was at this time eager to explore the effects of attachments and emotional availability. It seemed at the very least to offer a tonic to the poetic imagination.

If, as appears to be the case, "Hermione" was written as early as 1841, an explanation would be needed as to why it did not appear in the *Dial*, and, further, how Sturgis could have been surprised—and not altogether pleasantly—on reading it, evidently for the first time, in the 1847 *Poems*. When she mentioned her displeasure to Emerson on 11 February 1847, the poet was abashed. He wrote to her a few days later:

I have had many regrets & much more than regrets, since I saw you, in recalling what I said of my poems,—that they were not historic, &c: for, on remembering certain poems, to which I make no doubt you alluded, it is quite plain what their meaning was when they were written. I have only to say in explanation . . . that such pieces are consciously fabulous to any actual life & purposes of mine, when I write them, & so manifestly, that, after a short time, they take rank in my memory with other people's poetry, as intellectual exercises, &, after a little while, are as readily exposed to other eyes as odes on Napoleon or Apollo. But the seeing you— suggested that these poems, which the day before were poems,— were personalities, & they instantly became unspeakably odious to me. I seem to have surprised myself in an offense which I never forgive in another. And that offence too against you. . . .

Yet there is for us a ground of absolute truth & confidence careless of occasions & interviews, & remaining unaltered through althe connections & histories into which we severally enter. And this is shaken by untruth, & by nothing else. The calling in by trumpeting poetry, of millions of witnesses, though it may be very idle, would be indifferent, so long as I am what I say & do not equivocate to myself. This friendship has been the solidest social good I have known, & it is my meaning to be true to it. (*L,* VIII, 106–107)

HERMIONE.

On a mound an Arab lay,
And sung his sweet regrets,
And told his amulets:
The summer bird
His sorrow heard,   5
And, when he heaved a sigh profound,
The sympathetic swallows swept the ground.

'If it be, as they said, she was not fair,
Beauty's not beautiful to me,
But sceptred genius, aye inorbed,   10
Culminating in her sphere.
This Hermione absorbed
The lustre of the land and ocean,
Hills and islands, cloud and tree,
In her form and motion.   15

'I ask no bauble miniature,
Nor ringlets dead
Shorn from her comely head,
Now that morning not disdains
Mountains and the misty plains   20
Her colossal portraiture;
They her heralds be,
Steeped in her quality,
And singers of her fame
Who is their Muse and dame.   25

'Higher, dear swallows! mind not what I say.
Ah! heedless how the weak are strong,
Say, was it just,
In thee to frame, in me to trust,
Thou to the Syrian couldst belong?   30

'I am of a lineage
That each for each doth fast engage;
In old Bassora's schools, I seemed
Hermit vowed to books and gloom,—
Ill-bested for gay bridegroom.   35
I was by thy touch redeemed;
When thy meteor glances came,
We talked at large of worldly fate,
And drew truly every trait.

'Once I dwelt apart,   40
Now I live with all;
As shepherd's lamp on far hillside
Seems, by the traveller espied,
A door into the mountain heart,
So didst thou quarry and unlock   45
Highways for me through the rock.

'Now, deceived, thou wanderest
In strange lands unblest;
And my kindred come to soothe me.

Southwind is my next of blood;   50
He is come through fragrant wood,
Drugged with spice from climates warm,
And in every twinkling glade,
And twilight nook,
Unveils thy form.   55
Out of the forest way
Forth paced it yesterday;
And when I sat by the watercourse,
Watching the daylight fade,
It throbbed up from the brook.   60

'River, and rose, and crag, and bird,
Frost, and sun, and eldest night,
To me their aid preferred,
To me their comfort plight;—
"Courage! we are thine allies,   65
And with this hint be wise,—
The chains of kind
The distant bind;
Deed thou doest she must do,
Above her will, be true;   70
And, in her strict resort
To winds and waterfalls,
And autumn's sunlit festivals,
To music, and to music's thought,
Inextricably bound,   75
She shall find thee, and be found.
Follow not her flying feet;
Come to us herself to meet."'

TEXTS

(A) MS printer's copy for B (present location unknown); (B) *Poems* (London, 1847), 119–122; (C) *Poems* (Boston, 1847), 151–155; (D) *Poems* (Boston, 1865), 154–158; (E) *Selected Poems* (Boston, 1876), 94–96; (F) *Poems* [Riverside] (Bos-

Hermione

ton, 1884), 89–92; (F²) *Poems* [Centenary] (Boston, 1904), 100–103. Reprintings of (C) exhibit plate damage resulting in the loss of terminal punctuation in lines 15 (1857 and 1858) and 61 (1858).

Format: No verse break after line 15 (A-B), which is the last line on the page in (C-D). (B) also lacks verse breaks after lines 39 and 60.

Pre-copy-text forms: Three drafts, all in pencil and all erased, occur in notebook X; these develop a first draft in notebook EF. See the discussion at *PN*, 814–815.

VARIANTS

2   regrets, (A-E) | regrets (F)

3   amulets: (C-F) | amulets, (A) | amulets; (B)

6   And, (C-F) | And (A-B)

7   swallows (A-B) | swallow (C-F)

8   'If (C-F) | If (A-B) || be, (C-F) | be (A-B) || fair, (C-F) | fair; (A-B)

10   genius, (C-F) | Genius (A-B)

14   cloud (C-F) | vine (A-B)

16   'I (C-F) | I (A-B) || bauble (A-B, F) | bawble (C-E)

19   disdains (C-F) | disdains,— (A-B)

20   plains (C-F) | plains— (A-B)

21   portraiture; (C-F) | portraiture: (A-B)

24   fame (C-F) | fame, (A-B)

25   Muse (C-F) | muse (A-B)

26   'Higher, (C-F) | Higher, (A-B) || swallows! (C-F) | swallows, (A-B)

28   just, (C-F) | just (A-B)

31   'I (E-F) | I (A-D)

32   engage; (C-F) | engage. (A-B)

33   schools, (C-F) | schools (A-B)

34   gloom,— (C-F) | gloom, (A-B)

35   bridegroom. (C-F) | bridegroom: (A-B)

36   redeemed; (B-F) | redeemed: (A)

38   fate, (C-F) | Fate, (A-B)

40   'Once (E-F) | Once (A-D)

42   hillside (D-E) | hillside, (A) | hill side, (B) | hill-side (C, F)

47   'Now, (E-F) | Now (A-B) | Now, (C-D) || deceived, (C-F) | deceived (A-B)

48   lands unblest; (C-F) | lands, unblest, (A-B)

49   me. (A, C-F) | me, (B)

50   Southwind (A, C-F) | South wind (B)

53   And (B-F) | And, (A)

55   form. (C-F) | form: (A-B)

57   yesterday; (C-F) | yesterday, (A-B)

58   And (C-F) | And, (A-B) || watercourse, (A, C-D, F) | watercourse, (B, E)

61   'River, (C-E) | River, (A-B) | 'River (F) || rose, (A-E) | rose (F) || crag, (A-E) | crag (F)

62   Frost, (A-E) | Frost (F) || sun, (A-E) | sun (F) || night, (C-F) | night (A-B)

64   plight;— (C-F) | plight: (A-B)

65   "Courage! (C-F) | 'Courage! (A-B) || allies, (A, C-F) | allies; (B)

66   wise,— (C-F) | wise, (A-B)

68   bind; (C-F) | bind: (A-B)

69   doest (C-F) | doest, (A-B)

72   waterfalls, (A-E) | waterfalls (F)

73   sunlit (A, C-F) | sun-lit (B)

77   feet; (C-F) | feet, (A-B)

78   meet."' (C-F) | meet.' (A-B)

33.   Bassora: Basra in Iraq, in the tenth and eleventh centuries a noted center of learning.

INITIAL, DÆMONIC, AND CELESTIAL LOVE.

This difficult suite of poems on love, allusive and esoteric by turns, has not attracted much comment beyond the observation that they express, from lowest to highest, the range of Plato's speculation on that subject in *Phaedrus* and the *Symposium*. Emerson's characteristic adherence to the Platonic schema is clear enough to make the poems seem, in effect, "Triple blossoms from one root," and yet the integrity of the whole is oddly problematic. When the work was first published, in the London edition of *Poems* (1847), it was collectively entitled, simply, "Ode," its subdivisions carrying the headings "I. Initial Love" and "II. Dæmonic and Celestial Love." The bracketing of the last two sections against the first is also reflected in the history of the critical commentary: John S. Harrison, in setting forth the Platonic and Neo-Platonic sources (*The Teachers of Emerson* [New York, 1910], 146–157), confined his remarks to the poem's last two-thirds, whereas Carl F. Strauch ("Emerson's Adaptation of Myth in 'The Initial Love,'" *American Transcendental Quarterly*, XXV [Winter 1975]: 51–65) dealt solely with the first third in discussing the literary and mythic sources. Evidence as to the period at which these poems were written is far from decisive, but there is reason to think, as Strauch held (57), that "The Initial Love" was probably composed before the end of 1840, while the whole design may have been arrived at as late as 1845.

The best evidence for the early date of "The Initial Love" is its apparent implication in the epistolary conversation on love and friendship carried on in the fall of 1840 among Emerson, Caroline Sturgis, and Margaret Fuller. The origins of this debate may well lie with Fuller's several readings of Plato's *Phaedrus* and the *Symposium* in 1839 (see Meg McGavran Murray, *Margaret Fuller: Wandering Pilgrim* [Athens, Ga., 2008], 164, 441 n. 8), and her interest, early in 1840, in what she called "the search after Eros" (*FuL*, II, 105, 107). Plato's influence on "The Initial Love" was also modulated through "Cupid's Conflict," a poem by the seventeenth-century Cambridge Platonist Henry More that Bronson Alcott had brought to Emerson's attention in early November. In a letter to Fuller of 4 November (*L*, II, 354–355) Emerson urged her to accept More's poem for publication in the *Dial* in place of any submission of Alcott's own—even at the "risk," he said, "of turning the Dial for once into a Retrospective Review." The letter conveying the poem (a complex Platonic rejection of Cupid's vulgar eroticism) was Emerson's first communication with Fuller after he had emphatically told her he would no longer entertain her increasingly impetuous discussion of their relationship. Fuller declared the poem "beautiful," but waited a year to publish it (*Dial*, II [October 1841]: 137–148). It is tempting, then, to see the poetic topos of Cupid in rather decidedly biographical terms, and as related (as "Hermione" was) to the emotionally supercharged period between the marriage of Samuel Gray Ward and Anna Barker in October 1840 and the marriage of Ellery Channing and Ellen Fuller the following September. Another bit of evidence supporting an early date for "The Initial Love"—overlooked by Strauch—is the occurrence of a draft of lines 11–12 in journal E ("He came late[;] he was shod like a traveller"), undated but probably from about October or November 1840 (*JMN*, VII, 406).

During Caroline Sturgis's extended visit to Concord in May and June 1845, when she boarded with the Hawthornes at the Old

Manse, Emerson promised to give her a copy of "the initial poem" before she left for Woburn in early June (*L,* VIII, 32n). Her visit had coincided with what Emerson described as an unusually productive "rhyming mania," so it may be that he was finishing the later sections at this time (*L,* III, 290). At some much later period, either in the late sixties or more probably in the early seventies, Emerson thought to include as an introduction to "The Initial Love" the ten lines eventually published as "Cupido" in *Selected Poems* (see CC5, p. 159). And yet this was never a firmly established intention, since he likewise thought of inserting the poem after line 189 of "The Celestial Love."

INITIAL, DÆMONIC, AND CELESTIAL LOVE.

I.

THE INITIAL LOVE.

Venus, when her son was lost,
Cried him up and down the coast,
In hamlets, palaces, and parks,
And told the truant by his marks,—
Golden curls, and quiver, and bow.   5
This befell how long ago!
Time and tide are strangely changed,
Men and manners much deranged:
None will now find Cupid latent
By this foolish antique patent.   10
He came late along the waste,
Shod like a traveller for haste;
With malice dared me to proclaim him,
That the maids and boys might name him.

Boy no more, he wears all coats,   15
Frocks, and blouses, capes, capotes;
He bears no bow, or quiver, or wand,
Nor chaplet on his head or hand.
Leave his weeds and heed his eyes,—
All the rest he can disguise.   20

In the pit of his eye's a spark
Would bring back day if it were dark;
And, if I tell you all my thought,
Though I comprehend it not,
In those unfathomable orbs   25
Every function he absorbs.
He doth eat, and drink, and fish, and shoot,
And write, and reason, and compute,
And ride, and run, and have, and hold,
And whine, and flatter, and regret,   30
And kiss, and couple, and beget,
By those roving eyeballs bold.

Undaunted are their courages,
Right Cossacks in their forages;
Fleeter they than any creature,—   35
They are his steeds, and not his feature;
Inquisitive, and fierce, and fasting,
Restless, predatory, hasting;
And they pounce on other eyes
As lions on their prey;   40
And round their circles is writ,
Plainer than the day,
Underneath, within, above,—
Love—love—love—love.
He lives in his eyes;   45
There doth digest, and work, and spin,
And buy, and sell, and lose, and win;
He rolls them with delighted motion,
Joy-tides swell their mimic ocean.
Yet holds he them with tortest rein,   50
That they may seize and entertain
The glance that to their glance opposes,
Like fiery honey sucked from roses.

He palmistry can understand,
Imbibing virtue by his hand   55
As if it were a living root;

The pulse of hands will make him mute;
With all his force he gathers balms
Into those wise, thrilling palms.

Cupid is a casuist, 60
A mystic, and a cabalist,—
Can your lurking thought surprise,
And interpret your device.
He is versed in occult science,
In magic, and in clairvoyance; 65
Oft he keeps his fine ear strained,
And Reason on her tiptoe pained
For aëry intelligence,
And for strange coincidence.
But it touches his quick heart 70
When Fate by omens takes his part,
And chance-dropped hints from Nature's sphere
Deeply soothe his anxious ear.

Heralds high before him run;
He has ushers many a one; 75
He spreads his welcome where he goes,
And touches all things with his rose.
All things wait for and divine him,—
How shall I dare to malign him,
Or accuse the god of sport? 80
I must end my true report,
Painting him from head to foot,
In as far as I took note,
Trusting well the matchless power
Of this young-eyed emperor 85
Will clear his fame from every cloud,
With the bards and with the crowd.

He is wilful, mutable,
Shy, untamed, inscrutable,
Swifter-fashioned than the fairies, 90

202

Substance mixed of pure contraries;
His vice some elder virtue's token,
And his good is evil-spoken.
Failing sometimes of his own,
He is headstrong and alone;   95
He affects the wood and wild,
Like a flower-hunting child;
Buries himself in summer waves,
In trees, with beasts, in mines, and caves;
Loves nature like a horned cow,   100
Bird, or deer, or caribou.

Shun him, nymphs, on the fleet horses!
He has a total world of wit;
O how wise are his discourses!
But he is the arch-hypocrite,   105
And, through all science and all art,
Seeks alone his counterpart.
He is a Pundit of the East,
He is an augur and a priest,
And his soul will melt in prayer,   110
But word and wisdom is a snare;
Corrupted by the present toy
He follows joy, and only joy.

There is no mask but he will wear;
He invented oaths to swear;   115
He paints, he carves, he chants, he prays,
And holds all stars in his embrace,
Godlike,—but 'tis for his fine pelf,
The social quintessence of self.
Well said I he is hypocrite,   120
And folly the end of his subtle wit!
He takes a sovran privilege
Not allowed to any liege;
For he does go behind all law,
And right into himself does draw;   125

203

For he is sovereignly allied,—
Heaven's oldest blood flows in his side,—
And interchangeably at one
With every king on every throne,
That no god dare say him nay,   130
Or see the fault, or seen betray:
He has the Muses by the heart,
And the Parcæ all are of his part.

His many signs cannot be told;
He has not one mode, but manifold,—   135
Many fashions and addresses,
Piques, reproaches, hurts, caresses,
Arguments, lore, poetry,
Action, service, badinage;
He will preach like a friar,   140
And jump like Harlequin;
He will read like a crier,
And fight like a Paladin.
Boundless is his memory;
Plans immense his term prolong;   145
He is not of counted age,
Meaning always to be young.
And his wish is intimacy,
Intimater intimacy,
And a stricter privacy;   150
The impossible shall yet be done,
And, being two, shall still be one.
As the wave breaks to foam on shelves,
Then runs into a wave again,
So lovers melt their sundered selves,   155
Yet melted would be twain.

TEXTS

(A) MS Am 82.5, Ralph Waldo Emerson Memorial Association deposit, Houghton Library, Harvard University, printer's copy for B; (B) *Poems* (London, 1847), 123–129; (C) *Poems* (Boston, 1847), 156–164; (D) *Poems* (Boston, 1865), 159–

166; (E) *Selected Poems* (Boston, 1876), 97–102; (F) *Poems* [Riverside] (Boston, 1884), 92–97; (G) *Poems* [Centenary] (Boston, 1904), 103–109.

Format: No verse break after line 32 (A-B, C [page break], D); none after line 53 ([page break in B-C], D-G); none after line 73 (E); none after line 113 ([page break in C], D). Line 102 inset (A). Verse break after line 133 (A-B, E-G) coincides with bottom of page in (C) and does not occur in (D).

Pre-copy-text forms: Drafts in poetry notebook X precede a manuscript fair copy in the Houghton Library (MS Am 1221 [49]). This last text was further revised in X, pp. 132–138, which in turn is the source for the London printer's copy (A). See *PN*, 838–839, for a discussion.

VARIANTS

Title: [*Variation in titles and subtitles is evidently owing to carelessness at first and house styling later; the present editors follow the authority of* (C).]

Below the title: "Insert / (The solid solid universe)" [*A reference to* "Cupido"] (CC5)

3   palaces, (A, C-E) I palaces (B, F-G)

4   marks,— (C-G) I marks, (A-B)

5   quiver, (A-E) I quiver (F-G) II bow. (C-G) I bow;— (A-B)

6   befell how long ago! (E-G) I befel long ago. (A-B) I befell long ago. (C-D) I befell long long ago. (CC1)

8   deranged: (C-G) I deranged; (A-B)

12   haste; (C-G) I haste, (A-B)

16   Frocks, (A-E) I Frocks (F-G) II capotes; (C-G) I capotes, (A) I capôtes, (B)

18   hand. (C-G) I hand<;>↑:↓ (A) I hand: (B)

19   eyes,— (C-G) I eyes, (A-B)

21   eye's (A, C-G) I eyes (B)

22   dark; (C-G) I dark, (A-B)

23   And, (C-G) I And,— (A-B)

24   not, (C-G) I not,— (A-B)

26   absorbs. (C-E) I absorbs; (A-B, CC4, F-G)

27   He doth (A-E) I Doth (F-G) I ["He" *is circled in* (CC4)]

32   eyeballs bold. (C-G) I eyeballs bold; (A) I eye-balls bold; (B)

33-34   [*Lines canceled*] (CC1, CC5)

35   creature,— (C-G) I creature, (A-B)

36   steeds, (C-G) I steeds (A-B) II feature; (C-G) I feature, (A-B)

38   hasting; (C-G) I hasting,— (A-B)

39   eyes (C-G) I eyes, (A-B)

40   lions (A-G) I ↑leaping?↓ lions (CC1) I leaping lions (CC4, CC5) II their (B-G) I the<re>ir (A)

41   writ, (C-G) I writ (A-B)

43   above,— (C-G) I above, (A-B)

44   Love—love—love—love. (C-G) I Love, love, love, love. (A-B)

45   eyes; (C-G) I eyes, (A-B)

50   holds he them (B-G) I holds ↑he↓ them (A) II tortest (A-C, E-F) I taughtest (D) I tautest (CC1, CC5, G)

51   seize (A, C-G) I sieze (B)

59   wise, (C-G) I wise (A-B)

61   cabalist,— (C-G) | cabalist, (A-B)
62   thought (C-G) | Thought (A-B)
63   device. (C-G) | device; (A-B)
64   He is (C-G) | Mainly (A-B)
65   In magic, (B-D) | ↑In↓ Magic
       (A) | In magic (E-G) || clairvoyance;
       (C-D) | clairvoyance. (A-B) |
       claivoyance, (E-G)
67   Reason (C-G) | reason (A-B) ||
       pained (C-G) | pained, (A-B)
68   aëry (C-G) | aery (A-B)
72   chance-dropped (C, E-G) |
       chance-dropt (A-B, D)
74   run; (C-G) | run, (A-B)
75   one; (C-G) | one, (A-B)
76   He spreads (C-G) | Spreads
       (A-B)
80   sport? (C-G) | sport?— (A-B)
86   cloud, (A-E) | cloud (F-G)
87   bards (C-G) | bards, (A-B)
90   fairies, (B-G) | faeries, (A)
91   contraries; (C-G) | contraries,
       (A-B)
93   evil-spoken. (C-G) | evil spoken.
       (A-B)
97   child; (C-G) | child, (A-B)
99   mines, (A-E) mines (F-G) ||
       caves; (C-D) | caves, (A-B, E-G)
100   horned (A-F) | hornèd (G)
101   caribou. (A, C-G) | cariboo.
       (B)
103   wit; (C-G) | wit,— (A-B)
106   And, (C-G) | And (A-B)
108   Pundit (B-G) | pundit (A) || East,
       (C-G) | east, (A-B)
111   is (C-G) | are (A-B)
112   toy (C-G) | <joy> toy, (A) | toy,
       (B)
114   wear; (C-G) | wear, (A-B)
115   swear; (C-G) | swear, (A-B)

117   embrace, (A-D) | embrace.
       (E-G)
118–121 [*Lines canceled* (CC1); *not
       present* (E-G)]
120   Well said I (A, C-D) | Well, said I,
       (B)
121   wit! (C-D) | wit, (A-B)
123   liege; (C-G) | liege, (A-B)
124   he does go (A-D) | Cupid goes
       (CC1, CC4, CC5, E-G)
125   draw; (C-G) | draw, (A-B)
126   sovereignly allied,— (C-G) |
       sov<ereign>↑ran↓ly allied. (A) |
       sovranly allied. (B)
127   side,— (C-G) | side, (A-B)
130   god (A, C-G) | God (B)
131   betray: (C-G) | betray; (A-B)
133   And the Parcæ [Parcae (A)] all
       are of (A-D) | And the stern Parcæ
       on (E-G) | The Parcæ (CC1, CC4,
       CC5)
134   told; (C-G) | told, (A-B)
135   mode, (A-D, F-G) | mood, (E) ||
       manifold,— (C-D) | manifold, (A-B,
       E-G)
137   caresses, (A-D), | caresses; (E) |
       caresses. (F-G)
138   [*Line not present* (A-B)]
138–139 [*Lines canceled* (CC1, CC5);
       not present (E-G)]
139   badinage; (C-D) | badinage, (A-
       B) | comedy (CC1)
141   And (A-G) | He will (CC1, CC4,
       CC5) || Harlequin; (C-G) |
       Harlequin, (A-B)
144   memory; (C-G) | memory, (A-B)
145   prolong; (C-G) | prolong, (A-B)
150   privacy; C-G) | privacy, (A-B)
152   And, (C-G) | And (A-B) || two,
       (C-G) | two (A-B)

NOTES

1.   The motif of the "hue and cry after Cupid" was first developed by Moschus, c. 150 B.C., in his first Idyl, "The Runaway Love"; see *The Greek Pastoral Poets, Theocritus, Bion, and Moschus*, trans. M. J. Chapman (London, 1836), 287–288. Important later treatments include Spenser, *The Faerie Queene*, III, vi, 11 ff., and Ben Jonson, *The Hue and Cry after Cupid* (1608), as well as "Cupid's Conflict," by Henry More, mentioned in the headnote. These sources, all but the first of which Emerson is known or is likely to have read, are discussed in Strauch, "Emerson's Adaptation of Myth."

40.   Strauch ("Emerson's Adaptation of Myth," 57) connects these lines with an 1838 journal passage: "Eyes are bold as lions [—] roving, running, leaping here & there; far, near; they wait for no introduction, they ask not leave of age or rank. They respect neither poverty nor riches[,] neither learning nor power nor virtue nor Sex but intrude & pierce & come again & go through & through you in a moment of time. . . . The power of eyes to charm down insanity or ferocity in beasts is a power behind the eye[;] it must be a victory first achieved in the will before it can be signified in the eye" (*JMN*, VII, 52). See also the note to line 65.

50.   In the entry for "tort," both the first and second edition of the *OED* condemn "tortest" as "an erroneous variant of tautest." Still, both editions cite this line of Emerson's to illustrate (without objection) the nineteenth-century variant spelling in the entry for "taut," a word, in either form, historically associated with nautical contexts.

65.   Clairvoyance: the paranormal ability of remote seeing. This is the earliest recorded American usage of the term, according to the *OED*. In the 1840s clairvoyance was associated with mesmerism, one of the "occult sciences."

108.   Pundit: A Hindu scholar, originally one who advised English colonial officials on points of Indian law.

INITIAL, DÆMONIC, AND CELESTIAL LOVE.

II.

THE DÆMONIC AND THE CELESTIAL LOVE.

When Emerson reprinted "The Dæmonic and the Celestial Love" in *Selected Poems* (1876), the second and third verse paragraphs of "The Dæmonic Love" were placed at the head of the poem's final division, thereby making them introductory to "The Celestial Love." The present edition retains these paragraphs in their original place (lines 23–48 below). Commenting in a note at the location from which the lines were taken, Edward said. "Here followed in the original the passage later rightly placed by Mr. Emerson at the beginning of 'The Celestial Love'" (*W*, IX, 438). The statement goes out of its way to assign responsibility for this change to the poet (as though there might otherwise have been reason to doubt), but Edward's emphatic approval may hint that the transfer had been effected to meet criticism from within the family. Since it is a main purpose of the lines to announce that the subject of a "higher" kind of love will now be introduced, the passage "works" in either location, but the removal vitiates the arguably well constructed Genesis context at the opening of the second section and seems to confess to a confusion in the structure of the whole similar to that which prompted the revisions in "May-Day" at the same time.

II.

THE DÆMONIC AND THE CELESTIAL LOVE.

Man was made of social earth,
Child and brother from his birth,
Tethered by a liquid cord
Of blood through veins of kindred poured.
Next his heart the fireside band   5
Of mother, father, sister, stand:
Names from awful childhood heard
Throbs of a wild religion stirred;—
Virtue, to love, to hate them, vice;
Till dangerous Beauty came, at last,   10
Till Beauty came to snap all ties;
The maid, abolishing the past,
With lotus wine obliterates
Dear memory's stone-incarved traits,
And, by herself, supplants alone   15
Friends year by year more inly known.
When her calm eyes opened bright,
All were foreign in their light.
It was ever the self-same tale,
The first experience will not fail;   20
Only two in the garden walked,
And with snake and seraph talked.

    But God said,
'I will have a purer gift;
There is smoke in the flame;   25
New flowerets bring, new prayers uplift,
And love without a name.
Fond children, ye desire
To please each other well;
Another round, a higher,   30

Ye shall climb on the heavenly stair,
And selfish preference forbear;
And in right deserving,
And without a swerving
Each from your proper state,   35
Weave roses for your mate.

'Deep, deep are loving eyes,
Flowed with naphtha fiery sweet;
And the point is paradise,
Where their glances meet: 40
Their reach shall yet be more profound,
And a vision without bound:
The axis of those eyes sun-clear
Be the axis of the sphere:
So shall the lights ye pour amain   45
Go, without check or intervals,
Through from the empyrean walls
Unto the same again.'

Close, close to men,
Like undulating layer of air,   50
Right above their heads,
The potent plain of Dæmons spreads.
Stands to each human soul its own,
For watch, and ward, and furtherance,
In the snares of Nature's dance;   55
And the lustre and the grace
To fascinate each youthful heart,
Beaming from its counterpart,
Translucent through the mortal covers,
Is the Dæmon's form and face.   60
To and fro the Genius hies,—
A gleam which plays and hovers
Over the maiden's head,
And dips sometimes as low as to her eyes.
Unknown, albeit lying near,   65

To men, the path to the Dæmon sphere;
And they that swiftly come and go
Leave no track on the heavenly snow.
Sometimes the airy synod bends,
And the mighty choir descends,   70
And the brains of men thenceforth,
In crowded and in still resorts,
Teem with unwonted thoughts:
As, when a shower of meteors
Cross the orbit of the earth,   75
And, lit by fringent air,
Blaze near and far,
Mortals deem the planets bright
Have slipped their sacred bars,
And the lone seaman all the night   80
Sails, astonished, amid stars.

Beauty of a richer vein,
Graces of a subtler strain,
Unto men these moonmen lend,
And our shrinking sky extend.   85
So is man's narrow path
By strength and terror skirted;
Also, (from the song the wrath
Of the Genii be averted!
The Muse the truth uncolored speaking,)   90
The Dæmons are self-seeking:
Their fierce and limitary will
Draws men to their likeness still.

The erring painter made Love blind,—
Highest Love who shines on all;   95
Him, radiant, sharpest-sighted god,
None can bewilder;
Whose eyes pierce
The universe,
Path-finder, road-builder,   100

Mediator, royal giver;
Rightly seeing, rightly seen,
Of joyful and transparent mien.
'Tis a sparkle passing
From each to each, from thee to me,   105
To and fro perpetually;
Sharing all, daring all,
Levelling, displacing
Each obstruction, it unites
Equals remote, and seeming opposites.   110
And ever and forever Love
Delights to build a road:
Unheeded Danger near him strides,
Love laughs, and on a lion rides.

But Cupid wears another face,   115
Born into Dæmons less divine:
His roses bleach apace,
His nectar smacks of wine.
The Dæmon ever builds a wall,
Himself encloses and includes,   120
Solitude in solitudes:
In like sort his love doth fall.
He is an oligarch;
He prizes wonder, fame, and mark;
He loveth crowns;   125
He scorneth drones;
He doth elect
The beautiful and fortunate,
And the sons of intellect,
And the souls of ample fate,   130
Who the Future's gates unbar,—
Minions of the Morning Star.
In his prowess he exults,
And the multitude insults.
His impatient looks devour   135
Oft the humble and the poor;

And, seeing his eye glare,
They drop their few pale flowers,
Gathered with hope to please,
Along the mountain towers,— 140
Lose courage, and despair.
He will never be gainsaid,—
Pitiless, will not be stayed;
His hot tyranny
Burns up every other tie. 145
Therefore comes an hour from Jove
Which his ruthless will defies,
And the dogs of Fate unties.
Shiver the palaces of glass;
Shrivel the rainbow-colored walls, 150
Where in bright Art each god and sibyl dwelt,
Secure as in the zodiac's belt;
And the galleries and halls,
Wherein every siren sung,
Like a meteor pass. 155
For this fortune wanted root
In the core of God's abysm,—
Was a weed of self and schism;
And ever the Dæmonic Love
Is the ancestor of wars, 160
And the parent of remorse.

III.

Higher far,
Upward into the pure realm,
Over sun and star,
Over the flickering Dæmon film, 165
Thou must mount for love;
Into vision where all form
In one only form dissolves;
In a region where the wheel
On which all beings ride 170

Visibly revolves;
Where the starred, eternal worm
Girds the world with bound and term;
Where unlike things are like;
Where good and ill,   175
And joy and moan,
Melt into one.
There Past, Present, Future shoot
Triple blossoms from one root;
Substances at base divided   180
In their summits are united;
There the holy essence rolls,
One through separated souls;
And the sunny Æon sleeps
Folding Nature in its deeps,   185
And every fair and every good,
Known in part, or known impure,
To men below,
In their archetypes endure.
The race of gods,   190
Or those we erring own,
Are shadows flitting up and down
In the still abodes.
The circles of that sea are laws
Which publish and which hide the cause.   195

Pray for a beam
Out of that sphere,
Thee to guide and to redeem.

O, what a load
Of care and toil,   200
By lying use bestowed,
From his shoulders falls who sees
The true astronomy,
The period of peace.
Counsel which the ages kept   205

Shall the well-born soul accept.
As the overhanging trees
Fill the lake with images,—
As garment draws the garment's hem,
Men their fortunes bring with them.   210
By right or wrong,
Lands and goods go to the strong.
Property will brutely draw
Still to the proprietor;
Silver to silver creep and wind,   215
And kind to kind.

Nor less the eternal poles
Of tendency distribute souls.
There need no vows to bind
Whom not each other seek, but find.   220
They give and take no pledge or oath,—
Nature is the bond of both:
No prayer persuades, no flattery fawns,—
Their noble meanings are their pawns.
Plain and cold is their address,   225
Power have they for tenderness;
And, so thoroughly is known
Each other's counsel by his own,
They can parley without meeting;
Need is none of forms of greeting;   230
They can well communicate
In their innermost estate;
When each the other shall avoid,
Shall each by each be most enjoyed.

Not with scarfs or perfumed gloves   235
Do these celebrate their loves;
Not by jewels, feasts, and savors,
Not by ribbons or by favors,
But by the sun-spark on the sea,
And the cloud-shadow on the lea,   240

The soothing lapse of morn to mirk,
And the cheerful round of work.
Their cords of love so public are,
They intertwine the farthest star:
The throbbing sea, the quaking earth,   245
Yield sympathy and signs of mirth;
Is none so high, so mean is none,
But feels and seals this union;
Even the fell Furies are appeased,
The good applaud, the lost are eased.   250

Love's hearts are faithful, but not fond,
Bound for the just, but not beyond;
Not glad, as the low-loving herd,
Of self in other still preferred,
But they have heartily designed   255
The benefit of broad mankind.
And they serve men austerely,
After their own genius, clearly,
Without a false humility;
For this is Love's nobility,—   260
Not to scatter bread and gold,
Goods and raiment bought and sold;
But to hold fast his simple sense,
And speak the speech of innocence,
And with hand, and body, and blood,   265
To make his bosom-counsel good.
For he that feeds men serveth few;
He serves all who dares be true.

TEXTS

(A) MS Am 82.5, Ralph Waldo Emerson Memorial Association deposit, Houghton Library, Harvard University, printer's copy for B; (B) *Poems* (London, 1847), 130–141; (C) *Poems* (Boston, 1847), 164–177; (D) *Poems* ["Fourth Edition"] (Boston, 1847), 164–177; (E) *Poems* (Boston, 1857), 164–177; (F) *Poems* (Boston, 1858), 164–177; (G) *Poems* (Boston, 1865), 167–180; (H) *Selected Poems*

Initial, Dæmonic, and Celestial Love

(Boston, 1867), 102–111; (I) *Poems* [Riverside] (Boston, 1884), 97–105; (J) *Poems* [Centenary] (Boston, 1904), 109–118.

Format: Line 23 set flush left (H-J) and line 196 indented (A). White line follows line 64 (A-B). White line after 93 (A-B) coincides with page break in (C), leading to loss of white line in (G-J). White line after line 114 (A) coincides with page break in (B-F), leading to loss of white line in (G-J). White line following lines 177 (G, I-J) and 188 (A-B). No white line following line 195 (B). White line after line 198 (A-B) coincides with page break in (C-F), leading to loss of white line in (G-J). No white line following line 216 (A-B).

Pre-copy-text forms: See *PN,* 767–768, 838–839.

VARIANTS

Title: [*Variation in titles and subtitles is evidently owing to carelessness at first and house styling later; the present editors follow the authority of* (C).]

2   birth, (C-J) | birth; (A-B)

4   poured. (C-J) | poured, (A-B)

6   stand: (C-G) | stand; (A-B, H-J)

7   Names from awful childhood heard (CC1, D-J) | [*Same except for* aweful (A)] | [*Same except for* heard, (B)] | These, like strong amulets preferred, (C)

8   stirred;— (C-J) | stirred, (A-B)

9   Virtue, to love, to hate them, vice; (C-J) | Their good was heaven, their harm was vice, (A-B)

10   [*Line supplied*] (CC10) | [*Line present*] (C-J) | [*Line not present*] (A-B)

11   ties; (C-J) | ties, (A-B)

13   lotus wine (C-J) | lotus-wine (A-B)

15   And, (C-J) | And (A-B) || herself, (C-J) | herself (A-B)

18   were (A-G) | else grew (H-J)

19   self-same (B-G, I-J) | selfsame (A, H)

20   first (C-J) | old (A-B) || fail; (C-J) | fail,— (A-B)

23–36   [*Lines canceled*] (CC3)

23–48   (A-G) | [*Lines bracketed in* (CC5) *and transferred to beginning of Part III* (H-J). *See discussion in the headnote.*]

23   said, (C-J) | said; (A-B)

24   'I (C-J) | I (A-B) || gift; (C-J) | gift, (A-B)

25   flame; (B-J) | flame (A)

35   state, (A-G, I-J) | state (H)

36   mate. (A-G, I-J) | mate.' (H)

37   'Deep, (C-G, I-J) | Deep, (A-B, H)

38   sweet; (C-J) | sweet, (A-B)

39   paradise, (C-G, I-J) | Paradise (A-B, H)

40   meet: (A-G, I-J) | meet; (H)

42   bound: (A-B, F, I-J) | bound; (C-E, G-H)

44   sphere: (C-J) | sphere; (A-B)

45   So (C-J) | Then (A-B)

46   Go, (C-J) | Go (A-B) || intervals, (B-J) | intervals (A)

47   walls (A, C-J) | walls, (B)

48   again.' (C-G, I-J) | again. (A-B, H)

54 watch, and ward, (A-H) I watch and ward (I-J) II furtherance, (C-J) I furtherance (A-B)

55 Nature's (C-J) I nature's (A-B)

57 To (E-J) I Which (A-D) I To (CC1) II youthful (C-J) I human (A-B)

58 its counterpart, (D-J) I another part, (A-B) I [its counterpart,] (C) I its counterpart, (CC1)

61 hies,— (C-J) I hies, (A-B)

64 eyes. (A-D, F, H-J) I eyes (E, G) I ["Insert a period"] (CC3) I eyes↑.↓ (CC4, CC5)

65 Unknown, (C-J) I Unknown,— (A-B) II near, (C-J) I near,— (A-B)

66 men, (C-J) I men (A-B) II sphere; (C-J) I sphere, (A-B)

67 go (C-J) I go, (A-B)

73 thoughts: (C-J) I thoughts. (A-B)

74 As, (C-J) I As (A-B)

77 far, (A, C-J) I far. (B)

78 Mortals deem the (B-J) I <As if> ↑Mortals deem↓ the <old> (A)

79 Have (B-J) I Ha<d>ve (A)

80 the lone seaman all the (B-J) I <wandering men at> ↑the lone seaman all the↓ (A)

81 Sails, astonished, amid (C-G, I-J) I <Walk> ↑Sails astonished amid↓ <the seeming> (A) I Sails astonished amid (B, H)

82–161 [*Lines canceled*] (CC3)

84 moonmen (C-J) I moon-men (A-B)

87 skirted; (C-J) I skirted, (A-B)

89 Also, (C-H) I Also (A-B, I-J)

90 uncolored (A, C-J) I uncoloured (B) II speaking,) (A-I) I speaking) (J)

91 self-seeking: (C-J) I selfseeking; (A) I self-seeking; (B)

94 blind,— (C-J) I blind, (A-B)

96 Him, (C-J) I Him (A-B) II god, (C-J) I god (A-B)

99 universe, (C-J) I Universe, (A-B)

100 Path-finder (B-J) I Pathfinder (A) II road-builder, (B-J) I <R>road-builder, (A)

101 giver; (C-J) I giver, (A-B)

102 Rightly seeing, rightly seen, (C-J) I Rightly-seeing, rightly-seen, (A-B)

103 mien. (A-H, J) I mien (I)

104 'Tis (B-J) I Tis (A)

105 thee to me, (C-J) I me to thee, (A-B)

106 To and fro perpetually; (CC10, C-J) I Perpetually, (A-B)

112 road: (C-J) I road; (A-B)

115 face, (C-J) I face (A-B)

116 Born (B-J) I <Poured> ↑Born↓ (A) II divine: (C-J) I divine, (A-B)

119–161 [*Lines canceled*] (CC4) I [*Lines bracketed*] (CC5)

120 encloses (C-J) I incloses (A-B)

123–126 [*Lines not present*] (H-J)

123 oligarch; (C-G) I oligarch, (A-B)

124 mark; (C-G) I mark, (A-B)

125 crowns; (C-G) I crowns, (A-B)

131 unbar,— (C-J) I unbar, (A-B)

133 [*Line inadvertently repeated, the second then canceled*] (A)

136 poor; (C-J) I poor, (A-B)

138 flowers, (C-J) I flowers (A-B)

139 please, (C-J) I please (A-B)

140 towers,— (C-J) I towers, (A-B)

142 gainsaid,— (C-J) I gainsaid, (A-B)

143 stayed; (C-J) I stayed. (A-B)

145 tie. (C-J) I tie; (A-B)

149 glass; (C-J) I glass, (A-B)

150 -colored (A, C-J) I -coloured (B)

151 Art (C-J) I art (A-B) II dwelt, (C-G) I dwelt (A-B, H-J)

152 zodiac's (C-J) I Zodiack's (A-B)

153 halls, (C-J) I halls (A-B)

154 siren (C-J) I Siren (A-B)

157 abysm,— (C-J) I abysm, (A-B)

158 schism; (C-J) I schism (A-B)

158–160 [*In* CC1 *lines canceled and*

recopied (*with inadvertent alterations*) *as
part of the transfer of lines 23–48.*]

159   Love (A-G, I-J) l love (H) l love
(CC1)

160   wars, (A-H) l wars (I-J) l wars
(CC1)

162–177 [*Lines canceled*] (CC1) [*Note
that these lines were in fact never dropped,
but Emerson's first idea for revision was
that the two transferred verse paragraphs
would replace this single verse
paragraph.*]

162   [*Lines 23–48, above, inserted here,
forming a new introduction to "The
Celestial Love"*] (H-J)

162–163 [*Lines combined into one:*]
Higher far into the pure realm, (H-J)

163   Upward (C-G) l Upward, (A-B)

164   and (C-J) l or (A-B)

166   love; (C-J) l love,— (A-B)

167   where (C-J) l which (A-B)

169   wheel (A, C-J) l wheel, (B)

170   ride (C-J) l ride, (A-B)

172   starred, (C-G, I-J) l starred (A-B,
H)

174   like; (C-J) l like, (A-B)

175–177 [*Lines canceled*] (CC3)

176   moan, (B-J) l moan (A)

178   Future (C-H) l Future, (A-B, I-J)

179   root; (C-J) l root, (A-B)

180–181 [*Lines canceled*] (CC3)

180   divided (A-H) l divided, (I-J)

181   united; (C-J) l united. (A) l
united, (B)

182   essence (C-J) l Essence (A-B)

183   souls; (C-J) l souls, (A-B)

185   Nature (C-J) l nature (A-B) ‖
deeps, (A-B, I-J) l deeps: (C-D) l
deeps (E-H)

186   good, (C-J) l good (A-B)

187   part, (C-J) l part (A-B) ‖ impure,
(C-J) l impure (A-B)

189–190 [*In* (CC5), *keyed to a horizontal
caret in the margin is the notation "*X

Solid?" *See the discussion in the headnote
to "The Initial Love."*]

190–193 [*Lines canceled*] (CC3)

194   laws (C-J) l laws, (A-B)

195   cause. (C-J) l Cause. (A-B)

196–204 [*Lines canceled*] (CC3)

197   sphere, (C-J) l sphere (A-B)

199   O, (C-J) l O (A-B)

200   toil, (C-J) l toil (A-B)

201   use (C-J) l Use (A-B)

202   falls (C-J) l falls, (A-B)

204   peace. (C-J) l Peace! (A) l peace!
(B)

205   kept (C-J) l kept, (A-B)

208   images,— (C-J) l images, (A-B)

209   hem, (A, C-J) l hem (B)

210   them. (C-J) l them; (A-B)

212   strong. (C-J) l strong; (A-B)

214   proprietor; (C-J) l proprietor,
(A-B)

216   kind. (A, C-J) l kind, (B)

220   seek, (C-J) l seek (A-B)

221   oath,— (C-J) l oath, (A-B)

222   both: (C-J) l both. (A-B)

223   fawns,— (C-J) l fawns, (A-B)

226   tenderness; (C-J) l tenderness,
(A-B)

227   And, (C-J) l And (A-B)

228   counsel (C-J) l purpose (A-B)

229   meeting; (C-J) l meeting, (A-B)

230   greeting; (C-J) l greeting, (A-B)

236   loves; (C-H) l loves, (A-B) l loves:
(I-J)

237   feasts, (A-H) l feasts (I-J) ‖
savors, (A, C-J) l savours, (B)

238   favors, (A, C-J) l favours, (B)

240   cloud-shadow (B-J) l
cloudshadow (A)

241   The (B-J) l <By the> ↑The↓ (A)

244   star: (C-J) l star. (A-B)

245   ↑(↓quaking↑)↓ (CC1) [*with a
question mark in the margin*]

246   Yield (B-J) l <Have> ↑Yield↓
(A)

248 union; (C-J) | union. (A-B)
251 faithful, (B-J) | faithful (A)
252 Bound (A-J) | /Bound/ Pledged/ (CC4)
253 as the low- (B-J) | as <is> the ↑low-↓ (A)
254 preferred, (B-J) | preferred (A)
260 Love's (A, C-J) | love's (B) ‖ nobility,— (C-J) | nobility, (A-B)

262 sold; (C-J) | sold, (A-B)
265 hand, (A-H) | hand (I-J) ‖ body, (A-H) | body (I-J)
266 good. (C-J) | good: (A-B)
267 For he (A-H) | He (I-J) | <For> he (CC4) ‖ men (C-J) | men, (A-B) ‖ few; (C-J) | few, (A-B)
268 all (C-J) | all, (A-B)

NOTES

76. The *OED,* defining "fringent" as "Exercising friction," cites no other example of its application than this by Emerson. Before the *OED* was published Gamaliel Bradford, Jr., condemned Emerson's use of the term as, probably, "a fault of style, though the dictionary gives me no clue to what it means" ("Emerson," *New Princeton Review,* V [March 1888]: 151). In fact, Emerson's brief description of meteors is better and more accurate than the scientists of his day could have supplied: the old view of the Scottish geologist James Hutton (1726–1797) that meteors were the product of lunar volcanoes enjoyed diminished support, though by 1845 astronomers had advanced few better ideas. See John Robie Eastman, *The Progress of Meteoric Astronomy in America* (Washington, D.C., 1890), 282 and passim.

THE APOLOGY.

On 12 March 1844 Emerson sent manuscripts of "The Dirge" and "The Poet's Apology" (as "The Apology" was then called) to his Philadelphia friend William H. Furness as contributions to an annual entitled *The Gift.* Of the former poem Emerson noted that it had been composed "years ago" (1838, as we know) and that he might have published those verses in the *Dial* "but for their per-sonality" (*L*, VII, 592). The fact that he offered no such history for the second poem might be taken to imply that it was recently written. The only light that the poetry notebooks shed on the question is that composition must in any event have occurred later than 1841 because it is inscribed over an erased draft of a poem, "The Park," of that date (see *PN*, 732–733). Because the fourth stanza of "The Apology" originally belonged to another poem, "Knows he who tills this lonely field" (*PN*, 844), Emerson was a little uncertain of its fitness: he gave Furness leave to omit or retain the stanza as he thought best (*L*, VII, 593).

THE APOLOGY.

Think me not unkind and rude
    That I walk alone in grove and glen;
I go to the god of the wood
    To fetch his word to men.

Tax not my sloth that I   5
    Fold my arms beside the brook;
Each cloud that floated in the sky
    Writes a letter in my book.

Chide me not, laborious band,
    For the idle flowers I brought;   10
Every aster in my hand
    Goes home loaded with a thought.

There was never mystery
    But 'tis figured in the flowers;
Was never secret history   15
    But birds tell it in the bowers.

One harvest from thy field
    Homeward brought the oxen strong;
A second crop thine acres yield,
    Which I gather in a song.   20

Poems (1847)

TEXTS

(A) *The Gift: A Christmas, New Year, and Birthday Present* (Philadelphia: Carey and Hart, 1845), 77; (B) MS Am 1280.235 (8), Ralph Waldo Emerson Memorial Association deposit, Houghton Library, Harvard University, printer's copy for C; (C) *Poems* (London, 1847), 142–43; (D) *Poems* (Boston, 1847), 178–79; (D²) *Poems* (Boston, 1858), 178–179; (D³) *Poems* (Boston, 1865), 181–182; (D⁴) *Poems* [Riverside] (Boston, 1884), 105–106; (D⁵) *Poems* [Centenary] (Boston, 1904), 119. In (D²), line 12, terminal punctuation is lost to plate damage. "The Apology" was not included in *Selected Poems* (Boston, 1876).

Format: Alternate indentation lacking in (C).

Pre-copy-text forms: Composed in poetry notebook P: see *PN*, 732–733.

VARIANTS

Title: THE APOLOGY. (B-D) | THE POET'S APOLOGY. (A)

1   rude (D) | rude, (A-C)
13   mystery (A, D) | mystery, (B-C)

14   'tis (A, C-D) | tis (B) || flowers; (D) | flowers, (A-C)
15   history (A, D) | history, (B-C)
18   strong; (B-D) | strong (A)

MERLIN.

I.

The origins of this poem can be traced to a conversation with Elizabeth Hoar on 21 June 1839 in the course of which Emerson came to the conclusion that although "you shall not speak truth in Prose,—you may in Verse." He felt then that he had access —through powers of concentration—to "that faculty of daring rhyme" that he most admired (*JMN*, VII, 218). A journal passage of a week later is recognizably the source of "Merlin I":

Rhyme; not tinkling rhyme but grand Pindaric strokes as firm as the tread of a horse. Rhyme that vindicates itself as an art, the stroke of the bell of a cathedral. Rhyme which knocks at prose & dulness with the stroke of a cannon ball. Rhyme which builds out into Chaos & Old night a splendid architecture to bridge the impassable, & call aloud on all the children of morning that the Creation is recommencing. I wish to write such rhymes as shall not suggest a restraint but contrariwise the wildest freedom. (*JMN*, VII, 219)

Possibly these thoughts had relation to Emerson's concurrent experience as editor of Jones Very's *Essays and Poems* (Boston, 1839), since within weeks of Very's visit to Concord on 16–17 June, when he agreed to undertake the project, he had culled sixty-six of the best sonnets from a sample of two hundred (*L*, II, 204, 209). It was not, however, until some years later that Emerson versified these ideas about strength and freedom in poetry and connected them to the figure of Merlin. Edward correctly assigned this belated effort to 1845 (*W*, IX, 440–441; cf. *JMN*, IX, 167–168), though, as we know from Emerson's statement to Elizabeth Hoar (*L*, III, 341), the poem, together with its companion, "Merlin II," was not finished until July 1846.

MERLIN.

I.

Thy trivial harp will never please
Or fill my craving ear;
Its chords should ring as blows the breeze,
Free, peremptory, clear.
No jingling serenader's art,   5
Nor tinkle of piano strings,
Can make the wild blood start
In its mystic springs.
The kingly bard
Must smite the chords rudely and hard,   10
As with hammer or with mace;
That they may render back

Artful thunder, which conveys
Secrets of the solar track,
Sparks of the supersolar blaze.   15
Merlin's blows are strokes of fate,
Chiming with the forest tone,
When boughs buffet boughs in the wood;
Chiming with the gasp and moan
Of the ice-imprisoned flood;   20
With the pulse of manly hearts;
With the voice of orators;
With the din of city arts;
With the cannonade of wars;
With the marches of the brave;   25
And prayers of might from martyrs' cave.

Great is the art,
Great be the manners, of the bard.
He shall not his brain encumber
With the coil of rhythm and number;   30
But, leaving rule and pale forethought,
He shall aye climb
For his rhyme.
'Pass in, pass in,' the angels say,
'In to the upper doors,   35
Nor count compartments of the floors,
But mount to paradise
By the stairway of surprise.'

Blameless master of the games,
King of sport that never shames,   40
He shall daily joy dispense
Hid in song's sweet influence.
Things more cheerly live and go,
What time the subtle mind
Sings aloud the tune whereto   45
Their pulses beat,
And march their feet,
And their members are combined.

By Sybarites beguiled,
He shall no task decline; 50
Merlin's mighty line
Extremes of nature reconciled,—
Bereaved a tyrant of his will,
And made the lion mild.
Songs can the tempest still, 55
Scattered on the stormy air,
Mould the year to fair increase,
And bring in poetic peace.

He shall not seek to weave,
In weak, unhappy times, 60
Efficacious rhymes;
Wait his returning strength.
Bird, that from the nadir's floor
To the zenith's top can soar,
The soaring orbit of the muse exceeds that journey's length. 65
Nor profane affect to hit
Or compass that, by meddling wit,
Which only the propitious mind
Publishes when 'tis inclined.
There are open hours 70
When the God's will sallies free,
And the dull idiot might see
The flowing fortunes of a thousand years;—
Sudden, at unawares,
Self-moved, fly-to the doors, 75
Nor sword of angels could reveal
What they conceal.

TEXTS

(A) MS HM 7624, by permission of the Huntington Library, San Marino, California (lines 1–40) and MS m.b., Berg Collection, by permission of the New York Public Library (lines 41–77), together printer's copy for B; (B) *Poems* (London, 1847), 143–149; (C) *Poems* (Boston, 1847), 180–184; (D) *Poems* ["Fourth Edition"] (Boston, 1847), 180–184; (E) *Poems* (Boston 1857), 180–184; (E²) *Poems*

Poems (1847)

(Boston, 1865), 183–187; (F) *Selected Poems* (Boston, 1867), 114–116; (G) *Poems* [Riverside] (Boston, 1884), 106–109; (H) *Poems* [Centenary] (Boston, 1904), 120–22.

Format: A verse break after line 65 (A-B) also occurs in pre-copy-text manuscripts but is not a feature of any American printing (C-H). The printer of (C) may have missed it if the long line 65 ran over in printer's copy, but lacking that manuscript the editors have elected to follow the authority of (C-H).

Pre-copy-text forms: A rough draft of the opening of the poem occurs in *JMN*, IX, 167–168. The Houghton MS, transcribed at *PN*, 687–689, lacks lines 39–42 and 63–64; it was clearly copied by Emerson from some intermediate draft, now lost.

VARIANTS

Title: MERLIN I. (A-E, G-H) | MERLIN. (F)

3   breeze, (A-E, G-H) | breeze (F)

6   strings, (B-H) | strings (A)

11   mace; (C-H) | mace, (A-B)

13   thunder, which (C-H) | thunder that (A-B)

17   forest tone, (C-E, G-H) | forest-tone, (A-B) | forest tone (F)

21   hearts; (C-H) | hearts, (A-B)

22   orators; (C-H) | orators, (A-B)

23   arts; (C-H) | arts, (A-B)

24   wars; (C-H) | wars, (A-B)

25   brave; (C-H) | brave, (A-B)

28   manners, (C-H) | manners (A-B) || bard. (C-H) | bard! (A-B)

30   number; (C-H) | number, (A-B)

33   rhyme. (C-H) | rhyme: (A-B)

34   'Pass (C-F, H) | Pass (A-B, G) || in,' the (C-H) | in, the (A-B)

35   'In (CC1, E-F, H) | In (A-D, G) || doors, (C-H) | doors; (A-B) [*In some late (1894) reprintings of* (G) *the quotation marks in lines 34 and 35 were restored*]

37   paradise (C-H) | Paradise (A-B)

38   surprise.' (CC1, E-H) | surprise. (A-D)

40   shames, (A, C-H) | shames (B)

43   Things (A-F) | ?Things/Forms?/ (CC1) | Forms (G-H)

45   Sings (C-H) | Plays (A-B)

49   beguiled, (C-H) | beguiled (A-B)

51   line (A, C-H) | line, (B)

52   reconciled,— (C-H) | reconciled, (A-B)

59   weave, (B-H) | weave (A)

60   weak, (C-H) | weak (A-B) || times, (B-H) | times (A)

61   rhymes; (A-E, G-H) | rhymes;— (F)

62   strength. (C-H) | strength; (A-B)

63   floor (C-H) | floor, (A-B)

64   can (C-H) | could (A-B) || soar, (A-F) | soar,— (G-H)

65   muse (B-H) | Muse (A) || length. (C-H) | length! (A-B)

66   Nor (C-H) | Nor, (A-B) || profane (A, C-H) | profane, (B)

67   that, (C-H) | that (A-B)

69   'tis (B-H) | tis (A)

71   God's (A, C-H) | god's (B)

72   idiot (B-H) | ideot (A)

73   years;— (C-H) | years; (A-B)

75   Self-moved, (C-H) | Self-moved (A-B) || doors, (A-B, D-H) | doors (C)

NOTES

58. The Welsh bards were especially connected with the ideal of peace: see Kenneth Walter Cameron, "The Potent Song in Emerson's Merlin Poems," *Philological Quarterly* XXXII (January 1953): 26, for Emerson's possible sources on this point.

70–77. In a lengthy 1835 description of his "First Philosophy," Emerson wrote: "But suddenly in any place, in the street, in the chamber, will the heaven open, and the regions of wisdom be uncovered, as if to show how thin the veil, how null the circumstances. As quickly, a Lethean stream washes through us and bereaves us of ourselves" (*JMN*, V, 275; cf. Cameron, "The Potent Song," 28).

MERLIN.

II.

In his note to this poem Edward Emerson expressed surprise that his father should have excluded it from *Selected Poems,* since it "well expressed his favorite idea of correspondence, universal rhyme and harmony in Nature, and compensation in life" (*W,* IX, 442). In illustration of this "favorite idea" Edward quoted from the article on Pythagoras that he had found in the *New American Cyclopædia* (1857–1866), edited by the Brook Farmers George Ripley and Charles Dana:

> The world subsists [according to Pythagoras] by the rhythmical order of its elements. Everywhere in Nature appear the two elements of the finite and the infinite which give rise to the elementary opposites of the universe, the odd and even, one and many, right and left, male and female, fixed and moved, straight and curved, light and darkness, square and oblong, good and bad.

Although the poem incorporates stray lines written in 1841 and 1842 (see notes to lines 24–25 and 50), its composition is not earlier than 1845; it was finished, as Emerson indicated to Elizabeth Hoar, along with its companion, in July 1846 (*L*, III, 341).

MERLIN.

II.

The rhyme of the poet
Modulates the king's affairs;
Balance-loving Nature
Made all things in pairs.
To every foot its antipode;   5
Each color with its counter glowed;
To every tone beat answering tones,
Higher or graver;
Flavor gladly blends with flavor;
Leaf answers leaf upon the bough;   10
And match the paired cotyledons.
Hands to hands, and feet to feet,
In one body grooms and brides;
Eldest rite, two married sides
In every mortal meet.   15
Light's far furnace shines,
Smelting balls and bars,
Forging double stars,
Glittering twins and trines.
The animals are sick with love,   20
Lovesick with rhyme;
Each with all propitious time
Into chorus wove.

Like the dancers' ordered band,
Thoughts come also hand in hand;   25
In equal couples mated,
Or else alternated;

Adding by their mutual gage,
One to other, health and age.
Solitary fancies go   30
Short-lived wandering to and fro,
Most like to bachelors,
Or an ungiven maid,
Not ancestors,
With no posterity to make the lie afraid,   35
Or keep truth undecayed.

Perfect-paired as eagle's wings,
Justice is the rhyme of things;
Trade and counting use
The self-same tuneful muse;   40
And Nemesis,
Who with even matches odd,
Who athwart space redresses
The partial wrong,
Fills the just period,   45
And finishes the song.

Subtle rhymes, with ruin rife,
Murmur in the house of life,
Sung by the Sisters as they spin;
In perfect time and measure they   50
Build and unbuild our echoing clay,
As the two twilights of the day
Fold us music-drunken in.

TEXTS

(A) MS, m.b., Berg Collection, by permission of the New York Public Library, printer's copy for B; (B) *Poems* (London, 1847), 147–149; (C) *Poems* (Boston, 1847), 185–187; (D) *Poems* ["Fourth Edition"] (Boston, 1847), 185–187; (D²) *Poems* (Boston, 1865), 188–190; (E) *Poems* [Riverside] (Boston, 1884), 109–110; (E²) *Poems* [Centenary] (Boston, 1904), 123–124. "Merlin II" was not included in *Selected Poems* (Boston, 1876).

Poems (1847)

Format: Stanza break following line 36 not present in (E); break occurs at bottom of page in (C-D).

Pre-copy-text forms: The earliest draft occupies three pages of poetry notebook X immediately before the draft of "Merlin I." The Houghton MS referred to above in relation to "Merlin I" also contains the complete text of "Merlin II," though it is largely devoid of punctuation.

VARIANTS

2   affairs; (C-E) | affairs, (A-B)

3   Nature (C-E) | nature (A-B)

5   antipode; (C-E) | antipode, (A-B)

6   color (A, C-E) | colour (B) || glowed; (C-E) | glowed, (A-B)

9   Flavor (A, C-E) Flavour (B) || flavor; (A, C-E) | flavour; (B)

10   bough; (C-E) | bough, (A-B)

12   hands, (B-E) | hand (A) || to feet, (C-E) | to feet (A-B)

13   In one body (B, D-E) | <Are> <Coeval> ↑In one body↓ (A) | Coeval (C)

14   Eldest rite, two (B-E) | ↑Eldest rite,↓ <T>two (A)

16   shines, (B-E) | shines (A)

21   Lovesick with rhyme; (A-E) | Sick with systematic rhyme; (CC4)

22   time (C-D) | Time (A-B, E)

25   hand; (C-E) | hand, (A-B)

26–27 [*Emerson abandoned an attempt to revise these two lines, inscribing "Or" in the margin by line 26, and "Or in train" in the margin by line 27, in which "Or else" is canceled*] (CC4)

27   alternated; (C-E) | alternated, (A-B)

28   gage, (C-E) | gage (A-B)

29   other, (C-E) | other (A-B)

31   Short-lived (B-E) | Short lived (A)

37   Perfect-paired (C-E) | Perfect paired (A-B) || wings, (B-E) | wings (A)

40   self-same (B-E) | selfsame (A)

47   rhymes, (C-E) | rhymes (A-B) || rife, (C-E) | rife (A-B)

50   measure (C-E) | measure, (A-B)

51   clay, (A-D) | clay. (E)

52   As (B-E) | <While> ↑As↓

NOTES

24–25.   Cf. "Thy thoughts come in bands / Sisters hand in hand," unused lines from an early (1842) draft of "Saadi" (*JMN,* VII, 480).

50.   Cf. "In perfect time & measure," from a poem, "Water," written in 1841 but not published during Emerson's lifetime (*JMN,* VIII, 112; *PN,* 960).

BACCHUS.

In his letter of 27 July 1846 to Elizabeth Hoar, who had gone to visit friends in New Haven, Emerson mentioned "Bacchus" as among the poems he had written "lately," adding that it was "not however translated from Hafiz" (*L*, III, 341). That point of clarification seems to acknowledge a general influence of the Persian poet on these verses. Emerson had acquired his copy of Joseph von Hammer's German translation of the *Diwan* just three months earlier and had become immediately fascinated by it. Elizabeth Hoar was no doubt familiar with Emerson's earliest efforts at translation from this work, including "Boy, bring the bowl full of wine" (*PN*, 750) and "Come let us strew roses / And pour wine in the cup" (*JMN*, IX, 398); hence the assurance that "Bacchus" was not yet another sign of his enthusiasm for the bibulous Hafiz. (In fact, of course, the wine of the *Diwan* is metaphorical, as it is in the Sufi tradition generally, though for the most part it lacks the eucharistic associations with which, here as in "Two Rivers," Emerson is so frequently concerned.)

Bacchus (or Dionysus), traditionally the god of wine and inspiration, had been a major figure for Margaret Fuller, who in 1839–1840 held out to her students in the Conversations the model of the Bacchantes, whose ecstatic chanting and dancing affirmed the god's passion (Murray, 164). Fuller biographer Charles Capper points out (I, 302) that "In one Conversation, [Elizabeth] Peabody reported Fuller's contrast of Apollo as 'Genius' with Bacchus as 'Geniality': '[Bacchus's] whole life was triumph. Born of fire; a divine frenzy; the answer of the earth to the sun,—of the warmth of joy to the light of genius. He is beautiful, also; not severe in youthful beauty, like Apollo; but exuberant,—and liable to excess'" (cf. *FuL*, II, 118). This element of exuberance and ecstasy is also alluded to in a sentence from the *Phaedrus* that Emerson entered as a motto to "Bacchus" in his correction copy of *Poems:* "The man who is his own master knocks in vain at the doors of poetry" (*W,* IX, 443; *JMN,* XI, 339; CC1; see also the use of this quotation in "Inspiration," *CW,* VIII, 153). The poem complexly interweaves the theme of the wine of inspiration and the psychology of ecstasy: "I take many stimulants," Emerson had confessed in his journal, "& often make an art of my inebriation" (*JMN,* VIII, 378; cf. *CW,* III, 15–17). Caroline Sturgis, who never favored reservedness, told Emerson that of all the many verses she had seen in manuscript that fall of 1846 she liked this poem best (*L,* VIII, 89).

It is unlikely that the Berg MS served as printer's copy for the London edition: it lacks the page numbers one would expect to find and there are many more variants between it and Chapman's text than one encounters in the case of manuscripts known to have been sent to England. More probably Emerson prepared the MS in July 1846 to show to Sturgis and other friends. It serves here as copy-text because it is the earliest coherent text of the poem. It has not hitherto been published.

BACCHUS.

Bring me wine, but wine which never grew
In the belly of the grape,
Or grew on vine whose tap-roots, reaching through
Under the Andes to the Cape,
Suffered no savor of the earth to scape.   5

Let its grapes the morn salute
From a nocturnal root,
Which feels the acrid juice
Of Styx and Erebus;
And turns the woe of Night,   10
By its own craft, to a more rich delight.

We buy ashes for bread;
We buy diluted wine;
Give me of the true,—

Whose ample leaves and tendrils curled   15
Among the silver hills of heaven,
Draw everlasting dew;
Wine of wine,
Blood of the world,
Form of forms, and mould of statures,   20
That I intoxicated,
And by the draught assimilated,
May float at pleasure through all natures;
The bird-language rightly spell,
And that which roses say so well.   25

Wine that is shed
Like the torrents of the sun
Up the horizon walls,
Or like the Atlantic streams, which run
When the South Sea calls.   30

Water and bread,
Food which needs no transmuting,
Rainbow-flowering, wisdom-fruiting
Wine which is already man,
Food which teach and reason can.   35

Wine which Music is,—
Music and wine are one,—
That I, drinking this,
Shall hear far Chaos talk with me;
Kings unborn shall walk with me;   40
And the poor grass shall plot and plan
What it will do when it is man.
Quickened so, will I unlock
Every crypt of every rock.

I thank the joyful juice   45
For all I know;—
Winds of remembering
Of the ancient being blow,

And seeming-solid walls of use
Open and flow.   50

Pour, Bacchus! the remembering wine;
Retrieve the loss of me and mine!
Vine for vine be antidote,
And the grape requite the lote!
Haste to cure the old despair,—   55
Reason in Nature's lotus drenched,
The memory of ages quenched;
Give them again to shine;
Let wine repair what this undid;
And where the infection slid,   60
A dazzling memory revive;
Refresh the faded tints,
Recut the aged prints,
And write my old adventures with the pen
Which on the first day drew,   65
Upon the tablets blue,
The dancing Pleiads and eternal men.

TEXTS

(A) MS, Berg Collection, by permission of the New York Public Library; (B) *Poems* (London, 1847), 149–152; (C) *Poems* (Boston, 1847): 188–191; (C²) *Poems* (Boston, 1865), 191–194; (D) *Selected Poems* (Boston, 1876), 117–119; (E) *Poems* [Riverside] (Boston, 1884), 111–113; (E²) *Poems* [Centenary] (Boston, 1904), 125–127.

Pre-copy-text forms: Only four lines of the poem occur in the single surviving draft, in poetry notebook X: see *PN*, 740–741.

VARIANTS

3   tap-roots, (C-E) | taproots (A-B)
|| through (B-E) | through, (A)
5   Suffered (A-E) | Suffer (CC4,

CC5) || savor (C-E) | savour (A-B) ||
earth (A, C-E) | world (B) || scape.
(A, C-E) | 'scape. (B)

6   morn (B-E) | Morn (A)

7   root, (C-E) | root (A-B)

9   Erebus; (C-E) | Erebus, (A-B)

10   woe (C-E) | wo (A-B) || Night, (C-E) | Night (A) | night, (B)

11   craft, (B-E) | craft (A)

12   bread; (C-E) | bread, (A-B)

13   wine; (B-E) | wine, (A)

14   true,— (C-E) | true, (A-B)

15   Whose ample (B-E) | <Of that w>Whose ↑ample↓ (A)

16   heaven, (B-D) | heaven (A, E)

17   dew; (B-E) | dew, (A)

20   forms, (A, C-E) | forms (B)

21   I (C-E) | I, (A-B)

23   through (B-E) | thro' (A) || natures; (C-E) | natures, (A-B)

25   well. (A-C, E) | well: (D)

28   walls, (C-E) | walls; (A-B)

29   streams, (C-E) | streams (A-B)

30   Sea (B-E) | sea (A)

31   bread, (A, C-E) | bread; (B)

32   transmuting, (B-E) | tra<s>nsmuting, (A)

33   wisdom-fruiting (C) | wisdom-fruiting; (A-B) | wisdom-fruiting, (D-E) [*The lack of punctuation in (C), carried over to the unsupervised edition (C²), may have resulted from plate damage, since the line occurs in a vulnerable position at the bottom of the page. Such damage, however, is more characteristic of later printings, and there is no sign here in the first-state printing even of a broken comma. What is at issue, of course, is whether line 33 modifies "wine" or "food."*]

36   Music is,— (A, C-E) | music is; (B)

37   wine (B-E) | Wine (A) || one,— (A, C-E) | one; (B)

39   Chaos (A, C-E) | chaos (B) || me; (C-E) | me, (A-B)

40   me; (A-E) | me, (A-B)

42   man. (C-E) | man, (A) | man: (B)

46   know;— (C-E) | know; (A-B)

49   seeming-solid (B-E) | seeming solid (A) || use (B-E) | Use (A) [*The MS situation here is difficult to express typographically: Emerson maintains a space between "seeming" and "solid" but the descender in the "g" connects to the ascender in the long "s" in "solid" (a situation that printers often interpreted as indicating a hyphenated compound). The "U" in "Use" is twice as tall as the average lower-case letters in the line, but the same height as the "s" that follows, making it difficult to determine whether Emerson intended a capital letter or not.*]

51   Bacchus! (C-E) | Bacchus, (A-B) || wine; (B-E) | wine, (A)

52   mine! (C-E) | mine; (A-B)

54   lote! (C-E) | lote. (A-B)

55   despair,— (C-E) | despair; (A) | despair, (B)

56   Nature's (A, C-E) | nature's (B)

57   quenched; (C-E) | quenched,— (A) | quenched;— (B)

58   shine; (A, C-E) | shine. (B)

59   undid; (C-E) | undid, (A-B)

61   revive; (C-E) | revive: (A) | revive. (B)

64   adventures (C-E) | adventures, (A-B)

65   Which (C-E) | Which, (A-B) || first day (B-E) | First Day (A) || drew, (C-E) | drew (A-B)

66   blue, (C-E) | blue (A-B)

67   Pleiads (C-E) | Pleiads, (A-B) || eternal (C-E) | the eternal (A-B)

NOTES

45–50. Bernard J. Paris, in "Emerson's 'Bacchus,'" *Modern Language Quarterly* XXIII (June 1962): 150–151, pointed out the connection between these lines and Emerson's explanation, in "Circles," of why "we value the poet": "In my daily work I incline to repeat my old steps, and do not believe in remedial force, in the power of change and reform. But some Petrarch or Ariosto, filled with the new wine of his imagination, writes me an ode, or a brisk romance, full of daring thought and action. He smites and arouses me with his shrill tones, breaks up my whole chain of habits, and I open my eye on my own possibilities. He claps wings to the sides of all the solid old lumber of the world, and I am capable once more of choosing a straight path in theory and practice" (*CW*, II, 185).

54. The "lote" (or λωτος) is the forgetfulness-inducing food of the Lotus-Eaters, mentioned in Book IX of *The Odyssey*. More specifically, the effect of feeding on the lotus is to lose the desire to return home.

67. The Pleiads (mentioned also in "Uriel," line 6, and "From Hafiz," line 8) are a cluster of seven stars in the constellation Taurus. According to Greek myth the stars correspond to the seven daughters of Atlas, who, in order to avoid pursuit by Orion, were translated into the heavens. Only six of the seven stars are visible to the naked eye, which gave rise to the myth of the "Lost Pleiad," the topic of a poem by the Welsh poet Felicia Hemans, that Emerson admired (*L*, I, 199; cf. *JMN*, XIV, 310). Paris (158–159) discusses Emerson's use of the myth.

LOSS AND GAIN.

On 9 May 1845 Emerson sent this poem, together with "A Fable" and "Forerunners," as his contribution to the gift book, *The Diadem*, edited by his life-long friend, William Henry Furness, Unitarian minister in Philadelphia (*L*, VIII, 26). He also, on 22 May, sent a copy of "Loss and Gain" to Caroline Sturgis's sister, Ellen Sturgis Hooper, whose poems Emerson had admired and had arranged to have published in the *Dial* (unpublished letter with enclosure, Beinecke Rare Book and Manuscript Library, by permission of Yale University).

LOSS AND GAIN.

Virtue runs before the Muse,
    And defies her skill;
She is rapt, and doth refuse
    To wait a painter's will.

Star-adoring, occupied,   5
    Virtue cannot bend her,
Just to please a poet's pride,
    To parade her splendor.

The bard must be with good intent
    No more his, but hers;   10
Must throw away his pen and paint,
    Kneel with worshippers.

Then, perchance, a sunny ray
    From the heaven of fire
His lost tools may overpay,   15
    And better his desire.

TEXTS

(A) *The Diadem for MDCCCXLVI* (Philadelphia, 1846), 9; (B) *Poems* (London, 1847), 153; (C) *Poems* (Boston, 1847), 192; (D) *Poems* (Boston, 1865), 195–96. Not included in any later editions.

Format: (B) prints all lines flush left.

Pre-copy-text forms: Two drafts occur in poetry notebook X, where they are indexed by Emerson under the heading "Virtue & Art" (see *PN*, 848). The MS sent to Ellen Hooper lacks indentations and has the following variant readings relative to the established text:

1   muse, *for* Muse,
3   rapt *for* rapt,
6   her *for* her,
10 hers, *for* hers;
11 or *for* and
13 Then perchance *for* Then, perchance,
15 will *for* may

VARIANTS

1   Muse, (C-D) | muse (A-B)
2   skill; (C-D) | skill, (A-B)
6   her, (A-B) | her (C-D)
8   splendor. (A, C-D) | splendour. (B)
10 hers; (C-D) | hers, (A-B)

11 Must throw (A, C-D) | Throw (B)
12 worshippers. (B-D) | her worshippers. (A)
14 fire (A, D) | fire, (B-C)
15 overpay, (C-D) | overpay (A) | over-pay, (B)

MEROPS.

As Edward Emerson notes (*W*, IX, 446), Merops was the mythological ruler of the Aegean island of Cos (or Κως), but a probably more relevant fact, first pointed out by Charles Eliot Norton, is that the name means "articulate speech" in Greek—or, perhaps more accurately, "endowed with speech."

238

MEROPS.

What care I, so they stand the same,—
    Things of the heavenly mind,—
How long the power to give them name
    Tarries yet behind?

Thus far today your favors reach,   5
    O fair, appeasing presences!
Yet taught my lips a single speech,
    And a thousand silences.

Space grants beyond his fated road
    No inch to the god of day;   10
And copious language still bestowed
    One word, no more, to say.

TEXTS

(A) *Poems* (London, 1847), 154; (B) *Poems* (Boston, 1847), 194; (B²) *Poems* (Boston, 1865), 197; (B³) *Poems* [Riverside] (Boston, 1884), 113; (B⁴) *Poems* [Centenary] (Boston, 1904), 127–128. "Merops" was not included in *Selected Poems* (Boston, 1876).

Format: (A) prints all lines flush left.

Pre-copy-text forms: The first draft, in notebook X, was transcribed inaccurately in *W*, IX, 445–446, and accurately in *PN*, 128. A revised fair copy, also in X, carries the title "Rhyme." See *PN*, 860.

VARIANTS

3   name (B) I fame (A)
5   today [*Eds., from MS form: see* PN, 202] I to-day (A-B) [*Probable house styling*] II favors (B) I favours (A)

6   presences! (B) I Presences! (A)
10   day; (B) I day, (A)

Poems (1847)

THE HOUSE.

Emerson shared this poem with Ellen Sturgis Hooper in a letter of 22 May 1845. It was evidently completed shortly before that date. Emerson's letter, which also enclosed copies of "The Forerunners" and "Loss and Gain," has not been published (Beinecke Rare Book and Manuscript Library, poem text quoted by permission of Yale University).

THE HOUSE.

There is no architect
    Can build as the Muse can;
She is skilful to select
    Materials for her plan;

Slow and warily to choose   5
    Rafters of immortal pine,
Or cedar incorruptible,
    Worthy her design.

She threads dark Alpine forests,
    Or valleys by the sea,   10
In many lands, with painful steps,
    Ere she can find a tree.

She ransacks mines and ledges,
    And quarries every rock,
To hew the famous adamant   15
    For each eternal block.

The House

She lays her beams in music,
    In music every one,
To the cadence of the whirling world
    Which dances round the sun;   20

That so they shall not be displaced
    By lapses or by wars,
But, for the love of happy souls,
    Outlive the newest stars.

TEXTS

(A) MS, m.b., Berg Collection, by permission of the New York Public Library, printer's copy for B; (B) *Poems* (London, 1847), 155–156; (C) *Poems* (Boston, 1847), 195–196; (C²) *Poems* (Boston, 1865), 198–199; (D) *Poems* [Centenary] (Boston, 1904), 128–29. No variants occur in later printings from the plates for C. "The House" was not included in *Selected Poems* (Boston, 1876) or *Poems* [Riverside] (Boston, 1884).

Format: Lines are flush left in (A-B).

Pre-copy-text forms: A partial and a complete draft of the poem are to be found in poetry notebook X: see *PN,* 818. The text sent to Ellen Sturgis lacks indentations and has the following variant readings relative to the established text:

    7   Cedars *for* Or cedar
  10   And *for* Or ‖ Sea, *for* sea,
  11   lands *for* lands,
  20   sun. *for* sun;
  23   But *for* But, ‖ souls *for* souls,

VARIANTS

  2   Muse (A, C-D) ǀ muse (B)
  8   design. (A-C) ǀ design, (D)
  9   forests, (A-C) ǀ forests (D)
 13   ledges, (A-C) ǀ ledges (D)
 15   adamant (C-D) ǀ adamant, (A-B)

 16   block. (A-C) ǀ block— (D)
 20   sun; (C) ǀ sun. (A-B) ǀ sun— (D)
 23   But, (C) ǀ But (A-B, D) ‖ souls,
        (C) ǀ souls (A-B, D)

SAADI.

Emerson knew of the Persian-inspired poems of Goethe's *West-östlicher Divan* as early as 1836 (*JMN*, V, 188), but his own poem "Saadi," written in 1842, is among the earliest indications that Orientalism would become a decisive element in his development as a poet. Emerson owned an 1808 edition of Saadi's *Gulistan; or, Rose Garden,* translated by Francis Gladwin, but it is not known how or just when he acquired the book (Walter Harding, *Emerson's Library* [Charlottesville, 1967], 236–237). His earliest dated reference to the great thirteenth-century Sufi poet Saadi (Mosharref od-Dīn ibn Mosleh od-Dīn Sa'di) occurs in a letter of 22 June 1841 (*L*, II, 407), where it already serves as the ideal name for his own poetic persona. "Saadi" was probably begun during the spring following this first invocation, especially if the reference to Saadi on 16 July 1842 (*JMN*, VIII, 188) alludes to the writing of the poem. A very rough draft of lines 145–150 (*JMN*, VIII, 469) was evidently written before February 1842. It is known, furthermore, that Emerson was at work on the poem's conclusion in August and September of that year, during one of Margaret Fuller's extended visits, and that she found the lines then added very moving (Joel Myerson, "Margaret Fuller's 1842 Journal: At Concord with the Emersons," *Harvard Library Bulletin,* XXI [July 1973]: 326, 338). It is possible that Emerson had little direct knowledge of the works of the Persian poet before October 1843, when he seems to have read the James Ross translation of the *Gulistan* in a copy from the Harvard College Library—in which, he says, "I find many traits which comport with the portrait I drew" (*JMN*, IX, 37; cf. *L*, III, 212). Years later, Emerson called Saadi "the poet of friendship, love, self-devotion, and serenity" ("Saadi," *Atlantic Monthly,* XIV [July 1864]: 34).

SAADI.

Trees in groves,
Kine in droves,
In ocean sport the scaly herds,
Wedge-like cleave the air the birds,
To northern lakes fly wind-borne ducks,   5
Browse the mountain sheep in flocks,
Men consort in camp and town,
But the poet dwells alone.

God, who gave to him the lyre,
Of all mortals the desire,   10
For all breathing men's behoof,
Straitly charged him, 'Sit aloof;'
Annexed a warning, poets say,
To the bright premium,—
Ever, when twain together play,   15
Shall the harp be dumb.

Many may come,
But one shall sing;
Two touch the string,
The harp is dumb.   20
Though there come a million,
Wise Saadi dwells alone.

Yet Saadi loved the race of men,—
No churl, immured in cave or den;
In bower and hall   25
He wants them all,
Nor can dispense
With Persia for his audience;
They must give ear,
Grow red with joy and white with fear;   30

But he has no companion;
Come ten, or come a million,
Good Saadi dwells alone.

Be thou ware where Saadi dwells;
Wisdom of the gods is he,—   35
Entertain it reverently.
Gladly round that golden lamp
Sylvan deities encamp,
And simple maids and noble youth
Are welcome to the man of truth.   40
Most welcome they who need him most,
They feed the spring which they exhaust;
For greater need
Draws better deed:
But, critic, spare thy vanity,   45
Nor show thy pompous parts,
To vex with odious subtlety
The cheerer of men's hearts.

Sad-eyed Fakirs swiftly say
Endless dirges to decay,   50
Never in the blaze of light
Lose the shudder of midnight;
Pale at overflowing noon
Hear wolves barking at the moon;
In the bower of dalliance sweet   55
Hear the far Avenger's feet;
And shake before those awful Powers,
Who in their pride forgive not ours.
Thus the sad-eyed Fakirs preach:
'Bard, when thee would Allah teach,   60
And lift thee to his holy mount,
He sends thee from his bitter fount
Wormwood,—saying, "Go thy ways,
Drink not the Malaga of praise,
But do the deed thy fellows hate,   65

And compromise thy peaceful state;
Smite the white breasts which thee fed;
Stuff sharp thorns beneath the head
Of them thou shouldst have comforted;
For out of woe and out of crime   70
Draws the heart a lore sublime."'
And yet it seemeth not to me
That the high gods love tragedy;
For Saadi sat in the sun,
And thanks was his contrition;   75
For haircloth and for bloody whips,
Had active hands and smiling lips;
And yet his runes he rightly read,
And to his folk his message sped.
Sunshine in his heart transferred   80
Lighted each transparent word,
And well could honoring Persia learn
What Saadi wished to say;
For Saadi's nightly stars did burn
Brighter than Dschami's day.   85

Whispered the Muse in Saadi's cot:
'O gentle Saadi, listen not,
Tempted by thy praise of wit,
Or by thirst and appetite
For the talents not thine own,   90
To sons of contradiction.
Never, son of eastern morning,
Follow falsehood, follow scorning.
Denounce who will, who will deny,
And pile the hills to scale the sky;   95
Let theist, atheist, pantheist,
Define and wrangle how they list,
Fierce conserver, fierce destroyer,—
But thou, joy-giver and enjoyer,
Unknowing war, unknowing crime,   100
Gentle Saadi, mind thy rhyme;

Heed not what the brawlers say,
Heed thou only Saadi's lay.

'Let the great world bustle on
With war and trade, with camp and town: 105
A thousand men shall dig and eat;
At forge and furnace thousands sweat;
And thousands sail the purple sea,
And give or take the stroke of war,
Or crowd the market and bazaar;   110
Oft shall war end, and peace return,
And cities rise where cities burn,
Ere one man my hill shall climb,
Who can turn the golden rhyme.
Let them manage how they may,   115
Heed thou only Saadi's lay.
Seek the living among the dead,—
Man in man is imprisonèd;
Barefooted Dervish is not poor,
If fate unlock his bosom's door,   120
So that what his eye hath seen
His tongue can paint as bright, as keen;
And what his tender heart hath felt
With equal fire thy heart shall melt.
For, whom the Muses smile upon,   125
And touch with soft persuasion,
His words like a storm-wind can bring
Terror and beauty on their wing;
In his every syllable
Lurketh nature veritable;   130
And though he speak in midnight dark,—
In heaven no star, on earth no spark,—
Yet before the listener's eye
Swims the world in ecstasy,
The forest waves, the morning breaks,   135
The pastures sleep, ripple the lakes,
Leaves twinkle, flowers like persons be,

And life pulsates in rock or tree.
Saadi, so far thy words shall reach:
Suns rise and set in Saadi's speech!'   140

And thus to Saadi said the Muse:
'Eat thou the bread which men refuse;
Flee from the goods which from thee flee;
Seek nothing,—Fortune seeketh thee.
Nor mount, nor dive; all good things keep   145
The midway of the eternal deep.
Wish not to fill the isles with eyes
To fetch thee birds of paradise:
On thine orchard's edge belong
All the brags of plume and song;   150
Wise Ali's sunbright sayings pass
For proverbs in the market-place;
Through mountains bored by regal art,
Toil whistles as he drives his cart.
Nor scour the seas, nor sift mankind,   155
A poet or a friend to find:
Behold, he watches at the door!
Behold his shadow on the floor!
Open innumerable doors
The heaven where unveiled Allah pours   160
The flood of truth, the flood of good,
The Seraph's and the Cherub's food:
Those doors are men: the Pariah hind
Admits thee to the perfect Mind.
Seek not beyond thy cottage wall   165
Redeemers that can yield thee all:
While thou sittest at thy door
On the desert's yellow floor,
Listening to the gray-haired crones,
Foolish gossips, ancient drones,—   170
Saadi, see! they rise in stature
To the height of mighty Nature,
And the secret stands revealed

Fraudulent Time in vain concealed,—
That blessed gods in servile masks   175
Plied for thee thy household tasks.'

TEXTS

(A) *Dial,* III (Oct. 1842): 265–269; (B) MS, m.b., Berg Collection, by permission of the New York Public Library, printer's copy for C; (C) *Poems* (London, 1847), 156–163; (D) *Poems* (Boston, 1847), 197–205; (E) *Poems* (Boston, 1865), 200–208; (F) *Selected Poems* (Boston, 1876), 34–39; (G); *Poems* [Riverside] (Boston, 1884), 114–119; (H) *Poems* [Centenary] (Boston, 1904), 129–135. No variants occur in later printings from the plates made for (D) apart from some loss of punctuation due to plate wear.

Format: The white line after line 16 (F-H; cf. *PN,* 87) coincides with page break in (A-B, D-E); it is not present in (C), which was set from (B).

Pre-copy-text forms: The first two drafts occur in notebook Dialling (*JMN,* VIII, 508–513), while a third draft is in poetry notebook P (*PN,* 86–89). Emerson expanded the third-draft text by borrowing lines from an abandoned poem, "Where the fungus broad & red," though no complete manuscript version survives earlier than printer's copy for the London edition of *Poems.* See the discussion at *PN,* 907–908.

VARIANTS

3   scaly (C-H) | finny (A) | <finny> ↑scaly↓ (B)
4   Wedge-like (C-H) | Wedgelike (A-B)
9   God, (A, D-H) | God (B-C)
11   all breathing men's (C-H) | all men's (A) | all ↑breathing↓ men's (CC8, B)
12   aloof;' (A-D) | aloof'; (E-H)
15   Ever, when (D-H) | When (A) | ↑Ever↓ <W>when (B) | Ever when (C) | ↑Ever↓ When (CC8)
16   Shall the harp (B-H) | The harp shall (A) | ↑Shall↓ The harp <shall> (CC8)
17   come, (A, C-H) | come (B)

18   sing; (A, C-H) | sing (B)
19   string, (A, C-H) | string (B)
20   dumb. (A, C-E, G-H) | dumb (B, F)
21   million, (A, D-H) | million (B-C)
24   churl, (D-H) | churl (A-C) || den; (D-H) | den,— (A-C)
28   audience; (C-H) | audience, (A-B)
30   joy (D-H) | joy, (A-C) || fear; (A, D-H) | fear, (B-C)
31   But (D-H) | Yet (A-C) || companion; (D-H) | companion, (A-C)
34   dwells; (D-H) | dwells, (A) | dwells<,>.— (B) | dwells. (C)

248

35 Wisdom of the gods is he,— (D-H) I Wisdom of the gods is he; (A) I <Wisdom of the gods is he,> (B) I [*Line not present*] (C)

36 Entertain it reverently. (A, D-H) I <Entertain it reverently.> (B) I [*Line not present*] (C)

41 they (B-H) I they, (A)

42 exhaust; (D-H) I exhaust: (A-C)

49 Sad-eyed (A, C-H) I Sadeyed (B)

50 decay, (A, D-H) I decay; (B-C)

51 Never (C-H) I Who never (A) I <Who n>Never (B, CC8)

52 midnight; (B-H) I midnight, (A)

53 Pale (D-H) I Who (A) I <Who,> ↑And↓ (CC8, B) I And (C) II noon (A, D-H) I noon, (B-C)

54 moon; (B-H) I moon, (A)

56 feet; (B-F) I feet. (A) I feet: (G-H)

57 Powers, (A, D-H) I Powers (B-C)

59 sad-eyed (A, C-H) I sadeyed (B) II preach: (D-H) I preach; (A-C)

60 teach, (B-H) I teach (A)

62 fount (A, D-H) I fount, (B-C)

63 Wormwood,— (D-H) I Wormwood; (A-C) II "Go (D-H) I Go (A-C) II ways, (A-F) I ways; (G-H)

64 Malaga (A, C-H) I malaga (B)

66 state; (D-H) I state. (A-C)

67 fed; (D-E) I fed, (A-C, F-H)

69 comforted; (D-H) I comforted. (A-C)

70 woe (D-H) I wo (A-C)

71 sublime.'" (D-H) I sublime.' (A-C)

73 tragedy; (B-H) I tragedy, (A)

75 contrition; (B-H) I contrition, (A)

76 whips, (B-H) I whips (A)

77 lips; (B-H) I lips, (A)

81 word, (D-H) I word. (A) I word; (B-C)

83 honoring (A-B, D-H) I honouring (C)

85 Dschami's (A-G) I Jami's (H)

86 Muse (D-H) I muse (A-C) II Saadi's (A, C-H) I Saadis (B) II cot: (D-H) I cot; (A-C)

87 'O (D-H) I O (A-C)

89 appetite (B-H) I appetite, (A)

91 contradiction. (B-H) I contradiction, (A)

92 son (A-B, D-H) I sun (C)

93 scorning. (D-H) I scorning, (A-C)

94 will deny, (A, D-H) I will, deny, (B-C)

95 sky; (B-H) I sky, (A)

97 list, (A, D-H) I list,— (B-C)

98 destroyer,— (A-B, D-H) I destroyer, (C)

99 thou, (D-H) I thou (A-C)

101 rhyme; (D-H) I rhyme, (A) I rhyme. (B-C)

103 Saadi's (A, C-H) I Saadis (B)

104 'Let (D-H) I Let (A-C)

105 town: (D-E) I town; (A, F-H) I town, (B) I town. (C)

106 eat; (A, D-H) I eat (B) I eat, (C)

107 sweat; (A, D-H) I sweat, (B-C)

108 sea, (B-H) I sea; (A)

109 war, (B-H) I war; (A)

110 bazaar; (A, D-H) I bazaar, (B) I bazaar. (C)

114 rhyme. (D-H) I rhyme; (A-C)

114–15 [*Between lines, the following canceled:*] <Masking wisdom with delight, / Toy with the bow, yet hit the white.> (B) [*See* PN, *852–853.*]

116 Saadi's (A, C-H) I Saadis (B)

117 dead,— (D-H) I dead, (A) I dead: (B-C)

118 imprisonèd; (H) I imprisoned, (A) I imprisonèd. (B) I imprisoned. (C) I imprisoned; (D-F)

120 door, (A-B, D-H) I door. (C)

121 seen (B-H) I seen, (A)

122   paint (A, D-H) | paint, (B-C) ||
keen; (A, D-H) | keen, (B-C)

123   felt (D-H) | felt, (A-C)

124–25   [*Between lines, the following
verses occur in* (A) *but are canceled in*
(CC8) *and* (B):] Now his memory is
a den, / A sealed [Sealèd (B)] tomb
from [<from> ↑to↓ (B)] gods and
men, / Whose rich secrets not
transpire; / Speech should be like air
and [& (B)] fire; / But to speak
when he assays, / His voice is bestial
and base; [base, (B)] / Himself he
heareth hiss or [& (B)] hoot, / And
crimson shame him maketh mute;
[mute. (B)]

125   For, (C-H) | But (A) | <But>
↑For,↓ (B) | <But> ↑For↓ (CC8) ||
Muses (D-H) | muses (A-C) || smile
(A, D-H) | shine (B-C) || upon, (B-H)
| upon (A)

128   beauty (B-H) | Beauty (A) ||
wing; (B-H) | wing, (A)

130   nature (A-G) | Nature (H)

131   dark,— (D-H) | dark, (A-C)

132   In heaven no star, on earth no
spark,— (D-H) | In heaven, no star;
on earth, no spark; (A-C)

139   Saadi, (D-H) | Saadi! (A-C) ||
reach: (D-H) | reach; (A-C)

140   speech!' (D-H) | speech. (A-C)

141   Muse: (D-H) | Muse; (A-B) |
muse; (C)

142   'Eat (D-H) | Eat (A-C)

144   nothing,— (D-H) | nothing;
(A-C)

146   deep. (A, D-H) | deep; (B-C)

148   paradise: (D-H) | paradise;
(A-C)

150   brags (A-B, CC2, CC10, CC11,
D-H) | brass (C)

152   market-place; (A, C-F) |
marketplace; (B) | market-place:
(G-H)

153   art, (A, D-H) | art (B-C)

156   find: (D-H) | find, (A) | find;
(B-C)

157   door! (D-H) | door, (A-C)

158   floor! (D-H) | floor. (A-C)

159   doors (A-B, D-H) | doors, (C)

160   pours (B-H) | pours, (A)

162   Seraph's (A-B, D-H) | seraph's
(C) || Cherub's (A-B, D-H) | cherub's
(C) || food: (D-E) | food, (A) | food;
(B-C) | food. (F-H)

163   men: (D-H) | men; (A-C) ||
Pariah hind (A-B, D-H) | pariah kind
(C)

166   Redeemers (A-B, D-H) |
Redeemer (C) || all: (D-H) | all.
(A-C)

167   door (A, D-H) | door, (B-C)

168   desert's (C-H) | desart's (A-B)

169   gray-haired (C-H) | grayhaired
(A) | gray haired (B)

170   drones,— (B-C) | drones, (A,
D-H)

171   Saadi, (B-H) | Saadi! (A) || see!
(D-H) | see, (A-C)

172   Nature, (A-B, D-H) | nature, (C)

173   revealed (B-H) | revealed, (A)

174   concealed,— (D-H) | concealed,
(A-C)

176   tasks.' (D-H) | tasks. (A-C)

NOTES

85.   Nur od-Dīn Abdul Rahmān Dschami (1414–1492), the last of the classic Sufi poets. In the Centenary edition, Edward Emerson emended the name to Jami, which was by then (1904) the more common English transliteration of the Arabic.

HOLIDAYS.

The germ of this poem is a passage in journal E written in early May 1841: "We must play sometimes. Six months, from October to April or May, the acorn lends itself as a plaything to the children; but now, in May, its game is over: would you lift the pretty fruit from the ground? behold, it is anchored to the spot by a stout & strenuous root of six inches or more & is already no acorn but an oak" (*JMN*, VII, 440). The theme of the preparation, in youthful playfulness, for the grounded round of duties in adult life is anticipated in journal entries of 12 and 16 April 1837 (*JMN*, V, 297–298), passages that stand also behind portions of "Each and All." Indeed the acorn passage puts a more positive construction on what, in "Each and All," Emerson had represented as the undoing of an initial "gay enchantment," as the free maiden becomes, in marriage, the closely constrained, anti-romantic wife and mother. The 1837 passages that treat this topic are developments of the point as Emerson's brother Charles had raised it, with much foreboding, in a letter to his fiancée Elizabeth Hoar (*JMN*, V, 157). Emerson had first been struck by this concern when he read through Charles's letters after his death in 1836. At the very moment of the acorn passage in 1841, Emerson had been re-reading Charles's letters, intrigued by the fact that "In every family is its own little body of literature, divinity, & personal biography" (*JMN*, VII, 443), and considering the revival of "my faded purpose of writing the oft requested Memoir of Charles" (*JMN*, VII, 445). Charles's anxious view of marriage and maturity (both eventually denied him) seems thus to have infected the family literature and by that route contributed to the debate on marriage held during the early 1840s among Emerson, Sturgis, and Fuller, ultimately affecting also Fuller's views as expressed in her *Dial* essay of 1843, "The Great Lawsuit," and *Woman in the Nineteenth-Century* two years later. In 1841 Emerson's third child, Edith, would be born.

HOLIDAYS.

From fall to spring the russet acorn,
    Fruit beloved of maid and boy,
Lent itself beneath the forest,
    To be the children's toy.

Pluck it now! In vain,—thou canst not;   5
    Its root has pierced yon shady mound;
Toy no longer—it has duties;
    It is anchored in the ground.

Year by year the rose-lipped maiden,
    Playfellow of young and old,   10
Was frolic sunshine, dear to all men,
    More dear to one than mines of gold.

Whither went the lovely hoyden?
    Disappeared in blessed wife;
Servant to a wooden cradle,   15
    Living in a baby's life.

Still thou playest;—short vacation
    Fate grants each to stand aside;
Now must thou be man and artist,—
    'Tis the turning of the tide.   20

TEXTS

(A) *Dial,* III (July 1842): 73; (B) MS, m.b., Berg Collection, by permission of the New York Public Library, printer's copy for C; (C) *Poems* (London, 1847), 164–65; (D) *Poems* (Boston, 1847), 206–07; (E) *Poems* (Boston 1865), 209–210; (F) *Poems* [Riverside] (Boston, 1884), 119–20; (F²) *Poems* [Centenary] (Boston, 1904), 136. No variants occur in printings from the plates made for (D). "Holidays" was not included in *Selected Poems* (Boston, 1876).

Format: All lines flush left (A-C).

Pre-copy-text forms: A fair copy in pencil occurs in poetry notebook P (*PN*, 96–97).

VARIANTS

1   spring (A-E) | spring, (F)

3   beneath the forest, (D, F) | beneath the forest (A-C, E) | by Walden Water, (CC3)

5   now! In vain,— (D-F) | now; in vain: (A-C) ‖ not; (A, D-F) | not, (B-C)

6   Its root has pierced yon shady mound; (D-F) | Its root has pierced yon shady mound, (B-C) | It has shot its rootlet down'rd: (A)

7   longer— (D-F) | longer, (A-C) ‖ duties; (B-F) | duties, (A)

8   in (A, C-F) | <to>in (B)

10   Playfellow (A-B, D-F) | Playfellow (C)

12   gold. (B-F) | gold; (A)

13   Wither went (C-F) | Whcre is now (A) | <Where is now> ↑Whither went↓ (B) ‖ hoyden? (A, D-F) | hoyden?— (B-C)

14   wife; (D-F) | wife, (A-C)

19   artist,— (D-F) | artist; (A-C)

20   'Tis (A, C-F) | Tis (B)

PAINTING AND SCULPTURE.

Public concern over issues of nudity in the fine arts flared conspicuously in the 1840s when Puritan and Victorian sensibilities in America were challenged by such sculptors as Hiram Powers and Horatio Greenough, among the earliest serious practitioners of the art in the United States. But the "scandals" with which they were associated—involving Powers' "Greek Slave" and Greenough's "George Washington"—were of a slightly later date than Emerson's brief poem. Sculptors dealt more freely than painters with the unclothed human subject because the art was still very largely beholden to the classical style of Greece and Rome—a style deliberately exemplified, if not enforced, by the plaster copies of European masterpieces that had been a staple at the Boston Athenaeum since 1823. Emerson had been interested in sculpture since his first visit to Italy in 1833, and one sees in his early lecture on Michelangelo (*EL*, I, 98–117) that the artist's sculpture, grounded in a deep study of anatomy, evident alike in the Italian originals and the Boston copies, was the occasioning basis for all of Emerson's subsequent thinking about art and aesthetics.

The attention of the Transcendentalists was especially drawn to the fine arts in 1839 when a major exhibition of the works of Washington Allston was mounted in Boston, and movement figures, including Margaret Fuller, Sarah Clarke, and Elizabeth and Sophia Peabody, as well as Samuel Gray Ward and James Freeman Clarke, could compare notes. Ward in particular, young though he was, seems actually to have known something about art, and the portfolio of engravings that he had just brought back from Europe proved, for Fuller and Emerson, an absorbing study. Emerson was writing his essay on "Art" at this time, published in *Essays* in 1841, while his "Thoughts on Art" appeared almost simultaneously in the *Dial* for January 1841.

PAINTING AND SCULPTURE.

The sinful painter drapes his goddess warm,
   Because she still is naked, being dressed:
The godlike sculptor will not so deform
   Beauty, which limbs and flesh enough invest.

TEXTS

(A) *Dial*, II (Oct. 1841): 205; (B) *Poems* (London, 1847), 165; (C) *Poems* (Boston, 1847), 208; (C²) *Poems* (Boston, 1865), 211. No variants occur in later printings from the plates made for C. "Painting and Sculpture" was not included in *Selected Poems* (Boston, 1876), nor did it appear in the Riverside and Centenary editions of *Poems*.

Format: The alternate indentation is a feature of (C) and its reprintings, though not of (C²), a new edition.

Pre-copy-text forms: Two drafts in pencil, the first erased, occur on the same page in poetry notebook P (*PN,* 67).

VARIANTS

2   naked, (B-C) | naked (A) ||
dressed: (C) | drest: (A) | drest; (B)

4   Beauty, (B-C) | Beauty (A) ||
limbs (A, C) | bones (B)

FROM THE PERSIAN OF HAFIZ.

This poem is Emerson's translation of "Sakiname, das Buch der Schenken," lines 1–238, from Joseph von Hammer's German translation of Hafiz, *Der Diwan von Mohammed Schemsed-din Hafis,* 2 vols. (Stuttgart and Tübingen, 1812–1813), II, 489–502. According to Account Book 4 Emerson purchased the volumes in April 1846. The number and extent of the differences between the Boston and London texts of 1847 are remarkable, as are the number of changes Emerson made in printer's copy for the London edition.

FROM THE PERSIAN OF HAFIZ.

The poems of Hafiz are held by the Persians to be allegoric and mystical. His German editor, Von Hammer, remarks on the following poem, that, 'though in appearance anacreontic, it may be regarded as one of the best of those compositions which earned for Hafiz the honorable title of "Tongue of the Secret."'

Butler, fetch the ruby wine
Which with sudden greatness fills us;
Pour for me, who in my spirit

Fail in courage and performance.
Bring this philosophic stone, 5
Karun's treasure, Noah's age;
Haste, that by thy means I open
All the doors of luck and life.
Bring to me the liquid fire
Zoroaster sought in dust: 10
To Hafiz, revelling, 'tis allowed
To pray to Matter and to Fire.
Bring the wine of Jamschid's glass,
Which glowed, ere time was, in the Néant;
Bring it me, that through its force 15
I, as Jamschid, see through worlds.
Wisely said the Kaisar Jamschid,
'The world's not worth a barleycorn:'
Let flute and lyre lordly speak;
Lees of wine outvalue crowns. 20
Bring me, boy, the veiled beauty,
Who in ill-famed houses sits:
Bring her forth; my honest name
Freely barter I for wine.
Bring me, boy, the fire-water;— 25
Drinks the lion, the woods burn;
Give it me, that I storm heaven,
And tear the net from the archwolf.
Wine wherewith the Houris teach
Souls the ways of paradise! 30
On the living coals I'll set it,
And therewith my brain perfume.
Bring me wine, through whose effulgence
Jam and Chosroes yielded light;
Wine, that to the flute I sing 35
Where is Jam, and where is Kauss.
Bring the blessing of old times,—
Bless the old, departed shahs!
Bring me wine which spendeth lordship,
Wine whose pureness searcheth hearts; 40

Bring it me, the shah of hearts!
Give me wine to wash me clean
Of the weather-stains of cares,
See the countenance of luck.
Whilst I dwell in spirit-gardens,   45
Wherefore stand I shackled here?
Lo, this mirror shows me all!
Drunk, I speak of purity,
Beggar, I of lordship speak;
When Hafiz in his revel sings,   50
Shouteth Sohra in her sphere.

Fear the changes of a day:
Bring wine which increases life.
Since the world is all untrue,
Let the trumpets thee remind   55
How the crown of Kobad vanished.
Be not certain of the world,—
'Twill not spare to shed thy blood.
Desperate of the world's affair
Came I running to the wine-house.   60
Bring me wine which maketh glad,
That I may my steed bestride,
Through the course career with Rustem,—
Gallop to my heart's content;
That I reason quite expunge,   65
And plant banners on the worlds.
Let us make our glasses kiss;
Let us quench the sorrow-cinders.
Today let us drink together;
Now and *then* will never agree.   70
Whoso has arranged a banquet
Is with glad mind satisfied,
'Scaping from the snares of Dews.
Woe for youth! 'tis gone in the wind:
Happy he who spent it well!   75
Bring wine, that I overspring

Both worlds at a single leap.
Stole, at dawn, from glowing spheres
Call of Houris to my sense:—
'O lovely bird, delicious soul,   80
Spread thy pinions, break thy cage;
Sit on the roof of seven domes,
Where the spirits take their rest.'

In the time of Bisurdschimihr,
Menutscheher's beauty shined.   85
On the beaker of Nushirvan,
Wrote they once in elder times,
'Hear the counsel; learn from us
Sample of the course of things:
The earth—it is a place of sorrow,   90
Scanty joys are here below;
Who has nothing has no sorrow.'
Where is Jam, and where his cup?
Solomon and his mirror, where?
Which of the wise masters knows   95
What time Kauss and Jam existed?
When those heroes left this world,
They left nothing but their names.
Bind thy heart not to the earth;
When thou goest, come not back;   100
Fools spend on the world their hearts,—
League with it is feud with heaven:
Never gives it what thou wishest.

A cup of wine imparts the sight
Of the five heaven-domes with nine steps: 105
Whoso can himself renounce
Without support shall walk thereon;—
Who discreet is is not wise.

Give me, boy, the Kaisar cup,
Which rejoices heart and soul.   110

Under wine and under cup
Signify we purest love.
Youth like lightning disappears;
Life goes by us as the wind.
Leave the dwelling with six doors,   115
And the serpent with nine heads;
Life and silver spend thou freely
If thou honorest the soul.
Haste into the other life;
All is vain save God alone.   120
Give me, boy, this toy of Dæmons:
When the cup of Jam was lost,
Him availed the world no more.
Fetch the wineglass made of ice;
Wake the torpid heart with wine.   125
Every clod of loam beneath us
Is a skull of Alexander;
Oceans are the blood of princes;
Desert sands the dust of beauties.
More than one Darius was there   130
Who the whole world overcame;
But, since these gave up the ghost,
Thinkest thou they never were?

Boy, go from me to the Shah;
Say to him, 'Shah, crowned as Jam,   135
Win thou first the poor man's heart,
Then the glass; so know the world.
Empty sorrows from the earth
Canst thou drive away with wine.
Now in thy throne's recent beauty,   140
In the flowing tide of power,
Moon of fortune, mighty king,
Whose tiara sheddeth lustre,
Peace secure to fish and fowl,
Heart and eye-sparkle to saints;—   145
Shoreless is the sea of praise;

I content me with a prayer:—
From Nisami's lyric page,
Fairest ornament of speech,
Here a verse will I recite,   150
Verse more beautiful than pearls:
"More kingdoms wait thy diadem
Than are known to thee by name;
Thee may sovran Destiny
Lead to victory day by day!'"   155

TEXTS

(A) MS, m.b., Berg Collection, by permission of the New York Public Library, printer's copy for B; (B) *Poems* (London, 1847), 166–172; (C) *Poems* (Boston, 1847), 209–216; (D) *Poems* (Boston, 1856), 209–216; (E) *Poems* (Boston, 1865), 212–219. The poem was not thereafter reprinted. The extensive excisions recorded in (CC4 and CC5) were evidently made to determine if an abridged version could be retained in later editions.

Format: Verse breaks following lines 73 and 92 (A-B). No verse break following line 109 (A-B), nor a break following line 133 (B).

Pre-copy-text forms: See *PN*, 799.

VARIANTS

Emerson's headnote: The poems . . . the Secret.'" (C-E) | The Poems of Hafiz are held by the Persians to be mystical & allegorical. The following ode, notwithstanding its anacreontic style, is regarded by his German editor, Von Hammer, as one of those which earned for Hafiz among his countrymen the title of 'Tongue of the Secret.' (A) | *Text as in* (A) *but with "and" for "&" and the whole enclosed in square brackets* (B)

1   wine (A, C-E) | wine, (B)

3   me, (C-E) | me (A-B)
4   courage (B-E) | <perf>courage (A) || performance. (A, C-E) | performance; (B)
5   this (C-E) | the (A-B)
6   age; (C-E) | life; (A-B)
9   to me the liquid fire (C-E) | me, boy, the fire-water (A-B)
10   dust: (C-E) | dust. (A-B)
11–24   [*Lines canceled*] (CC4)
11   Hafiz, revelling, (C-E) Hafiz revelling (A-B) || 'tis (B-E) | tis (A)
13   glass, (C-E) | glass (A-B)

14 Which glowed, (C-E) | That shone, (A-B) || Néant; (C-E) | Néant. (A-B)

15 Bring (C-E) | Give (A-B) || me, (B-E) | me (A) || force (C-E) | virtue (A-B)

17 Wisely said the Kaisar (C-E) | W<ell>isely said <Jamschid to> the Kaiser (A) | Wisely said the Kaiser (B)

18 'The (C-E) | This (A-B) || barleycorn:' (C-D) | barleycorn. / Bring me, boy, the nectar cup / Since it leads to Paradise (A) | barleycorn. / Bring me, boy, the nectar cup, / Since it leads to Paradise. (B) | barleycorn': (E)

19 Let flute (C-E) | Flute (A-B) || speak; (C-E) | speak (A) | speak, (B)

21 Bring me, boy, (C-E) | ↑Hither↓ Bring <me, boy,> (A) | Hither hring (B) | Hither bring (CC11) || beauty, (C-E) | beauty (A-B)

23 Bring (C-E) | <Bring> ↑Lead↓ (A) | Lead (B) || forth; (C-E) | forth: (A-B)

25 fire-water;— (C-E) | firewater, (A) | fire-water, (B) | liquid fire;— (CC4)

26 Drinks (B-E) | ↑—↓ Drinks (A) || lion, (C-E) | lion<,>— (A) | lion— (B) || burn; (C-E) | burn. (A-B)

27–32 [*Lines canceled*] (CC4)

28 And tear (C-E) | Tear (A-B) || from (B-E) | <of> ↑from↓ (A) || archwolf. (C-E) | arch-wolf. (A-B)

29 Wine (C-E) | Wine, (A-B)

30 Souls (C-E) | Angels (A-B) || paradise! (C-E) | Paradise. (A-B)

31 living (C-E) | glowing (A-B)

33–127 [*Lines canceled*] (CC5)

34 light; (C-E) | light: (A-B)

35 Wine, (B-E) | <Bring>Wine, (A)

37 times,— (C-E) | times; (A-B)

38 old, (C-E) | old (A-B) || shahs! (C-E) | Shahs; (A-B)

39–40 [*Lines not present*] (A-B)

41 it me, (A-E) | me wine, (CC4) || shah (C-E) | Shah (A-B) || hearts! (C-E) | hearts. (A-B)

42 Give (C-E) | Bring (A-B) || clean (A, C-E) | clean, (B)

43 weather-stains (B-E) | weatherstains (A) || cares, (C-E) | care, (A-B)

45 Whilst I dwell (C-E) | While I dwell (A-B) | Dwells my Soul (CC4)

46 stand (C-E) | sit (A-B)

47 Lo, (B-E) | <Drunk> ↑Lo↓, (A) || all! (C-E) | all. (A-B)

48 purity, (B-E) | purity; (A)

49 speak; (C-E) | speak. (A-B)

53 life. (C-E) | life, (A-B)

54–75 [*Lines canceled*] (CC4)

56 vanished. (B-E) | vanished. / <Seek in wine the heart's desire / Without wine there is not rest> (A)

57 world,— (C-E) | world; (A-B)

58 'Twill (B-E) | T'will (A)

59 affair (C-E) | affair, (A-B)

61 Bring (C-E) | Give (A-B)

63 Rustem,— (C-E) | Rustem, (A-B)

64 content; (C-E) | content. / Give me, boy, the ruby cup / Which unlocks the heart with wine, (A-B)

65 That I (A-E) | <That I> ↑Tiresome <↑Tedious↓>↓ (CC4) || expunge, (C-D) | renounce, (A-B)

67 Let (B-E) | <That> Let (A) || kiss; (C-E) | kiss, (A-B)

68 sorrow-cinders. (C-E) | sorrow-cinders: (A-B)

69 Today (A) | To-day (B-E) || together; (C-E) | together. (A-B) | [*Line canceled*] (CC4)

70 *Now* and *then* will never agree. (C-E) | [*Line not present*] (A-B)

71–75   [*Lines canceled*] (CC4)

71   arranged a banquet (C-E) I a
<feast assembled> ↑ banquet
dressed, ↓ (A) I a banquet dressed,
(B)

73   'Scaping (C-E) I Scaping (A-B)

74   Woe (C-E) I Alas (A-B) II 'tis (B-
E) I tis (A) II in the wind: (C-E) I in
wind,— (A-B)

75   well! (C-E) I well. (A-B)

76   Bring (C-E) I Give me (A-B) II
overspring (C-E) I o'erleap (A-B)

77   leap. (C-E) I spring. (A) I spring,
(B)

78   Stole, (C-E) I Stole (A-B) II dawn,
(C-E) I dawn (A-B)

79   my sense:— (C-E) I mine ear;
(A-B)

80   lovely bird, (C-E) I happy bird!
(A-B) II soul, (C-E) I soul! (A-B)

81   Spread (C-E) I 'Spread (A-B) II
pinions, (C-E) I pinion, (A-B) II thy
(C-E) I the (A-B)

82   Sit (C-E) I 'Sit (A-B) II of seven
(C-E) I of the seven (A-B)

83   Where (C-E) I 'Where (A-B) II
the spirits take their (C-E) I the
spirits take (A) I the spirit takes (B) II
rest.' (C-E) I repose.' (A-B)

85   shined. (C-E) I shined, (A-B)

88   counsel; (C-E) I counsel, (A) I
Counsel, (B)

89   [*In a copying error in* (A), *line 89
is written out twice and the second
instance canceled*] II Sample (C-E) I
'Sample (A-B) II things: (C-E) I
things; (A-B)

90   The earth— (C-E) I 'Earth, (A-
B) I <The> earth (CC4)

91   Scanty (C-E) I 'Scanty (A-B) II
below; (C-E) I below, (A-B)

92   Who (C-E) I 'Who (A-B) II
nothing (C-E) I nothing, (A-B) II
sorrow.' (B-E) I sorrow." (A)

94   Solomon (C-E) I Solomon, (A-
B) II mirror, (C-E) I mirror (A-B)

97–112   [*Lines canceled*] (CC4)

98   They left (D-E) I Left they
(A-C)

99   earth; (C-E) I earth, (A-B)

100   back; (C-E) I back. (A-B)

101   spend (D-E) I squander (A-C) II
hearts,— (C-E) I hearts, (A) I hearts.
(B)

102   League with it is feud with
heaven: (C-E) I <There at home &
remote from heaven.> ↑ League with
it, is feud with heaven; ↓ (A) I League
with it, is feud with heaven; (B)

106   renounce (C-E) I renounce,
(A-B)

107   shall (B-E) I <can> ↑ shall ↓ (A)
II thereon;— (C-E) I thereon. (A-B)

108   discrete is (C-E) I <is> discrete
↑ is, ↓ (A) I discrete is, (B)

109   Kaisar (A, C-E) I Kaiser (B) II
cup, (B-E) I cup (A)

110   soul. (C-E) I soul; (A-B)

111   wine and under (C-E) I <wine>
type of wine & (A) I type of wine and
(B)

113   disappears; (C-E) I disappears,
(A-B)

114   wind. (C-E) I wind; (A) I wind:
(B)

115–125   [*Lines canceled*] (CC4)

117   freely (C-E) I freely, (A-B)

118   honorest (C-E) I <lovest well>
↑ honourest ↓ (A) I honourest (B)

120   vain (C-E) I nought (A-B)

121   Dæmons: (C-E) I daemons. (A) I
dæmons. (B)

124   wineglass (A, C-E) I wine-glass
(B) II ice; (C-E) I ice, (A-B)

126   beneath (C-E) I below (A-B)

129   Desert (B-E) I Desart (A)

132   But, (C-E) I But (A-B)

134–155   [*Lines canceled*] (CC5)

134 Shah; [eds.] | Shah (E) | Shah, (A-B) | shah; (C-D)
135 him, 'Shah, (C-E) | him; Shah (A-B)
136 Win (B-E) | <Seek> ↑Win↓ (A)
138–155 [*Lines canceled*] (CC4)
138 the earth (B-E) | this earth (A)
141 power, (B-E) | power, / <Lord of earth, & prince of times,> (A)
145 saints;— (C-E) | saints; (A-B)
146 praise; (C-E) | praise,— (A-B)
147 prayer:— (C-E) | prayer. (A-B)
148 lyric page, (C-E) | poet-works, (A-B)
149 Fairest (C-E) | Highest (A-B)
150 Here a verse (B-E) | | ↑Here a↓ Verse<s three> (A)
151 Verse more (C-E) | Verse<s>

↑as↓ (A) | Verse as (B) || than pearls: (C-E) | as pearls: (A) | as pearls. (B)
152 "More (A, C-E) | 'More (B) || wait thy diadem (C-E) | <mayst thou subdue> ↑wait thy diadem, ↓ (A) | wait thy diadem, (B)
153 Than (C-E) | "Than (A) | 'Than (B) || are known to thee by name; (B-E) | <thyself canst think> ↑are known to thee by name;↓ (A)
154 Thee may (CC11, C-E) | "May the (A) | 'May the (B) || Destiny (C-E) destiny (A-B)
155 Lead to victory day by day!'" (C-E) | "Grant a victory every morn!" (A) | 'Grant a victory every morn!' (B)

NOTES

5. In the (originally Arabic) alchemical tradition, the philosopher's stone turned the base or mundane into the divine or valuable.

6. Karun: in Persian folklore a figure of proverbially enormous wealth. In "Persian Poetry" Emerson refers to him as "the Persian Crœsus" and cites as his source the *Shah Nameh* of Abul Kasim Mansur Firdusi (c. 950–c. 1020) (*CW*, VIII, 126). Noah, whose righteousness was rewarded with long life, received special attention in the heretical (mystical) interpretations of the Gnostics that may in turn be reflected in Sufi beliefs. On this point see Elaine Pagels, *The Gnostic Gospels* (1979; rpt. New York, 1989), 54–55; Irenaeus, *Against Heresies*, in *Ante-Nicene Fathers* [1885; rpt. Peabody, Mass., 1994], I, 356; and *The Apocryphon of John*, in James M. Robinson, ed., *The Nag Hammadi Library in English* (San Francisco, 1990), 121.

10. Zoroaster: sixth-century Persian prophet whose views are set forth in the *Zend-Avesta*. Zoroastrianism, a dualistic theology, was the principal religion in Persia before Islam.

13. Jamschid's glass: A mythical king of ancient Persia, Jamschid was reputed to have a cup bearing a representation of the entire world, in which all future events could be discerned. This is one of many of the traditions associated with Jamschid discussed in the *Shah Nameh*. In "Persian Poetry" Emerson refers to

Jamschid, "whose reign lasted seven hundred years," as "the binder of demons" (*CW,* VIII, 126).

14. Néant: French term for nothingness, referring to the primordial Chaos from which all things emerged.

28. Archwolf: Possibly an allegorical reference to Alexander the Great, who is so called in a story told by Demosthenes, and recorded in Plutarch's life of Demosthenes.

29. Houris: The nymphs of Paradise in Islamic teaching.

34. Jam and Chosroes: For Jam, see note to l. 13. Chosroes I, also known as Nushirvan (see l. 86), was a great Zoroastrian shah of Persia, who presided over a sixth-century golden age.

36. Kauss, son of Kobad, a legendary king of ancient Persia.

51. Sohra: In Persian mythology a figure of chastity, comparable to Artemis or Diana.

56. Kobad: Mythological king of early Persia, reputed founder of Ecbatana (modern Hamadan), and father of Kauss.

63. Rustem: One of the great heroes in Persian mythology, a counterpart of the Greek Hercules.

73. Dews, or Daevas: demons in service to Ahriman, the Devil-figure in Zoroastrianism.

94. Solomon's mirror was an object used for black magic divination and a means of summoning the aid of the angel Anael. The device was first described in *Grimorium Verum* (1517). Emerson refers to this mirror in the course of discussing Solomon's place in Persian mythology (*CW,* VIII, 126).

127. Alexander the Great conquered the Persian empire when he defeated Darius III in the battles of Issus and Gaugamela in 333 and 331 B.C., respectively.

128. The Persian empire had reached its zenith under Darius.

148. Nisami was a Persian poet of the twelfth century.

GHASELLE:

FROM THE PERSIAN OF HAFIZ.

This poem is a translation of Hafiz, Book III, Ode XL from the *Diwan von Mohammed Schemsed-din Hafis,* 2 vols. (Stuttgart and Tübingen, 1812–1813), I, 106–107. Emerson was drawn to the antinomian strain in mystical thought wherever he found it, as here in the Sufi tradition. See the discussion of the oriental influence on Emerson in the Historical Introduction, in which the present poem is instanced.

GHASELLE:

FROM THE PERSIAN OF HAFIZ.

Of Paradise, O hermit wise,
    Let us renounce the thought;
Of old therein our names of sin
    Allah recorded not.

Who dear to God on earthly sod   5
    No rice or barley plants,
The same is glad that life is had,
    Though corn he wants.

O just fakir, with brow austere,
    Forbid me not the vine;   10
On the first day, poor Hafiz' clay
    Was kneaded up with wine.

Thy mind the mosque and cool kiosk,
    Spare fast and orisons;

Mine me allows the drinking-house,   15
    And sweet chase of the nuns.

He is no dervise, Heaven slights his service,
    Who shall refuse
There in the banquet to pawn his blanket
    For Schiraz' juice.   20

Who his friend's skirt or hem of his shirt
    Shall spare to pledge,
To him Eden's bliss and angel's kiss
    Shall want their edge.

Up! Hafiz, grace from high God's face   25
    Beams on thee pure;
Shy thou not hell, and trust thou well,
    Heaven is secure.

TEXTS

(A) MS, m.b., Berg Collection, by permission of the New York Public Library, printer's copy for B; (B) *Poems* (London, 1847), 173–174; (C) *Poems* (Boston, 1847), 217–218; (D) *Poems* (Boston, 1865), 220–221; (E) *Poems* (Boston, 1866), 217–218. The poem was not included in *Selected Poems* (Boston, 1876) or in either the Riverside or Centenary editions.

Format: (A-B) lack alternate indentation. See the note to lines 9–16 below regarding the order of the stanzas.

Pre-copy-text forms: Three drafts occupy pp. 174–180 in poetry notebook X: see *PN,* 208–211 and 801–802.

VARIANTS

Title: GHASELLE: FROM THE PERSIAN OF HAFIZ. (C, E) I From the Persian of Hafiz. (A) I FROM THE PERSIAN OF HAFIZ. (B) I GHASELLE. FROM THE PERSIAN OF HAFIZ. (D)

2   thought; (C-E) I thought. (A-B)

6   rice or barley (CC9, E) I corn-grain (A-D)

9–16   [*Order of stanzas as here given*]

(C-E) | [*Order of stanzas 3 and 4 reversed*] (A-B) [*Note: The first order (A-B) observes the sequence of the source in Von Hammer; in the belief that the transposition was deliberate, however, the editors adopt the revised sequence.*]

9   fakir, (C-E) | fakeer, (A-B)

11   poor Hafiz' (C-E) | <w>poor Hafiz' (A) | poor Hafiz (B)

14   fast (C-E) | fast, (A-B)

19   banquet (C-E) | banquet, (A-B)

20   Schiraz' (A, C-E) | Schiraz's (B)

21   friend's skirt (CC10, C-E) | friend's skirt, (A) | friend's shirt (B) || his shirt (C-E) | his shirt, (A-B)

23   angels's (C-E) | Angel's (A-B)

25   Up! Hafiz, (C-E) | Up, Hafiz; (A-B)

27   Shy thou (A, CC10, C-E) | Shy then (B)

XENOPHANES.

The first draft of this poem, in pencil, partially erased, is dated "21 March" (poetry notebook P, p. 21; *PN*, 25); the ink fair copy on the preceding page may have been inscribed long afterward, and carries an evidently incorrect dateline: "Concord 1834." Since Emerson was in New Bedford on 21 March 1834, the editors of *PN* speculate, based on several relevant journal passages of two years later, that the correct date is actually 1836 (see *PN*, 977–978). On 11 March of the latter year, for example, Emerson wrote in his journal, "All is in Each. Xenophanes complained in his old age that all things hastened back into Unity[,] Identity. He was weary of seeing the same thing in a tedious variety of forms" (*JMN*, V, 136). Five years earlier Emerson had said the same thing apropos of Heraclitus (*JMN*, III, 266), but the source of the anecdote—the *Histoire comparée des systèmes de philosophie,* by Joseph-Marie de Gérando (Paris, 1822–1823), I, 460—clearly associates it with Xenophanes. Emerson had been studying Xenophanes (c. 576–c. 480 B.C.) and the Eleatic school of philosophers in that source as early as 1830 (*JMN*, III, 368). Indeed he was familiar with the idea of the "All in Each in Nature"—as Madame de Stael derived it from Goethe—as early as 1821 when Mary Moody Emerson brought it to his attention (*Selected Letters of Mary Moody Emerson*, ed. Nancy Craig Simmons [Athens Ga., 1993], 142). These several distinct influences converged on 21 March 1836 in his discovery of a sentence in Goethe which was, he said, "a comment and consent to my speculations on the All in Each in Nature of this last week" (*JMN*, V, 138). For a discussion of the poem's sources in Gérando, see Carl F. Strauch, "The Year of Emerson's Poetic Maturity: 1834," *Philological Quarterly*, XXXIV (October 1955): 365–369.

Emerson was long fascinated with the idea expressed in this poem, and he found a variety of applications for it. If the emphasis here is on the tedium of universal self-similarity, the notion nevertheless, in a slightly different guise, authorizes the metonymic structure of Emerson's poetry. In his lecture on "Poetry and English Poetry" (1854), Emerson said that "this metonomy [*sic*], or seeing the same sense in divers things, gives a pure pleasure. Every one of a million times we take pleasure in the metamorphosis. It makes us dance and sing. It delights all. All men are poets" (*LL*, I, 303; cf. *CW*, VIII, 12–13).

XENOPHANES.

By fate, not option, frugal Nature gave
One scent to hyson and to wall-flower,
One sound to pine-groves and to waterfalls,
One aspect to the desert and the lake.
It was her stern necessity: all things   5
Are of one pattern made; bird, beast, and flower,
Song, picture, form, space, thought, and character
Deceive us, seeming to be many things,
And are but one. Beheld far off, they part
As God and devil; bring them to the mind,   10

Xenophanes

They dull its edge with their monotony.
To know one element, explore another,
And in the second reappears the first.
The specious panorama of a year
But multiplies the image of a day,—   15
A belt of mirrors round a taper's flame;
And universal Nature, through her vast
And crowded whole, an infinite paroquet,
Repeats one note.

TEXTS

(A) MS, m.b., Berg Collection, by permission of the New York Public Library, printer's copy for B; (B) *Poems* (London, 1847), 175; (C) *Poems* (Boston, 1847), 219–220; (D) *Poems* ["Fourth Edition"] (Boston, 1847), 219–220; (E) *Poems* (Boston, 1865), 222–223; (F) *Selected Poems* (Boston, 1876), 163; (G) *Poems* [Riverside] (Boston, 1884), 120–121; (G²) *Poems* [Centenary] (Boston, 1904), 137. There are no variants in printings from the plates made for (C) after (D).

Pre-copy-text forms: See *PN,* 977–978.

VARIANTS

1   fate, (B-G) | fate (A) || option, (B-G) | option (A) || Nature (C-G) | nature (A-B)
2   wall-flower, (C-G) | wallflower, (A-B)
3   pine-groves (B-G) | pinegroves (A) || waterfalls, (A-D, F-G) | waterfalls (E)
4   desert (B-G) | desart (A) || lake. (C-G) | lake, (A-B)
5   necessity: all (C-G) | necessity. All (A-B)
6   beasts, (A-F) | beasts (G) || flower, (C-G) | plant, (A-B)
7   thought, (A-F) | thought (G) || character (A, F-G) | character, (B-E)

9   part (A-B, D-G) | differ (C)
10   devil; (C-G) | Devil; (A-B)
12   one element, (C-G) | the old element (A-B) || explore another, (C-G) | <we> explore a new, | explore a new, (B)
15   day,— (C-G) | day, (A-B)
16   flame; (C-G) | flame, (A-B)
17   Nature, through (C-G) | nature thro' (A) | nature through (B)
18   paroquet, (B-G) | parroquet, (A)
19   one note. (CC10, C-G) | one <tedious> ↑cricket↓ note. (A) | one cricket note. (B)

Poems (1847)

THE DAY'S RATION.

The relation of "The Day's Ration" to "Alphonso of Castile" is suggested by its prose source, a journal entry of December, 1842:

The gods having closed their senate departed. The men met. They thought that the parsimony which for a long time had characterized the government of Olympus, could not be sufficiently reprobated. It was stingy, it was shabby, it deserved worse names. We were no better than bread & water prisoners. One gentleman had said that he must call it a bread & water system. One lady had said,
   "Ask! must I ask? The gods above should give;
   They have enough, & we do poorly live."
Must I enter into particulars, said the orator? I call it the wineglass policy. With the heaven & earth to give away; and, according to the received maxims, a heaven & earth to be bestowed totally on each child, and the same universe entire to every child, for the world was like manna which being consumed today was whole again tomorrow; to every man was left his desire for the whole,—. . . this hunger as of Space to be filled with planets; this cry & famine as of devils for Souls: Then for the satisfaction;—to each man was administered a few drops, say a wineglass, full of vital power, every day; a cup as large as Space, and one drop of water *per diem;* Each man woke in the morning with an appetite that could eat the Solar System like a cake, with a spirit for action & passion without bounds, he could lay his hand on the morning star, he could wrestle with Orion, or try conclusions with Gravitation, or Chemistry, but on trial hands, feet, & senses would not serve him, he was an Emperor deserted by his states, and left to whistle by himself . . . (*JMN,* VII, 474–475; cf. the headnote, above, to "Alphonso of Castile").

THE DAY'S RATION.

When I was born,
From all the seas of strength Fate filled a chalice,
Saying, 'This be thy portion, child; this chalice,
Less than a lily's, thou shalt daily draw
From my great arteries,—nor less, nor more.'   5
All substances the cunning chemist Time
Melts down into that liquor of my life,—
Friends, foes, joys, fortunes, beauty, and disgust.
And whether I am angry or content,
Indebted or insulted, loved or hurt,   10
All he distils into sidereal wine
And brims my little cup; heedless, alas!
Of all he sheds how little it will hold,
How much runs over on the desert sands.
If a new Muse draw me with splendid ray,   15
And I uplift myself into its heaven,
The needs of the first sight absorb my blood,
And all the following hours of the day
Drag a ridiculous age.
Today, when friends approach, and every hour   20
Brings book, or starbright scroll of genius,
The little cup will hold not a bead more,
And all the costly liquor runs to waste;
Nor gives the jealous lord one diamond drop
So to be husbanded for poorer days.   25
Why need I volumes, if one word suffice?
Why need I galleries, when a pupil's draught
After the master's sketch fills and o'erfills
My apprehension? why seek Italy,
Who cannot circumnavigate the sea   30
Of thoughts and things at home, but still adjourn
The nearest matters for a thousand days?

Poems (1847)

TEXTS

(A) MS, m.b., Berg Collection, by permission of the New York Public Library, printer's copy for B; (B) *Poems* (London, 1847), 176–177; (C) *Poems* (Boston, 1847), 221–222; (C²) *Poems* (Boston, 1865), 224–225; (D) *Selected Poems* (Boston, 1876), 167–168; (E) *Poems* [Riverside] (Boston, 1884), 121–122; (E²) *Poems* [Centenary] (Boston, 1904), 138–139.

Format: Line 1 is flush left in (A-B) and (C²)

Pre-copy-text forms: The only surviving draft of the poem is in *JMN*, XIV, 4–6.

VARIANTS

3 'This (C-E) | This (A-B)

5 arteries,— (C-E) | <flood> ↑arteries↓; (A) | arteries; (B) || more.' (C-E) | more. (A-B)

7 life,— (C-E) | life, (A-B)

8 beauty, (A-D) | beauty (E) || disgust. (C-E) | disgust, (A-B)

11 wine (C-E) | wine, (A-B)

14 desert (B-E) | desart (A)

15 Muse (C-E) | muse (A-B)

16 its (C-E) | her (A-B)

20 Today (A) | To-day (B-E)

21 book, (A, C-E) | book (B) ||

starbright (A-C, E) | star-bright (D) || genius, (B-E) | Genius, (A)

22 little (C-E) | tiny (A-B)

23 waste; (C-E) | waste, (A-B)

24 lord (C-E) | time (A-B)

28 sketch (C-E) | sketch, (A-B)

29 why (A, C-E) | Why (B) || seek Italy, (C-E) | should I roam, (A-B)

31 thoughts (B-E) | tho'ts (A)

32 for a thousand days? (C-E) | to another moon? / Why see new men / Who have not understood the old? (A-B)

BLIGHT.

The position of the journal draft of this poem suggests that it was written between 10 and 16 July 1843, about six months before it was published in the *Dial* with the title "The Times. A Fragment." Possibly the alteration of the title in 1846 when Emerson was preparing his first volume of poems had to do with a journal entry written, apparently, in April of that year: "Some times I seem to move in a constellation. I think my birth has fallen in the thick of the Milky Way: and again I fancy the American Blight & English narrowness & German defectiveness & French surface have bereaved the time of all worth" (*JMN*, IX, 359).

BLIGHT.

Give me truths;
For I am weary of the surfaces,
And die of inanition. If I knew
Only the herbs and simples of the wood,
Rue, cinquefoil, gill, vervain, and agrimony,   5
Blue-vetch, and trillium, hawkweed, sassafras,
Milkweeds, and murky brakes, quaint pipes, and sundew,
And rare and virtuous roots, which in these woods
Draw untold juices from the common earth,
Untold, unknown, and I could surely spell   10
Their fragrance, and their chemistry apply
By sweet affinities to human flesh,
Driving the foe and stablishing the friend,—
O, that were much, and I could be a part
Of the round day, related to the sun   15
And planted world, and full executor
Of their imperfect functions.
But these young scholars, who invade our hills,
Bold as the engineer who fells the wood,
And travelling often in the cut he makes,   20
Love not the flower they pluck, and know it not,
And all their botany is Latin names.
The old men studied magic in the flowers,
And human fortunes in astronomy,
And an omnipotence in chemistry,   25
Preferring things to names, for these were men,
Were unitarians of the united world,
And, wheresoever their clear eye-beams fell,

They caught the footsteps of the SAME. Our eyes
Are armed, but we are strangers to the stars, 30
And strangers to the mystic beast and bird,
And strangers to the plant and to the mine.
The injured elements say, 'Not in us;'
And night and day, ocean and continent,
Fire, plant, and mineral say, 'Not in us,' 35
And haughtily return us stare for stare.
For we invade them impiously for gain;
We devastate them unreligiously,
And coldly ask their pottage, not their love.
Therefore they shove us from them, yield to us 40
Only what to our griping toil is due;
But the sweet affluence of love and song,
The rich results of the divine consents
Of man and earth, of world beloved and lover,
The nectar and ambrosia, are withheld; 45
And in the midst of spoils and slaves, we thieves
And pirates of the universe, shut out
Daily to a more thin and outward rind,
Turn pale and starve. Therefore, to our sick eyes,
The stunted trees look sick, the summer short, 50
Clouds shade the sun, which will not tan our hay,
And nothing thrives to reach its natural term;
And life, shorn of its venerable length,
Even at its greatest space is a defeat,
And dies in anger that it was a dupe; 55
And, in its highest noon and wantonness,
Is early frugal, like a beggar's child;
Even in the hot pursuit of the best aims
And prizes of ambition, checks its hand,
Like Alpine cataracts frozen as they leaped, 60
Chilled with a miserly comparison
Of the toy's purchase with the length of life.

Blight

TEXTS

(A) *Dial,* IV (Jan. 1844): 405–406; (B) MS, m.b., Berg Collection, by permission of the New York Public Library, printer's copy for C; (C) *Poems* (London, 1847), 178–180; (D) *Poems* (Boston, 1847), 223–226; (E) *Poems* (Boston, 1857), 223–226; (E²) *Poems* (Boston, 1865), 226–229; (F) *Poems* [Riverside] (Boston, 1884), 122–124; (F²) *Poems* [Centenary] (Boston, 1904), 139–141. Not included in *Selected Poems* (Boston, 1876).

Pre-copy-text forms: The only manuscript rough drafts occur in Journal R (*JMN,* VIII, 435–437).

VARIANTS

Title: BLIGHT. (B-F) | THE TIMES. A FRAGMENT. (A) | < THE TIMES. A FRAGMENT.> ↑Blight↓ (CC8)

1 truths; (D-F) | truths, (A-C)

5 agrimony, (A, D-F) | pimpernel, (B-C)

6 Blue-vetch, (A-E) | Blue-vetch (F)

7 Milkweeds (A-E) | Milkweed (F) || pipes, (A-B, D-E) | pipes (C, F)

14 O, (D-F) | O (A-C)

15 sun (A, D-F) | sun, (B-C)

18 scholars, (D-F) | scholars (A-C)

23 flowers, (A-B, D-F) | flower, (C)

28 And, (D-F) | And (A-C) || eyebeams (A, D-F) | eyebeams (B-C)

29 SAME. (A, D-F) | same. (B-C)

32 mine. (D-F) | mine; (A-C)

33 'Not (D-F) | Not (A-C) || us;' (D-F) | us; (A-C)

35 plant, (A-E) | plant (F) || mineral (B-F) | mineral, (A) || 'Not (D-F) | Not (A-C) || us,' (D-E) | us, (A-C) | us;' (F)

37 gain; (D-F) | gain, (A-C)

39 love. (A-B, D-F) | love, (C) || [*In* (CC8) *Emerson notes that this line corresponds to the first line on p. 225 of* (D)]

45 ambrosia, (D-F) | ambrosia (A-C)

49 Therefore, (A, D-F) | Therefore (B-C)

51 hay, (A, D-F) | hay. (B-C)

52 term; (D-F) | term, (A-C)

54 space (D-F) | space, (A-C)

55 dupe; (A, D-F) | dupe, (B-C)

56 And, (B-F) | And (A)

57 frugal, (A, D-F) | frugal (B-C)

57–58 child; / Even (E-F) | child; / With most unhandsome calculation taught, / Even (A, D) | child: / With most unhandsome calculation taught, / Even (B-C)

60 cataracts (D-F) | cataracts, (A-C)

NOTES

17. Edward's note at *W,* IX, 450, calls attention to a passage in "The Poet": "He [the poet] uses forms according to the life, and not according to the form. This

is true science. The poet alone knows astronomy, chemistry, vegetation, and animation, for he does not stop at these facts, but employs them as signs" (*CW*, III, 13).

19–20.   "Can you believe it, the little town is full of Irish ready to cut a railroad through Walden Woods this very month?" (Emerson to Caroline Sturgis on the construction of the Fitchburg Railroad, 3 May 1843; *L*, VII, 540).

27.   When Emerson asserted in 1846 that Johannes Kepler was "'an unitarian of the united world'" (*JMN*, IX, 360), he was probably quoting himself.

52.   Reference may in part be to the death of Emerson's son Waldo little more than a year earlier, at the age of five; and yet Emerson would also have had in mind the death of the brilliant Charles Stearns Wheeler (1816–1843), news of which he conveyed to Margaret Fuller, even as the poem was being written, on 11 July (*L*, III, 182–183).

MUSKETAQUID.

"Musketaquid" is the Indian name for the notoriously languid Concord River, on whose banks, before the Revolution, Emerson's grandfather had built "The Old Manse," northward of Concord center. It was from there, probably on 21 February 1835, that Emerson wrote to his fiancée, Lydia Jackson, at Plymouth, hoping to make her think well of the town, his family's ancestral home, and urging that it become their marital home as well. He pointed out that he had "promised" to write a poem in the river's honor— "whenever the tardy, callow muse shall new moult her feathers. River large & inkstand little, deep & deep would blend their voices" (*L*, I, 440; see *L*, VII, 237–238, for the correction of the conjectured date for this letter). Emerson did not fulfill the promise immediately, and when eventually he did—probably in 1843 or 1844—the river was no longer the main focus. When he sent the poem to John Chapman, his London publisher, on 30 October 1846, he said that it had "declined very much in my good graces by keeping" (*L,* III, 359), implying that it had been completed at a much earlier date. Emerson's estimate of the poem must have improved over time, however, since it survived the winnowing process and was included in *Selected Poems* in 1876.

MUSKETAQUID.

Because I was content with these poor fields,
Low, open meads, slender and sluggish streams,
And found a home in haunts which others scorned,
The partial wood-gods overpaid my love,
And granted me the freedom of their state,   5
And in their secret senate have prevailed
With the dear, dangerous lords that rule our life,
Made moon and planets parties to their bond,
And through my rock-like, solitary wont
Shot million rays of thought and tenderness.   10
For me, in showers, in sweeping showers, the spring
Visits the valley;—break away the clouds,—
I bathe in the morn's soft and silvered air,
And loiter willing by yon loitering stream.
Sparrows far off, and nearer, April's bird,   15
Blue-coated,—flying before from tree to tree,
Courageous, sing a delicate overture
To lead the tardy concert of the year.
Onward and nearer rides the sun of May;
And wide around, the marriage of the plants   20
Is sweetly solemnized. Then flows amain
The surge of summer's beauty; dell and crag,
Hollow and lake, hill-side, and pine arcade,
Are touched with genius. Yonder ragged cliff
Has thousand faces in a thousand hours.   25

Beneath low hills, in the broad interval
Through which at will our Indian rivulet
Winds mindful still of sannup and of squaw,

Whose pipe and arrow oft the plough unburies,
Here in pine houses built of new-fallen trees, 30
Supplanters of the tribe, the farmers dwell.
Traveller, to thee, perchance, a tedious road,
Or, it may be, a picture; to these men,
The landscape is an armory of powers,
Which, one by one, they know to draw and use. 35
They harness beast, bird, insect, to their work;
They prove the virtues of each bed of rock,
And, like the chemist mid his loaded jars,
Draw from each stratum its adapted use
To drug their crops or weapon their arts withal. 40
They turn the frost upon their chemic heap,
They set the wind to winnow pulse and grain,
They thank the spring-flood for its fertile slime,
And, on cheap summit-levels of the snow,
Slide with the sledge to inaccessible woods 45
O'er meadows bottomless. So, year by year,
They fight the elements with elements,
(That one would say, meadow and forest walked,
Transmuted in these men to rule their like,)
And by the order in the field disclose 50
The order regnant in the yeoman's brain.

What these strong masters wrote at large in miles,
I followed in small copy in my acre;
For there's no rood has not a star above it;
The cordial quality of pear or plum 55
Ascends as gladly in a single tree
As in broad orchards resonant with bees;
And every atom poises for itself,
And for the whole. The gentle deities
Showed me the lore of colors and of sounds, 60
The innumerable tenements of beauty,
The miracle of generative force,
Far-reaching concords of astronomy
Felt in the plants, and in the punctual birds;

Better, the linked purpose of the whole,   65
And, chiefest prize, found I true liberty
In the glad home plain-dealing nature gave.
The polite found me impolite; the great
Would mortify me, but in vain; for still
I am a willow of the wilderness,   70
Loving the wind that bent me. All my hurts
My garden spade can heal. A woodland walk,
A quest of river-grapes, a mocking thrush,
A wild-rose, or rock-loving columbine,
Salve my worst wounds.   75
For thus the wood-gods murmured in my ear:
'Dost love our manners? Canst thou silent lie?
Canst thou, thy pride forgot, like nature pass
Into the winter night's extinguished mood?
Canst thou shine now, then darkle,   80
And being latent feel thyself no less?
As, when the all-worshipped moon attracts the eye,
The river, hill, stems, foliage are obscure,
Yet envies none, none are unenviable.'

TEXTS

(A) MS, m.b., Berg Collection, by permission of the New York Public Library, printer's copy for B; (B) *Poems* (London, 1847), 181–184; (C) *Poems* (Boston, 1847), 227–231; (D) *Poems* (Boston, 1865), 230–234; (E) *Selected Poems* (Boston, 1876), 164–166; (F) *Poems* [Riverside] (Boston, 1884), 124–127; (G) *Poems* [Centenary] (Boston, 1904), 141–144.

Format: Additional line breaks occur at lines 10 and 67 (A-B).

Pre-copy-text forms: Only snatches and fragments survive from the early drafts: ll. 1–8, 24–25, and 68–84 are in journal Books Small (*JMN*, VIII, 458, 465–466), while ll. 13–18, 11–12, and 20–21 are in poetry notebook P (*PN*, 26, 77). Lines 26–31, corresponding to the text added at the last minute to (C), is in notebook Phi (*JMN*, XII, 279–280, 284).

Poems (1847)

VARIANTS

2 Low, (C-G) I Low (A-B)
4 wood-gods (B-G) I woodgods (A)
7 dear, (C-G) I dear (A-B)
9 And through my rock-like, solitary (C-G) I And↑, pitying,↓ through my <rock-like> solitary (A) I And pitying though my solitary (B)
11 me, (C-G) I me (A-B) II spring (A-E) I Spring (F-G, CC5)
12 valley;— (C-G) I valley:— (A-B) II clouds,— (C-G) I clouds, (A-B)
15 and (C-G) I and, (A-B) II April's bird, (C-G) I yonder bird (A-B)
16 Blue-coated,— (C-G) I Blue-coated, (A-B) II before (C-G) I before, (A-B)
17 Courageous, (C-E) I Courageous (A-B, F-G) II overture (C-G) I overture, (A-B)
19 Onward (C-G) I Onward, (A-B) II rides (C-G) I draws (A-B) II May; (C-G) I May, (A-B)
20 around, (C-G) I around (A-B)
21 solemnized. Then (C-G) I solemnized; then (A-B)
23 hill-side, (C-D) I hillside, (A, E) I hill side, (B) I hill-side (F) I hillside (G)
26–31 [These six lines in (C-G) replace the following two in (A-B):] Here friendly landlords, men ineloquent, / Inhabit, and subdue the spacious farms.
29 [The comma after "unburies" is present in first two printings of (F), but is lost to plate damage beginning with the third (or large-paper) printing (Myerson A 18.6.c₁).]
30 new-fallen (E-G) I new fallen (C-D)

32 Traveller, (C-G) I Traveller! (A-B)
33 Or, it may be, a picture; (C-G) I Or soon forgotten picture,— (A-B) II men, (C-G) I men (A-B)
34 armory (C-G) I armoury (A-B)
35 [The period after "use" is present in the first two printings of (F), but is lost to plate damage beginning with the third (or large-paper) printing (Myerson A 18.6.c₁).]
38 the (C-G) I a (A-B) II mid (C, E-F) I 'mid (A-B, D, G)
39 use (C-G) I use, (A-B)
40 crops (C-G) I crops, (A-B)
41 heap, (C-G) I heap; (A-B)
42 pulse (C-G) I vetch (A-B) II grain, (C-G) I grain; (A-B)
43 slime, (C-G) I slime; (A-B)
44 And, (A-D, F-G) I Earlier, (E)
45 woods (C-G) I woods, (A-B)
47 with elements, (A-F) I with elements (G)
48 walked, (C-G) I walked (A-B)
49 Transmuted in these men (C-G) I Upright in human shape (A-B) II like,) (A, C-F) I like.) (B) I like), (G)
50 And (B-G) I <Thus> ↑And↓ (A) II disclose (C-G) I <they hint> ↑disclose↓ (A) I disclose, (B)
52 miles, (A-D, F-G) I miles (E)
53 acre; (C-G) I acre: (A-B)
56 tree (C-G) I tree, (A-B)
59 deities (C-G) I Mother of all (A-B)
60 colors (C-G) I colours (A-B) II sounds, (C-G) I sounds; (A-B)
61 beauty, (C-G) I beauty; (A-B)
62 force, (C-G) I force; (A-B)
64 plants, (C-E) I plants (A-B, F-G)

65 Better, (C-G) | Mainly, (A-B) ||
whole, (C-G) | whole; (A-B)
66 liberty (C-G) | liberty, (A-B)
67 In the glad home plain-dealing
(C-G) | The home of homes plain
dealing (A-B) || nature (C-E) | Nature
(A-B, F-G)
69 vain; for still (C-G) | vain: (A-B)
72 garden spade (C-G) | garden-
spade (A-B)
73 A quest of river-grapes, a
mocking thrush, (C-G) | [*Line not
present*] (A-B)
74 wild-rose, (C-G) | wild rose,
(A-B)
75 wounds. (C-G) | wounds<.>, ↑&
leave no cicatrice.↓ (A) | wounds,
and leave no cicatrice. (B)
76 ear: (C-G) | ear, (A-B)
77 'Dost (C-G) | Dost (A-B)
78 nature (A-F) | Nature (G)
81 And (B-G) | And, (A) || latent
(C-E) | latent, (A-B, F-G)
82 As, (C-D, F-G) | As (A-B, E)
83 foliage (C-G) | foliage, (A-B) ||

obscure, (A-B, E-G) | obscure (C-D)
[*Note: some copies of* (C) *have the
reading* "obscure,"]
84 unenviable.' (C-G) | unenviable.
(A-B)
[*Following l. 84,* (A) *has 14 canceled
lines:*]
    <Oft when I scan fond pictures
poets drew / Of rural joy <I> how
gladly I can spare / These hollow
charities of paint & song. / What
prayers & dreams of youthful genius
feign, / I bodily dwell in, and am not
so blind / But I can see the elastic
tent of day / Proffers a wider
hospitality / Than my few needs
exhaust, and bids me read /
Profounder emblems on its arches
blue. / Yet nature will not be in full
possessed, / And they who trueliest
love her, heralds are / And
harbingers of a majestic race, / Who,
having more absorbed, more largely
yield, / And walk on earth as the sun
walks in the sphere.>

NOTES

Title: In his "Historical Discourse at Concord" (1835), Emerson noted that the Indian term Musketaquid meant "Grassy Brook" (*W,* XI, 32). He derived this information from Lemuel Shattuck, who cited authorities in his *History of the Town of Concord* (Boston, 1835) to argue that the word meant "grassy brook" when applied to the river and "grass-ground" when applied to the land adjacent (5). This was close to Thoreau's understanding also, as evidenced by the first sentence of his *Week on the Concord and Merrimack Rivers* (1849), though several years later he learned from Indian guides that the word in fact meant "Dead Stream" or "Dead-water" (*The Maine Woods*, ed. Joseph J. Moldenhauer [Princeton, 1974], 142, 169).

24–25. In a detached journal notation of c. 28 September 1842, Emerson wrote, "The Cliff / Has thousand faces in a thousand hours" (*JMN,* VIII, 458).

The "Cliff" was a hill near Walden Pond, used by locals as a picnic ground: see "Woodnotes II," line 251.

26–31.   Thoreau quoted these lines as the epigraph to the introductory chapter of his *Week on the Concord and Merrimack Rivers* (1849).

DIRGE.

On 12 March 1844, in conveying these verses to his old friend William Henry Furness for publication in *The Gift* for 1845, Emerson wrote:

> I send you a rude dirge which was composed or rather hummed by me one afternoon, years ago, as I walked in the woods & on the narrow plain through which our Concord River flows, not far from my grandfather's house, and remembered my brothers Edward & Charles, to whom as to me this place was in boyhood & youth all "the country" which we knew. At the time of this walk, I was thirty five years old, and the verses began in a different metre,—

> > I reached the middle of the mount,
> > Up which the incarnate soul must climb,
> > And paused for them & looked around
> > With me who walked through space & time.

> So it went on for a verse or two more, then the metre changed into that which I send you, & a critical ear will easily find varieties in that. My sister Elizabeth Hoar, who first persuaded me to print some rhymes, is fond of these verses, so I draw them out of their sad recess for you. Their cadence was so agreeable that I should

have printed them in the Dial but for their personality. (*L*, VII, 592)

"Dirge," written in 1838, memorializes Emerson's younger brothers Charles Chauncy, who died in 1836, and Edward Bliss, who died in 1834, and recalls their many summer visits, as children, to the home of their step-grandfather, Ezra Ripley, in Concord. In *Emerson in Concord* (Boston, 1889), the poet's son pointed out that the family took refuge there for an extended period during the War of 1812, when prices in Boston spiked and poverty threatened. The boys in their play favored the great meadows east of the Old Manse, and liked as well "Cæsar's Woods" and "Peter's Field," retired places nearby named for slaves who had lived there before the Revolution (18–19; for Cæsar Robbins, see Franklin B. Sanborn, *Henry D. Thoreau* [Boston, 1884], 104–105, and William Emerson, *Diaries and Letters,* ed. Amelia Forbes Emerson [Boston, 1972], 74). At the time the poem was written, two other brothers were alive, William (1801–1868) and Robert Bulkeley (1807–1859). See Ronald A. Bosco and Joel Myerson, *The Emerson Brothers: A Fraternal Biography in Letters* (New York, 2006).

The poem's appearance in the anonymously edited *Memory and Hope,* an 1851 publication of Ticknor, Reed, and Fields, probably (but not certainly) represents an unauthorized reprinting from the *Gift* text, with which it has a number of unique readings in common and only seven differences, all in the accidentals. According to *The Cost Books of Ticknor and Fields* (Tryon and Charvat, eds.) the editor was Marianne C. D. Silsbee of Salem. Emerson knew her, and while it is possible that he provided a manuscript for the occasion, there is no direct evidence.

DIRGE.

Knows he who tills this lonely field,
   To reap its scanty corn,
What mystic fruit his acres yield
   At midnight and at morn?

In the long sunny afternoon,
　　The plain was full of ghosts;
I wandered up, I wandered down,
　　Beset by pensive hosts.

The winding Concord gleamed below,
　　Pouring as wide a flood
As when my brothers, long ago,
　　Came with me to the wood.

But they are gone,—the holy ones
　　Who trod with me this lovely vale;
The strong, star-bright companions
　　Are silent, low, and pale.

My good, my noble, in their prime,
　　Who made this world the feast it was,
Who learned with me the lore of time,
　　Who loved this dwelling-place!

They took this valley for their toy,
　　They played with it in every mood;
A cell for prayer, a hall for joy,—
　　They treated nature as they would.

They colored the horizon round;
　　Stars flamed and faded as they bade;
All echoes hearkened for their sound,—
　　They made the woodlands glad or mad.

I touch this flower of silken leaf,
　　Which once our childhood knew;
Its soft leaves wound me with a grief
　　Whose balsam never grew.

Hearken to yon pine-warbler
　　Singing aloft in the tree!

Dirge

Hearest thou, O traveller,   35
    What he singeth to me?

Not unless God made sharp thine ear
    With sorrow such as mine,
Out of that delicate lay could'st thou
    Its heavy tale divine.   40

'Go, lonely man,' it saith;
    'They loved thee from their birth;
Their hands were pure, and pure their faith,—
    There are no such hearts on earth.

'Ye drew one mother's milk,   45
    One chamber held ye all;
A very tender history
    Did in your childhood fall.

'Ye cannot unlock your heart,
    The key is gone with them;   50
The silent organ loudest chants
    The master's requiem.'

TEXTS

(A) *The Gift: A Christmas, New Year, and Birthday Present.* Edited by William Henry
Furness (Philadelphia: Carey and Hart, 1845), 94–96; (B) MS, m.b., Berg Col-
lection, by permission of the New York Public Library, printer's copy for C (with
"1838" written in the upper left corner of page 1); (C) *Poems* (London, 1847),
185–187; (D) *Poems* (Boston, 1847), 232–235; (E) *Memory and Hope* (Boston:
Ticknor, Reed, and Fields, 1851), 237–239; (F) *Poems* (Boston, 1865), 235–238;
(G) *Selected Poems* (Boston, 1876), 188–189; (H) *Poems* [Riverside] (Boston,
1884), 127–129; (I) *Poems* [Centenary] (Boston, 1904), 145–147.

Format: Alternate indentation lacking in (B-C).

Pre-copy-text forms: A version of the poem, consisting of the third through the
thirteenth stanzas, was composed on consecutive pages (185–192) of poetry
notebook P; the first and second stanzas were transferred from an abandoned

poem (cf. "Peter's Field," *W*, IX, 363–364), drafted on pages 205–207 of P, which also included lines eventually used in "The Apology," a companion poem in several respects. These two draft segments of "The Dirge" were combined in a fair copy on pages 14–16 of P, and there dated 1838. The date likely refers to the early drafts rather than to the fair copy, which may very well have been inscribed in 1844. See, further, the discussion in *PN*, 773–774.

VARIANTS

The following lines are added (from the fair copy in poetry notebook P [see PN, 21–22]) before line 1 in (H-I):

I reached the middle of the mount / Up which the incarnate soul must climb, / And paused for them, and looked around, / With me who walked through space and time. / [*white line*] / Five rosy boys with morning light / Had leaped from one fair mother's arms, / Fronted the sun with hope as bright, / And greeted God with childhood's psalms.

1 field, (D-G) I field (A-C, H-I)

5 afternoon, (B-D, F-G) I afternoon (A, E, H-I)

6 ghosts; (D-I) I ghosts, (A-C)

11 brothers, (A-B, D-I) I brothers (C)

13 gone,— (A-D, F-I) I gone— (E) II ones (A, D-I) I ones, (B-C)

14 lovely (D, F-I) I lonely (A-C, E) II vale; (D, F-I) I vale, (A-C, E)

15 star-bright (A, C-I) I starbright (B)

16 pale. (A-D, F-I) I pale,— (E)

20 dwelling-place! (D, F-I) I dwelling-place. (A, C, E) I dwellingplace (B)

21 toy, (A, D-I) I toy (B-C)

22 mood; (D, F-I) I mood, (A-C, E)

23 joy,— (D, F-I) I joy, (A-C, E)

24 nature (C-H) I Nature (A-B, I)

25 colored (D-I) I coloured (A-C) II the horizon (C-D, F-I) I the whole horizon (A, E) I the <whole> horizon (B) II round; (D, F-I) I round, (A-C, E)

26 bade; (D, F-G) I bade, (A-C, E, H-I)

27 sound,— (D, F-I) I sound, (A-C, E)

28 glad (A, C-I) I <merry> ↑ glad ↓ (B)

29 leaf, (D, F-I) I leaf (A-C, E)

30 knew; (D, F-I) I knew, (A-C, E)

33 pine-warbler (D, F-I) I pine warbler, (A, E) I pinewarbler (B) I pine warbler (C)

34 tree! (D, F-I) I tree; (A-C, E)

35 traveller, (D, F-I) I traveller! (A-C, E)

39 lay (A-D, F-I) I lay, (E) II could'st (D, H-I) couldst (A-C, E-G)

40 Its heavy tale (A, D-I) I The heavy dirge (B-C)

41 'Go, (D, F-I) I "Go, (A, E) I Go, (B-C) II man,' (D, F-I) I man," (A, E) I man, (B-C) II it (A, C-I) I <he> ↑ it ↓ (B) II saith; (D, F-I) I saith, (A-C, E)

42 'They (D, F-I) I "They (A, E) I They (B-C) II birth; (D, F-I) I birth,

(A-C, E) [*Note: semicolon in* (F) *battered*]

43   faith,— (D, F-I) | faith, (A-C, E)

45–48   [*Lines not present in* (G)]

45   'Ye (D, F, H-I) | "Ye (A, E) | Ye (B-C) || milk, (A, C-F, H-I) | milk (B)

46   all; (C-D, F, H-I) | all (A, E) | all: (B)

49   'Ye (D, F) | "Ye (A, E) | Ye (B-C) | 'You (CC1, CC5, G-I)

51   loudest chants (C-I) | loudest chaunts (A) | <best doth> ↑<loudest> loudest↓ chant↑s↓ (B)

52   requiem.' (D, G-I) | requiem." (A, E) | requiem. (B-C, F)

NOTES

29–32.   Edward identifies this flower as the lespedeza, "which, in after years, Mr. Emerson seldom passed without a tender word for it to his children" (*W*, IX, 452).

51.   When Charles died, his estate was valued at $886, including $300 as the estimated value of an organ, clearly his one extravagant possession (*L*, II, 42, 58).

THRENODY.

Emerson's eldest son and first-born child, Waldo, died at 8:15 P.M. on Thursday, 27 January 1842 at the age of five. On the previous Sunday Emerson had taken him through inclement weather to services at the First Parish Church, just then reopened after extensive renovations. On Monday the child came down with what at first looked like a cold, and Lidian supposed he had contracted it on his excursion of the day before, either provoking the quickly developing crisis or making that crisis, in the end, more difficult to survive. Waldo's symptoms grew rapidly more alarming (despite doses of castor oil), and so Dr. Josiah Bartlett, the family physician, was called in. On the 27th, Lidian, still not quite suspecting the dismal prognosis, asked the doctor if her son would soon recover, but Bartlett, who had diagnosed the Scarlet Fever, and who now saw that his patient was nearly delirious, could only respond with an anguished indirection: "I had hoped to be spared this" (Ellen T. Emerson, *Life of Lidian Emerson,* ed. Delores Bird Carpenter [Boston, 1980], 88). Scarlet Fever, or Scarletina, as milder versions were sometimes called, generally attacked children of Waldo's age and a little older and was a fearsome diagnosis for parents to hear. Doctors scarcely knew what the disorder was. In a treatise of the period it was defined as "a febrile disease, dependent on a specific miasm, resulting from unknown external influences" (Caspar Morris, *Lectures on Scarlet Fever* [Philadelphia, 1851], 49). Treatment varied between cold compresses to break the fever (67) and rubbing of the body with suet and lard to assuage the rash (68); lemonade and biscuits called "dried rusk" were particularly recommended (64–65). Under such conditions of medical information the mortality rate from the disease was high; many years later its character as a bacterial infection came to be understood, and eventually antibiotics easily controlled it.

Emerson had dealt before with the loss of loved ones, but the death of a child, his then only son, was an ordeal for which it was impossible fully to prepare. In 1838, two years after the death of his brother Charles, four years after the death of his brother Edward, and seven years after the death of his much-beloved first wife, Ellen, Emerson told the poet Jones Very "that I have never suffered, & that I could scarce bring myself to feel a concern for the safety & life of my nearest friends that would satisfy them: that I saw clearly that if my wife, my child, my mother, should be taken from me, I should still remain whole with the same capacity of cheap enjoyment from all things. I should not grieve enough, although I love them. But could I make them feel what I feel—the boundless resources of the soul,—remaining entire when particular threads of relation are snapped,—I should then dismiss forever the little remains of uneasiness I have in regard to them" (*JMN,* VII, 132). This was very much the position that the death of Waldo tested, as "Threnody" shows. In the immediate aftermath of the catastrophe Emerson could scarcely comprehend the extent of his loss. In the privacy of his journals and in letters to friends he captured a few characteristic incidents of the young life that was gone; in public, he stoically went about his business, lecturing, for example, in Providence, Rhode Island, as soon as 11 February.

Just when Emerson began to compose "Threnody" is difficult to say. Edward's notes imply a family tradition that the poem's first half, the lament, was written fairly soon after the event and probably in 1842, and that the second half was deferred a year or two for the ebbing of the grief, by which time Emerson could more clearly appreciate the consolations of his philosophy. But the evidence of the manuscript drafts in journal Book Small (*JMN*, VIII, 451–457, 473–474) and notebook Trees [A] (*JMN*, VIII, 530), tends to show that the poem was written inconsecutively in various stints, no earlier at any point than October 1842 and much more probably in the spring of 1843. Portions of the second half of "Threnody" can confidently be assigned to 1843: the material at *JMN*, VIII, 473 follows drafts of "To Rhea" and "Pericles" and the date "21 May [1843]," while lines 270–283 occur in a notebook (Trees [A]) that was not used before January 1843. The first half of the poem is set during the spring, the time of the returning and reviving "South-wind," and yet it is unlikely, despite the family tradition, that Emerson was ready to frame a poem on this subject quite so soon after the event. In June 1842 Charles King Newcomb, a Brook Farm friend of Margaret Fuller's, lifted Emerson's spirits by sending him a story, "The Two Dolons," that drew on his fond recollections of Waldo: "when I carried his MS story to the woods, & read it in the armchair of the upturned root of a pinetree I felt for the first time since Waldo's death some efficient faith again in the repairs of the Universe, some independency of natural relations whilst spiritual affinities can be so perfect & compensating" (*JMN*, VIII, 179). It is doubtful that the poem could have been in progress at this point. It was well along, however, by the following spring, though it was not complete even as late as January 1844, when Margaret Fuller requested "a copy of your poem about [Waldo], even if it is not finished," evidently implying that portions had earlier been read to her. Emerson offered to make and send the copy (*L*, III, 236, 239; *FuL*, III, 176).

Often praised as one of Emerson's finest poems, and arguably one of the great nineteenth-century elegies, it has, in the opinion of Oliver Wendell Holmes, "the dignity of 'Lycidas' without its refrigerating classicism" (*Ralph Waldo Emerson* [Boston, 1884], 333).

THRENODY.

The South-wind brings
Life, sunshine, and desire,
And on every mount and meadow
Breathes aromatic fire;
But over the dead he has no power,   5
The lost, the lost, he cannot restore;
And, looking over the hills, I mourn
The darling who shall not return.

I see my empty house,
I see my trees repair their boughs;   10
And he, the wondrous child,
Whose silver warble wild
Outvalued every pulsing sound
Within the air's cerulean round,—
The hyacinthine boy, for whom   15
Morn well might break and April bloom,—
The gracious boy, who did adorn
The world whereinto he was born,
And by his countenance repay
The favor of the loving Day,—   20
Has disappeared from the Day's eye;
Far and wide she cannot find him;
My hopes pursue, they cannot bind him.
Returned this day, the South-wind searches,
And finds young pines and budding birches;   25
But finds not the budding man;

Nature, who lost, cannot remake him;
Fate let him fall, Fate can't retake him;
Nature, Fate, men, him seek in vain.

And whither now, my truant wise and sweet,   30
O, whither tend thy feet?
I had the right, few days ago,
Thy steps to watch, thy place to know;
How have I forfeited the right?
Hast thou forgot me in a new delight?   35
I hearken for thy household cheer,
O eloquent child!
Whose voice, an equal messenger,
Conveyed thy meaning mild.
What though the pains and joys   40
Whereof it spoke were toys
Fitting his age and ken,
Yet fairest dames and bearded men,
Who heard the sweet request,
So gentle, wise, and grave,   45
Bended with joy to his behest,
And let the world's affairs go by,
Awhile to share his cordial game,
Or mend his wicker wagon-frame,
Still plotting how their hungry ear   50
That winsome voice again might hear;
For his lips could well pronounce
Words that were persuasions.

Gentlest guardians marked serene
His early hope, his liberal mien;   55
Took counsel from his guiding eyes
To make this wisdom earthly wise.
Ah, vainly do these eyes recall
The school-march, each day's festival,
When every morn my bosom glowed   60
To watch the convoy on the road;

The babe in willow wagon closed,
With rolling eyes and face composed;
With children forward and behind,
Like Cupids studiously inclined;   65
And he the chieftain paced beside,
The centre of the troop allied,
With sunny face of sweet repose,
To guard the babe from fancied foes.
The little captain innocent   70
Took the eye with him as he went;
Each village senior paused to scan
And speak the lovely caravan.
From the window I look out
To mark thy beautiful parade,   75
Stately marching in cap and coat
To some tune by fairies played;—
A music heard by thee alone
To works as noble led thee on.

Now Love and Pride, alas! in vain,   80
Up and down their glances strain.
The painted sled stands where it stood;
The kennel by the corded wood;
The gathered sticks to stanch the wall
Of the snow-tower, when snow should fall;   85
The ominous hole he dug in the sand,
And childhood's castles built or planned;
His daily haunts I well discern,—
The poultry-yard, the shed, the barn,—
And every inch of garden ground   90
Paced by the blessed feet around,
From the roadside to the brook
Whereinto he loved to look.
Step the meek birds where erst they ranged;
The wintry garden lies unchanged;   95
The brook into the stream runs on;
But the deep-eyed boy is gone.

On that shaded day,
Dark with more clouds than tempests are,
When thou didst yield thy innocent breath 100
In birdlike heavings unto death,
Night came, and Nature had not thee;
I said, 'We are mates in misery.'
The morrow dawned with needless glow;
Each snowbird chirped, each fowl must crow; 105
Each tramper started; but the feet
Of the most beautiful and sweet
Of human youth had left the hill
And garden,—they were bound and still.
There's not a sparrow or a wren, 110
There's not a blade of autumn grain,
Which the four seasons do not tend,
And tides of life and increase lend;
And every chick of every bird,
And weed and rock-moss is preferred. 115
O ostrich-like forgetfulness!
O loss of larger in the less!
Was there no star that could be sent,
No watcher in the firmament,
No angel from the countless host 120
That loiters round the crystal coast,
Could stoop to heal that only child,
Nature's sweet marvel undefiled,
And keep the blossom of the earth,
Which all her harvests were not worth? 125
Not mine,—I never called thee mine,
But Nature's heir,—if I repine,
And seeing rashly torn and moved
Not what I made, but what I loved,
Grow early old with grief that thou 130
Must to the wastes of Nature go,—
'Tis because a general hope
Was quenched, and all must doubt and grope.
For flattering planets seemed to say

This child should ills of ages stay, 135
By wondrous tongue, and guided pen,
Bring the flown Muses back to men.
Perchance not he but Nature ailed,
The world and not the infant failed.
It was not ripe yet to sustain 140
A genius of so fine a strain,
Who gazed upon the sun and moon
As if he came unto his own,
And, pregnant with his grander thought,
Brought the old order into doubt. 145
His beauty once their beauty tried;
They could not feed him, and he died,
And wandered backward as in scorn,
To wait an æon to be born.
Ill day which made this beauty waste, 150
Plight broken, this high face defaced!
Some went and came about the dead;
And some in books of solace read;
Some to their friends the tidings say;
Some went to write, some went to pray; 155
One tarried here, there hurried one;
But their heart abode with none.
Covetous death bereaved us all,
To aggrandize one funeral.
The eager fate which carried thee 160
Took the largest part of me:
For this losing is true dying;
This is lordly man's down-lying,
This his slow but sure reclining,
Star by star his world resigning. 165

O child of paradise,
Boy who made dear his father's home,
In whose deep eyes
Men read the welfare of the times to come,
I am too much bereft. 170

The world dishonored thou hast left.
O truth's and nature's costly lie!
O trusted broken prophecy!
O richest fortune sourly crossed!
Born for the future, to the future lost!   175

The deep Heart answered, 'Weepest thou?
Worthier cause for passion wild
If I had not taken the child.
And deemest thou as those who pore,
With aged eyes, short way before,—   180
Think'st Beauty vanished from the coast
Of matter, and thy darling lost?
Taught he not thee—the man of eld,
Whose eyes within his eyes beheld
Heaven's numerous hierarchy span   185
The mystic gulf from God to man?
To be alone wilt thou begin
When worlds of lovers hem thee in?
To-morrow, when the masks shall fall
That dizen Nature's carnival,   190
The pure shall see by their own will,
Which overflowing Love shall fill,
'Tis not within the force of fate
The fate-conjoined to separate.
But thou, my votary, weepest thou?   195
I gave thee sight—where is it now?
I taught thy heart beyond the reach
Of ritual, bible, or of speech;
Wrote in thy mind's transparent table,
As far as the incommunicable;   200
Taught thee each private sign to raise,
Lit by the supersolar blaze.
Past utterance, and past belief,
And past the blasphemy of grief,
The mysteries of Nature's heart;   205

And though no Muse can these impart,
Throb thine with Nature's throbbing breast,
And all is clear from east to west.

'I came to thee as to a friend;
Dearest, to thee I did not send   210
Tutors, but a joyful eye,
Innocence that matched the sky,
Lovely locks, a form of wonder,
Laughter rich as woodland thunder,
That thou might'st entertain apart   215
The richest flowering of all art:
And, as the great all-loving Day
Through smallest chambers takes its way,
That thou might'st break thy daily bread
With prophet, savior, and head;   220
That thou might'st cherish for thine own
The riches of sweet Mary's Son,
Boy-Rabbi, Israel's paragon.
And thoughtest thou such guest
Would in thy hall take up his rest?   225
Would rushing life forget her laws,
Fate's glowing revolution pause?
High omens ask diviner guess;
Not to be conned to tediousness.
And know my higher gifts unbind   230
The zone that girds the incarnate mind.
When the scanty shores are full
With Thought's perilous, whirling pool;
When frail Nature can no more,
Then the Spirit strikes the hour: 235
My servant Death, with solving rite,
Pours finite into infinite.

'Wilt thou freeze love's tidal flow,
Whose streams through nature circling go?
Nail the wild star to its track   240
On the half-climbed zodiac?

Light is light which radiates,
Blood is blood which circulates,
Life is life which generates,
And many-seeming life is one,—   245
Wilt thou transfix and make it none?
Its onward force too starkly pent
In figure, bone, and lineament?
Wilt thou, uncalled, interrogate,
Talker! the unreplying Fate?   250
Nor see the genius of the whole
Ascendant in the private soul,
Beckon it when to go and come,
Self-announced its hour of doom?
Fair the soul's recess and shrine,   255
Magic-built to last a season;
Masterpiece of love benign;
Fairer that expansive reason
Whose omen 'tis, and sign.
Wilt thou not ope thy heart to know   260
What rainbows teach, and sunsets show?
Verdict which accumulates
From lengthening scroll of human fates,
Voice of earth to earth returned,
Prayers of saints that inly burned,—   265
Saying, *What is excellent,*
As God lives, is permanent;
Hearts are dust, hearts' loves remain;
Heart's love will meet thee again.
Revere the Maker; fetch thine eye   270
Up to his style, and manners of the sky.
Not of adamant and gold
Built he heaven stark and cold;
No, but a nest of bending reeds,
Flowering grass, and scented weeds;   275
Or like a traveller's fleeing tent,
Or bow above the tempest bent;
Built of tears and sacred flames,
And virtue reaching to its aims;

Built of furtherance and pursuing, 280
Not of spent deeds, but of doing.
Silent rushes the swift Lord
Through ruined systems still restored,
Broadsowing, bleak and void to bless,
Plants with worlds the wilderness; 285
Waters with tears of ancient sorrow
Apples of Eden ripe to-morrow.
House and tenant go to ground,
Lost in God, in Godhead found.'

TEXTS

(A) bMS Am 82.5 (1), Ralph Waldo Emerson Memorial Association deposit, Houghton Library, Harvard University, printer's copy for B; (B) *Poems* (London, 1847), 188–199; (C) *Poems* (Boston, 1847), 236–249; (D) *Poems* ["Fourth Edition"] (Boston, 1847), 236–249; (E) *Poems* (Boston, 1865), 239–252; (F) *Selected Poems* (Boston, 1876), 190–199; (G) *Poems* [Riverside] (Boston, 1884), 130–138; (H) *Poems* [Centenary] (Boston, 1904), 148–158. There are no variants in printings from the plates made for (C) after (D). In 1861, Emerson's publisher James T. Fields anonymously edited a collection of short works by several hands (*Favorite Authors* [Boston, Ticknor and Fields, 1861], reissued by J. R. Osgood in 1873) that included Emerson's "Threnody" (240–248). However, none of the eleven variants in this text has authority.

Format: Emerson indicated in (A) that a "double white line" should follow after line 175. No verse break after line 73 (C-H); none after line 79 (A-B); none after line 97 (F); none after line 115 (A-D, F-H); none after line 237 (B, G-H); none after line 248 (C-H). Lines 98, 166, and 249 inset (A-B).

Pre-copy-text forms: Houghton bMS Am 1280.236 (1) is a single-sheet MS containing lines 54–73, together with several canceled and unused lines. Other passages, as indicated in the discussion above, occur in *JMN,* VIII, 451–457, 473–474, and 530.

VARIANTS

1   South-wind (C-E, G-H) |
southwind (A) | south-wind (B, F)
2   sunshine, (A-F) | sunshine
(G-H)

4   fire; (C-H) | fire, (A-B)
6   lost, he (C-H) | lost he (A-B) ||
restore; (C-H) | restore, (A-B)
10   boughs; (C-H) | boughs, (A-B)

11   he, (C-H) | he,— (A-B)

14   round,— (C-H) | round, (A-B)

16   break (C-H) | break, (A-B) || bloom,— (C-G) | bloom, (A-B, H)

20   favor (C-H) | favour (A-B) || Day,— (C-H) | Day, (A-B)

21   eye; (B-H) | eye, (A)

22   him; (C-H) | him, (A-B)

24   day, (C-H) | day (A-B) || Southwind (H) | southwind (A) | southwind (B, E-F) | south wind (C-D, G) || searches, (C-H) | searches (A-B)

25   birches; (C-H) | birches, (A-B)

27   Nature, (C-H) | Nature (A-B) || lost, (CC1, D-H) | lost him, (A-C)

29   men, (A-B, D-H) | Men, (C)

30   wise and (B-H) | ↑wise and ↓ (A)

31   O, (C-H) | O (A-B)

33   know; (A-F) | know: (G-H)

42   ken, (C-H) | ken;— (A-B)

44   request, (C-H) | request (A-B)

45   wise, (A-F) | wise (G-H)

46   behest, (A-F) | behest (G-H)

48   Awhile (A-F) | A while (G-H)

49   wagon-frame, (C-H) | wagon frame, (A-B)

51   hear; (C-H) | hear, (A-B)

55   mien; (C-H) | mien, (A-B)

58   Ah, (C-H) | Ah! (A-B)

61   road; (C-H) | road;— (A-B)

63   composed; (C-H) | composed, (A-B)

65   inclined; (C-H) | inclined, (A-B)

66   he (C-H) | he, (A-B) || chieftain (C-H) | Chieftain, (A-B)

70   captain (C-H) | Captain (A-B)

71   went; (C-H) | went, (A-B)

75   parade, (C-H) | parade (A-B)

77   played;— (C-H) | played; (A-B)

80   Love (C-H) | love (A-B) || Pride, (C-H) | pride, (A-B) || alas! (C-H) | alas, (A-B)

82   stood; (C-H) | stood, (A-B)

83   wood; (C-H) | wood, (A-B)

84   The (A-F) | His (CC1) [*Perhaps not in Emerson's hand*] | His (G-H) || stanch (C-H) | staunch (A-B)

85   fall; (C-H) | fall, (A-B)

87   planned; (C-H) | planned. (A-B)

88   discern,— (C-H) | discern, (A-B)

89   poultry-yard, (C-H) | poultry yard, (A-B) || barn,— (C-H) | barn, (A-B)

92   roadside (A, C-H) | road side (B) || brook (C-H) | brook, (A-B)

94   birds (A-F) | fowls (CC1, CC5 [*Perhaps in neither case in Emerson's hand*], G-H) || ranged; (C-H) | ranged, (A-B)

95   unchanged; (C-H) | unchanged, (A-B)

96   on; (C-H) | on, (A-B)

97   boy (C-H) | Boy (A-B)

101   birdlike (C-H) | bird-like (A-B)

102   thee; (C-H) | thee,— (A-B)

103   'We (C-H) | We (A) | we (B) || misery.' (C-H) | misery. (A-B)

104   glow; (C-H) | glow, (A-B)

105   snowbird (C-H) | snow-bird (A-B) || crow; (C-H) | crow, (A-B)

106   started; (C-H) | started,— (A-B)

109   still. (A-D, F-H) | still (E)

112   tend, (A-F) | tend (G-H)

113   lend; (C-H) | <b>lend, (A) | lend, (B)

115   rock-moss (B-H) | rock moss (A)

116   ostrich-like (C-H) | <foul> ↑<parent's> ostriches' ↓ (A) | ostriches' (B)

120   host (A, C-H) | host, (B)

123   [*In* (A) *followed by two canceled lines:*] <And save her hope, her last & best, / From ruin by that scarlet pest,>

125   harvests (B-H) | <kingdoms> ↑harvests↓ (A)

126   mine,— (C-H) | mine, (A-B)

127   Nature's (C-H) | nature's (A-B)

128   And (C-H) I And, (A-B) II moved (C-H) I moved, (A-B)

129   loved, (A, C-H) I loved. (B)

130   thou (A, CC10, CC11, C-H) I then (B)

131   Nature (C-H) I nature (A-B)

132   'Tis (B-H) I Tis (A)

133   grope. (B-H) I grope<,>. (A)

134   planets (B-H) I <nature> ↑planets↓ (A) II say (C-H) I say, (A-B)

135   This child should (B-H) I <He> ↑This child↓ should <the> (A) II stay, (C-H) I stay,— (A-B)

136   tongue, (C-H) I tongue (A-B) II pen, (C-H) I pen (A-B)

137   Muses (A, C-H) I muses (B) II men. (C-H) I men.— (A-B)

138   Perchance (C-H) I Perchance, (A-B) II he (C-H) I he, (A-B) II Nature (C-H) I nature (A-B)

139   world (C-H) I world, (A-B) II failed. (C-H) I failed, (A-B)

140   yet (C-H) I yet, (A-B)

144   And, (A, C-H) I And (B)

146   His beauty once (C-H) I Awhile his beauty (A-B) II tried; (C-H) I tried, (A-B)

148   scorn, (C-H) I scorn (A-B)

149   æon (C-H) I aeon (A) I Æon (B)

150   beauty (A-E, G-H) I fleauty (F) II waste, (C-H) I waste<!>; (A) I waste; (B)

152   dead; (C-H) I dead, (A-B)

153   read; (C-H) I read, (A-B)

154   say; (C-H) I say, (A-B)

155   pray; (C-H) I pray, (A-B)

156   one; (C-H) I one, (A-B)

158   all, (C-H) I all (A-B)

160   fate (C-H) Fate (A-B)

161   me: (C-H) I me. (A-B)

162   dying; (C-H) I dying, (A-B)

163   down-lying, (B-H) I downlying, (A)

164   his (A, CC10, C-H) I is (B)

166   paradise, (C-H) I Paradise! (A-B)

167   home, (A, C-H) I home (B)

169   come, (A, C-H) I come; (B)

170   bereft. (C-H) I bereft; (A-B)

171   dishonored (C-H) I dishonoured (A-B) II left. (C-H) I left; (A-B)

172   truth's (C-H) I truths (A-B) II costly lie! (C-H) I I ↑costly↓ lie! (A) I costly lie; (B)

173   trusted (C-H) I trusted, (A-B)

176   'Weepest (C-H) I Weepest (A-B)

177   Worthier (B-H) I <Nearer> ↑Worthier↓ (A) II wild (A, C-H) I wild, (B)

179   pore, (C-H) I pore (A-B)

180   eyes, (C-H) I eyes (A-B) II before,— (C-H) I before? (A-B)

183   thee— (C-H) I thee,— (A-B) II eld, (B-H) I eld (A)

187   alone (C-H) I alone, (A-B) II begin (C-H) I begin, (A-B)

188   lovers (B-H) I <dreamers> ↑lovers↓ (A)

189   To-morrow, (B-H) I Tomorrow, (A)

190   Nature's (C-H) I nature's (A-B)

191   see (C-H) I see, (A-B)

192   Love (C-H) I love (A-B) II fill, (C-H) I fill,— (A-B)

193   'Tis (B-H) I Tis (A) II fate (C-H) I Fate (A-B)

195   votary, (B-H) I <envoy> ↑votary↓, (A)

196   sight— (C-H) I sight, (A-B)

199   table, (C-H) I table (A-B)

201   raise, (C-F) I raise (A-B, G-H)

203   utterance, (C-H) I utterance (A-B)

205   Nature's heart; (C-H) I nature's heart,— (A-B)

206   Muse (C-H) I muse (A-B)

207   Nature's (C-H) I nature's (A-B)

209   'I (C-H) | I (A-B) || friend; (C-H)
| friend, (A-B)
214   thunder, (C-H) | thunder; (A-B)
216   art: (C-H) | art; (A-B)
220   prophet, (C-H) | Prophet, (A-B)
|| savior, (D-F) | Saviour, (A-B) |
Savior, (C) | savior (G-H)
223   paragon. (C-H) | Paragon:
(A-B)
226   her (C-H) | its (A-B)
228   guess; (C-H) | guess, (A-B)
229   tediousness. (A-G) | tediousness
(H)
230   know (C-H) | know, (A-B)
231   mind. (C-H) | mind, (A-B) || [*In
(A) there follow two canceled lines:*] <My
servant Death with solving rite /
Pours finite into infinite.> [*cf. lines
236–237*]
233   perilous, (C-H) | perilous (A-B)
|| pool; (C-H) | pool, (A-B)
234   more, (C-H) | more,— (A-B)
235   Spirit (A, C-H) | spirit (B) ||
hour: (C-H) | hour, (A-B)
236   Death, (C-H) | Death (A-B) ||
rite, (C-H) | rite (A-B)
238   'Wilt (C-F) | Wilt (A-B, G-H) [*In
(G-H) the quotation mark is omitted
because there is no new verse paragraph*]
239   nature (A-G) | Nature (H)
240   the wild star (C-H) | the star
struggling (A-B)
241   zodiac? (C-H) | Zodiack? (A-B)
246   Wilt thou transfix and (B-H) |
<Heedless, w>Wilt thou ↑transfix
&↓ (A) || none? (C-H) | none, (A-B)
247   force (C-H) | stream (A-B)
248   bone, (A-G) | bone (H)
249   thou, uncalled, interrogate, (C-
H) | thou ↑uncalled↓ interrogate
(A) | thou uncalled interrogate (B)
250   Fate? (C-H) | fate? (A-B)
251   genius (C-H) | <needs>

↑<Empire> Genius↓ (A) | Genius
(B)
253   Beckon (B-H) | Beckon<ing>
(A)
254   Self-announced (B-H) | <Itself>
<And> self-announced (A) || doom?
(C-H) | doom. (A-B)
255   recess (B-H) | <closet> ↑recess↓
(A)
256   built (C-H) | built, (A-B) ||
season; (C-H) | season, (A-B)
257   benign; (C-E) | benign! (A-B) |
benign (F) | benign, (G-H)
259   'tis, (B-H) | tis, (A)
260   ope thy heart to know (C-H) |
<with credit pay> ↑ope thy heart to
know↓ (A) | ope this heart to know
(B)
261   teach, (C-H) | teach (A-B) ||
show? (C-H) | <say> show, (A) | show,
(B)
263   lengthening (A, C-H) |
lengthened (B)
265   saints (C-H) | hearts (A-B) ||
burned,— (C-H) | burned; (A-B)
267   *permanent;* (C-H) | *permanent,*
(A-B)
268   *hearts'* (B-H) | *heart's* (A) ||
remain; (C-E, G-H) | *remain,* (A-B, F)
273   cold; (C-H) | cold, (A-B)
275   grass, (C-F) | grass (A-B, G-H) ||
weeds; (C-H) | weeds, (A-B)
277   bent; (CC10, CC11, C-H) | bent,
(A) | pent, (B)
281   doing. (B-H) | doing<;>.
284   Broadsowing, (C-H) | Broad-
sowing, (A-B)
285   wilderness; (C-H) | wilderness,
(A-B)
287   to-morrow. (C-H) | tomorrow;
(A) | to-morrow; (B)
288   ground, (B-H) | ground; (A)
289   found.' (A, C-H) | found. (B)

Poems (1847)

59.   Waldo, together with the children of several neighbors, attended school in a small building near the home of Samuel Hoar on Main Street kept by Mary Russell of Plymouth, whom Emerson had brought to Concord for this purpose in the summers of 1840 and 1841 (Ellen T. Emerson, *The Life of Lidian Jackson Emerson,* ed. Dolores Bird Carpenter (Boston, 1980), 78; *L,* II, 402; *JMN,* VIII, 165).

165.   Emerson may here be recalling a bit of mythopoesis by Charles Emerson in a letter to Ralph Waldo of 29 October 1834 concerning the recent death of their brother Edward: "When he was born into rational thought & affection, he lifted up his eyes, & a bright circle of stars bent their aspect on him & he said in his heart, These will watch over me even to the end—But star after star shoots from its place & sets untimely, & he feels alone, & the new constellations wear not such eyes of love to him" (quoted in Bosco and Myerson, *The Emerson Brothers* [New York, 2006], 147).

177–178.   Emerson held this paradox in common with Thoreau, who wrote on 2 March to Lidian's sister, Lucy Brown, "As for Waldo, he died as the mist rises from the brook, which the sun will soon dart his rays through. Do not the flowers die every autumn? He had not even taken root here. I was not startled to hear that he was dead;—it seemed the most natural event that could happen. His fine organization demanded it, and nature gently yielded its request. It would have been strange if he had lived" (*The Correspondence of Henry David Thoreau,* ed. Walter Harding and Carl Bode [New York, 1958], 63). Thoreau was also grieving for his brother John, who had died from lockjaw just two weeks before Waldo's death.

214.   "The babe cheers me with his hearty & protracted laugh which sounds to me like thunder in the woods" (20 August 1837, *JMN,* V, 371).

CONCORD HYMN

SUNG AT THE COMPLETION
OF THE BATTLE MONUMENT,
JULY 4, 1837.

The first battle of the American Revolution occurred on 19 April 1775 at Concord's North Bridge between British troops sent out from Boston by General Thomas Gage and a body of hastily assembled minute-men from Concord and the nearby towns of Acton and Lincoln. This bridge, located half a mile from Concord center, lay virtually in Emerson's grandfather's backyard—that is, immediately behind the historic Old Manse, which William Emerson, the town's minister, had built in 1769. He was present on the fateful day, "to animate and encourage his people," according to Concord historian Lemuel Shattuck (*A History of the Town of Concord* [Boston, 1835], 105; see also *Diaries and Letters of William Emerson*, ed. Amelia Forbes Emerson [Boston, 1972], 71–75). Two months later he was with the American troops at Bunker Hill. He then served as an army chaplain, fell ill at Fort Ticonderoga, and died in Rutland, Vermont, in October 1776, while trying to get home to Concord. Following his death his place in the Concord pulpit was taken by Ezra Ripley, who several years later married Emerson's widow and occupied the Manse until his own death in 1841. Many of the residents took an interest in the town's Revolutionary history because its minister did. Ripley published his *History of the Fight at Concord* in 1827, provoked thereto by recently developed claims from the citizens of Lexington that the Revolution had in fact begun there. Ripley asserted that during the predawn encounter in neighboring Lexington only the British had fired, killing several, and that the local militia had obeyed the orders of its commander, Captain John Parker (Theodore Parker's grandfather), not to fire. And so it was at Concord that Britain was first forcibly and effectually resisted. The celebrated lawyer and politician Samuel Hoar, Elizabeth's father, concurred: neither he nor his own father, a member of the Lincoln company at the Fight, had ever heard of Lexington having resisted (50). It was in this spasm of local feeling that Ezra Ripley organized a project to place a memorial at the site of the battle bridge, the original bridge having been taken down without fanfare in 1778. To assure that this monument, an obelisk, would actually be installed, he donated to the town the plot of land where the engagement had occurred. The memorial committee wrangled at length, however, over the wording of the inscription, rejecting submissions from Ripley, Shattuck, and Emerson himself (all too long for the space available on the shaft), before accepting a revised version composed by physician Edward Jarvis (Jarvis, *Traditions and Reminiscences of Concord, Massachusetts, 1779–1878,* ed. Sarah Chapin [Amherst, 1993], 223). In consequence of these delays, the dedication, originally scheduled for 19 April 1836, had to be put off yet another year, to 4 July 1837. For that occasion, Emerson, who had already described the battle in his "Historical Discourse" in 1835, was asked to supply a hymn, which he wrote sometime in June (*L,* II, 85, n. 121). Its performance as a hymn, sung to the tune of Old Hundred, was entrusted to a choir of townsmen at the dedication, though because the text was printed on slips of paper and distributed to the large crowd, others no doubt joined in. Emerson himself did not, because he and Lidian happened to be absent that day at Plymouth. Thoreau, however, home from Harvard, sang as a member of the choir, as did John Shepard Keyes, who years later recalled the occasion:

> It was a very hot, sunny, July day. After the noon salute and bell ringing the village became as quiet as of a Sunday. About three o'clock the procession, escorted by the military companies, . . . came slowly along the Common and passed up the road to the old North Bridge. There were assembled about the Monument two or three hundred, seated on the grass, who listened to a prayer by Mr.

Concord Hymn

[Barzillai] Frost, an oration by Samuel Hoar, and then Mr. Emerson's hymn was sung by all who could join in full chorus. The hymn was printed on slips of paper about six inches square and plentifully supplied to the audience. . . . Rev. John Wilder prayed, and Dr. Ripley gave a very solemn benediction—for was not his life's work and effort accomplished in this Monument, erected and dedicated on the spot he had selected? (quoted in Walter Harding, *The Days of Henry Thoreau* [New York, 1965], 48).

Emerson's first draft of the hymn in poetry notebook P occurs in close relation to drafts of "In Memoriam. E.B.E.," the initial section of which offers a rather different and more somber view of the battle. Lacking the nearly seamless integrity of the hymn, "In Memoriam" was cannibalized for mottoes used in *Essays: Second Series* (1844) and was not published in full until *May-Day* (1867).

The hymn's title changed with nearly every edition: reference is, first, to the completion of the "Concord Monument," said erroneously (beginning in *Poems*) to have occurred on 19 April 1836. Emerson's recollection, when he crafted the formal title nine years after the event, was simply faulty: Jarvis's inscription on the monument, which Emerson saw innumerable times during this period, gives the date as 1836, but the dedication did not take place until the year following. This inaccuracy was not corrected until 1904. The substitution of "Battle Monument" for "Concord Monument" in the title as it appears in the Riverside and Centenary editions tacitly acknowledged the arrival, in 1875, of a second monument, the popular Minuteman statue by Concord sculptor Daniel Chester French. The momentary choice of "Concord Fight" as the title in *Selected Poems* seems a concession to local idiom. In 1860 Samuel Ripley Bartlett, son of the Emerson family physician Josiah Bartlett, published *Concord Fight*, a lengthy poem that directly engaged (and at one point quoted from) Emerson's work. In 1875, a year before the publication of *Selected Poems*, the Reverend Grindall Reynolds, minister at Ezra Ripley's old church, published *Concord Fight, April 19, 1775*, a prose account. Simultaneously, in the May 1875 issue of *Harper's Monthly* (L, 777–805), Concord resident Frederic Hudson published his own account, "The Concord Fight," which included, at p. 778, an engraved facsimile of Emerson's poem, lacking a title and with the first two and last two stanzas reversed. None of the titles for Emerson's poem, in short, satisfactorily combines factual accuracy with respect for the author's intention. This best known, perhaps, of all of Emerson's poems is commonly referred to, simply and appropriately, as "Concord Hymn."

This "perfect little poem," as Oliver Wendell Holmes called it (*Ralph Waldo Emerson* [Boston, 1885], 332), has long been a staple in the schoolroom, though not because its crystal clarity exempts it from being misread. Bliss Perry cited an instance:

> As for the Concord Hymn, my recollection is that a student came up after a class-room discussion of the poem, and said: "My teacher in the Normal School told us that there were four mistakes in the first stanza:
>
> 1. The bridge had no arch. It was laid on flat stringers.
> 2. We don't know that there was any flag.
> 3. There was no battle-array to justify the word 'embattled'; just a straggling crowd of farmers.
> 4. The farthest point at which the shots were heard was South Acton." (quoted in Strauch, Diss., 554).

One effect of this joke is to recoup a sense of Emerson's audaciousness in the figurative language of line 4, largely lost to us through too frequent quotation. In one of the four surviving copies of the broadside printing, one of the hundred or so original singers underscored that line and wrote next to it in the margin a single word—"poetical" (*The Parkman Dexter Howe Library, Part II*, ed. Sidney Ives [Gainesville, 1984], Plate 2).

CONCORD HYMN

SUNG AT THE COMPLETION OF
THE BATTLE MONUMENT,
JULY 4, 1837

By the rude bridge that arched the flood,
    Their flag to April's breeze unfurled,
Here once the embattled farmers stood,
    And fired the shot heard round the world.

The foe long since in silence slept;   5
    Alike the conqueror silent sleeps;
And Time the ruined bridge has swept
    Down the dark stream which seaward creeps.

On this green bank, by this soft stream,
    We set today a votive stone,   10
That memory may their deed redeem,
    When, like our sires, our sons are gone.

Spirit, that made those heroes dare
    To die, and leave their children free,
Bid Time and Nature gently spare   15
    The shaft we raise to them and thee.

TEXTS

(A) Broadside printing, 1837; (B) MS, SLV/105/13, Sterling Library, by permission of the University of London, printer's copy for C; (C) *Poems* (London, 1847), 200; (D) *Poems* (Boston, 1847), 250–251; (E) *Poems* (Boston, 1863), 250–251; (F) *Poems* (Boston, 1865), 253–254; (G) *Selected Poems* (Boston, 1876), 202; (H) *Poems* [Riverside] (Boston, 1884), 139; (I) *Poems* [Centenary] (Boston, 1904), 158–159.
    [*Note:* Reprintings of the poem in the *Concord Freeman* and the (Concord) *Yeoman's Gazette* on 8 July 1837 exactly reproduce the text of the broadside, except

that the former carries the title "HYMN." and the latter omits the title. Emerson produced a number of post-publication fair copies as specimens to give to friends and acquaintances—as, for example, the copy presented to Annie Fields, wife of Emerson's publisher, James T. Fields, now in the Pierpont Morgan Library, and the one provided to Frederic Hudson, apparently in 1875, as indicated in the headnote (see, further, *PN,* 764). The few variants these items contain have no textual significance.]

Format: Alternate indentation lacking in (B-C).

Pre-copy-text forms: The principal drafts occur in poetry notebook P: see the discussion in *PN,* 763-764.

VARIANTS

Title: CONCORD HYMN / SUNG AT THE COMPLETION OF THE BATTLE / MONUMENT, JULY 4, 1837 (I) | ORIGINAL HYMN. (A) | Hymn Sung at the Completion of <the> Concord Monument, April 19, 1836. (B) | HYMN. / SUNG AT THE COMPLETION OF CONCORD MONUMENT, / APRIL 19, 1836. (C) | HYMN: / SUNG AT THE COMPLETION OF THE CONCORD MONUMENT, / April 19, 1836. (D-F) | CONCORD FIGHT. / HYMN SUNG AT THE COMPLETION OF THE CONCORD / MONUMENT, APRIL 19, 1836. (G) | CONCORD HYMN: / SUNG AT THE COMPLETION OF THE BATTLE MONUMENT, / APRIL 19, 1836. (H)

3 Here once (B-I) | Here, once, (A) || stood, (A-H) | stood (I)

5 foe long since (B-I) | foe, long since, (A) || slept; (A, D-I) | slept, (B-C)

6 Alike (B-I) | Alike, (A) || conqueror (A, D-I) | Conqueror (B-C) || sleeps; (A, D-I) | sleeps, (B-C)

10 set today (B) | set to-day (C-I) | place with joy (A) || stone, (A-C) | stone; (D-I)

12 When, (A, D-I) | When (B-C) || sires, (A, D-I) | sires (B-C)

13 Spirit, that (D-I) | O Thou who (A) | Spirit! who (B-C) || heroes (A, D-I) | freemen (B-C)

14 die, and (CC1, CC3, CC4, CC5, E, G-I) | die, or (A, C-D, F) | die or (B) || free, (B-I) | free,— (A)

15 Time (A, D-I) | time (B-C) || Nature (A, D-I) | nature (B-C)

16 thee. (D-F, H-I) | Thee. (A-C, G)

MAY-DAY AND OTHER PIECES
(1867)

MAY-DAY.

[1867 VERSION]

The earliest trace of the poem is a 41-line version in notebook Z, probably written about 1838 (*JMN*, VI, 296–297). Over the years Emerson wrote additional short fragments on the subject of Spring, several of which eventually found their way into the poem, but there seems to have been no concerted effort to expand, revise, or complete the work until the Civil War years, and even then progress was slow. Early in April 1865, "after the fall of Richmond," Emerson read a long version of the poem at the home of Mr. and Mrs. James T. Fields, who for some years had heard intriguing references to certain unfinished "verses on Spring." But when the reading was ended, Emerson declared that the work was still "too fragmentary to satisfy him" and would not consent to publication (Annie Fields, "Glimpses of Emerson," *Harper's New Monthly Magazine* 68 [February 1884]: 461; rpt. in Fields, *Authors and Friends* [Boston, 1897], 82).

At about the same time (evidently also in April 1865) Emerson wrote the first draft of a 67-line poem, unpublished during his lifetime, to which he gave the title "May-Day," the principal and longer poem having all the while remained without title, its several drafts indexed under "Spring." This shorter poem, referred to in *PN* as "May-Day [Invitation]," seemed to address a lacuna in the longer one, since it dealt with the actual May-Day folk ritual, cast as a taunt from the countryside to the city, but in the end it supplied to the published poem no more than its title.

May-Day and Other Pieces (1867)

"May-Day," the title piece in Emerson's second collection of verse—published in 1867, twenty years after the first—was much the longest poem that Emerson ever wrote, and perhaps for that reason, and because it was not all written at once, its structure proved unsatisfactory, above all to its author and his children. Famously, the poem was rearranged and revised for inclusion in the *Selected Poems* of 1876 (mostly by Ellen Emerson with her father's cooperation), and yet again, by Edward, for the Riverside edition. The feeling was general within the Emerson household that the original order of the sections did not closely enough track the natural onset of Spring, though other violations of organic unity must also have made themselves felt. There was no time, for example, when lines 480–602 did not constitute a very distinct section of the poem. In the major draft in notebook KL[A] these lines occupy pages of their own (pp. 39–47) in the midst of what is otherwise an essentially continuous inscription. Likewise, in the printer's copy for the 1867 volume, pages 31-[39] are exclusively devoted to this section, pages that are in fact separately numbered 1 through 9. And yet it was not until 1876 and the publication of *Selected Poems* that these lines were extracted and published by themselves under the title of "The Harp." If "May-Day [Invitation]" never quite worked its way into the poem, "The Harp" clearly worked its way out, as if to acknowledge how poorly it fit within the larger poetic unit. It has also been noticed that at various points Emerson seems to recall passages from certain of his earlier poems, such as "The Snow-Storm" and "Days." Similarly, the 1849 motto to *Nature* (*CW*, I, 7) is repeated here (see *PN*, 181, 866, and *JMN*, IX, 163), contributing further to the retrospective and allusive—not to say valedictory—feel that the poem is capable of generating at times.

In the notes to the poem the editors have paid special attention to the journal sources because, in providing chronological points of reference, these passages shed much light on the atypical history of the poem's composition. Indeed the evidence shows how misleading was Edward Emerson's long-credited statement that "May-Day" "was probably written in snatches in the woods on his afternoon walks, through many years" (*W*, IX, 455). It now seems clear that relatively few lines are of an early date and that these show no signs of belonging from inception to a large project. The poem likely had no conceptual existence much before 1859 and was very largely the work of 1862–1866. Emerson was still adding lines in the fall of 1866, even as the poem was being set in type.

The 1876 and 1884 texts of the poem have very little textual significance, though the latter, because it was the basis for the 1904 printing in the Centenary edition, has a certain virtue of familiarity. They are excluded from the present edition of the 1867 version, but are taken up in a separate Appendix at the end of the volume.

MAY-DAY.

Daughter of Heaven and Earth, coy Spring,
With sudden passion languishing,
Maketh all things softly smile,
Painteth pictures mile on mile,
Holds a cup with cowslip-wreaths,   5
Whence a smokeless incense breathes.
Girls are peeling the sweet willow,
Poplar white, and Gilead tree,
And troops of boys
Shouting with whoop and hilloa   10
And hip, hip, three times three.
The air is full of whistlings bland;
What was that I heard
Out of the hazy land?
Harp of the wind, or song of bird,   15
Or clapping of shepherd's hands,
Or vagrant booming of the air,
Voice of a meteor lost in day?
Such tidings of the starry sphere
Can this elastic air convey.   20
Or haply 'twas the cannonade
Of the pent and darkened lake,
Cooled by the pendent mountain's shade,

Whose deeps, till beams of noonday break,
Afflicted moan, and latest hold   25
Even into May the iceberg cold.
Was it a squirrel's pettish bark,
Or clarionet of jay? or hark,
Where yon wedged line the Nestor leads,
Steering north with raucous cry   30
Through tracts and provinces of sky,
Every night alighting down
In new landscapes of romance,
Where darkling feed the clamorous clans
By lonely lakes to men unknown.   35
Come the tumult whence it will,
Voice of sport, or rush of wings,
It is a sound, it is a token
That the marble sleep is broken,
And a change has passed on things.   40

Beneath the calm, within the light,
A hid unruly appetite
Of swifter life, a surer hope,
Strains every sense to larger scope,
Impatient to anticipate   45
The halting steps of aged Fate.
Slow grows the palm, too slow the pearl:
When Nature falters, fain would zeal
Grasp the felloes of her wheel,
And grasping give the orbs another whirl.   50
Turn swiftlier round, O tardy ball!
And sun this frozen side,
Bring hither back the robin's call,
Bring back the tulip's pride.

Why chidest thou the tardy Spring?   55
The hardy bunting does not chide;
The blackbirds make the maples ring
With social cheer and jubilee;
The redwing flutes his *o-ka-lee,*

314

The robins know the melting snow;   60
The sparrow meek, prophetic-eyed,
Her nest beside the snowdrift weaves,
Secure the osier yet will hide
Her callow brood in mantling leaves;
And thou, by science all undone,   65
Why only must thy reason fail
To see the southing of the sun?

As we thaw frozen flesh with snow,
So Spring will not, foolish fond,
Mix polar night with tropic glow,   70
Nor cloy us with unshaded sun,
Nor wanton skip with bacchic dance,
But she has the temperance
Of the gods, whereof she is one,—
Masks her treasury of heat   75
Under east-winds crossed with sleet.
Plants and birds and humble creatures
Well accept her rule austere;
Titan-born, to hardy natures
Cold is genial and dear.   80
As Southern wrath to Northern right
Is but straw to anthracite;
As in the day of sacrifice,
When heroes piled the pyre,
The dismal Massachusetts ice   85
Burned more than others' fire,
So Spring guards with surface cold
The garnered heat of ages old:
Hers to sow the seed of bread,
That man and all the kinds be fed;   90
And, when the sunlight fills the hours,
Dissolves the crust, displays the flowers.

The world rolls round,—mistrust it not,—
Befalls again what once befell;
All things return, both sphere and mote,   95

And I shall hear my bluebird's note,
And dream the dream of Auburn dell.

When late I walked, in earlier days,
All was stiff and stark;
Knee-deep snows choked all the ways,   100
In the sky no spark;
Firm-braced I sought my ancient woods,
Struggling through the drifted roads;
The whited desert knew me not,
Snow-ridges masked each darling spot;   105
The summer dells, by genius haunted,
One arctic moon had disenchanted.
All the sweet secrets therein hid
By Fancy, ghastly spells undid.
Eldest mason, Frost, had piled   110
With wicked ingenuity
Swift cathedrals in the wild.
The piny hosts were sheeted ghosts
In the star-lit minster aisled.
I found no joy: the icy wind   115
Might rule the forest to his mind.
Who would freeze in frozen brakes?
Back to books and sheltered home,
And wood-fire flickering on the walls,
To hear, when, 'mid our talk and games,   120
Without the baffled north-wind calls.
But soft! a sultry morning breaks;
The cowslips make the brown brook gay;
A happier hour, a longer day.
Now the sun leads in the May,   125
Now desire of action wakes,
And the wish to roam.

The caged linnet in the Spring
Hearkens for the choral glee,
When his fellows on the wing   130

Migrate from the Southern Sea.
When trellised grapes their flowers unmask,
And the new-born tendrils twine,
The old wine darkling in the cask
Feels the bloom on the living vine,   135
And bursts the hoops at hint of Spring:
And so perchance, in Adam's race,
Of Eden's bower some dream-like trace
Survived the Flight, and swam the Flood,
And wakes the wish in youngest blood   140
To tread the forfeit Paradise,
And feed once more the exile's eyes;
And ever when the happy child
In May beholds the blooming wild,
And hears in heaven the bluebird sing,   145
'Onward,' he cries, 'your baskets bring,—
In the next field is air more mild,
And o'er yon hazy crest is Eden's balmier Spring.'

Not for a regiment's parade,
Nor evil laws or rulers made,   150
Blue Walden rolls its cannonade,
But for a lofty sign
Which the Zodiac threw,
That the bondage-days are told,
And waters free as winds shall flow.   155
Lo! how all the tribes combine
To rout the flying foe.
See, every patriot oak-leaf throws
His elfin length upon the snows,
Not idle, since the leaf all day   160
Draws to the spot the solar ray,
Ere sunset quarrying inches down,
And half way to the mosses brown;
While the grass beneath the rime
Has hints of the propitious time,   165
And upward pries and perforates

Through the cold slab a thousand gates,
Till green lances peering through
Bend happy in the welkin blue.

April cold with dropping rain   170
Willows and lilacs brings again,
The whistle of returning birds,
And trumpet-lowing of the herds.
The scarlet maple-keys betray
What potent blood hath modest May.   175
What fiery force the earth renews,
The wealth of forms, the flush of hues;
Joy shed in rosy waves abroad
Flows from the heart of Love, the lord.

Hither rolls the storm of heat;   180
I feel its finer billows beat
Like a sea which me infolds;
Heat with viewless fingers moulds,
Swells, and mellows, and matures,
Paints, and flavors, and allures,   185
Bird and briar inly warms,
Still enriches and transforms,
Gives the reed and lily length,
Adds to oak and oxen strength,
Boils the world in tepid lakes,   190
Burns the world, yet burnt remakes;
Enveloping heat, enchanted robe,
Wraps the daisy and the globe,
Transforming what it doth infold,
Life out of death, new out of old,   195
Painting fawns' and leopards' fells,
Seethes the gulf-encrimsoning shells,
Fires gardens with a joyful blaze
Of tulips, in the morning's rays.
The dead log touched bursts into leaf,   200
The wheat-blade whispers of the sheaf.
What god is this imperial Heat,

Earth's prime secret, sculpture's seat?
Doth it bear hidden in its heart
Water-line patterns of all art,   205
All figures, organs, hues, and graces?
Is it Dædalus? is it Love?
Or walks in mask almighty Jove,
And drops from Power's redundant horn
All seeds of beauty to be born?   210

Where shall we keep the holiday,
And duly greet the entering May?
Too strait and low our cottage doors,
And all unmeet our carpet floors;
Nor spacious court, nor monarch's hall,   215
Suffice to hold the festival.
Up and away! where haughty woods
Front the liberated floods:
We will climb the broad-backed hills,
Hear the uproar of their joy;   220
We will mark the leaps and gleams
Of the new-delivered streams,
And the murmuring rivers of sap
Mount in the pipes of the trees,
Giddy with day, to the topmost spire,   225
Which for a spike of tender green
Bartered its powdery cap;
And the colors of joy in the bird,
And the love in its carol heard,
Frog and lizard in holiday coats,   230
And turtle brave in his golden spots;
We will hear the tiny roar
Of the insects evermore,
While cheerful cries of crag and plain
Reply to the thunder of river and main.   235

As poured the flood of the ancient sea
Spilling over mountain chains,
Bending forests as bends the sedge,

319

Faster flowing o'er the plains,—
A world-wide wave with a foaming edge 240
That rims the running silver sheet,—
So pours the deluge of the heat
Broad northward o'er the land,
Painting artless paradises,
Drugging herbs with Syrian spices, 245
Fanning secret fires which glow
In columbine and clover-blow,
Climbing the northern zones,
Where a thousand pallid towns
Lie like cockles by the main, 250
Or tented armies on a plain.
The million-handed sculptor moulds
Quaintest bud and blossom folds,
The million-handed painter pours
Opal hues and purple dye; 255
Azaleas flush the island floors,
And the tints of heaven reply.

Wreaths for the May! for happy Spring
Today shall all her dowry bring,
The love of kind, the joy, the grace, 260
Hymen of element and race,
Knowing well to celebrate
With song and hue and star and state,
With tender light and youthful cheer,
The spousals of the new-born year. 265
Lo Love's inundation poured
Over space and race abroad!

Spring is strong and virtuous,
Broad-sowing, cheerful, plenteous,
Quickening underneath the mould 270
Grains beyond the price of gold.
So deep and large her bounties are,
That one broad, long midsummer day

Shall to the planet overpay
The ravage of a year of war.   275

Drug the cup, thou butler sweet,
And send the nectar round;
The feet that slid so long on sleet
Are glad to feel the ground.
Fill and saturate each kind   280
With good according to its mind,
Fill each kind and saturate
With good agreeing with its fate,
Willow and violet, maiden and man.

The bittersweet, the haunting air   285
Creepeth, bloweth everywhere;
It preys on all, all prey on it,
Blooms in beauty, thinks in wit,
Stings the strong with enterprise,
Makes travellers long for Indian skies,   290
And, where it comes, this courier fleet
Fans in all hearts expectance sweet,
As if tomorrow should redeem
The vanished rose of evening's dream.
By houses lies a fresher green,   295
On men and maids a ruddier mien,
As if Time brought a new relay
Of shining virgins every May,
And Summer came to ripen maids
To a beauty that not fades.   300

The ground-pines wash their rusty green,
The maple-tops their crimson tint,
On the soft path each track is seen,
The girl's foot leaves its neater print.
The pebble loosened from the frost   305
Asks of the urchin to be tossed.
In flint and marble beats a heart,

The kind Earth takes her children's part,
The green lane is the school-boy's friend,
Low leaves his quarrel apprehend,   310
The fresh ground loves his top and ball,
The air rings jocund to his call,
The brimming brook invites a leap,
He dives the hollow, climbs the steep.
The youth reads omens where he goes,   315
And speaks all languages the rose.
The wood-fly mocks with tiny noise
The far halloo of human voice;
The perfumed berry on the spray
Smacks of faint memories far away.   320
A subtle chain of countless rings
The next unto the farthest brings,
And, striving to be man, the worm
Mounts through all the spires of form.

I saw the bud-crowned Spring go forth,   325
Stepping daily onward north
To greet staid ancient cavaliers
Filing single in stately train.
And who, and who are the travellers?
They were Night and Day, and Day and Night,   330
Pilgrims wight with step forthright.
I saw the Days deformed and low,
Short and bent by cold and snow;
The merry Spring threw wreaths on them,
Flower-wreaths gay with bud and bell;   335
Many a flower and many a gem,
They were refreshed by the smell,
They shook the snow from hats and shoon,
They put their April raiment on;
And those eternal forms,   340
Unhurt by a thousand storms,
Shot up to the height of the sky again
And danced as merrily as young men.

I saw them mask their awful glance
Sidewise meek in gossamer lids,   345
And to speak my thought if none forbids,
It was as if the eternal gods,
Tired of their starry periods,
Hid their majesty in cloth
Woven of tulips and painted moth.   350
On carpets green the maskers march
Below May's well-appointed arch,
Each star, each god, each grace amain,
Every joy and virtue speed,
Marching duly in her train,   355
And fainting Nature at her need
Is made whole again.

'Twas the vintage-day of field and wood
When magic wine for bards is brewed;
Every tree and stem and chink   360
Gushed with syrup to the brink:
The air stole into the streets of towns,
And betrayed the fund of joy
To the high-school and medalled boy:
On from hall to chamber ran,   365
From youth to maid, from boy to man,
To babes, and to old eyes as well.
'Once more,' the old man cried, 'ye clouds,
Airy turrets purple-piled,
Which once my infancy beguiled,   370
Beguile me with the wonted spell.
I know ye skilful to convoy
The total freight of hope and joy
Into rude and homely nooks,
Shed mocking lustres on shelf of books,   375
On farmer's byre, on meadow-pipes,
Or on a pool of dancing chips.
I care not if the pomps you show
Be what they soothfast appear,

Or if yon realms in sunset glow   380
Be bubbles of the atmosphere.
And if it be to you allowed
To fool me with a shining cloud,
So only new griefs are consoled
By new delights, as old by old,   385
Frankly I will be your guest,
Count your change and cheer the best.
The world hath overmuch of pain,—
If Nature give me joy again,
Of such deceit I'll not complain.'   390

Ah! well I mind the calendar,
Faithful through a thousand years,
Of the painted race of flowers,
Exact to days, exact to hours,
Counted on the spacious dial   395
Yon broidered zodiac girds.
I know the pretty almanac
Of the punctual coming-back,
On their due days, of the birds.
I marked them yestermorn,   400
A flock of finches darting
Beneath the crystal arch,
Piping, as they flew, a march,—
Belike the one they used in parting
Last year from yon oak or larch.   405
Dusky sparrows in a crowd,
Diving, darting northward free,
Suddenly betook them all,
Every one to his hole in the wall,
Or to his niche in the apple-tree.   410
I greet with joy the choral trains
Fresh from palms and Cuba's canes.
Best gems of Nature's cabinet,
With dews of tropic morning wet,
Beloved of children, bards, and Spring,   415
O birds, your perfect virtues bring,

Your song, your forms, your rhythmic flight,
Your manners for the heart's delight,
Nestle in hedge, or barn, or roof,
Here weave your chamber weatherproof,   420
Forgive our harms, and condescend
To man as to a lubber friend,
And, generous, teach his awkward race
Courage, and probity, and grace!

Poets praise that hidden wine   425
Hid in milk we drew
At the barrier of Time,
When our life was new.
We had eaten fairy fruit,
We were quick from head to foot,   430
All the forms we looked on shone
As with diamond dews thereon.
What cared we for costly joys,
The Museum's far-fetched toys?
Gleam of sunshine on the wall   435
Poured a deeper cheer than all
The revels of the Carnival.
We a pine-grove did prefer
To a marble theatre,
Could with gods on mallows dine,   440
Nor cared for spices or for wine.
Wreaths of mist and rainbows spanned,
Arch on arch, the grimmest land;
Whistle of a woodland bird
Made the pulses dance,   445
Note of horn in valleys heard
Filled the region with romance.

None can tell how sweet,
How virtuous, the morning air;
Every accent vibrates well;   450
Not alone the wood-bird's call,
Or shouting boys that chase their ball,

Pass the height of minstrel skill,
But the plowman's thoughtless cry,
Lowing oxen, sheep that bleat,   455
And the joiner's hammer-beat,
Softened are above their will.
All grating discords melt,
No dissonant note is dealt,
And though thy voice be shrill   460
Like rasping file on steel,
Such is the temper of the air,
Echo waits with art and care,
And will the faults of song repair.

So by remote Superior Lake,   465
And by resounding Mackinac,
When northern storms the forest shake,
And billows on the long beach break,
The artful Air doth separate
Note by note all sounds that grate,   470
Smothering in her ample breast
All but godlike words,
Reporting to the happy ear
Only purified accords.
Strangely wrought from barking waves,   475
Soft music daunts the Indian braves,—
Convent-chanting which the child
Hears pealing from the panther's cave
And the impenetrable wild.

One musician is sure,   480
His wisdom will not fail,
He has not tasted wine impure,
Nor bent to passion frail.
Age cannot cloud his memory,
Nor grief untune his voice,   485
Ranging down the ruled scale
From tone of joy to inward wail,
Tempering the pitch of all

In his windy cave.
He all the fables knows, 490
And in their causes tells,—
Knows Nature's rarest moods,
Ever on her secret broods.
The Muse of men is coy,
Oft courted will not come; 495
In palaces and market squares
Entreated, she is dumb;
But my minstrel knows and tells
The counsel of the gods,
Knows of Holy Book the spells, 500
Knows the law of Night and Day,
And the heart of girl and boy,
The tragic and the gay,
And what is writ on Table Round
Of Arthur and his peers, 505
What sea and land discoursing say
In sidereal years.
He renders all his lore
In numbers wild as dreams,
Modulating all extremes,— 510
What the spangled meadow saith
To the children who have faith;
Only to children children sing,
Only to youth will spring be spring.

Who is the Bard thus magnified? 515
When did he sing? and where abide?

Chief of song where poets feast
Is the wind-harp which thou seest
In the casement at my side.

Æolian harp, 520
How strangely wise thy strain!
Gay for youth, gay for youth,
(Sweet is art, but sweeter truth,)

In the hall at summer eve
Fate and Beauty skilled to weave.   525
From the eager opening strings
Rung loud and bold the song.
Who but loved the wind-harp's note?
How should not the poet doat
On its mystic tongue,   530
With its primeval memory,
Reporting what old minstrels said
Of Merlin locked the harp within,—
Merlin paying the pain of sin,
Pent in a dungeon made of air,—   535
And some attain his voice to hear,
Words of pain and cries of fear,
But pillowed all on melody,
As fits the griefs of bards to be.
And what if that all-echoing shell,   540
Which thus the buried Past can tell,
Should rive the Future, and reveal
What his dread folds would fain conceal?
It shares the secret of the Earth,
And of the kinds that owe her birth.   545
Speaks not of self that mystic tone,
But of the Overgods alone:
It trembles to the cosmic breath,—
As it heareth, so it saith;
Obeying meek the primal Cause,   550
It is the tongue of mundane laws.
And this, at least, I dare affirm,
Since genius too has bound and term,
There is no bard in all the choir,
Not Homer's self, the poet sire,   555
Wise Milton's odes of pensive pleasure,
Or Shakspeare, whom no mind can measure,
Nor Collins' verse of tender pain,
Nor Byron's clarion of disdain,
Scott, the delight of generous boys,   560
Or Wordsworth, Pan's recording voice,—

Not one of all can put in verse,
Or to this presence could rehearse,
The sights and voices ravishing
The boy knew on the hills in Spring   565
When pacing through the oaks he heard
Sharp queries of the sentry-bird,
The heavy grouse's sudden whirr,
The rattle of the kingfisher;
Saw bonfires of the harlot flies   570
In the lowland, when day dies;
Or marked, benighted and forlorn,
The first far signal-fire of morn.
These syllables that Nature spoke,
And the thoughts that in him woke,   575
Can adequately utter none
Save to his ear the wind-harp lone.
And best can teach its Delphian chord
How Nature to the soul is moored,
If once again that silent string,   580
As erst it wont, would thrill and ring.

Not long ago, at eventide,
It seemed, so listening, at my side
A window rose, and, to say sooth,
I looked forth on the fields of youth: 585
I saw fair boys bestriding steeds,
I knew their forms in fancy weeds,
Long, long concealed by sundering fates,
Mates of my youth,—yet not my mates,
Stronger and bolder far than I,   590
With grace, with genius, well attired,
And then as now from far admired,
Followed with love
They knew not of,
With passion cold and shy.   595
O joy, for what recoveries rare!
Renewed, I breathe Elysian air,
See youth's glad mates in earliest bloom,—

Break not my dream, obtrusive tomb!
Or teach thou, Spring! the grand recoil 600
Of life resurgent from the soil
Wherein was dropped the mortal spoil.

Soft on the south-wind sleeps the haze:
So on thy broad mystic van
Lie the opal-colored days, 605
And waft the miracle to man.
Soothsayer of the eldest gods,
Repairer of what harms betide,
Revealer of the inmost powers
Prometheus proffered, Jove denied; 610
Disclosing treasures more than true,
Or in what far tomorrow due;
Speaking by the tongues of flowers,
By the ten-tongued laurel speaking,
Singing by the oriole songs, 615
Heart of bird the man's heart seeking;
Whispering hints of treasure hid
Under Morn's unlifted lid,
Islands looming just beyond
The dim horizon's utmost bound;— 620
Who can, like thee, our rags upbraid
Or taunt us with our hope decayed?
Or who like thee persuade,
Making the splendor of the air,
The morn and sparkling dew, a snare? 625
Or who resent
Thy genius, wiles, and blandishment?

There is no orator prevails
To beckon or persuade
Like thee the youth or maid: 630
Thy birds, thy songs, thy brooks, thy gales,
Thy blooms, thy kinds,
Thy echoes in the wilderness,

Soothe pain, and age, and love's distress,
Fire fainting will, and build heroic minds.   635

For thou, O Spring! canst renovate
All that high God did first create.
Be still his arm and architect,
Rebuild the ruin, mend defect;
Chemist to vamp old worlds with new,   640
Coat sea and sky with heavenlier blue,
New-tint the plumage of the birds,
And slough decay from grazing herds,
Sweep ruins from the scarped mountain,
Cleanse the torrent at the fountain,   645
Purge alpine air by towns defiled,
Bring to fair mother fairer child,
Not less renew the heart and brain,
Scatter the sloth, wash out the stain,
Make the aged eye sun-clear,   650
To parting soul bring grandeur near.
Under gentle types, my Spring
Masks the might of Nature's king,
An energy that searches thorough
From Chaos to the dawning morrow;   655
Into all our human plight,
The soul's pilgrimage and flight;
In city or in solitude,
Step by step, lifts bad to good,
Without halting, without rest,   660
Lifting Better up to Best;
Planting seeds of knowledge pure,
Through earth to ripen, through heaven endure.

TEXTS

(A) MS, Wake Forest University Library, by permission, printer's copy for B; (B) *May-Day* (Boston, 1867), 3–39; (C) *May-Day* (London, 1867), 5–41.

May-Day and Other Pieces (1867)

Format: The 1867 printing indents the first line of each of the poem's 31 verse paragraphs, with the exception of the first, which begins with a drop cap. In (A), however, Emerson clearly indents on only seven occasions, in lines 1, 55, 68, 93, 98, 358, and 391, and of these, lines 1, 55, 93, and 391 coincide with the first lines on their respective pages. The editors have regularized to reflect Emerson's scribal practice, eliminating the indentations, but retaining the white lines (or line spaces) with which Emerson regularly distinguished his verse paragraphs.

Pre-copy-text forms: The several major drafts and the numerous brief draft passages that contributed to the text are discussed in *PN*, 853–856. A significant draft of lines 98–126 was subsequently published from notebook Orientalist in *TN,* II, 122.

VARIANTS

1 Daughter ... Spring, (B-C) | Io paean! The darling Spring (A)
2–11 [*Lines canceled*] (CC7)
3 Maketh all things softly (A-C) | Teaching barren moods to (CC7)
4 Painteth pictures (A-C) | Painting pictures (CC7)
5 cowslip-wreaths, (B-C) | cowslips wreathed, (A)
6 breathes. (B-C) | breathed, / Dripping dew cold daffadillies, / Making drunk with wine of lilies, (A)
7 sweet (B-C) | <gree>sweet (A)
8 white, (B-C) | white (A) || Gilead tree, (A) | Gilead-tree (B-C)
10 hilloa (A) | hilloa, (B-C)
11 hip, hip, (A-B) | hip, hip (C) || times three. (B-C) | times three (A)
12 bland; (B-C) | bland (A)
[*inscription runs off page edge*]
14 land? (A-C) | strands? (CC7)
16 shepherd's hands, (B-C) | shepherds' hands; (A)
18 day? (B-C) | day, (A)
19 sphere (B-C) | space (A)
20 convey. (B-C) | convey: (A)
21 'twas (B-C) | twas (A)
22 lake, (B-C) | lake (A)
26 into (A-B) | unto (C)

27 bark, (B-C) | bark (A)
29 leads, (B-C) | leads (A)
37 [*Line canceled*] (CC7)
40 things. / [*white line*] (B-C) | things. / [*end of page*] (A) || [*Line canceled*] (CC7)
47 pearl: (B-C) | pearl, (A)
49 felloes (B-C) | spondyls (A)
50 orbs (B-C) | tires (A)
59 *o-ka-lee,* (B-C) | o-ka-lee, (A)
60 snow; (B-C) | snow, (A)
61 The sparrow meek, (B-C) | And song-sparrow, (A)
62 Her (B-C) | Its (A) || snowdrift (A) | snow-drift (B-C)
64 Her (B-C) | Its (A)
68 foolish fond, (A-C) | her time forerun, (CC7)
70 glow, (B-C) | glow (A)
74 one,— (B-C) | one: (A)
81 Southern (B-C) | southern (A) || Northern (B-C) | northern (A)
90 fed; (B-C) | fed, (A)
91 And, (B-C) | She (A) || sunlight fills (B-C) | sun fulfils (A)
92 flowers. (B-C) | flowers [*inscription runs off page edge*] (A)
93 round,— (B-C) | round, (A) || not,— (B-C) | not, (A)

332

94 befell; (B-C) | befel; (A)

97 the (B-C) | <a>the (A)

100 Knee-deep (B-C) | Kneedeep (A)

101 spark; (B-C) | spark: (A)

102 Firm-braced (B-C) | Firmbraced (A) || ancient (B-C) | Ancient (A)

103 roads; (B-C) | <w>roads; (A)

104 desert (B-C) | desart (A)

105 Snow-ridges (B-C) | Snowridges (A) || spot; (B-C) | spot, (A)

110 piled (A) | piled, (B-C)

111 ingenuity (A) | ingenuity, (B-C) | [*Line canceled*] (CC7)

112 wild. (A) | wild; (B-C)

117 in frozen brakes? (A-C) | on frozen lakes? (CC7)

121 north-wind (B-C) | northwind (A)

122 breaks; (B-C) | breaks, (A)

123 gay; (B-C) | gay, (A)

124 day. (B-C) | day,— (A) | day; (CC7)

128 Spring (A, C) | spring (B)

131 Sea. (A) | Sea; (B-C)

135 vine, (B-C) | <w>vine, (A)

136 Spring: (A, C) | spring: (B)

137 so (A) | so, (B-C)

144 wild, (B-C) | wilde, (A)

146 'Onward,' (A) | "Onward," (B-C) || 'your (A) | "your (B-C)

148 Spring.' (A, C) | spring." (B)

153 Zodiac (B-C) | Zodiack (A)

154 are (B-C) | <were>are (A)

163 half way (A) | half-way (B-C)

175 May. (A) | May; (B-C)

177 hues; (B-C) | hues, (A)

179 lord. (A) | Lord. (B-C)

185 flavors, (A-B) | flavours, (C)

186 briar [*Ed.*] | briar<s> (A) | brier (B-C)

190–193 [*Lines bracketed*] (CC7)

191 remakes; (B-C) | remakes, (A)

194 infold, (B-C) | enfold, (A) [*cf. line 182*]

198 gardens (A-B) | garden (C)

199 tulips, (A-B) | tulips (C)

201 of (B-C) | <to>of (A) || sheaf. (B-C) | sheaf (A) [*inscription runs off page edge*]

203 seat? (B-C) | seat<,>? (A)

205 Water-line (B-C) | Waterline (A)

206 graces? (B-C) | graces, (A) | [*Line bracketed*] (CC7)

214 floors; (B-C) | floors, (A)

215 hall, (B-C) | hall (A)

219 broad-backed (B-C) | broadbacked (A)

224 trees, (B-C) | trees (A)

227 cap; (B-C) | cap: (A)

228 colors (A-B) | colours (C)

229 heard, (B-C) | heard (A)

231 spots; (B-C) | spots: (A)

234 of (A-C) | from (CC7)

235 main. (A, C, CC7) | main (B)

239 plains,— (B-C) | plains, (A)

241 sheet,— (B-C) | sheet, (A)

245 Drugging . . . spices, (B-C) | Retouching old with quaint surprises, (A)

247 clover-blow, (B-C) | cloverblow; (A)

255 dye; (B-C) | dye, (A)

259 Today (A) | To-day (B-C)

263 song (B-C) | song, (A) || hue (B-C) | hue, (A) || star (B-C) | star, (A)

265 new-born (B-C) | newborn (A)

266–267 [*Lines bracketed*] (CC7)

267 abroad! (B-C) | abroad. (A) [*Note: The manuscript page continues with a white line followed by six canceled lines, later repeated as lines 276–81. Then follows an inserted leaf (blue, lined paper) bearing lines 268–281.*]

268 Spring (B-C) | She (A)

269 Broad-sowing, cheerful, (B-C) | Cheerful, broadsowing, (A)

271 gold. (B-C) | gold; (A)

273 broad, (B-C) | broad (A)

274   Shall (B-C) | Will (A)

277   nectar (B-C) | madness (A)

283–284 fate, / Willow (B-C) | fate,—/ Willow (A) | fate, / ↑ and soft perfection of its plan, ↓ / Willow (CC7)

285   bittersweet, (A) | bitter-sweet, (B-C) || air (A-B) | air, (C)

291   And, (A) | And (B-C) || comes, (A) | comes (B-C)

293   tomorrow (A) | to-morrow (B-C)

297   Time (A) | time (B-C)

298   virgins (B-C) | Virgins (A)

301   green, (B-C) | green (A)

306   tossed. (A) | tost. (B-C)

308   Earth (B-C) | earth (A)

321–324 A subtle . . . form. (B-C) | [*Lines not present*] (A)

328   single (B-C) | singly (A)

333   snow; (B-C) | snow, (A)

335   bell; (B-C) | bell, (A)

339   on; (B-C) | on, (A)

340   forms, (B-C) | forms (A)

341   storms, (B-C) | storms (A)

342   again (A) | again, (B-C)

345   lids, (A) | lids; (B-C)

347   gods, (B-C) | gods (A)

348   periods, (B-C) | periods (A)

358   'Twas (B-C) | Twas (A) || wood (A) | wood, (B-C)

361   brink: (A) | brink. (B-C)

362–363 towns, / And (A-C) | towns, / Refreshed the wise, reformed the clowns, / And (CC7)

367   well. (B-C) | well; (A)

368   more,' (B-C) | more', (A)

370   beguiled, (B-C) | beguiled (A)

371   wonted spell. (B-C) | <self [?]>wonted spell (A)

376   meadow-pipes, (B-C) | grassy pipes, (A) | pasture rude, (CC7)

377   Or on a pool of dancing chips. (A-C) | And stony pathway to the wood. (CC7)

390   complain.' (B-C) | complain. (A)

391   Ah! (B-C) | Ah, (A) || calendar, (B-C) | calendar (A)

396   zodiac (B-C) | zodiack (A)

403   march,— (B-C) | march, (A)

405   larch. (A) | larch; (B-C)

410   apple-tree. (B-C) | appletree. (A)

411   greet with joy the choral (B-C) | <hailed> ↑greet↓ with joy the <flying> ↑choral↓ (A)

412   palms and Cuba's canes. (B-C) | <ricefield> ↑<the> palms↓ & Cuba's canes<;—> ↑.↓ (A)

413   Best (B-C) | <O> ↑Best↓ (A)

415   bards, (B-C) | bard<,>s, (A)

416   O birds, your perfect virtues (B-C) | ↑O birds,↓ Your perfect <chorus hither> ↑virtues↓ (A)

420   weatherproof, (A) | weather-proof, (B-C)

422   man (A) | man, (B-C)

423   his (B-C) | <our> ↑his↓ (A)

442   rainbows (A) | rainbow (B-C) || spanned, (B-C) | spanned (A)

443   arch, (B-C) | arch (A)

448   sweet, (B-C) | sweet (A)

449   virtuous, (B-C) | virtuous (A) || air; (B-C) | air, (A)

451   Not (B-C) | Not, (A)

453   height of minstrel (B-C) | <learned minstrels> ↑height of minstrel↓ (A)

454   plowman's (A) | ploughman's (B-C)

456   hammer-beat, (B-C) | hammer-beat (A)

457–458 will. / All (B-C) | will, / <Take tones from groves they wandered through / Or flutes which passing angels blew.> / All (A) [*The cancellation is in pencil, as is a note ("not in text") not in Emerson's hand.*]

462   air, (B-C) | air (A)

467   the forest (A-B) | and forest (C)

469   Air (B-C) | air (A) ‖ doth (A-C) |
will (CC7)

475–476 Strangely . . . braves,— (B-C) |
Music daunts the Indian brave (A)

477   Convent-chanting (A-C) |
Convent-chanting, (CC7)

491   tells,— (B-C) | tells (A)

492   moods, (B-C) | moods (A)

494   Muse (B-C) | muse (A)

495   come; (B-C) | come, (A)

497   Entreated, (B-C) | Entreated (A)
‖ dumb; (B-C) | dumb. (A)

500   of Holy Book the spells, (B-C) |
<the spell> of Holy Book<,> ↑ the
spells ↓ (A)

502   girl and boy, (B-C) | girl<s> &
boy<s> (A)

504   Table Round (B-C) | Round
Table (A)

510   extremes,— (B-C) | extremes
(A)

512   children who have faith; (B-C) |
child ↑ ren ↓ who <has>have faith.
(A)

513   children children (A-C) |
children, children (CC7)

516   sing? (A-B) | sing, (C)

517   poets feast (B-C) | Poets feast,
(A)

518   wind-harp (B-C) | Wind-harp
(A)

520   Æolian harp, (B-C) | Aeolian
harp (A)

522   youth, gay (A-C) | youth, bard
(CC7)

523   (Sweet (B-C) | Sweet (A) ‖
truth,) (B-C) | truth. (A)

525   Fate (B-C) | Life (A)

528   but loved (B-C) | loved not (A) ‖
wind-harp's (B-C) | windharp's (A)

529   should (B-C) | <could>should
(A) ‖ doat (B-C) | <dote>doat (A)

530   tongue, (B-C) | tongue<,>? (A)

532   said (A-C) | told (CC7)

533   within,— (B-C) | within, (A)

535   air,— (B-C) | air, (A)

537   cries (B-C) | <f>cries (A)

540–552 And what . . . dare affirm, (B-
C) | ↑ And what . . . dare affirm, ↓
(A) [*Added by Emerson on a separate
sheet of paper, with directions to the
printer as to their location.*]

540   shell, (B-C) | shell (A)

543   dread folds (A-C) | folds (CC7)

544   Earth, (A) | earth, (B-C)

547   Overgods (B-C) | overgods (A)

549   saith; (B-C) | saith, (A)

552   [*In* (A) *this is the last line of the
12-line insert; at the top of the next page,
Emerson has left uncanceled:* And more
than this I dare affirm,]

553   too has bound and term, (B-C) |
<also> ↑ too ↓ has <its> ↑ bound
& ↓ term, (A)

554   choir, (B-C) | quire, (A)

561   Wordsworth, Pan's recording
voice,— (B-C) |
Wordsworth<'s> ↑, ↓ Nature's
nearest voice, (A)

562   can (B-C) | can can (A) ‖ verse,
(B-C) | verse (A)

563   rehearse, (B-C) | rehearse (A)

565   Spring (A) | spring, (B) | Spring,
(C)

568   whirr, (A, C) | whir, (B)

570   flies (B-C) | flies, (A)

572   marked, (B-C) | saw, (A)

577–578 lone. / And (A-C) | lone. /
[*Added lines: see note to ll. 99–102 of*
"The Harp"] / And (CC7)

578   Delphian (B-C) | <d>Delphian
(A)

582   Not . . . eventide, (B-C) | ↑ Not
. . . eventide, ↓ (A)

583   It seemed, so (B-C) | <Me>
↑ I ↓ thought, <thus> ↑ so ↓ (A)

587   fancy weeds, (B-C) | fancy-weeds,
(A)

588   Long, (B-C) I Long (A)

596–602 O joy, . . . spoil. (B-C) I ↑O
joy, ↑ ! ↓ . . . spoil, ↓ (A) [*The lines are
added on an inserted sheet of blue lined
paper, with Emerson's directions to the
printer indicating their location.*]

600   Or teach (B-C) I Teach (A) II
Spring! (B-C) I O Spring! (A)

602   spoil. (B-C) I spoil, (A)

603   south-wind (B-C) I southwind
(A) II haze: (B) I haze (A) I haze! (C)

605   opal-colored days, (B) I opal-
colored days (A) I opal-coloured
days, (C)

607   gods, (B-C) I gods (A)

608   Repairer . . . betide, (B-C) I
<Herald of joy that shall betide>
↑Repairer . . . betide ↓ (A)

612   tomorrow (A) I to-morrow (B-C)

614   laurel (B-C) I lily (A)

620   bound;— (B-C) I bound; (A)

621   upbraid (A) I upbraid, (B-C)

624   splendor (A-B) I splendour (C)
II air, (B-C) I air (A)

625   dew, (B-C) I dew (A)

628   prevails (B-C) I ↑ ↑prevails ↓ (A)

629   To (B-C) I <Can> ↑To ↓ (A)

631   Thy (B-C) I <Nor morn nor eve
thy music fails;> / Thy (A)

633   wilderness, (B-C) I wilderness
(A)

634   Soothe (B-C) I <Heal>
↑Soothe ↓ (A)

635   build (B-C) I /feed/rebuild/
(A)

636   thou, O Spring! canst renovate
(B-C) I thou <fair>O Spring!
<hast> ↑ canst ↓ renovate<d> (A)

637   did first create. (B-C) I <at>
↑did ↓ first create<d>, (A)

638   Be still his arm and architect, (B-
C) I <<Gods> ↑His ↓ steward
thou,> ↑Be still his arm ↓ &
architect (A)

639   defect; (B-C) I defect, (A)

640   worlds (B-C) I <stuff>
↑worlds ↓ (A)

642–643 New-tint . . . herds, (B-C) I
↑To ↓ Slough decay from grazing
herds / <Coat> New tint the
plumage of the birds, (A)

648   brain, (B-C) I brain (A)

649   Scatter the (B-C) I Drive out (A)

650   sun-clear, (B-C) I sun-clear (A)

651   [*Following this line, at the bottom of
the page in* (A), *is a canceled notation in
Emerson's hand:* "Two or three lines to
be added here." *Then follows, on the
next page, twelve unused lines:* "Nor less
the golden time / Spoke to the eye
with optic chime / By the hill-bound
woodland lake, / When flaws of wind
the water whipt / Into fleets of
ripples gay; / The swift slight
spiritual drift / More like northern
meteor's play / Than any spectacle
of day / [*white line*] / How easily doth
youth persuade / Its children to
delight! / What happy fools an image
made, / A sounding verse, a ballad
right!" *The next manuscript page is
headed* "Conclusion of 'May Day'" *and
contains the poem's final 16 lines.*]

653   king, (B-C) I King, (A) I King
(CC7)

655–656 morrow; / Into (B-C) I
morrow<;>. / If wisest prophets
truly teach, / Deeper far its virtues
reach, / Into (A)

657–658 flight; / In (B-C) I flight; /
Informs with grace all elements, /
Bane to benefit ferments; / In (A)

659   good, (B-C) I good; (A)

663   Through earth to ripen,
through heaven (B-C) I Ripening
harvests that (A)

NOTES

5.   Cf. Thoreau: "The marsh marigold—caltha palustris improperly called cow-slip" (*J*, III, 236).

12.   "The air is full of whistlings" occurs as a fragment in journal V (1844–1845): see *JMN*, IX, 169.

21–22.   "Apr. 5, [1856.] Walden fired a cannonade yesterday of a hundred guns, but not in honor of the birth of Napoleon" (*JMN*, XIV, 62; versified in 1861: see *JMN*, XV, 124). Edward cites this journal passage (*W*, IX, 457), but supposes that it refers to a literal cannonading by the Concord Artillery Company—and yet the reference is surely to the breaking up of the ice on Walden Pond.

27–35.   These lines were written in the spring of 1863: see *JMN*, XV, 341. In line 29 Emerson puns on Nestor, the aged counsellor or guide in the Homeric poems—and creatures that build nests.

49.   Felloes are the curved elements that, joined together at the end of the spokes, form the rim of a wooden wheel. Emerson originally wrote "spondyls," but these, the joints between the felloes, of course cannot be grasped. In the next line Emerson substituted "orbs" for "tires": in the metaphoric context of wooden wheels, tires would refer to the iron band affixed to the outside of the rim.

55–67.   A journal entry of April 1862: "Spring. Why complain of the cold slow spring? the bluebirds don't complain, the blackbirds make the maples ring with social cheer & jubilee, the robins know the snow must go & sparrows with prophetic eye that these bare osiers yet will hide their future nests in the pride of their foliage. And you alone with all your six feet of experience are the fool of the cold of the present moment, & cannot see the southing of the sun" (*JMN*, XV, 249–250).

67.   Emerson's astronomy is at fault here: he should say "northing," as Edward noticed (*W*, IX, 458).

85–86.   An 1863 journal entry reads: "How all magnifies New England & Massachusetts! A. said, her ice burns more than others' fire" (*JMN*, XV, 406). "A." has not been identified.

94.   The line occurs by itself on a page in journal VA, written in 1863: see *JMN*, XV, 308.

97.   The allusion is at once to the "Sweet Auburn" of Oliver Goldsmith's popular "Deserted Village" (1770), and to a wooded area in Cambridge, Mass., which Emerson knew prior to its development as Mount Auburn Cemetery. Ellen Emerson observed: "I know that he delighted in Mount Auburn which in his day

was called Sweet Auburn, a name he liked very much. It pleased him to have it named for the deserted village, and he objected much to the change to *Mount Auburn*. It was then [when Emerson attended Harvard, beginning in 1817] a wild tract and very pretty and full of flowers; the graves in it were few. It was his walking-ground almost every day when he was in Cambridge" ("What I Can Remember about Father," 1902, MS Am 1280.227, p. 14: Ralph Waldo Emerson Memorial Association deposit, Houghton Library, Harvard University. Emerson, who with his brother Charles attended the dedication of the cemetery in 1831 (*Chronology*, 64), later recalled the "voice of the bluebird and the witchcraft of the Mount Auburn dell in those days! (*W*, IX, 458).

98–103.   Evidently these lines are based on the same journal entry (3 March 1862) that describes Emerson's encounter with the titmouse in snow-choked Walden woods (see *JMN*, XV, 241, and "The Titmouse").

110–112.   "Winter builds / Sudden cathedrals in the wilds" occurs as a detached fragment in journal V, perhaps written in 1844 or 1845: see *JMN*, IX, 169.

127.   In an 1863 journal entry Emerson wrote: "The delight in the first days of spring, the 'wish to journeys make,' seems to be a reminiscence of Adam's Paradise, & the longing to return thither" (*JMN*, XV, 319; cf. lines 137–142, below).

132–136.   In his note to these lines, Edward Emerson associates them with his father's visit, during a lecture tour, to the Cincinnati winery of Nicholas Longworth. Moncure Conway, a Unitarian minister in the city at the time, described the visit in his *Autobiography*. He and Emerson were told by the German mastervintner that they had to keep an eye on the new bottles: "We find out about them when the vines in the vintage begin to flower; then the wine ferments and some bottles break"—adding that some of the casks would burst in the spring as well. Conway's recollection of the date of this visit seems confused: it probably occurred in 1857 (*Autobiography: Memories and Experiences of Moncure Daniel Conway*, 2 vols. [Boston, 1904], I, 283–284).

137–142.   These lines were written in 1863: see *JMN*, XV, 318–319.

164–169.   An observation made in 1859: see *JMN*, XIV, 336.

170–173.   These lines were written in 1859: see *JMN*, XIV, 245.

205.   Water-line: it is unclear whether Emerson refers to water-marks in paper or to longitudinal cross-section plans for the building of ships. The term could refer to either.

278–279.   The prose germ for these lines is a journal entry of 15 March 1845: "How gladly, after three months sliding on snow, our feet find the ground again!" (*JMN*, IX, 150; versified on 169).

338

297–300. These lines were written in 1854: see *JMN*, XIII, 318, 411, and 491–492.

307–316. Compare a journal entry of 1848: "The earth takes the part of her children so quickly & adopts our thoughts, affections, & quarrels. The schoolboy finds every step of the ground on his way to school acquainted with his quarrel, & smartly expressing it. The ground knows so well his top & ball, the air itself is full of hoop-time, ball-time, swimming, sled, & skates. So ductile is the world. The rapt prophet finds it not less facile & intelligent. 'Tis Pentecost all, the rose speaks all languages. . ." (*JMN*, XI, 61–62). This entry is the source also of the poetic motto to the 1849 edition of *Nature*, which takes lines 315–316 and 321–324 (see the discussion in the headnote).

465. In 1866 Emerson recorded an anecdote from his brother-in-law, Dr. Charles T. Jackson, who had conducted a geological survey in Michigan twenty years earlier: "Dr. Jackson said, he was at Pulpit rock, Lake Superior, when he heard music, like rhythmical organ or vocal chanting, & believed it to come from some singers. But going on a little further, it ceased; in another direction, heard it again; & by & by perceived that it was the beating of the waves on the shore deprived of its harshness by the atmosphere" (*JMN*, XVI, 46). Edward Emerson claimed—obviously incorrectly—that his father heard this anecdote in 1874 (*W*, IX, 460).

469–474. The draft of this passage in poetry notebook KL[A] has been cross-referenced by Emerson to a passage in notebook S (Salvage): "Tis because Nature is an instrument so thoroughly musical, that the most aukward hand cannot draw a discord from it. A devil struck the chords in defiance, & his spite was punished by a sweeter melody than the angels made" (see *PN*, 575, and *TN*, III, 126).

570. Harlot flies: a very rare term for fireflies. Emerson's only other reference to them is in a journal entry of 10 June 1838: "The little harlot flies of the lowlands sparked in the grass & in the air" (*JMN*, VII, 10). The entire entry was versified and eventually published in *W*, IX, 346–347, with the non-authorial title "Night in June" (see *PN*, 827).

THE ADIRONDACS.

The plan of an excursion into the primitive wilderness of New York's Adirondac region was formed between James Russell Lowell and a painter friend of his, William James Stillman, who had recently moved to Cambridge following his founding and brief editorship in New York of *The Crayon*, America's first art journal. Stillman quickly attracted notice for the landscapes he exhibited at this time, including one that he called "The Procession of the Pines," a sublime scene painted at Follansbee Pond in the manner of the Hudson River School artists, particularly his teacher, Frederick Edwin Church and his friend, Sanford R. Gifford. It was Gifford who had urged on him the advantages of painting in the seclusion of wild Adirondac scenery, and Stillman had accepted the hint fervently, for many years making annual pilgrimages to the northern wilderness. He may also have been influenced in going there by a book published in 1849 with the Thoreauvian title, *The Adirondack; Or, Life in the Woods*, by Joel T. Headley, like Stillman a graduate of Union College in Schenectady.

Stillman's circle of acquaintance in Cambridge and Boston expanded rapidly after a first visit in 1855, and Lowell, who befriended him and contributed poems to *The Crayon*, introduced him to his own friends in the recently-established Saturday Club. In 1857 Stillman organized the first of several camping trips to Follansbee Pond. On this trip Stillman escorted Lowell's brother-in-law, Dr. Estes Howe, together with Howe's best friend, John Holmes, brother of Oliver Wendell Holmes. This excursion was so successful that a second and more ambitious one was scheduled for the next summer. Howe and Holmes would return (Oliver Wendell, it seems, was too entirely a man of the city to consider going). Five new campers, including Emerson and Lowell, were members of the Saturday Club: Louis Agassiz, professor of natural history at Harvard; Judge Ebenezer Rockwood Hoar, of Concord,

soon to be elevated to the Supreme Judicial Court of Massachu-
setts; and the convivial Horatio Woodman, whose great success in
life was to have founded the Saturday Club. The remaining two
members of the group were, like Howe and Holmes, not mem-
bers of the Club. These were Jeffries Wyman, professor of anat-
omy at Harvard and president of the Boston Society of Natural
History, and Dr. Amos Binney—not the acclaimed author of the
posthumously published *Terrestrial Air-Breathing Mollusks of the
United States* (1851), but his twenty-eight year-old eldest son, of
the same name, a friend and patron of Stillman. Longfellow had
also been invited, but on hearing that Emerson had purchased a
double-barreled gun (a combination rifle and shotgun), he po-
litely but emphatically asked to be excused (Longfellow, *Letters*,
IV, 92). Nor was he the only one concerned on this point.

Setting out on Monday, 2 August 1858, Emerson, together with
most of the party, arrived by nightfall in the town of Lake George,
N.Y., at the southern end of the Champlain Valley. The next day
they traveled "down the Lake" to Burlington, Vt., crossed by
steamer to Port Kent, then by stage the short distance to Kee-
seville, N.Y., where they joined Stillman. There they were also
greeted by a large group of Keeseville folk hoping to get a glimpse
of Agassiz, who had been in the news lately for declining an invita-
tion from Louis Napoleon to head the natural history museum in
Paris, the Jardin des Plantes. On Wednesday morning, the party
set out, as Emerson records, "in strong country carts" down the
rough road along the Ausable River to the village of Saranac Lake,
the site of "Martin's Beach," as Emerson calls it. This was in fact a
hotel operated by William F. Martin, who specialized in outfitting
just such camping expeditions as this one. William H. H. Murray
wrote ten years later that "Martin is one of the few men in the
world who seem to know how 'to keep a hotel.' At his house you
can easily and cheaply obtain your entire outfit for a trip of any
length. Here it is that the celebrated Long Lake guides, with their
unrivalled boats, principally resort. Here, too, many of the Sara-
nac guides, some of them surpassed by none, make their head-
quarters" (*Adventures in the Wilderness; Or, Camp-Life in the Adiron-
dacks* [Boston, 1869], 47).

Provisioned, and with eight guides hired and assigned, the party traversed Lower Saranac Lake, then passed by the Saranac River to Round Lake, now known as Middle Saranac Lake. After crossing that, they were assisted by their guides over a portage to Upper Saranac Lake, the lower end of which they rowed across to a second portage, the mile-long "Indian Carry," at the end of which they found, at Stony Creek Ponds, the log house of Stephen C. Martin, William Martin's brother and Stillman's own favorite guide and life-long friend. The party rested there during a day of rainy weather before setting out, at 10 o'clock on Friday morning, paddling over the Ponds to the Raquette River and thence to the marshy inlet of Follansbee Pond, discovering there a good-sized lake hemmed on three sides by high wooded hills, themselves overseen by mountain peaks miles farther off. At Follansbee they occupied what Lowell dubbed "Camp Maple," in some part rustically constructed by Stillman less than a week before. The delighted visitors from Boston and Cambridge and Concord stayed about ten days, until 16 August (*L*, VIII, 573). Emerson's unpublished Account Books show that he was home by the evening of the 17th, bringing to a close what Paul Schneider has identified as a landmark in the history of American ecotourism (*The Adirondacks: A History of America's First Wilderness* [New York, 1997], 9).

Emerson made very few notes while in New York, but seems to have written at least an early version of the poem very quickly, since he read "Adirondac" to friends and family at the John Murray Forbes estate at Naushon Island no later than the last day of August (*ETE*, I, 148). The fact that he was giving private readings of the poem (see *JMN*, XV, 527, for another) while still withholding it from publication might imply that he hoped to expand the work by including verse portraits of his "fellow-travellers." Some such design may be indicated by the poem's four-line epigraph with its allusions to *The Canterbury Tales* and the *Decameron*. However that may be, Emerson actually did compose portraits for eight of his companions—all but the obscure Dr. Binney. (See *PN*, 724, for the evidence that these were written before 22 February 1859.) Emerson wrote the conclusion of the poem toward the end of October 1866, as may be inferred from the manuscript printer's copy prepared for *May-Day*. A notation on the next-to-last page ("Twelve lines are to be added here") was evidently written by a compositor: fourteen lines in fact follow on the late-supplied last leaf, headed "Conclusion of 'Adirondacs.'" in Emerson's hand and dated "Nov 1" by the compositor (see also *L*, IX, 251). On 20 October Emerson had withdrawn Henry M. Field's *History of the Atlantic Telegraph* (New York, 1866) from the Boston Athenæum (Kenneth Walter Cameron, *Ralph Waldo Emerson's Reading* (Raleigh, N.C., 1941), 38.

In *Emerson as Poet* (Princeton, 1974), Hyatt H. Waggoner suggested that "The Adirondacs" was among the very best of Emerson's late poems, though its "perfectly conventional blank verse" contributed nothing new, in a prosodical way, to his poetic achievement (109). Nevertheless Emerson's imperfectly regular blank verse has its surprises, the diction swings amusingly between the two rewards of the demotic and the gorgeous, and the poem becomes a travelogue taking the reader from prosaic Keeseville to loud Bog River, not omitting along the way "the midge, musquito, and the fly"—to come at last upon an "Oreads' fended Paradise" where "Some mystic hint accosts the vigilant." Of course the Paradise was "fended" in fact by brawny, unlettered Saranac guides, whose society put the scholars and professors to a radical test of relevance (the test of the "red flannel"), contributing largely to a sophisticated mock-heroic tone that one doesn't meet with everywhere in Emerson. And the sudden intrusion into wildest nature of the century's technological sublime (the presence of a future not quite arrived, in the midst of a past not quite gone) is the surprise that composes the poem structurally and accounts for much of its intellectual interest.

THE ADIRONDACS.
A JOURNAL.

DEDICATED TO MY FELLOW-TRAVELLERS
IN AUGUST, 1858.

Wise and polite,—and if I drew
Their several portraits, you would own
Chaucer had no such worthy crew,
Nor Boccace in Decameron.

343

We crossed Champlain to Keeseville with our friends,   5
Thence, in strong country carts, rode up the forks
Of the Ausable stream, intent to reach
The Adirondac lakes. At Martin's Beach
We chose our boats; each man a boat and guide,—
Ten men, ten guides, our company all told.   10

    Next morn, we swept with oars the Saranac,
With skies of benediction, to Round Lake,
Where all the sacred mountains drew around us,
Taháwus, Seward, MacIntyre, Baldhead,
And other Titans without muse or name.   15
Pleased with these grand companions, we glide on,
Instead of flowers, crowned with a wreath of hills,
And made our distance wider, boat from boat,
As each would hear the oracle alone.
By the bright morn the gay flotilla slid   20
Through files of flags that gleamed like bayonets,
Through gold-moth-haunted beds of pickerel flower,
Through scented banks of lilies white and gold,
Where the deer feeds at night, the teal by day,
On through the Upper Saranac, and up   25
Père Raquette stream, to a small tortuous pass
Winding through grassy shallows in and out,
Two creeping miles of rushes, pads, and sponge,
To Follansbee Water, and the Lake of Loons.

    Northward the length of Follansbee we rowed,   30
Under low mountains, whose unbroken ridge
Ponderous with beechen forest sloped the shore.
A pause and council: then, where near the head
On the east, a bay makes inward to the land
Between two rocky arms, we climb the bank,   35
And in the twilight of the forest noon
Wield the first axe these echoes ever heard.
We cut young trees to make our poles and thwarts,
Barked the white spruce to weatherfend the roof,
Then struck a light, and kindled the camp-fire.   40

The Adirondacs

The wood was sovran with centennial trees,—
Oak, cedar, maple, poplar, beech, and fir,
Linden and spruce. In strict society
Three conifers, white, pitch, and Norway pine,
Five-leaved, three-leaved, and two-leaved, grew thereby.   45
Our patron pine was fifteen feet in girth,
The maple eight, beneath its shapely tower.

'Welcome!' the wood god murmured through the leaves,—
'Welcome, though late, unknowing, yet known to me.'
Evening drew on; stars peeped through maple boughs,   50
Which o'erhung, like a cloud, our camping fire.
Decayed millennial trunks, like moonlight flecks,
Lit with phosphoric crumbs the forest floor.

Ten scholars, wonted to lie warm and soft
In well-hung chambers daintily bestowed,   55
Lie here on hemlock boughs, like Sacs and Sioux,
And greet unanimous the joyful change.
So fast will Nature acclimate her sons,
Though late returning to her pristine ways.
Off soundings, seamen do not suffer cold,   60
And, in the forest, delicate clerks, unbrowned,
Sleep on the fragrant brush, as on down beds.
Up with the dawn, they fancied the light air
That circled freshly in their forest dress
Made them to boys again. Happier that they   65
Slipped off their pack of duties, leagues behind,
At the first mounting of the giant stairs.
No placard on these rocks warned to the polls,
No door-bell heralded a visitor,
No courier waits, no letter came or went,   70
Nothing was ploughed, or reaped, or bought, or sold;
The frost might glitter, it would blight no crop,
The falling rain will spoil no holiday.
We were made freemen of the forest laws,
All dressed, like Nature, fit for her own ends,   75
Essaying nothing she cannot perform.

In Adirondac lakes,
At morn or noon, the guide rows bareheaded:
Shoes, flannel shirt, and kersey trousers make
His brief toilette: at night, or in the rain,
He dons a surcoat which he doffs at morn: 80
A paddle in the right hand, or an oar,
And in the left, a gun, his needful arms.
By turns we praised the stature of our guides,
Their rival strength and suppleness, their skill
To row, to swim, to shoot, to build a camp,   85
To climb a lofty stem, clean without boughs
Full fifty feet, and bring the eaglet down:
Temper to face wolf, bear, or catamount,
And wit to trap or take him in his lair.
Sound, ruddy men, frolic and innocent,   90
In winter, lumberers; in summer, guides;
Their sinewy arms pull at the oar untired
Three times ten thousand strokes, from morn to eve.

Look to yourselves, ye polished gentlemen!
No city airs or arts pass current here.   95
Your rank is all reversed: let men of cloth
Bow to the stalwart churls in overalls:
They are the doctors of the wilderness,
And we the low-prized laymen.
In sooth, red flannel is a saucy test   100
Which few can put on with impunity.
What make you, master, fumbling at the oar?
Will you catch crabs? Truth tries pretension here.
The sallow knows the basket-maker's thumb;
The oar, the guide's. Dare you accept the tasks   105
He shall impose, to find a spring, trap foxes,
Tell the sun's time, determine the true north,
Or stumbling on through vast self-similar woods
To thread by night the nearest way to camp?

Ask you, how went the hours?   110
All day we swept the lake, searched every cove,

346

North from Camp Maple, south to Osprey Bay,
Watching when the loud dogs should drive in deer,
Or whipping its rough surface for a trout;
Or bathers, diving from the rock at noon;   115
Challenging Echo by our guns and cries;
Or listening to the laughter of the loon;
Or, in the evening twilight's latest red,
Beholding the procession of the pines;
Or, later yet, beneath a lighted jack,   120
In the boat's bow, a silent night-hunter
Stealing with paddle to the feeding grounds
Of the red deer, to aim at a square mist.
Hark to that muffled roar! a tree in the woods
Is fallen: but hush! it has not scared the buck   125
Who stands astonished at the meteor light,
Then turns to bound away,—is it too late?

Sometimes we tried our rifles at a mark,
Six rods, sixteen, twenty, or forty-five;
Sometimes our wits at sally and retort,   130
With laughter sudden as the crack of rifle;
Or parties scaled the near acclivities
Competing seekers of a rumored lake,
Whose unauthenticated waves we named
Lake Probability,—our Carbuncle,   135
Long sought, not found.

                    Two Doctors in the camp
Dissected the slain deer, weighed the trout's brain,
Captured the lizard, salamander, shrew,
Crab, mice, snail, dragon-fly, minnow, and moth;
Insatiate skill in water or in air   140
Waved the scoop-net, and nothing came amiss;
The while, one leaden pot of alcohol
Gave an impartial tomb to all the kinds.
Not less the ambitious botanist sought plants,
Orchis and gentian, fern, and long whip-scirpus,   145
Rosy polygonum, lake-margin's pride,

Hypnum, and hydnum, mushroom, sponge, and moss,
Or harebell nodding in the gorge of falls.
Above, the eagle flew, the osprey screamed,
The raven croaked, owls hooted, the woodpecker   150
Loud hammered, and the heron rose in the swamp.
As water poured through hollows of the hills
To feed this wealth of lakes and rivulets,
So Nature shed all beauty lavishly
From her redundant horn.

                  Lords of this realm,   155
Bounded by dawn and sunset, and the day
Rounded by hours where each outdid the last
In miracles of pomp, we must be proud,
As if associates of the sylvan gods.
We seemed the dwellers of the zodiac,   160
So pure the Alpine element we breathed,
So light, so lofty pictures came and went.
We trode on air, contemned the distant town,
Its timorous ways, big trifles, and we planned
That we should build, hard-by, a spacious lodge,   165
And how we should come hither with our sons,
Hereafter,—willing they, and more adroit.

    Hard fare, hard bed, and comic misery,—
The midge, the blue-fly, and the musquito
Painted our necks, hands, ankles, with red bands: 170
But, on the second day, we heed them not,
Nay, we saluted them Auxiliaries,
Whom earlier we had chid with spiteful names.
For who defends our leafy tabernacle
From bold intrusion of the travelling crowd,—   175
Who but the midge, musquito, and the fly,
Which past endurance sting the tender cit,
But which we learn to scatter with a smudge,
Or baffle by a veil, or slight by scorn?

Our foaming ale we drunk from hunters' pans,   180
Ale, and a sup of wine. Our steward gave
Venison and trout, potatoes, beans, wheat-bread;
All ate like abbots, and, if any missed
Their wonted convenance, cheerly hid the loss
With hunters' appetite and peals of mirth.   185
And Stillman, our guides' guide, and Commodore,
Crusoe, Crusader, Pius Æneas, said aloud,
"Chronic dyspepsia never came from eating
Food indigestible":—then murmured some,
Others applauded him who spoke the truth.   190

Nor doubt but visitings of graver thought
Checked in these souls the turbulent heyday
'Mid all the hints and glories of the home.
For who can tell what sudden privacies
Were sought and found, amid the hue and cry   195
Of scholars furloughed from their tasks, and let
Into this Oreads' fended Paradise,
As chapels in the city's thoroughfares,
Whither gaunt Labor slips to wipe his brow,
And meditate a moment on Heaven's rest.   200
Judge with what sweet surprises Nature spoke
To each apart, lifting her lovely shows
To spiritual lessons pointed home.
And as through dreams in watches of the night,
So through all creatures in their form and ways   205
Some mystic hint accosts the vigilant,
Not clearly voiced, but waking a new sense
Inviting to new knowledge, one with old.
Hark to that petulant chirp! what ails the warbler?
Mark his capricious ways to draw the eye.   210
Now soar again. What wilt thou, restless bird,
Seeking in that chaste blue a bluer light,
Thirsting in that pure for a purer sky?

349

And presently the sky is changed; O world!
What pictures and what harmonies are thine!   215
The clouds are rich and dark, the air serene,
So like the soul of me, what if 'twere me?
A melancholy better than all mirth.
Comes the sweet sadness at the retrospect,
Or at the foresight of obscurer years?   220
Like yon slow-sailing cloudy promontory,
Whereon the purple iris dwells in beauty
Superior to all its gaudy skirts.
And, that no day of life may lack romance,
The spiritual stars rise nightly, shedding down   225
A private beam into each several heart.
Daily the bending skies solicit man,
The seasons chariot him from this exile,
The rainbow hours bedeck his glowing chair,
The storm-winds urge the heavy weeks along,   230
Suns haste to set, that so remoter lights
Beckon the wanderer to his vaster home.

With a vermilion pencil mark the day
When of our little fleet three cruising skiffs
Entering Big Tupper, bound for the foaming Falls   235
Of loud Bog River, suddenly confront
Two of our mates returning with swift oars.
One held a printed journal waving high
Caught from a late-arriving traveller,
Big with great news, and shouted the report   240
For which the world had waited, now firm fact,
Of the wire-cable laid beneath the sea,
And landed on our coast, and pulsating
With ductile fire. Loud, exulting cries
From boat to boat, and to the echoes round,   245
Greet the glad miracle. Thought's new-found path
Shall supplement henceforth all trodden ways,
Match God's equator with a zone of art,
And lift man's public action to a height

Worthy the enormous cloud of witnesses,   250
When linkèd hemispheres attest his deed.
We have few moments in the longest life
Of such delight and wonder as there grew,—
Nor yet unsuited to that solitude:
A burst of joy, as if we told the fact   255
To ears intelligent; as if gray rock
And cedar grove and cliff and lake should know
This feat of wit, this triumph of mankind;
As if we men were talking in a vein
Of sympathy so large, that ours was theirs,   260
And a prime end of the most subtle element
Were fairly reached at last. Wake, echoing caves!
Bend nearer, faint day-moon! Yon thundertops,
Let them hear well! 'tis theirs as much as ours.

   A spasm throbbing through the pedestals   265
Of Alp and Andes, isle and continent,
Urging astonished Chaos with a thrill
To be a brain, or serve the brain of man.
The lightning has run masterless too long;
He must to school, and learn his verb and noun,   270
And teach his nimbleness to earn his wage,
Spelling with guided tongue man's messages
Shot through the weltering pit of the salt sea.
And yet I marked, even in the manly joy
Of our great-hearted Doctor in his boat,   275
(Perchance I erred,) a shade of discontent;
Or was it for mankind a generous shame,
As of a luck not quite legitimate,
Since fortune snatched from wit the lion's part?
Was it a college pique of town and gown,   280
As one within whose memory it burned
That not academicians, but some lout,
Found ten years since the California gold?
And now, again, a hungry company
Of traders, led by corporate sons of trade,   285

Perversely borrowing from the shop the tools
Of science, not from the philosophers,
Had won the brightest laurel of all time.
'Twas always thus, and will be; hand and head
Are ever rivals: but, though this be swift,   290
The other slow,—this the Prometheus,
And that the Jove,—yet, howsoever hid,
It was from Jove the other stole his fire,
And, without Jove, the good had never been.
It is not Iroquois or cannibals,   295
But ever the free race with front sublime,
And these instructed by their wisest too,
Who do the feat, and lift humanity.
Let not him mourn who best entitled was,
Nay, mourn not one: let him exult,   300
Yea, plant the tree that bears best apples, plant,
And water it with wine, nor watch askance
Whether thy sons or strangers eat the fruit:
Enough that mankind eat, and are refreshed.

    We flee away from cities, but we bring   305
The best of cities with us, these learned classifiers,
Men knowing what they seek, armed eyes of experts.
We praise the guide, we praise the forest life;
But will we sacrifice our dear-bought lore
Of books and arts and trained experiment,   310
Or count the Sioux a match for Agassiz?
O no, not we! Witness the shout that shook
Wild Tupper Lake; witness the mute all-hail
The joyful traveller gives, when on the verge
Of craggy Indian wilderness he hears   315
From a log-cabin stream Beethoven's notes
On the piano, played with master's hand.
'Well done!' he cries, 'the bear is kept at bay,
The lynx, the rattlesnake, the flood, the fire;
All the fierce enemies, ague, hunger, cold,   320
This thin spruce roof, this clayed log-wall,
This wild plantation will suffice to chase.

352

The Adirondacs

Now speed the gay celerities of art,
What in the desart was impossible
Within four walls is possible again,—   325
Culture and libraries, mysteries of skill,
Traditioned fame of masters, eager strife
Of keen competing youths, joined or alone,
To outdo each other, and extort applause.
Mind wakes a new-born giant from her sleep.   330
Twirl the old wheels! Time takes fresh start again,
On for a thousand years of genius more.'

   The holidays were fruitful, but must end;
One August evening had a cooler breath;
Into each mind intruding duties crept;   335
Under the cinders burned the fires of home;
Nay, letters found us in our paradise;
So in the gladness of the new event
We struck our camp, and left the happy hills.
The fortunate star that rose on us sank not;   340
The prodigal sunshine rested on the land,
The rivers gambolled onward to the sea,
And Nature, the inscrutable and mute,
Permitted on her infinite repose
Almost a smile to steal to cheer her sons,   345
As if one riddle of the Sphinx were guessed.

TEXTS

(A) MS Am 82.12, Ralph Waldo Emerson Memorial Association deposit, Hough-ton Library, Harvard University, printer's copy for B; (B) *May-Day* (Boston, 1867), 41–62; (C) *Poems* [Riverside] (Boston, 1884), 159–170; (D) *Poems* [Centenary] (Boston, 1904), 182–194. [*Note:* Because the Houghton manuscript (A) is tightly bound, the editors were unable to recover end-of-line punctuation at the following points: 93, "ev"; 94, "gentlemen"; 96, "cloth"; 97, "overalls"; 100, "test"; 102, "oar"; 103, "he"; 296, "sublime"; 330, "wheels." (upper portion of exclamation point may be obscured).]

Format: The epigraph (lines 1–4) is on a separate page in (A) and is set, cen-tered, in a smaller font in (B-D), followed by a line space.

May-Day and Other Pieces (1867)

Pre-copy-text forms: The poem was principally composed in poetry notebook NP, as were the verse portraits of Louis Agassiz, Ebenezer Rockwood Hoar, John Holmes, James Russell Lowell, Jeffries Wyman, Horatio Woodman, Estes Howe, and William James Stillman. See *PN*, 722–724. A proof-sheet of the lines on John Holmes survives: see *PN*, [xxviii].

VARIANTS

Title: THE ADIRONDACS. / A JOURNAL. / DEDICATED TO MY FELLOW-TRAVELLERS IN AUGUST, 1858. (B-C) | *The Adirondacs.* [*A preliminary page containing the four-line epigraph has the heading* "Adirondac." *The verso of the next leaf is headed* "The Adirondacs." *slightly below* "August, 1858" *in the upper right corner*] (A) | THE ADIRONDACS / A JOURNAL / DEDICATED TO MY FELLOW TRAVELLERS IN AUGUST, 1858 (D)

1 Wise (B-D) | ——Wise (A)
5 [*Flush*] We (B-D) | [*Inset*] We (A)
8 lakes. At (B-D) | lakes ↑.↓ <a>At (A) || Beach (B-D) | beach, (A)
9 guide,— (B-D) | guide, (A)
10 guides, our company all told. (B-D) | guides. (A)
14 Seward, [*Ed.: see note.*] | Seaward, (A-D) || MacIntyre, (B-D) | Macintyre (A)
16 we glide on, (A-D) | gliding on, (CC7)
17 hills, (A-B) | hills. (C-D)
18 And (A-B) | We (CC7, C-D)
22 gold-moth-haunted (B-D) | purple (A) || pickerel flower, (A) | pickerel-flower, (B-D)
24 night, the teal by day, (B-D) | night, (A)

26 small (A-D) | short (CC7)
28 pads, (A-B) | pads (C-D)
29 Water, (A-B) | Water (C-D)
30 [*Inset*] Northward (B-D) | [*Flush*] Northward (A)
33 then, (B-D) | then ↑,↓ [*added in pencil*] (A)
34 On the (A-B) | Due (CC7, C-D) || east, (A) | east (B-D)
35 arms, (B-D) | a<l>rms, (A) || bank, (B-D) | bank (A)
40 light, (A-B) | light (C-D)
41 trees,— (B-D) | trees (A)
42 beech, (A) | beech (B-D)
44 pitch, (A-B) | pitch (C-D)
45 leaved, three-leaved, and two-leaved, (B) | leaved three-leaved & two-leaved (A) | leaved, three-leaved and two-leaved, (C-D)
46 girth, (B-D) | girth (A)
47 eight, beneath its shapely tower. (B-D) | measured eight.— (A)
48 [*Inset*] 'Welcome!' (B-D) | [*Flush*] "Welcome!" (A) || wood god (A-B) | wood-god (CC7, C-D) || leaves,— (B-D) | leaves, (A)
49 'Welcome, (B-D) | "Welcome, (A) || me.' (B-D) | me." (A)
50 on; (B-D) | on, (A) || maple boughs, (A) | maple-boughs, (B-D)
54 scholars, (B-D) | scholars (A)
56 hemlock boughs, (A) | hemlock-boughs, (B-D)

60   cold, (A) I cold; (B-D)

62   the fragrant brush, (B-D) I the <hemlock boughs> ↑fragrant brush↓, (A) II down beds. (A) I down-beds. (B-D)

66   off (B-D) I of↑f↓ [*added in pencil*] (A)

69   door-bell (B-D) I doorbell (A) [*The* OED *lists no nineteenth-century authority for writing the word without the hyphen.*] II visitor, (B-D) I visiter (A) [*Emerson wrote this word both ways throughout his life, developing, however, a late preference for the less archaic form.*]

75   dressed, (B-D) I drest, (A)

78   trousers (B-D) I trowzers (A)

82   And (B-D) I And, (A)

88   or (B-D) I <&>or (A)

90   Sound, (B-D) I Sound (A)

96   reversed: (A-B) I reversed; (C-D)

99   *They* (B-D) I They (A)

103 Truth tries pretension here. (B-D) I ↑Truth pricks all bubbles he ↓ [*end of inscription not recoverable*] (A)

104 thumb; (B-D) I thumb, (A)

106 He shall impose, to find (B-D) I <He shall impose—to find a spring,> / He<'ll set you,—> ↑shall impose, to↓ find (A)

107 Tell the sun's time, determine (B-D) I Tell <<time> ↑hours↓ by the sun> ↑the sun's time,↓ <point> ↑determine↓ (A)

108 Or stumbling on (B-D) I Stumbling ↑rush↓ (A)

109 To thread (B-D) I To <find> ↑</tread/grope/> ↑thread↓ ↓ (A)

111 lake, searched every cove, (B-D) I lake↑,↓ <with oars> ↑searched every cove,↓ (A)

112 south (B-D) I <S>south (A)

115 Or (A-B) I Or, (C-D)

119 pines; (B-D) I Pines; (A)

121 boat's bow, [*Ed.*] I ↑boat's↓ bow↑s,↓ <of the boat>, (A) I boat's bows, (B-D)

122 feeding grounds (A) I feeding-grounds (B-D)

128 [*Inset*] Sometimes we (B) I [*Flush*] Sometimes we (A) I [*Inset*] Our heroes (CC7, C-D) II our (A-B) I their (CC7, C-D)

129 forty-five; (B-D) I forty five; (A)

130 our (A-B) I their (CC7, C-D)

132 acclivities (B-D) I declivities (A)

133 Competing seekers of (B-D) I <To seek> ↑Competing seekers of↓ (A)

135 Carbuncle, (A) I carbuncle, (B-D)

136 sought, not found. (B-D) I sought, /ne'er/not/ found. <Two> (A) ["not" *added in pencil*]

137 Dissected the slain (B-D) I Dissect the new-killed (A)

139 dragon-fly, (B-D) I dragonfly, (A) [*Only the hyphenated and two-word forms are acknowledged by the* OED.] II minnow, (A-B) I minnow (C-D)

141 scoop-net, (B-D) I scoopnet, (A) [*Only the hyphenated and two-word forms are acknowledged by the* OED.]

142 one (B-D) I a (A)

143 an (B-D) I <one> ↑an↓ (A)

145 fern, (A-B) I fern (C-D)

147 Hypnum, (A) I Hypnum (B-D) II sponge, (A-B) I sponge (C-D)

150 hooted (B-D) I hoot<ed> (A)

151 Loud hammered, (B-D) I Hammered, (A)

153 To feed this wealth (B-D) I To <fill> ↑feed↓ this <chain> ↑wealth↓ (A)

155 Lords of this realm, (B-D) I Masters of this green empire (A)

160 zodiac, (B-D) I Zodiack, (A)

161 Alpine (B-D) I ↑alpine↓ (A)

162   pictures came (B-D) | pictures
       <—>came (A)

163   town, (B-D) | <T>town, (A)

165   build, hard-by, a spacious lodge,
       (B-C) | build a rooftree in the woods,
       (A) | build, hard-by, a spacious lodge
       (D)

167   willing . . . adroit. (B-D) |
       ↑willing . . . adroit.↓ (A)

168   Hard (B-D) | Hard<f> (A) ||
       bed, (A-B) | bed (C-D)

169   blue-fly, (B) | blue fly, (A) | blue-
       fly (C-D) || musquito (A) | mosquito
       (B-D)

175   crowd,— (B-D) | crowd, (A)

176   musquito, (A) | mosquito, (B) |
       mosquito (C-D)

179   veil, or slight by scorn? (B-D) |
       veil<?>↑, or slight by scorn?↓
       (A)

180   [*Inset*] Our (B-D) | [*Flush*] Our
       (A) || drunk (A-B) | drank (CC7,
       C-D)

184   cheerly (B-D) | ↑cheerly↓ (A)

185   appetite (B-D) | appetite, (A)

186   guide, (B-D) | Guide, (A)

191   visitings of (B-D) | ↑visitings
       <at>of↓ (A)

193   'Mid (B-D) | Mid (A)

196   tasks, (A-B) | tasks (C-D)

197   fended Paradise, (B-D) |
       ↑fended↓ Paradise<.>, (A)

199   brow, (A-B) | brow (C-D)

202   lifting (B-D) | <turning>
       ↑lifting↓ (A)

203   home. (A-B) || home, (C-D)

204   night, (B-D) | night (A)

205   So (B-D) | <By>So (A)

206   the vigilant, (B-D) | <us> ↑the
       vigilant,↓ [*addition in pencil*] (A)

208   with old. (B-D) | with <the> old
       (A)

210   ways to (B-D) | ways <as if> to
       (A)

217   me, what if (B-D) | me, ↑what
       if↓ (A)

218   mirth. (B-D) | mirth<;>. (A)

218–219 [*One line canceled in* (A):]
       <Sometimes restoring heavy
       youthful days.>

221   yon slow-sailing cloudy
       promontory, (B) | yon<der> ↑slow-
       ↓ sailing cloud↑y promontory,↓ (A)
       yon slow-sailing cloudy promontory.
       (C) | yon slow-sailing cloudy
       promontory (D)

223   skirts. (B-D) | skirts— (A)

228   seasons (B-D) | Seasons (A)
       [*Emerson emphasized the upper-case "S"
       by double-underlining in* (A); *"Hours" in
       line* 229 *is equally unambiguous, but he
       may have changed his mind in proofs,
       seeing that "weeks" (lower-case in line
       230 in each text) could not be capitalized
       without making the allegory too
       obtrusive.*]

229   hours (B-D) | Hours (A)

230   storm-winds (B-D) | stormwinds
       (A)

232–233 [*Ten lines canceled in A:*] <For
       well we know, the crowning gift /
       The best of life, is presence of a muse
       / Who does not wish to wander,
       comes by stealth, / Divulging to the
       heart she sets on flame / No popular
       tale or toy, no cheap renown, /
       When the wings grow that draw
       ↑the↓ gazing eyes / <Unbalanced>
       ↑Ofttimes poor↓ Genius fluttering
       near the earth / Is wrecked upon the
       turrets of the town: / But lifted till he
       meets the steadfast gales / Calm
       blowing from the everlasting west.>
       [*For these lines, a versification of a
       passage in Mary Moody Emerson's
       Almanacks, see* PN, 743.]

239   Caught (B-D) | <Big>Caught
       (A)

243   on our (B-D) | on <the>our (A)

244   Loud, (B-D) | Loud (A)

246   new-found (B-D) | new found (A)

249   a (B-D) | <the>a (A)

250–251 witnesses, / When linkèd [*corrected to* linkèd *in* (D)] hemispheres attest his deed. (B-D) | witnesses / <He summons to assist him. > / ↑When linkèd <continents>hemispheres attest his deed.↓ (A)

253   there grew,— (B-D) | <were ours,> ↑the<n>re grew.↓ (A)

255   joy, (B-D) | joy (A)

256   intelligent; (B-D) | intelligent, (A) || rock (B-D) | rock, (A)

257   grove (B-D) | grove, (A) || cliff (B-D) | cliff, (A)

258   This feat of wit, this triumph of mankind; (B-D) | The triumph of mankind, this day of days, (A)

262   Wake, (B-D) | Wake (A)

263   Yon (B-D) | yon (A)

264   'tis (B-D) | tis (A)

269   long; (B-D) | long, (A)

270   school, (A-B) | school (C-D) || noun, (A-B) | noun (C-D)

273–274 sea. / And (B-D) | sea / And (A) [*It is likely that lines 265–273, which occupy the upper two-thirds of p. "19" in* (A) *replace a longer passage. The page that follows, beginning with line 274, is numbered "21" at the top, apparently in Emerson's hand, and "20" at the bottom, apparently in a different hand.*]

275   boat, (A-B) | boat (C-D)

276   erred,) (A-B) | erred), (C-D) || discontent; (B-D) | discontent, (A)

282   lout, (B-D) | lout (A)

283   gold? (B-D) | gold. (A)

286   Perversely borrowing (B-D) | ↑Perversely↓ Borrowing (A)

287   the (B-D) | ↑the↓ (A)

289   'Twas (B-D) | <twas>T'was (A) || thus, and will be; (B-D) | thus ↑& will be↓; <the> (A)

290   though (B-D) | tho' (A)

295   cannibals, (B-D) | Cannibals ↑,↓ (A) [*addition in pencil*]

296   free race (B-D) | free <wise> race (A)

297   too, (B-D) | too (A)

298   feat, and lift humanity. (B-D) | feat.<——> ↑& lift humanity.↓ (A)

300   Nay, (B-D) | Nay (A) || let (B-D) | <L>let (A)

304   eat, (A-B) | eat (C-D)

308   life; (A-B) | life: (C-D)

309   dear-bought (B-D) | dearbought (A)

310   books and arts (B-D) | books, & <trained experiment>arts (A)

313   Lake; (B-D) | lake; (A)

315   Of craggy Indian (B-D) | Of Indian (A)

316   log-cabin (A-C) | log cabin (D)

317   On the piano, played with master's hand. (B-D) | <Masterly played.> / On the piano, <heedless of the wolf> ↑played with master's hand↓. (A)

318   'Well done!' (B-D) | "Well done!" (A) || cries, (A) | cries; (B-D) || 'the (B-D) | "the (A)

319   fire; (B-D) | fire, (A)

320   ague, hunger, cold, (B-D) | ↑ague,↓ hunger, <&> cold, (A)

323   art, (B-D) | Art, (A)

324   desart (A-B) | desert (C-D)

328   alone, (A) | alone (B-D)

329   other, (A-B) | other (C-D)

330   Mind wakes a new-born giant from her sleep. (B-D) | Genius is born once more. Twirl the old wheels. (A)

331   Twirl the old wheels! Time takes

(B-D) | Time makes (A) || again, (B-D) | again (A)

332   genius more.' (B-D) | Genius more, (A)

332–333 [*Notation not in Emerson's hand:*] Twelve lines to be added here. (A)

333   [*Inset*] The (B-D) | [*Flush*] The (A)

336   Under the cinders burned the fires of home; (B-D) | <For had we not left truest friends at home> ↑ Burned in each heart remembrances of home; ↓ (A)

337   paradise; (A-B) | paradise: (C-D)

339   camp, (A-B) | camp (C-D) || left (B-D) | <quit> ↑ left ↓ (A)

NOTES

10. There were only eight guides, since Stillman served as guide to Agassiz; nevertheless, as it turned out, he frequently relegated that duty to any of the hired eight who might happen to be unoccupied so that he could spend more time with Emerson. The names of the guides are listed in Emerson's notebook WA (*TN*, I, 277).

13–14. Taháwus, said to mean "cloudsplitter" or "he splits the sky" in some unspecified Indian language, was more probably the invention of New York writer Charles Fenno Hoffman to replace the more prosaic "Mt. Marcy" as the name of the tallest peak in the state (see Alfred L. Donaldson, *A History of the Adirondacks* [New York, 1921], I, 47, and *JMN*, XV, 361). Just as Mt. Marcy was named for New York's anti-abolitionist Senator William L. Marcy, Franklin Pierce's Secretary of State, so Mt. Seward was named for New York's anti-slavery Senator William Henry Seward, subsequently Secretary of State under Lincoln. In the published text of "The Adirondacs" the name of the latter mountain comes out as "Seaward," and Stillman has suggested that Emerson "repudiated" its official form ("The Philosophers' Camp," in *The Old Rome and the New and Other Studies* [London, 1897], 273). In the manuscript draft in poetry notebook NP, the name is "Seward." Politics aside, it is unlikely that Emerson could have seen all of these mountains from any one point along his route.

26. Stillman believed that the Raquette River had been named for "one of the first of the Jesuit explorers of the northern states, Pere Raquette" ("The Philosophers' Camp," 268). But this explorer is unknown to history, and the fact that his name is French for "snowshoe" casts further doubt on the identification.

29. The name has since been standardized as Follensby. Numerous early guidebooks claim that the pond was so called after a certain Captain Follansbee, an English expatriate, who set up as a hermit at that location around 1820.

33. In fact Emerson and his party entered Follansbee Pond from the north end and rowed due south. An entry in notebook WA may acknowledge Emer-

son's tendency to be confused on this point. "It soon comes out in the woods," he wrote, "whether you know where the north is" (*TN*, I, 275).

34.   Consistent with Emerson's disorientation, this bay, since named Agassiz Bay, is actually on the west side of Follansbee.

39.   Citing *The Tempest,* V, i, 10, the *OED* claims that "weatherfend" was a neologism of Shakespeare's and that it has remained ever since a literary locution.

41–43.   Stillman corrected Emerson's catalogue: "There is no oak, linden, or poplar in these forests. He had passed them in the Ausable valley on his way up, and probably forgot their exact habitat" ("The Philosophers' Camp," 274). Indeed, Emerson knew better, having made a notation on the spot: "The pond is totally virgin soil without a clearing in any point, & covered with primitive woods, rock-maple, beech, spruce, white cedar, arbor vitae" (*JMN*, XIII, 56).

45.   In notebook WA Emerson identifies the five-leaved, three-leaved, and two-leaved varieties as, respectively, *Pinus strobus, Pinus rigida,* and *Pinus resinosa* (*TN*, I, 274).

50–53.   "As the water is poured out lavishly to fill all the hollows of those mountains, making an endless chain of lakes, so is beauty poured out profusely everywhere. The stars peeped through our maple boughs which oerhung like cloud our camping fire and old decaying trunks the forest floor lit with phosphoric crumbs" (*TN*, I, 276). See also lines 152–155.

56.   Emerson rarely indulged in puns in his published writing, tending rather to relish them in the privacy of his journals. Here, it seems, he has depicted his circle of artists and scholars as, with a nice accuracy, "Saxon Sioux." Michael West in *Transcendental Wordplay: America's Romantic Punsters and the Search for the Language of America* (Athens, Ohio, 2000) has much to say about the mid-century popularity of punning, an art—or vice—nearly perfected, as West points out, by such Saturday Club members as Holmes, Lowell, and Thomas Gold Appleton. Actual punning contests are spoken of, including one between Stillman and Lowell (Edward Wagenknecht, *James Russell Lowell: Portrait of a Many-Sided Man* [New York, 1971], 141). Perhaps this accounts for some of the hilarity of the Follansbee campers.

77–78.   "And how could prose go on all-fours more unmetrically than this?" (Oliver Wendell Holmes, *Ralph Waldo Emerson* [Boston, 1884], 327).

87.   "On the top of a large white pine in a bay was an osprey's nest around which the ospreys were screaming, 5 or 6. We thought there were young birds in it, & sent [William] Preston to the top. This looked like an adventure. The tree must be 150 ft. high at least; 60 ft. clean straight stem, without a single branch &, as Lowell & I measured it. . . , 14 ft 6 inches in girth. Preston took advantage of a hemlock close by it & climbed till he got on the branches, then went to the top of the pine & found the nest empty, though the great birds wheeled & screamed

about him." The next morning Lowell returned to the scene alone and duplicated Preston's feat (*JMN*, XIII, 34, 56).

100–101.   "Our party when assembled in costume were a remarkable set, considering who they were, and I think any one of them would have been convicted of piracy on very slight evidence, especially Mr. Emerson" (Judge Ebenezer Rockwood Hoar, quoted in Moorfield Storey and Edward Waldo Emerson, *Ebenezer Rockwood Hoar: A Memoir* [Boston, 1911], 148.

103.   To "catch a crab" in rowing is to have the water catch and push the oar rather than vice versa as normally; a sign of incompetence in the activity.

104.   Sallow is a variety of willow wood. In the notebook source Emerson specified a Scottish synonym: "The saugh knows the basketmaker's thumb, and the oar knows the guide's" (*TN*, I, 276). At *JMN*, VII, 407, "The saugh kens the basketmaker's thumb" is identified as a Scottish proverb.

110–127.   Emerson is describing the two styles of deer-hunting used in the camp, "hounding" and "jacking." In hounding, the hunter waited in his boat while a guide took a dog into the woods and drove the deer out. The hunter was to shoot while the deer was swimming. In jacking, the hunter took to the water at night equipped with a light with a forward-pointing shade (a "jack"). With the light shining shoreward over the bow of the boat, leaving the hunter in darkness, any deer feeding on lily pads in the shallows could be closely approached. Emerson's one experience with jacking failed because his night vision was impossibly poor. "I was to aim at a square mist. I knew not whether it were a rock or a bush. Stillman fired & shot the deer. We fired at another square mist, and a deer bounded from the shore up into the forest, crying ahaish! ahaish! to the resounding woods" (*TN*, I, 275). He had better luck in daylight, both in target practice with "some dozens of ale-bottles" (an activity that Thoreau judged "rather Cockneyish") and in bagging a "peetweet," or spotted sandpiper, for Agassiz to dissect (Thoreau, *Journals*, ed., Bradford Torrey and Francis H. Allen, 14 vols. [Boston, 1906], XI, 119–120).

119.   "The tall white pines, which when full grown rise from one hundred and fifty to two hundred feet, towering nearly half their height above the mass of deciduous trees, and beyond the protection which the solid forest gives against the dominant west winds, acquire a leaning to the east; and as they grew in long lines along the shores, or followed the rocky ridges up the mountain sides, they seemed to be gigantic human beings moving in procession to the east. I had the year before painted a picture of the subject, and Emerson had been struck by it at the [Boston] Athenæum exhibition; and when we were established in camp, almost the first thing he asked to see was the 'procession of the pines'; and our last evening on the lake was spent together watching the glow dying out behind a noble line of the marching pines on the shore of Follansbee Water" (Stillman, "The Philosophers' Camp," 283).

135.   The legend of the "Great Carbuncle," a treasure guarded in the wilderness by evil spirits, was long current in the region of the White Mountains. It was the basis for "The Great Carbuncle" by Nathaniel Hawthorne, who claimed to have encountered the legend in James Sullivan's *History of the District of Maine* (1795), but who seems also to have heard it from Ethan Allen Crawford, the famous story-telling innkeeper at the Notch of the White Mountains. A very similar tale is told in Chapter 19 of Walter Scott's *The Pirate* (1821), which locates the gem in the mountains of Hoy Island in the Orkneys. These sources are discussed by Raymond I. Haskell in "The Great Carbuncle," *New England Quarterly* 10 (1937): 533–535, and by Neal Frank Doubleday in *Hawthorne's Early Tales: A Critical Study* (Durham, N.C., 1972), 145–151.

136.   The two doctors were Agassiz, founder of Harvard's Museum of Comparative Zoology, and Jeffries Wyman, first curator of Harvard's Peabody Museum.

145–147.   Included in Emerson's list is the common bullrush (*Scirpus validus*), also called the bull whip, here referred to as the "long whip-scirpus." Polygonum is a genus in the buckwheat family, some species of which produce dense clusters of small pink flowers (e.g., *Polygonum pennsylvanicum*, or pink smartweed). Hypnum is a widespread genus of moss, and hydnum is the name of a genus of fungi, including the hedgehog mushroom (*Hydnum repandum*), common throughout North America.

148.   "On the gorge of the Ausable River was the harebell. Campanula rotundifolia" (*TN*, I, 276). Emerson would have seen this near Keeseville.

152–155.   See the note to lines 50–53.

155.   Emerson evokes the cornucopia, or horn of plenty, derived from the Greek myth of Zeus and Amalthea.

164–167.   This "planning" led to the formation of the Adirondack Club comprised of shareholders in the purchase of an immense tract of wilderness—some 22,500 acres, including Ampersand Pond—that Stillman actually acquired at an Albany sheriff's sale for $600 in back taxes. The intention of club members seems to have been to ward off development and keep the wilderness pristine while ensuring access to themselves and their children. In the summer of 1859 Samuel Gray Ward, his son, and Edward Emerson were among those who came to the first annual on-site "meeting" of the club, but plans foundered thereafter. Emerson himself continued to pay assessments on the property until 1862, but the Civil War killed the project, and the land reverted to state ownership. See Edward Emerson, *Early Years of the Saturday Club*, 131, Rusk, *Life*, 541 n. 401, and *L*, X, 184. Stillman's celebrated painting of the encampment—later purchased by Judge Hoar and donated to the Concord Free Public Library—is entitled "The Philosophers' Camp," but when Edward reproduced it in *The Early Years of the Saturday Club*, he took the liberty of calling it "The Adirondack Club," contributing to a confusion between actual Club members and the excursion party of 1858.

184.   The *OED* identifies "convenance," as, in this sense, a non-naturalized French word, and cites only two nineteenth-century deployments, both by Emerson: this passage and one in "The Visit" (line 24). The meaning is conventional propriety or usage.

187.   The Latin epithet "pius," applied by Virgil to the hero Æneas, does not mean "pious"—at least not in the modern sense—but denotes the Roman virtue of *pietas,* implying faithfulness to duties and loyalty to friends, family, and the gods.

197.   The Oreads were the fabled nymphs of the mountains, associated with hunting as companions of Diana the huntress.

204.   The "watches of the night" refers to the system of watches set by the ancient Israelites between sunset and sunrise; though the exact phrase does not occur in the English Bible, it is common in English poetry, where the Biblical reference is generally retained, as in Isaac Watts' popular hymn beginning "'Twas in the watches of the night, I thought upon thy power," or John Wesley's "Thee in the watches of the night."

216–223.   These lines versify two passages from Mary Moody Emerson's Almanacks: "The clouds are rich & dark,—air serene,—so like the soul of me, t'were me" (MME, II, 170; *PN,* 723), and "Is sadness on me at retrospection?—or at prospect of darker years, like the cloud on which the purple iris dwells in beauty,—superior to its gaudy colors?" (MME, II, 181; *PN,* 723).

224–232.   Cf. *Nature* (*CW,* I, 8–9): "One might think the atmosphere was made transparent with this design, to give man, in the heavenly bodies, the perpetual presence of the sublime. Seen in the streets of cities, how great they are! If the stars should appear one night in a thousand years, how would men believe and adore; and preserve for many generations the remembrance of the city of God which had been shown! But every night come out these envoys of beauty, and light the universe with their admonishing smile."

233–246.   According to Emerson's entry in journal DO, he, Agassiz, and Woodman, together with their guides, set out on the morning of Wednesday, 11 August, down the Raquette River for fourteen miles into "Big Tupper" Lake, then "6 miles to Jenkins's near the Falls of the Bog River" (*JMN,* XIII, 56). While this is clearly the excursion Emerson memorializes, there is no mention in the journal entry of hearing about the Transatlantic cable. News that the cable had been successfully laid between Ireland and Newfoundland was first announced in the New York *Herald* on 5 August in an article widely reprinted over the next several days. The excitement with which the news was received was quite as profound and universal as Emerson indicates. In a *Herald* article on 6 August, for example, it was said that "No man can estimate the full importance of this event, which will be the starting point of the civilization of the latter half of the nineteenth century, as Fulton's first trip up the Hudson in the little steamer Claremont was its starting point in the first half thereof" ("The Atlantic Cable—The World Revolution Begun," p. 4, cols. 2–3). In fact, the cable ceased to function the following month and was not restored until 1866: see John Steele Gordon, *A Thread Across the Ocean: The Heroic Story of the Transatlantic Cable* (New York, 2002).

250.   "Cloud of witnesses": see Hebrews 12:1.

283.   On 24 January 1848 James Wilson Marshall, a carpenter, discovered gold at the sawmill he was constructing with John Sutter on the American River at Coloma, California. Agassiz, whose geological studies began in Europe in the 1830s with his investigations of glaciers, performed a number of important geological surveys in the United States following his arrival from Switzerland in 1846. His 1848 survey in Michigan did not discover the important Michigan copper deposits (these were already known), but in due course his son Alexander became wealthy by developing the Hecla and Calumet mines there. He was also involved in supervising mining activities for Emerson's friend, the railroad magnate John Murray Forbes.

OCCASIONAL AND MISCELLANEOUS PIECES.

BRAHMA.

In July 1845 Emerson took a leisurely trip to Middlebury, Vermont, where he was to address the Philomathesian Society of Middlebury College (*LL*, I, 81–100). His reading during this time away from home consisted of *The Vishńu Puráńa, a System of Hindu Mythology and Tradition,* trans. H. H. Wilson (London, 1840), a copy of which he had on loan from James Elliot Cabot (*L*, III,

293). He wrote to Cabot after returning that he had "read [the book] with wonder in the mountains" (ibid.). Perhaps at that time—though more probably a little later—Emerson took notes from it, which he entered in journal Y, including an item from p. 139: "What living creature slays or is slain? What living creature preserves or is preserved? Each is his own destroyer or preserver, as he follows evil or good" (*JMN*, IX, 319).

Some time during March or April 1847 Emerson copied these sentences into journal AB, and probably at the same time versified the source in four lines, the draft of which occurs, out of chronological order, at the very end of journal Y (*JMN*, IX, 354). At this point, Emerson was trying to express the source in a quatrain, as shown both by this draft and two subsequent ones in poetry notebooks EF (*PN*, 307) and EL (*PN*, 361).

In the summer of 1856 Emerson took a fresh approach with the poem, producing a sixteen-line version entitled "Song of the Soul" in two drafts, one in journal SO (*JMN*, XIV, 102–103) and another, nearly contemporaneous, in poetry notebook EF (*PN*, 315). He was prompted to this revision by reading an English translation of the Upanishads by Dr. Edward Röer, published in Calcutta in 1853, in a copy given to him by Thoreau (*L*, V, 70–71). Emerson's notes from this volume surround the draft of "Song of the Soul" in journal SO (*JMN*, XIV, 101–107). Yet another, coinciding source is from the *Bhăgvăt-Gēētă*, a volume that Emerson first saw in 1845 but that he may have quoted from much later (*L*, III, 288):

> The man who believeth that it is the soul which killeth, & he who thinketh that the soul may be destroyed, are both alike deceived; for it neither killeth, nor is it killed. It is not a thing which a man may say, it hath been, it is about to be, or is to be hereafter; for it is a thing without birth; it is ancient constant & eternal, & is not to be destroyed in this its mortal frame. (Notebook Orientalist, *TN*, II, 131).

When "Brahma" was published in the inaugural issue of the *Atlantic Monthly* in November 1857, it met with a good deal of incomprehension and derision and is still accounted one of Emerson's most challenging poems. In his note in the Centenary edition Edward tried to counter this widespread and, by then, longstanding objection to the poem's impenetrability. He offered an anecdote of the schoolgirl who, not having been forewarned that it was a puzzle or that its author was heterodox, chose it for recitation because it was "easy"—that its message was, simply, "God everywhere" (*W,* IX, 467).

BRAHMA.

If the red slayer think he slays,
    Or if the slain think he is slain,
They know not well the subtle ways
    I keep, and pass, and turn again.

Far or forgot to me is near;   5
    Shadow and sunlight are the same;
The vanished gods to me appear;
    And one to me are shame and fame.

They reckon ill who leave me out;
    When me they fly, I am the wings;   10
I am the doubter and the doubt,
    And I the hymn the Brahmin sings.

The strong gods pine for my abode,
    And pine in vain the sacred Seven;
But thou, meek lover of the good!   15
    Fine me, and turn thy back on heaven.

TEXTS

(A) *AM,* I (November 1857): 48; (B) *May-Day* (Boston, 1867), 65–66; (B²) *Selected Poems* (Boston, 1876), 73; (B³) *Poems* [Riverside] (Boston, 1884), 170–171; (B⁴) *Poems* [Centenary] (Boston, 1904), 195.

Format: Alternate indentation introduced in B.

Pre-copy-text forms: In addition to the drafts mentioned above, several additional versions and fair copies are discussed in *PN,* 750–751.

VARIANTS

5   near; (B) I near, (A)   7   appear; (B) appear, (A)
6   same; (B) I same, (A)

NOTES

9   In his early lecture on the "Humanity of Science" (1836), Emerson cited as a proverb: "he counts without his host who leaves God out of his reckoning" (*EL,* II, 30).

13   Edward identifies the "strong gods" as "Indra, god of the sky and wielder of the thunderbolt; Agni, the god of fire; and Yama, the god of death and judgment" (*W,* IX, 466); but compare Emerson's list at *JMN,* XIII, 434: Indra (firmament), Agni (fire), Vritra (cloud), Maruts (winds), and Aswins (waters). Emerson derived this list in May 1855 from H. H. Wilson, trans., *Rig-veda Sanhitá. A Collection of Ancient Hindú Hymns,* 4 vols. (London, 1850–1866), vols. 1–2.

NEMESIS.

The manuscript histories of the two stanzas are quite distinct, as though they were two poems on one theme, brought at last together. The first stanza, lacking lines 5–6, was written in poetry notebook EF and slightly revised in X; lines 5–6 originate in the draft of the complete first stanza at NP, p. 74. The second stanza, the only portion of the poem for which evidence regarding the date of composition is available, was entirely composed in topical notebook EO, largely a collection of entries on the subject of fate. The final four lines were drafted first, on pages 95, 106, and 139 of EO (*TN,* I, 72, 73, and 79); those on page 139 immediately follow a draft of "Fate" ("Deep in the man"), which could not have been written before the spring or early summer of 1855 (see *PN*, 788). When the entire second stanza was worked out on pp. 37–38 of EO, it was prefaced by the sentence "The thunderbolt goes to its mark." This sentence, the source for line 11, had been copied from journal NO (*JMN*, XIII, 434), where it was a note (or quotation) taken in the course of Emerson's reading of H. H. Wilson's translation of the *Rig-veda Sanhitá,* in May 1855.

It cannot be determined how much time elapsed before Emerson made fair copies in poetry notebooks NP and Rhymer, though the substitution in line 14 of the NP text of "Nemesis" for "Savage Fate" confirms the sequence of the two copies. These have, respectively, the titles "Fate" and "Destiny," so the introduction of the term "Nemesis" is the last significant verbal alteration that the author made, both in the title and the body of the poem. It may reflect Emerson's old stricture on Byron's apostrophe to Nemesis in Canto IV of *Childe Harold's Pilgrimage,* which he copied into topical notebook RT in 1858 or 1859 (*TN*, II, 185).

NEMESIS.

Already blushes in thy cheek
The bosom-thought which thou must speak;
The bird, how far it haply roam
By cloud or isle, is flying home;
The maiden fears, and fearing runs   5
Into the charmed snare she shuns;
And every man, in love or pride,
Of his fate is never wide.

   Will a woman's fan the ocean smooth?
Or prayers the stony Parcæ sooth,   10
Or coax the thunder from its mark?
Or tapers light the chaos dark?
In spite of Virtue and the Muse,
Nemesis will have her dues,
And all our struggles and our toils   15
Tighter wind the giant coils.

TEXTS

(A) *May-Day* (Boston, 1867), 67–68; (B) *Poems* [Centenary] (Boston, 1904), 196. The poem was not included in *Selected Poems* or the Riverside edition of *Poems*.

Pre-copy-text forms: See *PN,* 870, and the headnote above.

VARIANTS

1	in (A) I on (B)	9	[*Inset*] (A) I [*Flush*] (B)
2	bosom-thought (A) I bosom thought (B)	10	sooth, (A) I soothe, (B)

NOTES

10.   In notebook EO, on the page before the draft of the second stanza, Emerson quoted a few lines from *The Suppliants* by Æschylus: "Whatever is fated, that will take place. The great immense mind of Jove is not to be transgressed. O mighty Jove, defend me from the nuptials of the Sons of Ægyptus. That indeed would be best: but you would soothe a deity not to be soothed" (*TN,* I, 64–65).

FATE.

Emerson had surprisingly little to say, anywhere, about Oliver Cromwell, who was a very great hero to his friend Thomas Carlyle. It seems inconceivable that Emerson would have failed to read Carlyle's magisterial two-volume edition of the Lord Protector's *Letters and Speeches* (1845), and yet the journals do not contain notes from it, nor is there record of its ever being in Emerson's library. When, having corresponded with Carlyle for a dozen years, Emerson renewed his personal acquaintance on a second trip to England in 1847 and 1848, the two men found that they had grown apart both intellectually and temperamentally, with the result that their friendship, though not quite broken, would never thereafter be the same. Carlyle's continually advancing respect for discipline and dictatorship, a response to the social and political affronts of modernity in the period leading up to the revolutionary disturbances of 1848, caused him to magnify the virtues of Cromwell and to insist upon them, at times emphatically, as a cultural panacea. In December 1847, as Emerson recalled, a conversation on the subject of Cromwell turned ugly: "I differed from him . . . in his estimate of Cromwell's character, & he rose like a great Norse giant from his chair—and, drawing a line with his finger across the table, said, with terrible fierceness: Then, sir, there is a line of separation between you and me as wide as that, & as deep as the pit" (quoted in *CEC*, 36; cf. Richardson, *Emerson: The Mind on Fire*, 444–445, and *L*, III, 460).

Even eight years later in 1855—when, as nearly as can be determined, "Fate" was written—the subject of Cromwell's character could not have been separated in Emerson's mind from his dramatic clash with Carlyle. The first draft of the poem, in notebook EO, is headed "Hutchinson" (*TN*, I, 79), a reference to the *Memoirs of the Life of Colonel Hutchinson . . . Written by His Widow Lucy*, of which Emerson owned a copy of the 1822 fourth edition (Harding, *Emerson's Library*, 145). This account of John Hutchinson's activities during the English civil war (he signed the death warrant of Charles I) is not very directly concerned with Oliver Cromwell, but its few references to him are not laudatory. Emerson read this book in April or May, 1855 (*JMN*, XIII, 427).

FATE.

Deep in the man sits fast his fate
To mould his fortunes mean or great:
Unknown to Cromwell as to me
Was Cromwell's measure or degree;

Unknown to him, as to his horse,   5
If he than his groom be better or worse.
He works, plots, fights, in rude affairs,
With squires, lords, kings, his craft compares,
Till late he learned, through doubt and fear,
Broad England harbored not his peer: 10
Obeying Time, the last to own
The Genius from its cloudy throne.
For the prevision is allied
Unto the thing so signified;
Or say, the foresight that awaits   15
Is the same Genius that creates.

TEXTS

(A) *May-Day* (Boston, 1867), 69; (B) *Poems* [Riverside] (Boston, 1884), 171; (C) *Poems* [Centenary] (Boston, 1904), 197. The poem was not included in *Selected Poems*.

Pre-copy-text forms: The manuscript history of this poem—and especially its origin in notebook EO—associates it with "Nemesis," as one of several poetic by-products of the long gestation of the essay "Fate." Lines 13–16 of this poem were first published as lines 11–14 of "Fate" ("Delicate omens"), the motto to "Fate" in *The Conduct of Life* (Boston, 1860), xi. See, further, *PN,* 788.

VARIANTS

2   fortunes (A-B) | fortunes, (C)   11   Time, (A-B) | time, (C)
5   him, (A) | him (B-C)

FREEDOM.

In a letter of 7 August 1853 Julia Griffiths, secretary of the Rochester (New York) Ladies' Anti-Slavery Society, invited Emerson to contribute to the second volume of her *Autographs for Freedom*, a fundraising effort in support of the work of her friend Frederick Douglass and other abolitionists in the Rochester area. It was also one of the first designedly interracial literary projects in American history. Responding in a letter of 24 October (*L*, VIII, 379), Emerson sent the poem, "On Freedom," which was duly published over a facsimile of his signature when the volume, bearing the anticipatory date of 1854 on the title page, appeared in December for the Christmas and New Year's trade. Presumably, then, the poem was written between August and October 1853.

Emerson had for some time been of the opinion that much talking on the slavery question was both fatally easy and morally superfluous and that overwrought rhetoric and long discourses ought to be left entirely to the doomed party, the defenders of slavery (*JMN*, IX, 126–128). At the funeral of abolitionist Charles T. Torrey in 1846, it had seemed to Emerson "almost too late to say anything for freedom,—the battle is already won" (*JMN*, IX, 400). Certainly it had never been enough for Emerson in his capacity either as poet or orator simply to say what others had already said—which would be to mistake the point of speaking at all. The poet's contribution would be to enlarge and transform the meanings that had been in play in casual and unconsidered ways in anti-slavery discourse. In one of his topical notebooks Emerson quoted some striking lines by Caroline Sturgis on the radical indirection of the poet's relation to slavery:

> Toil not to free the slave from chains,
> Strive not to give the laborer rest,

Unless rich beauty fill the plains,
The freeman wanders still unblest. (*TN*, I, 120)

FREEDOM.

Once I wished I might rehearse
Freedom's pæan in my verse,
That the slave who caught the strain
Should throb until he snapped his chain.
But the Spirit said, 'Not so;   5
Speak it not, or speak it low;
Name not lightly to be said,
Gift too precious to be prayed,
Passion not to be expressed
But by heaving of the breast: 10
Yet,—wouldst thou the mountain find
Where this deity is shrined,
Who gives to seas and sunset skies
Their unspent beauty of surprise,
And, when it lists him, waken can   15
Brute or savage into man;
Or, if in thy heart he shine,
Blends the starry fates with thine,
Draws angels nigh to dwell with thee,
And makes thy thoughts archangels be;   20
Freedom's secret wilt thou know?—
Counsel not with flesh and blood;
Loiter not for cloak or food;
Right thou feelest, rush to do.'

TEXTS

(A) *Autographs for Freedom*, ed. Julia Griffiths (Auburn, N.Y., 1854), 235–236; (B) *May-Day* (Boston, 1867), 70–71; (B²) *Poems* [Riverside] (Boston, 1884), 172; (B³) *Poems* [Centenary] (Boston, 1904), 198. The poem was not included in *Selected Poems*.

Pre-copy-text forms: The first four drafts occur in notebook HO (*JMN*, XIII, 229–32). In *W,* IX, 468, Edward Emerson reconstructed an unrevised form of the first draft. Lines 22–23, composed some time after 1853 in poetry notebook EL (*PN*, 369), were added to the fair copy in Rhymer (*PN*, 442), which was, in turn, the basis for the 1867 text. See also *PN*, 796.

VARIANTS

Title: FREEDOM. (B) | On Freedom. (A)

4 snapped (B) | snapt (A)

5 'Not (B) | "Not (A)

9 expressed (B) | exprest (A)

10 breast: (B) | breast; (A)

11 wouldst (B) | would'st (A)

13 to (B) | the (A) || sunset skies (B) | sunset-skies (A)

16 or (B) | and (A)

21 wilt (B) | would'st (A)

22–23 *Lines added in* (B)

24 feelest, rush to do.' (B) | feelest rashly do. (A)

NOTES

4. In "Poetry and Imagination" from *Letters and Social Aims* (*CW*, VIII, 33), Emerson quotes the boast of an unnamed "Runic bard": "I know a song which I need only to sing when men have loaded me with bonds: when I sing it, my chains fall in pieces and I walk forth in liberty." This passage, in fuller form, is also among the sources for Emerson's "Merlin's Song": see the headnote to that poem.

ODE SUNG IN THE TOWN HALL, CONCORD, JULY 4, 1857.

Emerson wrote this poem in June 1857, shortly before it was printed as a broadside and then sung at the breakfast celebration of Independence Day, at Concord Town Hall, 4 July 1857. The event had an additional purpose in raising money for the new Sleepy Hollow cemetery on Bedford Street, a project with which Emerson had been closely associated for the past two years. On 29 September 1855, as a member of the cemetery's board of directors, he had spoken at the dedication ceremonies (*W,* XI, 427–436). He had also hired and no doubt instructed the landscape architect, Horace W. S. Cleveland. As all evidence shows, the two men agreed, as Emerson put it, "that there is no ornament, no architecture alone, so sumptuous as well disposed woods and waters" (ibid., 431). Such romantic aesthetics would ally Sleepy Hollow with the nineteenth-century "rural cemetery" movement, launched in America at Mt. Auburn in Cambridge in 1831 (see Daniel Joseph Nadenicek, "Commemoration in the Landscape of Minnehaha: 'A Halo of Poetic Association,'" in Joachim Wolschke-Bulmahn, ed., *Places of Commemoration: Search for Identity and Landscape Design* [Washington, D.C., 2001], 55–80). Four days after the celebration at which the "Ode" was sung, Emerson had the remains of his mother (who had died in 1853) and his son Waldo (who had died in 1842) reinterred in the new cemetery on what became "Author's Ridge," in the plot where, in 1882, he would himself be buried (*JMN,* XIV, 154).

Nature, serene and conscious, provides the context in the opening and close of the Ode, but the poem is otherwise concerned with Fourth-of-July themes and the meaning of freedom.

ODE SUNG IN THE TOWN HALL, CONCORD, JULY 4, 1857.

O tenderly the haughty day
    Fills his blue urn with fire;
One morn is in the mighty heaven,
    And one in our desire.

The cannon booms from town to town,   5
    Our pulses are not less,
The joy-bells chime their tidings down,
    Which children's voices bless.

Ode Sung in the Town Hall, Concord, July 4, 1857

For He that flung the broad blue fold
    O'er-mantling land and sea,   10
One third part of the sky unrolled
    For the banner of the free.

The men are ripe of Saxon kind
    To build an equal state,—
To take the statute from the mind,   15
    And make of duty fate.

United States! the ages plead,—
    Present and Past in under-song,—
Go put your creed into your deed,
    Nor speak with double tongue.   20

For sea and land don't understand,
    Nor skies without a frown
See rights for which the one hand fights
    By the other cloven down.

Be just at home; then write your scroll   25
    Of honor o'er the sea,
And bid the broad Atlantic roll,
    A ferry of the free.

And, henceforth, there shall be no chain,
    Save underneath the sea   30
The wires shall murmur through the main
    Sweet songs of LIBERTY.

The conscious stars accord above,
    The waters wild below,
And under, through the cable wove,   35
    Her fiery errands go.

For He that worketh high and wise,
    Nor pauses in his plan,

Will take the sun out of the skies
   Ere freedom out of man.   40

TEXTS

(A) *Fourth of July Breakfast and Floral Exhibition, at the Town Hall, Concord, for the Benefit of Sleepy Hollow Cemetery* [Broadside, 1857]; (B) *May-Day* (Boston, 1867), 72–74; (C) *Selected Poems* (Boston, 1876), 207–208; (D) *Poems* [Riverside] (Boston, 1884), 173–174; (D²) *Poems* [Centenary] (Boston, 1904), 199–200. The broadside printing (A) exists in two states, both illustrated by Joel Myerson in his *Ralph Waldo Emerson: A Descriptive Bibliography* (Pittsburgh, 1982), 264 and 266; the only difference between them is the presence, in second state, of the author's name. It is unlikely that Emerson had anything to do with the poem's publication in an unidentified Boston-area newspaper of 30 July or 1 August 1866, where it appeared under the title "The Atlantic Cable"—as if to celebrate the recent restoration of cable service after the Civil War. This text was reproduced by Kenneth Walter Cameron in his lengthy and useful article, "Emerson, Thoreau, and the Atlantic Cable," *Emerson Society Quarterly*, no. 26 (1st Quarter 1962): 45–86 (55). Apart from the new title, the text differs from (A) only in accidentals, having "O'er mantling" in line 10; "State;" in line 13; "plead—" in line 17; "under-song—" in line 18; "Go" in line 19; "skies" and "frown" in line 22; "home," in line 25; "sea;" in line 26; "through" in line 31; "LIBERTY." in line 32; and "through" in line 35. Cameron's speculation cannot be ruled out that whoever was responsible for this publication may have had access to a manuscript.

Pre-copy-text forms: Drafts of the poem occur in notebook WO Liberty (*JMN*, XIV, 424–427), mingled with lines from "Boston." Three rejected stanzas, drafted in WO Liberty (*JMN*, XIV, 427–428) and originally intended for the "Ode," were revised as an independent poem, "O sun! take off thy hood of clouds," in journal VO (*JMN*, XIV, 153). Fair copies of this poem, but not of the "Ode," occur in the poetry notebooks (see *PN*, 879–880).

VARIANTS

Title: ODE SUNG IN THE TOWN
HALL, CONCORD, JULY 4, 1857.
(B-C) | ODE. (A) | ODE. SUNG IN
THE TOWN HALL, CONCORD,
JULY 4, 1857. (D)
2   fire; (B-D) | fire, (A)
6   are (A-C) | beat (CC7, D)

14   state,— (B-D) | state; (A)
15   mind, (A-C) | mind (D)
22   skies (B-D) | skies, (A) || frown
(B-D) | frown, (A)
25   write your scroll (B-D) | reach
beyond (A)

26 Of honor (B-D) | Your charter (A)

27 bid (B-D) | make (A) || roll, (B, D) | pond (A) | roll (C)

29 And, henceforth, (A-C) | And henceforth (D)

30 Save (B-D) | Save, (A) || sea (B-D) | sea, (A)

31 through (B-D) | thro' (A)

32 LIBERTY. (A-C) | liberty. (D)

34 below, (B-D) | below (A)

35 through (B-D) | thro' (A)

NOTES

13–16. Interrupting the draft of the poem in notebook WO Liberty is a prose passage, evidently written out to facilitate composition of this stanza: "Saying to you men of this land I give a new law[:] Be strong through freedom. Make your duty your fate & see that you cling to it while you live" (*JMN*, XIV, 427).

25. At some point between 1865 and 1867 Emerson made three attempts to revise this stanza (*TN*, III, 328), all differing from the form finally adopted in the *May-Day* text.

27–28. At the time the poem was written England and America had naval squadrons on the west coast of Africa to interdict the smuggling of slaves to the New World.

29. At the head of the drafts in WO Liberty is the sentence "The heavy blue chain of the sea didst thou just man endure," followed by a versification of the same (*JMN*, XIV, 423; cf. *W*, IX, 376, and *PN*, 813). Emerson found the sentence in the "Preiddeu Annwn," or "Spoils of the Deep," by the British bard Taliessin, and in "Poetry and Imagination" (W, VIII, 59) indicated the context, saying that it was addressed to "an exile on an island." Perhaps the precise location of this sentence in WO Liberty associates it more closely with drafts of the contemporaneously written "Boston," but it reminds us that here in the "Ode" as well as in "Boston," lines 17–18, Emerson is characteristically occupied with freedom and the image of the sea. That "chain" would have the sort of metaphoric extension that Taliessin gave it, is perhaps license enough for Emerson to use it here in ironically associating the chain of the slave with the "chain" (or cable) that, in linking England and America, would help to make the Atlantic a "ferry of the free." Although the Atlantic cable would not be completed until August 1858—as Emerson noted in "The Adirondacs"—the project had been long been eagerly anticipated.

BOSTON HYMN.

On the afternoon of New Year's Day, 1863, as Abraham Lincoln's signing of the Emancipation Proclamation gave it legal effect, a great jubilee was held in Boston's Music Hall. Emerson there read his poem to a crowd of three thousand as a last-minute surprise addition to the festivities, serving as prologue to the orchestra's performance of works by Beethoven, Rossini, and others. Henry James, Jr., who was present, recalled "the momentousness of the occasion, the vast excited multitude, the crowded platform and the tall, spare figure of Emerson, in the midst, reading out the stanzas . . . I well remember the immense effect with which his beautiful voice pronounced the lines—

'Pay ransom to the owner
And fill the bag to the brim.
Who is the owner? The slave is owner,
And ever was. Pay *him!*' ("Emerson," *Partial Portraits* [London, 1888], 27–28)

The old proposal to end slavery by compensating slave-owners who were being deprived of their "property"—a plan that as late as 1855 even Emerson looked upon favorably (*LL*, II, 13–14; cf. *W*, IX, 469)—had become official U. S. policy on 10 April 1862, when a Congressional joint resolution committed the government to pay for slaves wherever and whenever a state might adopt a policy of gradual emancipation (*Statutes at Large, Treaties, and Proclamations, of the United States*, vol. 12 [Boston, 1863], 617). It was a conservative anti-slavery measure, one that acknowledged the legitimacy of slave-owners' property rights and even accepted their estimates of the cash value of African-Americans. It was widely supposed that uncompensated emancipation would necessarily involve an unconstitutional taking and as such would have no legal foundation. The Emancipation Proclamation, issued by Lincoln in his capacity as Commander in Chief (as ostensibly a matter of military necessity) freed slaves in the ten states then in rebellion. The Border States kept their slaves and the Southern Confederacy ignored the Proclamation. Only in New England, in such places as Boston, was there rejoicing, and then only when the measure was seen—as Emerson presented it—as a magnificent vehicle of justice and equity and not (as it was regarded in many quarters) as an act of dubious legality, announced for purely pragmatic reasons, impossible to enforce, and, therefore, of wholly uncertain effect. Emerson's direct criticism of compensation to the slave-owners in the poem's most notable lines had, as James said, an "immense effect,"—equally in Boston's Music Hall and among black troops in occupied South Carolina—precisely because it asserted the moral case for emancipation. In this way Emerson's "Boston Hymn" directly helped to establish the towering prestige of Lincoln's Proclamation as a classic American document.

Emerson had been asked by his old friend John Sullivan Dwight sometime in middle of the previous month to compose an original poem for the Music Hall celebration, which Dwight was organizing. Dwight, whom Emerson had first met at Transcendental Club meetings in 1837 and whom he now saw at gatherings of the Saturday Club, had long since left the Unitarian ministry and was presently the highly regarded editor of *Dwight's Journal of Music*. Emerson was pleased with the invitation but hard-pressed to write the poem, given the many late-December lecture engagements to which he was already committed. He doubted whether the requisite inspiration would arrive in time. On 23 December he advised Dwight to print the program without the poem and without mentioning his name—though he still had hopes of finishing (*L*, IX, 89–90). As Carl F. Strauch has demonstrated, the poem, begun on the evening of 18 December, was finally put into shape on Wednesday, 31 December, a day before the event ("The Background for Emerson's 'Boston Hymn,'" *American Literature*, XIV [March 1942]: 40–41; *L*, IX, 90–91; and *PN*, 747–749).

At the tap of the conductor's baton at 3 P.M., Josiah Quincy, Jr., arose and announced to the audience that Emerson had written a prologue to the musical celebration and that he would now read it. A number of witnesses reported that as Emerson approached the podium he dropped his papers and there was some little delay as he got them back in order. Apart from that, Emerson's performance was entirely successful—and received with special warmth by the many abolitionists in the crowd, who, like William Lloyd Garrison, then seated in the gallery, had worked for so many years for emancipation. Harriet Beecher Stowe, who also bore some responsibility, likewise sat in the gallery and tearfully acknowledged the cheers of the people. Dwight called the poem he had commissioned "a hymn of Liberty and Justice, wild and strong, and musical and very short," noting that "in his rich tones [Emerson] spellbound the great assembly" (*Dwight's Journal of Music*, XXII [10 January 1863]: 327).

That evening Emerson attended a party at the home of George Luther Stearns and his wife Mary at Medford, Massachusetts, where a recently completed marble bust of John Brown by the sculptor Edwin A. Brackett was to be unveiled. Among those present were Wendell Phillips, W. L. Garrison, Samuel Gridley Howe and his wife Julia Ward, Bronson Alcott, Samuel Longfellow (brother of the poet), the sculptor Brackett, and Judge Martin F. Conway, a Kansas colleague of John Brown. At the request of some guests who had not been able to hear him at the Music Hall, Emerson read his poem again. This second, more private celebration made it clear how much of the credit for Emancipation was felt—especially by this group, which included two of the "Secret Six"—to be owing to the martyr Brown. Indeed the Brown connection offers an explanation for Emerson's decision to cast his poem as a moral and political charge delivered by God to the Pilgrims. Brown consciously modeled the Pilgrim mythology, believing as he did that he was descended from the Peter Brown who in 1620 arrived in America on the Mayflower. So he famously told the Stearnses' son in an autobiographical letter that Emerson admired, and which in turn became part of the Brown mythology when it was published in James Redpath's *Public Life of Capt. John*

Brown (1860), a book dedicated to Brown partisans Emerson, Wendell Phillips, and Henry Thoreau (see Richard J. Hinton, *John Brown and His Men* [New York, 1894], 28).

BOSTON HYMN.

READ IN MUSIC HALL, JANUARY 1, 1863.

The word of the Lord by night
To the watching Pilgrims came,
As they sat by the seaside,
And filled their hearts with flame.

God said, I am tired of kings,   5
I suffer them no more;
Up to my ear the morning brings
The outrage of the poor.

Think ye I made this ball
A field of havoc and war,   10
Where tyrants great and tyrants small
Might harry the weak and poor?

My angel,—his name is Freedom,—
Choose him to be your king;
He shall cut pathways east and west,   15
And fend you with his wing.

Lo! I uncover the land
Which I hid of old time in the West,
As the sculptor uncovers the statue
When he has wrought his best;   20

I show Columbia, of the rocks
Which dip their foot in the seas
And soar to the air-borne flocks
Of clouds, and the boreal fleece.

I will divide my goods; 25
Call in the wretch and slave:
None shall rule but the humble,
And none but Toil shall have.

I will have never a noble,
No lineage counted great: 30
Fishers and choppers and plowmen
Shall constitute a state.

Go, cut down trees in the forest,
And trim the straightest boughs;
Cut down trees in the forest, 35
And build me a wooden house.

Call the people together,
The young men and the sires,
The digger in the harvest-field,
Hireling, and him that hires; 40

And here in a pine state-house
They shall choose men to rule
In every needful faculty,
In church, and state, and school.

Lo, now! if these poor men 45
Can govern the land and sea,
And make just laws below the sun,
As planets faithful be.

And ye shall succor men;
'Tis nobleness to serve; 50
Help them who cannot help again:
Beware from right to swerve.

I break your bonds and masterships,
And I unchain the slave:

Free be his heart and hand henceforth   55
As wind and wandering wave.

I cause from every creature
His proper good to flow:
As much as he is and doeth,
So much he shall bestow.   60

But, laying hands on another
To coin his labor and sweat,
He goes in pawn to his victim
For eternal years in debt.

Today unbind the captive,   65
So only are ye unbound;
Lift up a people from the dust,
Trump of their rescue, sound!

Pay ransom to the owner,
And fill the bag to the brim.   70
Who is the owner? The slave is owner,
And ever was. Pay him.

O North! give him beauty for rags,
And honor, O South! for his shame;
Nevada! coin thy golden crags   75
With Freedom's image and name.

Up! and the dusky race
That sat in darkness long,—
Be swift their feet as antelopes,
And as behemoth strong.   80

Come, East and West and North,
By races, as snow-flakes,
And carry my purpose forth,
Which neither halts nor shakes.

My will fulfilled shall be, 85
For, in daylight or in dark,
My thunderbolt has eyes to see
His way home to the mark.

TEXTS

(A) *Dwight's Journal of Music*, XXII (24 January 1863): 337; (A²) *AM*, XI (February 1863): 227–228 [*text identical to* A *except for having* O *at line 73 rather than* Oh]; (B) Clipping from unidentified newspaper, text identical to (A) with respect to substantives, but with Emerson's holograph corrections, pasted into poetry notebook Rhymer, p. 95 (*PN*, 452); (C) "Emerson's New England Hymn," *New England Loyal Publication Society*, No. 108 (c. August 1863); (D) *May-Day* (Boston, 1867), 75–80; (D²) *Selected Poems* (Boston, 1876), 203–206; (E) *Poems* [Riverside] (Boston, 1884), 174–177; (F) *Poems* [Centenary] (Boston, 1904), 201–204.

Pre-copy-text forms: Two contradictory accounts of the poem's composition have been advanced, reflecting different inferences from the abundant if rather confusing evidence. Carl F. Strauch's seminal article, "The Background for Emerson's 'Boston Hymn,'" *American Literature* XIV (March 1942): 36–47, posits a different sequence of draft versions and offers an apparently less accurate census of manuscripts than is given in *PN*, 747–749. There is disagreement, for example, as to whether the composition to which Emerson gave the title "The Pilgrims" (see *PN*, 696–697) was the first or an intermediate draft of "Boston Hymn" or whether it was a separate conception that contributed its title and some of its lines to the latest draft in the notebooks. The two accounts seem to agree, however, on an essential point later in the poem's genesis: that at the Stearns party Emerson gave away the copy from which he had read at the Music Hall, and that it was thus not the source of printer's copy for *Dwight's Journal* or the *Atlantic Monthly*. Both of these printings lack the seventeenth stanza—which is strong evidence that printer's copy in both instances derived anew from the final draft in poetry notebook EL (*PN*, 356–359), where Emerson, having reordered the stanzas by numbering them, simply overlooked the seventeenth, which, crowded in at the bottom of a page, remained unnumbered. It is possible that Ellen or Edith, acting on their father's instructions, produced the defective printer's copy, since Emerson left on 2 January—earlier than scheduled—for his western lecture tour. The copy that Emerson read from, which did include the seventeenth stanza (see *L*, IX, 122–123), was given at the Stearns party to Samuel Longfellow, who, it seems, delivered it to his brother the next day. On 2 January H. W. Longfellow, explicitly referring to the manuscript, quoted three stanzas in a letter to Charles Sumner (*LLet*, IV, 307). Rather more improbably, there is a suggestion that this original manuscript had actually been divided at the party, the last leaf going to John Weiss, whose diary, now at the Massachusetts Historical Society, indeed still contains it. (The principal difficulty here is that Longfellow quoted the last stanza, which appears on Weiss's leaf.) A final source of confusion is Emerson's note of instruction to Edith, directing her to make a copy for "Miss Dunkin" (Rebecca Duncan) and to send "the original copy" to Mrs. Stearns "at once by mail" (*L*, V, 303). The most satisfactory sense that can be made of this is that the manuscript read from, which, as we have seen, was no longer in his possession, was not the only "original." If this was sent to Mary Stearns after copies were produced from it for the magazines, it probably also lacked the seventeenth stanza, which might in turn account for the fact that nearly a year later Emerson wrote out for her a new fair copy on specially provided paper; this she combined with other contributions from other attendees to make up the "John Brown Album" commemorating the 1 January party (see *L*, IX, 122–123). The Album is now in the Lilly Library at Indiana University.

VARIANTS

3   seaside, (D-F) | sea-side, (A-C)

5   said, (D-F) | said,— (A, C) | said— (B)

13   angel,— (A, C-F) | angel— (B) || Freedom,— (D-F) | Freedom, (A-C)

15   west, (A-D) | west (E-F)

19   the (C-F) | his (A) | <his> ↑the↓ (B) || statue (C-F) | statue, (A-B)

20   best; (D-F) | best. (A-C)

22   seas (A-C, E-F) | seas, (D)

24   clouds, (A-D) | clouds (E-F)

25   goods; (D-F) | goods, (A-C)

30   great: (A-B) | great, (C) | great; (D-F)

31   plowmen [*Ed., from the mss*] | ploughmen (A-F)

32   state. (D-F) | State. (A-C)

33   forest, (A-D) | forest (E-F)

35   forest, (A-D) | forest (E-F)

39   harvest-field, (A-B, F) | harvest field, (C-E)

40   Hireling, (A-D) | Hireling (E-F) || hires; (D-F) | hires. (A-C)

44   church, and state, (A, C-D) | church, and State, (B) | church and state (E-F)

46   sea, (A-D) | sea (E-F)

51   again: (C-F) | again; (A-B)

55   henceforth (D-F) | henceforth, (A-B) | henceforth. (C)

59   As (C-F) | So (A) | <So> ↑As↓ (B)

60   bestow. (A-F) | bestow; (CC7)

61   laying hands (C-F) | laying his hands (A) | laying <his> hands (B)

65–68 [*Lines not present in* (A); *added in the margin in* (B); *present in* (C-F)]

65   Today (B) | To-day (C-F) || captive, (B, D-F) | captive. (C)

69   owner, (A-D) | owner (E-F)

71   owner, (A-B, D-F) | owner. (C)

81   East (C-F) | East, (A-B) || West (D-F) | West, (A-C)

82   snow-flakes, (A-B, D-F) | snowflakes, (C)

NOTES

5–6. In *The Letters of Alexander von Humboldt to Varnhagen von Ense,* trans. Friedrich Kapp (New York, 1860), 193, Emerson read the comment of a "wise Counsellor" to Philip II: "Should God once be tired of monarchies, he will give another form to the political world." Emerson jotted this down in journal CL in 1860 under the heading "God getting tired of Kings" (*JMN,* XIV, 356; cf. *JMN,* XV, 338).

19–20. The lines evidently anticipate the unveiling of the John Brown bust at the Stearns house on the evening of 1 January 1863.

40. Asserting the political equality of the hireling and "him that hires" belongs to the abolitionist argument that a (Southern) slave and a (Northern) person employed at wages occupy radically different situations, from both a moral and an economic standpoint. The proslavery side to this argument was at its most intense at the time Emerson wrote, and might be said to have reached a crescendo with Thomas Carlyle's notorious squib, "The American Iliad in a Nutshell," published in August 1863, which equated chattel slavery with "hiring for life." The statement drew angry rejoinders from several of the Transcendentalists.

50. "Ich dien. I serve, is a truly royal motto" (*W,* XI, 297); identified in "Boston" (*W,* XII, 205) as the "most noble motto" of the Prince of Wales.

65–66. Emerson may well be thinking of John Brown here, but in June 1854 he said of Thomas Wentworth Higginson, who had tried to liberate the fugitive slave Anthony Burns, then in federal custody: "It is only they who save others, that can themselves be saved" (*L,* IV, 449).

75. The Comstock Lode was discovered in 1859 at Virginia City, in what was then Utah. By 1861 instreaming Californians had wrested the area from Mormon control, and Nevada Territory was created. The Comstock mines supplied the U. S. Mint in San Francisco; the one at Carson City, Nevada, did not begin operation until 1870.

78. The phrase "to sit in darkness" occurs several times in the Bible: see, e.g., Matthew 4:16 and Luke 1:79.

VOLUNTARIES.

The title of this poem was suggested to Emerson by James T. Fields, to whom Emerson read portions of the unfinished work at the Parker House in Boston, most probably in August 1863 (Annie Fields, *Authors and Friends* [Boston, 1896], 84–85). As a collective noun for volunteer soldiers the term was obsolete, according to the *OED*, but it was familiar enough in that sense to readers of Shakespeare and other writers of the seventeenth century. The term might equally refer, however, to the somber organ solos heard in church, fit for a dirge or for sacred things in general. Emerson's "Voluntaries" memorializes the gallantry and sacrifice of Colonel Robert Gould Shaw, the twenty-five-year-old commanding officer of the Massachusetts Fifty-Fourth Infantry Regiment, who died with 116 of his men in the assault on Fort Wagner, at Charleston harbor, on 18 July 1863. The Massachusetts Fifty-Fourth was, famously, the first Union regiment composed of free Northern blacks. Its existence was largely owing to the efforts of Massachusetts governor John Albion Andrew, who persuaded the Lincoln administration to admit African-American soldiers into the army's ranks. But those most active in organizing and supporting the regiment included a number of wealthy Boston abolitionists, including some Saturday Club members, who were friends and acquaintances of Emerson—men like John Murray Forbes, George Luther Stearns, Wendell Phillips, and, most significantly, Francis George Shaw, father of the regiment's volunteer leader, the quickly martyred Colonel Shaw.

In many respects the first months' history of the Fifty-Fourth, culminating in the demonstration at Fort Wagner, was the rolling out of a Transcendentalist and reform mythology, grounded in the more than lingering example of John Brown, of the sacrificial white leader who dies for the freedom of slaves, who expiates the guilt accrued from long years of cowardly inaction. It was a cultur-ally decisive mythology, immensely helpful to the war effort, and one to which, in the end, even the history of Lincoln himself was assimilated.

One of the emotional keys to the poem's meaning lies in the curious fact that when Governor Andrew wished to appoint young Shaw to the command of the new regiment—having chosen him for his staunch abolitionism and prior experience in the military —he put the question first to Shaw's father, who was requested, if he approved, to forward the enclosed commission to his son. This makes Frank Shaw a crucial unnamed presence in the work and the occasion of the poem's important economy of fathers and sons. Indeed it was in a literal sense to the elder Shaw in his capac-ity as father that Emerson addressed the work, having sent a copy to him on 10 September (*L*, IX, 113–114).

Emerson had known Francis George Shaw since the late 1820s when he and Emerson's younger brothers attended Harvard to-gether. They remained in touch after Shaw left college early, in 1828, to look after some of his father's very extensive foreign busi-ness interests—those especially in the Caribbean (Bosco and My-erson, *The Emerson Brothers*, 145). The Shaw family controlled one of the greatest mercantile fortunes of this period in Boston and had a way of marrying into other such fortunes, and yet Frank Shaw gradually turned away from the culture of capitalism (un-der the influence of Emerson's sermons, his biographer suggests) and became an increasingly active social reformer and abolition-ist (Lorien Foote, *Seeking the One Great Remedy: Francis George Shaw and Nineteenth-Century Reform* [Athens, Ohio, 2003], 30–32). Early drawn to Transcendentalism, he and his wife, Sarah Blake Sturgis (sister of Caroline Sturgis), moved from Boston to Roxbury in 1841 to be near Brook Farm, which they supported financially, and to cultivate the friendships in particular of Margaret Fuller and Theodore Parker. Frank Shaw, a Fourierist, contributed fre-quently to the *Harbinger,* translated Charles Pellarin's life of Fou-rier and the novel *Consuelo* by George Sand. When Brook Farm ceased operations Shaw and his family removed to Staten Island, began attending the Brooklyn church of Henry Ward Beecher, and got to know his sister, Harriet Beecher Stowe, whose *Uncle Tom's Cabin* (1852) was an enduring point of fascination for their young son Robert. It was apparently at this time that Frank Shaw made the acquaintance of Emerson's friend Henry James, Sr., whose son Garth Wilkinson James, while serving as adjutant under R. G. Shaw, was wounded at Fort Wagner.

Emerson felt multiply connected to the project of the Massachusetts Fifty-Fourth: when asked by one of Shaw's Roxbury relatives to speak at a recruiting and fundraising rally on its behalf, he did so—at Chickering Hall on 20 March 1863, though it is likely that he was acting also at the suggestion of George L. Stearns and with the encouragement of his own daughters, who knew Robert's sister Pauline (*L*, V, 318, 320; *JMN*, XV, 210–213; Len Gougeon, *Virtue's Hero: Emerson, Antislavery, and Reform* [Athens, Ga., 1990], 295–296). The fact that Emerson's frail son Edward was clamoring to leave Harvard and enlist was surely an emotional complication.

It is difficult to appreciate the cultural significance that attached to the death of young Robert Gould Shaw—at a time, at the height of the Civil War just weeks after Gettysburg and Vicksburg, when death was so prolific and indiscriminate. The commemorative volume assembled by his parents in 1864—*Memorial RGS*—offers a context for Emerson's poem more helpful and indicative than its first public appearance in the *Atlantic Monthly*. In that privately printed volume, together with official documents tracing the history of events, Emerson's poem figures among tributes from family members George W. Curtis and James Russell Lowell, both of whom contributed poems; from Sarah Shaw's close friends Lydia Maria Child and Harriet Martineau; from their pastor, Henry Ward Beecher, and from his sister Harriet Beecher Stowe; from Saturday Club members Louis Agassiz, T. W. Higginson, and the historian J. L. Motley; from William Lloyd Garrison, Charles Sumner, and the elder Henry James; from black abolitionists Henry Highland Garnet, Charlotte Forten, and (conveyed at secondhand by Sumner and Child respectively) from Joshua B. Smith and Harriet Jacobs. In July 1863 General Rufus Saxton, of Greenfield, Massachusetts, military governor of South Carolina, whose father had contributed to the *Dial* and sent another son to school at Brook Farm, suggested that a monument to Shaw be erected at Fort Wagner; Higginson's own regiment of freed slaves, the First South Carolina Volunteers, soon raised nearly $3000 for the purpose (Foote, 120). The aforementioned J. B. Smith, an escaped slave from North Carolina, had been taken in and employed by the Shaw family; later and for many years he was a successful caterer in Boston and an active member of the city's Vigilance Committee; still later he headed the fundraising for the high-relief bronze memorial to Shaw and his black troops executed by Augustus Saint-Gaudens and installed on Boston Common facing the State House.

VOLUNTARIES.

I.

Low and mournful be the strain,
Haughty thought be far from me;
Tones of penitence and pain,
Moanings of the tropic sea;
Low and tender in the cell   5
Where a captive sits in chains,
Crooning ditties treasured well
From his Afric's torrid plains.
Sole estate his sire bequeathed—
Hapless sire to hapless son—   10
Was the wailing song he breathed,
And his chain when life was done.

What his fault, or what his crime?
Or what ill planet crossed his prime?
Heart too soft and will too weak   15
To front the fate that crouches near,—
Dove beneath the vulture's beak;—
Will song dissuade the thirsty spear?
Dragged from his mother's arms and breast,
Displaced, disfurnished here,   20

His wistful toil to do his best
Chilled by a ribald jeer.
Great men in the Senate sate,
Sage and hero, side by side,
Building for their sons the State, 25
Which they shall rule with pride.
They forbore to break the chain
Which bound the dusky tribe,
Checked by the owners' fierce disdain,
Lured by "Union" as the bribe. 30
Destiny sat by, and said,
'Pang for pang your seed shall pay,
Hide in false peace your coward head,
I bring round the harvest-day.'

II.

Freedom all winged expands, 35
Nor perches in a narrow place;
Her broad van seeks unplanted lands;
She loves a poor and virtuous race.
Clinging to a colder zone
Whose dark sky sheds the snow-flake down, 40
The snow-flake is her banner's star,
Her stripes the boreal streamers are.
Long she loved the Northman well;
Now the iron age is done,
She will not refuse to dwell 45
With the offspring of the Sun;
Foundling of the desert far,
Where palms plume, siroccos blaze,
He roves unhurt the burning ways
In climates of the summer star. 50
He has avenues to God
Hid from men of Northern brain,
Far beholding, without cloud,
What these with slowest steps attain.
If once the generous chief arrive 55

To lead him willing to be led,
For freedom he will strike and strive,
And drain his heart till he be dead.

III.

In an age of fops and toys,
Wanting wisdom, void of right,   60
Who shall nerve heroic boys
To hazard all in Freedom's fight,—
Break sharply off their jolly games,
Forsake their comrades gay,
And quit proud homes and youthful dames,   65
For famine, toil, and fray?
Yet on the nimble air benign
Speed nimbler messages,
That waft the breath of grace divine
To hearts in sloth and ease.   70
So nigh is grandeur to our dust,
So near is God to man,
When Duty whispers low, *Thou must,*
The youth replies, *I can.*

IV.

O, well for the fortunate soul   75
Which Music's wings infold,
Stealing away the memory
Of sorrows new and old!
Yet happier he whose inward sight,
Stayed on his subtile thought,   80
Shuts his sense on toys of time,
To vacant bosoms brought.
But best befriended of the God
He who, in evil times,
Warned by an inward voice,   85
Heeds not the darkness and the dread,
Biding by his rule and choice,
Feeling only the fiery thread
Leading over heroic ground,

Walled with mortal terror round,   90
To the aim which him allures,
And the sweet heaven his deed secures.
Peril around all else appalling,
Cannon in front and leaden rain,
Him Duty through the clarion calling   95
To the van called not in vain.

Stainless soldier on the walls,
Knowing this,—and knows no more,—
Whoever fights, whoever falls,
Justice conquers evermore,   100
Justice after as before,—
And he who battles on her side,
God, though he were ten times slain,
Crowns him victor glorified,
Victor over death and pain;   105
Forever: but his erring foe,
Self-assured that he prevails,
Looks from his victim lying low,
And sees aloft the red right arm
Redress the eternal scales.   110
He, the poor foe, whom angels foil,
Blind with pride, and fooled by hate,
Writhes within the dragon coil,
Reserved to a speechless fate.

V.

Blooms the laurel which belongs   115
To the valiant chief who fights;
I see the wreath, I hear the songs
Lauding the Eternal Rights,
Victors over daily wrongs:
Awful victors, they misguide   120
Whom they will destroy,
And their coming triumph hide
In our downfall, or our joy:
They reach no term, they never sleep,

In equal strength through space abide;   125
Though, feigning dwarfs, they crouch and creep,
The strong they slay, the swift outstride:
Fate's grass grows rank in valley clods,
And rankly on the castled steep,—
Speak it firmly,—these are gods,   130
All are ghosts beside.

TEXTS

(A) MS, Emerson Miscellaneous Manuscript File, Rutherford B. Hayes Presidential Center, Fremont, Ohio, by permission, printer's copy for B; (B) *AM*, XII (October 1863): 504–506; (C) *Memorial RGS* (Cambridge, 1864), 161–164; (D) *May-Day* (Boston, 1867), 81–88; (E) *Selected Poems* (Boston, 1876), 209–213; (F) *Poems* [Riverside] (Boston, 1884), 178–182; (G) *Poems* [Centenary] (Boston, 1904), 205–209. Several early reprintings, lacking textual authority, are listed in *PN*, 959.

Pre-copy-text forms: The drafts in poetry notebook EL (pp. 104–112 and 120–131) suggest that the poem was composed in two stints. Lines 124–129, added to the published text in 1867, are present from the poem's inception in EL. Holographic copy for the *Atlantic* printing (A) was in James T. Fields' hands no later than 3 September 1863. Emerson mentions in a letter of 7 September that he has made some corrections, hopes shortly to add a pair of "closing lines," and concurs with Fields' suggestion that superfluous "indentations" should be removed (*L*, IX, 113). Fields retained the manuscript and eventually donated it to the Mississippi Valley Sanitary Fair, which in turn sold it in October 1864 to raise money for soldiers' medical care. The copy that Emerson sent to Francis G. Shaw on 10 September has not been traced; the presumption is that the text in *Memorial: RGS* (C) was set from this MS, but it may have been imperfectly adjusted to conform to the *Atlantic* text. See, further, *PN*, 958–959.

VARIANTS

4   tropic (A, C-G) | Tropic (B)
9   bequeathed— (B-E) |
bequeathed,— (A, F-G)
10   son— (B-E) | son,— (A, F-G)
13   [*Flush*] What (A-C, E) | [*Inset*]
What (D, F-G) [*possibly inset in* D *to*

compensate for the loss of the white
line, line *12 falling at the bottom of the
page*]
14   [*Line present*] (B-G) | [*Line
missing*] (A)
23   sate, (A-B, D-G) | sat, (C)

28 tribe, (A-B, D-G) | tribe; (C)

30 "Union" (A-F) | 'Union' (G)

31 said, (A-B, D-G) | said: (C)

32 'Pang (D-G) | "Pang (A-C) || pay, (A-B, D-G) | pay; (C)

34 harvest-day.' (A, D-E) | harvest-day." (B-C) | harvest day.' (F-G)

36 place; (D-G) | place, (A-C)

37 van (B-G) | wing (A) || lands; (D-G) | lands, (A-C)

39 Clinging (B-G) | <Long she clung> ↑Clinging↓ (A) || a (D-G) | the (A-C) || zone (B-G) | zone<,> (A)

40 snow-flake down, (B-F) | snowflake down; (A) | snowflake down, (G)

41 snow-flake (A-F) | snowflake (G)

46 Sun; (D-G) | Sun. (A, C) | Sun (B)

47 desert (B-G) | desart (A)

48 plume, siroccos (D-G) | plume and siroccos (A-C)

52 Hid from (B-G) | <Unknown to> ↑Hid from↓ (A) || Northern (D-G) | northern (A-C)

56 him (A-B, D-G) | him, (C) || led, (B-G) | led,— (A)

58 drain (B-G) | give (A)

62 fight,— (B-G) | fight? (A)

63 Break sharply off (B-G) | To put aside (A)

64 Forsake (B-G) | To leave (A) || gay, (A-E) | gay (F-G)

65 And (B-G) | To (A) || dames, (A-E) | dames (F-G)

66 toil, (A-E) | toil (F-G)

67 benign (B-G) | & fine (A)

68 messages, (B-G) | mesages, (A)

70 in (B-G) | <of> ↑in↓ (A)

71 nigh (B-G) | <near>nigh (A)

73 *must,* (B-G) | *must;* (A)

74 youth (B-G) | Youth (A)

75 [*Flush*] O, (D-G) | [*Inset*] O (A) | [*Flush*] Oh, (B-C)

76 infold, (B-G) | enfold, (A)

79 he (B, D-G) | he, (A, C) || sight, (B-G) | sight (A)

80 Stayed on his subtile thought, (B-G) | <Fixed> ↑Stayed↓ on his <guiding> ↑subtile↓ thought (A)

82 brought. (A-B, D-G) | brought; (C)

83 God (A-B, D-G) | God, (C)

84 He (B-G) | He, (A)

88 thread (B-G) | thread<,> (A)

90 round, (B-G) | round. (A)

93–96 Peril . . . vain. (E-G) | [*Lines not present*] (A-D) | [*Lines added, with terminal punctuation lacking in ll. 93 and 96*] (CC7) [*MS authority: see* PN, *959*]

93 around (E) | around, (F-G)

94 rain, (E) | rain (F-G)

95 Duty (E) | duty (F-G)

97 [*Flush*] Stainless (A-E) | [*Inset*] Stainless (F-G) || soldier (B-G) | Soldier (A)

98 more,— (B-G) | more— (A)

100 evermore, (B, D-G) | <as of yore> ↑evermore↓, (A) | evermore; (C)

102 side, (A-B, D-G) | side— (C)

103 God, (D-G) | ↑—↓God,— (A) | —God— (B) | God— (C) || slain, (D-G) | slain,— (A) | slain— (B-C)

105 pain; (B-E) | pain. (A, F-G)

106–114 Forever: . . . fate. (A-E) | [*Lines canceled* (CC7), *and omitted* (F-G)]

106 Forever: but his erring (B-E) | <But his mistaking> ↑Forever: but his erring↓ (A)

107–114 Self-assured . . . fate. (B-E) | [*Three canceled lines, followed by eight lines added on an inserted leaf:*] <Though he fancies he prevails, /

Sleeps within the dragon coil /
Reserved to a crueller fate> ↑ Self-
assured . . . fate.↓ (A)
114   speechless (B-E) | crueller (A)
123   downfall, (B-G) | downfal<, &>
(A)

124–129 They reach . . . steep,— (D-G)
| [*Lines not present*] (A-C)
130   firmly,— (A-C) | firmly, (D-G)

NOTES

35–42.   In an 1862 journal entry, Emerson wrote: "Wherever snow falls, man is free. Where the orange blooms, man is the foe of man" (*JMN*, XV, 178). And, again: "Freedom does not love the hot zone. The snow-flakes are the right stars of our flag, & the Northern streamers the stripes" (*JMN*, XV, 246; cf. 250).

109.   The judicial image of God's "red right arm" originates with Horace and was probably best known to Emerson through Milton's adaptation of it in *Paradise Lost,* II, 174, and through Byron's translation of Horace, *Odes,* 3.3, though the crucial phrase "*rubente dextera*" actually occurs in *Odes,* 1.2.

126.   "I have read in our old Norse bible of the Edda, that the God *Freye,* or *Freedom,* had a sword so good that it would itself strew a field with carnage, whenever the owner ordered it—Yet I think dwarves killed him once" (*PN,* 311).

128–129.   Edward Emerson (*W,* IX, 470–471) points out this passage from *Representative Men:* "The word Fate or Destiny expresses the sense of mankind in all ages that the laws of the world do not always befriend, but often hurt and crush us. Fate in the shape of *Kinde* or Nature, grows over us like grass" (*CW,* IV, 100).

LOVE AND THOUGHT.

None of the notebook drafts offers evidence about the date of composition. The central conceit, however, may be related to an idea that Emerson expressed in a letter of 24 January 1843 to

Samuel Gray Ward when he said, "I think the two first friends must have been travellers" (*L,* VII, 521). He was writing in a lonely mood from a city (Philadelphia) that he found nearly barren of interest and that contained none, he complained, with whom he could intelligently converse. "If the world was all Philadelphia," he explained to Ward, "although the poultry- & dairy-market would be admirable, I fear suicide would exceedingly prevail."

LOVE AND THOUGHT.

Two well-assorted travellers use
The highway, Eros and the Muse.
From the twins is nothing hidden,
To the pair is naught forbidden;
Hand in hand the comrades go   5
Every nook of nature through:
Each for other they were born,
Each can other best adorn;
They know one only mortal grief
Past all balsam or relief,   10
When, by false companions crossed,
The pilgrims have each other lost.

TEXTS

(A) *May-Day* (Boston, 1867), 89; (B) *Poems* [Centenary] (Boston, 1904), 210. The poem was not included in *Selected Poems* (Boston, 1876) or *Poems* [Riverside] (Boston, 1884). A letter from Edward Emerson to James Eliot Cabot of 25 October 1883 suggests that the omission from the Riverside edition of "Love and Thought," "Lover's Petition," and "Una"—poems appearing consecutively on pp. 89–93 of *May-Day,* but omitted from *Selected Poems*—may have been the result of the printers' mishandling of the copy they had been given of the earlier volume. Edward registers surprise and some regret that "Love and Thought" does not appear in the Riverside proofs ("I do not greatly care but I think it better than the other two") and gives Cabot the option, which he did not exercise, of restoring it (MS Am 1280.226 [297]: Ralph Waldo Emerson Memorial Association deposit, Houghton Library, Harvard University).

Pre-copy-text forms: The five drafts in the poetry notebooks are identified and discussed in *PN,* 849.

VARIANTS

6   nature (A) I Nature (B)   10   relief, (A) I relief; (B)

LOVER'S PETITION.

Emerson provided this poem in celebration of the wedding of Henry Morton Lovering and Isabel Francelia Morse at St. Thomas's Church in Taunton, Massachusetts, 28 June 1864, though it was in fact written nearly twenty years earlier. As a gift to the bride and groom, their friend Abijah Metcalf Ide, Jr. (1825–1875), Taunton postmaster and editor of the Taunton *Democrat,* compiled a privately printed booklet entitled *Over-Songs,* that included poetic contributions from Emerson, Jean Ingelow, Bayard Taylor, Theodore Tilton, George W. Curtis, Lucy Larcom, and Ide himself. This booklet is a considerable rarity since the edition consisted of no more than ten copies, the contributors receiving one copy each and the bride and groom two more. As a young aspiring poet in 1843, Ide had written to Edgar Allan Poe for professional advice and ended up publishing a number of poems in magazines with which Poe was connected. Throughout his life Ide cultivated contact with well known American poets, and as director of the Taunton Lyceum invited many of them to come to lecture, including Bayard Taylor, Lucy Larcom (who taught at the nearby Wheaton Female Seminary) and Emerson, who spoke at Taunton on at least seven occasions (*Chronology,* passim). It appears that Emerson made the bride's acquaintance at one of these events, but it is certain that he knew none of the wedding party so well as he knew Ide, who solicited the contribution. On 9 June

1864, Emerson complied with the request, sending Ide "a few rough verses" along with "all kind wishes to your friends as to yourself" (see Melanie L. Bauer, "Emerson's Acquaintance with Abijah Metcalf Ide, Jr.: Six Unpublished Emerson Letters," *Resources for American Literary Study*, XVII, 2 [1991]: 258–262).

LOVER'S PETITION.

Good Heart, that ownest all!
I ask a modest boon and small:
Not of lands and towns the gift,—
Too large a load for me to lift,—
But for one proper creature, 5
Which geographic eye,
Sweeping the map of Western earth,
Or the Atlantic coast, from Maine
To Powhatan's domain,
Could not descry. 10
Is 't much to ask in all thy huge creation,
So trivial a part,—
A solitary heart?
Yet count me not of spirit mean,
Or mine a mean demand, 15
For 't is the concentration
And worth of all the land,
The sister of the sea,
The daughter of the strand,
Composed of air and light, 20
And of the swart earth-might.
So little to thy poet's prayer
Thy large bounty well can spare.
And yet I think, if she were gone,
The world were better left alone. 25

TEXTS

(A) *Over-Songs* (Cambridge, Mass., 1864), rectos of leaves 10–11; (B) *May-Day* (Boston, 1867), 90–91. Not included in any subsequent collection; see textual note to "Love and Thought."

Pre-copy-text forms: The first two drafts occur in journal Y and appear to date from 1845 (*JMN*, IX, 277–278 and 283–284). For the subsequent revisions and fair copies, see *PN*, 850.

VARIANTS

1	Heart, (B) I Heart! (A)		11	ask (B) I ask, (A)
2	small: (B) I small! (A)		24	yet (B) I yet, (A)
8	the (B) I th' (A) II coast, (B) I			
coast (A)				

UNA.

The first drafts of "Una" occur in pencil in journal Z[A], partly erased and partly overwritten by material dating to mid-March 1843 (*JMN*, VIII, 343–348). It is likely, therefore, that the verses were written shortly before—or very shortly after—Emerson's return home, on 9 March, from a two-month lecture tour to Baltimore, Philadelphia, and New York.

In his note to the poem Edward Emerson acknowledged that the "solution of the pleasing riddle 'Una' . . . cannot be given with authority" (*W*, IX, 471).

UNA.

Roving, roving, as it seems,
Una lights my clouded dreams;
Still for journeys she is dressed;
We wander far by east and west.

In the homestead, homely thought;   5
At my work I ramble not;
If from home chance draw me wide,
Half-seen Una sits beside.

In my house and garden-plot,
Though beloved, I miss her not;   10
But one I seek in foreign places,
One face explore in foreign faces.

At home a deeper thought may light
The inward sky with chrysolite,
And I greet from far the ray,   15
Aurora of a dearer day.

But if upon the seas I sail,
Or trundle on the glowing rail,
I am but a thought of hers,
Loveliest of travellers.   20

So the gentle poet's name
To foreign parts is blown by fame;
Seek him in his native town,
He is hidden and unknown.

TEXTS

(A) *May-Day* (Boston, 1867), 92–93; (B) *Poems* [Centenary] (Boston, 1904), 210–211. Not included in *Selected Poems* (Boston, 1876) or *Poems* [Riverside] (Boston, 1884); see textual note to "Love and Thought."

Pre-copy-text forms: After the drafts in journal Z[A], copies occur in poetry notebooks P, X, and Rhymer: see *PN,* 954.

VARIANTS

5 thought; (A) | thought, (B)

NOTES

14. Chrysolite: another term for peridot, a clear green semi-precious stone. Cf. the passage on gems in "Beauty," from *The Conduct of Life:* "Polarized light showed the secret architecture of bodies; and when the *second-sight* of the mind is opened, now one color or form or gesture, and now another, has a pungency, as if a more interior ray had been emitted, disclosing its deep holdings in the frame of things" (*CW,* VI, 162; cf. *JMN,* XIV, 33).

LETTERS.

On 23 March 1862 Emerson sent a manuscript fair copy of this poem to Oliver Wendell Holmes, Jr.—the future Supreme Court justice—who was then recovering at his father's home on Charles Street, Boston, from severe wounds suffered in the battle of Ball's

Bluff. As Emerson mentioned in the cover letter, he was responding to an earlier request from the young Holmes for an autograph (*L*, IX, 71). It is likely that the poem was written some years earlier, but the precise date of composition cannot be fixed.

LETTERS.

Every day brings a ship,
Every ship brings a word;
Well for those who have no fear,
Looking seaward well assured
That the word the vessel brings   5
Is the word they wish to hear.

TEXTS

(A) *May-Day* (Boston, 1867), 94; (A²) *Selected Poems* (Boston, 1876), 78; (A³) *Poems* [Riverside] (Boston, 1884), 188; (B) *Poems* [Centenary] (Boston, 1904), 217.

Pre-copy-text forms: The first draft occurs in poetry notebook X, written over an erased draft of a translation from Hafiz; this is followed by a fair copy in Rhymer (see *PN*, 845–846). Several separate manuscripts, like the one given to Holmes (Houghton Library, MS Am 1234.8 [1]), appear to have been written out for autograph-seekers. Another at the Houghton Library (MS Am 1280.235 [172]) and one at the Humanities Research Center, University of Texas, Austin, are textually identical to (A). Another, at the Clifton Waller Barrett Library, University of Virginia, signed by but not otherwise in the hand of Emerson, lacks punctuation in lines 1–2.

VARIANTS

4   seaward (A) | seaward, (B) [*The comma is also present in the Rhymer fair copy, see* PN, *435.*]

403

RUBIES.

Emerson's experience in the early 1840s with certain younger friends—notably including Margaret Fuller and Caroline Sturgis —confirmed his belief that his constitutionally cool personality made him less helpful, less available, and less an object of genuine affection than he would have preferred. Among his many expressions of this feeling is a journal entry of 11 November 1842, in which Emerson said of the "selfish man,"

> That which he wishes most of all is to be lifted to some higher platform so that he may see beyond his present fear the trans-alpine good, so that his fear, his coldness, his custom may be broken up like fragments of ice melted & carried away in the great stream of goodwill. . . . We desire to be made great: we desire to be touched with that fire that shall command all this ice to stream; that I shall be a benefit thoroughly, thoroughly. (*JMN*, VIII, 253; cf. "New England Reformers," *CW*, III, 163)

Probably the poem's inception dates back as far as 1844 or 1845 when Emerson inscribed a couplet in journal V: "Friends to me are frozen wine / I wait the sun shall on them shine" (*JMN*, IX, 165; cf. *TN*, III, 345), which was posthumously published among the "Fragments on Nature and Life" in *W*, IX, 352). The phrase "frozen wine," which occurs by itself at *JMN*, IX, 169, was expanded in poetry notebook EF to "Rubies are but frozen wine" sometime after 1851 (*PN*, 281). Interestingly, this development of the idea attributes coolness to Emerson's friends rather than to himself—a position attested to from time to time in the letters (see, e. g., *L*, II, 330).

The draft of lines 5–8 that Emerson wrote in his pocket diary for 1855 (*JMN*, XIII, 507) occurs in pencil upside down at the bottom of the page for 14 May. Clearly it was not inscribed on that day. It more probably belongs to August, since the next pencil inscription, also out of chronological order, about "the right elevation of man," is a version of an entry in journal NO (*JMN*, XIII, 464) that Emerson made on 11 August 1855, shortly after returning home from a lecture at Amherst College. The text at poetry notebook EF, p. 53 (*PN*, 293–294), is written over a draft of "Days," which means that it could not be earlier than 1851. While evidence as to the date of composition of "Rubies" is spotty, what there is points to the last half of the decade of the 1850s.

RUBIES.

They brought me rubies from the mine,
    And held them to the sun;
I said, they are drops of frozen wine
    From Eden's vats that run.

I looked again,—I thought them hearts   5
    Of friends to friends unknown;
Tides that should warm each neighboring life
    Are locked in sparkling stone.

But fire to thaw that ruddy snow,
    To break enchanted ice,   10
And give love's scarlet tides to flow,—
    When shall that sun arise?

TEXTS

(A) *May-Day* (Boston, 1867), 95; (A²) *Poems* [Riverside] (Boston, 1884), 188; (A³) *Poems* [Centenary] (Boston, 1904), 217–218. "Rubies" was not included in *Selected Poems* (Boston, 1876).

Pre-copy-text forms: See the discussion of the several partial and complete drafts of the poem in *PN*, 905–906. In that discussion, the suggestion that the pocket diary text of lines 5–8 may have been written "from memory" presupposes that the poem was in finished form before 1855, which may not be the case.

MERLIN'S SONG.

"Merlin's Song" is the primary example in Emerson's work of what Kenneth Walter Cameron called the "potent song" motif, which finds expression also in the three other Merlin poems as well as in "Woodnotes II," "Freedom," "Solution," "Two Rivers," and a few other places (Cameron, "The Potent Song in Emerson's Merlin Poems," *Philological Quarterly*, XXXII [January 1953]: 22–28). The motif is a principal point of contact between Emerson and the bardic tradition, with which he first became acquainted toward the end of 1816, when, according to the Boston Library Society charging records, the first volume of William Godwin's four-volume *Life of Geoffrey Chaucer* was being read in the Emerson home (Cameron, 23). In June 1820 Emerson copied the crucial passage from this book:

> I know a song by which I soften & inchant the arms of my enemies & render their weapons of none effect. I know a song which I need only to sing when men have loaded me with bonds for the moment I sing it my chains fall in pieces & I walk forth at liberty. I know a song useful to all mankind; for as soon as hatred inflames the sons of men, the moment I sing it they are appeased. I know a song of such virtue, that were I caught in a storm, I can hush the winds, & render the air perfectly calm. (*JMN*, I, 371)

Eight months later, it would seem that Emerson found this passage again, quoted this time in the November 1807 issue of his father's old *Monthly Anthology and Boston Review*, where it was turned into verse by an unidentified contributor as "The Song of a Runic Bard" (quoted in Cameron, 24). On 26 July 1847 Emerson borrowed from the Harvard College library an edition of Paul Henri Mallet's *Northern Antiquities* in the translation by Bishop

Percy. Either at this time or when he subsequently acquired a copy of his own (Harding, *Emerson's Library,* 181), he discovered the source from which Godwin had quoted, "The Runic Chapter, or the Magic of Odin" (Cameron, 27). It was from this source that Emerson quoted the passage once more, in journal VS, in 1853 (*JMN,* XIII, 171), as part of his protracted research for *English Traits.* In 1856, in journal SO (*JMN,* XIV, 73–74), Emerson produced three brief prose imitations based on the already quoted portions of "The Runic Chapter," followed by two lines of verse:

Yet they who hear it shed their age
And take their youth again.

In none of these locations is the "potent song" yet associated with Merlin: Cameron persuasively argues that in making the connection Emerson was influenced by that character's depiction in Book III of Edmund Spenser's *Faerie Queene* (Cameron, 26; cf. headnote to the poem "Merlin," above).

Cameron's conclusion (28) is that the potent song motif allowed Emerson to set forth his conception of the transformative, immortality-conferring effect of inspired poetry, that such poetry "works" by bringing into play the divine indwelling Reason, disarming the ordinary, mundane functions of the Understanding, and so producing the kind of mystical restoration to wholeness and perfection announced by the Orphic Poet in the conclusion of *Nature* (1836). This immensely aggrandized estimate of the capacities of language—and hence the highest conception of the uses of poetry—is certainly not limited to the bardic tradition, though Emerson finds it, time and again, conveniently and appealingly expressed there. In most esoteric and all Gnostic systems of belief, a certain (nonstandard or "poetic") way of knowing is in itself redemptive. One finds this principle memorably expressed, for example, in the Gnostic *Gospel of Thomas,* when Jesus says, "Whoever finds the interpretation of these sayings will not experience death" (James M. Robinson, ed., *The Nag Hammadi Library in English,* 3rd ed. [San Francisco, 1990], 126). When we speak of the "vitality" of some poetic expression—because we have an *experi-*

ence of it—we have some version of this meaning in mind. See also: Nelson F. Adkins, "Emerson and the Bardic Tradition," *PMLA*, LXIII (1948): 662–677.

MERLIN'S SONG

Of Merlin wise I learned a song,—
Sing it low, or sing it loud,
It is mightier than the strong,
And punishes the proud.
I sing it to the surging crowd,— 5
Good men it will calm and cheer,
Bad men it will chain and cage.
In the heart of the music peals a strain
Which only angels hear;
Whether it waken joy or rage, 10
Hushed myriads hark in vain,
Yet they who hear it shed their age,
And take their youth again.

TEXTS

(A) *May-Day* (Boston, 1867), 96; (B) *Poems* [Centenary] (Boston, 1904), 218. Not in *Selected Poems* (Boston, 1876) or *Poems* [Riverside] (Boston, 1884).

Pre-copy-text forms: After the draft of lines 12–13 in journal SO (*JMN*, XIV, 74), the poem developed through several drafts in poetry notebook EL prior to the ink fair copy in Rhymer (see *PN*, 859–60).

VARIANTS

Title: MERLIN'S SONG. (A) |
  MERLIN'S SONG / I (B) [Paired in
  (B) with "Considerations by the
  Way," retitled by Edward Emerson
  "Merlin's Song II."]

2   low, (A) | low (B)
7   cage. (A) | cage— (B)
10 rage, (A) | rage (B)

THE TEST.

In offering this poem to James Russell Lowell for publication in the *Atlantic Monthly*, Emerson explained that "My riddle, you see, is not very deep, & admits, like other riddles, of several solutions. Mine is, five national poets, Homer, Dante, Shakspeare, Swedenborg, & Goethe. A German can, if he will, interpret it, Bach, Mozart, Handel, Haydn, & Beethoven. If you choose to print it, I can put my solution into rhyme in another number" (14 November 1860; *L*, V, 230). "The Solution," however (see below), was much delayed.

THE TEST.

(Musa loquitur.)

I hung my verses in the wind,
Time and tide their faults may find.
All were winnowed through and through,
Five lines lasted sound and true;
Five were smelted in a pot   5
Than the South more fierce and hot;
These the siroc could not melt,
Fire their fiercer flaming felt,
And the meaning was more white
Than July's meridian light.   10
Sunshine cannot bleach the snow,
Nor time unmake what poets know.
Have you eyes to find the five
Which five hundred did survive?

TEXTS

(A) *AM,* VII (January 1861): 85; (B) Ms.E.9.1 no. 68, by permission of the Boston Public Library, printer's copy for C; (C) *May-Day* (Boston, 1867), 97; (C²) *Poems* [Riverside] (Boston, 1884), 189; (C³) *Poems* [Centenary] (Boston, 1904), 220. Not included in *Selected Poems* (Boston, 1876).

Pre-copy-text forms: The first drafts occur in journal Z among Emerson's translations of passages from Goethe's *Nachgelassene Werke,* done in the late 1830s—though the verses are probably of a later date, possibly the early 1850s (*JMN,* VI, 298–299). A draft of the first twelve lines follows in poetry notebook EL, while a copy of the whole is in Rhymer. There the lines are entitled "Purging," while in the subtitle, "Phoebus Apollo" is canceled in favor of "Musa." (The "subtitle" is in dramatic form and means "the Muse speaks.") It is possible that the text sent to Lowell derived not from the Rhymer text, which has the *May-Day* reading in line 14, but rather from NP, p. 107, where an ink fair copy has been torn out of the notebook. See *PN,* 933–934.

VARIANTS

Subtitle: (Musa loquitur.) (B-C) I *Musa loquitur.* (A)
1   wind, (B-C) I wind; (A)
3   through, (B-C) I through; (A)
6   hot; (B-C) I hot. (A)
7   the (A, C) I ↑the↓ (B) II siroc (B-C) I Siroc (A)

9   the (B-C) I their (A)
12   time (C) I Time (A-B)
14   hundred did (B-C) I thousand could (A)

SOLUTION.

With the exception of lines 41–42, which were written many years earlier in journal Books Small (*JMN,* VIII, 463), "Solution" was composed in four drafts in poetry notebook X sometime between late 1860 and the fall of 1866. It had not been written when Emerson sent "The Test" (see above) to *Atlantic* editor J. R. Lowell, but the manuscript printer's copy for its first publication, in *May-Day,* carries a compositor's notation showing that it was set in type on 10 November of the latter year. The fact that the poem did not follow soon after "The Test" in the *Atlantic*—together with the evidence of the four drafts in X—suggested to Carl F. Strauch (Diss., 80) that the poem had cost Emerson "great labor" and that it was probably not finished much before its publication in *May-Day.* But four drafts are not necessarily a sign of difficulty or an indicator of delay. Lists in poetry notebook NP, however, imply some indecision about the artists to be commemorated: originally Emerson thought of including either Milton or Robert Burns in the place finally occupied by Emanuel Swedenborg (*PN,* 523, 524; cf. *L,* V, 230).

SOLUTION.

I am the Muse who sung alway
By Jove, at dawn of the first day.
Star-crowned, sole-sitting, long I wrought
To fire the stagnant earth with thought:
On spawning slime my song prevails,   5
Wolves shed their fangs, and dragons scales;
Flushed in the sky the sweet May-morn,
Earth smiled with flowers, and man was born.
Then Asia yeaned her shepherd race,
And Nile substructs her granite base,—   10
Tented Tartary, columned Nile,—
And, under vines, on rocky isle,
Or on wind-blown sea-marge bleak,
Forward stepped the perfect Greek:
That wit and joy might find a tongue,   15
And earth grow civil, HOMER sung.

   Flown to Italy from Greece,
I brooded long, and held my peace,
For I am wont to sing uncalled,

And in days of evil plight   20
Unlock doors of new delight;
And sometimes mankind I appalled
With a bitter horoscope,
With spasms of terror for balm of hope.
Then by better thought I lead   25
Bards to speak what nations need;
So I folded me in fears,
And DANTE searched the triple spheres,
Moulding nature at his will,
So shaped, so colored, swift or still,   30
And, sculptor-like, his large design
Etched on Alp and Appenine.

    Seethed in mists of Penmanmaur,
Taught by Plinlimmon's Druid power,
England's genius filled all measure   35
Of heart and soul, of strength and pleasure,
Gave to the mind its emperor,
And life was larger than before:
Nor sequent centuries could hit
Orbit and sum of SHAKSPEARE's wit.   40
The men who lived with him became
Poets, for the air was fame.

    Far in the North, where polar night
Holds in check the frolic light,
In trance upborne past mortal goal   45
The Swede EMANUEL leads the soul.
Through snows above, mines underground,
The inks of Erebus he found;
Rehearsed to men the damned wails
On which the seraph music sails.   50
In spirit-worlds he trod alone,
But walked the earth unmarked, unknown.
The near by-stander caught no sound,—
Yet they who listened far aloof
Heard rendings of the skiey roof,   55

412

Solution

And felt, beneath, the quaking ground;
And his air-sown, unheeded words,
In the next age, are flaming swords.

In newer days of war and trade,
Romance forgot, and faith decayed,   60
When Science armed and guided war,
And clerks the Janus-gates unbar,
When France, where poet never grew,
Halved and dealt the globe anew,
GOETHE, raised o'er joy and strife,   65
Drew the firm lines of Fate and Life,
And brought Olympian wisdom down
To court and mart, to gown and town;
Stooping, his finger wrote in clay
The open secret of today.   70

So bloomed the unfading petals five,
And verses that all verse outlive.

TEXTS

(A) MS Barrett 6248-a, Clifton Waller Barrett Library, by permission of the University of Virginia, printer's copy for B; (B) *May-Day* (Boston, 1867), 98–102; (C) *Poems* [Riverside] (Boston, 1884), 189–191; (D) *Poems* [Centenary] (Boston, 1904), 220–223. Not included in *Selected Poems* (Boston, 1876).

Format: Lines 17, 33, 43, 59, and 71 are indented in (B-D); in (A) only lines 71–72 are indented.

Pre-copy-text forms: See *PN,* 919–920, for a discussion of the interrelation of drafts in X.

VARIANTS

6   dragons scales; (B-D) I dragons, scales. (A)
10   base,— (B-D) I base, (A)
17   Greece, (B-D) I Greece (A)

18   long, (A-B) I long (C-D)
19   uncalled, (B-D) I uncalled (A)
21   delight; (B-D) I delight (A)

23   horoscope, (B-D) | horoscope (A)

24   With (B-D) | <With>Bring (A) [*Possibly a printer's error, but more likely Emerson reverted in proof to the original reading.*]

26   need; (B-D) | need[?] (A) [*End-line punctuation unrecoverable in MS.*]

27   fears, (B-D) | fears (A)

29   nature (A-C) | Nature (D)

32   Appenine (A) | Apennine (B-D)

40   SHAKSPEARE'S (B-D) | SHAKSPEARES (A)

49   damned (A-C) | damnèd (D)

51   spirit-worlds (B-D) | spirit worlds, (A)

52   unknown. (B-D) | unknown, (A)

53   by-stander (A-C) | bystander (D)

55   skiey (A) | skyey (B-D)

65   o'er (B-D) | oer (A)

66   Life, (A-B) | Life (C-D)

68   to gown (B-D) | to <town &> gown (A) || town; (A-B) | town (C) | town. (D)

70   today (A) | to-day (B-D)

71   bloomed (A-B) | bloom (C-D)

NOTES

32.   More commonly spelled Apennines, the major mountain range in Italy. The *OED* accepts Emerson's spelling, but probably the *Atlantic Monthly* did not.

33–34.   Penmanmaur and Plinlimmon are mountain peaks in Wales.

47.   Swedenborg had considerable expertise in mining and metallurgy.

48.   Erebus: the ante-chamber to Hades. Swedenborg was the author of *Heaven and Hell* (1758).

51.   Somewhat as Dante had done, Swedenborg claimed to have traveled to heaven and conversed with angels and the spirits of the departed. This claim was co-opted by American spiritualists, beginning with Andrew Jackson Davis in 1847, and provided a rationale of access to the "spirit-world."

62.   The Roman temple of the Argilentum, sacred to the worship of Janus, had massive double gates, the so-called Gates of War, which were closed during times of peace and opened only when war raged.

70.   The phrase "open secret" translates Goethe's "das öffentliche Geheimnis." In all likelihood Emerson first encountered it in the letter he received from Thomas Carlyle in 1837 praising his new book, *Nature:* "It is the true Apocalypse this when the 'open secret' becomes revealed to a man" (*CEC,* 157, and Joseph Slater, "Goethe, Carlyle, and the Open Secret," *Anglia,* LXXVII [1958]: 422–428).

NATURE AND LIFE.

NATURE.

I.

The composition of this poem is decidedly atypical, having been assembled from fragments composed at different times without apparent reference to one another. When the fragments at last came together, Emerson's impulse was to invent a larger structure for the poem to be a part of.

Lines 12–15 were written first, as an independent quatrain—possibly as early as the 1830s since it originates in poetry notebook P. A revised text of these lines entitled "Beware!" occurs on the verso of a sheet that Emerson used to insert new matter into the lecture "The Humanity of Science," delivered several times between 1836 and 1848 (see *EL*, II, 382, and *Chronology*, 117, 221, 225). The quatrain retained its independence at least until February 1849, when Emerson wrote it out for an autograph-seeker (*PN*, 867).

Lines 16–21 begin their development in journal Books Small among passages of which the only datable ones belong to 1843 (*JMN*, VIII, 446). Yet another distinct segment, including lines 9–11, appears to have been rejected from a draft of "The World-Soul," a poem completed in 1846 (*PN*, 134). Lines 7–8 originate in notebook JK (*JMN*, X, 383), which Emerson used between 1843 and 1847.

Above the ink fair copy of "Nature I" inscribed on p. 212 of notebook X and consisting of lines 1–6 and 9–15, Emerson inserted a "I" in pencil, indicating that it was to be the first element in a three-part poem (*PN*, 228–229). Part "II," on p. 211, was the poem posthumously published with the supplied title "The Walk":

see *Poems* [Riverside] (Boston, 1884), 304, and *Poems* [Centenary] (Boston, 1904), 366. Part "III," on p. 213, was a ten-line version of "Fate" ("Delicate omens"). The three parts, in the indicated order, were copied into poetry notebook NP, where lines 7–8 of "Nature I" were at last added (*PN*, 494). The combination of the three poems, for all the appearance of accident in the assembly, works surprisingly well as a "variations-on-a-theme" experiment, of a kind that Emerson did not attempt elsewhere. Still, in publishing "Nature I" in a subsequent combination with "Nature II" in *May-Day*, Emerson chose not to bring this effort to a conclusion.

NATURE.

I.

Winters know
Easily to shed the snow,
And the untaught Spring is wise
In cowslips and anemonies.
Nature, hating art and pains,   5
Baulks and baffles plotting brains;
Casualty and Surprise
Are the apples of her eyes;
But she dearly loves the poor,
And, by marvel of her own,   10
Strikes the loud pretender down.
For Nature listens in the rose,
And hearkens in the berry's bell,
To help her friends, to plague her foes,
And like wise God she judges well.   15
Yet doth much her love excel
To the souls that never fell,
To swains that live in happiness,
And do well because they please,
Who walk in ways that are unfamed,   20
And feats achieve before they're named.

TEXTS

(A) *May-Day* (Boston, 1867), 105–106; (B) *Poems* [Riverside] (Boston, 1884), 193; (B²) *Poems* [Centenary] (Boston, 1904), 225. Not included in *Selected Poems* (Boston, 1876).

Pre-copy-text forms: See *PN,* 867–868.

VARIANTS

12	rose, (A) l rose (B)		18	happiness, (A) l happiness (B)
13	bell, (A) l bell (B)			

NATURE.

II.

The second draft of this poem was inscribed over a draft portion of Emerson's speech at the Robert Burns Centenary, which he gave on 25 January 1859 (*W,* XI, 437–443). None of the three manuscript versions of the poem gives indication of a relationship to or combination with the earlier poem published as "Nature I" (see above).

NATURE.

II.

She is gamesome and good,
But of mutable mood,—
No dreary repeater now and again,

She will be all things to all men.
She who is old, but nowise feeble, 5
Pours her power into the people,
Merry and manifold without bar,
Makes and moulds them what they are,
And what they call their city way
Is not their way, but hers, 10
And what they say they made today,
They learned of the oaks and firs.
She spawneth men as mallows fresh,
Hero and maiden, flesh of her flesh;
She drugs her water and her wheat 15
With the flavors she finds meet,
And gives them what to drink and eat;
And having thus their bread and growth,
They do her bidding, nothing loath.
What's most theirs is not their own, 20
But borrowed in atoms from iron and stone,
And in their vaunted works of Art
The master-stroke is still her part.

TEXTS

(A) *May-Day* (Boston, 1867), 107–108; (A²) *Poems* [Riverside] (Boston, 1884), 194; (A³) *Poems* [Centenary] (Boston, 1904), 226. Not included in *Selected Poems* (Boston, 1876). The Riverside and Centenary editions of *Poems* follow (A).

Pre-copy-text forms: Two drafts occupy poetry notebook NP, pp. 206–209. A fair copy is in Rhymer (see *PN,* 868). Printer's copy for (A) does not survive, but a sheet of paper apparently used to blot a page containing lines 1–14 is in the Clifton Waller Barrett Library at the University of Virginia, where it has long served as backing for a photograph of Emerson. Unfortunately the mirror image of the inscription is not legible enough—particularly with regard to the punctuation—to be useful here.

VARIANTS

11   today, [*MS form: see* PN, *456,*
535] | to-day, (A) [*Probable house*
styling.]

NOTES

18.   The word is "breed" in the first two drafts in poetry notebook NP, changed to "bread" in the Rhymer fair copy and so printed.

20–23.   In his note to the poem in *W,* IX, 478, Edward Emerson directed the reader's attention to a passage in "Thoughts on Art," published in the *Dial* in 1841 and reprinted as "Art" in *Society and Solitude:* In the fine arts, according to Emerson, "the prominent fact is subordination of man. His art is the least part of his work of art. A great deduction is to be made before we can know his proper contribution to it" (*CW,* VII, 21).

THE ROMANY GIRL.

Emerson's interest in Gypsies had been sparked by the works of the English linguist and travel-writer George Henry Borrow (1803–1881). In 1842 Emerson reviewed *The Zincali; or, An Account of the Gypsies of Spain* (1841) in the *Dial* and published a shorter notice of Borrow's *The Bible in Spain* (1843) a year later. His library eventually included Borrow's *Lavengro, the Scholar, the Gypsy, the Priest* (1851) and its sequel, *The Romany Rye* (1857). In March 1843, about the time he would have been reading *The Bible in Spain,* Emerson set down in his journal an impression that years later would re-emerge in the second stanza of "The Romany Girl": "Gypsies & militia captains, paddies & Chinese, all manner of cunning & pragmatical men and a few fine women, a strange world made up of such oddities; the only beings that belong to the horizon being the fine women" (*JMN,* VIII, 345). In his remarks on *The Zincali,* Emerson gave his opinion that Borrow overstated the wretchedness and isolation of the Gypsies, that he did not disclose the "resources and compensation" that must exist. "It is an aristocracy of rags, and suffering, and vice, yet as exclusive as the patricians of wealth and power. . . . The condition of the Gypsy may be bad enough, tried by the scale of English comfort, and yet appear tolerable and pleasant to the Gypsy, who finds attractions in his out-door way of living, his freedom, and sociability, which the Agent of the Bible Society [i.e., Borrow] does not reckon" (*Dial*, III [July 1842]: 128).

Emerson continued to refer to Borrow, generally enlisting him in support of a romantic view of noble savagery against the effete manners of the hypercivilized. "I much prefer the heathenism of Indians & Gipsies," he wrote in 1853, recalling "Borrow's story of the squinting gypsies to whom he read St John's gospel" (*JMN*, XIII, 158). Two years later he listed "Lavengro" first among illustrations of "Real power" (*JMN*, XIII, 394). A few pages later, Emerson began to identify and formulate that power, first in what appears to be prose: "The sun goes down, & with it the coarseness of my attire: the moon rises, and with it the power of my beauty"— and then, on consecutive pages, in drafts of the poem's first stanza (*JMN*, XIII, 396–397). Thus the poem was begun in 1855. The only reason to question Edward Emerson's claim that it was finished at that time as well (*W*, IX, 479) is the presence in Emerson's manuscript Account Book 6 for March 1857 of what is evidently an early version of the final stanza: "We bide by market & moors / Fortunes we can spae & spell / We know life's taste tho' not indoors / Pale men's fortunes reading well" (see *PN*, 904).

"The Rommany Girl," as Emerson, following Borrow, at first spelled the title (see *CW*, V, 386), was among the poems he offered for the first issue of the *Atlantic Monthly*. He returned proof on 24 September 1857, having, he said, "no correction to make," and declining to accept editor James Russell Lowell's suggestion that changing "under" to "beneath" in line 13 would help with the rhythm (*L*, VIII, 532–533). Ten years later, in the publication of *May-Day*, Emerson would resolve this problem with a different choice.

The poem was an especial favorite of Emerson's daughter Ellen, who was gratified on one occasion to hear a friend remark that "Your Father's 'Romany Girl' is better Gypsy, infinitely!" than George Eliot's 1868 poem, "The Spanish Gypsy" (*ETE*, I, 503).

THE ROMANY GIRL.

The sun goes down, and with him takes
The coarseness of my poor attire;
The fair moon mounts, and aye the flame
Of Gypsy beauty blazes higher.

Pale Northern girls! you scorn our race;   5
You captives of your air-tight halls,
Wear out in-doors your sickly days,
But leave us the horizon walls.

And if I take you, dames, to task,
And say it frankly without guile,   10
Then you are Gypsies in a mask,
And I the lady all the while.

If, on the heath, below the moon,
I court and play with paler blood,
Me false to mine dare whisper none,—   15
One sallow horseman knows me good.

Go, keep your cheek's rose from the rain,
For teeth and hair with shopmen deal;
My swarthy tint is in the grain,
The rocks and forest know it real.   20

The wild air bloweth in our lungs,
The keen stars twinkle in our eyes,
The birds gave us our wily tongues,
The panther in our dances flies.

You doubt we read the stars on high,   25
Nathless we read your fortunes true;
The stars may hide in the upper sky,
But without glass we fathom you.

May-Day and Other Pieces (1867)

TEXTS

(A) MS Autograph File, E, Houghton Library, Harvard University, printer's copy for B; (B) *AM*, I (November 1857): 46–47; (C) *May-Day* (Boston, 1867), 109–110; (C²) *Selected Poems* (Boston, 1876), 86–87; (D) *Poems* [Riverside] (Boston, 1884), 195–196; (E) *Poems* [Centenary] (Boston, 1904), 227–228.

Pre-copy-text forms: See *PN*, 904. The last version before printer's copy (A) is the fair copy in poetry notebook Rhymer, where it bears the title "Gypsy's Song."

VARIANTS

Title: THE ROMANY GIRL. (C-E) | *The Rommany Girl.* (A) | THE ROMMANY GIRL. (B) |
4   Gypsy (C-E) | gypsy (A-B)
5   Northern (C-F) | northern (A-B) || race; (B-E) | race, (A)
6   You (B-E) | You, (A)
7   in-doors (A-D) | indoors (E)

11   Gypsies (C-E) | gypsies (A-B)
13   If, (B-C) | If (A, D-E) || heath, (B-E) | heath (A) || below (C-E) | under (A-B)
15–16   none,—/ One (B-E) | none, /—One (A)
18   deal; (B-E) | deal, (A)

NOTES

5.   In 1840 (*JMN*, VII, 536) and again in 1853 (*JMN*, XIII, 268) Emerson quoted line 132 of "L'Apparition" by Hégésippe Moreau (1810–1838): "Pâles filles du Nord! vous n'êtes pas mes sœurs" (*Œuvres Complètes de Hégésippe Moreau* (Paris, 1890), 60. See also *W*, IX, 479.

DAYS.

Emerson did not often comment in his journals on his own poems, but early in 1852 he made the following remarkable entry: "I find one state of mind does not remember or conceive of another state. Thus I have written within a twelvemonth verses ("Days") which I do not remember the composition or correction of, & could not write the like today, & have only for proof of their being mine, various external evidences as, the MS. in which I find them, & the circumstance that I have sent copies of them to friends, &c &c. Well, if they had been better, if it had been a noble poem, perhaps it would have only more entirely taken up the ladder into heaven" (*JMN*, XIII, 10). The passage firmly assigns the date of composition to 1851, but there is also the valuable strangeness of its estimating the quality of a poem by the degree to which its author has forgotten that he ever struggled with the writing of it. This creative amnesia may indeed be the secret to the poem's widely-acknowledged success, for as Robert D. Richardson, Jr., has noted, "The perception behind 'Days,' the nagging regretful sense that the days are gods, each one laden with gifts we are never quite able to take, was expressed scores of times in Emerson's notes, letters, and journals" (178). By the time he committed the poem to paper, Emerson had been revolving the idea so constantly and for so long a period, that he had in a sense come to inhabit it.

The early, fragmentary anticipations of "Days" seem each to explore some salient but subordinate aspect of the finished poem—as, for example, among the earliest, some lines of 1825 that depict Emerson's commitment to a career in the church as removing him from an ordinary history of hopes and disappointment:

May-Day and Other Pieces (1867)

Days that come dancing on fraught with delights
Dash our blown hopes as they limp heavily by. (*JMN*, II, 405; cf. *W*,
IX, 384–385)

Two years later, in sickness and discouragement, he implicitly
compared his case to that of Job: "My days run onward like the
weaver's beam [cf. Job 7:6]. They have no honour among men,
they have no grandeur in the view of the invisible world. It is as if
a net of meanness were drawn around aspiring men thro' which
their eyes are kept on mighty objects but the subtile fence is for-
ever interposed" (*JMN*, III, 78–79; cf. Richardson, 78–79). The
imagery here may serve to remind us that a "pleached" garden
(line 7) is one fenced off from the world by the interwoven
branches of a hedge, a boundary established, for good or ill, by
the art of the gardener. Emerson experimented with the more
morbid developments of the idea in poems of this period, includ-
ing a sonnet, "My days roll by me" (*JMN*, III, 36), and a quatrain,
"The days pass over me" (*W*, IX, 395; *PN*, 770)—the latter dis-
cussed by Egbert S. Oliver as a source for "Days" ("Emerson's
'Days,'" *New England Quarterly*, XIX (December, 1946): 518–524.
   In "Doctrine of the Hands," a lecture first given on 13 Decem-
ber 1837, Emerson redirected the evolving mythology toward the
comic possibilities:

> Silent and passive and as it were sulkily nature offers every morn-
> ing her wealth to man. She is immensely rich: he is welcome to her
> entire goods; but she speaks no word, will not beckon or cough,
> only leaves all her doors ajar—hall, storeroom, and cellar. He may
> do as he will: if he takes her hint and uses her goods, she speaks no
> word; if he blunders and starves, she says nothing. (*EL*, II, 235)

In a letter to Margaret Fuller in October 1840, with his mind on
reform and the Brook Farm experiment, he supposed that "The
morning & evening cannot touch us with their delicate fingers,
[&] the finer hints of all beneficent spirits are lost on the flannel
& buckram customs in which we wrap ourselves warm." Here "cus-

tom" is the old "subtile fence" that keeps a bountiful providence
at bay. "Heaven walks among us ordinarily muffled in such triple
or tenfold disguises that the wisest are deceived & no one suspects
the days to be gods" (*L,* II, 342). That heaven should be so deeply
disguised—that it should not plainly show itself for what it is—
makes "hypocrites" of its avatars in days.

In 1844 Emerson tried out on his Aunt Mary the idea that the
days are "gods" and found her willing to concede that, yes, they
were "(little) gods," originating, like us, with their Father, yet not-
ing, with characteristically free orthography, "how many of them
in touching our earth instead of strenght receive dingy feeble
aspects some robed like harliquins, some habited like gaity or
pomp" (*The Selected Letters of Mary Moody Emerson,* ed. Nancy Craig
Simmons [Athens, Ga., 1993], 455).

In a letter to Lidian of 3 September 1846, written as he was as-
sembling his volume of *Poems,* he gave this old idea a Gnostic twist,
saying that "though days go smoothly enough they do not bring
me in their fine timely wallets the alms I incessantly beg of them."
He goes on to stipulate what, just then in particular, he hoped the
days would bring him, and it turns out to be a version of the "po-
tent song" of the Merlin poems: "Where are the melodies, where
the unattainable words, where the efficacious rhymes, that make
night & day alike, good luck & bad, and abolish all that is called
fortune or glory, before the serenity & security of him that heareth
these? Where? Where? If Eddy knows them, send him back by car
or boat or cloud. No, he is only the theme of these. One day that
strange revolution & Declaration of Independence which occurs
in human breasts may befal in his, & he may know himself & these,
and begin to murmur incantations of his own" (*L,* III, 344). As in
the Gnostic religion, so in Emerson's, self-knowledge is the key
to world-knowledge, both alike are redemptive, and both sustain
the language of poetry. It should also be noted here that F. O.
Matthiessen discovered an allusion to Shakespeare's *Troilus and
Cressida* (III, iii, 145–146) in the reference to Time's "wallet" as a
source of "alms" (*American Renaissance* [New York, 1941], 59–60);
in annotating Emerson's letter Rusk independently identified a

second allusion to the same play. The whole of Matthiessen's discussion of the poem (57–64) remains valuable.

On 24 May 1847, Emerson wrote in his journal: "The days come & go like muffled & veiled figures sent from a distant friendly party, but they say nothing, & if we do not use the gifts they bring, they carry them as silently away" (*JMN*, X, 61; used in "Works and Days," *CW*, VII, 85). The notion of a "distant friendly party" conveys something of Aunt Mary's humor, but it begins also to draw attention to a conceptual rift between the eternal and temporal aspects of the question—particularly whether we deal with days, in time, as exemplary of what Emerson called "succession," or whether, instead, we deal *through* days with what is beyond time. This distinction was closer to the fore in a journal entry two years later:

> How difficult to deal erect with the Days! Each of these events which they bring,—this Concord thieving, the muster, the ripening of plums, the shingling of the barn, all throw dust in your eyes, & distract your attention. He is a strong man who can look them in the eye, see through this superficial juggle, feel their identity & keep his own; know surely that one will be like another to the end of the world, nor permit bridal or funeral, earthquake or church, election or revolution[,] to draw him from his task. (*JMN*, XI, 154)

So it is not wrong to be suspicious of the miscellaneous particular gifts that the "endless file" of days provides: the great enabling gift to which the soul is entitled as by birthright—the gift beyond suspicion or hypocrisy—is, as it must be, singular and out of time, not plural or in time. Emerson once represented this possibility mythologically, effectively placing it out of time by framing it as a dream:

> I dreamed that I floated at will in the great Ether, and I saw this world floating also not far off, but diminished to the size of an apple. Then an angel took it in his hand & brought it to me and said "This must thou eat." And I ate the world. (*JMN*, VII, 525; cf. Richardson, 342).

Days

The world-apple represents the soul's unbounded entitlement, which is forfeit in every tragic, subsiding settlement for less. The gifts of days may be petty decoys into time, where sight of the real is proportionately lost. It is a possibility recurrently insisted upon in the world's transcendental mythologies, as, for example, in the "Hymn of the Pearl" from the apocryphal *Acts of the Apostle Thomas:* "They mixed me drink with their cunning and gave me to taste of their meat. I forgot that I was a king's son, and served their king. I forgot the Pearl for which my parents had sent me. Through the heaviness of their nourishment I sank into deep slumber" (quoted in Hans Jonas, *The Gnostic Religion*, 2nd ed. [Boston, 1963], 69).

DAYS.

Daughters of Time, the hypocritic Days,
Muffled and dumb, like barefoot dervishes,
And marching single in an endless file,
Bring diadems and fagots in their hands.
To each they offer gifts after his will,   5
Bread, kingdoms, stars, or sky that holds them all.
I, in my pleached garden, watched the pomp,
Forgot my morning wishes, hastily
Took a few herbs and apples, and the Day
Turned and departed silent. I, too late,   10
Under her solemn fillet saw the scorn.

TEXTS

(A) *AM,* I (November 1857): 47; (B) MS MA 925.3, by permission of the Pierpont Morgan Library, printer's copy for C; (C) *May-Day* (Boston, 1867), 111; (D) *May-Day* (Boston, 1868), 111; (E) *Selected Poems* (Boston, 1876), 172; (F) *Poems* [Riverside] (Boston, 1884), 196; (F²) *Poems* [Centenary] (Boston, 1904), 228.

Pre-copy-text forms: See *PN,* 769–770. As noted in *PN,* there exist a number of separate manuscript copies other than the *May-Day* printer's copy. One, the so-called Storrer MS at the Houghton Library (MS Am 82.10), was probably originally conveyed to Elizabeth Hoar. Others, of no direct textual significance, were prepared from time to time for autograph seekers: see, for example, *L,* VI, 290.

VARIANTS

1   Daughters (A, CC6, CC7, E-F) |
Damsels (B-C) | Daughter (D)
2   dumb (B-F) | dumb, (A)
4   hands. (A, C-F) | hands. <—>
(B)

5   gifts (B-F) | gifts, (A) || will, (C-
F) | will,— (A) | will, <—> (B)
6   and (B-F) | or (A)
7   pleached (A-D, F) | pleachéd
(E)

NOTES

1. The *May-Day* reading of "Damsels" follows Emerson's holograph printer's copy and some of the earlier drafts, but by 1867 had been rejected. After the publication of the volume Emerson wrote to James Elliot Cabot, "I read with amazement the word 'Damsels' which slipped into the new text, I know not how. 'Daughters' was right & shall be" (*L*, V, 518). Emerson ordered the correction to be made in the 1868 printing of *May-Day*, but the resulting plate-correction read "Daughter"—a reading that persisted in later printings within the edition. Some antecedents for the phrase "daughters of Time" have been noted: Nelson F. Adkins suggested some lines from Night VIII of *Night Thoughts* (1742–1745) by Edward Young ("Time's daughters, true as those of men, deceive us; / Not one, but puts some cheat on all mankind"); and William Sloane Kennedy suggested "The Mystic" (1830) by Tennyson ("The silent congregated hours, / Daughters of time, divinely tall, beneath / Severe and youthful brows"), both referenced by Carl F. Strauch, "The MS Relationships of Emerson's 'Days,'" *Philological Quarterly*, XXIX (April 1950): 199–200.

1. When, on 24 September 1857, Emerson returned proofs to F. H. Underwood, Lowell's assistant at the *Atlantic*, he conceded that "about the word 'hypocritical,' he [Lowell] is right again, but I cannot mend it to-day" (*L*, VIII, 533). The editors of *The Poetry Notebooks* and of the *Letters* appear to have assumed that Emerson originally had "hypocritical" in printer's copy, and that Lowell, objecting, suggested "hypocritic." In fact the reverse is more likely, since the reading "hypocritic" is the invariable form in the drafts. Lowell must have objected to the word-choice, preferring "hypocritical" as the more correct or less unusual term, though its introduction would upset the meter. It is the latter consideration that caused Emerson to say that he could not "mend it to-day." Emerson gave Lowell permission to make such a change at this point as suited him, but evidently the editor left the line as he found it.

5. Possibly there is a recollection here of St. Paul's discussion of the diversity of spiritual gifts in I Corinthians 12:11: "But all these worketh that one and self-same Spirit, dividing to every man severally as he will."

7.   The term "pleached" is explained in the headnote above. Holmes noted appreciatively that the word was "an heir-loom from Queen Elizabeth's day" (*Ralph Waldo Emerson* [Boston, 1884], 313). Emerson probably gave it a two-syllable pronunciation to judge from the acute accent over the final e in the Storrer manuscript and the *Selected Poems* text.

THE CHARTIST'S COMPLAINT.

The first draft of this poem (*JMN*, X, 49), written in the late winter or early spring of 1847, has even less to do with actual Chartists than the version that Emerson completed some time after his return from England in 1848. Carl F. Strauch (Diss., 572–575) makes a convincing case that "The Chartist's Complaint" and "Days" were companion poems, both essentially brought to completion in 1851: their subject matter, the history and sequence of their manuscripts, and—for the most part—their publication history bear out Strauch's argument. It is clear, however, that "Days" proved to be much the more popular poem, and Emerson did not insist on pairing it with "The Chartist's Complaint" (indeed he dropped that poem entirely) in *Selected Poems*.

Draft copies of the poem had a number of titles, beginning with "Fine Days," then "Villeggiatura," then "Chartism" (canceled in favor of "Janus"). Only the final fair copy, in poetry notebook Rhymer, had the title as published. In 1848, during his trip to England, Emerson had some first-hand experience of the radicals known as "Chartists" for their advocacy of the six points of the so-called People's Charter: annual parliaments, universal male suffrage, abolition of property requirements for members of the House of Commons, secret ballot, equally sized electoral districts, and salaries for MPs. Emerson's enumeration of these points in his journal (*JMN*, X, 567) suggests that he was very slow in taking notice of the reformers' particular demands. He had been generally aware of the movement at least since 1840 when he was sent a copy of a pamphlet that Carlyle had written on the subject (*CEC*, 256). Carlyle and Emerson both sympathized with the oppressed laboring classes, but differed sharply in their views on how the problems they saw should be addressed, Carlyle insisting that the aristocracy do its duty by the poor and govern more forcibly, Emerson finding in a laissez-faire position a remedy far more in the American democratic vein. Indeed, like many of his countrymen, Emerson considered the European revolutions of 1848 a function of the historical inevitability that American-style democracy would assert itself successfully against monarchical and aristocratic models. In *English Traits* (1856), he wrote that "The English dislike the American structure of society, whilst yet trade, mills, public education, and chartism are doing what they can to create in England the same social condition" (*CW*, V, 85; see also Richardson, 451–456).

In "The Chartist's Complaint," however, which came so near to having a different title, English politics are nowhere to be seen. The more universal case of the inequities of class difference, of the widely varying perceptions of nature and days that follow as sequels from wealth or poverty—these are Emerson's themes, and they betray not only a sense of brutal unfairness, but a measure of personal guilt as well. On the day of the grand Chartist demonstration in London, 10 April 1848, Emerson was present as workers rioted and the Duke of Wellington defended the city. The next day, as he would later learn, there was a devastating fire at "a rich man's wood and lake," when the Irish-built Fitchburg Railroad set the bucolic Walden woods ablaze (*L*, IV, 109–110).

THE CHARTIST'S COMPLAINT.

Day! hast thou two faces,
Making one place two places?
One, by humble farmer seen,
Chill and wet, unlighted, mean,

Useful only, triste and damp,   5
Serving for a laborer's lamp?
Have the same mists another side,
To be the appanage of pride,
Gracing the rich man's wood and lake,
His park where amber mornings break,   10
And treacherously bright to show
His planted isle where roses glow?
O Day! and is your mightiness
A sycophant to smug success?
Will the sweet sky and ocean broad   15
Be fine accomplices to fraud?
O Sun! I curse thy cruel ray:
Back, back to chaos, harlot Day!

TEXTS

(A) MS formerly at the Edward Lawrence Doheney Memorial Library, St. John's Seminary, Camarillo, California; sold to an unknown buyer in 1987, probably printer's copy for B; (B) *AM*, I (November 1857): 47; (C) *May-Day* (Boston, 1867), 112–113; (C²) *Poems* [Riverside] (Boston, 1884), 197; (C³) *Poems* [Centenary] (Boston, 1904), 232. Not included in *Selected Poems* (Boston, 1876).

Pre-copy-text forms: See *PN*, 758.

VARIANTS

2	places? (B-C) I places; (A)	13	Day! (B-C) I day! (A)
5	triste (B-C) I triste, (A)	17	ray: (C) I ray; (A) I ray! (B)
6	lamp? (B-C) I lamp: (A)	18	Day! (B-C) I day! (A)
7	side, (B-C) I side (A)		

NOTES

8.   Appanage: a provision for the maintenance of the younger sons of royalty or the aristocracy.

MY GARDEN.

"My Garden" celebrates the extensive woodlot at Walden Pond that Emerson purchased in 1845 and that he described in a letter to Carlyle of 14 May 1846:

> I . . . have a new plaything, the best I ever had—a woodlot. Last fall I bought a piece of more than forty acres on the border of a little lake half a mile wide & more, called Walden Pond—a place to which my feet have for years been accustomed to bring me once or twice in a week at all seasons. My lot to be sure is on the further side of the water, not so familiar to me as the nearer shore. Some of the wood is an old growth, but most of it has been cut off within twenty years & is growing thriftily. In these May days, when maples poplars oaks birches walnut & pine are in their spring glory, I go thither every afternoon, & cut with my hatchet an Indian path through the thicket all along the bold shore, & open the finest pictures. My two little girls know the road now though it is nearly two miles from my house & find their way to the spring at the foot of a pine grove & with some awe to the ruins of a village of shanties all overgrown with mullein which the Irish who built the railroad left behind them. At a good distance in from the shore the land rises to a rocky head, perhaps sixty feet above the water. Thereon I think to place a hut, perhaps it will have two stories & be a petty tower, looking out to Monadnoc & other New Hampshire Mountains. (*CEC,* 399)

In *Emerson in Concord,* Edward noted that "The garden at home was often a hindrance and care, but he soon bought an estate which brought him unmingled pleasure, first the grove of white pines on the shore of Walden [where Thoreau built his hut], and later the large tract on the farther shore running up to a rocky pinnacle [the "ledge" mentioned in the poem] from which he could look down on the Pond itself, and on the other side to the

432

Lincoln woods and farms, Nobscot blue in the South away beyond Fairhaven and the river gleaming in the afternoon sun" (58).

Emerson made two attempts to express in verse what he felt about his "garden." This one—"My Garden"—was completed to his satisfaction late in 1866 and published in the *Atlantic Monthly* shortly before its appearance in *May-Day*. The other effort, untitled, is referred to in *The Poetry Notebooks* as "In my garden three ways meet": it was first published, after Emerson's death, in the Riverside edition of *Poems,* with the supplied title "Walden." Edward's note to that poem a little misleadingly calls it "the early form of *My Garden*" (307 n.), and even more misleadingly states elsewhere that the two "were originally one poem" (*Emerson in Concord,* 59 n.). There is certainly a close relation between the manuscript drafts of these two works, and it is also true that "My Garden" arrived at final form only when certain verses were extracted from the other poem. And yet they are quite separate conceptions.

"My Garden" seems to have been particularly well received by James T. Fields when it was submitted to the *Atlantic Monthly.* Emerson claimed that this encouraging response allayed some personal doubts about the waning of his talent as publication of *May-Day* loomed (*L,* V, 479–480).

MY GARDEN.

If I could put my woods in song,
And tell what's there enjoyed,
All men would to my gardens throng,
And leave the cities void.

In my plot no tulips blow,— 5
Snow-loving pines and oaks instead;
And rank the savage maples grow
From spring's faint flush to autumn red.

My garden is a forest ledge
Which older forests bound; 10

The banks slope down to the blue lake-edge,
Then plunge to depths profound.

Here once the Deluge ploughed,
Laid the terraces, one by one;
Ebbing later whence it flowed,   15
They bleach and dry in the sun.

The sowers made haste to depart,—
The wind and the birds which sowed it;
Not for fame, nor by rules of art,
Planted these, and tempests flowed it.   20

Waters that wash my garden side
Play not in Nature's lawful web,
They heed not moon or solar tide,—
Five years elapse from flood to ebb.

Hither hasted, in old time, Jove,   25
And every god,—none did refuse;
And be sure at last came Love,
And after Love, the Muse.

Keen ears can catch a syllable,
As if one spake to another,   30
In the hemlocks tall, untamable,
And what the whispering grasses smother.

Æolian harps in the pine
Ring with the song of the Fates;
Infant Bacchus in the vine,—   35
Far distant yet his chorus waits.

Canst thou copy in verse one chime
Of the wood-bell's peal and cry,
Write in a book the morning's prime,
Or match with words that tender sky?   40

434

Wonderful verse of the gods,
Of one import, of varied tone;
They chant the bliss of their abodes
To man imprisoned in his own.

Ever the words of the gods resound;   45
But the porches of man's ear
Seldom in this low life's round
Are unsealed, that he may hear.

Wandering voices in the air,
And murmurs in the wold,   50
Speak what I cannot declare,
Yet cannot all withhold.

When the shadow fell on the lake,
The whirlwind in ripples wrote
Air-bells of fortune that shine and break,   55
And omens above thought.

But the meanings cleave to the lake,
Cannot be carried in book or urn;
Go thy ways now, come later back,
On waves and hedges still they burn.   60

These the fates of men forecast,
Of better men than live today,
If who can read them comes at last,
He will spell in the sculpture, 'Stay.'

TEXTS

(A) *AM*, XVIII (December 1866): 665–666; (B) MS HM 45717, by permission of the Huntington Library, San Marino, California, printer's copy for C; (C) *May-Day* (Boston, 1867), 114–118; (D) *Selected Poems* (Boston, 1876), 173–175; (E) *Poems* [Riverside] (Boston, 1884), 197–200; (F) *Poems* [Centenary] (Boston, 1904), 229–231. An unmarked proof sheet laid in notebook Rhymer (see *PN,*

424), prepared for *May-Day* and containing all of "My Garden," differs from printer's copy (B) at lines 38 (wood-bells'), 45 (resound;), 48 (unsealed,), 50 (wold,), and 62 (to-day,).

Pre-copy-text forms: See *PN*, 864–865 (for "My Garden"), and 836 (for "In my garden three ways meet"). A proof sheet containing lines 1–32 of "In my garden three ways meet," evidently prepared in conjunction with *May-Day*, is reproduced in *PN*, xxix.

VARIANTS

1   song, (A-D) | song (E-F)

5   blow,— (B-F) | blow, (A)

6   instead; (B-F) | instead, (A)

8   spring's (A, C-D) | Spring's (B, E-F) || autumn (A, C-D) | Autumn (B, E-F) | [*A notation in* (CC7) *questioned whether these words should be capitalized*]

9   forest ledge (B-F) | forest-ledge, (A)

12   to (B-F) | in (A)

14   by one; (A, C-F) | by one, (B)

17   depart,— (B-F) | depart, (A)

20   these, (B-F) | these (A)

21   garden side (C-E) | garden-side (A, F) | garden side<s> (B)

23   They (A, C-F) | <H>They (B)

25   hasted, (A, C-F) | hasted (B) || time, (A, C-F) | time (B)

29   syllable, (A, C-F) | syllable (B)

30   another, (B-F) | another (A)

38   cry, (B-F) | cry? (A)

42   import, (A, C-F) | import (B) || tone; (A, C-F) | tone, (B)

43   chant (A, C-F) | <sing>chant (B)

45   resound; (C-F) | resound, (A-B)

47   this (A-F) | our (CC7)

48   unsealed, (C-F) | unsealed (A-B)

49   air, (A-D) | air (E-F)

50   wold, (A, C-D) | wold (B, E-F)

60   burn. (B-F) | burn (A)

62   today, (B) | to-day; (A, C-F)

63   who (A, C-F) | <he>who (B) || last, (A-C) | last (D-F)

64   'Stay.' (D-F) | "Stay." (A) | "Stay!" (B) | 'Stay!' (C)

NOTES

5.   In his journal Emerson refers to the small garden-plot on the south side of his Concord house, in which his wife's tulips, imported from her native Plymouth, vied all too successfully with Emerson's vegetables: "The young minister did very well, but one day he married a wife, and after that he noticed that though he planted corn never so often, it was sure to come up tulips, contrary to all the laws of botany" (quoted in Edward Emerson, *Emerson in Concord*, 66).

24. "The rising and falling of Walden's waters are curiously independent of dry or wet seasons. Its watershed is small; it is fed by springs at its bottom,—its clear water being more than one hundred feet in depth" (Edward Emerson's note, *W,* IX, 481). See Thoreau, *J,* VIII, 90.

THE TITMOUSE.

The titmouse, also known as the black-capped chickadee (*Penthestes atricapillus*), has been the official state bird of Massachusetts since 1941. It is a small, energetic creature and, at least in Concord woods in the days of Emerson and Thoreau, more apt to show a friendly confidence in human beings than a fear of them. That was part of the point of the anecdote that Thoreau had included in *Walden* (1854) about his friend, the Canadian woodchopper Alek Therien: "as he sat on a log to eat his dinner the chicadees would sometimes come round and alight on his arm and peck at the potato in his fingers; and he said that he 'liked to have the little *fellers* about him'" (*Walden,* ed. J. Lyndon Shanley [Princeton, N.J., 1971], 146). The fact was offered as a sign of the man's "animal spirits" and of his admirable willingness to rest in nature. Emerson read the passage in *Walden* of course, but he also discussed it with the dying Thoreau late in the winter of 1862. Shortly after Thoreau's death on 6 May, Emerson, reading through his friend's journals, came upon the entry on which the *Walden* anecdote was based (see *JMN,* XV, 283). By then "the antidote to fear" in the face of death had been well worked out and "The Titmouse" written—a poem that R. A. Yoder has aptly called Emerson's "indirect tribute to Thoreau" (*Emerson and the Orphic Poet in America* [Berkeley, 1978], 157).

Emerson's own journal VA suggested to his son Edward that the poem was based on a particular event in the late spring of 1862:

> March 3, 1862. The snow still lies even with the tops of the walls across the Walden road, and, this afternoon, I waded through the woods to my grove. A chicadee came out to greet me, flew within reach of my hands, perched on the nearest bough, flew down into the snow, rested there two seconds, then up again, just over my head, & busied himself on the dead bark. I whistled to him through my teeth, and, (I think in response,) he began at once to whistle. I promised him crumbs, & must not go again to these woods without them. I suppose the best food to carry would be the meat of shag-barks or castille nuts. Thoreau tells me that they are very sociable with wood-choppers, & will take crumbs from their hands. (*JMN*, XV, 241)

But Edward is certainly mistaken in believing that this March sighting was the occasion for the poem, since his father mentioned the work almost two weeks earlier, in a letter of 19 February to Margaret Perkins Forbes, the sister of Emerson's friend, John Murray Forbes. It reads in part: "I have a little neighbor who, I am sure, is also a neighbor of yours, the black-capped titmouse, of whose qualities I think highly. If I can get my poem to him fairly copied out, I will send it to you with this: if not, soon" (*L*, IX, 71). The manuscript copy that Emerson promised may, then, have been conveyed with this letter, but more probably he brought it to the Forbes home in Milton, Massachusetts, on 16 March, at which time, according to a notation on the manuscript, it was "read aloud in our parlor by him." This manuscript is exceptionally interesting as it was generated contemporaneously with—though, evidently, very slightly earlier than—the manuscript sent to James Russell Lowell for printing in the *Atlantic*. Emerson's account book for 1859–1864 shows that the $50 Lowell paid for the poem was received on 14 March (*L*, IX, 72n).

Edward Emerson was clearly miffed that Matthew Arnold should have singled out "The Titmouse" as a characteristic failure in the lecture on Emerson that he gave in Boston in 1883. "One never quite arrives at learning what the titmouse actually did for him at all," Arnold complained, "though one feels a strong interest and desire to learn it; but one is reduced to guessing, and cannot be quite sure that after all one has guessed right" ("Emerson," *Discourses in America* [London, 1885], 158). Edward alluded to this objection in his note to the poem in the Centenary edition (*W*, IX, 483), adding that the "American reader will hardly find the poem so obscure." As if unable to let the matter lie, he recurred to the Englishman's critical befuddlement once again, in *The Early Years of the Saturday Club* (407). Arnold's Boston lecture, which marked the beginning of the posthumous reconsideration of Emerson's significance, undoubtedly affected the reputation of this poem in particular—adversely and for a long while. It was not until 1974, when a stronger and more sympathetic reader, Hyatt Waggoner, identified "The Titmouse" as one of the best of Emerson's later poems, that it began to attract serious critical attention (Waggoner, *Emerson as Poet* [Princeton, 1974], 109, 136; cf. Yoder, 159).

THE TITMOUSE.

You shall not be overbold
When you deal with arctic cold,
As late I found my lukewarm blood
Chilled wading in the snow-choked wood.
How should I fight? my foeman fine   5
Has million arms to one of mine:
East, west, for aid I looked in vain,
East, west, north, south, are his domain.
Miles off, three dangerous miles, is home;
Must borrow his winds who there would come.   10
Up and away for life! be fleet!—
The frost-king ties my fumbling feet,
Sings in my ears, my hands are stones,
Curdles the blood to the marble bones,
Tugs at the heart-strings, numbs the sense,   15
And hems in life with narrowing fence.
Well, in this broad bed lie and sleep,

The punctual stars will vigil keep,
Embalmed by purifying cold,
The winds shall sing their dead-march old,   20
The snow is no ignoble shroud,
The moon thy mourner, and the cloud.

Softly,—but this way fate was pointing,
'Twas coming fast to such anointing,
When piped a tiny voice hard by,   25
Gay and polite, a cheerful cry,
Chic-chic-a-dee-dee! saucy note
Out of sound heart and merry throat,
As if it said, 'Good day, good sir!
Fine afternoon, old passenger!   30
Happy to meet you in these places,
Where January brings few faces.'

This poet, though he live apart,
Moved by his hospitable heart,
Sped, when I passed his sylvan fort,   35
To do the honors of his court,
As fits a feathered lord of land;
Flew near, with soft wing grazed my hand,
Hopped on the bough, then, darting low,
Prints his small impress on the snow,   40
Shows feats of his gymnastic play,
Head downward, clinging to the spray.

Here was this atom in full breath,
Hurling defiance at vast death;
This scrap of valor just for play   45
Fronts the north-wind in waistcoat gray,
As if to shame my weak behavior;
I greeted loud my little saviour,
'You pet! what dost here? and what for?
In these woods, thy small Labrador,   50
At this pinch, wee San Salvador!

What fire burns in that little chest,
So frolic, stout, and self-possest?
Henceforth I wear no stripe but thine;
Ashes and jet all hues outshine.   55
Why are not diamonds black and gray,
To ape thy dare-devil array?
And I affirm, the spacious North
Exists to draw thy virtue forth.
I think no virtue goes with size;   60
The reason of all cowardice
Is, that men are overgrown,
And, to be valiant, must come down
To the titmouse dimension.'

      'Tis good will makes intelligence,   65
And I began to catch the sense
Of my bird's song: 'Live out of doors
In the great woods, on prairie floors.
I dine in the sun; when he sinks in the sea,
I too have a hole in a hollow tree;   70
And I like less when summer beats
With stifling beams in these retreats,
Than noontide twilights which snow makes
With tempest of the blinding flakes.
For well the soul, if stout within,   75
Can arm impregnably the skin;
And polar frost my frame defied,
Made of the air that blows outside.'

      With glad remembrance of my debt,
I homeward turn; farewell, my pet!   80
When here again thy pilgrim comes,
He shall bring store of seeds and crumbs.
Doubt not, so long as earth has bread,
Thou first and foremost shalt be fed;
The Providence that is most large   85
Takes hearts like thing in special charge,

Helps who for their own need are strong,
And the sky doats on cheerful song.
Henceforth I prize thy wiry chant
O'er all that mass and minster vaunt;   90
For men mis-hear thy call in spring,
As 't would accost some frivolous wing,
Crying out of the hazel copse, *Phe—be!*
And, in winter, *Chic-a-dee-dee!*
I think old Cæsar must have heard   95
In northern Gaul my dauntless bird,
And, echoed in some frosty wold,
Borrowed thy battle-numbers bold.
And I will write the annals new,
And thank thee for a better clew,   100
I, who dreamed not when I came here
To find the antidote of fear,
Now hear thee say in Roman key,
Pæan! Veni, vidi, vici.

TEXTS

(A) MS Am 82.2, Ralph Waldo Emerson Memorial Association deposit, Houghton Library, Harvard University, printer's copy for C; (B) bMS Am 1280.235 (602) ["The Forbes MS"], Ralph Waldo Emerson Memorial Association deposit, Houghton Library, Harvard University; (C) *AM*, IX (May 1862): 585–587; (D) MS MA 565, by permission of the Pierpont Morgan Library, printer's copy for E; (E) *May-Day* (Boston, 1867), 119–124; (E²) *Selected Poems* (Boston, 1876), 62–65, identical to (E) except for "behaviour" in line 47; (F) *Poems* [Riverside] (Boston, 1884), 200–203; (G) *Poems* [Centenary] (Boston, 1904), 233–236. The poem's first appearance in a book was in *Good Company for Every Day in the Year*, ed. James T. Fields (Boston: Ticknor and Fields, 1866), 284–287, published late in 1865; it lacks authority, however, being merely a reprint of the *Atlantic* text, with one possibly fortuitous correction (sir! for Sir! in line 29) and one error (the omission of the comma after Labrador in line 50). No notice is here taken of various pencil inscriptions in (B) that record variants from (E); these were probably made by someone in the Forbes family. A proof sheet containing the first thirteen lines of the poem, identical to the (D) text, is laid in poetry notebook Rhymer (see *PN*, 424).

The Titmouse

Pre-copy-text forms: See *PN,* 945–946. The principal drafts are in poetry note-book NP, 43–57, and journal VA (*JMN,* XV, 242–243).

VARIANTS

1   [*Flush*] You (B-G) | [*Inset*] You
(A) || overbold (A-B, D-G) | over-bold
(C)

4–5 wood. / How (B-G) | wood. /
[*white line*] How (A)

6   to (A, C-G) | for (B) || mine: (A-
B, D-G) | mine. (C)

7   vain, (A-B, D-G) | vain; (C)

8   domain. (A, C-G) | domain (B)

9   off, (A, C-G) | off,— (B) || miles,
(C, E-G) | miles (A-B, D) || home; (C,
E-G) | home, (A-B, D)

11   fleet!— (B, D-G) | fleet! (A, C)

12   The frost-king (B-G) | <Alas!
he> ↑The frost-king↓ (A)

12–13 feet, / Sings (B-G) | feet. /
<All aid remote, the foe is nigh, /
Shoots from the ground, drops from
the sky,> / Sings (A)

15   heart-strings (D-G) | heartstrings
(A-C)

16   And hems (B, D-G) | Hems
(A, C) || life (B, D-G) | the life (A,
C)

16–17 fence. / [*Flush*] Well, (E-G) |
fence. / [*White line*] / [*Inset*] Well,
(A-C) | fence. / [*Flush*] Well (D)

17   sleep, (A, C-E) | sleep: (B) |
sleep,— (F-G)

18   keep, (A, C-E) | keep; (B) |
keep,— (F-G)

19   by (B-G) | <in>by (A) || cold,
(A-E) | cold; (F-G)

20   dead-march (C-G) | dead march
(A-B) || old, (A, C-G) | old; (B)

23   [*Inset*] Softly,— (D-G) | [*Flush*]
Softly,— (A-C)

24   'Twas (C-G) | Twas (A-B)

25   voice (A, C-G) | <bird>voice
(B) || hard by, (A, C, E-G) | hard-by,
(B, D)

26   Gay (B-G) | Gay, (A)

27   *Chic-chic-a-dee-dee!* (B, G) |
Chicadeedee! (A) | *"Chic-chic-a-dee-
dee!"* (C) | *Chic-chicadeedee!* (D-F) ||
note (B, D-G) | note, (A, C)

28   throat, (B-G) | throat (A)

29   'Good (A-B, D-G) | "Good (C) ||
sir! (A-B, D-G) | Sir! (C)

32   few faces.' (D-G) | few men's
faces. (A) | few men's faces.' (B) | few
men's faces." (C)

33   [*Inset*] This poet, though he live
apart, (E-G) | [*Flush*] This hermit,
though he live apart, (A) | [*Inset*]
The little hermit perched apart (B) |
[*Flush*] This poet, though he live
apart, (C-D)

34   Moved by his (D-G) | <Lodges>
↑Moved by↓ a (A) | Hastes, out of
(B) | Moved by a (C)

35   Sped, when I passed (C-G) |
Hastes, when <you> ↑I↓ pass (A) |
Soon as I pass (B) || fort, (A, C-G) |
fort (B)

36   court, (A, C-G) | court. / <Flies
down with soft wing sweeps my
hand> (B)

37   of land; (D-G) | of the land, (A)
| of land, (B-C)

38   Flew near, (C-G) | Flies near, (A)
| Flies down, (B) || grazed my hand,
(C-G) | sweeps <your> ↑my↓ hand
(A) | sweeps my hand, (B)

39   Hopped (C-G) I Hops (A-B) II
then, (A, C, E-G) I then (B, D)
41   play, (B-G) I play (A)
42   clinging (B-G) I cling<s>ing
(A)
42–43   spray. / [*White line*] / [*Inset*]
Here (B, E-G) I spray / [*Page break*] /
[*Inset*] <The little Esquimaux in gray
/ Mounted at ease each icy spray.> /
Here (A) I spray. / Here (C) I spray.
/ [*White line*] / [*Flush*] Here (D)
43   breath, (B, E-G) I breath (A,
C-D)
44   death; (B, E-G) I death, (A, C-D)
46   north-wind (C, E-G) I northwind
(A, D) I North wind (B) II gray, (B-G)
I gray (A)
47   behavior; (B, D-G) I behavior:
(A) I behavior. (C)
48   saviour, (D-E) I savior, (A, F-G) I
saviour. (B) I saviour: (C)
49   'You (A, E, G) I You (B, F) I
"Thou (C) I "You (D) [L, *IX,* 72,
*shows that Emerson only grudgingly
accepted the emendation in* (C) *suggested
by* Atlantic Monthly *editor, James T.
Fields*]
51   pinch, wee (B-G) I pinch [*space*]
wee (A)
52   chest, (A-C) I chest (D-G)
53   stout, (A-E) I stout (F-G)
53–54   self-possest? / Henceforth (D-
G) I selfpossest? / Didst steal the
glow that lights the west? /
Henceforth (A) I self-possest? / Didst
. . . West? / Henceforth (B-C) [*The
omission may have been an oversight
when Emerson prepared* (D), *but the fact
that the line is the weak last third of a
triplet, never subsequently restored, is
evidence of deliberate authorial
emendation.*]
54   thine; (E-G) I thine (A) I thine,
(B, D) I thine: (C)

55   jet (D-G) I black (A-C)
56   gray, (B-C, E-G) I gray (A, D)
57   dare-devil (C-G) I daredevil
(A-B)
58   affirm, (D-G) I affirm (A, C) I
maintain (B) II North (B-G) I north
(A)
59   virtue (B-G) I Virtue (A)
60   size; (E-G) I size, (A-B, D) I size:
(C)
64   dimension.' (E-G) I dimension.
(A-B) I dimension." (C) I
<proportion>dimension. (D)
65   [*Inset*] 'Tis (E-G) I [*Inset*] Tis (A-
B, D) I [*Flush*] 'Tis (C) II good will
(A-B, G) I good-will (C, E-F) I
goodwill (D) II intelligence, (A, C-G)
I intelligence (B)
67   my (A, C-G) I the (B) II bird's (B-
G) I birds (A) II song: (C, E-G) I song;
(A, D) I song, (B) II 'Live (B, D-G) I
"Live (A, C) II doors (A-B, D-G) I
doors, (C)
68   woods, on (D-G) I woods, & (A) I
woods on (B) I woods, and (C) II
floors. (C-G) I floors; (A) I floors
(B)
69   sun; (A, C-G) I sun (B) II sea, (A,
C-G) I sea (B)
70   I too (A-B, D-G) I I, too, (C) II
tree; (D-G) I tree. (A, C) I tree (B)
71   summer (B-D) I Summer (A,
E-G)
72   retreats, (D-G) I retreats
(A-C)
74   flakes. (A-B, E-G) I flakes: (C) I
flakes.' (D)
75–78   [*Not present in* (D)]
76   skin; (C, E-G) I skin (A) I skin,
(B)
77   frost (A, C, E-G) I blasts (B) II
defied, (C, E-G) I defied (A-B)
78   outside.' (E-G) I outside (A) I
outside. (B) I outside." (C)

444

79   [*Inset*] With (B, D-G) | [*Flush*] With (A, C)

80   turn; (A, D-G) | go; (B) | turn. (C) || farewell, (E-G) | Farewell, (A, C-D) | farewell (B)

81   comes, (B-G) | comes (A)

82   He shall bring (A, C-G) | He brings thee (B) || crumbs. (B-G) | crumbs / <Nor doubt, so long as earth yields bread, / Thou first & foremost shalt be fed. / The Providence that is most large / Takes hearts like thine in special charge / Helps who for their own need are strong / And <g>God & man love cheerful song.> (A)

83–88   [*Lines present,* (E-G) *only*]

89   Henceforth (A, C-G) | Henceforth, (B) || chant (A-C, E-G) | chaunt (D)

90   O'er (B-G) | Oer (A) || and (C-G) | or (A-B) [*this emendation was suggested by James T. Fields: see* L, IX, 72] || vaunt; (D-G) | vaunt. (A-B) | vaunt: (C)

91   mis-hear (A-B, D-G) | mishear (C) || spring, (B-E) | spring (A) | Spring, (F-G)

92   't would (C, F-G) | <if it> ↑t' ↓would (A) | t'would (B, D-E) || wing, (B-G) | wing (A)

93   the hazel copse, (B-G) | the copse, (A) || *Phe-be!* (E-G) | Phe-be! (A) | *Phe-be,* (B) | *"Phe-be!"* (C) | *Phe-be* (D)

94   And, (A-B, D-G) | And (C) || *Chic-a-dee-dee!* (D-G) | chic a dee dee! (A) | *chic a dee dee.* (B) | *"Chic-a-dee-dee!"* (C)

96   northern (D-G) | Northern (A-C)

98   battle-numbers (B-G) | battle numbers (A)

99   And (B-G) | <But> ↑And↓ (A) || will (D-G) | shall (A-C)

100   clew, (A-B, D-G) | clew: (C)

101   I, (B-G) | I (A) || not (B, D-G) | not, (A, C) || here (A-B, D-G) | here, (C)

103   key, (C-G) | key (A-B)

104   *Pæan! Veni, vidi, vici.* (E-G) | Paean! Ve-ni vi-di, vi-ci. (A) | Paean! Veni, vidi, vici. (B) | *"Pæan! Ve-ni, Vi-di, Vi-ci."* (C) | *Paean! Veni vidi vici.* (D)

NOTES

84.   Emerson seems to have noticed that it was habitual with Thoreau to speak of the chickadee's song as "wiry": see, e.g., *J*, V, 112, 203, 421. In 1838 Emerson listed "the thin note of the titmouse & his bold ignoring of the bystander" as among the things that poets had not yet recorded (*JMN*, V, 469; cf. *JMN*, IV, 273).

104.   Pæan refers to a hymn of praise, thanksgiving, or deliverance, originally addressed to Apollo in his guise as the healer, Pæan, physician to the gods. Later, in a Roman context, it was a song in celebration of a military victory. "Veni, vidi, vici" (I came, I saw, I conquered) is famously associated with Julius Cæsar.

SEA-SHORE.

On 31 July and 1 August 1855 Emerson visited with his old friend the Unitarian minister and Transcendental Club member Dr. Cyrus A. Bartol at his seaside cottage at Pigeon Cove on the tip of Cape Ann (*L*, VIII, 447; *L*, IV, 524). He must have enjoyed the sea-baths on the rocky shore, the cool ocean breezes, the winds through the immense westward depth of pine forest, the tower atop Bartol's cottage, and the private observatory next door. The following summer he brought his family and stayed a week:

> 23 July [1856]. Returned from Pigeon Cove, where we have made acquaintance with the sea, for seven days. 'Tis a noble friendly power, and seemed to say to me, "Why so late & slow to come to me? Am I not here always, thy proper summer home? Is not my voice thy needful music; my breath thy healthful climate in the heats; my touch, thy cure? Was ever building like my terraces? Was ever couch so magnificent as mine? Lie down on my warm ledges and learn that a very little hut is all you need. I have made thy architecture superfluous, and it is paltry beside mine. Here are twenty Romes & Ninevehs & Karnacs in ruins together, obelisk & pyramid and Giants' Causeway here they all are prostrate or half piled." And behold the sea, the opaline, plentiful & strong, yet beautiful as the rose or the rainbow, full of food, nourisher of men, purger of the world, creating a sweet climate, and, in its unchangeable ebb & flow, and in its beauty at a few furlongs, giving a hint of that which changes not, & is perfect. (*JMN*, XIV, 100–101)

This magic destination was reachable by train to the village of Rockport, north of Gloucester, then by coach or carriage the last two miles along the scenic ocean road skirting the several granite quarries that may well have suggested the imagery of Nineveh ruins. Though Emerson thinks of himself as a belated "Pilgrim" (line 2), he comes to the rock-bound coast of New England from the land side, in comfort, in search of more comfort, not a re-enactor of Puritan settlement, but as a pioneer of the American summer vacation. Pigeon Cove began to attract attention in the early 1840s when the family of the elder Richard Henry Dana stayed there. By the time Emerson arrived it had become a distinctly fashionable resort, its seasonal residents then and later including James Freeman Clarke, Ezra Stiles Gannett, Edwin Percy Whipple, Junius Brutus Booth, T. W. Higginson, E. H. Chapin, Thomas Starr King, and James T. Fields.

Emerson's poem bears some relation to accounts of the region offered by such local promoters as Henry C. Leonard, according to whom,

> Gentlemen, whether with or without families, came to Pigeon Cove . . . for rest and quiet and healthful pastimes; for ocean-view and seaside ramble; for good air from over the brine, and healing whiffs from the balsamic pines; and for all the pure and sweet pleasures which can be had where rural and marine attractions and charms are so singularly and happily brought together. (*Pigeon Cove and Vicinity* [Boston, 1873], 45)

Actual swimming was as yet an uncommon activity for Yankees, especially in the cold waters of Cape Ann. The "bathing" that early accounts refer to (including Emerson's) was generally, at its most venturesome, what we would call "wading," and was done for many years at Pigeon Cove by holding on to ropes anchored in the rocks. Anxiety about being too freely in the natural environment was clearly an issue in New England's emergent vacation grounds, and Leonard was pleased to be able to say, as late as 1873, that "the first case of drowning has not yet occurred" (136).

But the poem has more serious meanings as well, developing in the direction of "Days," for example, as it considers the overlooked or unrealized "gifts" of the "sea-gods," who become benefactors to the "wise" in prodigal economies of "Force."

Edward Emerson's note to the poem (*W,* IX, 484–485) contains a few errors (such as placing the event in 1857 rather than 1856), but it also contains a personal recollection that his father, on the day after returning home, was surprised to find that his prose journal entry was almost a poem already, and that he read it as such to the gathered family. Thus the first draft in notebook EL would date from late July 1856. Emerson made additional revisions some eight years later—those in KL and in the manuscript printer's copy—when the poem was sent off for publication in *The Boatswain's Whistle,* a circular that appeared daily between 9 and 19 November 1864, at the National Sailors' Fair in Boston. The fair was a way of raising money for the National Sailors' Home, a facility for Navy veterans disabled in the Civil War that in fact opened in August of 1866 in Quincy, Massachusetts. *The Boatswain's Whistle* was the patriotic project of Julia Ward Howe, though Emerson's contribution was evidently solicited by one of her "Editorial Council," Edwin Percy Whipple, late of Pigeon Cove (*L,* IX, 156).

SEA-SHORE.

I heard or seemed to hear the chiding Sea
Say, Pilgrim, why so late and slow to come?
Am I not always here, thy summer home?
Is not my voice thy music, morn and eve?
My breath thy healthful climate in the heats,   5
My touch thy antidote, my bay thy bath?
Was ever building like my terraces?
Was ever couch magnificent as mine?
Lie on the warm rock-ledges, and there learn
A little hut suffices like a town.   10
I make your sculptured architecture vain,
Vain beside mine. I drive my wedges home,
And carve the coastwise mountain into caves.
Lo! here is Rome, and Nineveh, and Thebes,
Karnak, and Pyramid, and Giant's Stairs,   15
Half piled or prostrate; and my newest slab
Older than all thy race.

           Behold the Sea,
The opaline, the plentiful and strong,
Yet beautiful as is the rose in June,

Fresh as the trickling rainbow of July;   20
Sea full of food, the nourisher of kinds,
Purger of earth, and medicine of men;
Creating a sweet climate by my breath,
Washing out harms and griefs from memory,
And, in my mathematic ebb and flow,   25
Giving a hint of that which changes not.
Rich are the sea-gods:—who gives gifts but they?
They grope the sea for pearls, but more than pearls:
They pluck Force thence, and give it to the wise.
For every wave is wealth to Dædalus,   30
Wealth to the cunning artist who can work
This matchless strength. Where shall he find, O waves!
A load your Atlas shoulders cannot lift?

    I with my hammer pounding evermore
The rocky coast, smite Andes into dust,   35
Strewing my bed, and, in another age,
Rebuild a continent of better men.
Then I unbar the doors: my paths lead out
The exodus of nations: I disperse
Men to all shores that front the hoary main.   40

    I too have arts and sorceries;
Illusion dwells forever with the wave.
I know what spells are laid. Leave me to deal
With credulous and imaginative man;
For, though he scoop my water in his palm,   45
A few rods off he deems it gems and clouds.
Planting strange fruits and sunshine on the shore,
I make some coast alluring, some lone isle,
To distant men, who must go there, or die.

TEXTS

(A) MS Barrett 6248-a, Clifton Waller Barrett Library, by permission of the University of Virginia, printer's copy for B; (B) *Boatswain's Whistle* (Boston), No. 9,

May-Day and Other Pieces (1867)

18 November 1864, p. 65; (C) corrected clipping from B inserted in poetry notebook Rhymer (*PN,* 455); (D) *May-Day* (Boston, 1867), 125–127; (E) *Selected Poems* (Boston, 1876), 112–113; (F) *Poems* [Riverside] (Boston, 1884), 207–209; (G) *Poems* [Centenary] (Boston, 1904), 242–243.

Pre-copy-text forms: See *PN,* 912.

VARIANTS

Title: SEA-SHORE. (B-F) | Sea-Shore. (A) | SEASHORE (G)

2   Say, (B-G) | Say,— (A)

3   summer (A, D-G) | Summer (B-C)

4   my voice thy music, morn and eve? (B-G) | <thy>my voice <my>thy <cradle song> ↑music, morn & eve ↓? (A)

6   antidote, (D-G) | antidote; (A-C)

8   as (B-G) | <like>as (A)

12   mine. I . . . home, (D-G) | mine:—[*End of line*] (A-C)

13   And . . . caves. (D-G) | [*Line omitted*] (A-B) | ↑I carve . . . caves ↓ [*In pencil*] (C)

14   Rome, (A-E) | Rome (F-G) || Nineveh, (A-E) | Nineveh (F-G)

15   Karnak, (A-E) | Karnak (F-G) || Pyramid, (A-E) | Pyramid (F-G) || Giant's (D-G) | Giants' (A-C) || Stairs, (A-E) | Stairs (F-G)

16   Half piled (B-G) | Half-piled (A) || and (B-G) | <but> ↑and ↓ (A)

17   thy (B-G) | <your> ↑thy ↓ (A) || race. [*White line*] Behold (A-C, F-G) | race. [*No white line*] Behold (D-E)

20   July; (D-G) | July: (A-C)

24   Washing . . . memory, (D-G) | [*Line omitted*] (A-B) | ↑Washing . . . memory, ↓ [*In pencil*] (C)

27   sea-gods:—who (D-G) | sea-gods:—Who (A) | Sea-gods:—who (B-C)

30   Dædalus, (D-G) | Dædalus,— (A-C)

34   [*Inset*] I (A, D-G) | [*Flush*] I (B-C)

36   bed, (A-D, F-G) | bed; (E)

38   the (B-G) | <my>the (A) || my (B-G) | <thy>my (A)

41   too have arts (B-G) | ↑too ↓ have <my> arts (A)

43   spells (A, D-G) | shells (B) | <shells> ↑spells ↓ [*Correction in pencil*] (C)

44   credulous and imaginative man; (D-G) | credulous imaginative man. (A) | credulous, imaginative man. (B-C)

49   men, (D-G) | men (A-C)

NOTES

8.   Robert H. Woodward has pointed out that Emerson echoes ll. 32–33 of "Thanatopsis," by William Cullen Bryant ("nor couldst thou wish / Couch more

magnificent"). Various structural and prosodic features (i.e., the soothing address of Nature, the choice of blank verse) also recall Bryant: see Woodward, "Emerson's 'Seashore' and Bryant's Poetic Theory in Practice," *Emerson Society Quarterly*, no. 19 (II Q 1960): 21–22.

15. The "Giant's Stairs" (or "Causeway") refers to a volcanic formation on the coast of Northern Ireland consisting of thousands of hexagonal basalt columns. The "Giant," its putative builder, was the legendary Finn McCool.

27–33. At the end of the journal source for the poem (see headnote), Emerson added a cross-reference to "CD 7" (*JMN*, X, 62), an entry made in the summer of 1847: "On the seashore at Nantucket I saw the play of the Atlantic with the coast. Here was wealth: every wave reached a quarter of a mile along shore as it broke. There are no rich men, I said, to compare with these. Every wave is a fortune. One thinks of Etzlers [J. A. Etzler, author of *The Paradise within the Reach of All Men* (Pittsburgh, 1833), proposed harnessing energy from wind and tides] and great projectors who will yet turn this immense waste strength to account and save the limbs of human slaves." An 1842 London reprint of Etzler's work was the subject of Thoreau's "Paradise (to Be) Regained" in the *Democratic Review* for November 1843.

47–49. Tennyson's dreamy "Lotos-Eaters" (1832) may have had something to do with Emerson's ideas about the shore as a place for idling. In July 1868, following a trip to the beach at Newport, Rhode Island, he wrote in a scrap of verse that the waves "give my guest eternal afternoon" (*JMN*, XVI, 104).

SONG OF NATURE.

The earliest hint of this poem—in a sense its germ—is the detached phrase "the sportive sun" (line 3), rejected from a draft of "The Humble-Bee" in 1837 (*PN*, 136) and copied into journal Y (*JMN*, IX, 292) in 1845. There and in several later locations, where it is joined by other fragments on the topic of Spring, it seemed destined for inclusion in "May-Day," and indeed many of the lines in early drafts of "Song of Nature" were gravitationally drawn to a second inspiration, to a poem never entirely finished, though published after Emerson's death under the title "Cosmos" (*W*, IX, 366–367; see also *PN*, 970). The "sportive sun," however, seems to have had its own strong gravitational force and progressively organized the lines that belonged to it, culminating in a work, "Song of Nature," that has been called "the crown of Emerson's subjective evolutionary humanism" (Strauch, "The Sources of Emerson's 'Song of Nature,'" *Harvard Library Bulletin*, IX [Autumn 1955]: 300). Published in January 1860, almost simultaneously with Charles Darwin's *On the Origin of Species*, Emerson's poem offers a theory of—that is to say, a way of thinking about—the ameliorating force of Nature and of the relation of constant physical change and eternal spiritual constancy.

The erotic or generative connotation of the term "sportive" would be labeled archaic by the *OED* or even obsolete by later dictionaries, but it was a meaning perennially evoked in poetic representations of the sun, and here emphasized in the mating of the "sportive sun" with the swelling, female "gibbous moon." But the special fitness of the word may lie in the crypto-Darwinian meaning which the *OED* supplies in its application to plants: "liable to sport or vary unusually from the true type"—which is to say, to develop by free accidents of mutation. In his important and subtle essay on the poem, Strauch insisted that the phrase was "Emerson's own" (320), yet provided a convincing source in a work that Emerson was reading at the time, the *Miscellaneous Essays* of Henry T. Colebrooke (London, 1837), I, 128, where an ancient philosopher is quoted: "The parent of all beings produced all states of existence, for he generates and preserves all creatures: therefore is he called the generator. Because he shines and sports, because he loves and irradiates, therefore is he called resplendent or divine. . . . We meditate on the light, which, existing in our minds, continually governs our intellects in the pursuits of virtue, wealth, love, and beatitude" (Strauch, 324). Emerson's science had more in common with such poetic, pagan formulations than with the modern forms of empiricism because he was radically attuned to the interdependence of the observer and the showy old Not-Me of outward Nature. The "sportive sun" is the generative force in

Nature, but Emerson has turned the old argument from design on its head by insisting that the meaning of Nature was not a function of authorship, but lay, as it were, on the other side, with the adequate audience (the tarrying man-child) whom all its splendid forms predicted.

The poem, as Strauch indicates, was substantially written in 1859. Emerson sent a copy of lines 14–72 to his brother William in New York, perhaps early in October, and got back an encouraging response (see *PN*, 921). On 23 October, he indicated that he had finished the poem "by writing six more quatrains, & sent it to Lowell, who has it, he says, already in print. It shall be mended, I hope, when the proof comes to me" (*L*, V, 178). If the last sentence implies some criticism from William, it may have to do with the suppression of the seventeenth stanza (lines 65–68), present in the manuscripts but missing in the *Atlantic* text. The Accounts Books show that Emerson was paid $50 for the poem.

SONG OF NATURE.

Mine are the night and morning,
The pits of air, the gulf of space,
The sportive sun, the gibbous moon,
The innumerable days.

I hide in the solar glory,   5
I am dumb in the pealing song,
I rest on the pitch of the torrent,
In slumber I am strong.

No numbers have counted my tallies,
No tribes my house can fill,   10
I sit by the shining Fount of Life,
And pour the deluge still;

And ever by delicate powers
Gathering along the centuries

453

From race on race the rarest flowers,   15
My wreath shall nothing miss.

And many a thousand summers
My apples ripened well,
And light from meliorating stars
With firmer glory fell.   20

I wrote the past in characters
Of rock and fire the scroll,
The building in the coral sea,
The planting of the coal.

And thefts from satellites and rings   25
And broken stars I drew,
And out of spent and aged things
I formed the world anew;

What time the gods kept carnival,
Tricked out in star and flower,   30
And in cramp elf and saurian forms
They swathed their too much power.

Time and Thought were my surveyors,
They laid their courses well,
They boiled the sea, and baked the layers   35
Of granite, marl, and shell.

But he, the man-child glorious,—
Where tarries he the while?
The rainbow shines his harbinger,
The sunset gleams his smile.   40

My boreal lights leap upward,
Forthright my planets roll,
And still the man-child is not born,
The summit of the whole.

Must time and tide forever run? 45
Will never my winds go sleep in the west?
Will never my wheels which whirl the sun
And satellites have rest?

Too much of donning and doffing,
Too slow the rainbow fades, 50
I weary of my robe of snow,
My leaves and my cascades;

I tire of globes and races,
Too long the game is played;
What without him is summer's pomp, 55
Or winter's frozen shade?

I travail in pain for him,
My creatures travail and wait;
His couriers come by squadrons,
He comes not to the gate. 60

Twice I have moulded an image,
And thrice outstretched my hand,
Made one of day, and one of night,
And one of the salt-sea-sand.

One in a Judæan manger, 65
And one by Avon stream,
One over against the mouths of Nile,
And one in the Academe.

I moulded kings and saviours,
And bards o'er kings to rule;— 70
But fell the starry influence short,
The cup was never full.

Yet whirl the glowing wheels once more,
And mix the bowl again;

Seethe, Fate! the ancient elements,   75
Heat, cold, wet, dry, and peace, and pain.

Let war and trade and creeds and song
Blend, ripen race on race,
The sunburnt world a man shall breed
Of all the zones and countless days.   80

No ray is dimmed, no atom worn,
My oldest force is good as new,
And the fresh rose on yonder thorn
Gives back the bending heavens in dew.

TEXTS

(A) MS Lowell 14, Houghton Library, Harvard University, printer's copy for B;
(B) *AM*, V (January 1860): 18–20; (C) *May-Day* (Boston, 1867), 128–133; (D)
Selected Poems (Boston, 1876), 159–162; (E) *Poems* [Riverside] (Boston, 1884),
209–212; (E²) *Poems* [Centenary] (Boston, 1904), 244–247.

Format: (B) indents even numbered lines; all other printings are flush left
throughout. In (A) line 1 is indented.

Pre-copy-text forms: See *PN*, 920–922. The evolution of the drafts is made yet
more complicated by the intermingled presence of lines later developed in the
unfinished poem to which Edward Emerson gave the title "Cosmos" (*W*, IX,
366–367). A large portion of Strauch's "Sources of Emerson's 'Song of Nature'"
actually concerns "Cosmos."

VARIANTS

5   solar (C-E) I blinding (A-B)
6   am dumb (C-E) I lurk (A-B)
8   In slumber I am (C-E) I Nor less
in death am (A) I In death, new-born
and (B)
11   Life, (C-D) I life, (A-B) I Life
(E)
12   still; (C-E) I still. (A-B)
15   rarest (C-E) I fairest (A-B) II
flowers, (B-E) I flowers (A)

18   apples (A-C) I harvests (D) I
gardens (CC7, E)
25   rings (B-E) I rings, (A)
26   stars (B-E) I stars, (A)
28   anew; (C-E) I anew. (A-B)
35   boiled (A-C, E) I poured (D) II
and baked (A-D) I they piled (CC7) I
and piled (E)
36   marl, (A-D) I marl (E)
37   he, (C-E) I him— (A-B) II man-

child (B-E) | manchild (A) ||
glorious,— (C-E) | glorious, (A-B)

43   man-child (B-E) | manchild (A)

46   west? (A, C-E) | West? (B)

47   wheels (A, C-E) | wheels, (B)

48   satellites (C-E) | satellites, (A-B)

50   fades, (C-E) | fades; (A-B)

52   leaves (C-E) | leaves, (A-B) ||
cascades; (C-E) | cascades. (A-B)

55   What (C-E) | What, (A-B) || him
(C-E) | him, (A-B)

59   squadrons, (B-E) | <thousands>
↑squadrons↓ (A)

63   day, (A-D) | day (E) || night, (A-
D) | night (E)

64   salt-sea-sand. (A-B) | salt sea-
sand. (C-E)

65–68   [*Lines present*] (A, C-E) | [*Lines
omitted*] (B)

65   Judæan (C-E) | Judaean (A) |
Judean (CC7)

68   in (C-E) | <by>in (A)

69   kings and saviours, (B-D) |
tuneful poets, (A) | kings and saviors,
(E)

70   bards o'er kings (B-E) | captains
born (A) || rule;— (C-E) | rule;
(A-B)

74   again; (C-E) | again, (A-B)

76   wet, dry, and peace, (C-E) | dry,
wet, and peace (A-B)

77   war (B-E) | war, (A) || trade (B-
E) | trade, (A) || creeds (B-E) |
creeds, (A)

78   race, (C-E) | race,— (A-B)

80   zones (B, D-E) | Zones, (A) |
zones, (C)

NOTES

5.   Carl F. Strauch has noted the dependence of a number of single-line frag-
ments in poetry notebook NP on two essays by Plutarch in the *Morals:* "Why the
Oracles Cease to Give Answers" and "Of Isis and Osiris, or Of the Ancient Reli-
gion and Philosophy of Egypt" ("Sources," 315–318). The relationship helps to
account for the second stanza, particularly in its first-draft form, though in its fi-
nal form only line 5 retains a clear trace of its origin in the second of these essays
(*Morals* [London, 1718], IV, 115), in the reference to Osiris as the god "who lies
hidden in the Arms of the Sun."

18.   Emerson was a considerable orchardist, selling upwards of a hundred bar-
rels of apples per year in addition to pears and other fruits. Strauch points out
that Emerson knew of the theories of the Belgian horticulturalist Jean-Baptiste
van Mons through Andrew J. Downing, *Fruits and Fruit Trees of America,* the 1846
edition of which Emerson owned. Improvements in apples and pears (coming
to a "state of amelioration") were effected by intelligent channeling of natu-
ral forces ("Sources," 312–313; *JMN,* X, 156). Late substitutions of "harvests"
(1876) and "gardens" (1884) for "apples" in line 18 have been resisted in part
to preserve the genetic history of the idea. See *W,* IX, 485, for Edward's state-
ment that his father "hesitated long" before "substituting 'gardens' [i.e., in the
correction copy] for the more lively image" of "apples"; he does not mention the
intervening reading, "harvests."

25–28.   As Strauch pointed out, Emerson had been reading of "celestial phenomena which have been discovered since the time of Newton," including changes in the rings of Saturn and "twenty-seven small planets" between the orbits of Mars and Jupiter (i.e., the asteroid belt), supposed to be detritus from the ancient breaking up of a large planet there. Emerson's source was Sir David Brewster's *Memoirs of the Life, Writings, and Discoveries of Sir Isaac Newton* (Edinburgh, 1855), borrowed from the Boston Athenaeum on 25 July 1855 (Strauch, "Sources," 313–314).

35.   Emerson would appear to have been dissatisfied with the verbs in this line, which do not especially comport with the trope of "surveyors" introduced in line 33. It was scarcely an improvement when "boiled" was changed to "poured" in the *Selected Poems* text, especially since "baked" was retained. In the Riverside edition Edward changed "baked" to "piled," accepting his father's emendation from a correction copy—though at the same time he restored the "boiled" reading, oddly declining the alliterative possibilities of "poured" and "piled." The revisions, in other words, were never coherent: the best sense that can be made is that the original diction of cookery is an effort to express, metaphorically, the kind of constructive manipulation for which, in a different context, surveyors are the designers.

37.   The "man-child" is related to the figure of the same name in "The Sphinx," but also to the "fireeyed child" who "has yet [to be] born," but who will usher in "a new age & adequate to Nature"—of whom mention is made in Emerson's letter of 13 October 1857 to Caroline Sturgis (*L*, V, 86).

45–56.   Strauch was the first to note the dependence of stanzas 12–14 on a passage from Aunt Mary Moody Emerson's Almanacks: "1834 x x x x x I forget what I meant to say—likely, that Doctor Ripley would not live. But he has to return, & willingly. Ah! as I walked there just now, so sad was wearied nature, that I felt her whisper, 'Even these leaves you use to think my better emblems—have lost their charm on me too, & I weary of my pilgrimage,—tired that I must again be clothed in the grandeurs of winter, and anon be bedizened in flowers & cascades. Oh if there be a Power superior to me, (& that there is, my own dread fetters proclaim,) when will he let my lights go out,—my tides cease to an eternal ebb,—my wheels which whirl this ceaseless rotation of suns & satellites stop the great chariot of their maker in mid career?" (quoted in "Sources," 322–323).

61.   As in the case of "saviours" in line 69, Emerson's "moulded" is a British usage—among the few that he inconsistently allowed himself. Some American dictionaries of the period, including Webster's, deemed "mould" "an incorrect orthography," and referred readers to the entry for "mold."

65–68.   The references here are to Jesus, Shakespeare, Moses, and Plato. In his note to these lines, Edward Emerson professed to be uncertain about the third identification, claiming that his father "would have been far more likely to refer to one of the great Alexandrian Neo-platonists" (*W,* IX, 486), implying, presumably, Plotinus. He also suggested (magnifying the ambiguity) that "over against the mouths of Nile" might conceivably point to Italy and thus to Dante.

TWO RIVERS.

The central conceit of this poem—that a natural fact (Concord's Musketaquit River) can and does present itself as the symbol of a spiritual fact (the flow of spirit or divinity through the world) concisely illustrates a central point of Transcendental doctrine, as Emerson had announced it in the early manifesto *Nature* (*CW,* I, 17). The imagery that Emerson chose in "Two Rivers" has an especially rich and resonant history in the Judeo-Christian tradition, as Edward Emerson intimated in pointing out the relevance to the poem of the remarks of Jesus to the Samaritan woman in the fourth chapter of John (*W,* IX, 488). There Jesus says, "If thou knewest the gift of God, and who it is that saith to thee, Give me to drink; thou wouldest have asked of him, and he would have given thee living water" (John 4: 10). Referring then to the water she had come to draw from Jacob's well, Jesus says, "Whosoever drinketh of this water shall thirst again: But whosoever drinketh of the water that I shall give him shall never thirst; but the water that I shall give him shall be in him a well of water springing up into everlasting life" (4: 13–14). This metaphoric structure, in which water under the sign of spirit is played off against water as an element of the natural world, was held in common by orthodox and Gnostic writers, but seems to have been especially emphasized by the latter. One begins to get a sense of the resonances of the motif in the so-called *Excerpts of Theodotus,* a Gnostic or Montanist text from the second century:

Now regeneration is by water and spirit, as was all creation: "For the Spirit of God moved on the abyss." And for this reason the Saviour was baptized, though not Himself needing to be so, in order that He might consecrate the whole water for those who were being regenerated. Thus it is not the body only, but the soul, that we cleanse. It is accordingly a sign of the sanctifying of our invisible part, and of the straining off from the new and spiritual creation of the unclean spirits that have got mixed up with the soul.

"The water above the heaven." Since baptism is performed by water and the Spirit as a protection against the twofold fire,—that which lays hold of what is visible, and that which lays hold of what is invisible; and of necessity, there being an immaterial element of water and a material, is it a protection against the twofold fire. And the earthly water cleanses the body; but the heavenly water, by reason of its being immaterial and invisible, is an emblem of the Holy Spirit, who is the purifier of what is invisible, as the water of the Spirit, as the other of the body. (*Ante-Nicene Fathers* [1886; rpt. Peabody, Mass., 1994], VIII, 44)

It seems that in orthodox texts of this period the language has already lost much of its metaphorical quality, so that, for example, the early second-century *Didache* directs that baptism be done in "running water" [i.e., "living" water or water infused with spirit], though if that is not available "ordinary water" will do (*Early Christian Writings,* trans. Maxwell Staniforth [London, 1968], 230–231).

Hans Jonas quotes from a Gnostic (Mandaean) creation myth:

They brought living water and poured it into the turbid water; they brought shining light and cast it into the dense darkness. They brought the refreshing wind and cast it into the scorching wind. They brought the living fire and cast it into the devouring fire. They brought the soul, the pure Mana, and cast it into the worthless body. (*The Gnostic Religion,* 2nd ed. [Boston, 1963], 58–59)

Jonas further points out that the heretical Mandaeans, who especially venerated John the Baptist, insisted more pointedly than the orthodox that their central rite of baptism could only be performed in flowing streams ("all of which the Mandaeans called

'Jordans'") because only flowing or "living" water was divine (97–98). It is not too much to say that the Gnostics above all other groups asserted the metaphoric or "poetic" uses of water, some trace of which continues to the present day to inform its profounder meanings in religious or spiritual contexts.

In *Freedom and Fate,* Stephen Whicher offered a darker, post-Transcendental reading of the poem by equating Emerson's Musketaquit with Robert Frost's "West-Running Brook" as "The stream of everything that runs away." In Whicher's still influential view, Emerson's poem was a sign of resignation if not discouragement, a "small concession" that "his spiritual life was subject to time" ([Philadelphia, 1953], 98–99).

TWO RIVERS.

Thy summer voice, Musketaquit,
Repeats the music of the rain;
But sweeter rivers pulsing flit
Through thee, as thou through Concord Plain.

Thou in thy narrow banks art pent: 5
The stream I love unbounded goes
Through flood and sea and firmament;
Through light, through life, it forward flows.

I see the inundation sweet,
I hear the spending of the stream   10
Through years, through men, through nature fleet,
Through love and thought, through power and dream.

Musketaquit, a goblin strong,
Of shard and flint makes jewels gay;
They lose their grief who hear his song,   15
And where he winds is the day of day.

So forth and brighter fares my stream,—
Who drink it shall not thirst again;

No darkness stains its equal gleam,
And ages drop in it like rain.   20

TEXTS

(A) *AM,* I (January 1858): 311; (A²) *May-Day* (Boston, 1867), 134–135; (B) *Selected Poems* (Boston, 1876), 156; (B²) *Poems* [Riverside] (Boston, 1884), 213; (C) *Poems* [Centenary] (Boston, 1904), 248.

Pre-copy-text forms: The first several drafts occur in journals SO (*JMN,* XIV, 65–67, 94) and VO (*JMN,* XIV, 140–141), dating from 1856 and 1857 respectively, followed by a fair copy in poetry notebook Rhymer: see the discussion at *PN,* 954.

VARIANTS

11   nature (A-B) | Nature (C)   12   love and (B-C) | passion, (A)

NOTES

5–8.   In *Nature* (1836), Emerson had written: "The river, as it flows, resembles the air that flows over it; the air resembles the light which traverses it with more subtile currents; the light resembles the heat which rides with it through space" (*CW,* I, 27). In an 1840 journal entry he wrote: "We see the river glide below us but we see not the river that glides over us & envelopes us in its floods" (*JMN,* VII, 499). In "The Over-Soul" (1841), he developed the proposition that "Man is a stream whose source is hidden" by saying, "When I watch that flowing river, which, out of regions I see not, pours for a season its streams into me, I see that I am a pensioner; not a cause, but a surprised spectator of this ethereal water; that I desire and look up, and put myself in the attitude of reception, but from some alien energy the visions come" (*CW,* II, 159–160).

19.   "George Fox saw that there was 'an ocean of darkness and death but withal an infinite ocean of light and love which flowed over that of darkness'" ("Montaigne," *Representative Men, CW,* IV, 103; cf. *EL,* I, 171).

WALDEINSAMKEIT.

The title means "woodland solitude." The poem was conceived and the first draft written in August 1857 during Emerson's brief visit (the first of many) to Naushon Island, situated between New Bedford and Martha's Vineyard. This island, seven miles long, wooded, stocked with deer, and accessible by yacht, was the recently purchased private estate of Emerson's friend John Murray Forbes, railroad tycoon and fellow Saturday Club member (*L*, V, 80–81; *Letters and Recollections of John Murray Forbes* [Boston, 1899], I, 16–27 and passim). Undoubtedly the prose germ of the poem was written on the island:

> I do not count the hours I spend in the woods, though I forget my affairs there & my books. And, when there, I wander hither & thither; any bird, any plant, any spring, detains me. I do not hurry homewards for I think all affairs may be postponed to this walking. And it is for this idleness that all my businesses exist. (*JMN*, XIV, 145)

The poem received contributions from memories of other walks closer to home and was so far finished by January or February of the following year that Emerson submitted it, with others, to J. R. Lowell at the *Atlantic,* allowing him to choose which of the batch he would publish. "He took the other pieces, & rejected this, I continuing to fancy this," Emerson explained in a letter to his hostess Mrs. Forbes. "Wishing yet to give my poor rhymes a chance with a selectest audience, I wrote them in your book"—referring to the guest-book at Naushon, in which he entered the poem on 2 September (MS privately owned; see also *ETE*, I, 147–148). He was completely surprised, therefore, when, within a few weeks, the poem appeared in the issue of the *Atlantic* for October, 1858, a clear violation of his rule that nothing of his was to be published unless he had seen proofs. When Emerson inquired about the matter, Francis Underwood, the *Atlantic*'s "sub-editor," explained that he had found the manuscript and had printed it while his supervisor, Lowell, and his author, Emerson, were off camping together in the Adirondacs. The poet was chagrined that what, as a gift, was to have been entirely private had thus been made public. He asked Mrs. Forbes to excise the poem "with a sharp pair of scissors," promising to replace it with something else (*L*, V, 118–119). Mrs. Forbes, of course, did no such thing.

WALDEINSAMKEIT.

I do not count the hours I spend
In wandering by the sea;
The forest is my loyal friend,
Like God it useth me.

In plains that room for shadows make   5
Of skirting hills to lie,
Bound in by streams which give and take
Their colors from the sky;

Or on the mountain-crest sublime,
Or down the oaken glade,   10
O what have I to do with time?
For this the day was made.

Cities of mortals woe-begone
Fantastic care derides,
But in the serious landscape lone   15
Stern benefit abides.

Sheen will tarnish, honey cloy,
And merry is only a mask of sad,
But, sober on a fund of joy,
The woods at heart are glad.   20

Waldeinsamkeit

There the great Planter plants
Of fruitful worlds the grain,
And with a million spells enchants
The souls that walk in pain.

Still on the seeds of all he made   25
The rose of beauty burns;
Through times that wear, and forms that fade,
Immortal youth returns.

The black ducks mounting from the lake,
The pigeon in the pines,   30
The bittern's boom, a desert make
Which no false art refines.

Down in yon watery nook,
Where bearded mists divide,
The gray old gods that Chaos knew,   35
The sires of Nature, hide.

Aloft, in secret veins of air,
Blows the sweet breath of song,
O, few to scale those uplands dare,
Though they to all belong!   40

See thou bring not to field or stone
The fancies found in books;
Leave authors' eyes, and fetch your own,
To brave the landscape's looks.

Oblivion here thy wisdom is,   45
Thy thrift, the sleep of cares;
For a proud idleness like this
Crowns all thy mean affairs.

TEXTS

(A) MS *Island Book*, 172–175, privately owned; (B) *AM*, II (October 1858): 550–551; (C) *May-Day* (Boston, 1867), 136–139; (D) *Selected Poems* (Boston, 1876), 157–158; (E) *Poems* [Riverside] (Boston, 1884), 214–15; (E²) *Poems* [Centenary] (Boston, 1904), 249–251. The holograph copy in the Naushon guest-book, signed by Emerson and dated "Sept. 2. 1858," is adopted as copy-text both because it is the earliest coherent form of the text and because it has not previously been published.

Format: In (B) alternate lines are indented.

Pre-copy-text forms: See *PN*, 960.

VARIANTS

2   sea; (B-E) I sea, (A)
4   Like God it useth (A-C, E) I A Delphic shrine to (D) II me. (A-E) I me; (CC7)
8   Their (B-E) I The (A) II from (B-E) I of (A) II sky; (A, C-E) I sky, (B)
9   Or (B-E) I Or, (A) II mountain-crest (B-E) I mountain crest (A)
11   O (A, C-E) I Oh, (B) II time? (B-E) I time?— (A)
13   woe-begone (C-E) I wo-begone (A) I woebegone (B)
14   care (B-E) I Care (A)
18   sad, (C-E) I sad (A) I sad; (B)
19   But, (C-E) I But (A-B) II joy, (C-E) I joy (A-B)
22   grain, (B-E) I grain (A)
26   burns; (B-E) I burns, (A)
27   wear, (A-D) I wear (E)
31   desert (B-E) I desart (A)

33   nook, (B-E) I nook (A)
36   Nature, (B-E) I nature (A)
37   Aloft, (B-E) I Aloft (A) II air, (B-E) I air (A)
38   song, (C-E) I song; (A-B)
39   O, (C-E) I Ah! (A-B)
40   belong! (C-E) I belong. (A-B)
41–44   [*Eight lines canceled: these four and the four mentioned in the next note*] (CC7)
45   [*Four lines omitted*] (D-E) I And if, amid this dear delight, / My thoughts did home rebound, / I should reckon it a slight / To the high cheer I found. (A-C) [(A) *lacks punctuation in the first line;* (C) *has* "I well might" *for* "I should" *in the third line*]
46   thrift, (A, C-E) I thrift (B)
48   thy (C-E) I life's (A-B)

NOTES

1–2. Edward Emerson notes (*W*, IX, 489) that "Allah does not count the days spent in the chase" was "a favorite quotation" with his father. Indeed it occurs under the heading "Holidays" in journal VS (*JMN*, XIII, 203) and appears several times in the published writings: in *English Traits* (*CW*, V, 38), and in the essays "Inspiration" (*CW*, VIII, 156) and "Concord Walks" (*W*, XII, 174).

13.   General references here and in line 24 may reflect the distress caused by the financial panic of 1857.

19–20.   In journal V are consecutive lines of jotting, probably entered in the spring of 1845: "The wood is soberness with a basis of joy / Sober with a fund of joy" (*JMN*, IX, 169).

26.   Cf. "See how the roses burn! / Bring wine to quench the fire! / Alas! the flames come up with us, / We perish with desire." The lines are Emerson's translation of Hafiz, *Diwan*, II, 198, first published in "Persian Poetry" (1858): see *TN*, II, 65, and *W*, VIII, 245.

33–36.   In September 1857, during a "valuable walk [with Thoreau] through the savage fertile houseless land" at Ebba Hubbard's swamp near Concord, Emerson "saw pigeons & marsh-hawks, &, ere we left it, the mists, which denote the haunt of the elder Gods, were rising" (*JMN*, XIV, 162).

41–44.   After a walk to Flint's Pond near Concord with Ellery Channing on 1 August 1857, Emerson wrote: "Reading is a languid pleasure and we must forget our books to see the landscape's royal looks." This is followed by the first draft of these lines in verse (*JMN*, XIV, 161).

TERMINUS.

In the spring of 1846, around the time of his forty-third birthday, Emerson wrote in his journal, "I grow old, I accept conditions;—thus far—no farther;—to learn that we are not the first born, but the latest born; that we have no wings; that the sins of our predecessors are on us like a mountain of obstruction" (*JMN*, IX, 363). A year later he wrote to his brother William ironically insisting that, like the enduringly profligate Falstaff, he meant "to

467

live within bounds. And I am taking in sail; and shall break out of slavery, if I can" (*L*, III, 390). Emerson's son, Edward, who does not cite these passages, always supposed that "Terminus" had been written much later, in 1866, because he first heard his father read it then, shortly before its publication:

> In the month of December, 1866, I, returning from six months on a Western railroad [in the employ of a family friend: see *ETE*, I, 391], met my father in New York just setting out for his winter's journey to the West, and we spent the night together at the St. Denis Hotel. He read me some poems that he was soon to publish in his new volume, May Day, and among them Terminus. I was startled, for he, looking so healthy, so full of life and young in spirit, was reading his deliberate acknowledgment of failing forces and his trusting and serene acquiescence. (*Emerson in Concord*, 183; cf. *W*, IX, 489–490)

One fair copy of the poem bears the heading "Climacteric" (*PN*, 702–703, 932), which might seem to refer the lines to Emerson's sixty-third year, which in fact commenced on 25 May 1866. And yet it is clear, as the researches of Carl F. Strauch have shown, that the first draft was inscribed before 1860, because it was overwritten in poetry notebook X by drafts of two quatrains ("Gardener" and "Nature in Leasts") published in that year (see "The Date of Emerson's *Terminus*," *PMLA*, LXV [June 1950]: 361; cf. *PN*, 224).

It remains an unsettled question just how long before 1860 the poem was begun. Strauch argues for the period 1850–1851, based largely on the tone of disgust regarding "politics" that the first draft develops and on the sense of personal mortality generated in Emerson by the death of Margaret Fuller in July of 1850. But as much or more evidence—including the journal entry about growing old and accepting conditions—favors 1846. The political themes that figure in the first draft but that are largely absent from the poem as published shed some considerable light on its inception, and these themes, reminiscent of the stance adopted in the "Ode to Channing," point also to 1846 rather than the more engaged and combative position that Emerson assumed in 1851 following Webster's defection and the passage of the Fugitive Slave Law. In the former instance Emerson argued the case for getting out of "politics"; in the latter, he plunged passionately in. The passage in notebook X that Strauch (surely correctly) identified as the beginning of the poem is a fragment that eventually became lines 33–34:

> As the bird trims himself to the gale
> So I trim myself to the tempest of time
> And I shall find something pleasant in my last throb that I am getting
> out of mean politics (X, p. 198; *PN*, 222).

Emerson expanded these lines on X, p. 205, and, later, as indicated by its being inscribed further down on the same page, wrote "Cold Bangor / Where is no summer but a thaw" (*PN*, 224). Emerson was in Bangor, Maine, between 5 and 16 October 1846, delivering his Representative Men lectures and preparing the manuscript of *Poems* that he sent to John Chapman in London (*Chronology*, 208–209). He had not been in Bangor since 1834.

The successive drafts, as Strauch was the first to point out, present unusually rich and rewarding complications for the researcher. Some of the most significant evidence bearing on the question of the date of composition relates to portions excluded from "Terminus" as published, and so may be, perhaps, of slightly less interest here. For present purposes, therefore, it will suffice first to corroborate Strauch's conclusion that the poem was not originally about growing old (the final quatrain, for example, does not appear in the early drafts, but was probably added during the period 1864–1866), and, second, to endorse the conclusion of the *Poetry Notebooks* editors that the first draft was, with a high degree of probability, written between 1846 and 1851.

TERMINUS.

It is time to be old,
To take in sail:—
The god of bounds,
Who sets to seas a shore,
Came to me in his fatal rounds,   5

And said: 'No more!
No farther shoot
Thy broad ambitious branches, and thy root.
Fancy departs: no more invent,
Contract thy firmament   10
To compass of a tent.
There's not enough for this and that,
Make thy option which of two;
Economize the failing river,
Not the less revere the Giver,   15
Leave the many and hold the few.
Timely wise accept the terms,
Soften the fall with wary foot;
A little while
Still plan and smile,   20
And, fault of novel germs,
Mature the unfallen fruit.
Curse, if thou wilt, thy sires,
Bad husbands of their fires,
Who, when they gave thee breath,   25
Failed to bequeath
The needful sinew stark as once,
The Baresark marrow to thy bones,
But left a legacy of ebbing veins,
Inconstant heat and nerveless reins,—   30
Amid the Muses, left thee deaf and dumb,
Amid the gladiators, halt and numb.'

   As the bird trims her to the gale,
I trim myself to the storm of time,
I man the rudder, reef the sail,   35
Obey the voice at eve obeyed at prime:
'Lowly faithful, banish fear,
Right onward drive unharmed;
The port, well worth the cruise, is near,
And every wave is charmed.'   40

Terminus

TEXTS

(A) *AM*, XIX (January 1867): 111–112; (B) *May-Day* (Boston, 1867), 140–142; (C) *Selected Poems* (Boston, 1876), 186–187; (D) *Poems* [Riverside] (Boston, 1884), 216–217; (D²) *Poems* [Centenary] (Boston, 1904), 251–252.

Pre-copy-text forms: See the analysis at *PN*, 931–933, and the several drafts transcribed at *PN*, 702–704. The discussion of pre-publication drafts includes reference to one fair copy that may contain emendations inscribed later than the first published text yet never incorporated into any subsequent edition. The editors regard these as unsuccessful trial revisions.

VARIANTS

6 said: 'No (B-D) | said, "No (A)
7 farther shoot (CC7, C-D) | further spread (A) | farther spread (B)
8 root. (B, D) | root; (A) | root, (C)
15 revere (B-D) | adore (A)
21 And, (A-C) | And,— (D) || germs, (A-C) | germs,— (D)
22–23 [*No white line*] (B-D) | [*White line*] (A)

23 Curse, (B-D) | "Curse, (A)
32 numb.' (B-D) | numb." (A)
32–33 [*White line*] (A, C-D) | [*Coincides with page break*] (B)
33 [*Inset*] As (C-D) | [*Flush*] As (A-B)
36 eve (B-D) | eve, (A)
37 'Lowly (B-D) | "Lowly (A)
40 charmed.' (B-D) | charmed." (A)

NOTES

1–2. "Take in your canvass or clear your decks before the gale comes" (Journal F2, 1840; *JMN*, VII, 496). In "Montaigne," Emerson gives a portrait of the skeptic: "He is the Considerer, the prudent, taking in sail, counting stock, husbanding his means, believing that a man has too many enemies, than that he can afford to be his own foe" (*CW*, IV, 91).

12–13. "You must elect your work; you shall take what your brain can, and drop all the rest. Only so, can that amount of vital force accumulate, which can make the step from knowing to doing" ("Power," *The Conduct of Life, CW*, VI, 39).

23–32. In an 1847 journal entry Emerson wrote: "We have experience, reading, relatedness enough, o yes, & every other weapon, if only we had constitution enough. But, as the doctor said in my boyhood,—'You have no *stamina*'" (*JMN*, X, 110). Cf. "Fate": "How shall a man escape from his ancestors, or draw off from his veins the black drop which he drew from his father's or his mother's life?" (*CW,* VI, 5). In 1859 he wrote: "Shall I blame my mother, whitest of women, because she was not a gypsy, & gave me no swarthy ferocity? or my father, because he came of a lettered race, & had no porter's shoulders? (*JMN,* XIV, 283).

36.   It is important to Strauch's argument in behalf of an early date for "Terminus" that the first draft version of this line is "The voice at noon obeyed <in> ↑at↓ prime" (*PN,* 224).

THE PAST.

It was an almost accurate statement by Edward (*W,* IX, 492) that "No trace of the history of this poem remains." Indeed, all that can be said is that the first, partially erased pencil draft, in poetry notebook EL, is preceded on the page by a draft of "What flowing central forces," a posthumously published fragment that appears to date from the spring of 1863 (*PN,* 336–338).

THE PAST.

The debt is paid,
The verdict said,
The Furies laid,
The plague is stayed,
All fortunes made;   5
Turn the key and bolt the door,
Sweet is death forevermore.
Nor haughty hope, nor swart chagrin,
Nor murdering hate, can enter in.
All is now secure and fast;   10

The Past

Not the gods can shake the Past;
Flies-to the adamantine door
Bolted down forevermore.
None can re-enter there,—
No thief so politic,   15
No Satan with a royal trick
Steal in by window, chink, or hole,
To bind or unbind, add what lacked,
Insert a leaf, or forge a name,
New-face or finish what is packed,   20
Alter or mend eternal Fact.

TEXTS

(A) *May-Day* (Boston, 1867), 143–144; (A²) *Poems* [Riverside] (Boston, 1884), 221–222; (B) *Poems* [Centenary] (Boston, 1904), 257–258. Not included in *Selected Poems* (Boston, 1876).

Pre-copy-text forms: Three drafts occur in poetry notebook EL. Emerson added lines 6–9 to the latest draft, an otherwise complete fair copy. See *PN*, 892.

VARIANTS

4   stayed, (A) I stayed. (B)   14   re-enter (A) I reënter (B)

IN MEMORIAM.
E. B. E.

The period 1831 to 1842 included the deaths of Emerson's first wife, two younger brothers, and an infant son. It was at this time very decidedly the style not only of Emerson personally but of his entire family to discover death's uses for education. Each calamity was the means by which the survivors came, through mourning, into a self-conscious possession of the rhetorically adduced and enumerated virtues of the deceased. Death became in this way a provocation to eloquence. The family's domestic correspondence, as we find it sampled in Ronald A. Bosco and Joel Myerson, eds., *The Emerson Brothers* (New York, 2006), shows a consciously cultivated poetry of paradox in the face of death. Consolation lay in the most effective denial of death, and the loss of traditional Christian resources in the performance of that task drove the imagination in new directions. For example, Charles Chauncy Emerson responded to the loss of his brother Edward in a letter to fiancée Elizabeth Hoar in October 1834: "I say, He [is] the more Fortunate! His life darkly blighted as it was pleases me now. Because it was true to higher principles than a prosperous ambition. It was not he that was blighted, but only his fortunes" (Bosco and Myerson, 146). Charles took a slightly different approach when he wrote to Waldo a few days later: "A remarkable life," he said. "We see plenty of abuse of genius by the individual, but seldom does the Hand that lighted so overshadow & extinguish the torch. The Providence must be rich that can afford to waste such a rare piece of work—not sacrifice it to the All, but refuse & snatch it back" (146).

It was more true of the Emerson family than of most others that it developed its own literature, and the language of mourning un-

474

derlay the most complex of its genres. Following Edward's death, Aunt Mary Moody Emerson wrote to Charles:

> I think of you—now as connected with Edwards life & death. T'was for you more than any in the great web of w'h his meteoric existence made a flash that he lived—aspired—struggled—suffered—failed of all hope and died to gain what virtue not fame could give. Oh yes dear Edward thou are not walking among the haggard forms of eclipsed—dead renown—bending to earth looks of ire & disappointment—No thy sorrows & toils are weaving into thy shekinah unfading flowers—thro his influence I once knew thee to love. . . . Often may the wasted darkened form of his life & fortunes attend your side to point your brighter way or raise your head above the mists & storms of life. (145–146)

Emerson's "In Memoriam" falls into this private literature of eclipsed characters, of the young dead, who become ideals in the course of having it luminously said who and what they were.

The talented and graceful Edward Bliss Emerson, younger brother of Ralph Waldo, died in San Juan, Puerto Rico, on 1 October 1834. His life was a tragedy of promise unrealized. He had been at the very head of Harvard's Class of 1824—"not merely the first scholar . . . but first by a long interval," as Frederic Henry Hedge recalled (71)—taking the Bowdoin Prize and, to a remarkable extent, earning the respect and admiration of the faculty. Edward Everett paid tribute to his memory in 1837, noting that he was "of a very superior nature intellectually and morally" (69). Like his brother Charles, Edward hoped to combine a legal career with the sort of lyceum lecturing that Waldo did. Despite some early success, including a professional and social connection with Daniel Webster, the delicacy of his constitution proved his undoing: "all was given," as his brother would say in the present poem, "and only health denied" (line 72). He endured a nervous breakdown in 1828 and was for a time a patient at the McLean Asylum in Charlestown. Recovering mentally if not physically, Edward was admitted to the bar in 1829, then practiced briefly in the law office of his brother William in New York before, at last, sailing to the West Indies in December of 1830 (*L*, I, 313). At the time of his death he was working in a counting house in San Juan.

The first draft of the poem, in notebook P, was probably written in 1838 or 1839, since it is partly inscribed over a draft of "Concord Fight" and is closely related to "Dirge," composed in 1838. The evidence of the two lines in journal D (see the note to lines 101–102, below) must be regarded as inconclusive, as they may be a quotation from memory. Emerson seems to have left the P draft unfinished for many years, since the complete second draft was composed in notebook EL, which Emerson did not begin to use until 1849. Annie Fields, wife of James T. Fields, reported that in 1863 Emerson thought of publishing "In Memoriam" in the *Atlantic,* but that it was, even then, not finished to his satisfaction (*Authors and Friends* [Boston, 1896], 84–85).

When the poem was at last published in *May-Day* Emerson gave it an especially rich setting, since it followed "The Past"—verses that seem almost a deliberate gloss on line 109 of "In Memoriam" —and "The Last Farewell," a poem that Edward had written as he sailed from Boston harbor in October 1832, returning to Puerto Rico after a brief last visit home. These lines, which Emerson had first printed a quarter of a century earlier in the inaugural issue of the *Dial,* illustrate Edward's strength of character in accepting without complaint that the time for the writing and revising of history—activities he had seemed destined to accomplish—was at an end (see Bosco and Myerson, 135).

IN MEMORIAM.
E. B. E.

I mourn upon this battle-field,
But not for those who perished here.
Behold the river-bank
Whither the angry farmers came,
In sloven dress and broken rank,   5
Nor thought of fame.
Their deed of blood
All mankind praise;

Even the serene Reason says,
It was well done.   10
The wise and simple have one glance
To greet yon stern head-stone,
Which more of pride than pity gave
To mark the Briton's friendless grave.
Yet it is a stately tomb;   15
The grand return
Of eve and morn,
The year's fresh bloom,
The silver cloud,
Might grace the dust that is most proud.   20

   Yet not of these I muse
In this ancestral place,
But of a kindred face
That never joy or hope shall here diffuse.

   Ah, brother of the brief but blazing star!   25
What hast thou to do with these
Haunting this bank's historic trees?
Thou born for noblest life,
For action's field, for victor's car,
Thou living champion of the right?   30
To these their penalty belonged:
I grudge not these their bed of death,
But thine to thee, who never wronged
The poorest that drew breath.

   All inborn power that could   35
Consist with homage to the good
Flamed from his martial eye;
He who seemed a soldier born,
He should have the helmet worn,
All friends to fend, all foes defy,   40
Fronting foes of God and man,
Frowning down the evil-doer,

477

Battling for the weak and poor.
His from youth the leader's look
Gave the law which others took,   45
And never poor beseeching glance
Shamed that sculptured countenance.

    There is no record left on earth,
Save in tablets of the heart,
Of the rich inherent worth,   50
Of the grace that on him shone,
Of eloquent lips, of joyful wit;
He could not frame a word unfit,
An act unworthy to be done;
Honor prompted every glance,   55
Honor came and sat beside him,
In lowly cot or painful road,
And evermore the cruel god
Cried, "Onward!" and the palm-crown showed.
Born for success he seemed,   60
With grace to win, with heart to hold,
With shining gifts that took all eyes,
With budding power in college-halls,
As pledged in coming days to forge
Weapons to guard the State, or scourge   65
Tyrants despite their guards or walls.
On his young promise Beauty smiled,
Drew his free homage unbeguiled,
And prosperous Age held out his hand,
And richly his large future planned,   70
And troops of friends enjoyed the tide,—
All, all was given, and only health denied.

    I see him with superior smile
Hunted by Sorrow's grisly train
In lands remote, in toil and pain,   75
With angel patience labor on,

With the high port he wore erewhile,
When, foremost of the youthful band,
The prizes in all lists he won;
Nor bate one jot of heart or hope,   80
And, least of all, the loyal tie
Which holds to home 'neath every sky,
The joy and pride the pilgrim feels
In hearts which round the hearth at home
Keep pulse for pulse with those who roam.   85

    What generous beliefs console
The brave whom Fate denies the goal!
If others reach it, is content;
To Heaven's high will his will is bent.
Firm on his heart relied,   90
What lot soe'er betide,
Work of his hand
He nor repents nor grieves,
Pleads for itself the fact,
As unrepenting Nature leaves   95
Her every act.

    Fell the bolt on the branching oak;
The rainbow of his hope was broke;
No craven cry, no secret tear,—
He told no pang, he knew no fear;   100
Its peace sublime his aspect kept,
His purpose woke, his features slept;
And yet between the spasms of pain
His genius beamed with joy again.

    O'er thy rich dust the endless smile   105
Of Nature in thy Spanish isle
Hints never loss or cruel break
And sacrifice for love's dear sake,
Nor mourn the unalterable Days

479

That Genius goes and Folly stays.   110
What matters how, or from what ground,
The freed soul its Creator found?
Alike thy memory embalms
That orange-grove, that isle of palms,
And these loved banks, whose oak-boughs bold   115
Root in the blood of heroes old.

TEXTS

(A) *May-Day* (Boston, 1867), 148–154; (B) *Poems* [Riverside] (Boston, 1884), 224–227; (C) *Poems* [Centenary] (Boston, 1904), 261–265. Not included in *Selected Poems* (Boston, 1876).

Format: Line 73 set flush left (A).

Pre-copy-text forms: Inside the front cover of a journal (ST) that Emerson used between 1870 and 1877 is a slip of paper, date entirely uncertain, containing lines 37–37, 41–47 (*JMN*, XVI, 202). It has the reading "Flowed" for "Flamed" in l. 37 (a misreading of the manuscript), "evil doer" for "evil-doer" in l. 42, "Youth" for "youth" in l. 44, and "Countenance" for "countenance" in l. 47.

Lines 92–96 were published separately (from poetry notebook P, p. 244: see *PN*, 94) as the second of two mottoes for "Character" in *Essays: Second Series* (1844). This text has "commends" for "repents" and "grieves:" for "grieves," in l. 93, and "fact;" for "fact," in line 94 (see *CW*, III, 52).

A manuscript in the hand of Margaret Fuller gives, as a continuous passage, lines 46–47 and 92–96. This text has "Never" for "And never" in l. 46, "countenance;" for "countenance." in line 47, "What he had done" for "Work of his hand" in l. 92, and "<repents> ↑commends↓" for "repents" in l. 93. See *L*, II, 23, and *PN*, 835.

For additional details, including a discussion of the major drafts in P and EL, see *PN*, 835–836.

VARIANTS

52   wit; (A) | wit: (B-C)   59   showed. (A-B) | showed, (C)

NOTES

1–6.   For the engagement at Concord's North Bridge in 1775, see the notes to "Dirge" and "Concord Hymn."

39.   Emerson "had a romantic admiration" for his brother Edward, according to Emerson's son, "for he saw in him qualities that he missed in himself. Edward was handsome, graceful, had a military carriage and had been an officer in the college company; he had confidence and executive ability, great ambition and an unsleeping, goading conscience that would never let him spare himself" (*Emerson in Concord*, 51).

101–102.   In a journal entry of 11 March 1839, Emerson wrote, "Their peace profound his features kept / His purpose woke, his aspect slept;" (*JMN*, VII, 176).

ELEMENTS.

The selection and ordering of the following thirteen poems— all previously published mottoes to essays—were determined by Emerson on the occasion of their publication in *May-Day,* as was the collective title, "Elements." Emerson's choice of poems certainly indicates which works in this category he felt could best stand alone. These were the ones, as Edward stated, that his father "preferred" (*W*, IX, 494). What reasons he may have had for the order of their presentation, however, remain mysterious, as they are by no means chronologically arranged. While six items from the *May-Day* group were dropped in *Selected Poems,* the order of the remaining poems (not designated as "Elements" or otherwise distinguished from the non-epigraphic poems) was preserved in that edition. The present edition retains the *May-Day* ordering, while in each instance selecting the first published form as copy-text—with the exception of "Culture," where printer's copy survives. The alteration of the section title to "Elements and Mottoes" in the Centenary Edition has been rejected, as has Edward's unaccountable shifting of "Spiritual Laws" from the eleventh to the eighth position in the Centenary sequence. As a distinct subset among the "Pieces" offered in *May-Day,* the "Elements" resist being offered on an equal footing with the other poems, and indeed William Dean Howells, in a review of the volume, candidly confessed that "we do not expect to live long enough to enjoy some of them" (*AM,* XX [September 1867]: 378).

EXPERIENCE.

The only surviving draft of these verses is in journal V, in erased pencil, under an entry in ink dated 15 June 1844 (*JMN,* IX, 114–115). The poem was written to serve as the epigraph to "Experience" in *Essays: Second Series,* which was published in mid-October of that year. It was with this volume that Emerson initiated the practice of writing original verse epigraphs for his essays; he went back and supplied mottoes for the first series of *Essays* for the second edition of that title in 1847.

EXPERIENCE.

The lords of life, the lords of life,—
I saw them pass,
In their own guise,
Like and unlike,
Portly and grim,—   5

Experience

Use and Surprise,
Surface and Dream,
Succession swift and spectral Wrong,
Temperament without a tongue,
And the inventor of the game   10
Omnipresent without name;—
Some to see, some to be guessed,
They marched from east to west:
Little man, least of all,
Among the legs of his guardians tall,   15
Walked about with puzzled look.
Him by the hand dear Nature took,
Dearest Nature, strong and kind,
Whispered, 'Darling, never mind!
Tomorrow they will wear another face,   20
The founder thou; these are thy race!'

TEXTS

(A) *Essays: Second Series* (Boston, 1844), 47; (B) *Essays: Second Series* (Boston, 1850), 47; (C) *May-Day* (Boston, 1867), 157–158; (D) *Selected Poems* (Boston, 1876), 169; (E) *Poems* [Riverside] (Boston, 1884), 228; (F) *Poems* [Centenary] (Boston, 1904), 269. (B) was the first edition printed from stereotype plates and so became the origin of many later printings.

Pre-copy-text forms: JMN, IX, 114–115.

VARIANTS

2   pass, (A-D) | pass (E-F)
5   grim,— (C-F) | grim, (A-B)
8   swift (C-F) | swift, (A-B)
16   look. (C, E-F) | look:— (A-B) | look; (D)
17   Nature took, (C-F) | nature took; (A) | Nature took; (B)

18   Nature, (C-F) | nature, (A-B)
20   Tomorrow (A) | To-morrow (B-F) [*See CW, III, 251, for the argument that the hyphenated form was house-style and inconsistent with Emerson's scribal practice.*]
21   thou; (C-F) | thou! (A-B)

483

COMPENSATION.

The two poems comprising "Compensation" were brought together to serve as epigraphs to the essay of that title in the second edition of *Essays: First Series* in 1847. There is no reason to believe that they were written at that time or, indeed, at the same time. A manuscript draft of the first poem survives bearing the date 1841 (*PN,* 650), but this might simply and misleadingly refer to the date of the first printing of the essay with which it is associated. The evidence of the manuscript drafts of the second poem points to a date of 1847 for it.

The few emendations introduced in the *May-Day* printing were not transferred to the text in later printings of *Essays: First Series,* which retain the 1847 forms.

COMPENSATION.

I.

The wings of Time are black and white,
Pied with morning and with night.
Mountain tall and ocean deep
Trembling balance duly keep.
In changing moon and tidal wave   5
Glows the feud of Want and Have.
Gauge of more and less through space,
Electric star or pencil plays,
The lonely Earth amid the balls
That hurry through the eternal halls,   10
A makeweight flying to the void,
Supplemental asteroid,

Compensation

Or compensatory spark,
Shoots across the neutral Dark.

II.

Man's the elm, and Wealth the vine;   15
Stanch and strong the tendrils twine:
Though the frail ringlets thee deceive,
None from its stock that vine can reave.
Fear not, then, thou child infirm,
There's no god dare wrong a worm;   20
Laurel crowns cleave to deserts,
And power to him who power exerts.
Hast not thy share? On winged feet,
Lo! it rushes thee to meet;
And all that Nature made thy own,   25
Floating in air or pent in stone,
Will rive the hills and swim the sea,
And, like thy shadow, follow thee.

TEXTS

(A) *Essays: First Series* (Boston, 1847), 81–82; (B) *May-Day* (Boston, 1867), 159–160; (B²) *Poems* [Riverside] (Boston, 1884), 229; (B³) *Poems* [Centenary] (Boston, 1904), 270–271. Not included in *Selected Poems* (Boston, 1876).

Format: In (A) the two fourteen-line poems are printed on consecutive pages; in (B) they are printed together, but denoted "I." and "II." respectively. (B²-B³) eliminate the roman numerals.

Pre-copy-text forms: See *PN,* 762.

VARIANTS

5   moon and (B) I moon, in (A) II
wave (B) I wave, (A)
7   space, (B) I space (A)
8   or (B) I and (A) II plays, (B) I
plays. (A)

20   worm; (B) I worm. (A)
22   exerts. (B) I exerts; (A)

NOTES

23–24. Edward Emerson (*W,* IX, 494–495) notes the relevance to these lines of a journal entry of 25 September 1840: "I read today in [Simon] Ockley [*History of the Saracens*] a noble sentence of Ali, son-in-law of Mahomet; 'Thy lot or portion in life is seeking after thee; therefore be at rest from seeking after it'" (*JMN,* VII, 400).

POLITICS.

No drafts of this poem survive. Probably it was written shortly before its publication in 1844, but in fact no evidence bears on the question.

POLITICS.

Gold and iron are good
To buy iron and gold;
All earth's fleece and food
For their like are sold.
Hinted Merlin wise,   5
Proved Napoleon great,
Nor kind nor coinage buys
Aught above its rate.
Fear, Craft, and Avarice
Cannot rear a State.   10
Out of dust to build
What is more than dust,—
Walls Amphion piled

Phœbus stablish must.
When the Muses nine   15
With the Virtues meet,
Find to their design
An Atlantic seat,
By green orchard boughs
Fended from the heat,   20
Where the statesman ploughs
Furrow for the wheat,—
When the Church is social worth,
When the state-house is the hearth,
Then the perfect State is come,   25
The republican at home.

TEXTS

(A) *Essays: Second Series* (Boston, 1844), 215; (B) *May-Day* (Boston, 1867), 161–162; (C) *Poems* [Riverside] (Boston, 1884), 230; (C²) *Poems* [Centenary] (Boston, 1904], 271–272. The poem was not included in *Selected Poems* (Boston, 1876).

Pre-copy-text forms: None.

VARIANTS

5   Hinted (B) | Boded (A, C) [*Emerson emended to* "Hinted" *in his correction copy of* Essays: Second Series; *that reading then occurs in* The Prose Works *(Boston, 1870) and* Essays: Second Series *[Little Classic]* (Boston, 1876), *reverting to* "Boded" *in subsequent (posthumous) editions: see* CW, *III, 261.*]

6   great, (B-C) | great,— (A)
9   Craft, (A-B) | Craft (C)
22   wheat,— (B-C) | wheat; (A)

NOTES

1–2.   Perhaps suggested by the expression "They talk gold & give iron," quoted in an 1840 journal entry (*JMN*, VII, 402), which was undoubtedly derived from the admonition of Queen Elizabeth to the Earl of Essex, cited in Walter Savage

Landor, *Citation and Examination of William Shakespeare . . . before the Worshipful Sir Thomas Lucy . . . Now First Published from Original Papers* (London, 1834), 274.

13–14. Stones spontaneously assembled themselves into the walls of Thebes in response to the singing of Amphion, son of Zeus and Antiope, according to Horace, *Odes,* III, 11, in a passage that Emerson quoted in a college journal (*JMN,* I, 31). In a legend alluded to by Horace in *Odes,* III, 3, Phœbus Apollo was responsible for the walls of Troy.

HEROISM.

This poem, a motto to the essay "Heroism" in the second edition of *Essays: First Series,* was probably written in 1847. O. W. Firkins wittily pointed out that, the poem's "authentic inspiration" notwithstanding, "two questions might be put to the author with equal propriety: Why not half as many specifications? and Why not twice as many? and both questions are unanswerable. One says with Touchstone: 'I'll rhyme you so eight years together'" (*Ralph Waldo Emerson* [Boston, 1915], 281, 280).

HEROISM.

Ruby wine is drunk by knaves,
Sugar spends to fatten slaves,
Rose and vine-leaf deck buffoons;
Thunderclouds are Jove's festoons,
Drooping oft in wreaths of dread,   5
Lightning-knotted round his head;
The hero is not fed on sweets,
Daily his own heart he eats;

Chambers of the great are jails,
And head-winds right for royal sails.   10

TEXTS

(A) *Essays: First Series* (Boston, 1847), 221; (B) *May-Day* (Boston, 1876), 163; (C²) *Poems* [Riverside] (Boston, 1884), 231; (C³) *Poems* [Centenary] (Boston, 1904), 272. Not included in *Selected Poems* (Boston, 1876).

Pre-copy-text forms: Two drafts of "Heroism" occur in a 30-page insert at the back of poetry notebook X. See the discussion at *PN*, 815.

VARIANTS

4   Thunderclouds (A) | Thunder-   5   dread, (B) | dread (A)
clouds (B) [*Written as one word in both
manuscript drafts.*]

NOTES

2   Sugar cane, grown in Cuba, the West Indies, and the American Gulf coast, was a major staple in the economy of slavery. In the early nineteenth century the Quaker-led boycott of all products of slave labor tended to emphasize their status as luxury items.

CHARACTER.

In the Riverside edition the poem carries a note, presumably by Edward Emerson: "A part of this motto was taken from *The Poet,* an early poem never published by Mr. Emerson" (231). The

Centenary edition has a similar note and both refer the reader to the text of a long, chaotic composition with the editorially supplied title "The Poet," in which lines 1–6 of "Character" reappear as lines 134–139. In fact the manuscripts from which Edward derived "The Poet" ("concocted" is not too strong a word) actually represent Emerson's abortive effort in 1843 to expand an otherwise complete unpublished poem entitled "The Discontented Poet: a Masque" (see *PN*, 775–776). The draft of lines 1–6, independently composed in poetry notebook P at some earlier period, was momentarily swept up in this effort, but was never organically a part of any poem other than the motto to the 1844 essay on "Character."

CHARACTER.

The sun set, but set not his hope:
Stars rose; his faith was earlier up:
Fixed on the enormous galaxy,
Deeper and older seemed his eye;
And matched his sufferance sublime   5
The taciturnity of time.
He spoke, and words more soft than rain
Brought the Age of Gold again:
His action won such reverence sweet
As hid all measure of the feat.   10

TEXTS

(A) *Essays: Second Series* (Boston, 1844), 95; (B) *May-Day* (Boston, 1867), 164; (B²) *Poems* [Riverside] (Boston, 1884), 231; (B³) *Poems* [Centenary] (Boston, 1904), 273. Not included in *Selected Poems* (Boston, 1876). All printings of the poem as a motto to "Character" in *Essays: Second Series*—down to and including *CW*, III, 51—follow (A).

Pre-copy-text forms: A draft of the first six lines is in poetry notebook P, repeated in Houghton Library MS Am 1280.235 (73)—referred to in *PN* as Poems folder 73—where it occurs in an experimental combination with other verses. See, further, *PN*, 757 and the headnote above.

VARIANTS

1   set, (B) | set; (A)   9   sweet (B) | sweet, (A)
4   eye; (B) | eye: (A)

NOTES

6.   Emerson refers to "this reserve & taciturnity of Time" in a journal passage composed on or shortly after 30 January 1841 (*JMN*, VII, 546).

CULTURE.

It was a central informing feature of Emerson's career that he so constantly and so expressively anticipated the poet-messiah, the perfectly fit reader of the world, variously called the "fireeyed child" and the "central man," a figure who is owed to the world, who is promised by the age, and who yet remains unborn (*L*, V, 86). In his gloss on the word "impressional" in line 4 (*W*, IX, 495), Edward Emerson pointed to a passage in the essay "Fate" in which his father explained that "We are all impressionable, for we are made of them; all impressionable, but some more than others, and these first express them. . . . So the great man . . . is the impressionable man,—of a fibre irritable and delicate, like iodine to light. He feels the infinitesimal attractions. His mind is righter than others, because he yields to a current so feeble as can be felt only by a needle delicately poised" (*CW*, VI, 24). On the page in poetry notebook NP immediately preceding the first draft of "Culture" is a comment about the poet Jones Very that might be supposed to refer to just this kind of susceptibility: "V. could read the song of a bobolink into English sentences[,] but that is easier he could look at an apple tree in bloom & tell you accurately what it said to you & you wd listen & ponder & confess that he had said what you felt" (*PN*, 500). Elsewhere Emerson associates this fine impressionability with the powers of Eros:

> And what is specially true of love is, that it is a state of extreme impressionability; the lover has more senses and finer senses than others; his eye and ear are telegraphs; he reads omens on the flower, and cloud, and face, and form, and gesture, and reads them aright. In his surprise at the sudden and entire understanding that is between him and the beloved person, it occurs to him that they might somehow meet independently of time and place. How delicious the belief that he could elude all guards, precautions, ceremonies, means, and delays, and hold instant and sempiternal communication! (*CW*, VII, 154)

This is the culture of the "semigod whom we await," which cannot be regulated or taught, but which, as in the best poetry, frees communication from all friction, redeems it from all hindrance of time and space. It is noteworthy that Emerson does not in fact use the word "impressionable" in the poem (as Edward's gloss seems almost to assume), but chooses instead a new term, "impressional" associated with the diction of spiritualism. The *OED* cites Emerson's poem as the earliest instance of the word, but quotes Emerson's old acquaintance, Boston Mayor Josiah Quincy, Jr., as the author of the only other nineteenth-century use recorded: "The resemblance . . . could scarcely be called physical," Quincy wrote shortly before his death in 1882, "and I am loath to borrow the word 'impressional' from the vocabulary of spirit mediums." As also in lines 7–8 (cf. the discussion of "second-sight" at *CW*, VI, 292), Emerson associates in metaphor that which he means with that which the culture knows in popular spiritualist facsimile.

CULTURE.

Can rules or tutors educate
The semigod whom we await?

Culture

He must be musical,
Tremulous, impressional,
Alive to gentle influence   5
Of landscape and of sky,
And tender to the spirit-touch
Of man's or maiden's eye:
But, to his native centre fast,
Shall into Future fuse the Past,   10
And the world's flowing fates in his own mould recast.

TEXTS

There are no variants among the texts as published: (A) MS HM 1216, by per-
mission of the Huntington Library, San Marino, California, printer's copy for B;
(B) *The Conduct of Life* (Boston, 1860), 111; (B²) *May-Day* (Boston, 1867), 165;
(B³) *Poems* [Riverside] (Boston, 1884), 232; (B⁴) *Poems* [Centenary] (Boston,
1904), 273. Not included in *Selected Poems* (Boston, 1876). There are no variants
in later printings of *The Conduct of Life*.

Format: In (B⁴) lines 1–10 are inset, while the long eleventh, an Alexandrine, is
set flush left.

Pre-copy-text forms: A draft of the first six lines is in poetry notebook P, repeated
in Houghton Library MS Am 1280.235 (73)—referred to in *PN* as Poems folder
73—where it occurs in an experimental combination with other verses. See, fur-
ther, *PN*, 757 and the headnote above.

VARIANTS

11   [*Followed in* (A) *by five canceled
lines:*] <The sun & moon shall fall
amain, / Like sower's seeds, into his
brain, / There quickened to be born
again; / And Art's & Wisdom's
garnered power / Spring from his
hand a fresh-blown flower.> [*The
triplet (lines 1–3) often occurs separately
in the notebooks (EL, 103 and 148; NP,
296 and 300; ETE, 41 and 170; and*

*XO, 101) and was published
posthumously as lines 34–36 of "Mask
thy wisdom with delight," an editorially
assembled collection of verse fragments, in*
Poems [Riverside] (Boston, 1884), 268,
reprinted in Poems [Centenary] (Boston,
1904), 326 (cf. PN, 757–758). The
couplet (lines 4–5) has not been located
elsewhere in Emerson's writings.]

NOTES

3   "But, for the Poet,—/ Seldom in centuries / Comes the well-tempered / Musical man. / He is the waited-for" (lines 25–29 of Emerson's unpublished "Poet of poets," composed in 1849: see *PN*, 326).

FRIENDSHIP.

This poem was written in 1847 to serve as a motto for the essay "Friendship" in the second edition of *Essays: First Series.*

FRIENDSHIP.

A ruddy drop of manly blood
The surging sea outweighs,
The world uncertain comes and goes,
The lover rooted stays.
I fancied he was fled,—   5
And, after many a year,
Glowed unexhausted kindliness,
Like daily sunrise there.
My careful heart was free again,
O friend, my bosom said,   10
Through thee alone the sky is arched,
Through thee the rose is red;
All things through thee take nobler form,
And look beyond the earth,
The mill-round of our fate appears   15
A sun-path in thy worth.

494

Me too thy nobleness has taught
To master my despair;
The fountains of my hidden life
Are through thy friendship fair.   20

TEXTS

(A) *Essays: First Series* (Boston, 1847), 173; (B) *May-Day* (Boston, 1867), 166–167; (B²) *Selected Poems* (Boston, 1876), 177; (C) *Poems* [Riverside] (Boston, 1884), 232–233; (C²) *Poems* [Centenary] (Boston, 1904), 274. No notice is taken of several variants in the accidentals of later printings of *Essays: First Series*.

Pre-copy-text forms: See *PN,* 797.

VARIANTS

3   goes, (A-B) I goes; (C)
5   fled,— (B-C) I fled, (A)
7   kindliness, (B-C) I kindliness (A)
9   again, (B-C) I again,— (A)

12   red; (B-C) I red, (A)
15   The (B-C) I And is the (A) II fate appears (B-C) I fate (A)

BEAUTY.

The first ten lines of this poem developed through several drafts of "There are beggars in Iran & Araby," a sequel to "Saadi" that Emerson projected in late 1844: see the first draft in journal V (*JMN,* IX, 130) and the later drafts identified in *PN*, including the one in notebook QL, subsequently published in *TN*, III, 353. Lines 15–16, originating in journal VO in the spring of 1858

(*JMN*, XIV, 202), are the germ of the latter portion (lines 11–26), which would thus have been written (mostly in poetry notebook X) between 1858 and 1860, the date of publication.

BEAUTY.

Was never form and never face
So sweet to SEYD as only grace
Which did not slumber like a stone,
But hovered gleaming and was gone.
Beauty chased he everywhere,   5
In flame, in storm, in clouds of air.
He smote the lake to feed his eye
With the beryl beam of the broken wave;
He flung in pebbles well to hear
The moment's music which they gave.   10
Oft pealed for him a lofty tone
From nodding pole and belting zone.
He heard a voice none else could hear
From centred and from errant sphere.
The quaking earth did quake in rhyme,   15
Seas ebbed and flowed in epic chime.
In dens of passion, and pits of woe,
He saw strong Eros struggling through,
To sun the dark and solve the curse,
And beam to the bounds of the universe.   20
While thus to love he gave his days
In loyal worship, scorning praise,
How spread their lures for him in vain
Thieving Ambition and paltering Gain!
He thought it happier to be dead,   25
To die for Beauty, than live for bread.

TEXTS

(A) *The Conduct of Life* (Boston, 1860), 245; (B) *May-Day* (Boston, 1867), 168–169; (B²) *Selected Poems* (Boston, 1876), 178; (B³) *Poems* [Riverside] (Boston, 1884), 233–234; (B⁴) *Poems* [Centenary] (Boston, 1904), 275–276.

Format: Lines 8 and 10 indented (A).

Pre-copy-text forms: See *PN*, 742–743 ("Beauty"), and 935–937 ("There are beggars"). A corrected proof-sheet containing lines 1–10 as part of "There are beggars" and lines 11–26 as a separate poem was found with poetry notebook Rhymer. It seems to be intermediate between the manuscripts published in *PN*, 704–707, and the *May-Day* printing. It is illustrated in *PN*, [xxvi].

VARIANTS

3	stone, (B) | stone (A)	23	him (B) | him, (A) || vain (B) |
17	woe, (B) | wo, (A)		vain, (A)

NOTES

12. The word "nodding" seems to have been borrowed from line 21 of "There are beggars," the poem most closely associated with "Beauty" in the manuscripts ("Loved harebells nodding on a rock"). Line 146 of "The Adirondacs" ("Or harebell nodding in the gorge of falls") was also written in 1858.

MANNERS.

On 10 August 1840, Christopher Pearse Cranch and Theodore Parker made a social call on Emerson in Concord; during a walk in the woods that day, Emerson spoke with his visitors in warm praise of his promising young friend Thoreau (John Weiss, *Life and Correspondence of Theodore Parker*, 2 vols. [New York, 1864], I, 125; *FuL*, III, 162n4). A few days later, Emerson, in company with Margaret Fuller, visited Anna Barker in Cambridge, then escorted Fuller home to Jamaica Plain. There "she taxed me as often before . . . with inhospitality of soul. She & C[aroline Sturgis] would gladly be my friends, yet our intercourse is not friendship, but literary gossip" (*JMN*, VII, 509–10; cf. *L*, II, 325). Two days later Emerson was discussing with Bronson Alcott and George Ripley a plan to settle friends in Concord and so create a "college" where public lectures would be given. They hoped to involve Fuller and Parker, as well as Frederic Hedge, George P. Bradford, and a number more of their extended circle (*L*, II, 323–324; *L*, VII, 398–399). A couple of days after that, on 18 August, Emerson made an entry in his journal:

> Two or three men and three or four women rule the life of every mortal. He wishes their love as his chief good. He affects not to visit them but he converses with them in his solitude. He does not look at them when they are present, but fastens his eyes on the ground; yet the ground becomes a lookingglass & he still reads their faces thereon. He does not speak much to them but his voice trembles, & his heart dances, whilst he talks with them; they take from him his words & his wit. Unable to escape from these tyrants, he scuds behind a grave-stone at last, and if you go there to look, you shall find a tuft of fresher grass. (*JMN*, VII, 510)

The first draft of the poem follows, in pencil, on the next journal page, though it was probably not written on 18 August, the date inscribed at the top of that page in ink. The brief ink inscription, interestingly, includes the phrase "The Enchanters the enchanters," which may be a form of line 9 of "The Park," a poem composed about this time on a similar theme. At the end of the prose source on the previous page Emerson had written, "turned in a verse & printed," but just when that turning occurred is difficult to say, since it would not be "printed" for another twenty years.

The poem served as the motto to the essay "Behavior" in *The Conduct of Life*, but Emerson gave it the title "Manners" when he reprinted it in *May-Day*. In fact, "Manners" was the original title of the 1860 essay, canceled in favor of "Behavior" in the printer's copy (*CW*, VI, 361).

MANNERS.

Grace, Beauty, and Caprice
Build this golden portal;
Graceful women, chosen men,
Dazzle every mortal.
Their sweet and lofty countenance   5
His enchanted food;
He need not go to them, their forms
Beset his solitude.
He looketh seldom in their face,
His eyes explore the ground,—   10
The green grass is a looking-glass
Whereon their traits are found.
Little and less he says to them,
So dances his heart in his breast;
Their tranquil mien bereaveth him   15
Of wit, of words, of rest.
Too weak to win, too fond to shun
The tyrants of his doom,
The much-deceived Endymion
Slips behind a tomb.   20

TEXTS

(A) MS MA 1035, by permission of the Pierpont Morgan Library, printer's copy for B; (B) *The Conduct of Life* (Boston, 1860), 145; (C) *May-Day* (Boston, 1867), 170–171; (D) *Selected Poems* (Boston, 1876), 179; (E) *Poems* [Riverside] (Boston, 1884), 234; (E²) Poems [Centenary] (Boston, 1904), 276–277. (A) is printer's copy for the essay as well as the poem; it is described in *CW*, VI, 361. The first-edition text (B) is unaltered in later editions of *The Conduct of Life*, with the exception that the Centenary edition has portal, rather than portal; in line 2 (*W*, VI, 167).

Pre-copy-text forms: See *PN*, 851.

VARIANTS

Title: MANNERS. (C-E) |
<MANNERS> ↑BEHAVIOR. ↓ (A) |
BEHAVIOR. (B)
1   Grace, (B-E) | Grace (A) ||
Beauty, (B-D) | Beauty (A, E)
2   portal; (B-E) | portal (A)
3   women, (B-E) | women (A) ||
men, (C-E) | men (A-B)
4   mortal. (C-E) | mortal: (A-B)

6   enchanted (C-E) | enchanting
(A-B)
10   ground,— (C-E) | ground, (A-B)
13   Little and less he (C-E) | Little
he (A-B)
14   breast; (C-E) | breast, (A-B)
19   much-deceived (D) | much
deceived (A-C, E)

NOTES

19–20.   Endymion, a shepherd of Mt. Latmos, was beloved by Cynthia, the moon goddess, who put him permanently to sleep so that she might behold forever his unchanging beauty.

20.   Edward Emerson found a parallel to the poem in a passage from a letter to Samuel Gray Ward, written 1 March 1840 in which his father describes himself as "a devout student & admirer of persons. I cannot get used to them: they daunt & dazzle me still. . . . I see persons whose existence makes the world rich. But blessed be the Eternal power for those whom fancy even cannot strip of beauty, & who never for a moment seem to me profane" (*L,* VII, 370). Edward (*W,* IX, 496) accepted the date of 1 March 1841 mistakenly assigned to the letter in his source, Charles Eliot Norton, ed., *Letters of Emerson to a Friend* (Boston, 1899), 32.

ART.

This poem was written for the 1847 second edition of *Essays: First Series,* where it served as the epigraph for "Art," the final essay in the volume. The only relic of its composition is an ink fair copy in a sequence of these 1847 mottoes in poetry notebook X, where it is written over an erased pencil draft of "Mithridates," inscribed in 1846 (*PN*, 233–234).

ART.

Give to barrows, trays, and pans
Grace and glimmer of romance;
Bring the moonlight into noon
Hid in gleaming piles of stone;
On the city's paved street   5
Plant gardens lined with lilac sweet;
Let spouting fountains cool the air,
Singing in the sun-baked square;
Let statue, picture, park, and hall,
Ballad, flag, and festival,   10
The past restore, the day adorn,
And make to-morrow a new morn.
So shall the drudge in dusty frock
Spy behind the city clock
Retinues of airy kings,   15
Skirts of angels, starry wings,
His fathers shining in bright fables,
His children fed at heavenly tables.
'Tis the privilege of Art
Thus to play its cheerful part,   20
Man on earth to acclimate,
And bend the exile to his fate,
And, moulded of one element
With the days and firmament,
Teach him on these as stairs to climb,   25
And live on even terms with Time;
Whilst upper life the slender rill
Of human sense doth overfill.

TEXTS

(A) *Essays: First Series* (Boston, 1847), 315; (B) *May-Day* (Boston, 1867), 172–173; (B²) *Selected Poems* (Boston, 1876), 181–182; (C) *Poems* [Riverside] (Boston, 1884), 235; (C²) *Poems* [Centenary] (Boston, 1904), 277–278.

Pre-copy-text forms: See *PN,* 735.

VARIANTS

1	trays, (A-B) ǀ trays (C)		12	to-morrow (B-C) ǀ each morrow
5	paved (A-C) ǀ pavèd (CC7)			(A)
9	park, (A-B) ǀ park (C)		21	on earth (B-C) ǀ in Earth (A)
10	flag, (A-B) ǀ flag (C)			

SPIRITUAL LAWS.

The first draft of "Spiritual Laws" was written in journal O in late June or early July, 1846, which is to say in the immediate afterglow of the great burst of activity that so largely supplied the 1847 *Poems* (*JMN,* IX, 437–438). It is probable, therefore, that it was not written in the first instance to be a motto to "Spiritual Laws" in the 1847 second edition of *Essays: First Series,* though it was soon enough pressed into that service. In his note to the poem in the Centenary edition Edward observes that it sheds light on "Uriel" and "Brahma" (*W,* IX, 495), though its relation to the former poem is, of the two, much the more apparent, especially in lines 8–10. A few pages after the first draft of "Spiritual Laws" in journal O Emerson began to versify an old theme, most memorably treated in "Uriel": "Nature hating lines & walls / Rolls her matter into balls" (*JMN*, IX, 439), a couplet that in due course developed into the motto for the essay "Circles."

Edward, in the same note, acknowledged that "Spiritual Laws" was an especially difficult poem in consequence of the extreme condensation of its rhetoric. He supposed that he might elucidate some of its mysteries by quoting an earlier draft:

Heaven is alive
Self built & quarrying itself
Upbuilds eternal towers
Self commanded works
In vital cirque
By dint of being all
Its loss is transmutation
Fears not the craft of undermining days
Grows by decays
And by the famous might that's lodged
In reaction & recoil
Makes flames to freeze & ice to boil,
And thro' the arms of all the fiends
Builds the firm seat of Innocence (*PN*, 251)

SPIRITUAL LAWS.

The living Heaven thy prayers respect,
House at once and architect,
Quarrying man's rejected hours,
Builds therewith eternal towers;
Sole and self-commanded works,   5
Fears not undermining days,
Grows by decays,
And, by the famous might that lurks
In reaction and recoil,

Makes flame to freeze, and ice to boil;   10
Forging, through swart arms of Offence,
The silver seat of Innocence.

TEXTS

(A) *Essays: First Series* (Boston, 1847), 115; (A²) *May-Day* (Boston, 1867), 174; (B) *Poems* [Riverside] (Boston, 1884), 236; (B²) *Poems* [Centenary] (Boston, 1904), 275.

Pre-copy-text forms: The first two drafts are in journal O (*JMN*, IX, 437–438 and 442–443); later drafts occur in poetry notebooks X and EF (see *PN*, 925–926).

VARIANTS

10   freeze, (A) | freeze (B)

UNITY.

This poem was the second of two epigraphs to "The Over-Soul" in the 1847 second edition of *Essays: First Series*—the first being a five-line extract from the "Psychozoia" of the Cambridge Platonist Henry More (see *CW*, II, 157 and note).

UNITY.

Space is ample, east and west,
But two cannot go abreast,

Unity

Cannot travel in it two:
Yonder masterful cuckoo
Crowds every egg out of the nest,   5
Quick or dead, except its own;
A spell is laid on sod and stone,
Night and Day were tampered with,
Every quality and pith
Surcharged and sultry with a power   10
That works its will on age and hour.

TEXTS

(A) *Essays: First Series* (Boston, 1847), 241; (B) *May-Day* (Boston, 1867), 175; (B²) *Poems* [Riverside] (Boston, 1884), 236; (B³) *Poems* [Centenary] (Boston, 1904), 279. Not included in *Selected Poems* (Boston, 1867). The *May-Day* emendation (line 8) appears in the text of the motto in *The Prose Works* (Boston, 1870), I, 355, but the plates made for (A) were not altered.

Pre-copy-text forms: The first draft, in poetry notebook X, gives evidence of Emerson's intent (obviously abandoned) of continuing the poem by adding some otherwise unused verses on an adjacent page. Three other drafts are also discussed at *PN,* 955–956.

VARIANTS

Title: UNITY. (B) | [*untitled*] (A)   8   Day were (B) | Day 've been (A)

WORSHIP.

The prose source for the poem, occurring in journal CL, was probably written in the late spring or early summer of 1859:

Bridle him.
Yes, but he takes the bridle in his teeth
Scourge him
He is refreshed by blows.
Imprison him
No prison will hold him
He invented locks & bolts & can unlock his own. This is he who invented the electric horse. He can swim across the ocean, & arrive in Asia at an earlier date than he left New York.
Throw him to the lions. But this is Androcles, Van Amburg; the lions lick his feet.

Fire will not burn him, but plays the part of Saint Irenaeus' <Martyr> flames,—namely of a wall, or a vaulted shrine bending <ornamentally> around & over him, without harm<ing him>. (*JMN,* XIV, 297–298; see the notes there for the lion-tamer Isaac H. Van Amburgh and the second-century heresiologist, Irenaeus).

WORSHIP.

This is he, who, felled by foes,
Sprung harmless up, refreshed by blows:
He to captivity was sold,
But him no prison-bars would hold:
Though they sealed him in a rock,   5
Mountain chains he can unlock:
Thrown to lions for their meat,
The crouching lion kissed his feet:

Worship

Bound to the stake, no flames appalled,
But arched o'er him an honoring vault.   10
This is he men miscall Fate,
Threading dark ways, arriving late,
But ever coming in time to crown
The truth, and hurl wrongdoers down.
He is the oldest, and best known,   15
More near than aught thou call'st thy own,
Yet, greeted in another's eyes,
Disconcerts with glad surprise.
This is Jove, who, deaf to prayers,
Floods with blessings unawares.   20
Draw, if thou canst, the mystic line
Severing rightly his from thine,
Which is human, which divine.

TEXTS

(A) *The Conduct of Life* (Boston, 1860), 173; (B) *May-Day* (Boston, 1867), 176–177; (B²) *Selected Poems* (Boston, 1876), 183; (C) *Poems* [Riverside] (Boston, 1884), 237; (C²) *Poems* [Centenary] (Boston, 1904), 279–280. In 1864, at the request of agents for John Pendleton Kennedy, Emerson prepared an untitled fair copy (now in the Ralph Waldo Emerson Collection at the Harry Ransom Center, University of Texas Library) for a volume entitled *Autograph Leaves of our Country's Authors,* to be sold at a fair in Baltimore to raise money for wounded soldiers (see *L,* V, 353; *L,* IX, 131–133). The text was not prepared with great care (line 1, for example, lacks all punctuation), but has been consulted as a supplemental source of textual evidence regarding line 21.

Pre-copy-text forms: See *PN,* 975.

VARIANTS

8   feet: (A-B) | feet; (C)
14   wrongdoers (A) | wrong-doers (B-C)
21   line (B-C) | line, (A) [*the comma is probably house style, as it does not appear in any manuscript form, including the Texas copy*]

507

NOTES

2.   In his note in *CW,* VI, 253, Joseph Slater points out that "sprang" is now the more common form of the preterit, and that "harmless" in the sense of unharmed was called "rare" by the *OED,* which cited no example later than William Thackeray's *Vanity Fair* (1848). The sentence "He is refreshed by blows" occurs by itself in Emerson's notebook S Salvage (*TN,* III, 127) as well as in the source quoted in the headnote.

QUATRAINS.

S. H.

Samuel Hoar (1778–1856) was one of the most distinguished and accomplished Concordians of his day, a leading lawyer of Massachusetts, and a Federalist and Whig politician until the slavery issue prompted him to organize the state Free Soil Party in 1848, and, with Emerson, the state Republican Party in 1854. In 1844 he had been appointed by the Massachusetts governor to investigate the treatment of the state's black sailors who were being routinely incarcerated in South Carolina ports and sold into slavery if they could not pay the costs of their detention. But he had hardly arrived in Charleston before the locals determined that he was "a dangerous emissary of sedition" (*W,* X, 603). Then, together with his daughter Elizabeth, who had accompanied him, he was forcibly ejected from South Carolina—much to the subsequent encouragement of Northern antislavery feeling, including Emerson's.

The Hoar family lived across from the Thoreaus on Main Street.

S. H.

Apart from "The Squire," as Samuel Hoar was generally called, the family consisted of his wife, Sarah Sherman Hoar (daughter of Roger Sherman, Connecticut representative to the Continental Congress); several sons, including Ebenezer Rockwood Hoar, a member of the Adirondac excursion with Emerson in 1858 and, later, Grant's Attorney-General, and George Frisbie Hoar, long-time senator from Massachusetts, and author of *Autobiography of Seventy Years* (2 vols., 1903); and—most consequentially for Emerson—a daughter, Elizabeth Sherman Hoar, betrothed to Charles Chauncy Emerson before his untimely death in 1836, and ever after regarded by Ralph Waldo as his "sister." In his final years Charles had entered on the practice of law by moving to Concord and partnering with Samuel Hoar.

At the time of his death in 1856, Samuel Hoar was memorialized by Emerson in *Putnam's Monthly* and again a short while later, at the editor's request, in the *Monthly Religious Magazine*. The latter was the occasion for the first printing of the quatrain, though why it did not appear with the first notice remains something of a mystery. These two brief obituaries were combined in "Samuel Hoar," *W*, X, 435–448.

The first draft of the poem occurs in journal GO among entries of October 1852, suggesting that Emerson may have been moved to write it by the death of Daniel Webster, at Marshfield, on the 24th of that month, when Emerson happened to be lecturing ten miles away in Plymouth (*JMN*, XIII, 105, 111). Hoar had frequently argued cases against Webster and for many years greatly admired his talents—though he felt, as Emerson noted, "a proportionately deep regret at Mr. Webster's political course in his later years" (*W*, X, 448), when his support for the Fugitive Slave Law in 1850 destroyed his reputation with many. When Emerson wrote out a copy of the verses for George F. Hoar in 1877, he referred to them as having been "written I suppose twenty years ago,—though printed later" (*L*, VI, 304). The vague allusion to "twenty years" might seem to put composition at around the period of Squire Hoar's death, but the somewhat more definite recollection that some time elapsed between composition and publication offers additional evidence that the quatrain was written in late 1852.

S. H.

With beams December planets dart
His cold eye truth and conduct scanned,
July was in his sunny heart,
October in his liberal hand.

TEXTS

(A) "Character of Samuel Hoar," *The Monthly Religious Magazine and Independent Journal*, XVII (January 1857): 9; (B) *May-Day* (Boston, 1867), 181; (C) text included in letter of 19 April 1877 to George Frisbie Hoar (*L*, VI, 304). The (B) text is unaltered in the Riverside and Centenary editions of *Poems*, though the text included in "Samuel Hoar," at *W*, X, 448, follows (A).

Pre-copy-text forms: See *PN*, 906–907. Franklin B. Sanborn, in *The Personality of Emerson* (Boston, 1903), 65, reproduces a manuscript given to him by Emerson with readings in lines 1–2 close to first-draft form: "With beams that stars at Christmas dart / His cold eyes truth and conduct scanned;" lines 3–4 are as in (A-B). Sanborn comments: "Here the allusion to Christmas suggests the old-fashioned religion of this aged Christian, a true follower of Emerson's grandfather, Parson [Ezra] Ripley." Another manuscript not mentioned in *PN* is MS Am 1280.214 (13) [5] (Ralph Waldo Emerson Memorial Association deposit, Houghton Library, Harvard University) with a text identical to (B). On the verso Emerson has copied an 1851 passage from journal CO: "The man of men— the only man you have seen (if you have seen one) is he who is immov<e>ably centred. Yet there are all degrees of aplomb, & most kinds turn out to be reliance on companies less or larger, and what does not yet threaten the company does not disconcert him" (cf. *JMN*, XI, 438). Additionally Emerson noted: "Find the book ↑of mine↓ from which this was taken" (cf. *CW*, VI, 147); "Notes on Thoreau"; "Read to the Concord Saturday Club Nov. 77" (probably in fact 29 October: see *ETE*, II, 274); "With these were used the paper [on Thoreau] of June 1862."

VARIANTS

1 dart (B-C) | dart, (A)   3 was (A-B) | shined (C)
2 scanned, (B) | scanned; (A, C)

A. H.

By allowing "A. H." to follow "S. H." in *May-Day*, Emerson (perhaps accidentally) allowed the inference that the poems' subjects were related, lending force to the further inference (undoubtedly not mistaken) that they represented male and female avatars of the beauty of manners. The sequence and pairing seem to have been deliberately broken up in the Riverside and Centenary editions, but the attention in each of the poems to qualities of heart and eye remains striking. The subjects are not, of course, related, since "A. H." is Anna Sturgis Hooper, sister of Caroline Sturgis Tappan.

On 27 April 1855 Emerson wrote to Caroline, who was then about to sail for an extended trip to Europe, in part to say that he had recently visited Mrs. Hooper, "who received me with great kindness. Her manners & beauty will serve to vindicate America to you in England & Italy, and, whilst she stays at home, I shall reckon securely on your return.

> Far capitals & marble courts her eye seemed still to see,
> Minstrels, & dames, & highborn men, the princeliest that be." (*L*,
>   VIII, 430)

The second distich of the quatrain was the first written, as shown by drafts in journal NO (*JMN*, XIII, 407, 419–420) among notes for the lecture "Beauty" (or "Beauty and Manners") that he first gave in Concord, 28 March 1855 (*Chronology*, 306). One of those notes may relate to an earlier encounter with Mrs. Hooper: "Manners, Mrs. H. thought, as rare & as powerful as beauty" (*JMN*, XIII, 96, 394).

A. H.

High was her heart, and yet was well inclined,
Her manners made of bounty well refined;
Far capitals, and marble courts, her eye still seemed to see,
Minstrels, and kings, and high-born dames, and of the best
    that be.

TEXTS

(A) *May-Day* (Boston, 1867), 181; (B) *Poems* [Riverside] (Boston, 1884), 238;
(B²) *Poems* [Centenary] (Boston, 1904), 291.

  Pre-copy-text forms: See *PN*, 721–722.

VARIANTS

3   capitals, (A) I capitals (B)   4   Minstrels, and kings, (A) I
                                            Minstrels and kings (B)

"SUUM CUIQUE."

Edward Emerson associated this couplet with his father's dis-
cussion of debt in the essay "Compensation": see *W*, II, 400, and
CW, II, 65–66. The Yankee's instinctive thrift and horror of debt
are given a transcendental interpretation in several journal en-
tries from 1838, as, for example, *JMN*, V, 476, and VII, 144–145.

"Suum Cuique."

"Suum Cuique" appears among the "Quatrains" in *May-Day* and in the Riverside edition, but is removed from that section in the Centenary edition.

The title is a form of the phrase "Suum cuique tribuere," meaning "give to each his due" or "to each his own." It was a commonplace among Roman jurists: see, for example, Cicero, *De Officiis,* 1.5.15, and *De Finibus,* 5.23.67, and may be thought of as a contemporary secular equivalent of the dictum of Jesus, "Render unto Cæsar the things that are Cæsar's, and to God the things that are God's" (Mark 12:17).

"SUUM CUIQUE."

Wilt thou seal up the avenues of ill?
Pay every debt, as if God wrote the bill.

TEXTS

(A) *May-Day* (Boston, 1867), 182; (A²) *Poems* [Riverside] (Boston, 1884), 238; (B) *Poems* [Centenary] (Boston, 1904), 357.

Pre-copy-text forms: PN, 928–929, discusses the relation of the seven manuscript drafts and fair copies. Emerson arrived at the final form of the couplet in the course of three drafts in journal CL in 1859 (*JMN,* XIV, 324–325).

VARIANTS

Title: "SUUM CUIQUE." (A) | SUUM   2   debt, (A) | debt (B)
  CUIQUE (B)

HUSH!

Emerson's defense of free speech extended to the corollary belief that intimidation and censorship were futile and self-defeating—as intrinsically impossible, indeed, as keeping secrets. He wrote in "Compensation" that "Every lash inflicted is a tongue of fame; every prison a more illustrious abode; every burned book or house enlightens the world; every suppressed or expunged word reverberates through the earth from side to side" (*CW*, II, 69–70). Efforts by the government or other public institutions to control or delimit speech, especially in relation to the slavery question, were notably rife in the ante-bellum period. On one occasion in 1837 the Salem Lyceum invited Emerson to speak—on the sole condition that he avoid "exciting topics upon which the public mind is honestly divided": Emerson declined, as he declined a similarly encumbered invitation from the New Bedford Lyceum, quoting in his journal the words of Lady Mary Wortley Montague that "The motto on all palace gates is *Hush*" (*JMN*, V, 376).

HUSH!

Every thought is public,
Every nook is wide;
Thy gossips spread each whisper,
And the gods from side to side.

TEXTS

(A) *May-Day* (Boston, 1867), 182; (A²) *Poems* [Riverside] (Boston, 1884), 238; (A³) *Poems* [Centenary] (Boston, 1904), 291.

Pre-copy-text forms: The sequence of eight manuscript drafts and fair copies is discussed in *PN*, 820–821. The earliest of the drafts (*JMN*, VIII, 466–467) probably dates to 1842.

NOTES

3–4. Perhaps a reminiscence of Milton's assertion that his own "noble task" was one "Of which all Europe talks from side to side": see Sonnet XXII ["To Mr Cyriack Skinner upon his Blindness"], l. 12.

ORATOR.

This quatrain seems to have been written in the summer of 1846, to judge from the location of its first drafts in journal O (*JMN*, IX, 443). There it occurs in the midst of commentary on the oratory of the opponents of slavery and the Mexican War. Earlier that summer, in the same journal, Emerson had followed an entry entitled "Cunning" with another that began "To every creature its own weapon" (*JMN*, IX, 413).

The poem was one of several that, toward the beginning of 1860, Emerson sent to Moncure Conway, a young Virginia convert to Transcendentalism and antislavery, who was at the time determined to revive the old *Dial* in a new venue, Cincinnati.

ORATOR.

He who has no hands
Perforce must use his tongue;
Foxes are so cunning
Because they are not strong.

TEXTS

(A) *Dial* [Cincinnati], I (March 1860): 195; (B) *May-Day* (Boston, 1867), 182; (B²) *Poems* [Riverside] (Boston, 1884), 238; (B³) *Poems* [Centenary] (Boston, 1904), 291.

Format: (A) indents lines 2 and 4.

Pre-copy-text forms: See *PN,* 887–888.

VARIANTS

2   tongue; (B) | tongue: (A)

ARTIST.

The title given to this poem in one of the journal drafts, "To an Artist," offers little support for the otherwise plausible hypothesis that Emerson had Thoreau in mind for the subject. In 1847, when the first draft was composed, Thoreau left his cabin at Walden to board at "Bush," as the Emerson house was known; simultaneously, Emerson left Bush for an extended lecture tour in England.

ARTIST.

Quit the hut, frequent the palace,
Reck not what the people say;
For still, where'er the trees grow biggest,
Huntsmen find the easiest way.

TEXTS

(A) *Dial* [Cincinnati], I (March 1860): 195; (B) *May-Day* (Boston, 1867), 183; (B²) *Poems* [Riverside] (Boston, 1884), 239; (B³) *Poems* [Centenary] (Boston, 1904), 291.

Format: (A) indents lines 2 and 4.

Pre-copy-text forms: Lines 3–4 were written in the spring of 1847 (*JMN*, X, 33), and the entire quatrain in August 1852 (*JMN*, XIII, 80–81). Fair copies are in poetry notebooks NP and Rhymer: see *PN*, 736.

VARIANTS

1   palace, (B) I palace— (A)   3   still, (B) I still (A) II biggest, (B)
                                          I biggest (A)

POET.

The second and third drafts of this quatrain, in journal NO (*JMN*, XIII, 410, 411–412)—and probably the first, in poetry notebook EF, as well—were written in April 1855. Emerson signed a fair copy, possibly for presentation to an autograph seeker, in January 1860. This was about the time that Emerson sent a number of quatrains to Moncure Conway for publication in his new journal, the *Dial*, but if this manuscript was in fact sent to Conway, it appears not to have been published.

POET.

Ever the Poet *from* the land
Steers his bark, and trims his sail;

Right out to sea his courses stand,
New worlds to find in pinnace frail.

TEXTS

(A) *May-Day* (Boston, 1867), 183; (B) *Poems* [Riverside] (Boston, 1884), 239;
(B²) *Poems* [Centenary] (Boston, 1904), 292.

Format: (A) indents lines 2 and 4.

Pre-copy-text forms: Nine MS drafts and fair copies are discussed in *PN*, 894–895.
A tenth copy was subsequently discovered on the back flyleaf of Emerson's cor-
rection copy of *Poems* (Boston, 1847); this is identical to the text given above,
save that its only punctuation is the comma after "bark" (CC1).

VARIANTS

2   bark, (A) | bark (B)

POET.

The only substantive variant is word/words in the second line;
the singular form is present in five of the six surviving holograph
copies. The first draft appears to date to 1847.

POET.

To clothe the fiery thought
In simple word succeeds,
For still the craft of genius is
To mask a king in weeds.

TEXTS

(A) *Dial* [Cincinnati], I (March 1860): 195; (B) *May-Day* (Boston, 1867), 183; (C) William Ellery Channing, *Thoreau: The Poet-Naturalist* (Boston, 1873), 127; (D) *Poems* [Riverside] (Boston, 1884), 239; (D²) *Poems* [Centenary] (Boston, 1904), 292. The quatrain is also quoted in *W*, I, 408, in annotation of a passage in the "Language" chapter of *Nature*, and in *W*, VI, 415, to illustrate Emerson's proposition in the essay "Beauty" (*The Conduct of Life*), that "In rhetoric, this art of omission is a chief secret of power, and, in general, is proof of high culture to say the greatest matters in the simplest way."

Format: (A) and (C) indent lines 2 and 4.

Pre-copy-text forms: See *PN*, 895–896.

VARIANTS

2   word (A, C) | words (B, D) ||
succeeds, (B-D) | succeeds; (A)

BOTANIST.

The unusual double rhyme in lines 2 and 4 and the unusual rhyming syntax of lines 1 and 3 contribute substantially to the quatrain's meaning.

BOTANIST.

Go thou to thy learned task,
I stay with the flowers of Spring;
Do thou of the Ages ask
What me the Hours will bring.

TEXTS

(A) *Dial* [Cincinnati], I, (February 1860): 131; (B) *May-Day* (Boston, 1867), 184; (C) *May-Day* (Boston, 1868), 184; (D) William Ellery Channing, *Thoreau: The Poet-Naturalist* (Boston, 1873), 135; (E) *Poems* [Riverside] (Boston, 1884), 239; (F) *Poems* [Centenary] (Boston, 1904), 292.

Format: (A) indents lines 2 and 4; (D) indents lines 1 and 3.

Pre-copy-text forms: Six manuscript copies exist, consistent in wording, but differing in punctuation. In the earliest of the titled fair copies (Rhymer, 31), "Naturalist" is canceled in favor of "Botanist." See *PN,* 749–750.

VARIANTS

1   task, (B-F) I task; (A)
2   Spring; (A, D) I spring: (B-C, E) I Spring: (F)
3   Ages (D, F) I ages (A-C, E) II ask (A-C, E-F) I ask, (D)

4   me (A-C, E-F) I to me (D) II Hours (D, F) I hours (A, C, CC6, CC7, E) I flowers (B)

GARDENER.

In July 1840, through weeks of hottest weather—into the mid-90s, when "the dogstar raged" and dried the crops (*JMN,* VII, 384)—Emerson proposed to be, himself, "coolness & shade." On the 28th he wrote to Samuel Gray Ward, saying that "In the sleep of the great heats there was nothing for me but to read the Vedas, the bible of the tropics, which I find I come back upon every three or four years. It is sublime as heat & night and a breathless ocean. . . . It is of no use to put away the book: if I trust myself in the woods or in a boat upon the pond Nature makes a Bramin of me presently: Eternal necessity, eternal compensation, unfathomable power unbroken silence,—this is her creed. Peace, she saith to me, and purity & absolute abandonment—these penances expiate all sin & bring you to the beatitude of the 'Eight Gods'" (*L*, VII, 398). At this time and in this mood he wrote in his journal: "Go to the forest if God has made thee a poet and make thy life clean & fragrant as thy office

>True Bramin in the morning meadows wet
>Expound the Vedas in the violet

Thy love must be thy art. Thy words must spring from love, and every thought be touched with love. Only such words fly & endure. There are two ways of speaking—One, when a man makes his discourse plausible & round by considering how it sounds to him who hears it, and the other mode when his own heart loves & so infuses grace into all that drops from him. Only this is living beauty. Nature also must teach thee rhetoric. She can teach thee not only to speak truth, but to speak it truly. . . . In most compositions, there is one thought which was spontaneous, & many which were added & abutted; but, in the true, God writes every word" (*JMN*, VII, 386).

Emerson completed the quatrain in the draft in journal TU (*JMN*, XI, 158), evidently in September 1849.

GARDENER.

True Bramin, in the morning meadows wet,
Expound the Vedas of the violet,
Or, hid in vines, peeping through many a loop,
See the plum redden, and the beurré stoop.

TEXTS

(A) *Dial* [Cincinnati], I (March 1860): 195; (B) *May-Day* (Boston, 1867), 184; (C) *Poems* [Riverside] (Boston, 1884), 239; (C²) *Poems* [Centenary] (Boston, 1904, 292.

Pre-copy-text forms: See *PN*, 800–801.

VARIANTS

1   Bramin (B) | Brahmin (A, C). [*The reading in B is consistent with the manuscripts; presumably the spelling* change was made by Moncure Conway in (A) *and by Edward Emerson in* (C).]

4   redden, (B-C) | redden (A)

NOTES

4.   The beurré is a variety of pear, its name derived from the French word for butter. On 24 July 1847 Emerson wrote admiringly of the "Golden Buerre of Bilboa" that he had planted and that was just then sprouting vigorously in his orchard (*JMN*, X, 118).

FORESTER.

There is no evidence for dating this poem more precisely than to the period 1847–1860. Still, in 1853, when Emerson was writing a number of these quatrains, there is a journal entry about Henry Thoreau passing without permission, quietly and unespied, through his neighbors' streams and woods (*JMN*, XIII, 187). After Thoreau's death in 1862 Bronson Alcott published a eulogy in the *Atlantic Monthly* entitled "Forester."

FORESTER.

He took the color of his vest
From rabbit's coat or grouse's breast;
For, as the wood-kinds lurk and hide,
So walks the woodman, unespied.

TEXTS

(A) *Dial* [Cincinnati], I (February 1860): 131; (B) *May-Day* (Boston, 1867), 184; (B²) *Poems* [Riverside] (Boston, 1884), 240; (B³) *Poems* [Centenary] (Boston, 1904), 292.

Pre-copy-text forms: See *PN*, 795.

VARIANTS

2   breast; (B) | breast, (A)   4   woodman, (B) | woodman (A)

NORTHMAN.

In 1853 Emerson was much occupied with researches in English history, in preparation for writing *English Traits*. In June of that year he was reading Augustin Thierry's *History of the Conquest of England by the Normans* (London, 1841) in which, on p. 21, he found the paraphrase of a Viking song: "The force of the storm is a help to the arm of our rowers; the hurricane is in our service; it carries us the way we would go" (*JMN*, XIII, 172). Emerson may have been struck by the idea and the language because they echoed passages he had noticed and quoted years earlier: the line from Samuel Butler's *Hudibras,* "We only row we're steered by fate" (*JMN*, V, 33), and the observation by Edward Gibbon that "The winds & waves are always on the side of the ablest navigators" (*JMN*, V, 108). Robert D. Richardson shrewdly connects this poem with Emerson's inspection, on 14 June, of Donald McKay's immense new clipper ship, the *Great Republic,* under construction in the shipyard at East Boston (*Emerson: The Mind on Fire,* 516; *JMN,* XIII, 181). In fact, Emerson had withdrawn the Thierry volume from the Boston Athenaeum just the day before (*Chronology,* 285). It would appear that the source was versified a little more than a year later, since the first drafts of the quatrain occur among notes taken from the volume of Samuel Pepys's *Memoirs* that Emerson withdrew from the Athenaeum in September 1854 (*JMN,* XIII, 356, 360–361; *Chronology,* 297).

NORTHMAN.

The gale that wrecked you on the sand,
It helped my rowers to row;
The storm is my best galley hand,
And drives me where I go.

TEXTS

(A) *Dial* [Cincinnati], I (March 1860): 195; (A²) *May-Day* (Boston, 1867), 185; (B) *Poems* [Riverside] (Boston, 1884), 240; (B²) *Poems* [Centenary] (Boston, 1904), 293.

Format: (A) indents lines 2 and 4.

Pre-copy-text forms: Five drafts in journal IO (*JMN,* XIII, 356, 360–361) precede titled fair copies in journal DO (*JMN,* XIII, 19) and poetry notebooks Rhymer and NP: see *PN,* 872–873.

VARIANTS

3   hand, (A) I hand (B)

FROM ALCUIN.

When Alcuin was asked by Pepin, the father of Charlemagne, to provide a definition of the sea, the English monk replied that it was "Le chemin des audacieux, la frontière de la terre, l'hôtellerie des fleuves, la source des pluies" (A[uguste] Baron, *Histoire Abrégée de la Littérature Française,* 2nd ed. [Bruxelles: Librairie Universelles de Rozez, 1851], 340). According to a passage in Emerson's journal VS, entered shortly before 14 June 1853, "Alcuin called the Sea, the road of the bold; the frontier of the land; the hostelry of the rivers; & the source of the rains." His versification of the statement followed immediately (*JMN,* XIII, 180). Emerson wrote out an untitled fair copy of the quatrain on 20 May 1857 while visiting his brother William at Staten Island.

FROM ALCUIN.

The sea is the road of the bold,
Frontier of the wheat-sown plains,
The pit wherein the streams are rolled,
And fountain of the rains.

TEXTS

(A) *Dial* [Cincinnati], I (March 1860): 195; (B) *May-Day* (Boston, 1867), 185; (C) *Poems* [Riverside] (Boston, 1884), 240; (C²) *Poems* [Centenary] (Boston, 1904), 293.

Format: (A) indents lines 2 and 4.

Pre-copy-text forms: See *PN,* 797–798.

VARIANTS

3   rolled, (A-B) | rolled (C)

EXCELSIOR.

The first draft of this quatrain occurs in journal C (*JMN*, V, 483), immediately before an entry dated 1 May 1838.

EXCELSIOR.

Over his head were the maple buds,
And over the tree was the moon,
And over the moon were the starry studs,
That drop from the angels' shoon.

TEXTS

(A) *May-Day* (Boston, 1867), 185; (B) *Poems* [Riverside] (Boston, 1884), 240; (C) *Poems* [Centenary] (Boston, 1904), 293.

Pre-copy-text forms: The drafts in poetry notebooks NP and EF carry the titles "Excelsior, *a song of degrees*" and "Four Stories," respectively. An untitled version, perhaps written out for an autograph seeker, is dated "May, 1859." See *PN*, 784–785.

VARIANTS

3   studs, (A) | stubs (B) | studs (C) [*In later printing from the plates* *made for* (B) *the word is corrected to* "studs"]

BORROWING.

FROM THE FRENCH.

In an April 1852 entry in journal DO (*JMN*, XIII, 18), the first draft of this quatrain immediately follows the text of the French poem it translates:

Enfin ils ne sont pas venus
Ces maux dont vous craign[i]ez les rig[u]eurs inhumaines;
Mais qu'ils vous ont couté de peines,
Ces maux que vous n'avez pas eus!

There is nothing to indicate that Emerson ever knew who the author was; when he first published his translation, in *The Conduct of Life,* he referred to the original as, simply, "an old French verse." He may have encountered the lines as the anonymous epigraph for an essay, "À une Femme qui avait des vapeurs," in *Correspondence Littéraire, Philosophique et Critique, Addressée a un Souverain d'Allemagne . . . par le Baron de Grimm et par Diderot,* 3 vols. (Paris, 1813), III, 232. Authorship of the lines has been claimed for Stanislas, Chevalier de Boufflers (1738–1815) by Gaston Maugras in *La Marquise de Boufflers et son fils le Chevalier de Boufflers,* 8th ed. (Paris, 1907), 237.

BORROWING.

FROM THE FRENCH.

Some of your hurts you have cured,
And the sharpest you still have survived,
But what torments of grief you endured
From evils which never arrived!

TEXTS

(A) "Considerations by the Way," *The Conduct of Life* (Boston, 1860), 233; (B) *May-Day* (Boston, 1867), 186; (B²) *Poems* [Riverside] (Boston, 1884), 241; (B³) *Poems* [Riverside] (Boston, 1904), 294.

Format: In (A) lines 2 and 4 are indented.

Pre-copy-text forms: See *PN*, 745.

VARIANTS

Title: BORROWING. / FROM THE FRENCH. (A-B) I BORROWING<.> ↑Trouble.↓ / FROM THE FRENCH. (CC7)

1   hurts (B) I griefs (A)
2   survived, (B) I survived; (A)
3   grief (B) I pain (A)
4   which (B) I that (A)

NATURE.

The first three drafts, in journal TU, date to the summer of 1849 (*JMN*, XI, 118–119); they interrupt notes that Emerson was taking from Emanuel Swedenborg's *Economy of the Animal Kingdom*.

NATURE.

Boon Nature yields each day a brag which we now first behold,
And trains us on to slight the new, as if it were the old:
But blest is he, who, playing deep, yet haply asks not why,
Too busied with the crowded hour to fear to live or die.

Fate

TEXTS

(A) *Dial* [Cincinnati], I (March 1860): 195; (B) *May-Day* (Boston, 1867), 186; (C) William Ellery Channing, *Thoreau: The Poet-Naturalist* (Boston, 1873), 182. The Riverside (241) and Centenary (294) editions follow (B).

Pre-copy-text forms: The eight manuscript drafts are discussed in *PN*, 866–867.

VARIANTS

1 Boon Nature (A-B) | Born nature (C) [*Emerson corrected* "Born" *to* "Boon" *in his copy of* (C), Houghton Library *AC 85.Em345.Zy873c: Ralph Waldo Emerson Memorial Association deposit, Houghton Library, Harvard University).]

2 slight (B-C) | see (A) || new, (A-B) | new (C) || old: (B) | old; (A, C)
3 But (A-B) | And (C) || he, who, (A-B) | he who (C) || haply (B-C) | happy (A)
4 busied (B) | busy (A, C) || hour (A-B) | day (C)

FATE.

"Fate" was probably composed in 1859, though it was evidently not among the quatrains that Emerson sent to Moncure Conway in January 1860 for publication in the Cincinnati *Dial.* Given that Emerson had ample time to read proofs for *May-Day,* the inference must be that he approved the form of the quatrain there; nevertheless, intrusion of house styling cannot be ruled out: for example, in none of the seven notebook drafts did Emerson hyphenate "today"; in three of the drafts "Today" (line 1), "Morrow" (line 2), and "Being" (line 3) are capitalized.

FATE.

Her planted eye today controls,
Is in the morrow most at home,
And sternly calls to being souls
That curse her when they come.

TEXTS

(A) *May-Day* (Boston, 1867), 187; (A²) *Poems* [Riverside] (Boston, 1884), 241; (A³) *Poems* [Centenary] (Boston, 1904), 294.

Pre-copy-text forms: The titled fair copy in poetry notebook NP, p. 229 (*PN*, 540), was inscribed some time after mid-January 1859. See *PN*, 789 for a discussion of this and other drafts.

VARIANTS

1   today [*MS form: see headnote*] | to-day (A)

HOROSCOPE.

It was probably because the first draft of this quatrain occurs in notebook Orientalist (*TN*, II, 50) that Edward Emerson supposed that it was a translation (*W*, IX, 498), in spite of the fact that Emerson appended his initials to the poem, his regular way of indicating original composition. In Orientalist it follows, on the same page, a draft translation of "The Phoenix" which was inscribed no later than the fall of 1850. The prose source for lines 3–4 is a sentence written in journal AB in the spring of 1847: "When he comes forth from his mother's womb, the gate of gifts closes behind him" (*JMN*, X, 34). This sentence found its way into the essay "Fate" (*CW*, VI, 6), while its versified form was copied into topical notebook EO, mainly devoted to entries on the subject of Fate (*TN*, I, 68).

HOROSCOPE.

Ere he was born, the stars of fate
Plotted to make him rich and great:
When from the womb the babe was loosed,
The gate of gifts behind him closed.

TEXTS

(A) *May-Day* (Boston, 1867), 187; (A²) *Poems* [Riverside] (Boston, 1884), 241; (A³) *Poems* [Centenary] (Boston, 1904), 294.

Pre-copy-text forms: Among the five notebook drafts the variant titles "Fate" and "Nativity" occur. See *PN,* 818.

POWER.

This quatrain, untitled, was the motto for "Self-Reliance," one of the few mottoes included in the 1841 first edition of *Essays.* There seems to be a common source behind this poem and a passage from the lecture "The Poet," written later in the same year: "You may find it [poetic genius], though rarely, in Senates, when the forest has cast out some wild, black-browed bantling, some great boy, to show the same energy in the crowd of officials, which he had learned in driving cattle to the hills, or in scrambling through thickets in a winter forest, or through the swamp and river for his game. In the folds of his brow, in the majesty of his mien, nature shall vindicate her son; and even in that strange and perhaps unworthy place and company, remind you of the lessons taught him in earlier days by the torrent, in the gloom of the pine woods, when he was the companion of crows and jays and foxes, and a hunter of the bear" (*EL,* III, 362).

POWER.

Cast the bantling on the rocks,
Suckle him with the she-wolf's teat;
Wintered with the hawk and fox,
Power and speed be hands and feet.

TEXTS

(A) *Essays* (Boston, 1841), 36; (B) *Essays: First Series* (Boston, 1847), 38; (C) *May-Day* (Boston, 1867), 187; (C²) *Poems* [Riverside] (Boston, 1884), 242; (C³) *Poems* [Centenary] (Boston, 1904), 295.

Pre-copy-text forms: The only manuscript draft occurs in poetry notebook P: see *PN,* 898.

VARIANTS

2   teat; (B) I teat: (A) I teat, (C) [*The* (B) *reading is preferred because Emerson is known to have paid particular attention to mottoing the essays at this time: see* L, *III, 417, and* CW, *II, 278– 279.*]

NOTES

1.   A bantling is a child or infant. As the *OED* notes, it was "often used deprecia-
tively, and formerly as a synonym of *bastard.*" Lines 1–2 recall the situation of
Romulus and Remus in the legendary account of the founding of Rome.

CLIMACTERIC.

The situation of the first drafts in poetry notebook X points to
composition in 1847, which would seem too soon for complaints
about old age from the 44-year-old Emerson. The "grand climac-
teric" traditionally refers to one's sixty-third year and signifies the
onset of genuine old age, but "climacteric," without the modifier,
can refer to any critical period, turning point, or climax in life.
The complaint here, however, is that the grief that ages us—as,
for example, the death of a son—brings with it no epochal revela-
tions, no life-altering changes, no advancement. We do not "turn
the leaf."

CLIMACTERIC.

I am not wiser for my age,
Nor skilful by my grief;
Life loiters at the book's first page,—
Ah! could we turn the leaf.

TEXTS

(A) *Dial* [Cincinnati], I (February 1860): 131; (B) *May-Day* (Boston, 1867), 188;
(B²) *Poems* [Riverside] (Boston, 1884), 242; (B³) *Poems* [Centenary] (Boston,
1904), 295.

Format: In (A) lines 2 and 4 are indented.

Pre-copy-text forms: See *PN,* 759. Three manuscript drafts have an early form of line 4 ("And we never turn the leaf."), and four have the final form, including the copy that Emerson sent to Caroline Sturgis Tappan in a letter of 14 April 1853 (*L,* VIII, 364).

VARIANTS

3   page,— (B) I page— (A)   4   leaf. (B) I leaf! (A)

HERI, CRAS, HODIE.

The early drafts in journal NO (*JMN,* XIII, 413, 418, and 453) suggest composition in 1855. What appears to be an 1858 prose source in journal AC (*JMN,* XIV, 211) is probably copied, as other entries on that page are, from an earlier source. The passage reads: "Men are a farsighted people. We can see well into the Dark Ages; guess into the Future; but what is rolled & muffled in impenetrable <clouds> ↑folds↓, is Today."

The title derives from an anecdote that Emerson found in the *Memoirs of Samuel Pepys:* John Bridgeman, Bishop of Chester (1577–1652), having bought an estate previously owned first by the Lever family, then by the Ashton family, had four shields installed in the window of the great hall, representing the arms of the Levers ("Olim" ["Once"]), the Ashtons ("Heri" ["Yesterday"]), the Bridgemans ("Hodie" ["Today"]), and an empty shield ("Cras nescio cujus" ["I don't know whose"]). See *JMN,* XIII, 361.

HERI, CRAS, HODIE.

Shines the last age, the next with hope is seen,
Today slinks poorly off unmarked between:
Future or Past no richer secret folds,
O friendless Present! than thy bosom holds.

TEXTS

(A) *Dial* [Cincinnati], I (February 1860): 131; (B) *May-Day* (Boston, 1867), 188; (B²) *Poems* [Riverside] (Boston, 1884), 242; (B³) *Poems* [Centenary] (Boston, 1904), 295.

Pre-copy-text forms: The evidence of numerous manuscript versions is that lines 3–4 were arrived at first, though probably not much time elapsed between the earliest draft and the achievement of the final form. See *PN*, 814.

VARIANTS

Title: HERI, CRAS, HODIE. (B) | *Cras, heri, hodie.* (A)

2   Today [*The form in all the MS drafts: see* PN, *814*] | To-day (A-B) ||

between: (B) | between; (A)

MEMORY.

The first drafts of "Memory" were inscribed in journal F2 immediately before an entry of 16 August 1840 (*JMN*, VII, 508–509). These in turn relate to prior speculations in prose about sleep and dreams, topics that Emerson had named in *Nature* (1836) as among those held to be "not only unexplained but inexplicable" (*CW*, I, 8). Carlyle may have had something to do with Emerson's interest in the subject, having written in "Quæ Cogitavit":

> Memory and Oblivion, like Day and Night, and indeed like all other Contradictions in this strange dualistic Life of ours, are necessary for each other's existence: Oblivion is the dark page, whereon Memory writes her light-beam characters, and makes them legible; were it all light, nothing could be read there, any more than if it were all darkness. (*Fraser's Magazine*, VII [May 1833], 588)

On 6 February 1837, Emerson wrote that there is "one memory of waking, & another of sleep" (*JMN*, V, 285). An entry later that year shows that Emerson considered the relation between normal dreaming and the "directed dream" induced by mesmerists, and the relation of both to prophecy (*JMN*, V, 371). On 16 October 1837 he wrote: "Culture inspects our dreams also. The pictures of the night will always bear some proportion to the visions of the day" (*JMN*, V, 398). Emerson's thoughts may have been influenced by the concurrent speculations of Bronson Alcott in "Psyche," which Emerson read first in 1836, and then again in a somewhat different version in 1838: see Kenneth Walter Cameron, *Emerson the Essayist* (Hartford, 1945), II, 103 and 113, for the relevant passages. Many of Emerson's journal entries on this theme found their way into the lecture on "Demonology," first delivered in February 1839 as part of the "Human Life" series (*EL*, III, 151–171; cf. *W*, X, 1). In fact, most American romantic writers shared in this fascination with dreams: Margaret Fuller and James Freeman Clarke, for example, had been debating their significance since 1830, when Clarke held out for a Coleridgean identification of dreams with the imagination as a portal to the spiritual, and Fuller stressed their gothic and uncanny aspect (Capper, I, 107–108). Twenty years later Nathaniel Hawthorne's views on dreams and dreaming, as given in "The Birth-Mark," drew the attention of Herman Melville, who marked the passages in his copy of *Mosses from an Old Manse* (Jay Leyda, *The Melville Log* [New York, 1951], I, 380).

MEMORY.

Night-dreams trace on Memory's wall
Shadows of the thoughts of day,
And thy fortunes, as they fall,
The bias of the will betray.

TEXTS

(A) *May-Day* (Boston, 1867), 188; (A²) *Poems* [Riverside] (Boston, 1884), 242; (A³) *Poems* [Centenary] (Boston, 1904), 295.

Pre-copy-text forms: The three first drafts in journal F2 (*JMN*, VII, 508–509) are followed by two more in poetry notebook P. These five texts, all in pencil, are followed by four ink drafts in notebook X, where, mainly through revisions to the first line, the final form of the quatrain emerged. Additional copies occur in notebooks Rhymer, NP, and EO, as well as in a separate autographed MS in the Manuscript Division, New York Public Library. See *PN*, 857–858.

LOVE.

Emerson composed lines 3–4 first, in several trials in poetry notebook EF, and worked out the remainder of the quatrain in notebook NP. What thus became the second couplet was based on Shakespeare, *Two Gentlemen of Verona*, IV, ii, 19–20: "love / Will creep in service where it cannot go," a passage that Emerson seems to have noticed first in the quotation "Love will creep where it cannot go," found in the *Golden Remains of the Ever Memorable Mr. John Hales, of Eton College* (London, 1673). Emerson had withdrawn this book from the Harvard Divinity School Library on 30 November 1827 and entered the aphorism in notebook Encyclopedia (see *JMN*, VI, 180; cf. *L*, III, 131).

Emerson twice illustrated the meaning that the aphorism had for him—first as a principle in nature, then as a principle of human psychology. In an 1840 journal passage, he wrote:

> "Love will creep where it cannot go," will accomplish that by imperceptible original incalculable methods, being his own lever, fulcrum, & moving power, which force could never achieve. Have you not seen in the woods in a late autumn morning a poor little fungus, an agaric, a plant without any solidity, nay, that seemed nothing but a soft mush or jelly, yet by its constant, total, & inconceivably gentle pushing had managed to break its way up through the frosty ground & actually to lift a pretty hard crust on its head? (*JMN*, VII, 398)

In the essay "Nominalist and Realist" (1844), Emerson attributes solidity only to that which our attention acknowledges or makes real:

> As the ancient said, the world is a *plenum* or solid; and if we saw all things that really surround us, we should be imprisoned and unable to move. For, though nothing is impassible to the soul, but all things are pervious to it, and like highways, yet this is only whilst the soul does not see them. As soon as the soul sees any object, it stops before that object. Therefore, the divine Providence, which keeps the universe open in every direction to the soul, conceals all the furniture and all the persons that do not concern a particular soul, from the senses of the individual. Through solidest eternal things, the man finds his road, as if they did not subsist, and does not once suspect their being. (*CW*, III, 142–143)

Edward Emerson cited a parallel passage (*W*, IX, 499) which has not been located in the notebooks, but which is evidently the source for a passage in the essay "Success": "The passion [of love], alike everywhere, creeps under the snows of Scandinavia, under the fires of the equator, and swims in the seas of Polynesia. Lofn is as puissant a divinity in the Norse Edda as Camadeva in the red vault of India, Eros in the Greek, or Cupid in the Latin heaven" (*CW*, VII, 154; see *LL*, I, 101–106, which assigns the composition of this lecture to 1857–1858). The form of Emerson's quatrain was also shaped by a statement he entered into journal VO in 1857: "love eats his way through Alps of opposition" (*JMN*, XIV, 191). The poem would thus appear to have been written no earlier than 1857.

LOVE.

Love on his errand bound to go
Can swim the flood, and wade through snow,
Where way is none, 'twill creep and wind
And eat through Alps its home to find.

TEXTS

(A) *May-Day* (Boston, 1867), 189; (B) *Poems* [Riverside] (Boston, 1884), 242; (B²) *Poems* [Centenary] (Boston, 1904), 295.

Pre-copy-text forms: See *PN*, 849. The two sources mentioned above from *JMN*, VI, 180, and *JMN*, XIV, 191, recur in Emerson's unpublished topical notebook on the subject of love, L Camadeva—slight but additional evidentiary support for a date of composition shortly after 1857.

VARIANTS

2   flood, (A) | flood (B)

SACRIFICE.

In his note to the poem (*W*, IX, 499), Edward Emerson identi-fied the source as *Calebs Integrity in Following the Lord Fully, in a ser-mon preached at St. Margarets Westminster, before the Honourable House of Commons, . . . Novemb. 30th, 1642.* The sermon's author was Richard Vines (c. 1600–1656), a prominent English Presbyterian clergyman and one of the leaders of the Westminster Assembly (*DNB*). Emerson entered the quotation ("'Tis a man's perdition to be safe when he ought to perish for God") in journal VO (*JMN*, XIV, 191) in December 1857.

The draft of the quatrain in journal KL (*JMN*, XV, 438) was written in late September or early October 1864, presumably with a view to including it (as in fact he did) in the lecture on "Charac-ter," first delivered on New Year's Day, 1865. Emerson and his wife Lidian were the houseguests of James and Annie Fields in Boston on the day of the lecture (*Chronology*, 401); nevertheless, the per-formance proving offensive to conservative religious sensibilities, Fields, as editor of the *Atlantic*, refused to publish it: hence the oddity of its appearance—and the first publication of "Sacrifice" —in the *North American Review*, at that time edited by James Rus-sell Lowell and Charles Eliot Norton.

SACRIFICE.

Though love repine, and reason chafe,
There came a voice without reply,—
''Tis man's perdition to be safe,
When for the truth he ought to die.'

TEXTS

(A) "Character," *North American Review,* CII (April 1866): 359; (B) *May-Day* (Boston, 1867), 189; (B²) *Poems* [Riverside] (Boston, 1884), 243; (B³) *Poems* [Centenary] (Boston, 1904), 296. The text included in the Centenary reprinting of the essay "Character" (*W,* X, 96), follows (A) in all but line 2, which lacks the terminal dash.

Format: In (A) lines 2 and 4 are indented.

Pre-copy-text forms: See *PN,* 909. Of the eight manuscript versions the earlier ones have "I heard" in line 2.

VARIANTS

1	love (B)	Love (A) ‖ reason (B) ‖ Reason (A)	3	''Tis (B)	"'Tis (A)
		4	die.' (B)	die." (A)

PERICLES.

The source of this quatrain is the reply of Pericles when asked to swear falsely on behalf of a friend; as Emerson set it down in an 1826 notebook, "'I'm your friend,' said Pericles, 'as far as the altar'" (*JMN,* VI, 34)—or, in Plutarch's once familiar Latin phrase, "amicus usque ad aras" (*Moralia,* 528c). In a brief essay on the history of the phrase, G. L. Hendrickson pointed out that the Latin form—and the word "aras" in particular—introduced an ambiguity not present in the Greek, so that from the seventeenth century on it was increasingly taken to mean that Pericles was pledging friendship even to the grave. But Hendrickson noted that touching the altar was the equivalent, in Attic courts, of the modern

Judeo-Christian practice of swearing on the Bible. The sanction against perjury, in other words, was a specifically religious one, and Pericles was asserting that friendship, however strong, could not overset a higher or transcendental responsibility to the truth ("Amici usque ad aras," *The Classical Journal,* XLV [May 1950]: 395–397).

The first drafts of the quatrain (*JMN*, VIII, 473, and poetry notebooks P and X) were written in 1843.

PERICLES.

Well and wisely said the Greek,
Be thou faithful, but not fond;
To the altar's foot thy fellow seek,
The Furies wait beyond.

TEXTS

(A) *May-Day* (Boston, 1867), 189; (B) *Poems* [Riverside] (Boston, 1884), 243; (B²) *Poems* [Centenary] (Boston, 1904), 296.

Pre-copy-text forms: The drafts are discussed in *PN*, 893. Variant titles are "Friendship" and "*Usque ad aras.*"

VARIANTS

3   seek, (A) I seek,— (B)

CASELLA.

Casella, a Florentine composer and friend of Dante, sings of love at Dante's request in canto II of the *Purgatorio*. Emerson alluded to Casella's performance in a journal entry of 25 September 1838, adding that "A song of love that gave us to know & own the natural & the heavenly or divine—that were indeed uplifting music" (*JMN*, VII, 86; cf. *JMN*, X, 70). In July 1846 Emerson wrote: "Metre of the Poet again, is his science of love. Does he know that lore? Never was poet who was not tremulous with love-lore" (*JMN*, IX, 442; cf. *TN*, III, 167, 193, 195, and 204). More than a decade passed, however, before these sources were versified, late in 1857, in three drafts in journal VO (*JMN*, XIV, 188). As with the quatrain "Love," hints of the poem's prose sources occur in the lecture (and subsequently the essay) entitled "Success," where, in the course of a discussion of love, Emerson asserts that "genius is measured by its skill in this science" (*CW*, VII, 153; cf. *CW*, II, 100, 121).

There is an equal or perhaps greater likelihood that Emerson's attention was first drawn to the subject of Casella by Milton's reference to him in the sonnet, "To my Friend, Mr Henry Lawes, on his Airs":

> *Dante* shall give Fame leave to set thee higher
> Than his *Casella,* whom he woo'd to sing,
> Met in the milder shades of Purgatory.

Here Milton is particularly praising Lawes for his extraordinary sensitivity in setting words to music.

CASELLA.

Test of the poet is knowledge of love,
For Eros is older than Saturn or Jove;
Never was poet, or late or of yore,
Who was not tremulous with love-lore.

TEXTS

(A) *May-Day* (Boston, 1867), 190; (A²) *Poems* [Riverside] (Boston, 1884), 243; (A³) *Poems* [Centenary] (Boston, 1904), 296.

Pre-copy-text forms: See *PN,* 756.

SHAKSPEARE.

Carl Strauch suggested that this poem was most probably written in the 1840s, on the theory that the quatrains generally "show the influence of the Persians," whom Emerson first read in that decade (Diss., 474). In fact, however, the earliest preserved manuscript copy, in poetry notebook P at p. 7 (drawn from the erased pencil draft at P, p. 39) appears to belong to the notebook's first sequence and gives every indication of being contemporary—or nearly contemporary—with the surrounding inscriptions (*PN,* 19, 31). Notebook P was begun in December 1834.

The best clues as to the date of composition may be the prose journal entries. Although Emerson knew Shakespeare's works be-

544

ginning in childhood, and in college was accounted a considerable expert on the subject (Cameron, *Ralph Waldo Emerson's Reading*, 44), Shakespeare's importance for Emerson was significantly clarified in the mid-1830s, first when he developed his theory of language in the course of two lectures on the dramatist written and delivered in 1835 (*EL*, I, 287–319), and again, in the fall of 1838, when he read Jones Very's "Dissertation on Shakspeare" and the companion essay on *Hamlet* (*L*, II, 165). After discussing these works at length with their author, Emerson reread *Hamlet* and *King Lear* (*JMN*, VII, 140–141) and concluded, "Shakspeare fills us with wonder the first time we approach him . . . By & by we return, & there he stands immeasurable as at first" (*JMN*, VII, 143; cf. *JMN*, VII, 18). A few days later, on 12 November, he wrote:

> Shakspeare has for the first time in our time found adequate criticism if indeed he have yet found it. Coleridge, Lamb, Schlegel, Goethe, Very. ↑ Herder ↓ The great facts of history are four or five names, Homer—Phidias—Jesus—Shakspeare—. One or two names more I will not add but see what these names stand for. All civil history & all philosophy consists of endeavors more or less vain to explain these persons. (*JMN*, VII, 147)

If it seems that Emerson approaches idolatry in his romantic estimate of Shakespeare's importance, it should be noted that in this respect he differs hardly at all from Samuel Johnson, S. T. Coleridge, Thomas Carlyle—or for that matter from Harold Bloom. He believed not only that "all modern Criticism is a making of rules out of the beauties of Shakspeare" (*TN*, II, 185), but that the very shape of contemporary Western culture had been effectively determined by Germany's critical engagement with that iconic English genius ("Thoughts on Modern Literature," *Dial*, I [October 1840]: 142). See, further, Robert P. Falk, "Emerson and Shakespeare," *PMLA*, LVI (June 1941): 523–543, for a still useful overview of a capacious subject.

SHAKSPEARE.

I see all human wits
Are measured but a few,
Unmeasured still my Shakspeare sits,
Lone as the blessed Jew.

TEXTS

(A) *May-Day* (Boston, 1867), 190; (B) *Poems* [Riverside] (Boston, 1884), 243; (B²) *Poems* [Centenary] (Boston, 1904), 296.

Pre-copy-text forms: See *PN*, 914. The late fair copy mentioned as occurring in notebook LI (dating to the early 1860s) has since been published in *TN*, II, 199.

VARIANTS

2   few, (A) | few; (B) [*Both marks of punctuation find support in the MSS.*]

HAFIZ.

No source in Hafiz has been located for this poem, which would appear to be an original work by Emerson in the manner of Hafiz. J. D. Yohannan, who made the most extensive study to date of Emerson's Persian translations, says that it may have been "suggested" by Emerson's own rendering of Hafiz, *Diwan,* II, 110 (I, 1–20),

"By breath of beds of roses drawn," of which three drafts have been published from notebook Orientalist in *TN*, II, 95, 98–99, 115–116 (see Yohannan, "Emerson's Translations of Persian Poetry from German Sources," *American Literature*, XIV [January 1943]: 415–416). But the similarities are not very striking.

The first two drafts of "Hafiz" clearly date to 1855; the second has the name "Saadi" in place of "Hafiz" in line 2.

HAFIZ.

Her passions the shy violet
From Hafiz never hides;
Love-longings of the raptured bird
The bird to him confides.

TEXTS

(A) *May-Day* (Boston, 1867), 190; (A²) *Poems* [Riverside] (Boston, 1884), 243; (A³) *Poems* [Centenary] (Boston, 1904), 296.

Pre-copy-text forms: Ten manuscript versions are discussed in *PN*, 806, the earliest dating to 1855, the latest (*JMN*, XV, 464–465) to 1865.

NATURE IN LEASTS.

The first two lines of this quatrain had an independent existence for about a decade, between April 1842, when they were inscribed in journal K (*JMN*, VIII, 241), and October 1852, when the complete poem was inscribed in journal GO (*JMN*, XIII, 101).

Even after the poem had been completed Emerson would on occasion write out the first two lines for autograph-seekers, as he did, for example, on 26 January 1859 while lecturing in Providence, R.I. (Brown University MS). The source in Goethe for Emerson's poem "Each and All" (q.v.) may well stand behind these two lines as also behind an 1839 entry in journal E: "the World reproduce[s] itself in miniature in every event that transpires, so that all the laws of nature may be read in the smallest fact" (*JMN*, VII, 302–303; *CW*, II, 201).

The title (in first-printing form, "Natura in minimis") comes from a sentence by Marcello Malpighi, a seventeenth-century pioneer in medical and anatomical microscopy, in his work on the silkworm, *De Bombyce* (1669; rpt. London, 1687), p. 1: "Cum enim tota in minimis existat natura, si alicubi, magis equidem in *insectorum* moleculis id deprehendi par fuerit." Emerson did not read Malpighi, but found this sentence quoted by Emanuel Swedenborg in "The Way to a Knowledge of the Soul," published in a translation by James John Garth Wilkinson, *Posthumous Tracts* . . . (London, 1847), 4–5. Wilkinson provided Malpighi's Latin in a footnote and translated the gist of it: "Nature exists in totality in the smallest objects." Emerson found many occasions thereafter to refer to this observation of Malpighi's, and in *Representative Men* (1850), discussed its importance to Swedenborg's thought (*CW*, IV, 59, 64–65, 195–196). In the early 1860s (if not before) Emerson noticed the similarity of the idea to the proposition of Aristotle, quoted in Francis Bacon's *Advancement of Learning*, that "the nature of everything is best seen in its smallest portions" (see *JMN*, XV, 7). It seems sometimes to happen that a source proves poetically evocative for Emerson when it is doubled or "rhymed" by a coinciding source.

NATURE IN LEASTS.

As sings the pine-tree in the wind,
So sings in the wind a sprig of the pine;
Her strength and soul has laughing France
Shed in each drop of wine.

TEXTS

(A) *Dial* [Cincinnati], I (March 1860): 195; (B) *May-Day* (Boston, 1867), 191; (B²) *Poems* [Riverside] (Boston, 1884), 244; (B³) *Poems* [Centenary] (Boston, 1904), 297.

Format: Line 2 and 4 indented in (A).

Pre-copy-text forms: See *PN*, 868–869. The text there referred to as having been written on an insert in notebook Morals has since been published in *TN*, III, 348. The copy of lines 1–2 written out for the English banker John Mills on 2 March 1848 was published in Isabel Petrie Mills, *From Tinder-Box to the "Larger" Light: Threads from the Life of John Mills* (Manchester, 1899), 144; the manuscript itself is in the Houghton Library Autograph File.

VARIANTS

Title: NATURE IN LEASTS. (B) | *Natura in minimis.* (A)   1   pine-tree (B) | pine tree (A)

'ΑΔΑΚΡΨΝ ΝΕΜΟΝΤΑΙ ΑΙΩΝΑ.

The title is from Pindar, *Olympian Ode*, II, lines 66–67: "[All who were wont to rejoice in keeping their oaths,] share a life that knoweth no tears." Emerson used this phrase as the epigraph to his own notebook X, the principal poetry notebook of the 1840s (*PN*, 110), and also of his 1843 notebook Trees (*JMN*, VIII, 519). Its meaning for him is perhaps best indicated in a prose passage in notebook S Salvage where the phrase stands as heading or title: "Genius is good natured. . . . It is always gentle. Hence the safety we feel, whenever genius is entrusted with political or ecclesiastical power. There is no fanaticism as long as there is the creative muse. Genius is a charter of freedom, and as long as I hear one graceful modulation of wit, I know the genial soul, & do not smell fagots. The Bunyan, the Boehman is nearer far to Montaigne & Rabelais, than to Bloody Mary & Becket & the Inquisition. Scaliger said, 'Never was a man a poet, or a lover of the works of poets, who had not his heart in the right place.' They are not tainted by the worst company. Genius hath an immunity from the worst times, & drawing its life from that which is out of time & place, is serene & glad amid bigots & juntoes" (*TN*, III, 80). As in the "Ode to W. H. Channing," written at about the same time, Emerson here pleads the case for the serenity and geniality of the poet as against the contentious didacticism of the reformer.

Indeed the first draft of the poem follows in journal O almost immediately after an entry entitled "Mob" that points out how the ardent declamation of the anti-slavery speakers Abby Kelley and her husband Stephen Foster very naturally provoked crowds to drown them out with shouts and stamping of feet (*JMN*, IX, 396; the poem draft is on 396–397). A few pages later in journal O is the first of Emerson's translations from Hafiz, whose *Diwan* he had just purchased at Elizabeth Peabody's West Street bookshop:

> Come let us strew roses
> And pour wine in the cup
> Break up the roof of heaven
> And throw it into new forms. (*JMN*, IX, 398)

A few pages more, and we find Emerson saying that "Nature never draws the moral; but leaves it for the spectator" (*JMN*, IX, 407), which echoes Emerson's statement on the first page of poetry notebook X, that nature "never grieves or rejoices αδάκρυν αιωνα Surprise & Casualty are the apples of her eyes" (*PN*, 110).

'ΑΔΑΚΡΥΝ ΝΕΜΟΝΤΑΙ ΑΙΩΝΑ

'A new commandment,' said the smiling Muse,
'I give my darling son, Thou shalt not preach';—
Luther, Fox, Behmen, Swedenborg, grew pale,

And, on the instant, rosier clouds upbore
Hafiz and Shakspeare with their shining choirs.   5

TEXTS

(A) *May-Day* (Boston, 1867), 191; (A²) *Poems* [Riverside] (Boston, 1884), 244;
(A³) *Poems* [Centenary] (Boston, 1904), 297.

Pre-copy-text forms: The journal O draft was probably inscribed in April (the
month when Emerson purchased the Hafiz volume (see *JMN,* IX, 399n), or
shortly thereafter; it is followed by copies in poetry notebooks P, X, and Rhymer.
See *PN,* 722.

TRANSLATIONS.

SONNET OF MICHEL
ANGELO BUONAROTI.

Emerson knew the *Rime di Michelagnolo Buonarroti,* ed., Giam-
battista Biagioli (Paris, 1821), at least as early as 1834, when he
borrowed the volume from the Harvard College library (*L,* I, 428)
in order to complete his research for the lecture "Michel Angelo
Buonaroti," first delivered in February 1835 (*EL,* I, 98–117). At
this time he made rough prose translations of a few of the poems
(*JMN,* IV, 366; see also *JMN,* XV, 57). Twenty-five years later, when
he translated "Sonetto I" in four drafts in journal AC (*JMN,* XIV,
220–223), he had acquired his own copy of Biagioli's edition

551

(Harding, *Emerson's Library* [Charlottesville, 1967], 45). He found the poem on page 1 of that volume:

ARGOMENTO.

Sono in marmo in potenza tutte le forme, così in donna ogni bene e ogni male. Adunque se lo scultore cava del marmo altra che l'immaginata, se incolpi, come chi da quella non felicità ma tormento.

Non ha l' ottimo artista alcun concetto,
    Ch' un marmo solo in se non circoscriva
    Col suo soverchio, e solo a quello arriva
    La man che obbedisce all' intelletto.

Il mal ch' io fuggo, e 'l ben ch' io mi prometto,
    In te, donna leggiadra, altera, e diva,
    Tal si nasconde, e, perch' io più non viva,
    Contraria ho l' arte al desiato effetto.

Amor dunque non ha, nè tua beltate,
    O fortuna, o durezza, o gran disdegno,
    Del mio mal colpa, o mio destino, o sorte,

Se dentro del tuo cor morte e pietate
    Porti in un tempo, e che 'l mio basso ingegno
    Non sappia ardendo trarne altro che morte.

Christoph Irmscher interestingly compares Emerson's and Longfellow's translations of this poem in *Longfellow Redux* (Urbana, Ill., 2006), 218–224, where he appears to fault Emerson for being "More motivated to create an Emersonian poem than to produce a faithful translation of another writer's work" (222). It is probably true that what is most appealing about Emerson's translation is the surprising extent to which another writer's work can be revealed, by a strong reading, to be Emersonian after all.

SONNET OF MICHEL ANGELO BUONAROTI.

Never did sculptor's dream unfold
A form which marble doth not hold
In its white block; yet it therein shall find
Only the hand secure and bold
Which still obeys the mind.   5
So hide in thee, thou heavenly dame,
The ill I shun, the good I claim;
I alas! not well alive,
Miss the aim whereto I strive.

Not love, nor beauty's pride,   10
Nor Fortune, nor thy coldness, can I chide,
If, whilst within thy heart abide
Both death and pity, my unequal skill
Fails of the life, but draws the death and ill.

TEXTS

(A) *May-Day* (Boston, 1867), 195; (B) *Poems* [Riverside] (Boston, 1884), 244–245; (C) *Poems* [Centenary] (Boston, 1904), 298.

Pre-copy-text forms: In addition to the four drafts in journal AC mentioned above, there is another in poetry notebook NP. See *PN,* 923.

VARIANTS

Title: MICHEL (A, C) | Michael (B) || BUONAROTI. (A) | BUONAROTTI. (B) | BUONAROTTI (C)

9–10   strive. / [*white line*] / Not (A) | strive. / [*end of page*] / Not (B) | strive. / [*no white line*] / Not (C)

THE EXILE.

FROM THE PERSIAN OF KERMANI.

J. D. Yohannan, in "Emerson's Translation of Persian Poetry from German Sources," *American Literature* XIV (January 1943): 413, calls "The Exile" "the most astonishing of all of Emerson's Persian poems," pointing out that the twenty-four lines of the translation (in its longer, first published form) is an elaboration of only four distichs in the German-language source:

Willkommen Ambramorgenwind!	Du über Kerman's Erde wehst.
Willkommen mir, o Nachtigall!	Du in dem Vaterlande wohnst.
Wie kommt's, daß mich das hohe Loos	Von diesem reinen Land verbannt?
So lang ich bleibe zu Bagdad,	Fällt mir der Tigris nur ins Aug.

Emerson found the text of the poem by Khwaju Kermani (1280–1352), a contemporary of Hafiz, in Joseph von Hammer's anthology, *Geschichte der Schönen Redekünste Persiens, mit einer Blüthenlese aus zweihundert persischen Dichtern* (Vienna, 1818), 248—and yet only lines 9–16 and 23–24 of Emerson's translation derive from it. The relationship between source and finished translation is even slighter in view of the fact that Emerson dropped the original fourth stanza after the first publication in the *Atlantic* essay, "Persian Poetry."

The two drafts of the last stanza (lines 21–24) in notebook PY (*TN*, II, 265) derive from a draft of lines 23–24 (a version, of course, of lines 15–16) entered in journal IO in September 1854 (*JMN*, XIII, 357). The first stanza translates Hafiz, *Diwan*, II, 282: a draft of these lines occurs together with lines 9–16 in one draft, and with 5–24 in another (*TN*, II, 86–87 and 97–98). The association of much of the first two stanzas with Hafiz accounts for the poem's being attributed to Hafiz in Emerson's two fair copies. It would seem, so far as anyone has been able to determine, that

Sonnet of Michel Angelo Buonaroti

Emerson is solely responsible for lines 17–22. Yohannan suggests that lines 17–20 may reflect Emerson's having read, in von Hammer's preface, "the . . . famous story of the poet Hafiz's reluctant journeys away from his native Shiraz" (414).

THE EXILE.

FROM THE PERSIAN OF KERMANI.

In Farsistan the violet spreads
Its leaves to the rival sky;
I ask how far is the Tigris flood,
And the vine that grows thereby?

Except the amber morning wind,   5
Not one salutes me here;
There is no lover in all Bagdad
To offer the exile cheer.

I know that thou, O morning wind!
O'er Kerman's meadow blowest,   10
And thou, heart-warming nightingale!
My father's orchard knowest.

The merchant hath stuffs of price,
And gems from the sea-washed strand,
And princes offer me grace   15
To stay in the Syrian land;

But what is gold *for*, but for gifts?
And dark, without love, is the day;
And all that I see in Bagdad
Is the Tigris to float me away.   20

TEXTS

(A) "Persian Poetry," *AM*, I (April 1858): 732; (B) *May-Day* (Boston, 1867), 196–197; (B²) *Poems* [Riverside] (Boston, 1884), 245–246; (B³) *Poems* [Centenary] (Boston, 1904), 298–299.

Format: The whole is enclosed in quotation marks in (A), a feature of house style not further noticed here. In (A) alternate lines are indented.

Pre-copy-text forms: See *PN,* 785, for a somewhat fuller discussion of the manuscript drafts.

VARIANTS

Title: THE EXILE. / FROM THE PERSIAN OF KERMANI. (B) I THE EXILE. (A)

2   sky; (B) I sky,— (A)

3   ask how (B) I ask, How (A)

6   salutes (B) I saluted (A)

7   lover (B) I man (A) II Bagdad (A) I Bagdat (B)

9   wind! (B) I wind, (A)

10   Kerman's (A) I Kernan's (B) [*the erroneous reading occurs in two of the manuscript drafts as well.*]

11   nightingale! (B) I nightingale, (A)

12–13   knowest. / [*white line*] / The (B) I knowest. / [*white line*] / Oh, why did partial Fortune / From that bright land banish me? / So long as I wait in Bagdad, / The Tigris is all I see. / [*white line*] / The (A)

16   land; (B) I land: (A)

17   *for,* (B) I for (A)

18   dark, (B) I dark (A) II love, (B) I love (A)

19   Bagdad (A) I Bagdat (B)

NOTES

1.   Farsistan was the traditional name of the region in southern Persia (the province of Fars in modern Iran) whose capital, Shiraz, is the burial place of both Hafiz and Kermani.

3.   The Tigris River flows southeast from Bagdad (line 7) into the Persian Gulf just west of Farsistan and would thus represent the speaker's way home. The city of Bagdad (or Baghdad) had been thoroughly sacked by Mongol invaders in 1258, twenty years before Kermani's birth. It would not be a pleasant place for several centuries thereafter.

10.   The city of Kerman is the center of the province of Kerman, east of Farsistan. The family name "Kermani" signifies the place of their origin.

20.   Syrian: Emerson sometimes uses this name as an epithet, meaning, broadly, oriental, with overtones of desert heat. If his meaning is more specific, he may have known that during the Abbasid Caliphate, Damascus was ruled from Bagdad.

FROM HAFIZ.

Emerson here translates Hafiz, Book XXV, Ode X, lines 9–10 (*Diwan*, II, 327), beginning with a prose version in notebook L Camadeva: "O heaven! boast not of thy pomp, for, in the world of Love, ↑And estimation true,↓ <the> ↑the heaped up↓ harvest of the moon is worth <but> one barleycorn ↑at most↓, & the ↑Pleiads'↓ sheaf <of the Pleiads but two> ↑but two.↓" (*TN*, III, 346).

FROM HAFIZ.

I said to heaven that glowed above,
O hide yon sun-filled zone,
Hide all the stars you boast;
For, in the world of love
And estimation true,   5
The heaped-up harvest of the moon
Is worth one barley-corn at most,
The Pleiads' sheaf but two.

TEXTS

(A) *May-Day* (Boston, 1867), 197; (A²) *Poems* [Riverside] (Boston, 1884), 246; (A³) *Poems* [Centenary] (Boston, 1904), 299.

Pre-copy-text forms: The first four drafts occur in L Camedeva (*TN*, III, 346–347), with copies in NP and Rhymer: see *PN*, 798.

NOTES

7–8. The annual rising and setting of the star-cluster known as the Pleiades marked the beginning of winter and summer and was therefore associated in primitive farming cultures with sowing and harvest, and particularly with the gathering of the "first sheaf." The Pleiades, as a cluster, were themselves often figured as a sheaf, as in poems by Bushāq and Jami written in imitation of this ghazal of Hafiz, and discussed by Paul E. Losensky in *Welcoming Fighani: Imitation and Poetic Individuality in the Safavid-Mughal Ghazal* (Costa Mesa, Cal., 1998), 166–73. On the rituals of the Pleiads' sheaf, see Robert A. Segal, ed., *The Myth and Ritual Theory* (Oxford, 1998), 47. The present poem seems related to Emerson's somewhat hyperbolic assertion, in "Quotation and Originality," that "Hafiz furnished Burns with the song of 'John Barleycorn,'" though he cites another as the principal basis for the claim (*CW*, VIII, 98; cf. *TN*, II, 115, and *PN*, 312).

["IF MY DARLING SHOULD DEPART."]

Emerson never assigned a title to these lines, which are taken from trial translations of a longer, 28-line poem ("Lord my god these people"), consisting of lines 9–36 of Hafiz, Book IX, Ode II (*Diwan*, II, 4–5). Several draft translations of the longer version as well as a separate draft of the eight lines published in "Persian Poetry" in 1858 occur in notebook Orientalist (*TN*, II, 107–109).

["IF MY DARLING SHOULD DEPART."]

If my darling should depart,
And search the skies for prouder friends,
God forbid my angry heart
In other love should seek amends.

When the blue horizon's hoop   5
Me a little pinches here,

Epitaph

Instant to my grave I stoop,
And go find thee in the sphere.

TEXTS

(A) "Persian Poetry," *AM*, I (April 1858): 732; (B) *May-Day* (Boston, 1867), 198; (B²) *Poems* [Riverside] (Boston, 1884), 246; (B³) *Poems* [Centenary] (Boston, 1904), 300.

Format: The whole is enclosed in quotation marks in (A), a feature of house style not further noticed here. In (A) alternate lines are indented.

Pre-copy-text forms: See "Lord my god these people" in *PN*, 848.

VARIANTS

1   depart, (B) | depart (A)
4   amends. (B) | amends! (A)

7   Instant to my grave I stoop, (B) |
On the instant I will die (A)

EPITAPH.

Emerson introduced this quatrain in "Persian Poetry," by saying, "Here is a little epitaph that might have come from Simonides" (730)—suggesting that it was the poem's memorial conciseness that he admired. But the strong note of irony in this fragment by Hafiz (*Diwan*, II, 573) is quite alien to the mentality of Simonides of Ceos (c. 556-c. 468 B.C.), who is best remembered for his epigrammatic praise of the Greek heroes in their stand against the Persians at Thermopylae.

EPITAPH.

Bethink, poor heart, what bitter kind of jest
Mad Destiny this tender stripling played;
For a warm breast of maiden to his breast,
She laid a slab of marble on his head.

TEXTS

(A) "Persian Poetry," *AM*, I (April 1858): 730; (B) *May-Day* (Boston, 1867), 198; (B²) *Poems* [Riverside] (Boston, 1884), 246; (B³) *Poems* [Centenary] (Boston, 1904), 300.

Format: The whole is enclosed in quotation marks in (A), a feature of house style not further noticed here. In (A) alternate lines are indented.

Pre-copy-text forms: See *PN*, 781.

VARIANTS

Title: EPITAPH. (B) | [Untitled] (A)   3   maiden (B) | ivory (A)
2   played; (B) | played: (A)

["THEY SAY . . ."]

This untitled quatrain translates Hafiz, Book VIII, Ode LXXVI, lines 5–8 (*Diwan*, I, 316). It is cited in "Persian Poetry" as an instance of the "amatory poetry of Hafiz," of which "we must be very sparing in our citations, though it forms the staple of the 'Divan'" (731).

["THEY SAY. . ."]

They say, through patience, chalk
Becomes a ruby stone;
Ah, yes! but by the true heart's blood
The chalk is crimson grown.

TEXTS

(A) "Persian Poetry," *AM,* I (April 1858): 731; (B) *May-Day* (Boston, 1867), 199;
(B²) *Poems* [Riverside] (Boston, 1884), 247; (B³) *Poems* [Centenary] (Boston, 1904), 300.

Format: The whole is enclosed in quotation marks in (A), a feature of house style not further noticed here. In (A) alternate lines are indented.

Pre-copy-text forms: Emerson translated most of this 24-line poem in notebook EF before revising the four opening lines in Orientalist and copying the result in Rhymer: see *PN,* 939.

VARIANTS

3   yes! (B) | yes, (A)
4   grown. (B) | grown, [*Because Emerson embeds the quatrain in a* *sentence of his own, the poem ends with a comma.*]

FRIENDSHIP.

In the summer of 1854 Emerson translated Hafiz, Book XIII, Ode I, lines 25–32 (*Diwan,* II, 91) in journal IO (*JMN,* XIII, 349–50). Of these eight lines, the first four were eventually published in "Persian Poetry" (1858) as "The chemist of love" (731), while the second four received further revision on the same page in IO and were eventually published without title at a different point in the same essay. What seems to be the latest copy of these verses, in Rhymer, carries the title "*Songs are for heroes*" (*PN*, 463).

FRIENDSHIP.

Thou foolish Hafiz! Say, do churls
Know the worth of Oman's pearls?
Give the gem which dims the moon
To the noblest, or to none.

TEXTS

(A) "Persian Poetry," *AM*, I (April 1858): 729; (B) *May-Day* (Boston, 1867), 199; (B²) *Poems* [Riverside] (Boston, 1884), 247; (B³) *Poems* [Centenary] (Boston, 1904), 300.

Format: The whole is enclosed in quotation marks in (A), a feature of house style not further noticed here.

Pre-copy-text forms: See *PN*, 797.

VARIANTS

Title: FRIENDSHIP. (B) | [*Untitled*] (A)   1   Say, (B) | say, (A)

["DEAREST, WHERE THY SHADOW FALLS."]

It is probable but not quite certain that the draft in journal LM (*JMN*, X, 341), which dates to July or August 1848, is the first. Emerson, at that location, plausibly attributes the poem to Hafiz, though the precise source has not been identified.

["DEAREST, WHERE THY SHADOW FALLS."]

Dearest, where thy shadow falls,
Beauty sits and Music calls;
Where thy form and favor come,
All good creatures have their home.

TEXTS

(A) "Persian Poetry," *AM*, I (April 1858): 728; (B) *May-Day* (Boston, 1867), 199; (C) *Poems* [Riverside] (Boston, 1884), 247; (C²) *Poems* [Centenary] (Boston, 1904), 301.

Format: The whole is enclosed in quotation marks in (A), a feature of house style not further noticed here.

Pre-copy-text forms: The "Dear friend" reading of the IO draft is revised to "Mirza!" in notebook Orientalist, and to "Dearest" in the Rhymer draft. "Mirza" is a Persian form of address to royalty or nobility, and is related to the term "emir." On the manuscripts, see, further, *PN*, 772.

VARIANTS

1   Dearest, (B-C) | Mirza! (A)   2   sits (A, C) | sits, (B)

["ON PRINCE OR BRIDE."]

In an 1850 journal entry Emerson provided a prose translation of a single line in "Sich selbst zum Rathe" by Enweri (or, more commonly, Anwari, a twelfth-century poet) from the source in *Geschichte*, 91: "On the neck of the young man <sits no>sparkles no gem so gracious as the spirit of adventure" (*JMN*, XI, 310). Successive drafts in notebook Orientalist expand the text first to two, then to four lines (*TN*, II, 47).

["ON PRINCE OR BRIDE."]

On prince or bride no diamond stone
Half so gracious ever shone,
As the light of enterprise
Beaming from a young man's eyes.

TEXTS

(A) "Persian Poetry," *AM*, I (April 1858): 726; (A²) *May-Day* (Boston, 1867), 200; (A³) *Poems* [Riverside] (Boston, 1884), 247; (A⁴) *Poems* [Centenary] (Boston, 1904), 301.

Format: The whole is enclosed in quotation marks in (A), a feature of house style not further noticed here.

Pre-copy-text forms: The Orientalist drafts and the Rhymer fair copy are discussed in *PN*, 885.

FROM OMAR CHIAM.

In the first paragraph of "Persian Poetry," Emerson predicted that "Omar Chiam" (as, following von Hammer, he rendered the name), was among the old Persian poets who "promise to rise in Western estimation" (724), and in so doing join the ranks of established masters like Firdousi, Enweri, Nisami, Dschelaleddin, Saadi, Hafiz, and Dschami. Within one year Edward FitzGerald would bring out the first edition of his anonymously translated (and fabulously popular) *Rubáiyát of Omar Khayyám, the Astronomer-Poet of Persia* (London, 1859), but Emerson's familiarity with this work dates from 1873, when Charles Eliot Norton provided him with a copy (*Letters of Charles Eliot Norton* [London and Boston, 1913], I, 508–509; Harding, *Emerson's Library* [Charlottesville, 1967], 204).

The text from which Emerson worked he found in von Hammer's *Geschichte*, 82:

> Wo Tulpen auf den Feldern sproßen,
> Trank jeder Fleck das Blut der Großen.
> Die Veilchen, die auf Wiesen prangen,
> Sind Muttermaale schöner Wangen.

FitzGerald's translation is quatrain XVIII in the 1859 sequence:

> I sometimes think that never blows so red
> The Rose as where some buried Cæsar bled;
>   That every Hyacinth the Garden wears
> Dropt in her Lap from some once lovely Head.

FROM OMAR CHIAM.

Each spot where tulips prank their state
Has drunk the life-blood of the great;
The violets yon field which stain
Are moles of beauties Time hath slain.

TEXTS

(A) "Persian Poetry," *AM,* I (April 1858): 731; (B) *May-Day* (Boston, 1867), 200; (C) *Poems* [Riverside] (Boston, 1884), 247; (D) *Poems* [Centenary] (Boston, 1904), 301.

Format: The whole is enclosed in quotation marks in (A), a feature of house style not further noticed here.

Pre-copy-text forms: Only one draft survives: in notebook Orientalist (*TN*, II, 87).

VARIANTS

Title: FROM OMAR CHIAM. (B) I   3   field (B-D) I fields (A)
[Untitled] (A) I FROM OMAR KHAY
YAM. (C) I FROM OMAR KHAYYAM
(D)

NOTES

4   A "mole" is a Roman mausoleum; according to the *OED,* the term is obsolete.

["HE WHO HAS A THOUSAND FRIENDS"]

Emerson seems to have known the source for this distich as early as 1849, referring to it in a journal entry in clipped form: "'He who has 1000 friends,' &c" (*JMN*, XI, 100). When he recorded the full prose version in journal NO in the spring of 1855 ("He who has a thousand friends, has not enough; and he who has one foe, has too many"), he identified the author as "Ali Ben Abi Taleb"—that is to say, Mohammed's son-in-law, the great fourth Caliph (*JMN*, XIII, 425–426; cf. *CW*, VI, 278). On the same journal page Emerson versified the apothegm.

["HE WHO HAS A THOUSAND FRIENDS."]

He who has a thousand friends has not a friend to spare,
And he who has one enemy will meet him everywhere.

TEXTS

(A) "Persian Poetry," *AM*, I (April 1858): 726; (B) "Considerations by the Way," *Conduct of Life* (Boston, 1860), 240; (C) *May-Day* (Boston, 1867), 200; (D) *Poems* [Riverside] (Boston, 1884), 248; (E) *Poems* [Centenary] (Boston, 1904), 302. There are no variants in later editions and reprintings of (B).

Format: The whole is enclosed in quotation marks in (A) and (B), a feature of house style not further noticed here.

Pre-copy-text forms: In addition to the first drafts in *JMN*, XIII, 426, two fair copies survive: see *PN*, 811. The printer's copy for (B) also survives: see the transcription of a canceled version of the lines at *CW*, VI, 407.

VARIANTS

Title: [*Untitled*] (A-D) | FROM ALI BEN   2   will (C-E) | shall (A-B)
ABU TALEB (CC6, E)

["ON TWO DAYS"]

According to von Hammer in *Geschichte,* 43, the original is by "Pindar aus Rei in Kuhistan"—or, as Joseph Slater explains in *CW,* VI, 177, "the Pindar of Rai (or Rhagae), a city in the province of Kuhistan, near the Caspian Sea." The first draft of Emerson's translation, in journal TU (*JMN,* XI, 103), was written in May 1849. Not included in "Persian Poetry," the quatrain was first published in the essay "Fate" in *The Conduct of Life* to illustrate the belief of "the Turk, the Arab, the Persian" in a rigorously foreordained destiny.

["ON TWO DAYS"]

On two days it steads not to run from thy grave,
The appointed, and the unappointed day;
On the first, neither balm nor physician can save,
Nor thee, on the second, the Universe slay.

TEXTS

(A) "Fate," *The Conduct of Life* (Boston, 1860), 3; (B) *May-Day* (Boston, 1867), 201; (B²) *Poems* [Riverside] (Boston, 1884), 248; (B³) *Poems* [Centenary] (Boston, 1904), 302.

Format: The whole is enclosed in quotation marks in (A), a feature of house style not further noticed here. In (A) alternate lines are indented.

Pre-copy-text forms: See *PN,* 886.

VARIANTS

Title: [*Untitled*] (A-B) | From Pindar of   1   days (B) | days, (A)
Rei in Cuhistan. (CC6)

FROM IBN JEMIN.

The author of this poem, which Emerson found in *Geschichte*, 239, is Emir Mahmoud Ben Jemin-eddin Ferjumendi, known as Ibn Jemin. It is not known when the translation was made.

FROM IBN JEMIN.

Two things thou shalt not long for, if thou love a mind serene;—
A woman to thy wife, though she were a crowned queen;
And the second, borrowed money,—though the smiling lender
    say
That he will not demand the debt until the Judgment Day.

TEXTS

(A) "Persian Poetry," *AM,* I (April 1858): 726; (B) *May-Day* (Boston, 1867), 201; (C) *Poems* [Riverside] (Boston, 1884), 248; (C²) *Poems* [Centenary] (Boston, 1904), 302.

Format: The whole is enclosed in quotation marks in (A), a feature of house style not further noticed here.

Pre-copy-text forms: See *PN,* 798.

VARIANTS

Title: FROM IBN JEMIN. (B-C) |
  [*Untitled*] (A)
  1   mind serene;— (B-C) | life
serene: (A)

2   to (B-C) | for (A)
3   And (B-C) | And, (A) ||
money,— (B-C) | money, (A) || say
(A, C) | say, (B)

THE FLUTE.

In "Persian Poetry," Emerson introduced this quatrain by saying, "A stanza of Hilali on a Flute is a luxury of idealism" (733). In fact it is not by Hilali at all, but by the great Sufi poet Mewlana Dschelaleddin Rumi, from a work entitled—in *Geschichte,* 197— "Proben aus dem Breviere der Derwische." Emerson's error of attribution is traceable to a draft version in notebook Orientalist, where it is written immediately below an unrelated fragment that Emerson correctly identified as Hilali's (*TN,* II, 89). The mistaken attribution, which became part of the poem's formal title in the *May-Day* printing, is here editorially emended.

The first draft, entitled "The Soul" by Emerson and correctly assigned to "Dchelaleddin" at Orientalist, 19, translates more of the source (*TN,* II, 48–49). Like other translations that occur in the first pages of that notebook, it was most likely written in 1850.

THE FLUTE.

Hark what, now loud, now low, the pining flute complains,
Without tongue, yellow-cheeked, full of winds that wail and sigh;
Saying, Sweetheart! the old mystery remains,—
If I am I; thou, thou; or thou art I?

TEXTS

(A) "Persian Poetry," *AM,* I (April 1858): 733; (B) *May-Day* (Boston, 1867), 202; (B²) *Poems* [Riverside] (Boston, 1884), 248; (B³) *Poems* [Centenary] (Boston, 1904), 303.

Format: The whole is enclosed in quotation marks in (A), a feature of house style not further noticed here. In (A) alternate lines are indented.

Pre-copy-text forms: See *PN,* 791–792.

VARIANTS

Title: THE FLUTE. [*Eds.*] | [*Untitled*] (A) | THE FLUTE. / FROM HILALI. (B)

1 Hark (B) | Hear (A)

2 sigh; (B) | sigh, (A)

3 Sweetheart! (B) | 'Sweetheart, (A) || remains,— (B) | remains, (A)

4 am I; thou, thou; (B) | am I, thou thou (A) || I? (B) | I.' (A)

TO THE SHAH.

FROM HAFIZ.

Emerson reminds his readers in "Persian Poetry" that Hafiz, Enweri, and the others were court poets, and offers a few examples of panegyric to demonstrate "the unimportance of your subject to success, provided only the treatment be cordial. In general, what is more tedious than dedications . . . addressed to grandees? Yet in the 'Divan' you would not skip them, since [the poet's] muse seldom supports him better" (728).

The present distich was extracted from a 28-line translation that Emerson made of a portion of Hafiz, Book VIII, Ode CLXVII (*Diwan,* I, 452–453). Only these two lines, corresponding to lines 53–54 in the source, were subject to revision.

TO THE SHAH.

FROM HAFIZ.

Thy foes to hunt, thy enviers to strike down,
Poises Arcturus aloft morning and evening his spear.

TEXTS

(A) "Persian Poetry," *AM,* I (April 1858): 728; (B) *May-Day* (Boston, 1867), 202; (B²) *Poems* [Riverside] (Boston, 1884), 249; (B³) *Poems* [Centenary] (Boston, 1904), 303. There are no variants in the text of the poem as included in later editions and printings of "Persian Poetry," *Letters and Social Aims* (1876).

Format: The whole is enclosed in quotation marks in (A), a feature of house style not further noticed here.

Pre-copy-text forms: See *PN,* 951–952.

VARIANTS

Title: TO THE SHAH. from hafiz. (B)
  | [*Untitled*] (A)

NOTES

2.   Arcturus, the brightest star in the constellation Boötes, means, in Greek, guardian of the bear (ἄρκτος), acknowledging its position close to Ursa Major and Ursa Minor. Its name in Arabic, *ar-Râmi,* means "spearman."

TO THE SHAH.

FROM ENWERI.

Emerson here translates line 5 of "Kaßide, zum Lobe Amadeddin Firußchahs" from *Geschichte*, 94. The first draft, in notebook Orientalist (*TN*, II, 54), appears to have been inscribed in 1850. In 1858 Emerson noted in his journal: "The panegyrics of Hafiz addressed to his Shahs & Agas show poetry, but they show deficient civilization. The finest genius in England or France would feel the absurdity of fabling such things to his queen or Emperor about their saddle, as Hafiz & Enweri do not stick at" (*JMN*, XIV, 196). Emerson explained his fascination with this form a little differently a few years later in speaking of the "insane compliments to the Sultan, borrowed from the language of prayer"; these, he felt, exemplified a characteristic Persian "wildness of license" ("Preface to the American Edition," *The Gulistan or Rose Garden*, trans. Francis Gladwin [Boston, 1865], iv, vi).

TO THE SHAH.

FROM ENWERI.

Not in their houses stand the stars,
But o'er the pinnacles of thine!

TEXTS

(A) "Persian Poetry," *AM*, I (April 1858): 728; (B) *May-Day* (Boston, 1867), 202; (C) William Ellery Channing, *Thoreau: The Poet-Naturalist* (Boston, 1873), 135. The Riverside and Centenary editions of *Poems* follow (B).

Format: The whole is enclosed in quotation marks in (A) and (C), a feature of house style not further noticed here.

Pre-copy-text forms: See *PN*, 951.

VARIANTS

Title: TO THE SHAH. FROM ENWERI.   2thine! (A-B) | thine. (C)
(B) | [*Untitled*] (A, C)

TO THE SHAH.

FROM ENWERI.

Emerson here translates rather freely from "An den Dichter Schedschaai" in *Geschichte,* 91. The lines were undoubtedly composed, like those preceding, in 1850.

TO THE SHAH.

FROM ENWERI.

From thy worth and weight the stars gravitate,
And the equipoise of heaven is thy house's equipoise.

TEXTS

(A) "Persian Poetry," *AM,* I (April 1858): 728; (B) *May-Day* (Boston, 1867), 203; (B²) *Poems* [Riverside] (Boston, 1884), 249; (B³) *Poems* [Centenary] (Boston, 1904), 303.

Format: The whole is enclosed in quotation marks in (A), a feature of house style not further noticed here.

Pre-copy-text forms: The manuscript drafts closely parallel those of the preceding poem: see *PN,* 951.

VARIANTS

Title: TO THE SHAH. FROM ENWERI.   2   equipoise. (B) | equipoise! (A)
(B) | [*Untitled*] (A)

SONG OF SEID NIMETOLLAH
OF KUHISTAN.

Arthur John Arberry, in *Classical Persian Literature* (1958; rpt., London, 1995), 412, says that "The Ni'mat-Allāhī order of dervishes, active to this day in parts of Persia, derives its name from Shāh Nūr al-Dīn Muhammad Ni'mat Allāh Vāli, . . . a renowned poet and a powerful saint who was born at Aleppo in 1330. . . . When twenty-four years of age he made the pilgrimage to Mecca and there came under the influence of the Sūfī teacher and biographer 'Abd Allāh al-Yāfi'ī, whose khalifa he eventually became." Seid Ni'mat Allāh (or Nimetollah) was the author of many short treatises on points of Sufi doctrine, but has always been best known for his *Diwan,* an extensive collection of lyric poems. Joseph von Hammer's German version of one of the many "Mystische Gasele"—the source of Emerson's "translation"—is to be found in *Geschichte,* 223:

Seid Nimetollah aus *Kuhistan,*

ein großer Scheich und ein mystischer Dichter, der, wie *Dewletschah* sich ausdrückt, ein Meer der Erkenntniß, ein Schacht des Wi∬ens, ein Sultan im Lande der Vervollkommnung, ein Re-

575

isender im Thale der Wahrheit, ein Jünger des Scheich *Jafii,* der auch den Hauch Gasali's empfangen.

Mystische Gasele.

So gestalt bin ich verwirret,	Daß ich Kopf von Hand nicht kenne,
Nicht das Herz von dem Geliebten,	Becher nicht vom Weine kenne.
Richte all mein Thun und La*ſſ*en	Nicht nach Aus*ſp*ruch des Verstandes;
Denn ich bin verwirrt und trunken,	Und allein mein Liebchen kenne.
Vom Gestad der Frommen bin ich	Zu des Sinnes Meer gekommen.
Was ist Land, und was sind Meere,	Da ich nur Juwelen kenne.
Seine Liebe ist das Feuer,	Herz und Seele ist das Rauchwerk.
Ha! ich flamme wie die Aloe,	Doch das Rauchfaß ich nicht kenne.
Ich bin wi*ſſ*end und unwi*ſſ*end,	Stehe nicht und sitze wieder.
Ach! Ich weine aus Betrübniß,	Weil ich Silber, Gold nicht kenne.
Wie das Aug' nach allen Seiten,	Wandt' ich mich nach jedem Winkel.
Weil verwüstet sind die Wangen,	Ich die Ansicht nicht erkenne.
Frage mich aus dem Gedächtniß,	Welches Haupstück dir beliebt.
Ich behalte all *Suren,*	Wenn ich gleich nicht Titel kenne.
Gottes Licht ist nun gekommen,	Was sind Gauern, was Moslimen!
Ich zwar folge den Rechtgläub'gen,	Doch Ungläub'ge ich nicht kenne.
Ich den Unterschied der Dinge	Wie der *Seid* gar nicht kenne.
Was zu sagen, da auf Erden,	Einen andern ich nicht kenne.

The headnote that Emerson appended to his own translation oddly slights the mystical content of the dervish's dance, or Sema, stressing instead the physical appearance of the performance, its orbital character, and the performer's relation to his sheik. But the poem makes it clear that the purpose here is not to compliment any human being, but instead to achieve an ecstatic transcendence of ego-awareness such that one's own rapt loving, wholly yielded to, can at last combine with God's love, all "difference" expiring in the act (line 26).

The best known of the so-called whirling dervishes comprise the Mevlavi Order of Sufis, which was founded by perhaps the greatest of all the Sufi poets, Mevlana Jelaluddin Rumi (1207–1273). The various orders of dervishes, however, all emphasized universal love as the pathway to God (the theme especially of the first stanza); like other Sufis, they were essentially Gnostic in their search for truth or divine wisdom (the theme of the second stanza). The jewel or signet ring of Solomon was a favorite trope of Sufi poets, as explained by Emerson's friend, William Rounseville Alger, a Boston Unitarian minister and amateur orientalist. In his 1856 book *The Poetry of the East* (an inscribed copy of which is in Emerson's library), Alger had written, "Such were the incredible virtues of [Solomon's] little talisman, that the touch of it exorcised all evil spirits, commanded the instant presence and services of the Genii, laid every secret bare, and gave its possessor almost unlimited powers of knowledge, dominion, and performance" (59–60). As Solomon had been preeminently a symbol of wisdom (or gnosis), so this jewel, lost by its first possessor, became a way of imagining its recovery. The third stanza stresses the Sufi independence from tradition and dogma in a manner common also to Gnostics and Transcendentalists. This privileging of meaning over reverence for textual authority is an important key to the poetics of mysticism in its various forms. The coda of Emerson's translation dramatically represents the transcendence that the dance—and the re-expression of the dance as poem—had set out to achieve.

It is a little uncertain whether the manuscript preserved at Brown University served as printer's copy for its publication in 1860. Since it is signed by Emerson and dated at Concord, December 1853, the presumptive recipient is Moncure Daniel Conway, then enrolled at the Harvard Divinity School. He had met Emerson for the first time the previous May, and, according to Conway's biographer, they studied the literature and religion of Persia during their time together (John d'Entremont, *Southern Emancipator* [New York, 1987], 80). In 1859, when Conway was editing a journal memorially entitled *The Dial*, he asked Emerson if he could publish this poem, which had "so long been in my treasury" (*L*, V, 181). The main difficulty in accepting the manuscript as printer's copy is the number of discrepancies between it and the *Dial* printing. Possibly Emerson supplied a fresh version along with his permission to publish the poem, which by then was at least six years old. That the 1853 manuscript belonged to Conway is further substantiated by a contemporary notation still with the document that it had been found in a scrapbook scrounged by a Union soldier at Fredericksburg, Virginia (Conway's home), on 15 December 1863, two days after a battle in which 18,000 combatants died.

SONG OF SEID NIMETOLLAH OF KUHISTAN.

[Among the religious customs of the dervishes is an astronomical dance, in which the dervish imitates the movements of the heavenly bodies, by spinning on his own axis, whilst at the same time he revolves round the Sheikh in the centre, representing the sun; and, as he spins, he sings the Song of Seid Nimetollah of Kuhistan.]

Spin the ball! I reel, I burn,
Nor head from foot can I discern,
Nor my heart from love of mine,
Nor the wine-cup from the wine.
All my doing, all my leaving,   5
Reaches not to my perceiving;
Lost in whirling spheres I rove,
And know only that I love.

I am seeker of the stone,
Living gem of Solomon;   10
From the shore of souls arrived,
In the sea of sense I dived;
But what is land, or what is wave,
To me who only jewels crave?
Love is the air-fed fire intense,   15
And my heart the frankincense;
As the rich aloes flames, I glow,
Yet the censer cannot know.
I'm all-knowing, yet unknowing;
Stand not, pause not, in my going.   20

Ask not me, as Muftis can,
To recite the Alcoran;

Song of Seid Nimetollah of Kuhistan

Well I love the meaning sweet,—
I tread the book beneath my feet.

Lo! the God's love blazes higher,   25
Till all difference expire.
What are Moslems? what are Giaours?
All are Love's, and all are ours.
I embrace the true believers,
But I reck not of deceivers.   30
Firm to Heaven my bosom clings,
Heedless of inferior things;
Down on earth there, underfoot,
What men chatter know I not.

TEXTS

(A) "Persian Poetry," *AM*, I (April 1858): 733–734; (B) MS, John Hay Library, by permission of Brown University, perhaps printer's copy for C; (C) *The Dial* [Cincinnati], I (January 1860), 37; (D) *May-Day* (Boston, 1867), 203–204. The Riverside and Centenary editions of *Poems* follow (D), except that each has the spelling "Seyd" for the *May-Day* form "Seid."

Format: The whole is enclosed in quotation marks in (A), a feature of house style not further noticed here.

Pre-copy-text forms: Four complete drafts occupy ten pages of notebook Orientalist, and a fair copy is in Rhymer. See *PN*, 922.

VARIANTS

Title: SONG OF SEID NIMETOLLAH OF KUHISTAN. (D) | [*Untitled*] (A) | ↑From the Persian ↓ / Song of the Dervish in the Sacred dance (B) | THE SACRED DANCE. / [From the Persian.] (C)

Headnote: [Among . . . Kuhistan.] (D) | Among . . . dervises, it seems, is . . . dervis imitates . . . bodies by . . .

whilst, . . . time, . . . sheikh . . . and as . . . Kuhistan:— (A) | [*None*] (B) | [The Dervish supposes that the inspired dance describes curves which exactly correspond with the orbits of the heavenly bodies. The Persians suppose that a magic gem was lost by Solomon on their coasts, and that some pearl-diver will one

579

day find it: this will explain the allusion in the ninth line of the verses.] (C)

4 wine. (A-B, D) | wine! (C)

5 leaving, (A-B, D) | leaving (C)

6 perceiving; (B-D) | perceiving. (A)

7 whirling (A, D) | whirl of (B-C)

8 only (A, C-D) | only— (B)

9 [*Flush*] I (A, C) | [*Inset*] I (B, D)

12 dived; (A-B, D) | dived: (C)

13 wave, (A-B, D) | wave (C)

14 me (A-B, D) | me, (C)

14–15 [*No white line*] (A-B, D) | [*White line*] (C)

15 Love is (B-D) | Love's (A)

16 And my heart (D) | My heart is (A-C) || frankincense; (A, D) | frankincense. (B) | frankincense: (C)

17 As the rich aloes flames, I glow, (A, D) | Ah! I flame as aloes do, (B) | Ah, I flame as aloes do, (C)

18 Yet (A-B, D) | But (C) || cannot (A-B, D) | can not (C) || know. (A-B, D) | know! (C)

19 unknowing; (A, C-D) | unknowing, (B)

20 going. (A-B, D) | going; (C)

20–21 [*White line*] (A-B, D) | [*No white line*] (C)

21 [*Flush*] Ask (A-C) | [*Inset*] Ask (D)

22 Alcoran; (A-B, D) | Alcoran: (C)

23 sweet,— (A-B, D) | sweet— (C)

24 book (A-B, D) | Book (C) || feet. (A-B, D) | feet! (C)

25 [*Flush*] Lo! (A-B) | [*Inset*] Lo! (D) | [*Flush*] Lo, (C)

26 difference (A-B, D) | differences (C) || expire. (A-B, D) | expire; (C)

27 Moslems? what (A, D) | Moslems? What (B-C)

28 Love's, (A-B, D) | love's (C) || ours. (A-B, D) | ours; (C)

31 Heaven (B-D) | heaven (A)

32 things; (A, D) | things. (B) | things: (C)

33 earth (A-B, D) | earth, (C) || underfoot, (A-B, D) | under-foot, (C)

NOTES

17. Although the fragrant wood of the Asian tree *Aquilaria agallocha* is called "aloes," it properly, if a little awkwardly, takes a singular verb, which undoubtedly accounts for Emerson's revision of this line.

SELECTED POEMS (1876)

THE HARP.

"The Harp" was originally a passage integral to the 1867 printing of "May-Day" (lines 480–603), occurring in a portion of that poem written in or after 1861. It was extracted for separate publication in *Selected Poems* in 1876 and reprinted in that form in the Riverside and Centenary editions. For the purpose of establishing the text of "The Harp," the original "May-Day" setting has been ignored and variants are not drawn from it.

An 1861 journal entry combines recollections of youth and satisfaction with melody, as produced both by the Æolian harp and by poetry:

> What came over me with delight as I sat on the ledge in the warm light of last Sunday, was the memory of young days at College, the delicious sensibility of youth, how the air rings to it! how all light is festal to it! how it at any moment extemporizes a holiday! I remember how boys riding out together on a fine day looked to me! ah there was a romance! How sufficing was mere melody! The thought, the meaning was insignificant; the whole joy was in the melody. For that I read poetry, & wrote it; and in the light of that memory I ought to understand the doctrine of the Musicians, that the words are nothing, the air is all.
>
> What a joy I found, & still can find, in the Aeolian harp! What a youth find I still in Collins's "Ode to Evening," & in Gray's "Eton College"! What delight I owed to Moore's insignificant but melodious poetry! That is the merit of Clough's "Bothie," that the joy of youth is in it. Ah the power of the spring! and, ah the voice of the bluebird! And the witchcraft of the Mount Auburn dell, in those days! (*JMN*, XV, 118)

Neighbor Julian Hawthorne recalled that Emerson had hung an enormous windharp in a tree in his front yard at Concord. It was "ten feet high," made from "sturdy limbs of pine," crossed with pine boughs. "No mortal hand could have drawn music from those strings; nor could any common breeze elicit sounds from them. . . . You would have come to the conclusion that Mr. Emerson's windharp was but a huge dummy, made to look at, with no life or soul of music in it. But wait until the great September gales began to blow! . . . Such were the moments for Mr. Emerson's windharp. It needed no careful listener to hear its voice then. The thunder could not drown it; the shriek of the gale only made it louder. Wild and vast rose the strains of the elemental music" (Quoted in Gary Scharnhorst, "Julian Hawthorne's Contributions to the Pasadena *Star-News,* 1923–1935," *Resources for American Literary Study,* XXXIII [2008]: 98).

THE HARP.

One musician is sure,
His wisdom will not fail,
He has not tasted wine impure,
Nor bent to passion frail.
Age cannot cloud his memory,   5
Nor grief untune his voice,
Ranging down the ruled scale
From tone of joy to inward wail,
Tempering the pitch of all
In his windy cave.   10
He all the fables knows,
And in their causes tells,—
Knows Nature's rarest moods,
Ever on her secret broods.
The Muse of men is coy,   15
Oft courted will not come;
In palaces and market-squares
Entreated, she is dumb;
But my minstrel knows and tells

The counsel of the gods, 20
Knows of Holy Book the spells,
Knows the law of Night and Day,
And the heart of girl and boy,
The tragic and the gay,
And what is writ on Table Round 25
Of Arthur and his peers,
What sea and land discoursing say
In sidereal years.
He renders all his lore
In numbers wild as dreams, 30
Modulating all extremes,—
What the spangled meadow saith
To the children who have faith;
Only to children children sing,
Only to youth will spring be spring. 35

    Who is the Bard thus magnified?
When did he sing? and where abide?

    Chief of song where poets feast
Is the wind-harp which thou seest
In the casement at my side. 40

    Æolian harp,
How strangely wise thy strain!
Gay for youth, gay for youth,
(Sweet is art, but sweeter truth,)
In the hall at summer eve 45
Fate and Beauty skilled to weave.
From the eager opening strings
Rung loud and bold the song.
Who but loved the wind-harp's note?
How should not the poet doat 50
On its mystic tongue,
With its primeval memory,
Reporting what old minstrels told

Of Merlin locked the harp within,—
Merlin paying the pain of sin,   55
Pent in a dungeon made of air,—
And some attain his voice to hear,
Words of pain and cries of fear,
But pillowed all on melody,
As fits the griefs of bards to be.   60
And what if that all-echoing shell,
Which thus the buried Past can tell,
Should rive the Future, and reveal
What his dread folds would fain conceal?
It shares the secret of the earth,   65
And of the kinds that owe her birth.
Speaks not of self that mystic tone,
But of the Overgods alone:
It trembles to the cosmic breath,—
As it heareth, so it saith;   70
Obeying meek the primal Cause,
It is the tongue of mundane laws.
And this, at least, I dare affirm,
Since genius too has bound and term,
There is no bard in all the choir,   75
Not Homer's self, the poet sire,
Wise Milton's odes of pensive pleasure,
Or Shakspeare, whom no mind can measure,
Nor Collins' verse of tender pain,
Nor Byron's clarion of disdain,   80
Scott, the delight of generous boys,
Or Wordsworth, Pan's recording voice,—
Not one of all can put in verse,
Or to this presence could rehearse
The sights and voices ravishing   85
The boy knew on the hills in spring,
When pacing through the oaks he heard
Sharp queries of the sentry-bird,
The heavy grouse's sudden whir,

The rattle of the kingfisher;   90
Saw bonfires of the harlot flies
In the lowland, when day dies;
Or marked, benighted and forlorn,
The first far signal-fire of morn.
These syllables that Nature spoke,   95
And the thoughts that in him woke,
Can adequately utter none
Save to his ear the wind-harp lone.
Therein I hear the Parcæ reel
The threads of man at their humming wheel,   100
The threads of life, and power, and pain,
So sweet and mournful falls the strain.
And best can teach its Delphian chord
How Nature to the soul is moored,
If once again that silent string,   105
As erst it wont, would thrill and ring.

    Not long ago, at eventide,
It seemed, so listening, at my side
A window rose, and, to say sooth,
I looked forth on the fields of youth: 110
I saw fair boys bestriding steeds,
I knew their forms in fancy weeds,
Long, long concealed by sundering fates,
Mates of my youth,—yet not my mates,
Stronger and bolder far than I,   115
With grace, with genius, well attired,
And then as now from far admired,
Followed with love
They knew not of,
With passion cold and shy.   120
O joy, for what recoveries rare!
Renewed, I breathe Elysian air,
See youth's glad mates in earliest bloom,—
Break not my dream, obtrusive tomb!

Or teach thou, Spring! the grand recoil   125
Of life resurgent from the soil
Wherein was dropped the mortal spoil.

TEXTS

(A) *Selected Poems* (Boston, 1876), 120–124; (B) *Poems* [Riverside] (Boston, 1884), 203–207; (B²) *Poems* [Centenary] (Boston, 1904), 237–241.

Pre-copy-text forms: See "May-Day."

VARIANTS

17   market-squares (A) | market squares (B)

26   peers, (A) | peers; (B)

39   Is (B) | In (A)

50   doat (B) | dote (A) [*"doat" is the less common variant spelling, but this is the form that occurs in the MS draft: see* PN, *577, and p. 335 above, variant for line 529*]

57   hear, (B) | hear,— (A)

84   rehearse (B) | rehearse, (A)

99–102 [*These lines were composed after 1867 as a revision of the* May-Day *text in* (CC6). *Nothing can be recovered from the erased draft at p. 33, but the version that Emerson copied at the bottom of p. 34 (intended for insertion after l. 577) reads:* <For in <thy> ↑its↓ voice at summer eve> / Therein I <over>hear the Parcae reel / The threads of man at their humming wheel, / The threads of life, and power, and pain, / So sweet and mournful falls the strain.]

100   humming wheel, (B) | humming-wheel, (A)

101   life, (A) | life (B) || power, (A) | power (B)

107   ago, (A) | ago (B)

NOTES

40.   A small Æolian harp hung in Emerson's study window (*W,* IX, 483).

47.   "Waldo asks if the strings of the harp open when he touches them?" (*JMN,* VII, 520; October 1840).

55–56. See Sir Thomas Malory, *The Byrth, Lyf, and Actes of King Arthur . . . and . . . Le Morte Darthur,* introduction and notes by Robert Southey, 2 vols. (London, 1817), I, xlvi-xlviii. Emerson borrowed these volumes from the Boston Athenaeum in 1860 (Kenneth Walter Cameron, *Ralph Waldo Emerson's Reading* [Raleigh, 1941], 32, 89). The story of Merlin's imprisonment is also given in "Poetry and Imagination" (*CW*, VIII, 34–35). The source is further discussed by B. J. Whiting in "Emerson and Merlin's 'Dungeon Made of Air,'" *PMLA*, LXIV (June 1949): 598–599.

81.   "Scott, crowned bard of generous boys," occurs as a detached line in journal ML, used between 1865 and 1869 (*TN*, III, 328).

APRIL.

Emerson was always attuned to the arrival of the temperate south-winds that marked the end of the New England winter. With the retreat of the snows and the greening of the Concord and Acton woods, Emerson each year celebrated returning life by recourse to versifying. The occasion for the writing of "April" was in fact an unseasonable thaw that occurred in February 1840, of which he wrote to Margaret Fuller:

> These spring winds are magical in their operation on our attuned frames. These are the days of passion when the air is full of cupids & devils for eyes that are still young; and every pool of water & every dry leaf & refuse straw seems to flatter, provoke, mock, or pique us. I who am not young have not yet forgot the enchantment, & still occasionally see dead leaves & wizards that peep & mutter. Let us surrender ourselves for fifteen minutes to the slightest of these nameless influences—these nymphs or imps of wood & flood of pasture & roadside, and we shall quickly find out what an ignorant pretending old Dummy is Literature who has quite omitted all that we care to know—all that we have not said ourselves. (21 February 1840; *L*, II, 255)

Emerson copied this passage—in all likelihood some years later —in his notebook S Salvage (*TN*, III, 173) under the heading "Spring." In the earliest draft of the poem, given among the "Additional Manuscripts" in *PN*, 620–621, there is an unused first line ("O southwinds have long memories") taken from "South Wind" (q.v.), a poem written on 20 September 1846. A collection of cross-references to passages on Spring, including one to the letter to Fuller at S Salvage 270, are noted in poetry notebook NP in the midst of drafts of "April": these cross-references (*PN*, 484) appear to have been copied from journal TU (*JMN*, XI, 114) where they were set down in 1849. The simplest explanation of these complexities is, therefore, that "April" was written after 1849.

APRIL.

The April winds are magical
And thrill our tuneful frames;
The garden walks are passional
To bachelors and dames.
The hedge is gemmed with diamonds,   5
The air with Cupids full,
The clews of fairy Rosamonds
Guide lovers to the pool.
Each dimple in the water,
Each leaf that shades the rock   10
Can cozen, pique, and flatter,
Can parley and provoke.
Goodfellow, Puck, and goblins
Know more than any book;
Down with your doleful problems,   15
And court the sunny brook.
The south-winds are quick-witted,
The schools are sad and slow,
The masters quite omitted
The lore we care to know.   20

April

TEXTS

(A) *Selected Poems* (Boston, 1876), 125; (B) *Poems* [Riverside] (Boston, 1884), 219; (B²) *Poems* [Centenary] (Boston, 1904), 255.

Pre-copy-text forms: The first draft, on a loose Houghton MS (*PN*, 620–621), is followed by three drafts in poetry notebook NP, then by fair copies in Rhymer (with the title "Spring Winds") and ETE (with the title "April"). See the discussion at *PN*, 733–734. The 1876 first printing closely follows the ETE copy, which is carefully punctuated.

VARIANTS

1   magical (B) | magical, (A)
3   garden walks (B) | garden-walks (A)
7   clews of fairy Rosamonds (A) | cobweb clues of Rosamond (B) [*Edward's text at* (B) *reverts to an early draft* (PN, *480*) *that Emerson subsequently revised* (PN, *485*).]

10   rock (B) | rock, (A)
11   pique, (A) | pique (B)
13   Puck, (A) | Puck (B) || goblins (A) | goblins, (B)
14   book; (A) | book. (B)

NOTES

7.   Rosamond de Clifford (c. 1140–1176), mistress to King Henry II of England, was the subject of numerous folkloric tales in prose and verse. She was said to have been installed by the king in a bower at the center of a complex labyrinth at the palace of Woodstock, near Oxford, a maze "so cunninglye contriv'd / With turnings round about, / That none but with a clue of thread, / Could enter in or out" (Thomas Delone, "Fair Rosamond" in *Percy's Reliques of Ancient English Poetry* [1765; rpt. London: J. M. Dent, (1912)], II, 22). According to certain traditions it was by such a "clue" that the queen, Eleanor of Aquitaine, discovered and confronted Rosamond—with results fatal to the younger woman.

9.   "Nature begins with the dimple in the whirlpool, the eye of the leaf, & runs up to man" (*PN*, 110). "What is the oldest thing? a dimple or whirlpool in water. That is Genesis, Exodus, & all" (*JMN*, X, 4).

13. Puck, or Robin Goodfellow, is a prankster sprite in English folklore who makes an appearance in Shakespeare's *Midsummer Night's Dream,* where he is ser-

vant to Oberon, king of the fairies. He is also the subject of "The Merry Pranks of Robin Goodfellow," a poem attributed, probably inaccurately, to Ben Jonson in *Percy's Reliques*, II, 313–317.

WEALTH.

"Wealth" appears as the epigraph to the essay of the same title in *The Conduct of Life* (1860), but it was not included in the group of such poems (called "Elements") gathered in *May-Day* (1867). It was first published separately from the essay in *Selected Poems* (1876). As an epigraph, it of course deals with themes expressed at large in Emerson's chapter on "Wealth," but because it also develops themes from the essay immediately preceding, entitled "Power," it functions as a point of connection and thematic transition. Emerson's views about the geologic evolution of the earth as a process subserving human intelligence—of providing a home for mind in matter—goes back at least as far as 1833 and his early lectures on natural history (*EL*, I, 1–83).

WEALTH.

Who shall tell what did befall,
Far away in time, when once,
Over the lifeless ball,
Hung idle stars and suns?
What god the element obeyed?   5
Wings of what wind the lichen bore,
Wafting the puny seeds of power,

Which, lodged in rock, the rock abrade?
And well the primal pioneer
Knew the strong task to it assigned,   10
Patient through Heaven's enormous year
To build in matter home for mind.
From air the creeping centuries drew
The matted thicket low and wide,
This must the leaves of ages strew   15
The granite slab to clothe and hide,
Ere wheat can wave its golden pride.
What smiths, and in what furnace, rolled
(In dizzy æons dim and mute
The reeling brain can ill compute)   20
Copper and iron, lead and gold?
What oldest star the fame can save
Of races perishing to pave
The planet with a floor of lime?
Dust is their pyramid and mole: 25
Who saw what ferns and palms were pressed
Under the tumbling mountain's breast,
In the safe herbal of the coal?
But when the quarried means were piled,
All is waste and worthless, till   30
Arrives the wise selecting will,
And, out of slime and chaos, Wit
Draws the threads of fair and fit.
Then temples rose, and towns, and marts,
The shop of toil, the hall of arts;   35
Then flew the sail across the seas
To feed the North from tropic trees;
The storm-wind wove, the torrent span,
Where they were bid the rivers ran;
New slaves fulfilled the poet's dream,   40
Galvanic wire, strong-shouldered steam.
The docks were built, and crops were stored,
And ingots added to the hoard.

But, though light-headed man forget,
Remembering Matter pays her debt: 45
Still, through her motes and masses, draw
Electric thrills and ties of Law,
Which bind the strengths of Nature wild
To the conscience of a child.

TEXTS

(A) Princeton MS, printer's copy for B; (B) *Conduct of Life* (Boston, 1860), 71–72; (C) *Selected Poems* (Boston, 1876), 170–171; (D) *The Conduct of Life* [Centenary] (Boston, 1904), 83–84; (E) *Poems* [Centenary] (Boston, 1904), 285–286. The poem was omitted from *May-Day* (Boston, 1867) and *Poems* [Riverside] (Boston, 1884), though it was included as the motto to the essay "Wealth" in later printings of *Conduct of Life*. Note that (A), which is 1860 printer's copy for both the motto and the essay, is described fully in *CW*, VI, 357–359.

Pre-copy-text forms: The several drafts in poetry notebook NP all begin with line 13 (see *PN*, 961–962). A version of lines 30–33 together with a first draft of line 8 in journal CL (*JMN*, XIV, 325), dates to 1859, suggesting that the whole poem was probably written shortly before copy for *The Conduct of Life* went to press.

VARIANTS

10	assigned, (C-E) I assigned (A-B)		41	wire, (B-E) I wires, (A)
11	through (B-E) I thro' (A)		43	hoard. (B-E) I hoard; (A)
34	Then temples rose, and towns, and marts, (B-E) I Then rose fair temples, town, & marts, (A)		44	But, (A-D) I But (E)
			45	debt: (B-E) I debt. (A)
39	bid (A-D) I bid, (E)		47	Law, (A-D) I law, (E)
40	slaves (B-E) I <might> ↑ slaves ↓ (A)			

NOTES

9–10. In *CW*, VI, 213, Joseph Slater explains that the assignment of this task to the lichen implies that "the original military meanings of 'pioneer' (sapper, miner, engineer) were still strong."

11.   Slater (ibid.) suspects an allusion here to *Paradise Lost*, V, 582–586, and, in both places, to the astronomical concept of the Platonic Year, which lasted 36,000 solar years.

23–25.   Limestone, the most widely used stone for architectural purposes (as in the block construction of the Egyptian pyramids or carved as in later mausoleums or "moles"), is a sedimentary rock, composed of calcite (calcium carbonate) originally belonging to the skeletal structure of marine life, including corals, and deposited on the sea bed over millions of years.

38–39.   Reference is to the harnessing of water power for the textile mills crucial to New England's industrial economy ("span" is an old-fashioned past tense for "spin").

40–41.   The use of electric wires, as in the recently laid Atlantic cable, facilitated commerce (especially the cotton trade) with England. Emerson insists that the North created wealth by the enlightened use of such "slaves" as electricity and steam, in implicit contrast to the use of the labor of human slaves at the South.

MAIDEN SPEECH OF THE ÆOLIAN HARP.

The tradition in the Emerson household, as in many New England households, was to exchange gifts on New Year's Day, though in later years the children and grandchildren were increasingly indulged on Christmas as well. The New Year's presents were often accompanied by verses, more or less humorous, so that all the members of the family became poets at least once a year (*ETE*, I, 458). A number of Emerson's own efforts of this sort survive in the archive at Harvard's Houghton Library, yet of these only one, the "Maiden Speech of the Æolian Harp," seemed to its author worthy of publication. When, on 2 January 1868 Emerson returned from a month-long lecture tour of the West, he arrived at the Milton, Massachusetts, home of his daughter Edith and her husband, Will Forbes, to find that "they had postponed New Year's one day for my sake" (*L*, VI, 3). The manuscript of the poem given to the Forbeses with the Æoleian harp has not been located, but a Photostat of it is preserved among the Emerson papers. It closely follows the last of the drafts in poetry notebook NP, which Emerson must have taken with him on his lecture tour.

MAIDEN SPEECH OF THE ÆOLIAN HARP.

Soft and softlier hold me, friends!
Thanks if your genial care
Unbind and give me to the air.
Keep your lips or finger-tips
For flute or spinnet's dancing chips;   5
I await a tenderer touch,
I ask more or not so much:
Give me to the atmosphere,—
Where is the wind, my brother,—where?
Lift the sash, lay me within,   10
Lend me your ears, and I begin.
For gentle harp to gentle hearts
The secret of the world imparts;
And not to-day and not to-morrow
Can drain its wealth of hope and sorrow;   15
But day by day, to loving ear
Unlocks new sense and loftier cheer.
I've come to live with you, sweet friends,
This home my minstrel journeying ends.
Many and subtle are my lays,   20
The latest better than the first,
For I can mend the happiest days
And charm the anguish of the worst.

TEXTS

(A) Photostat of MS; bMS Am 1280.235 (167), Ralph Waldo Emerson Memorial Association deposit, Houghton Library, Harvard University; (B) *Selected Poems* (Boston, 1876), 176; (C) *Poems* [Riverside] (Boston, 1884), 220; (C²) *Poems* [Centenary] (Boston, 1904), 256.

Pre-copy-text forms: See *PN*, 851.

VARIANTS

3   Unbind (B-C) | Unbinds (A) || give (B-C) | gives (A)
5   spinnet's (A-B) | spinet's (C)
9   wind, (C) | Wind (A) | wind (B)
11   Lend me your (B-C) | Lend your (A)
14   to-day (B-C) | to-day, (A)

18   [*Flush*] I've (B-C) | [*Inset*] I've (A)
19   home (B-C) | house (A) || minstrel journeying (B) | minstrel-journeying (A) | minstrel-journeyings (C)
22   days (C) | days, (A-B)

CUPIDO.

Edward Emerson's conjecture that this poem was written in 1843 (*W*, IX, 492) is evidently based on the appearance of an early draft, probably the first, in journal Z[A] (*JMN*, VIII, 345–346), where the poem is written over an erased pencil draft of "Una." Both "Una" and journal Z[A] date to 1843, while the page on which the draft is written is dated "March." Under the title "Cupido" or "Eros" Emerson wrote the poem out no fewer than eight times in various poetry notebooks over a period of more than twenty years. At one time Emerson considered making "Cupido" an introduction to "The Initial Love" (q.v.). In the draft contents for *Selected Poems* in ETE, the title is still given as "Eros" (see *PN,* 583).

CUPIDO.

The solid, solid universe
Is pervious to Love;
With bandaged eyes he never errs,
Around, below, above.
His blinding light   5
He flingeth white
On God's and Satan's brood,
And reconciles
By mystic wiles
The evil and the good.   10

TEXTS

(A) *Selected Poems* (Boston, 1876), 180; (A²) *Poems* [Riverside] (Boston, 1884), 221; (A³) *Poems* [Centenary] (Boston, 1904), 257.

Pre-copy-text forms: See *PN,* 766–767.

THE NUN'S ASPIRATION.

In "The Nun's Aspiration" Emerson versified several distinct and unrelated passages from the notebooks (or "Almanacks") of his Aunt Mary Moody Emerson. She had given these volumes to her nephew in 1859, in the expectation of her death—in fact she died in 1863 at the age of 89—and in the knowledge that over the years no member of the family had responded to her letters and diaries with such sympathetic appreciation as had Ralph Waldo, the son of her older brother William. In the course of transcribing excerpts from these volumes Emerson was struck, as he always had been, by the forceful and imaginative form his aunt's prose took, and, in the instance of this poem, gently prodded her language into verse.

The source for lines 1–6 occurs on p. 2 of Emerson's second book of transcripts, MME 2: "The yesterday does never smile, as I would; yet, in the name of the shepherd of mankind, I defy tomorrow. God himself cannot withdraw himself. Health feeble, alone, most alone, but I defy tomorrow." On pp. 13–14 of the same notebook is the source for lines 7–10: "And the simple principle which made me say in youth & laborious poverty, that, should He make me a blot on the fair face of his creation, I should rejoice in His will, has never been equaled [Emerson's note: "She means, that was the highwater mark in her history"],—though it returns in the long life of destitution, like an Angel." Emerson's 10-line versification of these passages was completed in 1859 (see *PN,* 876–877, for the evidence as to dating).

Ten years later Emerson versified other passages from the fourth MME notebook, which he was then reviewing in preparation for a talk he was to give before the New England Women's Club on his aunt's life. Lines 11–28 are based on passages from MME 4, pp. 110–112 and 113, originally written by Aunt Mary in 1832 and 1819 respectively:

Oh these mystic scenes of Autumn, when her solemn stole encircles us, it seems but a moment when the veil will be raised. Already the sublime dirge of Nature's funeral is hymned by the blasts of the mountains, & the sable pageantry of clouds is mourning the fallen beauty of the summer. How well do the emblems of sorrow in Nature correspond to that element of man's constitution. . . .These waves, these leaves tell their own tale of their Maker—if not, I feel unworthy to give them voice. No human language is so beautiful as their murmurs. But of these indefinable emotions so dear—too dear perhaps—of reasonings too nothing,—if the divine power of conscience is disregarded. On its altar hallowed by God's own erection, let every pleasure be sacrificed. Time enough for other pleasure, when this is secured in the immediate fruition of virtue.

A dull walk to see Mrs Thacher x x x, &, in the darker recollections of returning, what pleasure Byron gave me. And when *'my dust is as it should be,'* when the long sunken turf is forgotten amid splendid tombs, then, o then, where the recollections of my pigmy life will be? How peculiar the power to exert on the future,—to look at the present through the vista of ages.

The final lines of the poem have their source in a passage on pp. 41–42 of MME 4:

Shake not thy bald head at me, I defy thee to go too fast. Am I furry in sight,—fettered by age,—mired by climate—I wander beyond thee. I pass with the comet into space which mocks thy gnomons— which will exist by travellers who never heard thy earthly fugitive name. The frivolous now deny thee, and thy native home old space, any being. But I respect both—with them for modes of account or existence I shall unravel their labyrinths and explore their birth places. Neither shall I spurn them, I think, when able to look through all their boasted possessions—and remembering how drear the part I hold in the one—how tedious, how wasting the other.

In 1866, Emerson described the effect of reading Aunt Mary's writings: "They keep for me the old attraction; though, when I sometimes have tried passages on a stranger, I find something of fairy gold;—they need too much commentary, & are not as incisive as on me. They make the best example I have known of the power of the religion of the Puritans in full energy, until fifty years ago, in New England. The central theme of these endless diaries, is, her relation to the Divine Being; the absolute submission of her will, with the sole proviso, that she may know it is the direct agency of God, (& not of cold laws of contingency &c) which bereaves & humiliates her. But the religion of the diary, as of the class it represented, is biographical; it is the culture, the poetry, the mythology, in which they personally believed themselves dignified, inspired, judged, & dealt with, in the present & in the future. And certainly gives to life an earnestness, & to nature a sentiment, which lacking, our later generation appears frivolous" (*JMN*, XVI, 15–16). Emerson's intellectual relationship to his sibylline aunt, and especially, from earliest childhood, to her "eloquent theology" (*JMN*, XIV, 273), was a long and complex provocation: it is best described by Phyllis Cole in *Mary Moody Emerson and the Origins of Transcendentalism: A Family History* (New York, 1998).

THE NUN'S ASPIRATION.

The yesterday doth never smile,
Today goes drudging through the while,
Yet in the name of Godhead, I
The morrow front, and can defy;
Though I am weak, yet God, when prayed, 5
Cannot withhold his conquering aid.
Ah me! it was my childhood's thought,
If He should make my web a blot
On life's fair picture of delight,
My heart's content would find it right. 10
But O, these waves and leaves,—
When haply stoic Nature grieves,—
No human speech so beautiful
As their murmurs mine to lull.
On this altar God hath built 15
I lay my vanity and guilt;
Nor me can Hope or Passion urge
Hearing as now the lofty dirge
Which blasts of Northern mountains hymn,
Nature's funeral, high and dim,— 20
Sable pageantry of clouds,
Mourning summer laid in shrouds.
Many a day shall dawn and die,

Many an angel wander by,
And passing, light my sunken turf   25
Moist perhaps by ocean surf,
Forgotten amid splendid tombs,
Yet wreathed and hid by summer blooms.
On earth I dream;—I die to be:
Time! shake not thy bald head at me.   30
I challenge thee to hurry past,
Or for my turn to fly too fast.
Think me not numbed or halt with age,
Or cares that earth to earth engage,
Caught with love's cord of twisted beams,   35
Or mired by climate's gross extremes.
I tire of shams, I rush to Be,
I pass with yonder comet free,—
Pass with the comet into space
Which mocks thy æons to embrace;   40
Æons which tardily unfold
Realm beyond realm,—extent untold;
No early morn, no evening late,—
Realms self-upheld, disdaining Fate,
Whose shining sons, too great for fame,   45
Never heard thy weary name;
Nor lives the tragic bard to say
How drear the part I held in one,
How lame the other limped away.

TEXTS

(A) Lehigh University MS, possibly printer's copy for B; (B) *Selected Poems* (Boston, 1876), 184–185; (C) *Poems* [Riverside] (Boston, 1884), 217–218; (C²) *Poems* [Centenary] (Boston, 1904), 253–254.

Pre-copy-text forms: The various sources in Mary Moody Emerson's Almanacks are separately versified at numerous locations in Emerson's poetry notebooks and joined together only late in the compositional process. See the discussions in *PN*, 876–877, and Strauch, diss., 102–111. Several different titles are associated with the notebook drafts, including "The Nun's Prayer" and "Amita" (Latin for "aunt"); Emerson used the latter title for the sketch of her life that he gave as a talk before the New England Women's Club on March 1, 1869 (see *W,* X, 399–433, where the lecture was retitled "Mary Moody Emerson").

VARIANTS

2   Today (A) | To-day (B) | The day (C)

3   Yet (A-B) | Yet, (C)

11   O, (B-C) | Oh! (A)

12   haply (A) | happy (B-C) || grieves,— (A-B) | grieves, (C)

20   funeral, (A-B) | funeral (C)

23   [*Flush*] Many (B-C) | [*Inset*] Many (A)

26   ocean (B-C) | Ocean (A)

30   Time! (A-B) | Time, (C)

31   past, (A-B) | past (C)

37   Be, (A-B) | be: (C) [*It seems likely that Edward revised to emphasize the parallel to line 29.*]

45   shining (B-C) | shin<en>ing (A)

HYMN

SUNG AT THE SECOND CHURCH, AT THE ORDINATION OF REV. CHANDLER ROBBINS.

Emerson's successor as pastor of the Second Church of Boston was Chandler Robbins (1810–1882), at the time of his appointment a recent graduate of Harvard Divinity School and some years earlier a student of Emerson's brother Edward at his school in Roxbury (Charles C. Smith, *Memoir of the Rev. Chandler Robbins, D. D.* [Cambridge, 1884], 3). It is probable that Emerson was asked for a contribution to the ordination proceedings when, following his return from Europe, he preached from his old Hanover Street pulpit on 27 October 1833. He sent the verses by mail on

18 November 1833, addressed to Horace Scudder of Boston, evidently a lay member of the church with responsibilities for planning the event (*L*, I, 399). At the time Emerson was in New Bedford, supplying the church vacated by the Rev. Orville Dewey and entertaining the idea of permanent employment there. His duties at New Bedford kept him from attending Robbins' ordination on 4 December, an event described in the *Christian Examiner* for 7 December. The hymn, with original music composed by George Kingsley (1811–1884), was sung on the occasion from the broadside printing; its text was also included in the published form of the ordination sermon by Henry Ware, Jr., Emerson's erstwhile senior pastor. The hymn testifies to the affection that still subsisted between Emerson and his people at the Second Church.

In the spring of 1846 Samuel Longfellow, brother of the poet, asked Emerson for a copy of the poem for inclusion in a hymnal he was compiling together with his friend the Orientalist and Transcendentalist Samuel Johnson. Emerson obliged on 13 May, pointing out that "In transcribing it, I have mended it, I hope, a little; yet it is easy to see that a little labour would make it much better. But I am constrained today to let it go as it is, or not at all; and you shall print it or leave it, as you will" (*L*, VIII, 73). The 1846 Longfellow-Johnson printing omits the final stanza, restored, however, in the second edition in 1848. Emerson did not collect the hymn until *Selected Poems* (1876), at which time the text underwent final revisions. A signed, undated holograph fair copy of the text in this last version is at the Princeton University Library; it differs from the *Selected Poems* text only in having the single-word title, "Hymn."

HYMN

SUNG AT THE SECOND CHURCH, BOSTON, AT THE ORDINATION OF REV. CHANDLER ROBBINS.

We love the venerable house
  Our fathers built to God;
In heaven are kept their grateful vows,
  Their dust endears the sod.

Hymn

Here holy thoughts a light have shed   5
    From many a radiant face,
And prayers of tender hope have spread
    A perfume through the place.

And anxious hearts have pondered here
    The mystery of life,   10
And prayed the eternal Spirit to clear
    Their doubts, and aid their strife.

From humble tenements around
    Came up the pensive train,
And in the church a blessing found   15
    Which filled their homes again;

For faith and peace and mighty love
    That from the Godhead flow
Showed them the life of heaven above
    Springs from the life below.   20

They live with God, their homes are dust,
    But here the children pray,
And in this fleeting lifetime trust
    To find the narrow way.

On him who by the altar stands,   25
    On him the Spirit fall;
Speak through his lips thy pure commands,
    Thou Heart that lovest all!

TEXTS

(A) MS Am 1280.226 (2571), Ralph Waldo Emerson Memorial Association deposit, Houghton Library, Harvard University, probable printer's copy for B; (B) *Order of Services at the Ordination of Mr Chandler Robbins, as Pastor of the Second Church and Society in Boston* [Broadside] ([Boston]: I. R. Butts, [1833]); (B²) Henry Ware, Jr., *A Sermon Delivered at the Ordination of Rev. Chandler Robbins . . .* (Boston, 1833), 32; (C) MS LONG, 33705, Box 7, folder 7, courtesy National

Selected Poems (1876)

Park Service, Longfellow Historical Site, Cambridge, Mass., printer's copy for D, reproduced photographically by Kenneth Walter Cameron in "A Garland of Emerson Letters," *Emerson Society Quarterly*, no. 10 (1st Quarter 1958): 35–36; (D) *A Book of Hymns for Public and Private Devotion* [compiled by Samuel Longfellow and Samuel Johnson] (Cambridge: Metcalf, 1846), No. 423; (E) *A Book of Hymns . . .* "Second Edition" (Boston: William D. Ticknor, 1848), No. 423; (F) *Selected Poems* (Boston, 1876), 200–201; (F²) *Poems* [Riverside] (Boston, 1884), 192–193; (F³) *Poems* [Centenary] (Boston, 1904), 223–224. The text of (C) published in *L,* VIII, 74–75, contains several errors of transcription.

Format: (C) lacks the alternate indentation.

Pre-copy-text forms: Two drafts occur in Blotting Book IV (*JMN*, III, 370–372 and 372–375) and a third in Journal Q (*JMN*, IV, 97–98). The first draft differs so considerably from the second and third that Edward Emerson reproduced it separately in *W,* IX, 393–394, dating it June 1831 and calling it "probably the first trial" of the ordination hymn. He, however, took the date from the front cover verso of Blotting Book III (see *JMN*, III, 264), the notebook from which he erroneously supposed he had transcribed the text. This was the origin as well of Edward's otherwise unaccountable belief that the Robbins ordination had occurred in 1831 (see *W,* IX, 478).

VARIANTS

Title: HYMN SUNG AT THE SECOND CHURCH, BOSTON, AT THE ORDINATION OF REV. CHANDLER ROBBINS. (F; F³ omits "BOSTON,") | [*Untitled*] (A, C) | HYMN, BY REV. R. W. EMERSON. (B; B² omits "HYMN,") | THE HOUSE OUR FATHERS BUILT TO GOD (D-E)

2 God; (C-E) | God:— (A-B, F)

3 kept (C-F) | heard (A-B)

4 dust endears (C-F) | bones are in (A-B)

7 tender hope have spread (D-E) | humble virtue made (A-B, F) | <humble virtue made> ↑tender hope have spread↓ (C)

8 A perfume through (D-E) | The perfume of (A-B, F) | <The> ↑A↓ perfume <of> ↑through↓ (C)

11 eternal Spirit to (A, C) | eternal spirit (B) | Eternal Spirit (D-E) | eternal Light to (F)

12 doubts, (A-C, F) | doubts (D-E)

13 around (A, C-F) | around, (B)

15 church (A-B, D-F) | Church (C) || found (A-C, F) | found, (D-E)

16 Which (C-E) | That (A-B, F) || again; (A-B, F) | again, (C) | again. (D-E)

17 faith (A-C, F) | faith, (D-E) || peace (A-C, F) | peace, (D-E) || love (A-C, F) | love, (D-E)

18 That (A-B, D-F) | <W>That (C) || flow (C) | flow, (A-B, D-F)

19 Showed (A, C-F) | Show'd (B) || heaven (A-E) | Heaven (F)

21 God, (C-E) | God; (A-B, F) || dust, (C-E) | dust; (A-B, F)

22   But (A-E) | Yet (F) || the (A-C) | their (D-F)

23   And (A-B, F) | And, (C-E) || this (D-F) | their (A-B) | our (C) || lifetime (F) | life-time (A-B) | lifetime, (C-E) [*The 1846 emendation of MS* "our" *to* "this" *in the printed edition was probably at the instance of Samuel Longfellow, since it is unlikely that Emerson read proofs; nevertheless it is a decided improvement and was retained in* Selected Poems.]

25–28   [*Lines not present*] (D)

25   him (A, C, E-F) | HIM (B)

26   him the Spirit fall; (C) | him, thy spirit send, (A) || him, thy spirit send; (B) | him Thy blessing fall! (E) | him thy blessing fall, (F)

27   thy (A-C, F) | Thy (E)

28   Thou Heart that lovest all! (C) | Our Father and our Friend! (A) | Our Father and our friend. (B) | Thou Heart, that lovest all! (E) | Thou heart that lovest all. (F)

BOSTON.

The complicated manuscript history of this poem (see *PN*, 745–747) testifies to the difficulty Emerson had in arriving at a settled sense of its purpose. Edward Emerson was undoubtedly right in suggesting that the initial aim was simply celebratory (*W*, IX, 471–472): "I have a kind of promise," his father had declared in his journal in 1842, "to write one of these days a verse or two to the praise of my native city which in common days we often rail at, yet which has great merits to us ward[s]. That, too, like every city, has certain virtues, as a museum of the arts. The parlors of private collectors; the Athenaeum Gallery; & the College; become the city of the City. Then a city has this praise, that as the bell or band of music is heard outside beyond the din of carts, so the beautiful in architecture or in political & social institutions endures: all else comes to nought. So that the antiquities & permanent things in each city are good & fine" (*JMN*, VIII, 264–265). A few years later, he said again, "Boston deserves eulogy. It is the only city in which we can live. Those whom I love are its children" (*JMN,* VIII, 477).

But when, in the 1850s, he came to write the promised poem, Boston's recreancy on the subject of chattel slavery proved an altogether too stark flouting of the city's history of support for freedom. Beginning in 1851 with the passage of the Fugitive Slave Law, and the approval of it by Boston's old-line Whig elite, Emerson could only express amazement that heredity had somehow faltered: "It is the want perhaps of a stern & high religious training, like the iron Calvinism which steeled their fathers seventy five years ago. But though I find the names of old patriots still resident in Boston, it is only the present venerable Mr [Josiah] Quincy who has renewed the hereditary honour of his name by scenting tyranny in the gale. The others are all lapped in after[-]dinner dreams and are obsequious to Mr Webster as he is to the gentlemen of Richmond & Charleston" (*JMN,* XI, 353). Thus several stanzas discordantly interrupt the eulogy in an important early version titled "Trimountain" found in poetry notebook EL (*PN,* 408–411):

> O pity that I pause,—
> The song disdaining shuns
> To name the noble sires, because
> Of the unworthy sons. [etc.]

The five stanzas that introduced these chilling jeremiad notes in the 1859 draft were published by Edward in the annotations to "Boston" in both the Riverside and Centenary editions. Emerson had apparently tried, without success, to complete the poem as a forthright anti-slavery piece. Ellen Emerson, writing to her sister Edith, mentioned that their father had recited the poem's opening verses during a Sunday walk on 22 January 1859, implying that she had not heard the lines before. "While we walked along Father told us parts of a song he had tried to make for the Anti-Slavery Festival because he can't go to it. 'The rocky hill with summits 3 Looked Eastward from the Farms, And twice a day the flowing sea Took Boston in its arms.' Isn't that lovely? But I am afraid he will not finish it" (Gregg, I, 165; cf. Edward's recollection of this incident, *W,* IX, 472). Indeed, Emerson did not finish the poem. This "Trimountain" version proved hopelessly at cross purposes with itself and was abandoned, not to be taken up again until the Civil War had removed the slavery issue.

The occasion for resuming the work was an appeal from Annie Adams Fields, wife of Emerson's publisher James T. Fields. She, distantly related to the Revolutionary heroes John and Samuel Adams, wished to organize a centennial celebration of the Boston Tea Party, and so invited Emerson, together with others, to speak at Faneuil Hall on 16 December 1873. On 8 December, Emerson, daunted, tried to excuse himself: "my nerves shook at this invitation from you to this haughty anniversary" (*L,* X, 126). But he reversed his decision just two days before the celebration, telling Mrs. Fields that he had "read a page yesterday about the old times & thought of an old verse which made me a little penitent" (*L,* VI, 253). It would seem, then, that the stanzas concerning the Tea Party were written within a few days of the poem's public delivery.

The day after the event William Dean Howells, editor of the *Atlantic Monthly,* solicited the poem for publication. It was not until 5 January 1874, however, that Emerson complied, suggesting that "when you send me a proof, I can add a few couplets by way of refrains, or repeat some of those we have" (*L,* VI, 254). The delay in offering the manuscript, as Howells explained, caused him to miss the February number; Emerson a little huffily demanded the manuscript be returned: "it would be ridiculous," he told Howells, "to print so strictly occasional lines after two months, instead of one" (*L,* VI, 255). This contretemps probably reflected Emerson's dissatisfaction with the poem, with the imperfection of the system of "refrains," and with the residual incoherence of the work arising from its long and variously pointed evolution. "Boston" was eventually printed in the *Atlantic* two years later, in the February issue of 1876. It was the last poem Emerson published in that magazine.

As the most recently finished poem it also occupied last place in the 1876 *Selected Poems.* During the few months between its first magazine appearance and its collection in a book, Emerson received some helpful commentary from the public. Ellen mentions in March that her father "has had a letter on the Boston Ode from Mr [C. H. S.] Williams, our Concord minister, which he values very much, containing criticism & suggestions. He accepts two" (*ETE*, II, 198). During the compilation of *Selected Poems*, Emerson was getting accustomed to being advised, so possibly it was the Rev. Mr. Williams, pastor at the Trinitarian Church in Concord from 1868 to 1870, who suggested the most notable revision then undertaken, the reversing of the fifth and sixth stanzas.

BOSTON.

Sicut patribus, sit Deus nobis.

The rocky nook with hill-tops three
   Looked eastward from the farms,
And twice each day the flowing sea
   Took Boston in its arms;
     The men of yore were stout and poor,   5
     And sailed for bread to every shore.

And where they went on trade intent
   They did what freemen can,
Their dauntless ways did all men praise,
   The merchant was a man.   10
     The world was made for honest trade,—
     To plant and eat be none afraid.

The waves that rocked them on the deep
   To them their secret told;
Said the winds that sung the lads to sleep,   15
   "Like us, be free and bold!"
     The honest waves refused to slaves
     The empire of the ocean caves.

Old Europe groans with palaces,
   Has lords enough and more;—   20

Boston

We plant and build by foaming seas
   A city of the poor;—
      For day by day could Boston Bay
      Their honest labor overpay.

We grant no dukedoms to the few,   25
   We hold like rights, and shall;—
Equal on Sunday in the pew,
   On Monday in the mall.
      For what avail the plough or sail,
      Or land or life, if freedom fail?   30

The noble craftsman we promote,
   Disown the knave and fool;
Each honest man shall have his vote,
   Each child shall have his school.
      A union then of honest men,   35
      Or union nevermore again.

The wild rose and the barberry thorn
   Hung out their summer pride
Where now on heated pavements worn
   The feet of millions stride.   40

Fair rose the planted hills behind
   The good town on the bay,
And where the western hills declined
   The prairie stretched away.

What care though rival cities soar   45
   Along the stormy coast,
Penn's town, New York, and Baltimore,
   If Boston knew the most!

They laughed to know the world so wide;
   The mountains said, "Good day!   50

We greet you well, you Saxon men,
   Up with your towns and stay!"
     The world was made for honest trade,—
     To plant and eat be none afraid.

"For you," they said, "no barriers be,   55
   For you no sluggard rest;
Each street leads downward to the sea,
   Or landward to the West."

O happy town beside the sea,
   Whose roads lead everywhere to all;   60
Than thine no deeper moat can be,
   No stouter fence, no steeper wall!

Bad news from George on the English throne:
   "You are thriving well," said he;
"Now by these presents be it known,   65
   You shall pay us a tax on tea;
     'Tis very small,—no load at all,—
     Honor enough that we send the call."

"Not so," said Boston, "good my lord,
   We pay your governors here   70
Abundant for their bed and board,
   Six thousand pounds a year.
(Your Highness knows our homely word,)
     Millions for self-government,
     But for tribute never a cent."   75

The cargo came! and who could blame
   If *Indians* seized the tea,
And, chest by chest, let down the same
   Into the laughing sea?
     For what avail the plough or sail,   80
     Or land or life, if freedom fail?

The townsmen braved the English king,
    Found friendship in the French,
And Honor joined the patriot ring
    Low on their wooden bench.   85

O bounteous seas that never fail!
    O day remembered yet!
O happy port that spied the sail
    Which wafted Lafayette!
        Pole-star of light in Europe's night,   90
        That never faltered from the right.

Kings shook with fear, old empires crave
    The secret force to find
Which fired the little State to save
    The rights of all mankind.   95

But right is might through all the world;
    Province to province faithful clung,
Through good and ill the war-bolt hurled,
    Till Freedom cheered and the joy-bells rung.

The sea returning day by day   100
    Restores the world-wide mart;
So let each dweller on the Bay
    Fold Boston in his heart,
        Till these echoes be choked with snows,
        Or over the town blue ocean flows.   105

Let the blood of her hundred thousands
    Throb in each manly vein;
And the wit of all her wisest,
    Make sunshine in her brain.
        For you can teach the lightning speech,   110
        And round the globe your voices reach.

Selected Poems (1876)

And each shall care for other,
    And each to each shall bend,
To the poor a noble brother,
    To the good an equal friend.   115

A blessing through the ages thus
    Shield all thy roofs and towers!
God with the fathers, so with us,
    Thou darling town of ours!

TEXTS

(A) *AM*, XXXVII (February 1876): 195–197; (B) *Selected Poems* (Boston, 1876), 214–218; (C) *Poems* [Riverside] (Boston, 1884), 182–187; (D) *Poems* [Centenary] (Boston, 1904), 212–217.

Format: The refrains are set flush left in (C-D).

Pre-copy-text forms: The numerous surviving manuscripts are transcribed in *PN* and their relationships discussed in *PN*, 745–747.

VARIANTS

Epigraph: [*In italics*] (A-B) | [*In roman caps*] (C-D)

Note: [*Omitted*] (A, D) | READ IN FANEUIL HALL, ON DECEMBER 16, 1873, ON THE CENTENNIAL ANNIVERSARY OF THE DESTRUCTION OF THE TEA IN BOSTON HARBOR. (B) | [Read in Faneuil Hall, December 16, 1873; the Centennial Anniversary of the Destruction of the Tea in Boston Harbor.] (C)

1   hill-tops (A-C) | hilltops (D)

16   "Like us, (A) | "Like us (B-C) | 'Like us (D) || bold!" (A-C) | bold!' (D)

17   refused (C-D) | refuse (A-B)

20   enough (B-D) | enough, (A)

22   poor;— (B-D) | poor; (A)

25–36   [*Sequence of fifth and sixth stanzas as given* (B-D) | *Sequence reversed* (A); *internal revisions noted separately, below*]

26   rights, (A, C-D) | rights (B) || shall;— (B-D) | shall,— (A)

28   mall. (A-B) | mall, (C-D)

29–30   [*Lines present*] (B-D) | [*Not present*] (A)

35–36   A union then of honest men, / Or union nevermore again. (B-D, *with* never more *in* C *and* D) | For what avail the plow or sail, / Or land, or life, if freedom fail? (A)

38   pride (A-B) | pride, (C-D)

42   bay, (B-D) | bay; (A)

45   What care though rival cities soar (B-D) | What rival towers majestic soar (A)

46   coast, (B-D) | coast,— (A)

47   York, (A-B) | York (C-D) || Baltimore, (B-D) | Baltimore,— (A)

50   "Good day! (A) | 'Good day! (B) | "Good-day! (C) | 'Good-day! (D)

52   towns (B-D) | towns, (A) || stay!" (A, C) | stay!' (B, D)

55   "For you," (A-C) | 'For you,' (D) || "no (A-C) | 'no (D)

58   West." (A-B) | west." (C) | west.' (D)

62   stouter fence, (B-D) | steeper fence, (A) || steeper wall! (B-D) | better wall! (A) |

63   throne: (A-B) | throne; (C-D)

64   "You (A-C) | 'You (D) || well," (A-C) | well,' (D) || he; (B-D) | he, (A)

65   "Now (A-C) | 'Now (D) || known, (A-B) | known (C-D)

68   call." (A-C) | call.' (D)

69   "Not so," (A-C) | 'Not so,' (D) || Boston, (B-D) | Boston; (A) || "good (A-C) | 'good (D)

73   word,) (A-C) | word) (D)

74–75   [*Printed in roman*] (B-D) | [*Printed in italics*] (A)

75   cent." (B-C) | *cent.*" (A) | cent.' (D)

77   *Indians* (B-D) | Indians (A)

78   same (A-B) | same, (C-D)

80   plough (B-D) | plow (A) [*Emerson's MS form is consistently* plough]

81   land (B-D) | land, (A)

84   Honor (A-B) | honor (C-D)

94   State (B-D) | state (A)

108   wit (A-B) | wits (C-D) || wisest, (B-D) | wisest (A)

118   [*Printed in italics*] (A-B) | [*Printed in small caps after large capital* G] (C-D)

NOTES

Epigraph: The official motto of Boston. Emerson translates it in line 118.

17–18.   Reference is to the legal argument that because slavery is exclusively the creature of positive law, it cannot exist where that law does not extend, as, for example, over international waters. This principle was invoked in the Amistad and Creole cases in the 1840s. William Ellery Channing formulated the argument in "The Duty of the Free States" (1842): "The sea is the exclusive property of no nation. . . . No state can write its laws on that restless surface" (*The Works of William E. Channing*, 8th ed. [Boston, 1848], VI, 255). It is probable that Channing was getting advice on this point from Charles Sumner, who wrote—also in regard to the Creole case—that "the air of the ocean is too pure for slavery. There is the principle of manumission in its strong breezes,—at least, when the slave is carried there by the voluntary act of his owner" (quoted in Edward L. Pierce, *Memoir and Letters of Charles Sumner* [Boston, 1893], II, 200).

48.   Perhaps a reminiscence of a line from the *Iliad* (XIII, 355): "But Jove was the eldest born & knows most," quoted in a translation by Thomas Taylor at *JMN*, IX, 94 and 220. Emerson used this line in the first of his 1870 Harvard lectures on "The Natural History of the Intellect": see Ronald A. Bosco, "His Lectures Were Poetry . . . ," *Harvard Library Bulletin*, n.s, VIII (Summer 1997): 27, 55.

74–75.   In 1798 the French government secretly demanded a cash payment (i.e., a bribe) to settle its political differences with the young United States. The demand was rejected, and the comment by South Carolina Representative Robert Harper, "Millions for defense, but not one cent [or penny] for tribute," became the popular rendering of the American position in this scandal, known as the XYZ Affair.

88–89.   The Marquis de Lafayette landed at Boston, on his second trip to America, in 1780.

110–111.   The laying of the Atlantic Cable enabled telegraphic messages to be sent between the United States and England. After an initial success in 1858, the cable broke and was not fully restored until 1866.

UNCOLLECTED POEMS
(1829–1880)

WILLIAM RUFUS AND THE JEW.

Not much is known of the circumstances surrounding the appearance of three works by Emerson in *The Offering, for 1829* (Cambridge: Hilliard and Brown, 1829), a gift-book edited by Andrews Norton and sold "for the benefit of infant education." Emerson's unsigned and never-acknowledged contributions were two poems, "William Rufus and the Jew" and "Fame," along with a prose piece, "An Extract from Unpublished Travels in the East." The poems were the first by him to appear in print.

Emerson's authorship is certain, since the sole surviving draft of the poem occurs in his journal Wide World XIII, where it follows notes taken in the summer of 1824 from his reading of David Hume's *History of England* in the Philadelphia edition of 1810 (*JMN*, II, 267). It was there that Emerson found the story about King William II (c. 1060–1100), third son of William the Conqueror and his immediate successor to the throne of England. Known as William Rufus, he was regarded as impetuous and arrogant and was held in special contempt by the clergy for his impiety:

> As an instance of his irreligion, we are told, that he once accepted of sixty marks from a Jew, whose son had been converted to Christianity, and who engaged him by that present to assist him in bringing back the youth to Judaism. William employed both menaces and persuasion for that purpose; but finding the convert obstinate in his new faith, he sent for the father and told him, that as he had not succeeded, it was not just that he should keep the present; but as he had done his utmost, it was but equitable that he should be

paid for his pains; and he would therefore retain only thirty marks
of the money. (I, 256)

WILLIAM RUFUS AND THE JEW.

"May it please my lord the king,—there's a Jew at the door."
—"Let him in," said the king, "what's he waiting there for?"
—"I wot, Sir, you come from Abraham's loins,
Love not Christ, eat no pork, do no good with your coins."
"My lord the king! I do as Moses bids;   5
Eschewing all evil, I shut my coffer lids;
From the law of my fathers, God forbid I should swerve;
The uncircumcized Nazarite, my race must not serve;
But Isaac my son to the Gentiles hath gone over,
And no means can I find my first-born to recover.   10
I would give fifty marks, and my gabardine to boot,
To the Rabbi that would bring him from the Christian faith
     about;
But phylacteried Rabbins live far over sea,
I cannot go to them, and they will not come to me.
Will it please my lord the king, from the house of Magog,   15
To bring my son back to his own synagogue?"
—"Why I'll be the Rabbi,—where's a fitter Pharisee?
Count me out the fifty marks, and go send your son to me."
The king filled his mouth with arguments and jibes,
To win the boy back to the faith of the tribes,   20
But Isaac the Jew was so hard and stiff-necked,
That by no means could the king come to any effect;
So he paid the Jew back twenty marks of his gains;
Quoth he, "I think I'll keep the thirty for the payment of my
     pains."

TEXTS

(A)) *The Offering, for 1829* [Edited by Andrews Norton] (Cambridge, 1829),
17–18.

Pre-copy-text forms: see *JMN*, II, 267.

16   synagogue?" [Eds.] | synagogue."
 (A)

FAME.

In both the Riverside and Centenary editions Edward dates this poem to 1824, but the evidence from the drafts in the notebooks (*JMN*, II, 407–408, *JMN*, III, 11 and 90, and *PN*, 17) shows that "Fame" was begun in 1825 and probably completed in 1826 (though the final stanza may belong to 1827), during the time, that is to say, when Emerson was struggling with symptoms of tuberculosis and preparing for the ministry. His rather desultory work at the Harvard Divinity School brought him into contact with Andrews Norton, Dexter Professor of Sacred Literature: they would later cross swords over Emerson's controversial Divinity School Address, but in 1828 they were cordially comparing notes about the effect of New England weather on the life and health of the scholar (*L*, I, 229, 233). When Norton assembled his *Offering for 1829*, he included this poem, together with "William Rufus and the Jew," the first two poems Emerson ever published. See Ralph Thompson, "Emerson and *The Offering for 1829*," *American Literature*, VI (May 1934): 151–157, especially on the identification of Norton as the editor.

Ordinarily publication puts an end to a poem's manuscript history, but in this case Emerson included a variant version of "Fame" as the first entry in poetry notebook P, which he began to compile in December 1834 in order to "save my <live> verse" (*PN*, 16). During Emerson's lifetime the *Offering* text was reprinted only once: when Thomas Wentworth Higginson, having discovered Norton's rare old gift book and recognizing the poem's authorship, copied it in *The Radical,* IX (August 1871): 52. It would seem that Edward was unaware of these printings when he prepared the Riverside edition, so he reproduced, as if for the first time, the later text from notebook P, with, here and there, slight editorial interventions. In the present edition the 1829 printing serves as copy-text, but the 1834 MS version, while not always to be trusted in its accidentals, has considerable authority as to the substantives.

FAME.

Ah Fate! cannot a man
    Be wise without a beard?
East, West, from Beer to Dan,
    Say, was it never heard
That wisdom might in youth be gotten,   5
Or wit be ripe before 'twas rotten?

He pays too high a price
    For knowledge and for fame
Who sells his sinews to be wise,
    His teeth and bones to buy a name,   10
And crawls through life a paralytic
To earn the praise of bard and critic.

Were it not better done,
    To dine and sleep through forty years;
Be loved by few; be feared by none;   15
    Laugh life away; have wine for tears;
And take the mortal leap undaunted,
Content that all we asked was granted?

But Fate will not permit
    The seed of gods to die,   20
Nor suffer sense to win from wit
    Its guerdon in the sky,

Fame

Nor let us hide, whate'er our pleasure,
The world's light underneath a measure.

Go then, sad youth, and shine;   25
   Go, sacrifice to fame;
Put love, joy, health, upon the shrine,
   And life to fan the flame;
Being for Seeming bravely barter,
And die to Fame a happy martyr.   30

TEXTS

(A) *The Offering, for 1829* [Edited by Andrews Norton] (Cambridge, 1829), 52–53; (B) Notebook P, pp. 1–2, *PN,* 17; (C) *Poems* [Riverside] (Boston, 1884), 311–312; (D) *Poems* [Centenary] (Boston, 1904), 383–384. The Higginson reprint of the (A) text (see headnote above) was reproduced, a few months before the appearance of the Riverside edition, in Joel Benton, *Emerson as a Poet* (New York, 1883), 46–47. Both printings exhibit errors of transcription.

Pre-copy-text forms: See *PN,* 786–787.

VARIANTS

1   Fate! (A-B) | Fate, (C-D) || cannot (A, C-D) | Cannot (B)
3   East, West, from Beer (C-D) | East, West, from Beor (B) [*evidently an error*] | From East to West, from Beersheba (A)
4   Say, (A, C-D) | Say (B) || heard (B-D) | heard, (A)
5   gotten, (A, C-D) | gotten (B)
6   'twas (A, C-D) | t'was (B)
8   fame (B-D) | fame, (A)
9   sells (B-D) | gives (A) || sinews (B-D) | sinews, (A) || wise, (A, C-D) | wise (B)
10   bones (B-D) | bones, (A) || name, (A, C-D) | name (B)
11   paralytic (B-D) | paralytic, (A)

13   Were (B-D) | Is (A)
14   years; (B-D) | years, (A)
15   few; (B-D) | few, (A) || none; (B-D) | none, (A)
16   away; (B-D) | away, (A) || tears; (B-D) | tears, (A)
21   sense (B-D) | Sense (A) || wit (B-D) | Wit (A)
23   whate'er (A, C-D) | whateer (B)
24   measure. (A, C-D) | measure (B)
25   youth, (A, C-D) | youth! (B) || shine; (B-D) | shine! (A)
26   fame; (A) | Fame; (C-D) | Fame! (B)
27   love, (A) | youth, (B-D) || health,

(A-C) I health (D) II shrine, (A, C-D)   I Thy hapless self for praises (A) II
I Shrine (B)   barter, (A-C) I barter (D)
28   flame; (B-D) I flame! (A)   30   a happy (B-D) I an honored (A)
29   Being for Seeming bravely (B-D)   II martyr. (A, C-D) I martyr! (B)

NOTES

3.   "From Beersheba [or Be'er Sheva] to Dan," a biblical formula indicating the entire extent of Israel from south to north: see, e.g., I Chronicles 21:2.

6.   A play on the proverb "soon ripe, soon rotten."

24.   Cf. Matthew 5:15; Mark 4:21; Luke 11:33.

SILENCE.

Margaret Fuller's letter to Emerson of 19 July 1840, offering criticisms of his *Dial* submission, "Thoughts on Modern Literature," also asked if he could "send a distich to fit in here at the end of your piece" (*FuL,* II, 153). He obligingly provided "Silence" for that purpose, a poem presumably of recent vintage as it belongs evidently to the Emerson-Fuller debate on love and friendship, with the continuance of which Emerson was now beginning to express impatience. The prose source for the poem's first two lines, however, pre-dates that debate and relates to an earlier and rather different awkwardness: the controversy over the Divinity School Address and the demands then made that he explain and defend himself. On 9 October 1838 Emerson wrote in his journal, "They put their finger on their lip—the Powers above,—" (*JMN,* VII, 98). At the head of this entry, the date "October 6" is emended to "7," then to "8," and finally to "9," as though Emerson had wished to respond to his critics but was for several days balked and forbidden by the "Powers above." The journal entries of the previous week reveal both Emerson's deep chagrin that his Address, delivered in July and published in August, had disappointed so many, and his sense of how difficult (and ultimately how pointless) it had been to try to name and defend his position in public as opposed to living it privately with no converting designs on others.

The only evidence as to Margaret Fuller's reaction to "Silence" is that, as *Dial* editor, she placed it, as she expected to, at the end of Emerson's "Thoughts on Modern Literature." But apparently others found it problematical. Thomas Wentworth Higginson commented that "At the time of its first appearance the little verse was regarded as rather grotesque; and it will never, perhaps, be placed among his happiest efforts" (*Margaret Fuller Ossoli* [Boston, 1884], 159). This adverse response—and it is unclear how general it was—may not mean that the poem's personalities had been discovered; more likely the objection was to the verb "clip" in the third line. To clip is, simply, to embrace; but in Elizabethan poetic usage, as in the phrase "kiss and clip," a more specifically sexual embrace is implied (see Gordon Williams, *A Dictionary of Sexual Language and Imagery in Shakespearean and Stuart Literature* [London, 1994], q.v. "clip"). One had to be reasonably well acquainted with the older English poetry, as Higginson certainly was, in order to find coarseness or offense here, but if there were many such readers it may be that their reaction led Emerson to omit "Silence" from *Poems* (1847), making it one of three *Dial* poems thus ignored.

There seems to be no specific warrant for Edward's changing the title to "Eros" in the Riverside edition.

SILENCE.

They put their finger on their lip,—
    The Powers above;
The seas their islands clip,
The moons in Ocean dip,—
    They love but name not love.

TEXTS

(A) *Dial,* I (October 1840): 158; (B) *Poems* [Riverside] (Boston, 1884), 300; (B²) *Poems* [Centenary] (Boston, 1904), 362.

Pre-copy-text forms: The only MS text is in poetry notebook P: see *PN,* 916.

VARIANTS

Title: SILENCE. (A) I EROS. (B)
1   lip,— (A) I lip, (B)
2   above; (A) I above: (B)

4   Ocean dip,— (A) I ocean dip, (B)
5   love (A) I love, (B)

GRACE.

Early in January 1830 Emerson was reading Samuel Taylor Coleridge's *Aids to Reflection,* undoubtedly in the first American edition, published the previous year, with a preface by James Marsh, in Burlington, Vermont (*L,* I, 291). On page 256 of that volume Emerson encountered a poem by George Herbert, originally titled "Sinne," but here retitled by Coleridge "*Graces vouchsafed in a Christian Land*":

> Lord! with what care hast thou begirt us round!
> Parents first season us. Then schoolmasters
> Deliver us to laws. They send us bound
> To rules of reason. Holy messengers;
> Pulpits and Sundays; sorrow dogging sin;
> Afflictions *sorted;* anguish of all sizes;
> Fine nets and stratagems to catch us in!

Grace

Bibles laid open; millions of surprises;
Blessings beforehand; ties of gratefulness;
The sound of glory ringing in our ears:
Without, our shame; within, our consciences;
Angels and grace; eternal hopes and fears!
Yet all these fences, and their whole array,
One cunning BOSOM SIN blows quite away.

Several scholars have commented on the likelihood that Emerson was influenced by this poem in the writing of "Grace" (see N. A. Brittin, "Emerson and the Metaphysical Poets," *American Literature*, VIII [March 1936]: 1–21, and John C. Broderick, "The Date and Source of Emerson's 'Grace,'" *Modern Language Notes*, LXXIII [February 1958]: 91–95), but it was not until the publication of Emerson's sermons that the theory was strikingly confirmed. In Sermon 63, delivered on 24 January 1830, Emerson quoted Herbert's sonnet, asking rhetorically whether the poem did not, perhaps, effectively summarize "the history of the world":

> This would be disheartening indeed to all lovers of virtue, to all who hope well for man; this gloomy experience casts a shade over all the future and is only to be resisted by the consoling fact of a few glorious exceptions and by that strong hope that dwells in the bottom of the Soul (that spark that lives among the ashes of the past) that amendment is never late, (that with God all things are possible), the conviction that power is never wanting to us when we will be true to ourselves. (*CS*, II, 126)

The considerable fascination of Emerson's "Grace" has always consisted in its seeming denial of the poet's core doctrine of self-reliance, and yet here, in a contemporary statement, he makes his source an occasion for preaching truth to self rather than for pressing the case for conforming the criminal to law. Emerson understood the religious tenor of his time as determined by these contrary possibilities, and often, especially later in life, he would observe that the old Calvinist ideas (which he associated with his Aunt Mary Moody Emerson) and the newer, more spiritual views arising from Romantic individualism (which he associated with his brother Charles) were in a vital controversy, both sides of which, as it happened, were fairly represented in his own thinking. "Grace" might be said to capture the moment when the antinomian remembers that the other side must have its due. Thus, for example, Emerson could write in October 1832:

> It is awful to look into the mind of man & see how free we are—to what frightful excesses our vices may run under the whited wall of a respectable reputation. Outside, among your fellows, among strangers, you must preserve appearances,—a hundred things you cannot do; but inside,—the terrible freedom! (*JMN*, IV, 46)

This entry was Emerson's response to an article, "External Restraint," published by Sampson Reed in the Swedenborgian *New Jerusalem Magazine*. The article has been cited as a possible source for "Grace" (see C. P. Hotson, "A Background for Emerson's Poem, 'Grace,'" *New England Quarterly*, I [April 1928]: 124–132), but it might simply indicate Emerson's characteristic alertness to what was valuable and cautionary in the older views.

Emerson published the poem in the *Dial* in 1842, but never thereafter collected or reprinted it. He was surprised in 1852 to find that William Henry Channing had chosen it as an epigraph for his part of the *Memoirs of Margaret Fuller Ossoli*—and yet more surprised by Channing's attribution of the anonymous poem to George Herbert. Emerson noticed this flattering mistake—or so he thought it—when he was reading proofs for the book during his co-author's absence. His first impulse was to strike out the whole poem, but in the end he eliminated only Herbert's name in the American edition (*L*, VIII, 294–295). The incident has an additional importance in being one of the relatively few times we know for certain that Emerson read proofs for a particular poem.

GRACE.

How much, preventing God, how much I owe
To the defences thou hast round me set!
Example, custom, fear, occasion slow,—

Grace

These scorned bondmen were my parapet.
I dare not peep over this parapet   5
To gauge with glance the roaring gulf below,
The depths of sin to which I had descended,
Had not these me against myself defended.

TEXTS

(A) *Dial*, II (January 1842): 373; (B) *Memoirs of Margaret Fuller Ossoli* (Boston, 1852), II, 117; (C) *Poems* [Riverside] (Boston, 1883), 299; (C²) *Poems* [Centenary] (Boston, 1904), 359. The 1852 English edition of (B) differs from the American only in having "scornèd" in line 4 and, following the poem, the attribution to "HERBERT."

Format: Lines 2, 4, and 5 inset (B). The poem text in (B) is enclosed in double quotation marks, which is house style for chapter epigraphs in that work.

Pre-copy-text forms: Emerson wrote the first draft in pencil on the inside front cover of his copy of *A Selection from the English Prose Works of John Milton*, volume I (Boston, 1826): see the transcription at *PN*, 668. See also an interpretation of the importance of this draft by G. R. Elliott, "On Emerson's 'Grace' and 'Self-Reliance,'" *New England Quarterly*, II (January 1929): 93–104. An untitled fair copy is in poetry notebook P (*PN*, 89).

VARIANTS

1   preventing God, (B-C) | Preventing God! (A)
2   set! (B) | set: (A) | set; (C)
3   custom, fear, occasion (A, C) | Custom, Fear, Occasion (B)
4   bondmen (A, C) | bondsmen (B)
5   parapet (A, C) | parapet, (B)
6   gauge (B-C) | guage (A)

NOTES

1.   Emerson uses the word "preventing" in the old theological sense of prevenient or preventing grace. As the *OED* notes, the term does not imply restraint so much as the divine provision, before specific need arises, of spiritual strength or capacity ("to go before with spiritual guidance and help: said of God, or of his grace, anticipating human action or need"). In the Augustinian tradition, the

corrupt human will is first opened to choosing good by *gratia præveniens* (Herbert's "blessings beforehand") and is thereafter, in the converted soul, enabled to cooperate with divinity (*gratia cooperans*). See Joseph Pohle, "Grace," *The Catholic Encyclopedia*, 15 vols. (New York, 1907–1912), VI, 692. Margaret Fuller recalled Emerson's poem when she wrote an essay on "Thanksgiving" in the *New-York Daily Tribune*, 12 December 1844, p. 2, in which she said that "but for instruction, example, and the 'preventing God,' every sin that can be named might riot in our hearts" (*Margaret Fuller, Critic: Writings from the* New-York Tribune, ed. Judith Mattson Bean and Joel Myerson [New York, 2000], 12). Her point was that criminals in prison often did not have these advantages in life.

4–5. The use of the term "parapet" in an identical rhyme connecting the two quatrains may owe something to Thomas Jefferson's description of the sublime effect of the "Natural bridge" in *Notes on the State of Virginia:* "Though the sides of this bridge are provided in some parts with a parapet of fixed rocks, yet few men have resolution to walk to them, and look over into the abyss. You involuntarily fall on your hands and feet, creep to the parapet and peep over it. . . . If the view from the top be painful and intolerable, that from below is delightful in an equal extreme" (*Notes on the State of Virginia* [Boston, 1829], 21–22). Emerson was reading Jefferson's works in March 1830 (see *L*, I, 297, 300).

THE THREE DIMENSIONS.

The location of this poem's first draft in journal R dates it to late June or early July 1843, shortly before its submission to the *Dial*.

THE THREE DIMENSIONS.

"Room for the spheres!"—then first they shined,
And dived into the ample sky;
"Room! room!" cried the new mankind,

And took the oath of liberty.
Room! room! willed the opening mind,
And found it in Variety.

TEXTS

(A) *Dial,* IV (October 1843): 226. The poem was not collected during Emerson's lifetime, nor does it appear in the Riverside or Centenary editions. Its first book publication was in *The Poems of Ralph Waldo Emerson* (London and Newcastle-on-Tyne, 1886), volume 30 of *The Canterbury Poets,* p. 59, where it is, of course, reprinted from the *Dial.*

Pre-copy-text forms: The first draft occurs in journal R (*JMN,* VIII, 431) and a second in poetry notebook P (*PN,* 36), with the title "The three Spaces." See *PN,* 944.

THE PHŒNIX.

This poem translates the first 20 lines of Ode XXIV in Book XXIV of the *Diwan* by Hafiz (II, 308–309), though the earliest notebook drafts correspond to the full 28 lines of the original. A separate manuscript that never bore on the text as published nevertheless has readings in line 4 ("Fell his plumes, & pined his hope.") and lines 7–8 ("Till in that odorous niche of heaven / He nestle close again.") that may seem to some to be improvements (see *PN,* 695–696).

The Boston abolitionist Edmund Quincy had asked Emerson, probably in early September, for a contribution in prose or verse for the anti-slavery gift-book, *The Liberty Bell,* a volume to be sold as a fund-raiser at the annual bazaar in December. Emerson was at this time much occupied with the aftermath of Margaret Fuller's death, and specifically with the project of writing a memorial biography. He had difficulty coming up with anything suitable to send to Quincy, and advised him on 16 September that his muse was "absent, perhaps dead" (*L*, VIII, 260). On the 29th Quincy prodded him once more, suggesting that a reading of the recently enacted Fugitive Slave Bill might put some fight back into the poet's laggard muse (*L*, IV, 229). In the end, unable to produce anything truly apropos but not wishing to disappoint Quincy altogether, Emerson, on 24 October, sent a sheaf of "my translations, rather free, from Von Hammer's German literal versions of Hafiz," the first of which was "The Phœnix" (*L*, VIII, 264; see also Richard Tuerk, "Emerson as Translator—'The Phoenix," *ESQ*, LXIII [Spring 1971]: 24–26). It is unlikely that these translations were done at this time or especially for this occasion: another poem in the group, "Faith" (see below), had been sent to Lucretia Mott the previous April (*L*, VIII, 248–249).

Caroline Sturgis continued to be an appreciative audience for Emerson's poetry: on 19 January 1851 she mentioned that she had so much enjoyed "The Phœnix" and the other translations—probably in *The Liberty Bell*, but possibly in manuscript—that she had procured a copy of the *Diwan* for herself. Not immediately finding the originals, she flatteringly concluded that what Emerson assured her were "translations" were in fact "written by a modern Hafiz" (*L*, VIII, 268n).

In the *Liberty Bell* printing Emerson appended footnotes to the title and to the word "Tuba's" in line 10, the notes reading, respectively, "The Soul." and "The Tree of Life." This awkwardness was avoided in the version offered in the essay "Persian Poetry," where the untitled verses were introduced with the sentence, "In the following poem the soul is figured as the Phœnix alighting on the Tree of Life."

"The Phœnix" has not attracted much attention over the years, but its esoteric meaning was at least once discussed—by John Howard Carey, the anonymous author of a rare and strange work entitled *Restoration of the Earth's Lost History* (San Francisco, 1868). Carey's suggestion (119–120) that the tree of life in Genesis is also the tree of life in the Apocalypse and that its leaves are for "the healing of the nations" (Revelation 22:2) offers support for the view, advanced more recently by Len Gougeon (*Virtue's Hero: Emerson, Antislavery, and Reform* [Athens, Ga., 1990], 147–148), that Emerson's poem represents an undiscouraged view of reform, and is, after all, in some measure, an oblique response to the Fugitive Slave Law.

THE PHŒNIX.

My phœnix long ago secured
   His nest in the sky-vault's cope;
In the body's cage immured,
   He is weary of life's hope.

Round and round this heap of ashes   5
   Now flies the bird amain,
But in that odorous niche of heaven
   Nestles the bird again.

Once flies he upward, he will perch
   On Tuba's golden bough;   10
His home is on that fruited arch
   Which cools the blest below.

If over this world of ours
   His wings my phœnix spread,
How gracious falls on land and sea   15
   The soul-refreshing shade!

Either world inhabits he,
   Sees oft below him planets roll;
His body is all of air compact,
   Of Allah's love his soul.   20

TEXTS

(A) University of Texas MS, printer's copy for B; (B) *The Liberty Bell.* (Boston, 1851), 78–79; (C) "Persian Poetry," *AM,* I (April 1858): 730; (D) William Ellery

Channing, *Thoreau: The Poet-Naturalist* (Boston, 1873), 149 (lines 13–20 only); (E) "Persian Poetry," *Letters and Social Aims* (Boston, 1876), 229–230.

Format: (A, D) lack the alternate indentation. The whole is enclosed in quotation marks in (C, E), as are the two stanzas reproduced in (D), features of house style not further noticed here.

Pre-copy-text forms: Printer's copy for first publication was preceded by two drafts in poetry notebook X, one in EF, and a fair copy in Rhymer (see *PN,* 893–894). The separate manuscript mentioned above is related to revisions undertaken in notebook Orientalist, p. 23 (*TN,* II, 49–50), a draft overlooked by the editors of *PN.* Both of these appear to be post-copy-text.

VARIANTS

1   My phœnix long ago secured (C, E) | My bosom's phoenix has assured (A) | My bosom's Phœnix has assured (B)
2   cope; (C, E) | cope, (A-B)
3   cage (A, C, E) | eye (B) || immured, (C, E) | immured (A-B) ["eye" *is not an authorial revision, but a plausible misreading of Emerson's MS* "cage"]

4   is (A-C) | was (E) || life's (B-C, E) | lifes (A)
14   phœnix (C-E) | phoenix (A) | Phœnix (B)
15   falls on (A-C, E) | o'er (D)
17   Either world (B-E) | <In both> Either world<s> (A)
18   him (B-E) | <them>him (A)
20   love (C-E) | love, (A-B)

FAITH.

This poem corresponds to stanzas 7–9 of Emerson's otherwise unpublished translation of Hafiz, Book XXVII, Ode XVI (*Diwan,* II, 381–382), a poem beginning "Novice, hear me what I say" (see *PN,* 874–875). These three excerpted stanzas, given the title

"Faith," were among the poems that on 24 October 1850 Emerson sent to Edmund Quincy for publication in *The Liberty Bell:* see above, the headnote to "The Phœnix."

The shortened (eight-line) version published in the essay "Persian Poetry" (1858) serves purposes unique to that setting and cannot be supposed to represent Emerson's "final" intentions in regard to the poem. The twelve-line version was carelessly reprinted from *The Liberty Bell* in Charles Bigelow's edition of Emerson's *Uncollected Writings* (New York: Lamb, 1912), 187, which has "your" for "yon" in line 1 and lacks the second comma in line 10.

FAITH.

Plunge in yon angry waves,
    Defying doubt and care,
And the flowing of the seven broad seas
    Shall never wet thy hair.

Is Allah's face on thee   5
    Bending with love benign?
Thou too on Allah's countenance
    O fairest! turnest thine.

And though thy fortune and thy form
    Be broken, waste, and void,   10
Though suns be spent, of thy life-root
    No fibre is destroyed.

TEXTS

(A) University of Texas MS, printer's copy for B; (B) *The Liberty Bell* (Boston, 1851), 79–80; (C) "Persian Poetry," *AM,* I (April 1858): 732 (lines 1–8 only); (C²) "Persian Poetry," *Letters and Social Aims* (Boston, 1876), 234.

Format: Only (A) lacks the alternate indentation. The poem is set off by quotation marks in (C).

Pre-copy-text forms: It is difficult to establish a precise sequence in the MS drafts because Emerson appears to have transferred revisions from one draft to another at different times, rendering it unclear, for example, where a particular revision was initially made. The version of the first stanza that was sent to Lucretia Mott on 18 April 1850 (*L*, VIII, 249n) seems to be intermediate between the longer drafts in poetry notebooks X (*PN*, 250) and EF (*PN*, 268–269) on the one hand, where line 1 reads "Go leap into the waves," and the revisions in notebook Orientalist (*TN*, II, 50 and 106) on the other, which are closest to the MS sent to Quincy. Note that the discussion at *PN*, 786, omits reference to the second Orientalist draft.

VARIANTS

Title: FAITH. (B) | Faith. (A) | [*Untitled*] (C)

2   Defying (A-B) | Renouncing (C) || care, (A-B) | care; (C)

3   And the (A-B) | The (C)

6   benign? (A-B) | benign, (C)

7   Thou too on Allah's countenance (A-B) | And thou not less on Allah's eye (C)

9–12   [*Not present*] (C)

THE POET.

"The Poet" is a translation of Hafiz, Book XXIII, Ode LI, lines 33–44 (*Diwan,* II, 234–235). The verses offer a good illustration of the Gnostic aspect of Hafiz's Sufism. The comparison of knowledge (or gnosis) with gold and gems (to the advantage of the former) recalls such foundational texts of the ancient Jewish wisdom tradition as Proverbs 8.

In the *Liberty Bell* printing and in the case of its reprinting in Charles Bigelow's edition of Emerson's *Uncollected Writings* (New York: Lamb, 1912), 188, the poem is immediately followed by "I

truly have no treasure" (see below), as if it were a fourth stanza—
ignoring, in the first instance, the double rules by which Emerson
set it off in the MS printer's copy (A).

THE POET.

Hoard knowledge in thy coffers,
    The lightest load to bear;
Ingots of gold, and diamonds,
    Let others drag with care.

The devil's snares are strong,   5
    Yet have I God in need;
And if I had not God to friend,
    What can the devil speed?

Courage! Hafiz, though not thine
    Gold wedge and silver ore,   10
More worth to thee the gift of song,
    And the clear insight more.

TEXTS

(A) University of Texas MS, printer's copy for B; (B) *The Liberty Bell* (Boston,
1851), 80; (C) "Persian Poetry," *AM,* I (April 1858): 729 (lines 9–12 only); (C²)
"Persian Poetry," *Letters and Social Aims* (Boston, 1876), 228.

Format: Only (A) lacks the alternate indentation. The poem is set off by quota-
tion marks in (C).

Pre-copy-text forms: See *PN,* 895.

VARIANTS

9   Courage! Hafiz, (A-B) | High
heart, O Hafiz! (C)

10   Gold wedge (A-B) | Fine gold
(C) || ore, (A-B) | ore; (C)

["I HAVE NO HOARDED TREASURE."]

Emerson took this quatrain (lines 13–16) from Hafiz, Book VIII, Ode LV (*Diwan*, I, 285), which he first translated in 1847 in journal CD (*JMN*, X, 67–68). The revisions done separately on this quatrain in notebooks Orientalist and Rhymer probably date to 1850, in connection with the sheaf of translations that Emerson sent to Edmund Quincy in October. As pointed out in the headnote to "The Poet," above, this poem was printed in *The Liberty Bell* as if it were the conclusion of "The Poet"—and hence also in Emerson's *Uncollected Writings* (1912), p. 188.

["I HAVE NO HOARDED TREASURE."]

I have no hoarded treasure,
   Yet have I rich content;
The first from Allah to the Shah,
   The last to Hafiz went.

TEXTS

(A) University of Texas MS, printer's copy for B; (B) *The Liberty Bell* (Boston, 1851), 81; (C) "Persian Poetry," *AM*, I (April 1858): 729; (C²) "Persian Poetry," *Letters and Social Aims* (Boston, 1876), 228.

Format: Only (A) lacks the alternate indentation. The poem is set off by quotation marks in (C).

Pre-copy-text forms: See *PN*, 825–826.

VARIANTS

1   I have no hoarded (C) | I truly   2   content; (B-C) | content, (A)
have no (A-B)   4   went. (B-C) | went (A)

TO HIMSELF.

This quatrain translates Hafiz, Book XXVII, Ode II, lines 29–32
(*Diwan,* II, 358).

TO HIMSELF.

O Hafiz! speak not of thy need;
   Are not these verses thine?
Then all the poets are agreed,
   No man can less repine.

TEXTS

(A) University of Texas MS, printer's copy for B; (B) *The Liberty Bell* (Boston,
1851), 81; (C) "Persian Poetry," *AM,* I (April 1858): 729; (C²) "Persian Poetry,"
Letters and Social Aims (Boston, 1876), 228.

Format: Only (A) lacks the alternate indentation. The poem is set off by quota-
tion marks in (C).

Pre-copy-text forms: See *PN,* 948–949. The revisions in the Orientalist draft (*TN,*
II, 50–51) are post-copy-text, intermediate between the *Liberty Bell* version and
the "Persian Poetry" version.

VARIANTS

1   O Hafiz! (C) | Hafiz, (A-B) ||
need; (C) | need, (A-B)
3   Then (C) | Then, (A-B)

4   No man can less (C) | Thou
canst at nought (A-B)

FROM THE PERSIAN OF NISAMI.
WORD AND DEED.

This poem was among the translations that Emerson sent to Edmund Quincy in October 1850 for inclusion in the anti-slavery annual *The Liberty Bell* (see the headnote to "The Phœnix," above, for additional details). Nizami Ganjavi (c. 1141–c. 1209), a writer of romantic epics and didactic poems, and an admirer of Firdusi's *Shah Nameh,* or Book of Kings, is best known for the *Khamseh,* or "The Quintuplet." The German source of Emerson's translation is in Joseph von Hammer, *Geschichte,* 107–108.

FROM THE PERSIAN OF NISAMI.
WORD AND DEED.

While roses bloomed along the plain,
The nightingale to the falcon said,
"Why, of all birds, must thou be dumb?
With closed mouth thou utterest,
Though dying, no last word to man.   5
Yet sitt'st thou on the hand of princes,
And feedest on the grouse's breast,
Whilst I, who hundred thousand jewels

From the Persian of Nisami. Word and Deed

Squander in a single tone,
Lo! I feed myself with worms,   10
And my dwelling is the thorn."—
The falcon answered, "Be all ear:
Thou seest I'm dumb; be thou, too, dumb.
I, experienced in affairs,
See fifty things, say never one;   15
But thee the people prizes not,
Who, doing nothing, say'st a thousand.
To me, appointed to the chase,
The king's hand gives the grouse's breast;
Whilst a chatterer like thee   20
Must gnaw worms in the thorn. Farewell!"

TEXTS

(A) University of Texas MS, printer's copy for B; (B) *The Liberty Bell* (Boston, 1851), 156–157; (C) "Persian Poetry," *AM,* I (April 1858): 732; (C²) "Persian Poetry," *Letters and Social Aims* (Boston, 1876), 228. In both C and C² the poem is treated as an extract and enclosed in double quotation marks, so that dialogue within the poem is indicated by single quotation marks. Since this treatment is not intrinsic to the poem, but an effect of its being quoted, these features are not adopted into the final text. It is impossible to determine whether the omission of line 13 in C and C² was intentional. The reprinting of the *Liberty Bell* text in Emerson's *Uncollected Writings* (1912), 188–189, has, of course, no authority.

Pre-copy-text forms: The first two drafts are in journal AZ (*JMN,* XI, 208–209), where the inscription appears to date from January 1850 (see also *JMN,* XI, 223). A third draft occurs in notebook Orientalist (*TN,* II, 52).

VARIANTS

Title: [*As here*] (A-B) | [*Untitled*] (C)
1   While (C) | Whilst (A-B)
2   nightingale (A, C) | Nightingale (B) || falcon (A, C) | Falcon (B)
3   'Why, (C) | "Why (A-B) || birds, (C) | birds (A-B)

5   man. (C) | man: (A-B)
6   sitt'st (C) | sit'st (A-B) || princes, (C) | caliphs, (A-B)
7   breast, (C) | breast; (A-B)
11   the thorn.'— (C) || a thorn." (A-B)

12   falcon (A, C) | Falcon (B)
13   thou, too, (B) | thou too (A) |
[*line not present*] (C)
15   one; (C) | one. (A-B)

17   say'st a thousand. (C) | say a
hundred. (A-B)
19   breast; (C) | breast, (A-B)
21   thorn. (C) | thorns. (A-B)

["THE CUP OF LIFE."]

Carl F. Strauch devoted a lengthy discussion to establishing the order and date of the nine manuscript drafts and fair copies of this early poem (diss., 45–56), implying that it had a noteworthy place in the development of Emerson's mature poetic voice. To the extent that this rather slight poem can be seen as, on the one hand, breaking with the stilted eighteenth-century diction and rhythms of his juvenile verse and as constituting, on the other, a sort of unwitting prelude or proem to the group of verses written for Ellen Tucker between 1828 and 1832, Strauch's argument proves both canny and helpful.

Emerson wrote the second stanza of this poem first (see *JMN*, III, 83), either before or shortly after he returned from St. Augustine, Florida, where he had gone in the winter and spring of 1827 in response to flaring symptoms of tuberculosis. The fact that the stanza was inscribed on a page of journal 1826–1828 before some otherwise unrelated lines alluding to the Minorcan-run billiard rooms of St. Augustine (*L*, I, 189) might suggest that it was written while Emerson was still at the South. He returned home in the first week of June (*CS*, I, 42), and although he had gained more than ten pounds while in Florida (*JMN*, III, 75, 77), the still sliver-thin poet was not convinced that his health had significantly improved. With spirits therefore continuing depressed, he resumed his theological studies in Cambridge and his round of candidate and supply preaching.

The earliest text of the complete, two-stanza poem—finished, evidently, in a quite different mood—appears in notebook XVI (*JMN*, II, 410). This text was reproduced twice in the edition of the *Journals* prepared by Edward and his nephew Waldo Emerson Forbes (*J*, II, 132 and 219–20), where it was dated 1826 and 1827 respectively. Edward's note in the Centenary edition of *Poems* had assigned it a date of December 1827 so as to connect it with Emerson's first meeting, in Concord, New Hampshire, with Ellen Tucker (*W*, IX, 516). Nevertheless Strauch suggests, based mainly on its context in the notebook, that it could have been written as late as 1828, coinciding with Emerson's engagement with Ellen. The poem had no title at this time, nor did it have one when Ellery Channing published it in *Thoreau: The Poet-Naturalist* in 1873; but in the Centenary edition the title "Good Hope" was supplied.

["THE CUP OF LIFE."]

The cup of life is not so shallow
    That we have drained the best,
That all the wine at once we swallow
    And lees make all the rest.

Maids of as soft a bloom shall marry   5
    As Hymen yet hath blessed,
And fairer forms are in the quarry
    Than Angelo released.

TEXTS

(A) William Ellery Channing, *Thoreau: The Poet-Naturalist* (Boston, 1873), 132; (B) *Poems* [Centenary] (Boston, 1904), 387.

Pre-copy-text forms: The discussion of the nine manuscript, journal, and notebook drafts in *PN*, 941, draws on the detailed analysis in Carl F. Stauch's dissertation. Note that (B) is not a straightforward printing of any of the pre-copy-text forms but is in fact a conflation of texts found in poetry notebooks P and Rhymer.

Title: [*None*] (A) I GOOD HOPE (B)

   3   wine (B) I wines (A); *corrected to*
"wine" *by Emerson in his copy, Houghton*
Library, *AC 85.Em345.Zy873c (Ralph
Waldo Emerson Memorial Association

deposit, Houghton Library, Harvard
University) II swallow (B) I swallow,
(A)

   5   marry (B) I marry, (A)
   8   Angelo (A) I Phidias (B)

NOTES

8.   The allusion is to the doctrine associated with Michelangelo that the sculptor literally discovers the beautiful form in the marble rather than creates it. See Emerson's translation of "Sonnet of Michel Angelo Buonaroti" above. The substitution of "Angelo" for the original reading "Phidias" was probably done after Emerson's trip to Italy in 1833: it is characteristic of the last three pre-copy-text manuscripts.

["WHERE IS SKRYMIR?"]

   Skrýmir was the alias of Útgarða-Loki, the giant guardian and ruler of Utgarðar in Norse mythology, about whom, in 1847, Emerson read in *The Prose or Younger Edda Commonly Ascribed to Snorri Sturluson,* trans. George Webbe Dasent (Stockholm and London, 1842). The only publication of this poem during Emerson's lifetime was in William Ellery Channing's 1873 *Thoreau: The Poet-Naturalist,* evidently from an unlocated manuscript that took revi-

sion further than the latest of the surviving holographs, that being
a 10-line draft in poetry notebook P (*PN*, 49–50):

Where is Skrymir? Giant Skrymir?
Come transplant the woods for me!
Scoop up yonder aged ash,
Centennial pine, mahogany beech,
Oaks that grew in the dark ages
Heedful, bring them, set them straight,
In sifted soil, before my porch;
Now turn the river on their roots,
So the ↑new↓ top shall <never> ↑not↓ droop
His tall erected plume, nor a leaf wilt.

In 1847 Emerson had purchased from Charles Warren the lot im-
mediately to the east of his house and in April began to turn pas-
ture into orchard by a wholesale planting of fruit trees, recording
these efforts in two notebooks, Warren Lot and Trees. Emerson
could be satirical about the pride of the landowner (as, memora-
bly, in "Hamatreya"), but he could also indulge that pride himself,
especially in regard to the large-scale improvements that could
be made. In a journal entry of 1847 falling between the first two
drafts of this poem, Emerson marveled at his neighbor, Abel
Moore, "who danced a thousand tons of gravel from yonder blow-
ing sandheap on to the bog meadow beneath us where now the
English grass is waving over countless acres" (*JMN*, X, 101).

["WHERE IS SKRYMIR?"]

Where is Skrymir, giant Skrymir?
Come, transplant the woods for me!
Scoop up yonder aged ash,
Centennial fir, old boundary pine,
Beech by Indian warriors blazed,   5
Maples tapped by Indian girls,
Oaks that grew in the Dark Ages;
Heedful bring them, set them straight
In sifted soil before my porch,

Now turn the river on their roots,   10
That no leaf wilt, or leading shoot
Drop his tall-erected plume.

TEXTS

(A) William Ellery Channing, *Thoreau: The Poet-Naturalist* (Boston, 1873), 147.

Pre-copy-text forms: The first two drafts are in journal CD (*JMN*, X, 82 and 122). These precede the version in poetry notebook P, given in the headnote, above.

VARIANTS

1   [*The only emendation necessary in Channing's text is the correction of his misspelling of* Skrymir *as* Skymir.]

["THERE ARE BEGGARS IN IRAN AND ARABY."]

This poem was begun in 1844 as a sequel to "Saadi" (see *JMN*, IX, 130). In its most fully elaborated manuscript form it was 47 lines long (*PN*, 705–706), though Emerson seems to have abandoned it when he carved out ten lines to serve as the opening of the epigraph to "Beauty" in *The Conduct of Life* (1860). In the text published in *Thoreau: The Poet-Naturalist,* by William Ellery Channing, in 1873—the poem's only publication during Emerson's lifetime—the place of these transferred lines was taken by new verses, for which no manuscript drafts survive, from which negative evidence one might surmise that they were written in 1872 or 1873.

The manuscript history of the poem is very complicated, and the description in *PN*, 935–937, of the sequence of drafts may in some respects be faulty. The main line of development is somewhat uncertain, but the following is a plausible order: 1) Journal V (*JMN*, IX, 130, c. October-December 1844); 2) notebook QL (*TN*, III, 353, draft entitled "Saadi Again"); 3) poetry notebook P, draft headed "Saadi (new)," (*PN*, 101–102); 4) poetry notebook Rhymer (*PN*, 428–429); 5) a draft of added lines (Poems folder 79, MS 3, *PN*, 706–707); 6) a combination of the original poem (lacking the first ten lines) and the added lines just mentioned, in poetry notebook X (*PN*, 202–203); 7) the 47-line version (Poems folder 79, MS 2, *PN*, 705–706); 8) a version lacking lines 1–10 in poetry notebook NP (*PN*, 558); 9) the reduced, 32-line version, still retaining the lines eventually used in "Beauty" (Poems folder 79, MS 1, *PN*, 704–705); and, finally, the corrected proof sheet, textually identical to the preceding, found in poetry notebook Rhymer and photographically reproduced in *PN*, [xxvi]. The last item is unrelated to any actual publication, and must have been produced for Emerson privately, as a favor, probably by James T. Fields. All of these texts pre-date 1860 since they all contain the lines used in "Beauty."

A 57-line version was published by Edward Emerson in the 1884 Riverside edition as the first of the "Fragments on the Poet and the Poetic Gift"; this text was reprinted without alteration in the Centenary edition of 1904. Edward's text consists of a variant version of Channing's text together with 31 additional lines, all but eight of which have some authority in the surviving manuscripts. Given this fact—that Edward's 1884 text has about as much warrant in the manuscripts as does Channing's 1873 version—yet mindful of the difference it makes that the earlier text was published with Emerson's knowledge and permission, the present editors have chosen Channing's version as copy-text, reporting variants from the poem as Edward later published it. Where the two published texts differ, preference is given not necessarily to the copy-text form, but to the form favored by the preponderance of the manuscript evidence, where such evidence is available.

The motto chosen by Edward in 1904 to accompany "Society and Solitude" (*W,* VII, 1) consists of lines 19–34, 43–44, and 50–57 of this poem, according to its Riverside and Centenary lineation.

["THERE ARE BEGGARS IN IRAN AND ARABY."]

There are beggars in Iran and Araby,
SAID was hungrier than all;
Hafiz said he was a fly
That came to every festival,
He came a pilgrim to the Mosque   5
On trail of camel and caravan,
Knew every temple and kiosk
Out from Mecca to Ispahan;
Northward he went to the snowy hills,—
At court he sat in the grave Divan.   10
His music was the south-wind's sigh,
His lamp the maiden's downcast eye,
And ever the spell of beauty came
And turned the drowsy world to flame.
By lake and stream and gleaming hall,   15
And modest copse and the forest tall,
Where'er he went the magic guide
Kept its place by the poet's side.
Tell me the world is a talisman,
To read it must be the art of man;   20
Said melted the days in cups like pearl,
Served high and low, the lord and the churl;
Loved harebells nodding on a rock,
A cabin topped with curling smoke,
And huts and tents; nor loved he less   25
Stately lords in palaces,
Princely women hard to please,
Fenced by form and ceremony.

["There are beggars in Iran and Araby"]

TEXTS

(A) William Ellery Channing, *Thoreau: The Poet-Naturalist* (Boston, 1873), 161;
(B) *Poems* [Riverside] (Boston, 1884), 263–265; (B²) *Poems* [Centenary] (Boston, 1904), 320–322.

Pre-copy-text forms: See *PN*, 935–937.

VARIANTS

2   SAID (B) | Said (A)

3   Hafiz (B) | Men (A)

4   festival. (B) | festival, (A)

5   He came a pilgrim to the Mosque (B) | Also he came to the mosque (A)

6   On (B) | In (A) [*There is no MS precedent for Channing's reading ("In" without the definite article): Emerson alternated in the drafts between "In the" and "On," tending to favor "On" in the later MSS.*]

7   [*Line omitted in* (A), *a feature only of the earliest MSS.*]

8   Ispahan; (B) | Isphahan;— (A)

9   hills,— (A) | hills, (B)

10   Divan. (B) | divan. (A)

11   south-wind's (B) | south wind's (A)

12   lamp (A) | lamp, (B)

16   copse (B) | copse, (A)

17   went (A) | went, (B)

19–20   [*Lines not present in* (B).]

21   in cups like (A) | like cups of (B)

22   churl; (A) | churl, (B)

24   topped [*the reading in all pre-copy-text forms*] | hung (A, B)

25   tents; (B) | tents, (A)

27   [*Line not present in* (A)]

28   ceremony. [*End of poem*] (A) | ceremony, (B)

(B, B²) *continues:*

> Decked by courtly rites and dress
> And etiquette of gentilesse.   30
> But when the mate of the snow and wind,
> He left each civil scale behind:
> Him wood-gods fed with honey wild
> And of his memory beguiled.
> He loved to watch and wake   35
> When the wing of the south-wind whipt the lake
> And the glass surface in ripples brake
> And fled in pretty frowns away
> Like the flitting boreal lights,
> Rippling roses in the northern nights,   40
> Or like the thrill of Æolian strings
> In which the sudden wind-god rings.

649

In caves and hollow trees he crept
And near the wolf and panther slept.
He came to the green ocean's brim   45
And saw the wheeling sea-birds skim,
Summer and winter, o'er the wave,
Like creatures of a skiey mould,
Impassible to heat or cold.
He stood before the tumbling main   50
With joy too tense for sober brain;
He shared the life of the element,
The tie of blood and home was rent:
As if in him the welkin walked,
The winds took flesh, the mountains talked,   55
And he the bard, a crystal soul
Sphered and concentric with the whole.

[Note: Lines 35–42 derive from a prose source (*JMN,* XIV, 246) written in 1859, a passage copied into poetry notebook X and versified (*PN,* 176–177, 173), but not at that point obviously connected to "There are beggars." The manuscript authority for the remaining lines (29–34 and 43–57) is found in three locations: two separate manuscripts transcribed in *PN,* 705–707, and a draft in poetry notebook X (*PN,* 202–203). The source for lines 56–57 is an aphorism by Francis Bacon partly quoted in *EL,* I, 327, and alluded to by Charles Emerson in an 1833 letter to Elizabeth Hoar; see Elizabeth Maxfield-Miller, "Elizabeth of Concord: Selected Letters of Elizabeth Sherman Hoar . . . (Part Three)," *SAR, 1986* (Charlottesville, 1986), 119n. The relevant passage from this letter was excerpted in poetry notebook ETE Verses (*PN,* 584).]

["SAID SAADI,—WHEN
I STOOD BEFORE."]

According to the note provided by Edward Emerson in *W,* IX, 506, "Hassan the camel-driver was, without doubt, Mr. Emerson's sturdy neighbor, Mr. Edmund Hosmer, for whom he had great respect. The camels were the slow oxen, then universally used for farm-work, with which Mr. Hosmer ploughed the poet's fields for him." This identification is clearly correct, since a journal entry of 22 April 1842 compares Hosmer at the plow to historic conquerors on hard-fought campaigns (*JMN*, VIII, 238). Edward, in the same note, also points out the relevance of certain remarks in "Man the Reformer" (1841) praising manual labor and the education such labor indispensably provides to hands and feet (see *CW*, I, 150–152). The poem, like the lecture, owes much to Emerson's thinking about issues raised and addressed by the Brook Farm experiment. The location in the notebooks of the first draft of the poem points to composition in the spring or summer of 1842.

["SAID SAADI,—WHEN I STOOD BEFORE."]

Said Saadi,—When I stood before
Hassan the camel-driver's door,
I scorned the fame of Timour brave,—
Timour to Hassan was a slave.
In every glance of Hassan's eye   5
I read great years of victory.
And I, who cower mean and small
In the frequent interval
When wisdom not with me resides,
Worship toil's wisdom that abides.   10
I shunned his eye,—the faithful man's,
I shunned the toiling Hassan's glance.

TEXTS

(A) William Ellery Channing, *Thoreau: The Poet-Naturalist* (Boston, 1873), 167; (B) *Poems* [Riverside] (Boston, 1884), 265–266; (B²) *Poems* [Centenary] (Boston, 1904), 323.

Pre-copy-text forms: The first draft, in pencil in notebook Dialling (*JMN*, VIII, 513), is revised in a separate manuscript transcribed in *PN*, 701–702, and copied out in poetry notebooks X and ETE: see the discussion in *PN*, 909–910.

VARIANTS

1   Saadi,—When (A) | Saadi, "When (B)

3   brave,— (A) | brave; (B)

4   Timour (A) | Timour, (B) || Hassan (A) | Hassan, (B)

6   great (B) | rich (A) [*The* (B) *reading is that of all pre-copy-text versions.*] || victory. (A) | victory, (B)

8   interval (B) | interval, (A)

10   toil's (A) | Toil's (B) || abides. (B) | abides! (A)

11   eye,—the [*from pre-copy-text form*] | eyes,—the (A) | eyes, that (B) *[Note: The pre-copy-text forms differ casually as to punctuation, but all have singular "eye" and all have "the"]*

12   glance. (A) | glance." (B)

NOTES

3–4.   Timour, a variant of Tamburlaine or Tamerlane (c. 1336–1405), Islamic conqueror of central Asia and eastern Europe.

SOUTH WIND.

In the note to the poem in *W*, IX, 511, Edward claimed to be reproducing "the best version from the journals" rather than the text of the only previous complete printing, in Channing's *Thoreau: The Poet-Naturalist*, but in fact neither publication exactly matches any of the MS sources. Edward also gave the poem a new title, "September," having observed the evidence from poetry notebook X that the particular "gusty autumn day" when the poem had been written was 20 September 1846. On that day, a Sunday, Emerson had been out boating with Ellery Channing (*JMN*, IX, 455), who is perhaps referred to in lines 3–4.

Emerson's references to the South wind in his letters and journals are most often to its being in spring the bringer of warm weather. In April 1840, for example, he wrote to Margaret Fuller: "The North wind seems to have blown itself out at last and here is the bland warm wise poetic South whispering odes choruses cadences & wonderful caesuras from his lyrical wings. I hope he finds you happy & great. In these parts—be sure—he sings Georgics also & admonishes men of gardens & the planting of peas" (*L*, II, 282). Fuller may have had this language in mind when she wrote back in late May that she "cannot write down what the Southern gales have whispered" (*FuL*, II, 135). Emerson's "South Wind" would seem to merge spring and fall impressions.

SOUTH WIND.

In the turbulent beauty
Of a gusty autumn day,
Poet in a wood-crowned headland
Sighed his soul away.
Farms the sunny landscape dappled,   5
Swan-down clouds dappled the farms,
Cattle lowed in hazy distance
Where far oaks outstretched their arms.
Sudden gusts came full of meaning,
All too much to him they said;—   10
Southwinds have long memories,
Of that be none afraid.
I cannot tell rude listeners
Half the telltale Southwind said,

'Twould bring the blushes of yon maples   15
To a man and to a maid.

TEXTS

(A) Poetry notebook Rhymer, 59 (*PN,* 442), source, according to Emerson, for B; (B) William Ellery Channing, *Thoreau: The Poet Naturalist* (Boston, 1873), 183; (C) *Poems* [Riverside] (Boston, 1884), 310 (lines 9–16 only); (D) *Poems* [Centenary] (Boston, 1904), 361–362.

Format: As here presented (A-B); quatrains set off with white lines (stanza breaks) and alternate indentations (C-D).

Pre-copy-text forms: Lines 9–12 occur separately in poetry notebooks X and EF where the context suggests they were candidates for inclusion in "May-Day." Two drafts of the whole poem in X (dated 20 September 1846) precede the fair copy in Rhymer, where Emerson entitled the poem "South wind" and noted that it had been "printed in Channing's Life of Thoreau." See the discussion of the drafts in *PN,* 923–924.

VARIANTS

Title: South wind. (A) | [*untitled*] (B) | THE SOUTH WIND. (C) | SEPTEMBER (D)

2   autumn (A-B) | Autumn (D)

3   in a wood-crowned (A) | on a sunny (B-C) [*Emerson restored the* (A) *reading in his copy of* (B), *Houghton Library,* *AC 85.Em345.Zy873c *(Ralph Waldo Emerson Memorial Association deposit, Houghton Library, Harvard University)]*

6   Swan-down (A-B) | Swandown (D)

7   hazy (A) | hollow (B) | mellow (D)

10   said;— (A) | said, (B-D)

11   Southwinds (A) | South winds (B) | Oh, south winds (C-D)

14   telltale Southwind (A) | tell-tale south wind (B-C) | tell-tale South-wind (D) || said, (A-B) | said,— (C-D)

15   'Twould (B-D) | T'would (A)

ALMS.

In poetry notebook EF is a short list of proverbs, presumably from Persian sources, the first of which is "The sword will not cut off the giving hand," while the third reads "Alms is the waking of those that sleep" (*PN*, 277). On the next page of EF Emerson inscribed three drafts of this quatrain. A later fair copy, with the title "Alms" and an ascription to Hafiz, occurs in poetry notebook Rhymer (*PN*, 464). If the poem in fact derives from detached proverbs, then Emerson may have been mistaken in what was probably a much belated ascription. In any event, the source in Hafiz, if there is one, has not been located.

In the *Sketches and Reminiscences,* Mrs. John T. Sargent explains that the Radical Club would periodically hold "Poetical Picnics," at which members would read original verses; Emerson's untitled and undated lines are quoted among others for which a date of 1870 has been supplied. The context of the drafts, as explained in *PN*, 727, shows that the poem was composed some time after 1851.

ALMS.

The beggar begs by God's command,
    And gifts awake when givers sleep.
Swords cannot cut the giving hand,
    Nor stab the love that orphans keep.

TEXTS

(A) Mrs. John T. Sargent, ed., *Sketches and Reminiscences of the Radical Club of Chestnut Street, Boston* (Boston, 1880), 398; (B) *Poems* [Riverside] (Boston, 1884), 289; (C) *Poems* [Centenary] (Boston, 1904), 350.

Format: Alternate indentation occurs in (A-B), but not in (C) or in pre-copy-text forms.

Pre-copy-text forms: See *PN,* 727.

VARIANTS

Title: Alms. (Rhymer) | [*Untitled*] (A-C)   3   hand, (A) | hand (B-C)
  2   sleep. (A) | sleep, (B-C)

["THERE IS NO GREAT AND NO SMALL."]

This untitled quatrain was used as the first of two mottoes to "History" in *Essays* (1841). It did not appear in any collection of Emerson's poems during the author's lifetime, but in the Centenary edition it was combined with the second motto to "History," "I am owner of the sphere" (see below), as a two-part poem with sections "I" and "II." Edward Emerson gave to this combination the non-authorial title "The Informing Spirit" (*W,* IX, 282).

["THERE IS NO GREAT AND NO SMALL."]

There is no great and no small
To the Soul that maketh all:
And where it cometh, all things are;
And it cometh everywhere.

TEXTS

(A) *Essays* (Boston, 1841), 1; (B) *Essays: First Series* (Boston, 1847), 1; (C) *Poems* [Centenary] (Boston, 1904), 282. There are no variants in printings of the poem as motto to "History" after (B).

Pre-copy-text forms: An ink fair copy is in poetry notebook P (*PN,* 26) on the same page with the two other original quatrains used as mottoes in *Essays,* suggesting that they were all inscribed there shortly before publication (see *PN,* 937–938).

VARIANTS

Title: [*None*] (A-B) | THE INFORMING
SPIRIT / I (C)

4   everywhere. (B-C) | every where.
(A)

["I AM OWNER OF THE SPHERE."]

This quatrain, written in 1839 or 1840, was the second of two mottoes to "History" in *Essays* (1841). In the 1904 Centenary edition of *Poems* it was combined with the first motto, "There is no great and no small" (see above), and provided with the inclusive title "The Informing Spirit."

["I AM OWNER OF THE SPHERE."]

I am owner of the sphere,
Of the seven stars and the solar year,
Of Cæsar's hand, and Plato's brain,
Of Lord Christ's heart, and Shakspeare's strain.

TEXTS

(A) *Essays* (Boston, 1841), 2; (B) *Poems* [Centenary] (Boston, 1904), 282. There are no variants in later printings and editions of (A).

Pre-copy-text forms: The first draft occurs in notebook F No. I, an index notebook, where it is inscribed after passages dating to June 1839 (*JMN*, XII, 144); an ink fair copy is in poetry notebook P on the same page with the other two quatrains used as mottoes in 1841 (*PN*, 26; cf. *PN*, 821–822).

VARIANTS

Title: [*None*] (A) | THE INFORMING
   SPIRIT. . . / II (B)

NOTES

2.   The "seven stars" are the Pleiades.

NATURE.

   Although Emerson never collected this motto, it is probably his best known, partly because it came (in the 1849 second edition) to be attached to the most elaborate and most important of his early publications, the 1836 manifesto *Nature,* and because it was eventually understood (after 1859 and the publication of *On the Origin of Species*) as a singular anticipation of Darwinian evolution. *Nature* originally had as its motto a sentence from Plotinus: "Nature is but an image or imitation of wisdom, the last thing of the soul; nature being a thing which doth only do, but not know" (*CW*, I, 1). By 1849, when a second edition of *Nature* was called for, Emerson had firmly established the practice of including poetic mottoes of his own composition, a practice begun with *Essays: Second Series* in 1844 and continued with the introduction of similar mottoes in the 1847 revised edition of *Essays: First Series*. It is impossible to know whether Emerson had become dissatisfied with the sentence from Plotinus, or whether he thought it tactically important to offer a different philosophical context. Still, the substitution of his own motto was the most significant single revision in the second edition of *Nature*. In later years, when the "evolutionary" character of the poem was regularly a subject of comment, it seemed obvious that the substitution had been prompted by the energizing insight into scientific matters that Emerson gained in his 1847–1848 trip to England. But in fact the ascent of the "worm" or serpent draws mainly on the fanciful theories of the German scientist Lorenz Oken, of the Scottish surgeon and anatomist John Hunter (for the idea that Emerson called "arrested and progressive development"), and of a "poetic anatomist of our own day," John Bernhard Stallo, who "teaches that a snake, being a horizontal line, and man, being an erect line, constitute a right angle, and between the lines of this mystical quadrant all animated beings find their place." Emerson elaborates this idea most fully in "Swedenborg, or the Mystic" in *Representative Men* (*CW*, IV, 61; see also the note at pp. 196–197). The idea that nature is an organized aspiration after consciousness, a means of arriving at the human capacity for *knowing*, in fact repeats the major implication of the original epigraph from Plotinus.

NATURE.

A subtle chain of countless rings
The next unto the farthest brings;
The eye reads omens where it goes,

And speaks all languages the rose;
And, striving to be man, the worm   5
Mounts through all the spires of form.

TEXTS

(A) *Nature; Addresses, and Lectures* (Boston, 1849), vii; (A²) *Nature* (Boston, 1849), title-page [this volume was printed on 7 December 1849, two months after (A), mainly from the same plates, though the front matter, including the title page, was reset]; (A³) *Poems* [Centenary] (Boston, 1904), 281. There are no variants in the motto in any subsequent edition or reprinting. In (A³) it is conjoined with the unrelated motto to the 1844 essay "Nature."

Pre-copy-text forms: Lines 5–6 were probably drafted in 1845 (*JMN*, IX, 163; cf. 219); they were revised in poetry notebook X (*PN*, 254) and incorporated into "May-Day"—along with lines 1–4—in the same notebook (*PN*, 181). See *PN*, 853–856 and 866 for their further development in the "May-Day" drafts; they eventually figure as lines 315–316, 321–324 of the poem as published in 1867. The only surviving MS form of the discrete six-line motto occurs in Bronson Alcott's journal, where Emerson inscribed it on 5 August 1849, a little more than a month before it was published in (A). See *The Journals of Bronson Alcott*, ed. Odell Shepard (Boston, 1938), 211, and Shepard, *Pedlar's Progress: The Life of Bronson Alcott* (Boston, 1937), 459.

NOTES

4. In December 1848 Emerson commented in his journal on how thoroughly nature sympathizes with the various states of human consciousness: "'Tis Pentecost all, the rose speaks all languages[,] the sense of all affections" and is intelligible to all races (see *JMN*, XI, 62).

PRUDENCE.

This motto was published in 1847 as the epigraph for "Prudence" in the second edition of *Essays,* called *Essays: First Series.*

PRUDENCE.

Theme no poet gladly sung,
Fair to old and foul to young,
Scorn not thou the love of parts,
And the articles of arts.
Grandeur of the perfect sphere   5
Thanks the atoms that cohere.

TEXTS

(A) *Essays: First Series* (Boston, 1847), 199; (B) *Poems* [Centenary] (Boston, 1904), 280.

Pre-copy-text forms: A first draft and fair copy in journal O were apparently written in July 1846 (*JMN,* IX, 444).

VARIANTS

2   young, (A) | young; (B)

CIRCLES.

This motto was published in 1847 as the epigraph for "Circles" in the second edition of *Essays,* called *Essays: First Series.*

CIRCLES.

Nature centres into balls,
And her proud ephemerals,
Fast to surface and outside,
Scan the profile of the sphere;
Knew they what that signified,   5
A new genesis were here.

TEXTS

(A) *Essays: First Series* (Boston, 1847), 272; (A²) *Poems* [Centenary] (Boston, 1904), 282.

Pre-copy-text forms: Drafts of the poem occur in journal O and seem to date to June or July 1846 (*JMN,* IX, 439–440).

NOTES

2.   Ephemerals: i.e, human beings.

6.   The reference is probably an allusion to a theory that Bronson Alcott was at this time expounding in discussions with Emerson, a theory to which he gave the name "genesis." As described by Odell Shepard in *Pedlar's Progress* (Boston, 1937), 453–462, it was a restatement of the neo-Platonic doctrine as held by Plotinus and Philo that the reality of nature was mental, or, in other words, that the invisible, intelligible world of ideas—the real world—is perceived only by the mind and never by the senses.

INTELLECT.

These four lines were written between 1845 and 1847 as the third stanza of a poem, "Pale genius roves alone," not published during Emerson's lifetime, but included in *Poems* [Riverside] (Boston, 1884), 268–269, and *Poems* [Centenary] (Boston, 1904), 326–327. When Emerson needed a motto for the essay "Intellect" in the 1847 second edition of *Essays: First Series,* he took it from this poem, cancelling (or drawing a use mark through) this stanza in poetry notebook EL (see *PN,* 840).

INTELLECT.

Go, speed the stars of Thought
On to their shining goals;—
The sower scatters broad his seed,
The wheat thou strew'st be souls.

TEXTS

(A) *Essays: First Series* (Boston, 1847), 293; (B) *Essays: First and Second Series* (Boston, 1865), 253; (C) *Essays: First Series* [Centenary] (Boston, 1903), 323; (D) *Poems* [Centenary] (Boston, 1904), 283. Note that in the text of "Pale genius roves alone," the lines have the following variants from the text as printed above: l. 1 thought [Riverside]; l. 2 goals:—[Riverside and Centenary].

Pre-copy-text forms: See *PN,* 840.

VARIANTS

3   seed, (A) | seed,— (B) | seed; (C-D)   4   souls. (B-D) | souls (A)

THE POET.

Three drafts of this motto occur in pencil in journal R, over-written by an ink entry concerning a visit that Emerson made to Brook Farm on 21 June 1843 (*JMN*, VIII, 426–428). From this nineteen-line fragment ten lines were carved out to serve as the motto to the essay "The Poet." The full passage, in revised form, was eventually bundled together with similar passages by Edward Emerson to create the lengthy, non-authorial pastiche entitled "The Poet." The lines of the motto, in something like their original form, fall on p. 255 of the Riverside and p. 311 of the Centenary editions of *Poems*.

THE POET.

A moody child and wildly wise
Pursued the game with joyful eyes,
Which chose, like meteors, their way,
And rived the dark with private ray:
They overleapt the horizon's edge,   5
Searched with Apollo's privilege;
Through man, and woman, and sea, and star,
Saw the dance of nature forward far;
Through worlds, and races, and terms, and times,
Saw musical order, and pairing rhymes.   10

TEXTS

(A) *Essays: Second Series* (Boston, 1844), 1; (B) *Essays: Second Series* [Riverside] (Boston, 1883), 1; (B²) *Essays: Second Series* [Centenary] (Boston, 1903), 1.

Pre-copy-text forms: The only surviving drafts are those in journal R, mentioned above.

VARIANTS

7   star, (A) I star (B)   9   times, (A) I times (B)

GIFTS.

In the first draft form, written in the spring of 1842 (*JMN*, VIII, 514), the poem specified "Letters" in the first line, but Emerson changed the word to "Gifts" when he needed a motto for the essay of that title as collected in the 1844 *Essays: Second Series.*

GIFTS.

Gifts of one who loved me,—
'Twas high time they came;
When he ceased to love me,
Time they stopped for shame.

TEXTS

(A) *Essays: Second Series* (Boston, 1844), 171; (A²) *Essays: Second Series* (Boston, 1850), 153; (A³) *Essays: First and Second Series* (Boston, 1865), 413; (A⁴) *Essays: Second Series* [Centenary] (Boston, 1903), 157; (A⁵) *Poems* [Centenary] (Boston, 1904), 283.

Pre-copy-text forms: See *PN,* 802.

NATURE.

Early forms of lines 7–8 and 10 occur in isolated notations in journal Books Small (*JMN,* VIII, 462); otherwise no hints of the poem's composition survive. Among the mottoes written for *Essays: Second Series* (1844), this is one of several that develop the conceit of the physical and interpretive difficulties involved in looking at a "rounded world."

NATURE.

The rounded world is fair to see,
Nine times folded in mystery:
Though baffled seers cannot impart
The secret of its laboring heart,
Throb thine with Nature's throbbing breast,   5
And all is clear from east to west.
Spirit that lurks each form within
Beckons to spirit of its kin;
Self-kindled every atom glows,
And hints the future which it owes.   10

TEXTS

(A) *Essays: Second Series* (Boston, 1844), 181; (B) *Poems* [Centenary] (Boston, 1904), 281. In (B) the poem appears in editorial combination with the unrelated motto to the 1849 edition of *Nature.*

Pre-copy-text forms: See the headnote above.

VARIANTS

9   glows, (A) | glows (B)

NOMINALIST AND REALIST.

These lines, written for the essay "Nominalist and Realist" in *Essays: Second Series* (1844), were retitled by Edward Emerson in the 1904 Centenary edition of *Poems* on the grounds that the new title, "Promise," "seemed appropriate" (*W,* IX, 494), as perhaps it was.

NOMINALIST AND REALIST.

In countless upward-striving waves
The moon-drawn tide-wave strives;
In thousand far-transplanted grafts
The parent fruit survives;
So, in the new-born millions,   5
The perfect Adam lives.
Not less are summer-mornings dear
To every child they wake,
And each with novel life his sphere
Fills for his proper sake.   10

TEXTS

(A) *Essays: Second Series* (Boston, 1844): 243; (B) *The Prose Works of Ralph Waldo Emerson,* 2 vols. (Boston, 1870), I, 533; (C) *Poems* [Centenary] (Boston, 1904), 283–284.

Pre-copy-text forms: None.

VARIANTS

Title: NOMINALIST AND REALIST. (A-B) I PROMISE (C)

7   summer-mornings (A) I summer mornings (B-C)

NEW ENGLAND REFORMERS.

In the 1844 first edition of *Essays: Second Series,* "New England Reformers" had no motto, perhaps because it was generically a lecture, not an essay. The verse epigraph given below was, however, added in the 1850 second edition, though when it was first collected—in the Centenary edition of *Poems* (1904)—Edward Emerson gave it the title "Caritas." The whole question of Emerson's relation to reform continues to be debated, but it is clear from many sources, including this motto, that he took warning from the besetting jangle and discord of protest rhetoric, which had nothing in common with the beautiful renovations it claimed to promote.

NEW ENGLAND REFORMERS.

In the suburb, in the town,
On the railway, in the square,
Came a beam of goodness down
Doubling daylight everywhere:
Peace now each for malice takes,   5
Beauty for his sinful weeds,
For the angel Hope aye makes
Him an angel whom she leads.

TEXTS

(A) *Essays: Second Series* (Boston, 1850), 240; (A²) *Essays: Second Series* (Boston, 1903), 249; (B) *Poems* [Centenary] (Boston, 1904), 284.

Pre-copy-text forms: None.

VARIANTS

Title: NEW ENGLAND REFORMERS.
(A) | CARITAS (B)

NOTES

7–8.   Edward Emerson notes (*W,* III, 350) a similarity between the concluding lines of this poem and a posthumously published fragment that reads, "The archangel Hope / Looks to the azure cope, / Waits through dark ages for the morn, / Defeated day by day, but unto victory born" (*W,* IX, 354; cf. *PN,* 734). The fragment develops journal passages of June 1838 (*JMN,* VII, 10) and April 1842 (*JMN,* VIII, 228), of which the second, the source for the comment about being born to victory, is used also in "New England Reformers" (*CW,* III, 166).

FATE.

This poem served as the motto to "Fate" in *The Conduct of Life* (1860). Edward's note (*W,* VI, 337) states that "a fuller form of the motto, without the last four lines, which are rather explanatory than poetical, may be found in the Appendix to the *Poems* among the 'Fragments on the Poet'" (i.e., at *W,* IX, 326). This fragment, for which most of the manuscript history is lost, descends from an early form of the motto in poetry notebook EL (*PN,* 393). It reads:

The free winds told him what they knew,
Discoursed of fortune as they blew;

Omens and signs that filled the air
To him authentic witness bare;
The birds brought auguries on their wings,
And carolled undeceiving things
Him to beckon, him to warn;
Well might then the poet scorn
To learn of scribe or courier
Things writ in vaster character;
And on his mind as dawn of day
Soft shadows of the evening lay. (*W*, IX, 326; identical to *Poems*
    [Riverside] (Boston, 1884), 268)

The last four lines, which Edward deprecates, were borrowed
from "Fate" ("Deep in the man") shortly before the present po-
em's publication in 1860. They were restored to "Fate" ("Deep in
the man") when that poem was first published, in *May-Day,* in
1867.

FATE.

Delicate omens traced in air
To the lone bard true witness bare;
Birds with auguries on their wings
Chanted undeceiving things
Him to beckon, him to warn;   5
Well might then the poet scorn
To learn of scribe or courier
Hints writ in vaster character;
And on his mind, at dawn of day,
Soft shadows of the evening lay.   10
For the prevision is allied
Unto the thing so signified;
Or say, the foresight that awaits
Is the same Genius that creates.

TEXTS

(A) *The Conduct of Life* (Boston, 1860), xi; (A²) *The Prose Works of Ralph Waldo Emerson*, 2 vols. (Boston, 1870), II, 315; (B) *The Conduct of Life* [Centenary] (Boston, 1904), 1. [The first edition of *The Conduct of Life* exhibits three different configurations of the frontmatter, so that the motto to "Fate" appears in some copies on p. vi. Myerson notes (*Bibliography*, 271) that for the third printing of (A) all the intercalary verse was reset in a larger font size. This resetting did not, however, introduce any variants.]

Pre-copy-text forms: See *PN*, 788–789.

VARIANTS

1   air (A) | air, (B)   4   things (A) | things, (B)

POWER.

This poem is the motto to the essay "Power" in *The Conduct of Life* (1860). Emerson sent it to his publisher along with the motto for "Fate" on 26 April 1860 (*L*, IX, 15). The first draft of the motto occurs along with drafts of "The Song of Nature" in poetry notebook NP (writings clearly belonging to 1859) and may have originally been intended for inclusion in that poem (see *PN*, 493). Reprinting "Power" among the previously uncollected mottoes in the Centenary edition of *Poems*, Edward also separately reprinted the NP draft from the Riverside edition of *Poems* (274) in the Centenary edition (330):

I framed his tongue to music,
    I armed his hand with skill,

671

I moulded his face to beauty
And his heart the throne of Will.

POWER.

His tongue was framed to music,
And his hand was armed with skill,
His face was the mould of beauty,
And his heart the throne of will.

TEXTS

(A) *The Conduct of Life* (Boston, 1860), 43; (B) *The Conduct of Life* [Centenary] (Boston, 1904), 51; (B²) *Poems* [Centenary] (Boston, 1904), 284.

Pre-copy-text forms: See *PN,* 898.

VARIANTS

2   skill, (A) I skill; (B)

NOTES

2. Joseph Slater's notes to this motto (*CW,* VI, 198) offer a number of verbal parallels from Shakespeare, including one in extenuation of the pun in line 2, Exeter's speech in *Henry V:* "While that the armed hand doth fight abroad, / Th' advised head defends itself at home" (I, ii, 178–79).

ILLUSIONS.

This motto for the essay "Illusions" in *The Conduct of Life* (1860) consists of lines 32–68 of the unfinished and presumably abandoned 79-line poem entitled "Proteus," which Emerson composed, probably in the late 1840s or early 50s, in poetry notebook X over an erased draft of "The Dæmonic and Celestial Love" (see *PN*, 185–189).

ILLUSIONS.

Flow, flow the waves hated,
Accursed, adored,
The waves of mutation:
No anchorage is.
Sleep is not, death is not;   5
Who seem to die live.
House you were born in,
Friends of your spring-time,
Old man and young maid,
Day's toil and its guerdon,   10
They are all vanishing,
Fleeing to fables,
Cannot be moored.
See the stars through them,
Through treacherous marbles.   15
Know, the stars yonder,
The stars everlasting,
Are fugitive also,
And emulate, vaulted,
The lambent heat-lightning,   20
And fire-fly's flight.

When thou dost return
On the wave's circulation,
Beholding the shimmer,
The wild dissipation,   25
And, out of endeavor
To change and to flow,
The gas become solid,
And phantoms and nothings
Return to be things,   30
And endless imbroglio
Is law and the world,—
Then first shalt thou know,
That in the wild turmoil,
Horsed on the Proteus,   35
Thou ridest to power,
And to endurance.

TEXTS

(A) University of Virginia MS, printer's copy for B; (B) *The Conduct of Life* (Boston, 1860), 271–272; (C) *The Prose Works of Ralph Waldo Emerson,* 2 vols. (Boston, 1870), II, 481; (D) *Poems* [Centenary] (Boston, 1904), 287–288.

Format: Line 22 set flush left (D).

Pre-copy-text forms: The only surviving drafts are of the poem "Proteus": see *PN,* 833 and 900.

VARIANTS

3   mutation: (A-C) | mutation; (D)

9   Old (B-D) | <Days>Old (A)

12   fables, (B-D) | fables. (A)

16   [*Some copies of* (B) *lack the comma after* yonder]

20   lambent (B-D) | passing (A) ||

heat-lightning, (A-C) | heat lightning, (D)

21   fire-fly's (B-D) | fire fly's (A)

24   Beholding (A-C) | Behold (D)

28   become (A-B, D) | becomes (C)

NOTES

15.   In a note in *CW,* VI, 294, Joseph Slater suggests that the reference may be to a Roman temple, "false to its promise of permanence, through whose ruined roof the stars are visible." If the poem was written after June 1850, the reference could be to the illusion witnessed by Emerson at Mammoth Cave in Kentucky and memorably described in the essay "Illusions," whereby "stars" were made to appear on the vaulted roof of one of the darkened chambers (*CW,* VI, 165–166; cf. *JMN,* XIII, 59–60).

35.   Proteus: an elusive shape-shifting sea-god mentioned in Homer's *Odyssey.* See Emerson's development of "The Fable of Proteus" in *JMN,* V, 136–138 (cf. *CW,* I, 27). Emerson's objection to the symbol-system of Emanuel Swedenborg, who "fastens each natural object to a theologic notion," was that "The slippery Proteus is not so easily caught" (*CW,* IV, 68).

HENRY D. THOREAU
READS "THE SPHINX."

March 7th 8th 9th 10th 1841.
"The Sphinx"

The Sphinx is man's insatiable and questioning spirit, which still as of old, stands by the roadside in us and proposes the riddle of life to every passer.

The ancients represented this by a monster who was a riddle of herself, having a body composed of various creatures, as if to hint that she had no individual existence, but was nearly allied to and brooded over all. They made her devour those who were unable to explain her enigmas, as we are devoured by doubt, and struggle towards the light, as if to be assured of our lives. For we live by confidence and our bravery is in some moment when we are certain—to that degree that our certainty cannot be increased, as when a ray bursts through a gap in a cloud, it darts as far, and reaches the earth as surely as the whole sun could have done.

1 In the first four lines is described the mood in which the Sphinx bestirs herself in us. We must look on the world with a drowsy and half shut eye, that it may not be too much in our eye, and rather stand aloof from than within it. When we are awake to the real world, we are asleep to the actual. The sinful drowse to eternity—the virtuous to time. Menu says—that the "supreme omnipresent intelligence" is "a spirit which can only be conceived by a mind *slumbering.*" Wisdom and holiness always slumber—they are never active in the ways of the world. As in our nightdreams we are nearest to awakening—so in our daydreams we are near-

677

est to a supernatural awakening, and the plain and flat satisfactoriness of life becomes so significant as to be questioned.

The Sphinx hints that in the ages her secret is kept—but in the annihilation of ages alone is it revealed. So far from solving the problem of life, Time only serves to propose and keep it in. Time waits but for its solution to become eternity. Its lapse is measured by the successive failures to answer the incessant question, and the generations of men are the unskilful passengers devoured.

2. She hints generally at man's mystery. He knows only that he is, not what—nor whence. Not only is he curiously and wonderfully wrought, but with Daedalian intricacy. He is lost in himself as a labyrinth and has no clue to get out by. If he could get out of his humanity—he would have got out of nature. Daedalian expresses both the skill and the inscrutable design of the builder.

The insolubleness of the riddle is only more forcibly expressed by the lines—

> "Out of sleeping a waking,
> Out of waking a sleep,"

They express the complete uncertainty—and renunciation of knowledge of the propounder.

3–4–5–6. In these verses is described the integrity of all animate and inanimate things but man—how each is a problem of itself and not the solution of one—and presides over and uses the mystery of the universe as unhesitatingly as if it were the partner of God. How by a sort of *essential and practical faith* each understands all—for to see that we understand—is to know that we misunderstand. Each natural object is an end to itself—A brave undoubting life do they all live, and are content to be a part of the mystery which is God—and throw the responsibility on man of explaining them and himself too.

3—The outlines of the trees are as correct as if ruled by God on the sky—The motions of quadrupeds and birds nature never thinks to mend but they are a last copy—and the flourishes of his hand.

4—The waves lapse with such a melody on the shore as shows that they have long been at one with nature. Theirs is as perfect play as if the heavens and earth were not—they meet with a sweet difference and independently—as old play-fellows. Nothing do they lack more than the world—the ripple is proud to be a ripple and balances the sea.—The atoms which are in such a continual flux notwithstanding their minuteness—have a certain essential valor and independence—They have the integrity of worlds, and attract & repel firmly as such. The least has more manhood than Democritus.

5—So also in nature the perfection of the whole is the perfection of the parts—And what is itself perfect serves to adorn and set off all the rest. Her distinctions are but reliefs. Night veileth the morning for the morning's sake, and the vapor adds a new attraction to the hill. Nature looks like a conspiracy for the advantage of all her parts—when one feature shines all the rest seem suborned to heighten the charm. In her circle each gladly gives precedence to the other—Day gladly alternates with night—Behind these the vapor atones to the hill for its interference, and this harmonious scene is the effect of that at-one-ment.

6—In a sense the babe takes its departure from nature as the grown man his departure out of her, and so during its nonage is at one with her, and as a part of herself. It is indeed the very flower and blossom of nature—

> "Shines the peace of all being
> Without cloud in its eyes,
> And the *sum* of the world
> In soft *miniature* lies."

To the charming consistency of the palm and thrush, this universal and serene beauty is added—as all the leaves of the tree flower in the blossom.

7 But alas, the fruit to be matured in these petals is fated to break the stem which holds it to universal consistency. It passes *through nature* to manhood, and becomes unnatural—without being as yet quite supernatural. Man's most approved life is but conformity—not a simple and independent consistency, which would make all things conform to it. His actions do not adorn nature nor one another, nor does she exist in harmony but in contrast with them. She is not their willing scenery. We conc[e]ive that if a true action were to be performed it would be assisted by nature—and perhaps be fondled and reflected many times as the rainbow. The sun is a true light for the trees in a picture, but not for the actions of men. They will not bear so strong a light as the stubble—the universe has little sympathy with them, and sooner or later they rebound hollowly on the memory. The April shower should be as reviving to our life as to the garden and the grove, and the scenery in which we live reflect our own beauty, as the dew drop the flower. It is the actual man, not

the actual nature that hurts the romance of the landscape. "He poisons the ground". The haymakers must be lost in the grass of the meadow. They may be Faustus and Amyntas here—but near at hand they are Reuben and Jonas. The wood cutter must not be better than the wood lest he be *worse*—Neither will bear to be considered as a distinct feature. Man's works must lie in the bosom of nature, cottages be buried in trees, or under vines and moss, like rocks, that they may not outrage the landscape. The hunter must be dressed in Lincoln green, with a plume of eagle feathers—to imbosom him in nature. So the skilful painter secures the distinctness of the whole by the indistinctness of the parts.—We can endure best to consider our repose and silence. Only when—the city—the hamlet—or the cottage—is viewed from a distance does man's life seem in harmony with the universe, but seen closely his actions have no eagle feathers or Lincoln green to redeem them—The sunlight on cities at a distance is a deceptive beauty, but foretells the final harmony of man with nature.

Man as he is is not the subject of any art, strictly speaking—The naturalist pursues his study with love—but the moralist persecutes his with hate—In man is the material of a picture, with a design partly sketched—but nature is such a picture drawn and colored.—He is a studio—nature a gallery. If men were not idealists no sonnets to beautiful persons, nor eulogies on worthy ones would ever be written. We wait for the preacher to express *such* love for his congregation as the Botanist for his herbarium.

8 Man, however, detects something in the lingering ineradicable sympathy of nature which seems to side with him against the stern decrees of the soul. Her essential friendliness is only the more apparent to his waywardness, (for disease and sorrow are but a rupture with her). In proportion as he renounces his will, she repairs his hurts—and if she burns, does oftener warm, if she freezes oftener refreshes. This is the motherliness which the poet personifies—and the Sphinx or wisely inquiring man, makes express a real concern for him. Nature shows us a stern kindness and only we are unkind. She endures long with us, and though the serenity of her law is unrelaxed, yet its evenness and impartiality look relenting, and almost sympathize with our fault.

9–10–11–12–13–14. But to the poet there are no riddles, they are "pleasant songs" to him—his faith solves the enigmas which recurring wisdom does not fail to repeat. Poetry is the only solution time can offer. But the poet is soonest a pilgrim from his own faith. Our brave moments may still be distinguished from our wise. Though the problem is always solved for the soul, still does it remain to be solved by the intellect. Almost faith puts the question, for only in her light can it be answered. However true the answer it does not prevent the question—for the best answer is but plausible—and man can only tell his relation to truth, but render no account of truth to herself.

9.—Believe, and ask not—says the poet—

"Deep love lieth under
These pictures of time,
Thcy fade in the light of
Their meaning sublime."

Nothing is plain but love.

10–11–12–13. Man comes short because he seeks perfection. He adorns no world while he is seeking to adorn a better. His best actions have no reference to their actual scenery. For when our actions become of that worth that they might confer a grace on nature—they pass out of her into a higher arena—where they are still mean and awkward.

So that the world beholds only the rear of great deeds and mistakes them often for inconsistencies, not knowing with what higher they consist. Nature is beautiful as in repose—not promising a higher beauty tomorrow. Her actions are level to one another, and so are never—unfit or inconsistent. Shame and remorse, which are so unsightly to her, have a prospective beauty and fitness which redeem them. We would have our lover to be nobler than we, and do not fear to sacrifice our love to his greater nobleness[.] Better the disagreement of noble lovers than the agreement of base ones. In friendship each will be nobler than the other, and so avoid the cheapness of a level and idle harmony. Love will have its chromatic strains—discordant yearnings for higher chords—as well as symphonies. 13 Let us expect no finite satisfaction—who looks in the sun—will see no light else—but also he will see no shadow. Our life revolves unceasingly—but the centre is ever the same and the, same—and the wise will regard only the seasons of the soul.

14 The poet concludes with the same trust he began with, and jeers at the blindness which could inquire. But our sphinx is so wise as to put no riddle that can be answered. It is a great presumption—to answer conclusively a question which any sincerity has put. The wise answer no questions—(nor do they ask them—) She silences his jeers with the conviction that she is the eyebeam of his eye. Our proper eye never quails

before an answer. To rest in a reply—as a response of the oracle—that is error—but to suspect time's reply, because we would not degrade one of God's meanings to be intelligible to us—that is wisdom. We shall never arrive at his meaning, but it will ceaselessly arrive to us. The truth we seek with ardor and devotion will not reward us with a cheap acquisition. We run unhesitatingly in our career—not fearing to pass any goal of truth in our haste. We career toward her eternally.—A truth rested in stands for all the vice of an age—and revolution comes kindly to restore health.

16 The cunning Sphinx who had been hushed into stony silence and repose in us—arouses herself and detects a mystery in all things—in infancy—the moon—fire—flowers—sea—mountain—and,

17 in the spirit of the old fable, declares proudly—

"Who telleth one of my meanings
Is master of all I am.".

When some OEdipus has solved one of her enigmas, she will go dash her head against a rock.

———

You may find this as enigmatical as the Sphinx's riddle—Indeed I doubt if she could solve it herself.

(Henry David Thoreau, *Journal*, edited by John C. Broderick et al. [Princeton, 1981], I, 279–286. Quoted by permission.)

LATER VERSIONS
OF "MAY-DAY"

The text of "May-Day" in *Selected Poems* (Boston, 1876) exhibits relatively few intralinear revisions, but is characterized by large-scale cuts (reducing the original 30 verse paragraphs to 24) and by the reordering of sections, particularly in the first half of the poem. In the second half (verse paragraphs 16 through 24, corresponding to lines 325–663 in the 1867 text), apart from the excision of the lines published separately in *Selected Poems* as "The Harp," the text is essentially the same, including its order, as the 1867 text. The major changes are indicated in Chart I below, where the 24 verse paragraphs of the 1876 printing are matched with the line numbers from the 1867 text. Chart II lists the 24 verse paragraphs of the 1876 sequence in the rearranged order provided by Edward Emerson in the 1884 Riverside Edition. Again, paragraphs 16–24 are not rearranged and show very little emendation.

Chart I.	Chart II.
Selected Poems Order	*Poems* (1884) Order
1. 1–6, 12–40	1.
2. 98–122, 301–324	2. (Omitting the last ten lines.)
3. 128–169	3. (Divided into two verse paragraphs.)
4. 170–179	6.
5. 180–210	7.

6. 68–92	8.
7. 41–54	9.
8. 55–67	4.
9. 93–97	5.
10. 236–257	15.
11. 258–265	10.
12. 266–275	11.
13. 276–284	12.
14. 285–300	13.
15. 211–235	14.
16. 325–357	16.
17. 358–390	17.
18. 391–424	18.
19. 425–447	19.
20. 448–464	20.
21. 465–479	21.
22. 603–627	22.
23. 628–635	23.
24. 636–663	24.

What follows below is an unaltered reprinting of the *Selected Poems* text and not a critical edition. It serves here as the basis for referencing variants from the Riverside and Centenary editions, though it is to be understood in the first place that none of the variants has authority, and, in the second, that, because of the rearrangements, they occur at different points in the later editions of the poem. Line numbers below refer to the *Selected Poems* text; the corresponding lines in B and C can be ascertained by recourse to the charts above.

MAY-DAY.

[1.] Daughter of Heaven and Earth, coy Spring,
With sudden passion languishing,
Teaching barren moors to smile,
Painting pictures mile on mile,
Holds a cup with cowslip-wreaths   5
Whence a smokeless incense breathes.
The air is full of whistlings bland;
What was that I heard
Out of the hazy land?
Harp of the wind, or song of bird,   10

Or vagrant booming of the air,
Voice of a meteor lost in day?
Such tidings of the starry sphere
Can this elastic air convey,
Or haply 't was the cannonade   15
Of the pent and darkened lake
Cooled by the pendent mountain's shade
Whose deeps, till beams of noonday break,
Afflicted moan, and latest hold
Even into May the iceberg cold.   20
Was it a squirrel's pettish bark,
Or clarionet of jay? or hark
Where yon wedged line the Nestor leads,
Steering north with raucous cry
Through tracts and provinces of sky,   25
Every night alighting down
In new landscapes of romance
Where darkling feed the clamorous clans
By lonely lakes to men unknown.
Come the tumult whence it will,   30
It is a sound, it is a token
That the marble sleep is broken,
And the sun shall his orb fulfil.

[2.] When late I walked, in earlier days,
All was stiff and stark;   35
Knee-deep snows choked all the ways,
In the sky no spark;
Firm-braced I sought my ancient woods,
Struggling through the drifted roads;
The whited desert knew me not,   40
Snow-ridges masked each darling spot;
The summer dells, by genius haunted,
One arctic moon had disenchanted.
All the sweet secrets therein hid
By Fancy, ghastly spells undid.   45
Eldest mason, Frost, had piled
Swift cathedrals in the wild;
The piny hosts were sheeted ghosts
In the star-lit minster aisled.

685

I found no joy; the icy wind   50
Might rule the forest to his mind.
Who would freeze on frozen lakes?
Back to books and sheltered home,
And wood-fire flickering on the walls,
To hear, when, mid our talk and games,   55
Without the baffled north-wind calls.
But soft! a sultry morning breaks;
The ground-pines wash their rusty green,
The maple-tops their crimson tint,
On the soft path each track is seen,   60
The girl's foot leaves its neater print.
The pebble loosened from the frost
Asks of the urchin to be tost.
In flint and marble beats a heart,
The kind Earth takes her children's part,   65
The green lane is the school-boy's friend,
Low leaves his quarrel apprehend,
The fresh ground loves his top and ball,
The air rings jocund to his call,
The brimming brook invites a leap,   70
He dives the hollow, climbs the steep.
The youth reads omens where he goes,
And speaks all languages the rose.
The wood-fly mocks with tiny noise
The far halloo of human voice;   75
The perfumed berry on the spray
Smacks of faint memories far away.
A subtle chain of countless rings
The next unto the farthest brings,
And, striving to be man, the worm   80
Mounts through all the spires of form.

[3.] The caged linnet in the spring
Hearkens for the choral glee,
When his fellows on the wing
Migrate from the Southern Sea;   85
When trellised grapes their flowers unmask,
And the new-born tendrils twine,
The old wine darkling in the cask

Feels the bloom on the living vine,
And bursts the hoops at hint of spring: 90
And so perchance in Adam's race,
Of Eden's bower some dream-like trace
Survived the Flight and swam the Flood,
And wakes the wish in youngest blood
To tread the forfeit Paradise,   95
And feed once more the exile's eyes;
And ever when the happy child
In May beholds the blooming wild,
And hears in heaven the bluebird sing,
"Onward," he cries, "your baskets bring,—   100
In the next field is air more mild,
And o'er yon hazy crest is Eden's balmier spring."
Not for a regiment's parade,
Nor evil laws or rulers made,
Blue Walden rolls its cannonade,   105
But for a lofty sign
Which the Zodiac threw,
That the bondage-days are told,
And waters free as winds shall flow.
Lo! how all the tribes combine   110
To rout the flying foe.
See, every patriot oak-leaf throws
His elfin length upon the snows,
Not idle, since the leaf all day
Draws to the spot the solar ray,   115
Ere sunset quarrying inches down,
And half-way to the mosses brown;
While the grass beneath the rime
Has hints of the propitious time,
And upward pries and perforates   120
Through the cold slab a thousand gates,
Till green lances peering through
Bend happy in the welkin blue.

[4.] April cold with dropping rain
Willows and lilacs brings again,   125
The whistle of returning birds,
And trumpet-lowing of the herds;

687

The scarlet maple-keys betray
What potent blood hath modest May;
What fiery force the earth renews,   130
The wealth of forms, the flush of hues;
What Joy in rosy waves outpoured,
Flows from the heart of Love, the Lord.

[5.] Hither rolls the storm of heat;
I feel its finer billows beat   135
Like a sea which me infolds;
Heat with viewless fingers moulds,
Swells, and mellows, and matures,
Paints, and flavors, and allures,
Bird and brier inly warms,   140
Still enriches and transforms,
Gives the reed and lily length,
Adds to oak and oxen strength,
Transforming what it doth infold,
Life out of death, new out of old,   145
Painting fawns' and leopards' fells,
Seethes the gulf-encrimsoning shells,
Fires gardens with a joyful blaze
Of tulips, in the morning's rays.
The dead log touched bursts into leaf,   150
The wheat-blade whispers of the sheaf.
What god is this imperial Heat,
Earth's prime secret, sculpture's seat?
Doth it bear hidden in its heart
Water-line patterns of all art,   155
Is it Dædalus? is it Love?
Or walks in mask almighty Jove,
And drops from Power's redundant horn
All seeds of beauty to be born?

[6.] As we thaw frozen flesh with snow,   160
So Spring will not her time forerun,
Mix polar night with tropic glow,
Nor cloy us with unshaded sun,
Nor wanton skip with bacchic dance,
But she has the temperance   165

Of the gods, whereof she is one,—
Masks her treasury of heat
Under east-winds crossed with sleet.
Plants and birds and humble creatures
Well accept her rule austere;   170
Titan-born, to hardy natures
Cold is genial and dear.
As Southern wrath to Northern right
Is but straw to anthracite;
As in the day of sacrifice,   175
When heroes piled the pyre,
The dismal Massachusetts ice
Burned more than others' fire,
So Spring guards with surface cold
The garnered heat of ages old.   180
Hers to sow the seed of bread,
That man and all the kinds be fed;
And, when the sunlight fills the hours,
Dissolves the crust, displays the flowers.

[7.] Beneath the calm, within the light   185
A hid unruly appetite
Of swifter life, a surer hope,
Strains every sense to larger scope,
Impatient to anticipate
The halting steps of aged Fate.   190
Slow grows the palm, too slow the pearl:
When Nature falters, fain would zeal
Grasp the felloes of her wheel,
And grasping give the orbs another whirl.
Turn swiftlier round, O tardy ball!   195
And sun this frozen side,
Bring hither back the robin's call,
Bring back the tulip's pride.

[8.] Why chidest thou the tardy Spring?
The hardy bunting does not chide;   200
The blackbirds make the maples ring
With social cheer and jubilee;
The red-wing flutes his *o-ka-lee,*

689

The robins know the melting snow;
The sparrow meek, prophetic-eyed,   205
Her nest beside the snow-drift weaves,
Secure the osier yet will hide
Her callow brood in mantling leaves,—
And thou, by science all undone,
Why only must thy reason fail   210
To see the southing of the sun?

[9.] The world rolls round, mistrust it not,
Befalls again what once befell;
All things return, both sphere and mote,
And I shall hear my bluebird's note   215
And dream the dream of Auburn-dell.

[10.] As poured the flood of the ancient sea
Spilling over mountain-chains,
Bending forests as bends the sedge,
Faster flowing o'er the plains,—   220
A world-wide wave with a foaming edge
That rims the running silver sheet,—
So pours the deluge of the heat
Broad northward o'er the land,
Painting artless paradises,   225
Drugging herbs with Syrian spices,
Fanning secret fires which glow
In columbine and clover-blow.
Climbing the northern zones,
Where a thousand pallid towns   230
Lie like cockles by the main,
Or tented armies on a plain.
The million-handed painter pours
Opal hues and purple dye;
Azaleas flush the island floors,   235
And the tints of heaven reply.

[11.] Wreaths for the May! for happy Spring
To-day shall all her dowry bring,—
The love of kind, the joy, the grace,

Hymen of element and race,   240
Knowing well to celebrate
With song and hue and star and state,
With tender light and youthful cheer,
The spousals of the new-born year.

[12.] Spring is strong and virtuous,   245
Broad-sowing, cheerful, plenteous,
Quickening underneath the mould
Grains beyond the price of gold.
So deep and large her bounties are,
That one broad, long midsummer day   250
Shall to the planet overpay
The ravage of a year of war.

[13.] Drug the cup, thou butler sweet,
And send the nectar round;
The feet that slid so long on sleet   255
Are glad to feel the ground.
Fill and saturate each kind
With good according to its mind,
Fill each kind and saturate
With good agreeing with its fate,   260
The soft perfection of its plan—
Willow and violet, maiden and man.

[14.] The bitter-sweet, the haunting air
Creepeth, bloweth everywhere;
It preys on all, all prey on it,   265
Blooms in beauty, thinks in wit,
Stings the strong with enterprise,
Makes travellers long for Indian skies,
And where it comes this courier fleet
Fans in all hearts expectance sweet,   270
As if to-morrow should redeem
The vanished rose of evening's dream.
By houses lies a fresher green,
On men and maids a ruddier mien,
As if time brought a new relay   275

Of shining virgins every May,
And Summer came to ripen maids
To a beauty that not fades.

[15.] Where shall we keep the holiday,
And duly greet the entering May?   280
Too strait and low our cottage doors,
And all unmeet our carpet floors;
Nor spacious court, nor monarch's hall
Suffice to hold the festival.
Up and away! where haughty woods   285
Front the liberated floods:
We will climb the broad-backed hills,
Hear the uproar of their joy;
We will mark the leaps and gleams
Of the new-delivered streams,   290
And the murmuring rivers of sap
Mount in the pipes of the trees,
Giddy with day, to the topmost spire,
Which for a spike of tender green
Bartered its powdery cap;   295
And the colors of joy in the bird,
And the love in its carol heard,
Frog and lizard in holiday coats,
And turtle brave in his golden spots;
While cheerful cries of crag and plain   300
Reply to the thunder of river and main.

[16.] I saw the bud-crowned Spring go forth,
Stepping daily onward north
To greet staid ancient cavaliers
Filing singly in stately train.   305
And who, and who are the travellers?
They were Night and Day, and Day and Night,
Pilgrims wight with step forthright.
I saw the Days deformed and low,
Short and bent by cold and snow;   310
The merry Spring threw wreaths on them,
Flower-wreaths gay with bud and bell;
Many a flower and many a gem,

They were refreshed by the smell,
They shook the snow from hats and shoon,   315
They put their April raiment on;
And those eternal forms,
Unhurt by a thousand storms,
Shot up to the height of the sky again,
And danced as merrily as young men.   320
I saw them mask their awful glance
Sidewise meek in gossamer lids;
And to speak my thought if none forbids,
It was as if the eternal gods,
Tired of their starry periods,   325
Hid their majesty in cloth
Woven of tulips and painted moth.
On carpets green the maskers march
Below May's well-appointed arch,
Each star, each god, each grace amain,   330
Every joy and virtue speed,
Marching duly in her train,
And fainting Nature at her need
Is made whole again.

[17.] 'T was the vintage-day of field and wood,   335
When magic wine for bards is brewed;
Every tree and stem and chink
Gushed with syrup to the brink.
The air stole into the streets of towns,
Refreshed the wise, reformed the clowns,   340
And betrayed the fund of joy
To the high-school and medalled boy:
On from hall to chamber ran,
From youth to maid, from boy to man,
To babes, and to old eyes as well.   345
'Once more,' the old man cried, 'ye clouds,
Airy turrets purple-piled,
Which once my infancy beguiled,
Beguile me with the wonted spell.
I know ye skilful to convoy   350
The total freight of hope and joy
Into rude and homely nooks,

Shed mocking lustres on shelf of books,
On farmer's byre, on pasture rude,
And stony pathway to the wood.   355
I care not if the pomps you show
Be what they soothfast appear,
Or if yon realms in sunset glow
Be bubbles of the atmosphere.
And if it be to you allowed   360
To fool me with a shining cloud,
So only new griefs are consoled
By new delights, as old by old,
Frankly I will be your guest,
Count your change and cheer the best.   365
The world hath overmuch of pain,—
If Nature give me joy again,
Of such deceit I'll not complain.'

[18.] Ah! well I mind the calendar,
Faithful through a thousand years,   370
Of the painted race of flowers,
Exact to days, exact to hours,
Counted on the spacious dial
Yon broidered zodiac girds.
I know the trusty almanac   375
Of the punctual coming-back,
On their due days, of the birds.
I marked them yestermorn,
A flock of finches darting
Beneath the crystal arch,   380
Piping, as they flew, a march,—
Belike the one they used in parting
Last year from yon oak or larch;
Dusky sparrows in a crowd,
Diving, darting northward free,   385
Suddenly betook them all,
Every one to his hole in the wall,
Or to his niche in the apple-tree.
I greet with joy the choral trains
Fresh from palms and Cuba's canes.   390
Best gems of Nature's cabinet,

With dews of tropic morning wet,
Beloved of children, bards, and Spring,
O birds, your perfect virtues bring,
Your song, your forms, your rhythmic flight,   395
Your manners for the heart's delight,
Nestle in hedge, or barn, or roof,
Here weave your chamber weather-proof,
Forgive our harms, and condescend
To man, as to a lubber friend,   400
And, generous, teach his awkward race
Courage, and probity, and grace!

[19.] Poets praise that hidden wine
Hid in milk we drew
At the barrier of Time,   405
When our life was new.
We had eaten fairy fruit,
We were quick from head to foot,
All the forms we looked on shone
As with diamond dews thereon.   410
What cared we for costly joys,
The Museum's far-fetched toys?
Gleam of sunshine on the wall
Poured a deeper cheer than all
The revels of the Carnival.   415
We a pine-grove did prefer
To a marble theatre,
Could with gods on mallows dine,
Nor cared for spices or for wine.
Wreaths of mist and rainbows spanned,   420
Arch on arch, the grimmest land;
Whistle of a woodland bird
Made the pulses dance,
Note of horn in valleys heard
Filled the region with romance.   425

[20.] None can tell how sweet,
How virtuous, the morning air;
Every accent vibrates well;
Not alone the wood-bird's call,

Or shouting boys that chase their ball,   430
Pass the height of minstrel skill,
But the ploughman's thoughtless cry,
Lowing oxen, sheep that bleat,
And the joiner's hammer-beat
Softened are above their will.   435
All grating discords melt,
No dissonant note is dealt,
And though thy voice be shrill
Like rasping file on steel,
Such is the temper of the air,   440
Echo waits with art and care,
And will the faults of song repair.

[21.] So by remote Superior Lake,
And by resounding Mackinac,
When northern storms the forest shake,   445
And billows on the long beach break,
The artful Air will separate
Note by note all sounds that grate,
Smothering in her ample breast
All but godlike words,   450
Reporting to the happy ear
Only purified accords.
Strangely wrought from barking waves,
Soft music daunts the Indian braves,—
Convent-chanting which the child   455
Hears pealing from the panther's cave
And the impenetrable wild.

[22.] Soft on the south-wind sleeps the haze:
So on thy broad mystic van
Lie the opal-colored days,   460
And waft the miracle to man.
Soothsayer of the eldest gods,
Repairer of what harms betide,
Revealer of the inmost powers
Prometheus proffered, Jove denied;   465
Disclosing treasures more than true,
Or in what far to-morrow due;

Speaking by the tongues of flowers,
By the ten-tongued laurel speaking,
Singing by the oriole songs, 470
Heart of bird the man's heart seeking;
Whispering hints of treasure hid
Under Morn's unlifted lid,
Islands looming just beyond
The dim horizon's utmost bound;— 475
Who can, like thee, our rags upbraid,
Or taunt us with our hope decayed?
Or who like thee persuade,
Making the splendor of the air,
The morn and sparkling dew, a snare? 480
Or who resent
Thy genius, wiles, and blandishment?

[23.] There is no orator prevails
To beckon or persuade
Like thee the youth or maid: 485
Thy birds, thy songs, thy brooks, thy gales,
Thy blooms, thy kinds,
Thy echoes in the wilderness,
Soothe pain, and age, and love's distress,
Fire fainting will, and build heroic minds. 490

[24.] For thou, O Spring! canst renovate
All that high God did first create.
Be still his arm and architect,
Rebuild the ruin, mend defect;
Chemist to vamp old worlds with new, 495
Coat sea and sky with heavenlier blue,
New-tint the plumage of the birds,
And slough decay from grazing herds,
Sweep ruins from the scarped mountain,
Cleanse the torrent at the fountain, 500
Purge alpine air by towns defiled,
Bring to fair mother fairer child,
Not less renew the heart and brain,
Scatter the sloth, wash out the stain,
Make the aged eye sun-clear, 505

To parting soul bring grandeur near.
Under gentle types, my Spring
Masks the might of Nature's king,
An energy that searches thorough
From Chaos to the dawning morrow;   510
Into all our human plight,
The soul's pilgrimage and flight;
In city or in solitude,
Step by step, lifts bad to good,
Without halting, without rest,   515
Lifting Better up to Best;
Planting seeds of knowledge pure,
Through earth to ripen, through heaven endure.

TEXTS

(A) *Selected Poems* (Boston, 1876), 40–57; (B) *Poems* [Riverside] (Boston, 1884), 143–159; (C) *Poems* [Centenary] (Boston, 1904), 163–181.

VARIANTS (NOT INCLUDING REARRANGEMENTS)

5   cowslip-wreaths (A) | cowslip-wreaths, (B-C)
14   convey, (A) | convey. (B-C)
16   lake (A) | lake, (B-C)
17   shade (A) | shade, (B-C)
27   romance (A) | romance, (B-C)
30–31   will, / It (A) | will, / Voice of sport, or rush of wings, / It (B-C)
33   And . . . fulfil. (A) | And a change has passed on things. (B-C)
50   joy; (A) | joy: (B-C)
55   mid (A) | 'mid (B-C)
56   north-wind (A-B) | North-wind (C)
72–81   The youth . . . of form. (A) | [*Lines not present*] (B) | The youth sees omens where he goes, / And speaks all languages the rose, / The wood-fly mocks with tiny voice / The far halloo of human voice; / The perfumed berry on the spray / Smacks of faint memories far away. / A subtle chain of countless rings / The next into the farthest brings, / And, striving to be man, the worm / Mounts through all the spires of form. (C)
82   caged (A-B) | cagèd (C) || spring (A-B) | Spring (C)
90   spring: (A-B) | Spring: (C)
91   so perchance (A) | so, perchance, (B-C)
100   "Onward," (A-B) | 'Onward,' (C) || "your (A-B) | 'your (C)
102–103   spring." / [*Flush*] Not (A) | spring." / [*white line*] / [*Inset*] Not

(B) | spring.' / [*white line*] / [Inset] Not (C)

117   half-way (A-B) | halfway (C)

127   herds; (A) | herds. (B-C)

129   May; (A) | May, (B-C)

132   Joy (A) | joy (B-C) || outpoured, (A) | outpoured (B-C)

155   art, (A) |art? (B-C)

168   east-winds (A-B) | east winds (C)

185   light (A) | light, (B-C)

196   side, (A-B) | side. (C)

203   red-wing (A) | redwing (B-C)

212   round, mistrust it not, (A) | round,—mistrust it not,—(B-C)

215   note (A) | note, (B-C)

216   Auburn-dell. (A) | Auburn dell. (B-C)

218   mountain-chains, (A) | mountain chains (B-C)

228   clover-blow. (A) | clover-blow, (B-C)

232–233 plain. / The (A) | plain. / The million-handed sculptor moulds

/ Quaintest bud and blossom folds, / The (B-C)

238   bring,—(A) | bring, (B-C)

275   time (A-B) | Time (C)

283   hall (A) | hall, (B-C)

284   festival. (A, C) | festival (B)

323   forbids, (A) | forbids (B-C)

350   skilful (A, C) | skillful (B)

393   bards, (A) | bards (B-C)

402   Courage, and probity, (A) | Courage and probity (B-C)

434   hammer-beat (A) | hammer-beat, (B-C)

435–436 will. / All (A) || will, / Take tones from groves they wandered through / Or flutes which passing angels blew. / All (B-C)

443   [*inset*] So (A-B) | [*flush*] So (C)

458   south-wind (A-B) | South-wind (C)

482   wiles, (A) | wiles (B-C)

497   New-tint (A) | New tint (B-C)

SELECTED POEMS

The following list of the contents of *Selected Poems* (Boston: James R. Osgood, 1876) represents Emerson's judgment, as of that date, regarding the poems he thought best and most representative. Those drawn from *Poems* (Boston: Munroe, 1847) are marked by a single asterisk; those drawn from *May-Day and Other Pieces* (Boston: Ticknor and Fields, 1867) are marked by a double asterisk. Unmarked poems ("The Harp," "April," "Wealth," "Maiden Speech of the Æolian Harp," "Cupido," "The Nun's Aspiration," "Hymn [Sung at the Second Church]," and "Boston") had not previously been collected. Some of the longer works, such as "May-Day" and "Woodnotes, I and II," were abridged from their first-printing forms. Note that Emerson's organization of *Selected Poems* is generally chronological but is traversed by thematic groupings.

The Sphinx*; Each and All*; The Problem*; The Visit*; Uriel*; To Rhea*; The World-Soul*; Alphonso of Castile*; Mithridates*; Saadi*; May-Day**; The Rhodora*; The Humble-Bee*; The Titmouse**; The Snow-Storm*; Forerunners*; Hamatreya*; Brahma**; Astræa*; Etienne de la Boéce*; Forebearance*; Letters**; Sursum Corda*; Ode to Beauty*; Give All to Love*; The

Romany Girl**; Fate*; Guy*; To Eva*; The Amulet*; Hermione*; Initial, Dæmonic, and Celestial Love*; Sea-Shore**; Merlin, I* [reprinted as "Merlin"]; Bacchus*; The Harp [extracted from "May-Day"]; April; Woodnotes*; Monadnoc* [title given in 1876 as "Monadnock"]; Fable*; Two Rivers**; Waldeinsamkeit**; Song of Nature**; Xenophanes*; Musketaquid*; The Day's Ration*; Experience**; Wealth; Days**; My Garden**; Maiden Speech of the Æolian Harp; Friendship**; Beauty**; Manners**; Cupido; Art**; Worship**; The Nun's Aspiration; Terminus**; Dirge*; Threnody*; Hymn [Sung at the Second Church]; Concord Hymn [title given in 1876 as "Concord Fight"]*; Boston Hymn**; Fourth of July Ode**; Voluntaries**; Boston.

STANZA BREAKS

A line space (what Emerson regularly called a "white line") marking the break between stanzas, verse paragraphs, or other formal divisions of the poem, falls at the bottom of the page in this edition at the following locations:

Pages 37, 64, 69, 130, 183, 187, 194, 224, 240, 283, 292, 343, 344, 345, 348, 349, 374, 381, 383, 434, 454, 464, 604, 612, 613, 673.

INDEX

Index